ENGLISH DRAMATIC LITERATURE

WARD

A HISTORY

OF

ENGLISH DRAMATIC

LITERATURE

TO THE DEATH OF QUEEN ANNE

BY

ADOLPHUS WILLIAM WARD

VOL. III

1966

OCTAGON BOOKS, INC.

New York

Originally published 1875 by Macmillan and Co., Ltd. (London)

New and revised edition published 1899 by Macmillan and Co., Ltd. (London)

Reprinted 1966
by special arrangement with Macmillan and Co., Ltd. (London)

OCTAGON BOOKS, INC.
175 FIFTH AVENUE
NEW YORK, N.Y. 10010

LIBRARY OF CONGRESS CATALOG CARD NUMBER: 66-17496

Printed in U.S.A. by
NOBLE OFFSET PRINTERS, INC.
NEW YORK 3, N. Y.

ERRATA

p. 9, line 9 from top : *for* not *read* now.

p. 140, l. 4 from bottom : *for* instanee *read* instance.

p. 168, l. 7 from top : *for* 1 *read* 2.

p. 256, note 2, l. 3 from bottom : *for* Dryden *read* Dryden's age.

CONTENTS OF VOL. III

CHAPTER VIII.

THE END OF THE OLD DRAMA.

PAGE

PHILIP MASSINGER (1583–1640) 1-47

His life, 2: his difficulties, 3; Massinger and Fletcher, 4; his patrons, 6; his collision with the Licenser, 8; his relations with other dramatists, 9; his death, 10.—His religious and political tone, *ib.*—His character as a literary man, 11.—His plays: Massinger and Dekker's *The Virgin Martyr*, 12; Massinger's *The Duke of Milan*, 14; *The Unnatural Combat*, 15; *The Bondman*, 16; *The Renegado*, 17; *The Parliament of Love*, 18; *The Maid of Honour*, 19; *A New Way to Pay Old Debts*, 21; *The Roman Actor*, 24; *The Picture*, 27; *The Great Duke of Florence*, 28; *The Emperor of the East*, 29; *Believe as You List*, 31; *The City Madam*, 34; *The Guardian*, 35; *The Bashful Lover*, 36.—Joint plays by Massinger and Fletcher: *Henry VIII* and *The Two Noble Kinsmen*, 38; Massinger and Fletcher's (?) *A Very Woman, or The Prince of Tarent*, *ib.*—Joint plays by Massinger and other writers: Massinger and Field's *The Fatal Dowry*, 39; Middleton, William Rowley, and Massinger's (?) *The Old Law*, 41.—Massinger's characteristics: his moral earnestness an element in his dramatic power, *ib.*; his themes, and the principles illustrated by them, 42; his defectiveness in characterisation, *ib.*; in humour, 43; and in pathos, 44; rhetorical character of his genius, *ib.*; his diction, 45; Massinger and Shakspere, *ib.*; Massinger's versification, *ib.*; his constructive skill, 46; his various and frequently happy choice of subjects, *ib.*

NATHANIEL FIELD (1587–1633) 47-51

His life, and celebrity as an actor, 47.—His plays: *A Woman is a Weathercock*, 48; *Amends for Ladies*, 50.

JOHN WEBSTER (died 1650 c.) 51-65

His life, 51.—Data of his career as a dramatist, 52.—His co-operation with other playwrights, *ib.*—His literary friends and patrons, *ib.*—Joint and doubtful plays by Webster and others: Webster and William Rowley's *A Cure for a Cuckold*, 54; Webster (?) and William Rowley's (?) *The Thracian Wonder*, 55; Webster (?) and

PAGE

Dekker's (?) *The Weakest Goeth to the Wall,* 55.—Plays by Webster only : *The White Devil, or Vittoria Corombona,* 56 ; *The Duchess of Malfi,* 59 ; *The Devil's Law-Case,* 61 ; *Appius and Virginia,* 62.—Webster's chief characteristics as a dramatist : the intensity of his imagination, and the elaborateness of his workmanship, in the sphere of the Terrible, 63 ; his insight into human nature, *ib.* ; his humour, and poetic feeling, 64 ; Webster and Shakspere, *ib.* ; Webster deficient in characterisation, 65.

CYRIL TOURNEUR (*fl.* 1603–1613 c.) 66–71

His early productions, 66.—His plays : *The Atheist's Tragedy,* 67 ; *The Revenger's Tragedy,* 69.

JOHN FORD (1586–1640 c. or *post*) 71–89

His life and literary labours, 71.—Joint plays by Ford and other dramatists : Ford, Dekker, and William Rowley's *The Witch of Edmonton,* 74 ; other joint productions by Dekker and Ford, 75 ; Ford and Webster's *A Murder of a Son upon a Mother,* 76.—Plays written by Ford alone : *The Lover's Melancholy, ib.* ; *'Tis Pity She's a Whore,* 77 ; *The Broken Heart,* 79 ; *Love's Sacrifice,* 81 ; *The Fancies Chaste and Noble,* 83 ; *The Lady's Trial, ib.* ; *Perkin Warbeck,* 84 ; lost plays, 86.—Ford's characteristics as a dramatist : his want of comic power, *ib.* ; exceptional merits of his single historical drama, *ib.* ; his versification and construction, 87 ; his strength to be sought in the intensity of particular situations and passages, *ib.* ; contrasts of passion and sweetness, 88 ; his tragedy fails to purify the emotions, *ib.* ; his choice of themes at times as unsound as his treatment of them, 89.

JAMES SHIRLEY (1596–1666) 89–125

His life, 89.—His tragedies : *The Maid's Revenge,* 95 ; *The Traitor, ib.* ; *Love's Cruelty,* 97 ; *The Duke's Mistress, ib.* ; *The Politician, ib.* ; *The Cardinal,* 98.—General character of Shirley's other plays, 99. —Plays of an exceptional kind : *St. Patrick for Ireland, ib.* ; *Honoria and Mammon,* 101 ; *A Contention for Honour and Riches, ib.* ; *The Arcadia,* 102.—His comedies, *ib.* : *Love-Tricks,* 103 ; *The Wedding, ib.* ; *The Brothers,* 104 ; *The Witty Fair One, ib.* ; *The Grateful Servant,* 105 ; *Changes, or Love in a Maze, ib.* ; *Hyde Park,* 106 ; Shirley (and Chapman)'s *The Ball,* 107 ; *The Bird in a Cage,* 108 ; *The Young Admiral, ib.* ; *The Gamester,* 109 ; *The Example,* 111 ; *The Opportunity,* 112 ; Shirley's (and Fletcher's?) *The Coronation, ib.* ; *The Lady of Pleasure,* 114 ; *The Constant Maid, or Love will find out the Way, ib.* ; *The Royal Master,* 115 ; *The Doubtful Heir,* 116 ; *The Gentleman of Venice,* 117 ; *The Imposture, ib.* ; *The Sisters,* 118 ; *The Humorous Courtier, ib.* ; *The Court Secret,* 119.—Plays attributed to Shirley, 120.—Shirley's characteristics as a dramatist, *ib.* : the originality of his plots, and their unity, 121 ; the variety of his themes, 122 ; his debts to others not such as to interfere with his independence as a dramatic poet, *ib.* ; his numerous

PAGE

passages of poetic and picturesque beauty, 123 ; his comic powers,
ib. ; his comedy differs from that of the post-Restoration period,
124 ; his morality likewise differs from that of his successors, *ib.*

Minor dramatists of this period 125-164

RICHARD BROME (*d.* 1652-3), 125 : his modesty and his self-
consciousness as a dramatist, 127 ; his comedies of manners, 128 ;
his romantic comedies and dramas of intrigue, 129 ; *A Jovial Crew*
and *The Antipodes*, 130 ; Brome a type of the skilful playwright
without original genius, *ib.*—THOMAS RANDOLPH (1605-1635), 131 :
The Jealous Lovers, 133 ; *The Muses' Looking-Glass*, 134 ; *Amyntas*,
135 ; plays ascribed to Randolph on unsatisfactory evidence, 136.—
WILLIAM CARTWRIGHT (1611-1643), 137 ; his 'tragi-comedies':
The Royal Slave, 138 ; *The Lady Errant*, 139 ; *The Siege, ib.*; *The
Ordinary, ib.*—JASPER MAYNE (1604-1672), 140 : *The City-Match*,
141 ; *The Amorous War, ib.*—THOMAS MAY (1595-1650) : *The
Heir*, 142 ; *The Old Couple*, 143 ; his tragedies on classical subjects,
ib. ; May's (?) *Nero, ib.*—SIR JOHN SUCKLING (1609-1641 or 1642) :
The Goblins, 144 ; *Aglaura*, 145 ; *The Sad One, ib.*; *Brennoralt*,
146.—SHACKERLEY MARMION (1603-1639), *ib.* : *Holland's Leaguer*,
147 ; *A Fine Companion, ib.* ; *The Antiquary, ib.*—SIR JOHN DENHAM
(1615-1688) : *The Sophy*, 148.—WILLIAM HABINGTON (1605-1654),
149 : *The Queen of Arragon*, 150.—HENRY GLAPTHORNE (*temp.*
Charles I), 151. His plays : *Argalus and Parthenia, ib.* ; *The
Ladies' Privilege, ib.* ; *Albertus Wallenstein*, 152. His comedies :
The Hollander, 153 ; *Wit in a Constable, ib.* ; Glapthorne's (?) *The
Lady Mother*, 154. His fondness for poetic imagery, *ib.* ; his
connexion with the Court party, *ib.*—Other dramatists of the first
two Stuart reigns : Robert Daborne (*d.* 1628), 155 ; Lewis Machin
and Gervase Markham (1568-*c.* 1637), *ib.* ; Robert Tailor, 157 ;
Lodowick Barry, *ib.* ; Henry Shirley, *ib.* ; Robert Davenport, *ib.* ;
Thomas Goffe (1591-1629), 158 ; William Bowyer (?), 159 ; Lodo-
wick Carlell, 160 ; Thomas Rawlins, 161 ; William Heminge, *ib.* ;
Nathaniel Richards, 162 ; Joseph Rutter, *ib.* ; Lewis Sharpe, *ib.* ;
Henry Killigrew, 163 ; Sir William Berkeley, *ib.* ; Richard Lovelace, 164.

Dramatists who wrote both before and after the Civil War and Common-
    wealth periods 164-173

THOMAS KILLIGREW (1612-1683), 165.—SIR WILLIAM D'AVENANT
(1606-1668) : his life, 166 ; his ideas on dramatic composition, 167 ;
character of his earlier plays, 169 ; *Albovine, ib.* ; *The Cruel Brother*,
170 ; *The Just Italian, ib.* ; *The Platonic Lovers, ib.* ; *The Wits*, 171 ;
Love and Honour, 172 ; *The Unfortunate Lovers, ib.* ; *The Siege*,
173 ; *News from Plymouth, ib.* ; *The Fair Favourite, ib.*; *The Distresses, ib.* ; his masques, *ib.*

Academical plays 174-188

J. Tomkis' (?) *Lingua*, 174.—B. Holyday's *Technogamia*, 176.—

PAGE

J. Tomkis' *Albumazar*, 179. — Phineas Fletcher's *Sicelides*, 180. — J. Fisher's *Fuimus Troes*, 182. — P. Strode's *The Floating Island*, *ib.* — *The Sophister* and *Apollo's Shroving*, 183. — George Ruggle's *Ignoramus*, *ib.* — Abraham Cowley's *Naufragium Joculare*, 187. — Other academical plays in Latin, *ib.*

Masque-writers of the reigns of James I and Charles I .   .   . 188-206

THOMAS CAMPION (*d.* 1619-20), 189 : his masques, 190. — Other masque-writers of the period, 192. — THOMAS NABBES, 194: his *Microcosmus*, 195. — JOHN MILTON (1608-1674) : his life in the period 1632-1638, 196; his *Arcades*, 197; *Comus*, *ib.*; his dramatic designs, 201; *Samson Agonistes*, 203.

Historical review of the period from Shakspere to the Civil War .   206-229

Limits of the influence of Shakspere and the greatest of his fellow-dramatists, 206. — Approach of the Great Revolution, 207; the nation gradually divided into two parties, 208; the party chosen by the dramatists, *ib.* — The feebleness of the foreign policy of the age reflected in the drama, 209. — Elisabethan reminiscences, *ib.* — Isolated references to important transactions of contemporary European history, 210; the drama not allowed free comment on such topics, *ib.* — General public feeling, as reflected in the dramas, towards particular foreign nations, 211 : Germany, 212; the Dutch and the Danes, *ib.*; France, 213; Spain and the Spaniards, *ib.*; Italy, 214. — Faint reflexion in the drama of the political struggle at home, 215. — Absolutist sentiments of the dramatists, 216. — The drama and the royal family : under James I, 217; and Charles I, 218. — The loyalty of the dramatists, *ib.* — The drama and the national religion, 219. — Unbelief and superstition, 220. — Social views of the Court of James I and its surroundings, 221. — The growing importance and arrogance of London, *ib.*; reflected in the drama, 222. — Favourite social types of the drama, *ib.* — Prominent features in the manners of the times, 224 : extravagance, artificiality, and effeminacy in dress, 225; importation of foreign fashions, 226; partial advance of refinement in manners, *ib.* — Imperfect educational culture, 227. — Unsatisfactory relations between the sexes, *ib.* — The women of the period, 228.

The stage under James I and Charles I 229-257

Its relations with the King and the Royal Family, 230. — Legislation and official control of the stage, 233. — Puritan hostility to the theatre, 236 : slightness of its effect on administration or legislation, *ib.*; its intensity and bitterness, 237; its shortsightedness, 238; its powers and its prospects, *ib.* — Anti-theatrical literature (1616-25), 239 : Prynne's *Histriomastix*, 240; its consequences to the author, 243; its effect upon the theatre, 245. — The stage overwhelmed by the Revolution, *ib.* — Theatres closed (Sept. 2, 1642), 247. — Circumstances affecting dramatic productivity in this period : competition of other entertainments, *ib.*; and of foreign actors and actresses, 248. — Progress of the art of acting, *ib.* — Women's parts acted by

PAGE

boys, 251 ; earliest appearances of actresses in England, 252.—
Scenery and costume, 254.—The dramatists as appealing to their
patrons, 255 : Dedications, 256 ; Prologues and Epilogues, *ib.*

Summary of the literary history of the drama in this period .   . 257-269

Nature of the change in the next period, 257.—Obvious errors
traceable in the course of our dramatic literature in the period
under review, *ib.*—Its excessive productivity in the national
dramatic forms, 258.—Certain national species neglected : the
national historical drama, 259 ; the higher kind of historical drama
in general, 260.—Impoverishment of the tragic drama, *ib.*—Comedy
of character gives way to comedy of manners, *ib.*—Tendency to
rhetorical superficiality, 261 ; and conventional artificiality in style,
262.—Degeneration in moral tone, *ib.*—This decline of moral
sentiment not hopeless, 263.—Influence of foreign dramatic
literatures slight as a whole, 264 : Italian, *ib.* ; French, 265 ;
Spanish, *ib.*—Mutual indebtedness of the English dramatists in
non-essentials, 268.

Summary of the achievements of our dramatic literature in this
    period   269-276

Acknowledged pre-eminence of a few great writers, 269.—The
influence of Jonson, 270.—Achievements of Jonson and his contemporaries and successors in historic tragedy, *ib.*—Historic
tragedy neglected for romantic tragedy and 'tragi-comedy,' 271.—
Variety of subjects, and comparative paucity of motives, *ib.*—Excess
of passion, 272.—Distinctive merits and defects common to the
romantic tragedies of this period, *ib.*—Examples of Jonson and
Shakspere in comedy, 273.—Comic types of character elaborated,
and new types occasionally added, *ib.*—Progress in comedy of
manners, 274.—The Pastoral Drama and the Masque, *ib.*—Verse and
prose in the dramatic literature of this period, 275.—Conclusion, *ib.*

CHAPTER IX.

THE LATER STUART DRAMA.

The stage during the Civil War period and the Protectorate   . 277-291

Ordinance (Sept. 2, 1642) suppressing stage-plays, 277.—Relaxation of rules during the Protectorate, 280.—D'Avenant's devices,
281.—The re-opening of the theatres, 283.—Theatrical companies
after the Restoration, *ib.*—Flourishing condition of the art of
acting, 285.—Writers who published plays in the Commonwealth
period : Shirley, 286; Francis Quarles (1592–1642), *ib.*; Sir William
D'Avenant and the Killigrews, *ib.*; Sir Aston Cokayne (1608–1684),
287; William Chamberlayne (1619–1689), 289; Robert Baron, *ib.*;
Sir William Lower (*d.* 1662), 290.

PAGE

The Restoration and its effects upon the drama 291-301

The effects of the Restoration period upon a dramatic literature uncontrolled by the power of individual genius, 291.—The political results of the Restoration : as viewed by the Court party, 292 ; and by the great body of the dramatists of the age, *ib.*—The political and religious partisanship of the dramatists encouraged by the Restoration, 293 ; intensified in the latter part of the reign of Charles II, 294 ; moderated after the Revolution of 1688, 295 ; subsides in the reign of Queen Anne, 296.—Drawbacks to a patriotic enthusiasm for war, 297.—Social effects of the Restoration limited in their range, 298.—Literature and the stage no longer national, *ib.*—The moral tone of the stage not in sympathy with that of the people at large, 299.—The drama loses its full connexion with the national life, *ib.*—The influence of the Court of Charles II upon the drama : in what sense beneficial, 300 ; and in what sense pernicious, 301.

The influence of foreign dramatic literatures upon our own .   . 301-320

Encouragement given to foreign dramatic literature by the Court, 301.—Isolated followers of the ancients, 302.—Nature of contact with the Italian drama, *ib.*—Influence of later Spanish dramatists, 303.—English followers of the Spanish dramatists, 304 : George Digby, Earl of Bristol (1612-1676), 305 ; Sir Samuel Tuke (*d.* 1673), *ib.* ; Sir Richard Fanshawe (1607-1666), 306.—The French drama under Lewis XIV, *ib.*—Reaction towards refinement in higher French society and literature, 307.—The salons of the *Précieuses*, 308.—Chief French romances of this age, 309.—Relations between the French romances and the English drama, 312.—The French drama of this period, 313 : its relation to French national life, *ib.* ; its exotic elements, 314.—Influence of the French upon the English drama, 315.—Rime in French and in English tragedy, 316.—The spirit of French tragedy not communicated to English, 317.—The spirit and manner of Molière imperfectly communicated to English comedy, 318.

Other influences affecting the drama of this period   .   .   . 320-326

The Opera, 320 : Italian Opera in England, 321 ; French Opera, 322 ; English Opera, *ib.*—The Ballet, 324.—Scenes, machinery, and costume, 325.—Adaptations of earlier English plays, *ib.*

Dramatists who wrote both before the Revolution and after the Restoration   326-331

COWLEY: *Cutter of Coleman Street*, 327.—SIR WILLIAM D'AVENANT: his later plays : *The Siege of Rhodes*, 328 ; *The Siege*, 329 ; *The Playhouse to be Let*, 330 ; adaptations of old plays, *ib.* ; his position in our dramatic literature, 331.

Other dramatists who wrote both before and after the Restoration 332-340

The DUKE OF NEWCASTLE (1592-1676), 332.—The DUCHESS OF NEWCASTLE (*d.* 1676), *ib.*—LORD FALKLAND, 335.—SIR ROBERT STAPYLTON, 336.—JOHN WILSON (*d.* 1696), 337 ; his comedies :

PAGE

The Cheats, 338; The Projectors, ib.; his other plays: Andronicus
Comnenius, 339; Belphegor, or The Marriage of the Devil, ib.; his
sterling merits as a dramatist, ib.

ROGER BOYLE, EARL OF ORRERY (1621–1679) 340 345

The father of English heroic plays, 340.—His plays: their characteristics, 341; The History of Henry V, 342; Mustapha, 343;
The Black Prince, ib.; Tryphon, 344; Herod the Great, ib.; Altemira,
ib.; Guzman, 345.

JOHN DRYDEN (1631–1700) 346-392

His plays: The Wild Gallant, 346; The Rival Ladies, 347; Dryden
and Sir R. Howard's The Indian Queen, 348; Dryden's The Indian
Emperor, 349; Secret Love, or The Maiden Queen, 350; Sir Martin
Mar-All, 351; The Tempest, or The Enchanted Island, 352; An
Evening's Love, or The Mock Astrologer, ib.—Dryden's Essay of
Dramatic Poesy, 353: its preference of the English to the French
drama, 355; its plea for rime, ib.—Sir Robert Howard's Reply,
356.—Dryden's A Defence of an Essay of Dramatic Poesy, ib.—
Dryden's views as to rime in the English drama inadmissible, 357.
—Dryden's Tyrannic Love, or The Royal Martyr, 358; Almanzor
and Almahide, or The Conquest of Granada, 359.—The Defence of
the Epilogue, &c., 361.—The Duke of Buckingham and others
produce the burlesque of The Rehearsal, 362; nature and objects
of its satire, 364.—Dryden's Essay of Heroic Plays, 365.—His The
Assignation, or Love in a Nunnery, 366; Marriage à-la-Mode, ib.;
Amboyna, 367; The State of Innocence and Fall of Man, 368;
Aureng-Zebe, 370.—All for Love, or The World Well Lost, 372;
Dryden abandons the use of rime in tragedy, ib.; All for Love
and Antony and Cleopatra, ib.—Limberham, 373.—Dryden and
Lee's Œdipus, ib.—Dryden's Truth Found Too Late, 374; its
Preface, The Grounds of Criticism in Tragedy, 375; Dryden's change
of standpoint in his views of tragedy, ib.—The Spanish Friar, 376;
Lee and Dryden's The Duke of Guise, 377; Dryden's Albion and
Albanius, 380; King Arthur, or The British Worthy, 382; Don
Sebastian, ib.; Amphitryon, 384; Cleomenes, the Spartan Hero, ib.;
Love Triumphant, 385.—Epilogue, &c., for Fletcher's The Pilgrim,
ib.; Dryden's apology, ib.—His moral aberrations as a dramatist,
386.—Character and range of Dryden's dramatic powers, 387.—
His pre-eminence among the dramatists of his age, 390.—Dryden
the representative of the Restoration dramatist, ib.—His Prologues
and Epilogues, 391.

Other dramatists of the later Stuart period 393-407

SIR ROBERT HOWARD (1626–1698): his life and literary activity,
393; his tragedies: The Vestal Virgin, or The Roman Ladies, 394;
The Duke of Lerma, ib.—EDWARD HOWARD and JAMES HOWARD
(d. 1698), 396.—ELKANAH SETTLE (1648-1724), ib.—JOHN CROWNE
(d. 1703 or post), 398. His tragedies, 399: Juliana, or The Princess

PAGE

of Poland, 400; *The History of Charles VIII of France, ib.*; *The Destruction of Jerusalem, &c., ib.*; *The Ambitious Statesman, or The Loyal Favourite*, 401; *Thyestes*, 402; *Darius, King of Persia, ib.*; *Regulus*, 403; *Caligula, ib.* His comedies: *The Country Wit*, 404; *City Politics*, 405; *The English Friar, or The Town Spark, ib.*; *Sir Courtly Nice, or It Cannot Be*, 406; *The Married Beau, or The Curious Impertinent*, 407.

Other tragic dramatists of the period   407–442

NATHANIEL LEE (1653 *c.*–1692): his life, 407; his characteristics as a tragic dramatist, 408; his *Nero, Emperor of Rome, ib.*; *Sophonisba, or Hannibal's Overthrow, ib.*; *Gloriana, or The Court of Augustus*, 409; *The Rival Queens, or Alexander the Great, ib.*; *Mithridates*, 410; *Theodosius, or The Force of Love, ib.*; *Caesar Borgia, ib.*; *Lucius Junius Brutus, ib.*; *Constantine the Great*, 411; *The Princess of Cleve, ib.*; *The Massacre of Paris, ib.*; Lee's extravagance, 412.— THOMAS OTWAY (1651–1685), *ib.*: his life and works, 413; his *Alcibiades, ib.*; *Don Carlos, ib.*; *Titus and Berenice*, 414; *The Cheats of Scapin, ib.*; *Friendship in Fashion*, 415; *The History and Fall of Caius Marius, ib.*; *The Orphan, or The Unhappy Marriage, ib.*; *Venice Preserved, or A Plot Discovered*, 416: *The Atheist*, 418; Otway's end, *ib.*; progressive developement of his tragic genius, 419.—THOMAS SOUTHERNE (1660–1746), *ib.*: *The Loyal Brother, or The Persian Prince*, 420; comedies, 421; *Oroonoko, or The Royal Slave*, 422; *The Fate of Capua, ib.*; *The Spartan Dame*, 423; *Money's the Mistress, ib.*—GEORGE GRANVILLE, LORD LANSDOWNE (1667 *c.*–1735), *ib.*: his *Heroic Love*, 424; his comedies, *ib.*— AMBROSE PHILIPS (1675 *c.*–1740), 425.—JOHN DENNIS (1657–1733), 426: his *Appius and Virginia*, 427.—JOHN EVELYN (1620–1706), *ib.*—NAHUM TATE (1652–1715), *ib.*—CHARLES GILDON (1665–1724), 428.—JOHN OLDMIXON (1673–1742), *ib.*—JOHN BANKS, *ib.*: his *Cyrus the Great*, 429.—EDWARD RAVENSCROFT (*d.* 1692), *ib.*—JOHN HUGHES (1667–1720), 430.—AARON HILL (1685–1750), *ib.*—Other tragic writers, 431.—NICHOLAS ROWE (1674–1718), 433: his qualities as a tragic dramatist, *ib.*; his *The Ambitious Step-Mother*, 434; *Tamerlane, ib.*; *The Fair Penitent*, 435; *Ulysses*, 436; *The Royal Convert, ib.*; *Jane Shore* and *Lady Jane Grey*, 437.—JOSEPH ADDISON (1672–1719): his *Cato*, 439; circumstances of its production, *ib.*; its characteristics as a drama, 441.

Comic dramatists of the period   442–485

SIR GEORGE ETHEREDGE (1634–5 *c.*–1691 *c.*), 442; his comedies: *The Comical Revenge, or Love in a Tub*, 444; *She Would, if She Could*, 445; *The Man of Mode, or Sir Fopling Flutter*, 446.—SIR CHARLES SEDLEY (1639 *c.*–1728 *c.*), *ib.*; his tragedies, 447; his comedies: *The Mulberry Garden*, 448; *Bellamira, or The Mistress, ib.*; *The Grumbler, ib.*—JOHN LACY (*d.* 1681), actor and dramatist, 449; his adaptations, *ib.*; his *The Old Troop, or Monsieur Raggou*, 450; *Sir Hercules Buffoon, or The Poetical Squire, ib.*—EDWARD

PAGE

RAVENSCROFT (d. 1692), 451.—PETER ANTHONY MOTTEUX (1660–1718), ib.—MRS. APHRA BEHN (1640-1689), 452.—Other female comic dramatists, 453.—THOMAS D'URFEY (1653-1723), 454.—THOMAS SHADWELL (1640-1692): his life and politics, 455; his *The Sullen Lovers, or The Impertinents*, 456; *The Humourists, ib.*; *The Virtuoso, ib.*; *Epsom Wells, ib.*; *A True Widow*, 457; *The Woman-Captain, ib.*; *The Lancashire Witches and Tegue O'Divelly*, 458; *The Amorous Bigot, ib.*; *The Squire of Alsatia*, 459; *Bury Fair, ib.*; *The Scourers, ib.*; *The Volunteers, or The Stock-Jobbers, ib.*; Shadwell's characteristics as a dramatist, 460; Shadwell and Ben Jonson, *ib.*; Shadwell's merits and shortcomings, *ib.*—WILLIAM WYCHERLEY (1640-1715), 461 : his salient characteristics as a dramatist, 462; his comedies: *Love in a Wood, or St. James' Park*, 463; *The Gentleman Dancing-Master, ib.*; *The Country Wife*, 464; *The Plain-Dealer, ib.*; Wycherley's social satire, 466.—WILLIAM CONGREVE (1670-1729), 467: his wit, 468; his other merits as a comic dramatist, 470; his indecency, 471; his comedies: *The Old Bachelor, ib.*; *The Double-Dealer*, 472; *Love for Love*, 473; *The Way of the World*, 475; his tragedy, *The Mourning Bride*, 476.—SIR JOHN VANBRUGH (1666 c.-1726): characteristics of his comedy, 477; *The Relapse, or Virtue in Danger*, 478; *The Provoked Wife*, 479; *The False Friend, ib.*; *The Confederacy, ib.*; *The Mistake*, 480; *The Country House, ib.*; *A Journey to London* (unfinished), *ib.*; *Æsop, ib.*—GEORGE FARQUHAR (1678-1707): his merits and defects, 481; his plays: *Love and a Bottle*, 482; *The Constant Couple, or A Trip to the Jubilee, ib.*; *Sir Harry Wildair*, 483; *The Inconstant, or The Way to Win Him, ib.*; *The Twin-Rivals*, 484; *The Recruiting Officer, ib.*; *The Beaux' Stratagem, ib.*

Dramatists whose career extends beyond the reign of Anne . . 485-497

COLLEY CIBBER (1671-1757), 485: his *Love's Last Shift, or The Fool in Fashion*, 486; other earlier plays, *ib.*; *The Careless Husband, ib.*; *The Lady's Last Stake, or The Wife's Resentment*, 487.—MRS. CENTLIVRE (1667-1723): *The Perjured Husband, or The Adventures of Venice*, 488; characteristics of her comedies, *ib.*; *The Beau's Duel, or A Soldier for the Ladies*, 489; *The Basset-Table*, 490; *Love at a Venture, ib.*; *The Busy-Body* and *Marplot in Lisbon, ib.*; *The Wonder, or A Woman Keeps a Secret, ib.*; later plays, 491; Mrs. Centlivre's position as a comic dramatist, *ib.*—SIR RICHARD STEELE (1671-1729), *ib.*: his humour, and his politics, 493; Steele the real founder of sentimental comedy, *ib.*; *The Funeral, or Grief à-la-Mode*, 494; *The Lying Lover, or The Ladies' Friendship*, 495; *The Tender Husband, or The Accomplished Fools, ib.*; *The Conscious Lovers*, 496: consistency between Steele and Addison's plays and their essays, 497.

Concluding remarks on the later Stuart drama 497-518

Conditions under which the Restoration drama might have become a legitimate developement of the Elisabethan, 498; the later Stuart drama untrue to these conditions, *ib.*—Marked separation between

PAGE

tragedy and comedy, 498.—Summary of the history of tragedy in this period: Critical theories not consistently followed by their authors, 499; heroic plays, 500; developement of the species by Dryden, 501; by Lee and Otway, 502; decline of tragedy, *ib.*; extinction of English national tragedy as a literary growth, 503.— Comedy, *ib.*: its contact with the times, 504; extinction of romantic comedy and cognate species, *ib.*; perfection in this period of comic prose dialogue, *ib.*; licence of political comment, 505; English and foreign comedy, *ib.*; prevailing immorality of English comedy, 506; this immorality not imaginary or unreal, 507; anti-theatrical publications: Jeremy Collier and his predecessors, 509; effects of Collier's *Short View*, 511; beginnings of sentimental comedy, 515; later growths of English comedy, *ib.*; achievements of English comedy in this period, 516; comedy and the novel, 517.— Conclusion, *ib.*

APPENDIX 519
INDEX 521-599

ENGLISH DRAMATIC LITERATURE

CHAPTER VIII.

THE END OF THE OLD DRAMA.

HAVING in the previous Chapter spoken of Beaumont and Fletcher, I propose in the present to notice more briefly those other dramatic authors of mark whose earliest extant plays appeared after the death of Elisabeth, and whose activity as dramatists falls wholly, like theirs, or at all events in the main, within the period terminated by the outbreak of the Civil War. And the peculiarly intimate connexion between Fletcher and Massinger seems to render it imperative to give to the latter the first place among the writers discussed in this Chapter, although his can hardly be asserted to be the most commanding genius among them.

Yet among the secondary stars of the Elisabethan drama it may be questioned whether any has received a wider, and on the whole a more kindly, recognition than PHILIP MASSINGER. A sufficient proportion of the numerous plays of which he was sole author has been preserved to enable later generations to form a reasonably complete estimate of his gifts and powers; and his participation in the writing of a considerable number of further dramatic works has been established with practical certainty. Inasmuch as the plays which we owe to his unassisted hand have long since been competently edited, he has become the subject of a more exhaustive and appreciative criticism than has fallen to the lot of most of his contemporaries of a rank beneath the first, more especially since his relations to the political movements of his times have been placed in clearer relief.

Philip Massinger (1583–1640).

It is by no means impossible that his literary merits have thus come to be raised above the place properly due to them in a review of the chief writers of the Elisabethan drama ; yet it may safely be asserted that, little as we know of Massinger's life, few personalities in the gallery of our old dramatists are recognisable with greater distinctness in their works, and few commend themselves more signally to high-minded sympathy and esteem [1].

His life.   Philip Massinger, born at Salisbury in 1584 (the date of his baptism is November 24), was the son of Arthur Massinger, a gentleman of good family and a member of Parliament, who was attached to the service of Henry, second

---

[1] The standard edition of Massinger's dramatic works has long been that of Gifford (4 vols., 1805 ; second edition, 1813). On this is based Colonel Cunningham's one vol. edition (1870), which contains in addition the tragedy *Believe as You List*. An earlier edition is J. Monck Mason's (4 vols., 1779) ; and in 1840 Hartley Coleridge published a one vol. edition of the works of Massinger and Ford, with an Introduction. Mr. Arthur Symons in 1887 printed in the *Mermaid Series* five of Massinger's best-known plays, with an Introductory Essay. Gifford's edition contains a good essay on Massinger's dramatic writings by Dr. John Ferriar ; nor will Hallam's criticisms (in vol. iii of his *Literature of Europe*) be overlooked, since there was much in Massinger for which the historian entertained a genuine sympathy. A few caustic remarks by Hazlitt in his *Lectures*, &c. (p. 171) are also worth noticing. More recently Dr. S. R. Gardiner, in a paper in the *Contemporary Review* for August, 1876, reprinted in the *Transactions of the New Shakspere Society* of the same year, was the first to deal fully with *The Political Element in Massinger*; and Mr. Leslie Stephen contributed to *The Cornhill Magazine* for October, 1877, a general criticism of Massinger, which is all the more valuable, as Mr. Stephen has published so little concerning a field of literature which would benefit not a little by an occasional visitation on the part of so just a judge. The paper is republished in vol. ii of *Hours in a Library.*—See also a careful study *On Philip Massinger* by James Phelan (Halle, 1878).—Of the greatest importance for the establishment of definite results as to the dramatic collaboration of Fletcher and Massinger, and as to the characteristics of the versification and style of the latter, are the papers on *Beaumont, Fletcher and Massinger* contributed by Mr. R. Boyle to vols. v-x of *Englische Studien* and other periodicals, together with the elaborate statement of the case by the same writer in the *Transactions of the New Shakspere Society for* 1886. The first discussion of the subject had been Mr. Fleay's in the *Transactions for* 1874. Mr. Boyle is the author of the notice of Massinger in vol. xxxvii of *The Dictionary of National Biography* (1894), where the results arrived at are exhibited in a convenient form as established facts.—Mr. Fleay's conclusions are similarly re-stated in the section of his *English Drama* on Fletcher, Beaumont, Field and Massinger already cited.—As to the sources of Massinger's plays cf. E. Koeppel, *Quellen-Studien zu den Dramen Chapman's, Massinger's, und Ford's* (Strassburg, 1897).

Earl of Pembroke, and employed by him in both public and private business of importance. Whether or not, as was happily conjectured by Hartley Coleridge, Philip received his baptismal name in honour of Pembroke's famous brother-in-law, and was brought up as a page to the Countess of Pembroke herself[1], it is certain that he retained a sentiment of grateful attachment to the noble family with which his name, like that of a greater among our poets, is intimately associated[2]. The third Earl of Pembroke (the William Herbert known to Shakspere) succeeded to the title early in 1601 ; and in 1602 Massinger was entered at his father's college at Oxford, St. Alban Hall, which he appears to have quitted in 1606 without a degree. Possibly the reason was his father's death. From this circumstance, and from subsequent evidence of the straits in which Massinger is found in his London career, it may be fairly conjectured that no effective patronage was extended to him by the third Earl, who under James had taken a prominent position at Court. Gifford has thought a reason for this discoverable in the probability that Massinger, while at Oxford, was converted to the Roman Catholic faith. The internal evidence of some of Massinger's plays favours the supposition that Massinger sooner or later became a Catholic; but there is no evidence of the conversion having taken place at so early a date.

As to fifteen years—from 1606 to 1621, when *The Virgin Martyr* was, on December 7th, entered on the Stationers' Registers as by Dekker and Massinger[3],—we should be

His difficulties.

---

[1] This is suggested by Colonel Cunningham, who observes that Massinger's 'allusions to the position and minute duties of pages are perpetual.' The liveliest instance is little Ascanio (Maria) in *The Bashful Lover*.

[2] See the dedications of *The Bondman* and *A New Way to Pay Old Debts*, and the rather wooden lines *Sero sed serio* on the death of Charles Lord Herbert ; Cunningham, p. 628.

[3] *The Virgin Martyr* is the earliest play, so far as we know, openly associated with Massinger's name. *The Woman's Plot*, a comedy acted at Court in 1621, was described as Massinger's by Mr. Warburton, through whose servant it was lost with numerous other plays. (See below.) In 1653 a play was entered in the Registers under the name of *A Very Woman, or The Woman's Plot.* But it is extremely doubtful whether this was the same play as *A Very Woman, or The Prince of Tarent*, published as Massinger's in 1655. Cf. Fleay, vol. i. p. 215, and see *ante*, vol. ii. p. 743 and *note*, and below.

absolutely without knowledge of him based on any sort of external evidence, were it not that his name is appended to two documents of melancholy significance discovered by Malone and Collier respectively at Dulwich College. In the former of these, Nathaniel Field, Robert Daborne, and Philip Massinger address to their 'most loving friend Mr. Phillipp Hinchlow' a pitiful request for a loan of five pounds out of a sum of 'ten pounds more at least' to be received from him 'for the play,' declaring that he 'understands their unfortunate extremity,' and cannot be 'so void of Christianity, but that he would throw so much money into the Thames as they now request of him.' Field is the author of the main part of this document, which appeals both to Henslowe's heartstrings (to use a favourite phrase of Massinger's) and to his interests. For without the money 'we cannot be bailed, nor I play any more till this be dispatched. It will lose you twenty pound ere the end of the next week, beside the hindrance of the next new play.' But Daborne and Massinger each append a postscript Massinger's running as follows : ' I have ever found you a true loving friend to me, and in so small a suit, it being honest, I hope you will not fail us.' From a receipt given by the emissary of the three unfortunate suppliants, it further appears that Henslowe did not prove obdurate. The date of this letter is supposed to have been 1613 or 1614[1]. The other document, which was not known to Malone, consists of a bond to Henslowe from Daborne and Massinger for ' the full and entire sum of three pounds of lawful money of England,' and bears date July 4, 1615 [2]. Henslowe died in January, 1616.

Massinger and Fletcher. Malone's discovery furnishes another clue to Massinger's occupations as an author in the earlier part of his career. In his postscript to Field's petition, Daborne says: 'The money shall be abated out of the money' [which] ' remains for the play of Mr. Fletcher and ours.' Accordingly,

---

[1] This tripartite letter, which originally appeared in Malone's *Shakespeare*, is also given by Gifford, vol. i. p. 1; by Cunningham and others.

[2] It was printed by Collier in his *Memoirs of Edward Alleyn*, (Old) *Shakespeare Society's Publications*, 1841, p. 121.

some time—probably two or three years—before 1616
Fletcher had been assisted by Massinger as a playwright;
and since it is extremely probable that at all events after his
marriage in 1613 Beaumont had ceased writing for the
stage, his associate may about this time naturally have
resorted to other assistance.   Traces of Massinger's co-
operation with Beaumont and Fletcher have been thought
discoverable, dating 1611 or even 1610, but 1613 is the
earliest date which can with safety be assumed for his having
joined with Fletcher in dramatic composition.   From this
date onwards no reason suggests itself for assuming any
interruption, unless of a passing kind, in this relation between
them, although opinions may differ as to the number and
names of their joint plays.   The explicit and reiterated
testimony of Massinger's friend, Sir Aston Cokayne [1], leaves
no doubt whatever as to the notoriety, twenty years after
Massinger's death, of a literary association between the two
poets which should be taken into serious account in any
estimate of their respective achievements, although strangely
enough it has remained more or less obscured during more
than two centuries.

Throughout the greater part of their period of collaboration Fletcher and Massinger appear to have written for the
King's company of actors; but the earliest of the plays
which Massinger composed independently would appear
to have been written by him for another company (the

[1] In the lines addressed to the printer of the First Folio of Beaumont and
Fletcher, Sir Aston Cokayne complains of the injustice of designating the
volume as a whole under those two names:
    'For Beaumont (in those many) writ in few;
    And Massinger in other few; the Main
    Being sole Issues of sweet Fletcher's brain.'
In the *Epistle to Cotton* he says, in the same vein of censure, that
        'my good friend Old Philip Massinger,
    With Fletcher writ in some that we see there,'
viz. in the First Beaumont and Fletcher Folio. And in the *Epitaph on
Mr. John Fletcher and Mr. Philip Massinger* he records that
        'Plays they did write together, were great friends,
    And now one grave includes them in their ends.'
Cokayne's *Small Poems of Divers Sort* (1658), where all the above quotations
are to be found, contain further references to Massinger, from whom his
admirer in return took the hint for a play of his own (see below).

Queen's). After Fletcher's death, however, his services were
again given to the King's men, for whom, during the remaining fourteen years of his life, he produced a numerous series
of plays, partly extant, partly lost, and consisting in the main
either of compositions of his own, or of plays by Fletcher
which he had rewritten. Among that most unlucky
collection of old MS. plays, numbering together not less
than fifty-five, which were destroyed about the middle of
last century by the Omar of our early dramatic literature
execrated by posterity under the domestic designation of
'Warburton's cook,' were comprised not less than twelve
stated in the owner's list to have been written by Massinger;
and something like half that number may be concluded to
have been actual works of his, in whole or in part [1]. Inasmuch as several of the plays ascribed by Warburton to
Massinger are not mentioned in Sir William Herbert's Office-
book, the entries in which begin May 1622, the probability is
increased that Massinger had before that date been actively
engaged in the independent composition of dramatic works.

His patrons.   The rest of Massinger's biography must in the main be
built up from the internal evidence of his sentiments and
opinions derivable from his plays themselves, and from such
suggestions of facts as may be found in the Dedications to
his various patrons [2]. He appears to have cherished the
sentiment of his hereditary connexion with the house of
Herbert, whether or not it had been broken by his supposed
conversion to the Church of Rome or by any other cause,
continuing, as he says, to 'make a tender of all duties and
service' to the noble family in whose ancestral home he had
grown up. No opportunity of making the acquaintance
of Philip Earl of Montgomery and securing his good-will
appears to have offered itself until Massinger had learnt that
Montgomery had approved of his drama *The Bondman* and
helped to obtain a license for it [3]. The overture must

[1] Compare Gifford, *Introduction*, pp. xvii *seqq.*, with Mr. Boyle's conclusions. (Mr. Warburton, who held the office of Somerset Herald, had
left his collection to the care of his domestic, and intervened only at the
eleventh hour to save three plays from the doom of the companion MSS.)
[2] These have been collected by Mr. Fleay, *u. s.*, pp. 174-5.
[3] See the *Dedication* to *The Bondman*.

have been successful; for in 1634 Massinger is found
addressing a copy of verses entitled *Sero sed serio* to his
'good Lord and Patron,' who in 1630 had succeeded to
his brother's earldom of Pembroke, on the death of his
third son, Lord Charles Herbert. The Pembroke of the
Civil War and Commonwealth period—perhaps the best-
abused of that not very fortunate species, aristocrats who
seek to serve both themselves and Demos—is traditionally
known as a patron of letters and art, whose truest delight
was in the kennel and the cockpit, and as a friend of the
Puritans who scandalised the world by the flagrant immorality of his personal life. Massinger's relations with
him interest us because it has been thought that in his
political sympathies the poet, like his patron, inclined to
the popular party. In the play of *The Bondman* itself he
has been held to have satirised Buckingham and Middlesex,
to both of whom Pembroke was opposed; elsewhere he
seems to follow the turns in his patron's political attitude;
and in *Believe as You List* and in *The Maid of Honour* in
particular his support of the cause of the Palatinate, in
opposition to the mere opportunism of Weston, which the
Pembroke party from factious motives denounced, has been
thought perceptible beneath the veil of dramatic allegory [1].
Undoubtedly, as will be seen, Massinger's mind occupied
itself with political ideas and interests, and he was unable
to reconcile himself to the passive obedience theory which
was completely satisfactory to Beaumont and Fletcher. But
if, as there is reason to think probable, he was either actually
or at heart a Catholic, it is difficult to suppose that his and
Pembroke's political conceptions should have had very much
in common, or to regard any coincidence between them
as proving very much more than a natural wish on the part
of Massinger to suit his dramatic deliverances to the states-
manship of his hereditary patron.

Among the other patrons of Massinger, to whose good-
will he appeals in the Dedications of some of his plays, was
Robert Dormer, Earl of Carnarvon [2], who had been Pem-

---

[1] See Dr. Gardiner's paper cited above.
[2] See *Dedication* of *A New Way to Pay Old Debts*.

broke's ward and married his eldest daughter. Carnarvon, it may be noted, was not only a devoted royalist, who fell at the first battle of Newbury, but seems to have died a member of the Church of Rome, in which he had been originally brought up. To some of his other patrons Massinger complains, more or less bitterly, of the difficulties of his career. In the *Dedication* to *The Duke of Milan* (printed 1623) he speaks of his 'misfortunes'; in that to *The Roman Actor* his tone is similarly depressed; and in those to *The Maid of Honour* and *The Great Duke of Florence* (printed in 1632 and 1636 respectively) he explicitly declares that he 'had but faintly subsisted,' and that he 'had not to this time subsisted,' but for the bounty of those whom he addresses[1].

His collision with the Licenser.

During two years, more or less—from 1631 to 1632 or 1633—Massinger, whose means of subsistence must have, directly or indirectly, depended entirely upon the production of plays, had to 'bury his once-known name in silence[2].' It is not at all improbable, that this was due to *Believe as You List*, which in its original form the Master of the Revels had, in 1631, refused to license, on account of the 'dangerous matter' contained in it as to the deposition of Sebastian of Portugal, and as to Spanish policy in general, 'there being a peace sworn 'twixt the Kings of England and Spain[3].' It has been supposed that this indiscretion had been preceded by a previous offence of the same kind on the part of Massinger; but as a matter of fact no evidence exists to show, either that he was the author of *The Spanish Viceroy*, acted in 1624, or that the trouble in

---

[1] A secret dislike of these testimonials from author to patron seems to me discernible in some of the Dedications of Massinger's plays. In that of *The Picture* to 'my Honoured and Selected Friends of the Noble Society of the Inner Temple' he excuses himself for not mentioning their names on the ground that he 'had rather enjoy the real proofs of their friendship, than, mountebank-like, boast their numbers in a catalogue.'

[2] See the *Prologue* to *The Guardian*, which was licensed in October, 1633. Two plays are here mentioned as having suffered shipwreck; the other was doubtless *The Emperor of the East.*—As Gifford pointed out, *The City Madam* was licensed in May, 1632. Neither this play nor *The Guardian* was printed till many years afterwards.

[3] The Treaty of Madrid was signed on November 5, 1630.

which the actors were involved for originally performing that play without license, was aggravated by any allusion of political significance contained in it[1].   Henrietta Maria and the adversaries of Weston were so strongly opposed to the policy of amity with Spain that in 1634 the Queen may have had a special reason for gracing with her presence the performance of *Cleander*, a play by Massinger now lost[2]. When in 1638—the year before that of his death—another play of Massinger's which is now lost, called *The King and the Subject*[3], was before being licensed laid before King Charles I, he allowed its performance, but marked a passage in a speech by Don Pedro, King of Spain, as ' too insolent and to be changed.'

As to Massinger's relations with his fellow-dramatists, by whom as by poets of his age in general he was, according to Langbaine, ' extremely beloved,' we are without any more definite information extending beyond Henslowe's troublous *Memoranda* and Cokayne's statement as to the ' great friendship ' between Fletcher and his constant coadjutor. Whether Massinger was personally acquainted with Shak- *His relations with other dramatists.*

---

[1] The question to which reference has already been made *ante*, vol. ii. p. 530 *note*, is one of unusual complexity.   In December, 1624, the King's players were in trouble for having performed without license a play called *The Spanish Viceroy*, and humbly acknowledged their transgression to the Master of the Revels.   In 1653 an entry was made in the Stationers' Registers of a play bearing the same title, and the second title of *The Honour of Women*, and described as by Massinger.   But a play called *The Honour of Women* had been licensed, as by Massinger, in 1628 ; and it is a matter of speculation whether this was an original play by Massinger, or a revision by him of the 1624 play, and again whether the latter was written by him or by another author.   Mr. Fleay inclines to the last-mentioned opinion, and thinks that this author was Fletcher, whose original play he thinks recognisable in *A Very Woman, or The Prince of Tarent*, licensed in 1634, as by Massinger, and extant.   The entry in the Registers in 1653 of *A Very Woman, or The Woman's Plot* he regards as containing a printer's blunder, as the second title would be a misnomer as applied to the extant play.   In *A Very Woman* a Sicilian, or in other words a Spanish, Viceroy has a part ; but the play contains no trace of any allusion to Gondomar or Spanish affairs.

[2] Possibly an alteration by Massinger of the original *The Lovers' Progress* by Fletcher.   (See *ante*, vol. ii. p. 730.)

[3] Mr. Fleay, *u. s.*, p. 229, who thinks that this play was possibly the same as *The Tyrant* (one of the Warburton plays), tells us that the offensive passage ' was on the raising of supplies, &c.'

spere is a question that may be passed by ; even on the assumption that his hand is traceable in *Henry VIII*, it would be in the last degree improbable that the elder poet had any concern with this revision, supposing it to have been made in his lifetime [1].

Massinger was on terms of mutual respect and goodwill with Shirley [2]; and by still younger writers he came to be revered as a literary veteran, to judge from the instance of a droll divine whose reputation has perhaps suffered for the sins of others [3], and whom, according to the kindly literary fashion of the times, he was in the habit of calling his ' son.' With Fletcher he was to be once more associated, in his last

His death. resting-place. Massinger died in March, 1640, at his house in the Bankside, leaving behind him a widow and children ; to the former, Pembroke is stated to have continued the pension which he had allowed to her husband. He was buried, according to an epitaph by Cokayne, in the same grave as Fletcher, in St. Saviour's Church, Southwark ; but the precise spot has not been discovered [4].

*His re-
ligious and
political
tone.* What little can be added to this barren record of a fruitful life must consist entirely of deductions as to Massinger's character from the works which he has left to us. They seem to me to show that, whether or not subject during the years of his manhood to the influence of a more exacting faith than that of the national Church, he was a man of unusually sure

[1] In the mock romance of *Wit and Fancy in a Maze, or Don Zara del Fogo* (1656) cited by Gifford (*Introduction*, p. lxi, *note*), where an uproar is described among the English poets in Hades, Shakspere and Fletcher appear, accompanied by their Lifeguards, among whom Massinger and Dekker are named. The disturbance is caused by the vaunts of Ben Jonson; but the writer need not be supposed to have had in view any of the actual quarrels between Jonson and the *coterie* to which Dekker (who was associated with Massinger in the composition of *The Virgin Martyr*) belonged.

[2] See his hearty praise of Shirley's *The Grateful Servant,* and the complimentary lines addressed by Shirley to him on his *The Renegade.*

[3] James Smith, Canon of Exeter, best known by his contributions in *Wit's Recreations* and *Musarum Deliciae.*

[4] Cf. *ante*, vol. ii. p. 649.—A memorial window to Massinger was erected by public subscription in 1876 in St. Saviour's Church, which, thanks to the generous enterprise of the Rector, Dr. W. Thompson, is now further adorned by similar memorials to Shakspere, Beaumont and Fletcher, and Edward Alleyn.

and steady religious piety [1]. On the other hand, in his views of political relations he exhibits as a rule a moderate liberalism, if the term be permitted, by no means common among the dramatists, or indeed among the poets in general, of his age. With a lofty conception of the privileges and position of princes he combines a freedom from any slavish view of the difference between them and other men, and a tolerably distinct sense of the limits of their prerogative [2]. His views on foreign policy may have taken their colour from the interested designs of a faction; but to the deference formerly paid by Europe to the self-assertion of England he seems to have cast back a glance of lingering regret [3]. Experience had in any case taught him the necessity of caution; and there is no reason for supposing the powers that were to have apprehended any direct effect of his veiled allusions upon the public mind. Of such scholarship as he might have carried away from Oxford I find few traces in his plays [4]; but his versatility in the choice of dramatic

His character as a literary man.

[1] The subject of *The Virgin Martyr* naturally brings with it a flow of religious fervour. See, however, also the confession-scene in *The Emperor of the East* (act v. sc. 3) and in *The Bashful Lover* (act iv. sc. 2); and a striking tribute to a spirit of pious humility in *A Very Woman* (act ii. sc. 2 *ad fin.*). Nor is it probable that any but a Catholic would have devised the *dénouement* of *The Maid of Honour.*—No external evidence exists on the subject of Massinger's religious creed. Among his patrons one—Sir Francis Foljambe—was probably a Catholic; Sir Aston Cokayne, who was so warmly attached to his memory, certainly was one, and suffered heavy losses for the sake of his religion.

[2] See particularly *The Emperor of the East* (cf. the remarks below), and *The Maid of Honour* (act iv. sc. 5). In *The Great Duke of Florence* (see Charomonte's speech, act iv. sc. 2) it must be allowed that Massinger falls into the preposterous tone of Beaumont and Fletcher as to the demands of loyalty.

[3] See the striking passage in *The Maid of Honour* (act i. sc. 2):

> ' If examples
> May move you more than arguments, look on England,
> The empress of the European isles,
> And unto whom alone ours [Sicily] yields precedence;
> When did she flourish so, as when she was
> The mistress of the ocean, her navies
> Putting a girdle round about the world?
> When the Iberian quaked, her worthies named;
> And the fair flower-de-luce grew pale, set by
> The red rose and the white!'

[4] In the Prologue to *Believe as You List* he indeed expressly deprecates his being considered more than an ' English scholar.' But see below.

subjects seems to indicate that he was a man of considerable reading, and by no means willing to confine himself to the range of ideas with which most of his contemporaries were satisfied.   Whether his habit of self-repetition in phraseology be due to the rhetorical bent of his genius or not, it accords with other signs of a studious self-training. The severe apprenticeship through which a dramatist had to pass in this period was probably in few instances put to so conscientious a use as in that of Massinger, whose works almost uniformly bear the impress—and I think the term implies something besides a cavil—of genuine hard work. The tone of his addresses to the public is, moreover, usually characterised by a dignified modesty, contrasting with the arrogance which accompanies the book-learning of some of our dramatists.

*Mas-
singer's
plays.*
Before proceeding to notice those of Massinger's productions in which there is no reason for supposing him to have had before him a previous play by another writer, or to have joined hands with any such, it will be convenient to speak of the best known—by name at least—among his tragic works, of which a dramatist senior to himself was joint author.

*Massinger
and Dek-
ker's The
Virgin
Martyr
licensed
1620;
pr. 1621).*
The Virgin Martyr is reckoned among the earliest of Massinger's productions, a conjecture which internal evidence seems to support.   It was first printed in 1621; but already in 1620 it had been licensed, with alterations introduced into it for performance at the Red Bull.   It may be that by this we should understand that Massinger had revised an earlier play by Dekker, of whose fitful dramatic activity no other traces occur for some years before 1622 [1]. The popularity of the joint or revised play is proved by the fact that four quarto editions of it are extant, ranging in their dates from 1622 to 1661.

Dekker seems to have contributed the larger part of the play, including some very beautiful poetry as well as some

[1] Cf. Fleay, *English Drama*, vol. i. pp. 135 and 212.   Mr. Fleay suggests that the original play was *Dioclesian*, acted 1594, and not new then.

grossly ribald talk[1]. The action is simplicity itself; nor
is there the slightest attempt at refining upon the clear
purpose of the fable. The first four acts are concerned with
the martyrdom of Dorothea, whom the zealous persecutor
Theophilus in vain seeks to turn from Christianity by the
agency of his two daughters, themselves perverts. But
under her influence they are restored to the true faith;
whereupon they are put to death by their indignant father,
while the constancy of Dorothea herself is subjected to the
most material tests. The relation between her and Antoninus,
the heathen governor's son, is depicted with much pathos.
The repentance and martyrdom of Theophilus form a kind
of epilogue, which occupies the last act.

The language here and there rises to eloquence[2]; but,
upon the whole, the power of the execution is hardly equal
to the grandeur of the sentiment. As to the characters of
Hircius and Spungius, they are types of grovelling brutality;
their names have become proverbial, but they are not
drawn in the play with any extraordinary power. The
distinguishing merit of this tragedy lies in the grandeur
of the conception, which indicates a noble ambition
to rise above the level of the themes to which the
English tragedy of the age had accustomed itself and its
audiences.

Hallam suggested that the Spanish religious *autos* were
in all probability the model followed by Massinger; but
although these were the most long-lived examples of the
modern religious drama, the substance of his version of
the story of Theophilus had become the common property
of all who were acquainted with the martyrologies of
the Western Church. From some such popular source the
incidents and characters of *The Virgin Martyr* were in

---

[1] Already Charles Lamb conjectured that to Dekker is due the scene
between Dorothea and Angelo (act ii. sc. 1); and this scene, together
with the Hircius and Spungius scenes in general, is assigned to him by
Messrs. Fleay and Boyle.

[2] See particularly Dorothea's fine speech (act iv. sc. 3 : 'Thou fool,' &c.).
A beautiful passage in act iii. sc. 1, which may, like the scene just cited, be
safely ascribed to Massinger, contains an obvious reminiscence of Portia's
praise of mercy.

the main derived, with the exception of the twofold love-
story of Antoninus, and the comic adjuncts of Hircius and
Spungius.   The germ—but nothing more than the germ—
of the charming fancy of the guardian angel-page, Dorothea's attendant Angelo, may be discernible in the legend ;
Theophilus' secretary, the evil spirit Harpax, was a dramatic
invention to match [1].

The Duke of Milan *The Duke of Milan*, of which the first edition bears date
of Milan
(pr. 1623). 1623, and which was probably produced some three years
before, may be regarded as one of the earliest, if not the
earliest, of Massinger's original plays, and bears quite
unmistakeable marks of his authorship.   Although unrelieved either by pathos or by humour, this tragedy
powerfully depicts the operation of strong passions, while
suggesting a novel intermixture of public and private motives
of conduct.   The appalling effect of Francisco's versatile
villainy, like that of Iago's, remains unmitigated by the
existence of a motive for revenge (an invention of the
dramatist) ; but the change brought about in the bearing of
Marcelia by the discovery of her husband's unreasonably
selfish passion is not untrue to nature.   On the whole the
moral effect of the catastrophe exhibiting the ruinous results
of a lawless selfishness, is not impaired by what may seem
forced in the conditions of the plot ; and the skilfully contrived contrast between the politic wisdom of Duke Sforza's
public conduct with the headstrong rashness of his action in
private life introduces a welcome variation.   Yet effective
as the play is, we feel the atmosphere into which it introduces us to be overcharged, and a breath of humanity seems
wanting in order to render the treatment of such a subject
enjoyable as a work of art.   The suggestion of the horrible
scene in the last act where, imagining that she is alive, the
Duke seeks his own death from the poisoned lips of his
wife's corpse, Massinger owed to the source from which he

---

[1] Cf. Koeppel, pp. 82 *seqq.*, where a large Cologne Martyrology of the
year 1576 is shown to contain all the elements specified in the text.—In
the more ancient story (apparently Eastern in origin) of *Theophilus* (cf. *ante.*
vol. i. p. 330) the principal personage is a convert, and is served by an evil
spirit—no other in this instance than the Devil himself; but the events are
different.

took the story of his play; but he seems also to have followed in the footsteps of an earlier play [1]. It seems to bring before us the darkest aspects of the age of the later Italian Renascence; but in fact its plot was mainly founded upon a familiar episode of the Herodian period of Jewish history [2].

The Unnatural Combat (printed in 1639, and described by the author as 'an old tragedy,' and for this reason 'without prologue or epilogue') resembles *The Duke of Milan* in the horrible nature of its theme. The plot is of the gloomiest and ghastliest description, being in a word the story of a father who kills his son and entertains a guilty passion for his daughter [3]. Even more forced than the atrocity of this tragic complication is the humour, or

The Unnatural Combat (pr. 1639).

---

[1] *The Second Maiden's Tragedy* (cf. *ante*, vol. ii. p. 672 *note*), where however the effect, as if not quite adequate in itself, is eked out by the entrance of 'the Ghost, in the same form as the body in the chair.'

[2] See Koeppel, pp. 90 *seqq.* The background of the story is taken from Guiciardini's narrative of the historical conflicts between Ludovico Sforza and the Emperor Charles V, but Massinger has freely done violence to history. The true source of the plot, as was pointed out by Langbaine (p. 355), is Josephus' account (*De Antiquitatibus Judaïis*, bk. xv) of Herod the Great's deadly love for Mariamne. This theme has been frequently treated in the English as well as in other modern dramas; the earliest English handling of it seems to have been the dramatic poem in riming quatrains written by Spenser's kinswoman and patroness, Lady Elisabéth Carey or Carew, or—as seems probable—by her daughter and namesake, afterwards Lady Berkeley, and entitled *The Tragedie of Marian the faire Queene of Iewry*, printed 1613. (See *The Dictionary of National Biography*, vol. ix (1887), p. 64.) A tragedy by Gervase Markham and William Sampson, acted at the Red Bull, on the same subject, was printed in 1622. An adaptation of *The Duke of Milan* and Fenton's *Mariamne* (1723), produced in 1779, was attributed to Cumberland (Genest, vol. vi. p. 141); another adaptation of *The Duke of Milan* was performed in 1816.—F. L. Schmidt (*Denkwürdigkeiten*, vol. ii. pp. 28 *seqq.*) mentions a German version of Massinger's play, entitled *Alfonso von Ferrara*, composed map in hand by Schroeder, in order to preserve the unity of place, for which he was a great stickler.

[3] Dr. Koeppel, pp. 85 *seqq.*, has pointed out some striking resemblances between the plot of the play (the latter portion in particular) and the story of Beatrice Cenci, whose execution took place in 1599. Apart however from the absence of any indication of the form in which a report of the affair may have reached England, it would have been strange if Massinger had been at the pains of introducing material alterations into the story; nor am I satisfied that religious scruples or any other motive would have made him shrink from representing Beatrice as a parricide.

what is intended for the humour, of the 'poor captain' Belgarde ; the impertinence of the Page, on the other hand, has a lifelike ring. That there is some force in the depiction both of Malefort's endeavour to combat his own infatuation [1], and of the bestial villainy of his false friend Montreville, is undeniable ; but no robe of poetic beauty is thrown over the spectral outline of a revolting plot ; and the author, in compensation, as it were, for his inability to humanise so inhuman a theme, has to resort to a profusion of appalling effects, especially at the close, when Malefort, after being visited by the ghosts of his murdered wife and son, is killed by a flash of lightning.

The Bondman (acted 1623; pr. 1624).

The Bondman (first acted 1623, and printed in the following year [2]) is undoubtedly one of Massinger's more remarkable works. The historical background to the plot is the liberation of Syracuse from the Carthaginian danger by Timoleon, as narrated by Plutarch. After he and the youthful Leosthenes have led out the Syracusans to battle, the slaves rise and make themselves lords of the city, under the leadership of Marullo, the hero of the play. On his passion for Cleora, whom her lover Leosthenes has jealously bidden wear a kerchief over her eyes during his absence, the interest of the action turns. He controls his passion for her by a heroic effort, and thus gains her respect, which, on the return of the furiously jealous Leosthenes, passes by a natural transition into a more tender feeling. So far the intrigue is very interesting ; but when in the end it appears that the Bondman is a disguised gentleman of Thebes, whose object was to take vengeance for the desertion of his sister upon Leosthenes, till his fury was stayed by Cleora's beauty and virtue, the action loses the interest of novelty, and some of the force is taken out of the eloquent declamations on the wrongs of slaves. Of Massinger's rhetorical ability this play furnishes abundant evidence [3] ;

---

[1] See act iv. sc. 1.

[2] It was revived in 1719 by Betterton under the title of *The Bondman, or Law and Liberty* ; and again in 1779, with some alterations by Cumberland.

[3] See particularly Marullo's speech, act iv. sc. 2. The farcical flight, at the end of this scene, of the slaves, on hearing the crack of their returning masters' whips, is traced by Langbaine to a passage in Justin. Massinger's

and it is at the same time the first among his works that suggests a deliberate intention on the part of the dramatist to provoke an application to current events and characters of the invective put by him into the mouths of his characters[1].

In *The Renegado* (licensed in 1624 with the second title of *The Gentleman of Venice*[2], and printed in 1637) it is easy to recognise the influence of the religious sentiment traceable in so many Spanish dramas ; and the remembrance of the well-known fact of the five years' confinement of Cervantes at Algiers has led to the discovery of a fairly close resemblance to a Spanish play that owes much to the great novelist[3]. The scene of Massinger's drama lies at Tunis, where a Venetian Renegado, Grimaldi, has attained to a high degree of power—according to the wont of renegades in the fiction of this and of later ages. But he is disgraced, and is then with the help of a Jesuit priest reconverted to Christianity with the most satisfactory results. The vividly imagined previous history of Grimaldi—the sacrilegious act by which he became estranged both from his faith and from his native city[4]—is, so far as is known, the English poet's own invention. The Renegado however plays only a secondary part in the action, the main interest of which centres in the loves of the Venetian Vitelli and the Turkish princess Donusa. Overcome by passion, she at first tempts the Christian merchant (for as

The Renegado (licensed 1624 ; pr. 1637).

conception of the slaves shows that his popular sympathies did not carry him to excessive lengths.

[1] Dr. Gardiner has, *u. s.*, directed attention to passages alluding to Buckingham and Middlesex in act i. scenes 1 and 3, and *ib.* to the niggardliness of the House of Commons in granting money for war. Some of these passages were already pointed out by Dr. Ireland (see Gifford's edition).—According to Dr. Phelan, Archidamus' speech in act iii. sc. 1 was printed as a broadside and circulated at the time of Napoleon I's preparations for the invasion of England.

[2] The second title was changed or suppressed before the production, in 1639, of Shirley's play, *The Gentleman of Venice*.

[3] See Koeppel, pp. 97 *seqq.* Rapp first directed attention in this connexion to Cervantes ; Dr. Koeppel illustrates the use made by him of his Algiers experience in *Don Quixote* (the slave's story in Part i), and in the comedy *El Trato de Argel*. On this is said to be founded another comedy, *Los Baños de Argel*, printed in 1615, and, as it seems hardly possible to doubt, made use of by Massinger.

[4] See act i. sc. 1, and act iv. sc. 1.

such Vitelli has disguised himself), to stray from the
path of virtue ; but conscience and the influence of the
good Jesuit beckon him back ; and he is resisting her
seductions at the very moment when both are seized by
the jealous viceroy. The law offers her a chance of her
life being spared if she can make a renegade of her paramour ; instead of which she is by him converted to the
Christian faith, and baptised when both think their last
hour is at hand. The repentant Grimaldi however saves
them by a bold enterprise, and the play thus ends as
a tragi-comedy. The tone of this work is decidedly
Catholic ; and it is not a little surprising that a London
dramatist should at this date have ventured to make
a Jesuit the good angel of a stage-play. The humour of
Vitelli's servant Gazet, who in vain aspires to an office
of trust in the seraglio, is perhaps above the average of
Massinger's comic passages.

The Par-
liament of
Love (acted
1624).
Lightness of touch and vivacity of fancy might have
given an attractiveness which it cannot be said to possess
to *The Parliament of Love* (licensed for performance in
1624) ; but in truth the text has come down to us in so
imperfect a shape, that it is perhaps unjust to criticise as
it stands. This play, which has been unhesitatingly accepted
as that licensed by Massinger in 1624[1], must be the comedy
which was entered in the Stationers' Registers as by
William Rowley, and of which a MS. copy is said to
have been included in Warburton's unlucky batch. There
seems, however, no reason for concluding that Rowley had
any share in the extant work. It is manifestly, both in
its general conception and in one of its episodes, founded
upon a late French elaboration of the usage, so closely
associated with the art of the Troubadours, of Courts or
Parliaments of Love for the adjustment of questions arising
out of the cultivation of the tender passion[2]. Thus the
idea of this comedy recalls romantic conceptions belonging

---

[1] See Fleay, *History of the Stage*, p. 305.
[2] Gifford, in his Introduction to this play, referred to some of the *arrêts*
(decrees) of a Court of Love held at Troyes cited by de Sade in his
Mémoires pour la vie de François Petrarque ; but Dr. Koeppel, p. 103,

to an age very different from that which gave it birth.
Massinger was not the first or the last of our dramatists
to venture on this poetic ground[1]; but to him it was
a mere artificial enclosure. His love-cases are thus a mere
series of intrigues, hardly relieved by such conventionally
comic passages as he has managed to introduce; and the
result of his effort, which has only come down to us in a
fragmentary condition, cannot be described as pleasing from
any point of view.

The Maid of Honour was printed in 1632; but the date
of the first performance of this play can only be gathered
from internal evidence. This seems to point to the period
of the ascendancy of Buckingham, who must be at least
glanced at in the character of Fulgentio; while the allusions
to the troubles of the Elector Palatine and the hesitancy
of his royal father-in-law, which appear to underlie
the picture of the relations between the fugitive Duke
Ferdinand and the island king Roberto, suit the critical
position of affairs in 1621–2 more closely than the not
very dissimilar situation in 1634[2]. The heroine of this
well-constructed play, the story of which is adapted from
a story in Paynter's *Palace of Pleasure*, translated from the
Latin of Boccaccio[3], is the chaste Camiola. Faithful to
her love for Bertoldo, the Knight of Malta and the natural
brother of Roberto, King of Sicily, she rejects the imperious
advances of the king's favourite, Fulgentio. Bertoldo has
fallen into captivity in the course of an enterprise rashly
begun by him in a too ardent quest of glory, and sanctioned

*The Maid
of Honour
(pr. 1632).*

has shown that Massinger made direct use of the *Aresta Amorum*, a book
composed in French prose by Martial, called from his origin d'Auvergne,
about the close of the fifteenth century, and printed at Paris in 1555 with
a long Latin commentary.

[1] Dr. Koeppel refers to the trial presided over by Don Cupid (a figure
borrowed from Biron's speech in *Love's Labour's Lost*) in act v. sc. 1 of
Marston's *Parasitaster* (printed 1606); see also act iv. sc. 3 of Jonson's *The
New Inn* (acted 1629).

[2] Dr. Gardiner has assumed the later date.—Malone's assumption of the
identity of this play with *The Honour of Women* (licensed 1628, and
possibly identical with *The Spanish Viceroy*—cf. *ante*, p. 9, *note*—may be
regarded as untenable.

[3] *De Camiola Vidua* in his *De Claris Mulieribus*. See Koeppel,
p. 122.

by the king merely for the purpose of ridding himself of
his brother.   Although the king has forbidden the payment
of Bertoldo's ransom, fixed at an inordinate sum by the
captor, Camiola sends the money by a faithful follower—
and hopeless lover—of her own[1].   But the ransomed Bertoldo allows himself to be seduced from keeping his oath of
fidelity to Camiola—the condition of his ransom—by the
passionate advances of the Duchess Aurelia, against whose
interests his expedition was undertaken.   The solution of
this complication is of an unusual kind[2]; Camiola contents
herself with the repentance of Bertoldo, and takes the vows
of a nun, while he renounces all intentions of seeking a
dispensation from his own knightly obligation of celibacy.
This close adds a certain nobility to the play, and though
the solution arrived at would prove acceptable to very
few modern audiences[3], it appears to have provoked no
objection at a time when Catholic ideas might have been
expected to excite strenuous opposition.   *The Maid of
Honour* is beyond doubt to be reckoned among Massinger's
most attractive productions and those best according with
the bent of his own nature.   The comic character of 'Signior
Sylli, a foolish self-lover,' is at the same time unusually
diverting, especially in his references to his family traditions[4].

----

[1] Adorni is a fine character spoilt; Massinger, like other dramatists of his
period, works too rapidly to take much thought of his minor characters,
provided that they fit well into the action.

[2] 'For my part,' says Aurelia (act v. sc. 2), 'I cannot guess the issue';
and indeed the *dénouement* is only just sufficiently prepared to prevent it
from being what is so hazardous in a serious action,—a complete surprise.—
Dr. Koeppel, p. 123, points out that Massinger's habit of repeating himself
is exemplified by the resemblance between this Aurelia and her namesake
in *The Prophetess* (cf. *ante*, vol. ii. p. 727), in which this dramatist is supposed
to have had a hand.

[3] *The Maid of Honour* was acted at Covent Garden in 1785, in an adaptation by Kemble.   Mrs. Siddons was the Camiola, but Kemble took the part
not of Bertoldo, but of Adorni (Genest, vol. vi. p. 335).   Camiola was the
only part which Fanny Kemble, who revived the play at a later date, ever
selected for herself.   In her *Record of a Girlhood*, vol. ii. p. 118, will be
found a very able criticism of the play.

[4]   'But I, as I have ever done, deal simply;
          A mark of sweet simplicity, ever noted
          In the family of the Syllis.'   (Act i. sc. 2.)

The Page is a specimen of a type for which Massinger had a special predilection [1].

By far the best known comedy of Massinger is *A New Way to Pay Old Debts*, which was not printed till 1632, but was acted before 1626, probably in the preceding year [2]. Fletcher has, on metrical grounds, been supposed to have contributed to this play, more especially in the earlier part of it.   But the metrical evidence is not overwhelming [3], and though Fletcher had died in 1625, it is not likely that in 1632 Massinger would have assumed the entire credit of a work half written by his friend [4].   The play may be said to have more or less kept possession of the English stage since it was revived by Garrick in 1748 [5]. This enduring popularity is probably due in the main to two causes.   In the first place the chief and central personage in the comedy (Sir Giles Overreach) is a character drawn with genuine dramatic force, and is developed through a succession of effectively contrasted situations, from the height of triumph to the depth of overthrow. Secondly, this play is remarkable for a strong didactic

A New Way to Pay Old Debts (acted 1625; pr. 1632).

> ' *Fulg.*   I like a sharp wit well.
>   *Syll.*   I cannot endure it,
>   Nor any of the Syllis.'   (Act ii. sc. 2.)

[1] See *ib.*

[2] In act i. sc. 3 of *The Roman Actor* there is an unmistakeable allusion to this play, marked as such not only by the general subject of the ' covetous man,' but also by the quotation from *A New Way, &c.* (act iii. sc. 1), as to the land which it

> ' would tire
> A falcon's wings in one day to fly over.'

The Roman Actor was licensed in 1626.   On the other hand, in *A New Way, &c.* (act i. sc. 2) there is an explicit reference to the capture of Breda by Spinola in 1625.   Mr. Fleay thinks this passage was inserted by Massinger at a time subsequent to the original production of the play, and dates this before May 1622, as it is not mentioned in Herbert's entries.   It may, however, as Mr. Boyle points out, have been licensed in the interval indicated by the long gap which occurs in these entries in 1625.

[3] See Mr. Boyle's table in *Englische Studien*, vol. v. p. 92.

[4] See the Dedication to Lord Carnarvon.

[5] He did not, however, play Sir Giles himself (see Genest, vol. iv. p. 259), and the part is thus most memorably associated with Edmund Kean, who acted it in 1827.—A German adaptation by Achim von Arnim was acted at Berlin in 1821 (Goedeke, *Grundriss*, vol. iii. p. 949), and there exists also a German translation by Count Baudissin.

element, clothed in rhetoric of a very striking kind,—a combination which on the stage very frequently proves irresistible. It has been already noticed that for the general idea and the plot of this comedy its author was indebted to Middleton's *A Trick to Catch the Old One*[1]; but Massinger has adapted the progress of the action to the wholly original conception of the central character of his play.

Sir Giles Overreach is far from being a usurer of the ordinary type. As is said in the play[2]—

> 'To have a usurer that starves himself
> And wears a cloak of one and twenty years
> On a suit of fourteen groats, bought of the hangman,
> To grow rich, and then purchase, is too common ;
> But this sir Giles feeds high, keeps many servants,
> Who must at his command do any outrage ;
> Rich in his habit, vast in his expenses,
> Yet he to admiration still increases
> In wealth, and lordships.
>   He frights men out of their estates
> And breaks through all law-nets, made to curb ill men,
> As they were cobwebs. No man dares reprove him.
> Such a spirit to dare, and power to do, were never
> Lodged so unluckily.'

By encouraging his nephew's prodigality and obtaining bonds and mortgages from him, he has ruined the young man, as he has ruined every one with whom he has come into contact. He knows neither of scruples nor of pity; wisdom, except of the worldly kind, he holds in profound scorn—

> 'I would be worldly wise ; for the other wisdom
> That doth prescribe us a well govern'd life
> And to do right to others, as ourselves,
> I value not an atom[3].'

He goads his neighbours into law-suits in order that, his

---

[1] *Vide ante*, vol. ii. p. 516. The resemblances lie chiefly in the parallelism of the situations of Wellborn and Witgood, and in the behaviour of the creditors in both pieces before and after the turn in the fortunes of their debtor. Marrall the 'term-driver' in Massinger cannot be said to be borrowed from Dampit the 'trampler' in Middleton.—The name of the steward Order may possibly be taken from that of the 'Marshall of the hall' in *The Faerie Queene*, bk. v. canto ix. st. 23.

[2] Act ii. sc. 2.   [3] Act ii. sc. 1.

being the longer purse, he may be able to ruin them
and absorb their lands ; he keeps a Justice of the Peace in
his pay—   'So he serve
      My purposes, let him hang, or damn, I care not,
      Friendship is but a word[1] ;'—

he bids his henchman tempt the nephew whom he has
pauperised to crimes which may bring him to the gallows ;
in all his doings and schemes he is a ruthless fiend, without
even the one human fibre in his nature retained even by
a Shylock or a Barabas.   For the final purpose of his
ambition is, after making himself the owner of unbounded
wealth, to marry his daughter to a nobleman, and thus
to enjoy his triumph over the lords and ladies whom he
has beggared :   'There are ladies
      Of errant knights decay'd, and brought so low
      That for cast clothes and meat will gladly serve her.
      And 't is my glory, though I come from the city,
      To have their issue whom I have undone,
      To kneel to mine as bondslaves[2].'

But no love for his daughter is mixed in this design—and
in a scene which is infinitely the most powerful of the play,
although of a ghastly cynicism in its conception, he bids
her make light of her virgin purity in order to gain the end
which he has in view[3].

   Obviously, Massinger designed this character both with
the view of painting a monster of moral iniquity, and
with that of commenting on what seemed to him—perhaps

----

[1] Act ii. sc. i.
[2] *Ib.*   And cf. act iv. sc. i :
        'Now, for these other piddling complaints
      Breath'd out in bitterness ; as when they call me
      Extortioner, tyrant, cormorant, or intruder
      On my poor neighbour's right, or grand incloser
      Of what was common, to my private use ;
      Nay, when my ears are pierced with widows' cries,
      And undone orphans wash with tears my threshold,
      I only think what 't is to have my daughter
      Right honourable ; and 't is a powerful charm
      Makes me insensible of remorse, or pity,
      Or the least sting of conscience.'
[3] Act iii. sc. 2.

in part for reasons more personal than those which moved other dramatists of the age when they harped on the same string—a serious social evil.   Sir Giles Overreach is made to declare that there ever has been

'a feud, a strange antipathy
Between us and true gentry[1]'—

and it was thus sought to bring home by means of this terrible example the dangers threatening the nobility and gentry of the country from the usurpation of the wealthy commercial classes.   In the end, however, the devices of Overreach are overthrown; for, as it is finely said,

'Hard things are compass'd oft by easy means,
And judgment, being a gift derived from heaven,
Though sometimes lodged in the hearts of worldly men,
That ne'er consider from whom they receive it,
Forsakes such as abuse the giver of it.
Which is the reason that the politic
And cunning statesman, that believes he fathoms
The counsels of all kingdoms on the earth,
Is by simplicity oft over-reach'd[2].'

The nephew finds 'a new way to pay his old debts[3],' the daughter marries the husband of her choice, and the two agents of the usurer's overthrow, the good Lord Lovell and the kind Lady Allworth, appropriately pair off together. The vile tool of the usurer, Marrall, after tricking his master out of his bond, is kicked off the stage, and Sir Giles Overreach himself goes mad.   This last effect is introduced rather as an ultimate stage device than with any real intrinsic power.   Indeed, even in the finest passages of this play there is evidence of effort, such as is generally traceable in Massinger.   As for the comic character of Justice Greedy, it is too trite for its derivation to be worth enquiry.

The Roman Actor (acted in 1626[4], and printed in 1629)

---

[1] Cf. Heywood's *The Fair Maid of the Exchange*, act ii. sc. 2 :

'thou bloodhound, that dost hunt
The dear, dear life of noble gentry.'

Heywood was probably, like Massinger, born or (which is more to the point) bred a gentleman.

[2] Act v. sc. 1.   [3] Act iv. sc. 1.

[4] The allusions in the speech of Paris in act i. sc. 3 seem to show that

is one of the most interesting of its author's plays ; and it is *The*
easy to understand how it should have met with consider- *Roman*
able success on its first production, and, after being much *Actor*
lauded by contemporary poets, should have been revived by (*acted*
Betterton and at later dates[1]. Massinger himself declares 1626 ;
pr. 1629).
that he ' ever held it as the most perfect birth of his Minerva,'
and perhaps herein judged more correctly than is usual with
poets when determining the relative merits of their own
works. The subject is very happily chosen ; the authorities
(Suetonius and Dio Cassius) are used with a notable combination of care and freedom ; and the course of the action
is worked out with a sincerity of feeling for which it is not
difficult to account. There was a certain boldness in constituting an actor the hero of a tragedy, and in seeking to
show in his person how true a dignity of mind is sometimes
to be found where the world is least disposed to seek it.
Yet the experiment was not really so hazardous as it seems ;
for the glamour which surrounded the actor was as great in
the days of James as in those of Domitian, and quite independent of his social *status*, or perhaps all the more likely to
prove irresistible because of his supposed freedom from the
ordinary trammels of custom. We can hardly doubt that
Massinger, in part yielding to the temptation of the opportunity, in part seizing it in a spirit of earnestness to which
he was no stranger, not only delivered his soul on the theme
of the imputations so constantly cast on his profession, but
endeavoured to illustrate them from his own experience.
Of all the playwrights of his age, he perhaps most largely
exposed himself to the charge of endeavouring to

—' search into the secret of the time
And under feign'd names, on the stage, present
Actions not to be touch'd at ' ;

although this circumstance cannot of course invalidate the
justice of his defence that ' we cannot help it,' if what we

this play was produced after *A New Way to Pay Old Debts*, and probably
after a revision by Massinger of Middleton's *The Old Law.*

[1] It was performed (according to G:nest) in 1722 and 1796, and as a one-
act play, with the sub-title of *The Drama's Vindication*, for the benefit of
Edmund Kean, who took the part of Paris, on June 3, 1822 (*ib.*, vol. ix.
p. 132).

represent comes straight home to the individual spectator [1].
At any rate, a worthy conception of a noble profession is
here frankly and courageously assumed [2], and exemplified
in its representative, the Roman actor Paris.   After being
upheld by the favour of the Emperor Domitian against the
timorous censures of the Senate, he falls a victim to the
tyrant's jealousy, provoked (not unnaturally) by the infatuation with which the actor's art has inspired Domitian's
chosen mistress, Domitia, the divorced wife of Aelius Lamia.
But the despot himself respects the artist in the supposed
rival ; and takes his life, as it were deferentially, in the
course of a dramatic scene enacted by Paris and himself.
This device of a play within the play, or rather a scene
within the scene, is employed not less than thrice within
the compass of this tragedy [3]; and yet so ingeniously is
its use varied, and so effectively is the series brought to
a climax, that even in this respect the construction deserves
high praise.   The overthrow of Domitian himself, which
forms part of an episode of some power, though accompanied by an unnecessary apparition of ghosts, serves as
a fitting close ; and there is sufficient individuality in the
character of the tyrant, and sufficient reality of passion in
that of Domitia, to furnish impressive contrasts to the

---

[1] See the speech of Paris before the Senate, act i. sc. 3.   It is here that
occur the references to Massinger's own plays noticed above.

[2] ' *Aesop.*   For the profit, Paris,
          And mercenary gain, they are things beneath us. . . .
    Paris. Our aim is glory, and to leave our names
          To aftertime.' (Act i. sc. 1.)

[3] Act ii. sc. 1, where the ' Cure of Avarice, filch'd out of Horace ' (*Satires*,
bk. ii. 3. vv. 141 *seqq.*), fails to convert the old miser Philargus ; act iii. sc. 2,
where Paris as Iphis bewitches Domitia in an interlude taken from Ovid
(*Metamorphoses*, bk. xiv. vv. 698 *seqq.*); and act iv. sc. 2, where the Emperor,
determined to kill Paris, commands him to play

          ' but one short scene—that, where the lady
    In an imperious way commands the servant
    To be unthankful to his patron : when
    My cue 's to enter, prompt me.'—

As Dr. Koeppel suggests, *Hamlet* may have suggested the device; or, for
that matter, so may *The Spanish Tragedy.*—A curious parallel to Massinger's
use of it is mentioned by Ste. Beuve (*Port-Royal*, ed. 1867, vol. i. pp. 147
seqq.) In Rotrou's *Saint Génest comédien païen représentant le mystère d'Adrien*
the converted actor identifies himself with the martyr whom he enacts.

tranquil dignity of the hero of the tragedy, enhanced as it is by effective opportunities for the display of his artistic power.

In *The Picture* (licensed in 1629, and printed in the following year) we are once more taken back to one of those comedies of violent intrigue of which the drama of this period is so peculiarly prolific. The fable of this play may, as the old quarto asserts, be a 'true Hungarian story'; it was, however, taken in substance by Massinger from a novel by Bandello translated in Paynter's *Palace of Pleasure*[1]. Massinger has added the character of the ambitious Queen Honoria [2].

The Picture (acted 1629; pr. 1630).

The rather ingenious plot described below is not ineffectively worked out; though as usual Massinger has but little true pathos or humour at command for interesting us in the persons of the action, besides stimulating curiosity by the turns of the action itself. The honest old councillor Eubŭlus is a good representative of a type much affected by Beaumont and Fletcher, and indeed by many other dramatists.

---

[1] Bandello, i. 21; Paynter, ii. 28 (Koeppel).—Alfred de Musset used the same foundations for *Barberine*, a play written with his usual originality of manner.

[2] The plot deserves summarising.—Mathias, a poor knight of Bohemia, on sallying forth to relieve his poverty by the meed of warlike achievements, obtains from his friend Julio Baptista, a great, or as he is in the play (act i. sc. 1) still more appropriately termed, 'a general scholar,' a picture of his wife Sophia, which possesses the magic property of changing its hues according to the variations of sentiment and conduct in the conjugal fidelity of its original. Husband and wife are at heart true to one another; but their fidelity is in either case exposed to sore temptations. Mathias' heroic exploits in the service of the King of Hungary bring him to the notice of the imperious Queen Honoria, whose haughty temper brooks no rivalry, and who on hearing Mathias' praises of his wife is moved by pride—not by love —to tempt him in person to infidelity, while at the same time seeking to seduce Sophia from the path of virtue by means of two lying courtiers, sent to her with false reports of her husband's conduct. Sophia is thus made to waver in her constancy; and on the picture revealing to Mathias the condition of her mind, he is likewise about to give way to the supposed passion of the Queen. But Sophia's virtue is proof against the dangers by which it is beset; and the two courtiers are deservedly caught in their own toils. The Queen sees the error of her ways, and becomes the submissive wife of her uxorious husband; while Sophia, after reading Mathias a severe lesson on the wrongfulness of his jealous fears which caused him to provide himself with the test of the picture, is restored to happiness.

The rascally courtiers Ubaldo and Ricardo are too offensive to be amusing [1].

The Great Duke of Florence.

The Great Duke of Florence (licensed in 1627, and printed in 1635) exhibits a skilful treatment of a theme with which the English stage was already familiar; for there cannot be any doubt that Massinger in this instance transplanted into the favourite Italian soil the story of a popular English play [2]. But an air of refinement not usual in Massinger graces this re-fashioning of old material in a new and ampler form. Duke 'Cozimo' has magnanimously to pardon both his nephew and heir Giovanni and his favourite Sanazarro, each of whom had for his own purpose sought to hide from him the truth as to the charms and virtues of Giovanni's love, Lidia, the daughter of the young prince's tutor. The character of Lidia herself, although not wholly free from artificiality, reveals a true maidenly purity such as is but rarely imaged in the drama of this period; and passages in this play approach—it cannot perhaps be said that they attain—to poetic pathos [3]. The humour of Calandrino, Giovanni's servant and a would-be courtier, is a favourable specimen of a hackneyed, not to say exhausted, type [4]. The

---

[1] It is however a good touch when on their bringing to Sophia the news of her husband's safety and prosperity, and her returning thanks to Heaven, Ubaldo (full of evil thoughts) sagaciously observes,

> 'I do not like
> This simple devotion in her ; it is seldom
> Practised among my mistresses.
> *Ricardo.*   Or mine.
> *Would they kneel to I know not who,* for the possession
> Of such inestimable wealth, before
> They thank'd the bringers of it? the poor lady
> Does want instruction.' (Act iii. sc. 2.)

[2] See *ante*, vol. ii. pp. 609-10, as to *A Knacke to Knowe a Knave* (printed 1594).

[3] See *e. g.* Calandrino's speech (act i. sc. 1), 'For had I been your equal,' &c. ; and his fancied farewell to his hopes of happiness by her side (act v. sc. 3).

[4] See the conclusion of the play, where Calandrino obtains the Duke's consent to his marriage on the plea that a *desideratum* of the contemporary stage may be thus supplied :

> 'Why, the whole race
> Of such as can act naturally fools' parts
> Are quite worn out; and they that do survive
> Do only zany us.'

political allusions in this play, if they are such, are too casual and indirect to call for special comment.

The Emperor of the East (licensed in 1631, and printed in the same year) appears to have been at first ill received, but after being reproduced at Court, to have grown into favour[1]. Upon the whole, the earlier and less favourable judgment would seem to have been the more correct one. The plot of the play is a version—which towards the conclusion becomes extremely free—of a very curious chapter of Byzantine history. Part of this story might at first sight, according to Gibbon's expression, be 'deemed an incredible romance,' while an episode embroidered on it by Greek inventiveness—viz. the story of the migratory apple—is, in the opinion of the same historian, 'fit only for *The Arabian Nights*, where something not very unlike it may be found[2].' But Massinger has not made any very successful use of a strange and, in its way, fascinating story, or invested with any marked interest the character of the Empress Eudocia, which well deserved original dramatic treatment. The struggle for supremacy between Pulcheria, the sister of the Emperor Theodosius the Younger, and the youthful rival whom her influence had raised from a suppliant's place to a share of the imperial throne, forms merely an episode of the drama, instead of its central action. The Emperor's jealousy of his kinsman Paulinus, while trivial in its origin[3] and bombastic in the expression given

The Emperor of the East (acted and pr. 1631).

---

[1] See the *Prologue at Court*:
'And yet this poor work suffered by the rage
And envy of some Catos of the stage.'
It has already been pointed out that this was probably one of the two plays to whose ill-success reference is made in the *Prologue* to *The Guardian*.

[2] See Gibbon, *Decline and Fall*, ch. xxii, and cf. Finlay, *Greece under the Romans*, pp. 174–6 and *note* as to authorities.—Dr. Koeppel, *u. s.*, pp. 126 *seqq.* (who also refers to Gregorovius' monograph *Athenaïs*, 3rd ed. 1892), shows that Massinger may have used a French translation of Zonaras published in 1583, as in this writer and Cedrenus occur all the incidents in the first four acts of the play. The incident of the apple is in Cedrenus, but not in Zonaras. For its appearance in *The Arabian Nights* see *The Story of the Three Apples* in Dalziel's *Illustrated Arabian Nights' Entertainments*, pp. 141 *seqq.*—The story of Eudocia was again dramatically treated in Lee's *Theodosius, or The Force of Love* (see below).

[3] 'All this pother for an apple,' the flippant Flaccilla not inappropriately

to it [1], is strangely enough not permitted by the dramatist to bring about the tragic consequences which it historically entailed ; indeed his *dénouement* approaches the borders of comedy by representing the supposed paramour of the Empress as not only laid up with gout [2] but otherwise the reverse of dangerous. On the other hand, the scene in the last act in which Eudocia is confessed by her husband disguised as a friar, and thus enabled to vindicate her virtue to his satisfaction, is happily imagined, and seems to follow with the bent of the dramatist's mind in matters religious [3].

A scene of this play, where Massinger with some humour parodies the elaborate titles of Byzantine court etiquette, Pulcheria taking occasion to banish the ' Minion of the Suburbs ' and the ' Master of the Habit and Manners [4],' as well as the Projector, gives vigorous utterance to opinions which seem strange in a play received with favour at the Court of Charles I [5]. But perhaps the passage need not

observes (act i. sc. 5). Of course the operation of an apple, like that of a handkerchief, may be saved from triviality.

[1] See the speech of Theodosius (*ib.*) : ' What an earthquake I feel in me ! '

[2] This incident is taken from some of the Byzantine authorities. At this point of the action, a poor attempt is made to create a comic diversion in Jonson's manner by the introduction of an Empiric who professes to cure all diseases.

[3] Could it have been suggested by a scene which leads to a directly opposite result in Peele's *Chronicle of Edward I* (cf. *ante*, vol. i. p. 369 *note*) ?

[4] Of the ὀφφίκια τοῦ παλατίου τῆς Κονσταντινουπόλεως a full account will be found in J. H. Krause, *Die Byzantiner des Mittelalters*.

[5] ' *Pulch.*   Projector, I treat first
     Of you and your disciples ; you roar out,
     All is the King's, his will above his laws ;
     And that fit tributes are too gentle yokes
     For his poor subjects : whispering in his ear
     If he would have their fear, no man should dare
     To bring a salad from his country garden
     Without the paying gabel ; kill a hen,
     Without excise : and that if he desire
     To have his children or his servants wear
     Their heads upon their shoulders, you affirm
     In policy 'tis fit the owner should
     Pay for them by the poll ; or, if the prince want
     A present sum, he may command a city
     Impossibilities, and for non-performance
     Compel it to submit to any fine
     His officers shall impose. Is this the way
     To make our emperor happy ? ' &c.

be taken as showing more than that the surroundings of
the King were not so conscious as later historians have
been of the general tendencies of the financial policy
which he felt himself compelled to pursue. Elsewhere the
Emperor is made to give expression to a nobly-conceived
invective against the flattery which seeks to make kings
believe themselves omnipotent[1]. Finally, it may be noticed
that this play contains a lyric which appears to me of
a beauty very unusual in Massinger, whose compositions
of this kind are as a rule commonplace[2].

 Believe as You List was supposed to have been one of
the plays of Massinger irretrievably lost to posterity
through Warburton's cook, when it was fortunately recovered in 1844[3]. Beyond all doubt this play, which was
licensed in May 1631, was that which in the January preceding Sir Henry Herbert had refused to license, 'because
it did contain dangerous matter, as the deposing of Sebastian, King of Portugal, by Philip II, and there being a
peace sworn betwixt the Kings of England and Spain.'
Don Sebastian's adventures had been made known to English
readers in a pamphlet published so far back as 1601 by the
ingenious Anthony Munday, and an elaborate French
narrative, which was either used by Massinger or which was
based on the same original as his dramatic version of the
story, had appeared in 1605[4]. But the peace with Spain
was not quite two months old when this play first came
before the licenser. The trust of King Charles in the
promise of her moral support in his endeavours for the
restoration of the Palatinate was not shared by the great

Believe as You List (licensed 1631).

---

 [1] See Theodosius' speech (act v. sc. 2) :

'Wherefore pay you
Such adoration to a sinful creature?' &c.

 [2] Eudocia's song, which, like Desdemona, she sings before her expected
catastrophe : 'Why art thou slow, thou rest of trouble, Death?' (act v. sc. 3).

 [3] It was edited for the Percy Society in 1848 by Crofton Croker, and has
since been reprinted in a more correct form by Colonel Cunningham, to
whom is due the identification of its subject with the story of Don Sebastian
of Portugal (see *Introductory Notice*, p. xiv).—An examination of the text
will be found in a contribution to the (Old) *Shakespeare's Society's Papers*,
vol. iv (1849).

 [4] See the parallel passages cited by Koeppel, *u. s.*, pp. 155 *seqq.*

body of his subjects, and least of all by the opponents of his administration—opponents whose attention was by no means concentrated on constitutional questions ; and a widespread fear prevailed that he might be made the dupe of the same courteous but really immoveable diplomacy that had foiled the statecraft of his father [1]. The temptation was therefore great, while insinuating the applicability of the incidents of the play to 'a late and sad example,' to intermix allusions which might bear a still more closely interesting interpretation [2].

The hero of this tragedy is 'Antiochus, King of the Lower Asia, a fugitive' at Carthage, who after his defeat by the Romans is supposed to have taken flight to India, where he 'spent many years with the gymnosophists,' and who now after two-and-twenty years of wanderings re-appears to make his identity known. The Carthaginians are in doubt whether to place credit in him ; but the Roman ambassador Flaminius prevails, and King Antiochus has to seek a refuge with King Prusias of Bithynia. Pursued to this court by the Roman, he is delivered up to his implacable foe. Flaminius craftily endeavours to make him renounce his claims—employing the wiles of a courtesan for the purpose—but the royal sufferer remains firm. In the end he is recognised as the true Antiochus by a Roman proconsul and his wife, to whom he had of old showed high favour at his court. Flaminius is disgraced ; but the King himself is doomed to death [3].

---

[1] Like his father, too, he kept up an understanding with the other side,—in the person of Gustavus Adolphus, who had entered Germany in the summer of 1630.

[2] See *Prologue* ; and cf. Gardiner, *u. s.*, pp. 320 *seqq.*

[3] It is hardly worth while to observe that no such adventures ever befell any Antiochus, and that the historical names and relations mixed up in the action are a mere deception which 'any schoolboy' could expose. Indeed in his Prologue the author warns the audience that if they

> 'find what's Roman here,
> Grecian or Asiatic, draw too near
> A late and sad example, 'tis confest
> He's but an English scholar ; at his best
> A stranger to cosmography, and may err
> In the country's names, the shape and character
> Of the person he presents '—

The theme of *Believe as You List* is in itself eminently
suitable for tragic treatment, and indeed in some sense
belongs to a class of subjects which has proved attractive
to more than one dramatist of mark [1]. It will however be
observed that Massinger (notwithstanding the title of his
play) has no intention of leaving any doubt as to the true
royalty of his hero, upon whose martyr-like dignity he has
concentrated the interest of his drama, while the energy
of Flaminius and his 'intelligence department' is in its
turn held up to odium. The scene is powerfully conceived,
in which the famished King is touched by the supposed
compassion of his female visitor, till he recognises in her
a vile agent of his enemy's craft [2]; and considerable skill
is shown in the contrivance of the catastrophe, where, after
being recognised by Marcellus and his wife, the King is

---

and, as already observed, Antiochus is really no other than King Sebastian
of Portugal, the son of a daughter of Charles V, whose expedition against
Morocco ended in the terrible massacre of his whole army. Whether he
had himself fallen on the field of battle, remained doubtful; and not less
than four persons afterwards made their appearance in Portugal, which had
fallen into the hands of Spain, claiming to be the lost Sebastian. One of
these appeared twenty years after the battle, and after many strange
adventures was consigned to the galleys at Naples and died either here or
in imprisonment in Castile. The mysterious fate of Don Sebastian is referred
to in Beaumont and Fletcher's *Wit at Several Weapons* (act i. sc. 2).—As to
Dryden's *Don Sebastian* see below, chap. ix.—It is no doubt very probable
that many passages in *Believe as You List* are seasoned by allusions to the
Palatinate question and the hesitation (not very justly) imputed to Charles I
about doing his best on behalf of his unfortunate brother-in-law, then near
the close of his troubled course ; possibly too the energy of the ' Queen of
Prusias' may have been intended to reflect honourably upon Henrietta
Maria. But we should I think err in supposing that an appeal to popular
sentiment was designed by allusions so cautiously contrived that authority
could not have ventured to lay a finger upon them; at the utmost they
were to the address of a select few, whose perception of their meaning
could do little good to *any one*, except perhaps the author.—The author of
the contribution to the (Old) *Shakespeare Society's Papers*, cited above,
suggests that the application to which the Prologue refers is to the sufferings
of King Charles I, and that the Prologue was added to the play on a revival
after the Restoration.

[1] See below as to Ford's *Perkin Warbeck*.—' All ages,' says Flaminius
(act ii. sc. 2),   ' have been furnished
             With such as have usurped upon the names
             And persons of dead princes.'

[2] Act iv. sc. 5.

consigned to death by the very man who has been honourable enough to recognise his identity. The recovery of this play has certainly added to the list of Massinger's worthiest dramatic efforts.

The City Madam (acted 1632; pr. 1653).

The City Madam, licensed in 1632, was not printed till 1653. I cannot agree with the contention that either the versification or any other internal indication points to the authorship of any other writer than Massinger[1]; nor bring myself to believe that this play was not written by the author of *A New Way to Pay Old Debts*, with which it is distinctly cognate in sentiment. The character of Luke Frugal, although inferior in force to that of Sir Giles Overreach, is dramatically effective, and is said to have had a marked success in the hands of an eminent actor of our own day, whose Overreach is more generally remembered[2]. Luke Frugal, after leading the life of a prodigal, has become a recipient of his brother's charity. As such, he hypocritically assumes the character of a submissive and smooth-tongued dependant, and ingratiates himself impartially with the well-disposed and the evil-disposed alike[3]. But he is suddenly subjected to the crucial test of the inheritance of all the wealth of his brother, who has pretended retirement into a monastery. He is now at once transformed into a monster of selfish avarice, and on the promise of untold gains even consents to send his sister-in-law and her daughters to Virginia, to be offered up as sacrifices to the

[1] See, however, Fleay, *English Drama*, vol. ii. pp. 225-7. The passage in the *Prologue* to *The Guardian* already adverted to cannot, however, be very literally interpreted, if *The City Madam* was written by Massinger, and Mr. Fleay has adduced some plausible reasons for concluding that in its original form this play was produced at a much earlier date than 1632.

[2] The late Mr. Phelps.—*The City Madam*, after being revived in 1783, was brought out in 1810 in an adaptation by Sir John Bland Burges (who afterwards took the name of Lamb), under the title of *Riches, or The Wife and Brother*, who in his preface to the published play did scant justice to his original. (See Genest, vol. viii. pp. 163-4.) In this shape it was acted as late as 1822.—The characters in Thomas Thomson's *Mother Shipton, her Life*, printed about 1668, except those connected with Mother Shipton, are said by Halliwell-Phillipps to be taken from *The City Madam* and Middleton's *Chaste Maid in Cheapside*.

[3] His advice to the apprentices (act ii. sc. 1) comes very near to that of the Unjust Steward in the New Testament.

Devil himself. In the end his brief dream of wealth and
power of course collapses ; while the trials to which they
have been subjected effectually cure his brother's wife
(the ' City Madam [1] ') and her daughters of their ridiculous
pride and pretensions. The sketches of these frivolous
city ladies—a *famille Benoîton* of earlier days—of the idle
and worse than idle apprentices, and of divers other personages of varying degrees of disreputableness, are very
entertaining, and recall similar figures of Middleton's. By
way of contrast, the honest country-gentleman Plenty offers
a pleasing picture of the effect of those wholesome conditions of life towards which a decaying society is frequently
admonished by its censors to turn a hopeful glance [2].

The Guardian, as has been already seen, was produced
in 1633, after an interval of several months, during which
Massinger had abstained from bringing any production of
his on the stage ; and the *Epilogue* too betrays a certain
want of confidence in the success of this renewed effort.
This play, however, when repeated at Court early in 1634,
is said to have been ' well liked '—no proof of the refinement of the tastes prevailing there. The complications that
make up the plot of this farcical comedy are cleverly enough
unravelled ; but the species of which it is an example is not
pleasing to modern taste, and the bluff old gentleman
who gives its title to the play cannot be approved as the
exponent of a highly praiseworthy morality. The honourable system obtaining among the banished Severino's band
of outlaws recalls the traditions of Robin Hood ; the device
of the supposed saving miracle [3] seems to have been
borrowed by the dramatist from a more recent English
tale, or more probably from an English translation of an
Italian version of a collection of Indian fables [4].

*The
Guardian
(acted
1633;
pr. 1655).*

---

[1] In *The First Part* of *Edward the Fourth* by Thomas Heywood, Mistress
Blague says to Mistress Shore :
> ' The name of Mistrisse is a pretty thing,
> But Madam at each word doth glory bring.'

Both words have, however, had their vicissitudes.

[2] See Plenty's speech (act i. sc. 2) : ' 'Tis quite contrary,' &c.

[3] Act iii. sc. 9.

[4] Sir Thomas North's version (1579) of Doni's *Fables of Bidpai* (Koeppel,
p. 143).

The Bash-
ful Lover
(acted
1636;
pr. 1655).

The last of Massinger's plays preserved to us, *The Bashful Lover*, was licensed 1636 and printed in 1655. It is said to have been well received and to have been frequently acted[1]. No other of Massinger's plays commends itself by a more effective mixture of abundant incident and noble sentiment than this romantic drama, which from a theatrical point of view well deserved the success it achieved. Two plots are skilfully combined in it—the one (of unknown origin) being concerned with Honorio's modest love for the Princess Matilda, the other with the wronged Maria's recovery of her repentant seducer. In Honorio, whose timidly reverential love conceals a chivalrous spirit capable of great deeds, but who even after performing them is ready to renounce his reward for the sake of the lady of his heart, Massinger furnishes a nobler type of character than is usual either with him or with most of his contemporaries; and in the adventures of Ascanio-Maria, who, like Viola, can tell 'a pretty tale of a sister[2],' he has found a subject of which the pathos seemed to be unable to wear itself out. Some other more or less distinct reminiscences of Shakspere occur in this play. The course of the action is in both main- and bye-plot determined in favour of the right; and the conqueror of Matilda's father, who holds the Princess herself in his power, pays a tribute to virtue surpassing the traditional self-denial of Scipio. If, in spite of all this, the reader rises from a perusal of this play but moderately moved, the reason doubtless is that, even with so excellent a subject and in so skilful a treatment, the mainly rhetorical genius of Massinger was unable to pass beyond its bounds. In the dialogue there is too much argument, too much unction, and too much protesting; while, though so many opportunities are at hand, no single situation is seized and brought home with really impressive power. Yet the elevation of sentiment that marks Massinger's last work justly entitles

---

[1] It was unsuccessfully revived in 1798 in an adaptation entitled *Disinterested Love*, said to be by the actor and dramatist Thomas Hull. (See Genest, vol. vii. p. 370.)

[2] See the charming little scene, act ii. sc. 1.

it to a more than passing notice among the productions of
the later Elisabethan drama [1].

Of the numerous plays in which Massinger either co-
operated with another dramatist or dramatists, or which may
be taken to represent a more or less thorough recasting by
him of earlier works, by far the largest and most important
group has been dealt with in my previous chapter. Positive
external testimony shows that such plays were known to
exist [2]. They cannot in sum have fallen far short of a score,
if we may take them to comprise all those which were formerly ascribed to Fletcher, or to Beaumont and Fletcher,
but which are now assigned to Fletcher and Massinger, by
what in the majority of instances is an irresistible *consensus*
of modern critical opinion. As to the respective shares of
these two authors in the plays in question, the problem is
not always one that can be solved with certainty, even
by the application of tests in themselves reasonable and
useful. The metrical peculiarities of Fletcher and Massinger
respectively are not distinguishable with the same degree
of certainty. Fletcher indeed, in his later plays at all events,
had accustomed himself to a style which was no longer
capable of disguising itself; but Massinger's more sparing
resort to feminine endings, and his preference for the
practice (contrary to that habitually adopted by Fletcher)
of carrying on sense and sentence from line to line, are
only relatively characteristic, and very far from infallible,
marks. The mental and moral qualities of Massinger's
work are less easily mistakeable; but the brief review of
his unassisted plays attempted above will have sufficed to
show how often he assumed features that were not his own ;
and the critic is yet unborn whose power of divination will
enable him in every case to distinguish between Fletcher
and Massinger imitating him.

Joint plays by Massinger and Fletcher.

---

[1] It has been assumed that the application in act iv. sc. 2 of 'a late example'
of a merciless commander on whom the hand of Heaven has rested heavily, is
to Wallenstein, who was assassinated in February, 1634. The passage does
not fit Wallenstein particularly well; on the other hand, Tilly's death,
which had occurred as far back as April, 1632, can hardly be referred to.

[2] Cf. *ante*, p. 5.

HenryVIII and The Two Noble Kinsmen. To these plays I do not, with a single exception, propose to return, nor need I enter afresh into the question of Massinger's supposed association with Fletcher in *Henry VIII*, as that play is preserved to us, and in *The Two Noble Kinsmen*[1]. In the former case, I fail to see the necessity for complicating the difficulty as to Shakspere's sole authorship by introducing the supposition of a tripartite division. In the latter, I cannot deny that the hypothesis of Massinger's co-operation appears to me plausible. I am strongly disposed to believe that Fletcher was assisted by another writer, and incline to think that the writer in question was not Shakspere. But though in parts of this play I must suspect another hand than Fletcher's, the marks of Massinger which they have been held to display are not to my mind absolutely convincing[2].

Massinger and Fletcher's(?) A Very Woman, or The Prince of Tarent licensed 1634. Reference has already been made[3] to the difficult question as to the authorship of *A Very Woman, or The Prince of Tarent*, licensed in 1634 as by Massinger alone. Undoubtedly, not only the versification, but the passionate flow of language[4], in parts of this play, furnish a strong support to the supposition of Fletcher's co-operation. The psycho-

---

[1] Cf. *ante*, vol. ii. pp. 206, 242, 744, 746; and see Mr. R. Boyle's papers in *New Shakspere Society's Transactions*, 1880–6, Nos. xviii and xxi.

[2] Cf. above, p. 691, as to *Love's Cure, or The Martial Maid*, in the versification of which Fletcher's hand is most easily traceable, while the suggestion of Middleton's co-operation with Massinger has not met with acceptance.

[3] Cf. *ante*, vol. ii. p. 74; and vol. iii. p. 3, *note*.

[4] See, for instance, the speech of Cardenes (act i. sc. 1): ' No, I'll be plainer,' &c.; and most especially Antonio's narrative (act iv. sc. 3): ' Not far from where my father lives,' &c. I notice that Mr. Boyle ascribes both these passages to Massinger; but assuredly the latter, if anything in the play, bears the impress of Fletcher's style. The bold poetic beauty of Almira's answer to her cousin's attempt to convince her that Cardenes is not dead seems to me equally beyond Massinger, and appropriate to Fletcher:

> ' I know you,
> And that in this you flatter me; he's dead,
> As much as would die of him :—but look yonder!
> Amongst a million of glorious lights
> That deck the heavenly canopy, I have
> Discern'd his soul, transform'd into a star.
> Do not you see it?'

If the versification of the above is not strikingly Fletcherian, that of Almira's subsequent outburst of ' light-headedness' is I think unmistakeably such. The fine lines defining ' the height of Honour' (act iv. sc. 1), which are likewise attributed by Mr. Boyle to Massinger, seem to suit him well.

logical problem which the title announces, and the conditions of which are playfully indicated in the opening scene[1], turns on the change that may, against the laws of strict logic, be wrought in a woman's heart by patient devotion, even on the part of a lover previously rejected by her in favour of a rival. This theme is worked out with considerable power[2]. The Prince of Tarent, who in the first act has wounded —as he thinks, to death—his favoured rival Cardenes, contrives in the guise of a slave to win the love which as a prince he could not secure. Cardenes, on the other hand, is by his malady and its cure[3] converted to a philosophy which teaches him at once to resign and to forgive. The comic element in this play is supplied by the ill-regulated 'governess' Borachia, whose indomitable love of wine is presented after a most unsavoury fashion.

The tragedy of *The Fatal Dowry* was printed in 1632 with the initials of Massinger and Field, who in all probability took part in the performance of the play. This would fix the date of its production at a date not later than 1619[4],

Joint plays by Massinger and other writers: Massinger and Field's The Fatal Dowry (pr. 1632).

[1] Almira here declares herself loth to lose 'The privilege of my sex, which is my will,' in order ' to yield a reason like a man.'

[2] Dr. Koeppel, pp. 144 *seqq.*, following a suggestion of Rapp's, shows it to be probable that the dramatists made use of *El Amante Liberal*, one of the *Novelas Exemplares* of Cervantes.

[3] Having temporarily lost his senses, he is restored by the art of the physician Paulo. Massinger here finds another opportunity of extolling a profession in which he appears to have taken a strong interest. (Cf. *The Emperor of the East*, act iv. sc. 4, and *The Bashful Lover*, act v. sc. 1.) Paulo's request that a college for physicians of the right stamp may be founded as the only recompense which he asks for curing his prince, may contain an allusion to the Royal College of Physicians in London, which had been incorporated in 1518.—Massinger may possibly have derived the first idea of the episode of the prince's malady and cure from Ford's *The Lover's Melancholy* (1628) ; but as has been seen, *A Very Woman* is probably founded on an earlier original, and in any case Massinger's treatment of the incident differs altogether from Ford's.

[4] Field is not known to have acted after Burbage's death.—In act ii. sc. 2, a scene almost certainly as written by Field, the age of the actor who took the part of Florimel is referred to as thirty-one ; this would again suit 1619, as Field was baptised in October, 1587. See Fleay, *English Drama*, vol. i. p. 208, where it is suggested that the play as we have it is an alteration by Massinger of the earlier play of *The Judge*. In distributing the scenes o this play between the two authors, Collier thought Gifford had been hasty in setting down Field as the author of ' all that he thought unworthy of

which would also suit an incidental allusion. *The Fatal Dowry* has enjoyed considerable celebrity, owing largely to the fact that it was copied (without acknowledgment) by Rowe in a tragedy which long retained its popularity on the stage[1]. Massinger and Field's play has perhaps in consequence received at least as full a meed of admiration as was its due. If some of its characters possess more individuality than belongs to the large majority of Massinger's dramatic characters, the construction is less happy than in the case of many other plays of his. Our sympathy is to be sure powerfully engaged at the outset on behalf both of the noble Charolais, who, rather than allow his dead father's body to fall a prey to his creditors, himself submits to imprisonment[2], and of the generous Rochfort, who, in striking contrast to his worthless successor in office, takes pity on the young man, and not only redeems him from bondage, but bestows on him, with an ample dowry, the hand of his beloved daughter Beaumelle. Romont, Charolais' blunt, outspoken friend, is likewise a character drawn with much vigour, although of a sufficiently familiar type. But when, after this extremely promising opening, the action proper of the play commences, and Beaumelle falls a victim to the seductions of a contemptible fribble[3]—the son of the unjust judge Novall—her guilt remains so wholly without excuse or 'motive' as to find no atonement, in a dramatic sense, even in her repentance and death. Not but that in real life a Novall at times leads a Beaumelle astray; but such an amour is a moral excrescence, and a mightier wave of repentance than the authors had it in their power to image forth would be needed to wash

Massinger' (see Introduction to Field's *A Woman is a Weathercock* in *Five Old Plays*); but the prose at least may be safely attributed to Field. Messrs. Fleay and Boyle are substantially at one as to the distribution.

[1] See below as to *The Fair Penitent*.

[2] The idea of this sacrifice, as has been pointed out by several commentators, is clearly taken from the story of Cimon, the son of Miltiades.—In a long criticism of Massinger's and Rowe's plays (reprinted in Gifford's edition), Cumberland compares the very effective 'silence' of Charolais on his first appearance to that of Hamlet.

[3] A genuine Lord Foppington, down to the very 'O lard!' See act iv. sc. 1.

off so disfiguring a stain. But although the close of the
fourth act hardly meets so high a demand as this, yet
neither feeling nor power are absent from the great scene,
in which after a penitent confession Beaumelle is sentenced
by her father and slain by her husband. The fifth act, on
the other hand, in which Charolais justifies his conduct
before a bench of judges, is merely rhetorical in conception
and execution; the catastrophe, his death, is brought about
so to speak organically by the hand of a faithful follower of
the seduced ; and the moral drawn from the whole affair is
to the last degree trite and tame [1].

Of *The Old Law* (in which on the title-page of the comedy
as published in 1656 Massinger was said to have co-operated
with Middleton and William Rowley), mention has already
been made among Middleton's plays [2]. If Massinger had any
share in the revised version of this comedy, which was in all
probability originally produced three years before he was
entered at College, it cannot have been more than trifling.

Middleton, William Rowley, and Massinger's(?) The Old Law.

Some of his plays, lost by Warburton's domestic, have
been thought identifiable with other plays that are actually
in existence ; but into these conjectures, which from the
nature of the case must be hazardous, I forbear from
entering [3].

Massinger appears to me to furnish a signal illustration
of a connexion between cause and effect on which it is
unfortunately not superfluous to insist. The moral dignity
of his sentiment is at once the basis and the source of much of
his highest dramatic effectiveness. This observation seems
even more applicable to some of his later plays—including

Massinger's moral earnestness an element in his dramatic power.

---

[1] See the final speech of the advocate Charmi :
> ' We are taught
> By this sad precedent, how just soever
> Our reasons are to remedy our wrongs,
> We are yet to leave them to their will and power,
> That, to that purpose, have authority.'

[2] *Ante*, vol. ii. p. 501.

[3] See the list of 'Plays alleged to be lost' at the close of Mr. Boyle's
article in the *Dictionary of National Biography* ; and cf. the notes of
Mr. Fleay, especially as to *The Wandering Lovers, The Tyrant,* and *The
Spanish Viceroy.*

the last that is extant from his hand—than to such a production as *The Virgin Martyr*, where the nature of the subject almost necessarily implies the nature of its treatment. In Massinger we seem to recognise a man who firmly believes in the eternal difference between right and wrong, and never consciously swerves aside from the canon he acknowledges. It may be, as already said, that this frame of mind was in Massinger's case strengthened by the fact of his having sought the support of a form of Christianity which is more unwilling than any other to allow its adherents to walk alone. In any case Massinger's morality is solidly founded and consistently maintained.

His themes and the principles illustrated by them.

In Massinger's plays the conflict between lust and chastity is a frequent theme, though by no means so pre-eminently or even exclusively as in the case of other of our Elisabethan dramatists. Fortitude inspired by religious conviction; endurance steeled by the consciousness of a righteous cause; tyranny punished by its own excess; masculine self-control rising superior to the command of resistless authority; the spirit of honour calmly asserting itself amidst the collapse of fortune; a woman's renunciation of a love that she has recognised as unworthy of her; a man's victorious endeavour to quiet the tumult of imperious lust, or the siren voice that seeks to enervate the resistance that is in him,—such are, as he represents them, some of the moral forces that help to determine the crises of human life. And in truth, the poet— and the historian likewise—who fails to see that such forces as these must be reckoned with not less than gusts of passion on the one hand, and the operation of physical laws and the incalculable hazards of circumstance on the other, takes but a very one-sided view of human life. Massinger's strength— at least his relative strength among the dramatists of the age into which he had been born and bred—lies largely in his perception of these moral forces, and in his regard for them.

His defectiveness in characterisation;

In semblance, at least, the gusts of passion of which I have spoken are not missing in Massinger's repertory of dramatic effects. His male characters show avarice, jealousy, and their sister furies driving the victims of their influence towards death or confusion; and his women are frequently, though not

I think so exclusively as has been contended, thralls to the lower dictates of desire.   Hazlitt observes, with some point, if not without exaggeration, that Massinger's ' villains are a sort of *lusus naturae* ; his impassioned characters are like drunkards or madmen.'   Dr. Gardiner[1] concludes that Massinger is incapable of rising to a conception, at once simple and lofty, of virgin virtue—though if we were to search the literature of the stage, which directly appeals to the immediate impulses of its public, we should have to mount to rare heights before finding such a conception realised.   The truth simply is that Massinger fell short of conspicuous success in exhibiting the successive stages of a moral conflict, and in thus securing personal sympathy to his representation of its progress, by means of the developement of character in action.   Thus he fails to satisfy the highest test of dramatic power.   He constantly displays a laudable wish to present virtue under an attractive, and vice under an unlovely, aspect ; but he lacks variety of light and shade such as would induce us to take to our lesson as easily as we should to one of the stories without a purpose which he joined Fletcher in adapting to the stage.   In the plays where he had an entirely free hand, some of the chief personages seem labelled with the qualities they are intended to typify; there is no mistaking them as *dramatis personae* ; the sole difficulty lies in remembering that they are intended to stand for human beings like ourselves.   This want of the supreme power of characterisa- *in humour:* tion partly springs from the absence of humour noticeable in Massinger.   In comedy he is rarely successful, except in isolated figures of an intensity which resembles the kind of portraiture which we expect from the counsel for the Crown.   The character of Sir Giles Overreach is powerfully drawn, but with the sole purpose of irresistibly attracting our hatred ; Luke Frugal is an inferior, but still very successful, effort of the same sort.   Massinger's minor comic characters, except where they are to all intents and purposes conventional, are often merely repulsive.

[1] *History of England, &c.* (ed. 1884), vol. vii. pp. 327, 337.

and in pathos. If he lacks humour, he is almost equally deficient[1] in those deeper movements of feeling which we recognise or desiderate, as the case may be, where great dramatic opportunities are placed in readiness for them. No whirlwind of emotion seems to sweep through his most vehement declamations, no fire to burn beneath his most ample and at times luxurious eloquence. If the designs in which his villains lay to chastity are carried out with the deliberation that marked the military sieges of his age, so at times is the defence which they necessitate. A certain coldness seems to belong even to his noblest conceptions and to his most earnest moments. From the Virgin Martyr to the ill-starred royal fugitive (in *Believe as You List*) there is something wanting in the most powerful situations and in the most attractive characters of this author to excite the deepest sympathy,—to move the source of tears.

Rhetorical character of his genius. The genius of Massinger is, in a word, essentially rhetorical. In illustration of this contention, I may point to a curious peculiarity marking the construction of several of his plays. He seems to like nothing better than to work up the action to the reality or semblance of what may be described as a judicial issue, thus obtaining an excellent opportunity for indictment and defence, rebutter and rejoinder, and final judicial summary. Probably the consciousness of his special powers induced him so frequently to create such occasions for their exercise[2]. But he has another note of the rhetorician,— or, since it was detected in one of the great masters of eloquence[3], shall I say of the orator? This is his frequent recurrence to phrases and turns of expression which he may be said to have made his own, and the use of which came at all events to form part of his stock-in-trade[4]. It

---

[1] There are no doubt in Massinger characters and passages—as in *The Bashful Lover*—which have the ring of true pathos. But the ring is very like an echo.

[2] So besides *The Parliament of Love* (where a trial naturally springs out of the plot), in *The Great Duke of Florence*, in *The Maid of Honour*, and twice in *The Fatal Dowry*.

[3] 'Nolo irridere *rotam Fortunae* et *ius verrinum* et illud tertio quoque sensu in omnibus orationibus pro sententia positum " *esse videatur* ".' Tacitus, *De Oratoribus Dialogus*, c. 23 (of Cicero).

[4] My immediate reference is to such phrases as 'to wash in Aethiop';

may be urged that great poets have not been strangers to the habit of self-repetition in small things as well as in great; but few readers of Massinger can have failed to observe the extent to which he, as compared with our other Elisabethans, indulges in it. More careful investigation than that which had first led me to notice this peculiarity in him has proved that Massinger's usage of returning upon himself is altogether abnormal; and no real parallel to it is to be found in our poetical literature[1].

In general, the style of Massinger is strong rather than *His diction.* rich, and exhibits the qualities of an eloquence at once apt and intense rather than that of spontaneously impassioned poetry. Hallam compared the effect produced by the designed redundancy of his style to what by painters is, or was, called *impasto*. Fine and appropriate imagery is by no means rare in Massinger; but for much of this he *Massinger* may unhesitatingly be said to be indebted to Shakspere. *and* *Shakspere.* His familiarity with the plays of the greatest of his contemporaries is indeed astonishing; it has been said of Massinger with but slight exaggeration, that 'there is hardly a page of his writings but contains more than one allusion to his master[2].' And the indebtedness of the younger dramatist extends to almost every part or aspect of his dramatic work—to the formation of his plots, to the colouring of his characters, to his diction and to his versification.

In this last, he not so much holds the mean between *Mas-* Shakspere and Fletcher, as continues—in the sense in which *singer's* *versifica-* an inferior artist can be said to continue the manner of *tion.* a greater—Shakspere's last and maturest form of verse; nor can it be shown that he is wont to lapse into the more

---

an 'embryon' for an unperfected design; and the commonplace as to 'friends, though two bodies, having but one soul.'

[1] I cannot pretend to have examined the one-thousand parallel passages which Mr. Boyle has collected from Massinger's works—including of course passages in those parts of the 'Beaumont and Fletcher' plays in which he is held to have had a share,—or to follow the critic in all his deductions; but the general effect of the enquiry (*New Shakspere Society's Transactions* and *Englische Studien*) is extraordinary.

[2] See Mr. R. Boyle on *Massinger and the Two Noble Kinsmen, u. s.,* p. 373. Some of these Shaksperean reminiscences had been previously traced by Ferriar, in his essay printed by Gifford.

dissolved rhythm and monotonous cadence of his most frequent associate in composition. Hence, in critical questions, the great difficulty of determining whether a passage or section of a play be Shakspere's or Massinger's, unless it be remembered that the test of versification is, in the last *His con-* resort, only subsidiary and not decisive. In construc-
His con-
structive
skill.
tion Massinger appears to me a very skilful artist, and less prone than most of his contemporaries to a wearisome alternation in the conduct of two parallel plots to a combined issue; indeed many of his plays—and it is to their advantage—are virtually constructed on the lines of a single plot. He is more careful than Fletcher—whose voice may fairly be concluded to have been as a rule authoritative in the planning of the plays which the pair undertook in common— as to the use of materials discovered with the aid of a trained instinct; and he is more ready to apply, though not always successfully, his own inventive powers to the shaping of a satisfactory conclusion.

His various
and fre-
quently
happy choice
of subjects.
Finally, it should be pointed out, that the more Gifford's insufficient efforts to explore the sources of the subjects of Massinger's plays are supplemented by the researches of later scholars, the more the remarkable variety of these sources becomes evident. The learning which this dramatist expends upon the treatment of a subject unusual or remote in respect of place or circumstances—such as *The Roman Actor*, *The Emperor of the East*, *The Renegado*, or *Believe as You List*— is never in itself remarkable, and his fondness for 'applying' events and characters of the past to the politics of the present suffices to prove how little he has in him of the historic sense. But he has taught himself the art of surrounding the actions of his plays with an imposing drapery of period and place; and one of the causes of the long-continued attention commanded by his dramatic works is no doubt to be sought in the versatility and skill displayed by him in his choice of themes. Another lay in his openness to interests which the drama had long treated as outside its province, but which no writer who sought to interest his public could any longer ignore. But a permanent place is secured to him in our dramatic literature because of greater

qualities than these. He is not, I think, to be ranked among the most gifted of Shakspere's successors; but in the absence of high poetic genius he may be said to have compassed the noblest results which it lay within his power to achieve as a dramatist, and to have laboured in his art— take his works for all in all—in a spirit honourable both to that art and to himself.

NATHANIEL FIELD has already been mentioned as joint author with Massinger of *The Fatal Dowry*, and as involved in some of his and their friend Daborne's troubles in days when Henslowe's help was their common anchor of hope. He may be said to have been more conspicuous, or at least more active, as an actor than as an author[1]. He was born in the City of London in 1587 as the son of a minister who, four years previously, had taken the opportunity of a calamitous accident at Paris Garden (then used for the baiting of bears and bulls) to publish a diatribe against theatrical entertainments[2]. This John Field's elder son, Theophilus, ended as Bishop of Hereford, having largely devoted himself to the quest of preferment; as a poet he is obscure. The younger, Nathaniel, began his connexion with the stage as one of the Children of the Queen's Revels (afterwards known as the Children of the Chapel Royal); and in this capacity performed in 1600 and the following years in Jonson's *Cynthia's Revels* and in other of his plays. In 1607 he is found acting the important part of Bussy d'Ambois, the hero of Chapman's tragedy of that name; and this may help to account for the good-will displayed towards 'his loved son, Nat. Field' by Chapman in some rather crabbed commendatory lines (not devoid of a reference to Homer) prefixed to Field's first play, *A Woman is a Weathercock*, which must have been produced in or before 1610. He continued to perform in some of Jonson's plays, notably in

Nathaniel Field (1587– 1633). His life, and celebrity as an actor.

---

[1] The two plays by Field noticed in the text are printed, with Introductory Remarks, in Collier's *Five Old Plays* (1833) and in vol. xi of Hazlitt's *Dodsley*. For a biographical account of Field see the revised *Life* in Collier, vol. iii. pp. 345 *seqq.*, and the notice by Mr. Joseph Knight in vol. xviii of *The Dictionary of National Biography* (1889).

[2] The elder Field died a few months afterwards.

Catiline (1611) and in *Bartholomew Fair* (1614), in which latter play he is unequivocally complimented by the author[1]. Shortly after this he seems to have joined the King's Players, with whom he acted as the associate of Burbage till the death of the latter in 1619. Of his merits as an actor no doubt can be entertained, although as has been seen they were unable to preserve him, at all events before he had been admitted into the King's Company, from the vicissitudes so common to members of his profession[2]. His name is included in the list of ' the principal actors in all these plays ' prefixed to the First Folio edition of Shakspere.

Nothing certain is known of the later years of Field's career, except that he was married and had children. His conjugal life seems to have been unhappy, unless the point of an epigram beginning—

> ' Field is, in sooth, an actor—all men know it,
> And is the true Othello of the poet—'

ought to be set down to pure malice on the part of the facetious author[3]. He seems to have retired from the stage some time before 1625—probably some years earlier[4]; at all events his name is not included in the patent issued on the accession of Charles I to the throne. He died in February, 1633—in what circumstances, remains unknown.

His plays: A Woman is a Weather- cock (pr. 1612). Field's two extant plays were both produced while their author was still a young man and actively engaged in his profession as a player. The earlier of them, *A Woman is a Weathercock*, by the tone of its humorous *Dedication*[5] and *Address to the Reader*, as well as by the style of the

---

[1] 'Which is your Burbage now?' 'What mean you by that, sir?' 'Your best actor, your Field?' (act v. sc. 3).

[2] Cf. *ante*, p. 4.—In Flecknoe's *Short Discourse of the English Stage* (printed in 1664) the names of Burbage and Field are once more coupled, in a tribute such as any player might envy. 'In this time were poets and actors in their greatest flourish; Jonson and Shakespeare, with Beaumont and Fletcher, their poets, and Field and Burbage, their actors.' (Collier, vol. iii. p. 429 *note*.)

[3] The entire epigram is quoted by Collier, p. 437.

[4] See above, p. 39, as to the date of *The Fatal Dowry*.

[5] 'I did determine,' it begins, 'not to have dedicated my play to any body, because forty shillings I care not for'—certainly, as Collier remarks, a rather awkward boast under the light of Field's share in the application to Henslowe, made only a year or two afterwards.

comedy itself, bespeaks the confidence of youth. Both this play and *Amends for Ladies*, of which internal evidence proves the date of composition to have been 1610 and that of production 1610 or 1611 [1], are alike characterised by a curious combination of recklessness and *aplomb*, notwithstanding that the latter comedy professes, like another *Legende of Good Women*, to be antithetical in tendency to its predecessor. It is impossible to read either play, or for that matter the contributions by which Field cannot be said to have greatly enriched *The Fatal Dowry*, without perceiving that he knew his audience as well as he knew his stage, and could safely indulge in the freedom permitted to an acknowledged favourite.

Both these plays mingle serious elements with comic ; but in the earlier the serious passages are overlaid with an excess of rhetorical invective, while in each the comic are in part extremely coarse. The construction is, however, easy and effective in the later, and more complicated, as well as in the earlier drama ; and the wit of the writing is frequently very pointed and fresh. *A Woman is a Weathercocke*, printed in 1612, and first produced on the stage not long before its successor, tells the story of a faithless latterday Cressid. Her lover, however, brings her back to him by dint of persistency and with the aid of a tolerably unscrupulous friend, who had formerly substituted himself for the priest on the occasion of her marriage with the wealthy Count Frederick, and had thus rendered it a mock ceremony. Interwoven with this intrigue are two under-plots—in one of which the merchant Strange very vigorously brings to book Captain Ponts, who has aspersed his bride's honour; while in the other Sir Abraham Ninny (a kind of Sir Andrew Aguecheek—' my father is a Ninny, and my mother was a Hammer ') falls a victim to the energy of Mistress Wagtail. The progress of the main plot itself would be more interesting had the author been able to introduce an element of true pathos in the place of some of his hero's complaints against woman's fickleness.

A Woman is a Weathercock (acted by 1610 : pr. 1612).

[1] See Collier, vol. iii. p. 104, and cf. *ib.* 429 ; and Fleay, *English Drama*, vol. ii. p. 185.

Amends for Ladies (acted 1611; pr. 1612).

In order to make 'Amends' to a sex never very tolerant of satire against itself, Field, as he had promised in the *Dedication* to his earlier piece, produced his other comedy[1]. *Amends for Ladies* displays in the persons of the Ladies Honor, Perfect, and Bright the virtues most appropriate to their several conditions, by which they are called throughout the play,—of Maid, Wife, and Widow. While recognising the author's good intentions, the reader is not likely to find much pleasure in the means chosen for testing the excellence of the last two personages of the trio[2]; but the self-sacrificing fidelity of the Maid is touchingly exhibited. The treble plot is managed with considerable skill; and apart from objections on which there is no necessity for dwelling, the comedy merits high praise as an effective and in its design healthy work. A character with whom we have met before—the heroine of Middleton and Dekker's *Roaring Girle*—is quite superfluously introduced into one of the scenes by way of an incidental attraction (although she is here represented in an unfavourable light[3]). Another special gratification for the audience (which likewise seems to be referred to in the title-page of the edition of 1639) was doubtless intended by the scene[4] where Lord Feesimple is taught the art of 'roaring'—a scene the broad humour and the coarseness of which is hardly surpassed

---

[1] The Wife's complaint (act ii. sc. 2) might have without injustice been echoed by Frenchwomen, in a period of French dramatic literature of which the influence has not yet died out:

'Oh, men! what are you? why is our poor sex
Still made the disgrac'd subjects in these plays
For vices, folly and inconstancy,
When, were men look'd into with such critical eyes
Of observation,' &c. (Act ii. sc. 2.)

[2] Collier points out that the plot concerned with the Wife is borrowed from the story of the *Curioso Impertinente* in *Don Quixote*. This, unless Field read Spanish or French, helps to date the composition of the play. (Cf. *ante*, vol. ii. p. 680.)—It is conceivable that the general idea of this triple tribute was suggested to Field by Samuel Rowland's humorous dialogue *'Tis Merrie when Gossips Meete* (1602), which has in its turn been conjectured to have been possibly founded on the *Debate between a Wife, Widow and Maid* in Sir John Davies' *Poetical Rhapsodies* (also 1602).

[3] See act ii. sc. 1. This again points to a date in or near 1611.

[4] Act iii. sc. 4.

by anything similar in Smollett[1]. Good taste is, however, more signally offended by certain other passages in this play, excellent though it is in purpose and in many respects admirable in execution.

In passing onward to JOHN WEBSTER[2], we come into the presence of a poet to whom a foremost place has been rarely denied among the later writers of the great age of our drama, and in whom it is impossible not to recognise a genius of commanding originality, though apparently of not very versatile powers. It is most unfortunate that but few plays should have been preserved of which he was the sole author; for it is in these that his most distinctive gifts stand forth with incomparably the greatest clearness, and, as is pointed out by the most adequate of his modern critics, he seems, like Shakspere and Jonson, to have preferred to work alone.

John Webster (died 1650 c.).

Of Webster's life extremely little is known. From the Dedication to his *Monuments of Honour*, a pageant produced in 1624 in honour of a Lord Mayor who was a member of the Merchant Tailors' Company[3], Webster appears himself to have been 'one born free of' it. On the strength of this solitary fact, he has been provided with a father and a mother, as well as with a wife and a daughter. Gildon's statement that he held the office of clerk at St. Andrew's,

His life.

[1] Another nobleman who appears in this piece (Lord Proudly) is not a contemptible character; but there is a striking degree of severity in the comments (act iv. sc. 4) on the impunity attaching to noble offenders against the law in the matter of duels. Outbursts of this kind are so rare in this age as to make this vigorous passage worth noting.

[2] *The Works of John Webster; with some Account of the Author, and Notes.* By the Rev. A. Dyce. New edn. 1857.—*The Dramatic Works of John Webster.* Edited by William Hazlitt. 4 vols., 1857.—A selection of plays by Webster and Tourneur, with an Introduction and Notes by the late J. A. Symonds, forms one of the volumes of *The Mermaid Series.*—A brief notice of Webster by Mr. Swinburne is reprinted from *The Encyclopaedia Britannica* in his *Studies in Prose and Poetry* (1894). By far the best critical study of this dramatist with which I am acquainted is that by Mr. E. W. Gosse, reprinted in his *Seventeenth-Century Studies* (1883).

[3] This pageant concludes with a declaration on the part of the author, that he 'could a more curious and elaborate way have expressed himself,' had he not been desirous of avoiding to 'trouble my noble Lord' and 'puzzle the understanding of the common people.'

Data of his career as a dramatist. Holborn, remains unconfirmed by other evidence. Henslowe's *Diary* however supplies us with a few data as to the earlier part of Webster's career as a dramatist, which he must have begun before May, 1602, when he is found engaged together with Munday and others upon a play called *Caesar's Fall*[1]; other plays by several hands, now lost, with which his name is connected by Henslowe, are *The Two Harpies* (or whatever else may be the correct reading for the title '*too harpes*' given in the *Diary*) and *Christmas comes but once a Year.* Both belong to 1602.

His co-operation with other playwrights. Webster occasionally engaged in co-operation with other playwrights. He contributed to *The Famous History of Sir Thomas Wyatt*, or at least to the First Part of the play in two Parts called *Lady Jane*, of which *Sir Thomas Wyatt* appears to have been an abridgment[2]. He also joined Dekker in the composition of the two rollicking comedies, *Westward Ho* and *Northward Ho*[3]. A tragedy, now lost, by him and Ford[4] —perhaps an old play of his re-fashioned by the latter— called *A late Murther of the Sonn upon the Mother*, was licensed in 1624. It remains, as will be seen, a disputed point, whether he combined with William Rowley in at least one of the pieces attributed to their joint authorship. In 1604, he supplied the second edition of Marston's *Malcontent*, which was augmented by the author himself, with an Induction, and perhaps with other additions[5].

His literary friends and patrons. With his brother dramatists (as well as with the actors who appear in the Induction just referred to) he seems in general to have been on good terms. He 'ever' (as he says in the remarkable passage in the Address prefixed to *Vittoria Corombona*, where he gives a kind of estimate of several among his dramatic contemporaries) ' truly cherished his good opinion of other men's worthy labours'; he

---

[1] Mr. Fleay, *English Drama*, vol. ii. p. 269, states that the name Webster in the passage in Henslowe's *Diary* (November 3, 1601), where the play *The Gwisse* is mentioned, is a forged interlineation. (Collier, vol. iii. p. 202, says it is interlined ' perhaps in a different hand.') *The Guise* must therefore be Marlowe's *Massacre at Paris*, and Webster's play of the same name, mentioned in his Dedication of *The Devil's Law-Case*, must belong to a later date.—As to *The Weakest goeth to the Wall, vide infra.*

[2] Cf. *ante*, p. 468.   [3] Cf. *ante*, p. 469.
[4] Fleay, *u. s.* p. 273.   [5] Cf. *ante*, p. 483.

addresses some encomiastic lines, the versification of which
has been praised as in advance of their age, to Munday
(as a translator) and to Thomas Heywood (as author of the
Apology for Actors); in return, his brother dramatists,
Middleton, Rowley, and Ford, hail his masterpiece (*The
Duchess of Malfi*) with warm acknowledgments. Towards
the public Webster appears to have borne himself with
a conscious pride resembling in some degree that of Ben
Jonson; nor can a tendency to under-estimate his own
powers have been one of his weaknesses[1]. Whether he
enjoyed the favour of other patrons of rank besides those
to whom he dedicates one or two of his plays, we do
not know ; the lines in memory of Henry Prince of Wales
seem to point to some token of good-will having been
received from the Prince by their author[2].

These sparse *scintillae* convey all the information we
possess concerning the personal life of Webster[3]. The date
of his death is quite unknown, but no trustworthy trace of
him occurs later in date than his pageant in honour of his
brother Merchant-Tailor, the new Lord Mayor of the year
1604[4]. It is quite unlikely that he survived the suppression
of the theatres ; since it is ridiculous to suppose him, on
evidence which, short of identity of names, is nugatory, to
have been the author of two puritanical tracts and a volume
of sermons—all of which appeared in 1653–4, when the

---

[1] See the addresses prefixed to *The White Devil* and to *The Devil's Law-Case*.

[2] See *A Monumental Column, &c., ad fin.* The poem contains one or
two vigorous passages—in particular those in which slander and ' waste
elegies' are alike waved aside from the Prince's tomb, and a fine compliment is paid in passing to ' his sweet Homer and my friend'—Chapman.

[3] The supposition that he had at one time graduated at one of the Universities is based on the discredited identity to be referred to immediately. It
is therefore perhaps hardly worth while to observe that Webster seems
occasionally to manifest an acquaintance with University matters (see *The
Devil's Law-Case*, act ii. sc. 3, and cf. *ib.*, act i. sc. 2, the mention of a burden
which, unfortunately, for many a day to come was to continue to lie heavy
on our Colleges :

'Letters of commendations!
Why, 'tis reported that they are grown stale,
When places fall i' th' University').

[4] The will of ' John Webster, cloth-worker,' was made in August 1625,
and proved in the following October.

great dramatist may be computed to have been upwards of seventy years of age [1].

Among plays in which Webster had a hand, those in which he was associated with Dekker have been already noticed. *Sir Thomas Wyatt*, or Webster's share in it, can perhaps hardly be judged with fairness in the condition of the *congeries* which has come down to us. *Westward Ho* and *Northward Ho*, though by no means devoid of raciness of humour, would certainly fail of themselves to raise Webster's fame as a dramatist to a high level.

A Cure for a Cuckold, published in 1661 by the bookseller Kirkman as 'an excellent old play' by Webster and William Rowley, is thought by Dyce to be rightly assigned to their joint authorship [2]. Except on metrical grounds (which in this instance call for special caution), I should be disinclined to accept Mr. Gosse's conclusion that Webster's share in this play is so clearly distinguishable from Rowley's as to warrant its being separated off as an ' idyll,' for which he proposes the pleasing title of *Love's Graduate*. Undoubtedly this portion of the play exhibits a power of giving expression to an unusual refinement as well as elevation of sentiment ; and for the exercise of this power opportunity is most ingeniously furnished by the almost super-subtle con-

[1] See Dyce's *Introduction.* The titles of these productions were *The Saint's Guide* (1653), of which the author describes himself as an army-chaplain; *Academiarum Examen* (1654), to which there appeared two answers; and *The Judgment Set, and the Bookes Opened* (1654). To the *Academiarum Examen* two answers appeared. In the second of these, an anonymous ' reverend acute Logician,' who was joint author of the tract with Thomas Hall, says: 'This Mr. Webster (as I suppose), is that Poet whose Glory was once to be the Author of Stage-plaies (as *The Devil's Law-Case*), but now the Tutor of Universities.' Thomas Hall's assumption that this supposition is correct has evidently no critical value. And, as Dyce puts it, why were he and his coadjutor not at the pains of verifying their benevolent hypothesis? A further complication arises from the circumstance that the author of the *Examen* is unmistakeably identifiable with John Webster of Clitheroe, the author of *Metallographia* (1671) and *The Displaying of supposed Witchcraft* (1677), who was in all probability a Cambridge man and who records experiences singularly appropriate to an army-chaplain in time of war. Dyce's researches which have led to these results must not be passed by; lest the question as to the dramatist having written the three 1653-4 tracts should be regarded as still open.

[2] I confess myself at a loss to perceive on what grounds Mr. Fleay flatly denies Webster's joint authorship.

ception of the story of Clare and of her oracular injunction
to her lover[1]. There is no need for dwelling upon the
comic plot from which this comedy derives its ribald title;
but I can remember few pieces of the same description
which contain a more thoroughly diverting character than
that of the worthy mariner Compass, who returns from a
three years' voyage to find that many things beyond comment, although as it proves not beyond cure, have happened
during his absence. The whole business, including the
legal consultations with the attorneys Pettifog and Dodge
and a long-winded counsellor in the Three Tuns Tavern[2],
is extremely comical, and in parts resembles Molière's
most delectable expositions of the humours of ill-starred
husbands[3].

The same bookseller, Kirkman, to whom we owe (together with divers other services to our dramatic literature)
the preservation of the play just noted, in the same year put
forth *The Thracian Wonder* as a play written by Webster
and William Rowley. Dyce, Collier, and Fleay alike reject
the supposition that Webster had any hand in it; and, as
Collier suggests, Kirkman's assertion may have had its
origin in the fact that in 1617 one *William* Webster published a reproduction of the story of Argentile and Curan
from Warner's *Albion's England*, which story (itself connected with those of *Havelok the Dane* and of many later
romantic fictions) in some degree resembles the plot of *The
Thracian Wonder*. This 'comical history,' as it calls itself,
is uninteresting; the fulfilment of an obscure and complicated oracle being in any case ill adapted for the basis of
a dramatic action.

Webster (?) and William Rowley's (?) The Thracian Wonder (pr. 1661).

A play called *The Weakest Goeth to the Wall* (entered
on the Stationers' Registers in 1600; Hazlitt had however
seen no edition earlier than 1618) has been attributed, in
the first instance by Edward Phillips, to Webster conjointly

Webster (?) and Dekker's (?) The Weakest Goeth to the Wall (pr. 1600?).

[1] The resemblance (pointed out by Genest) of the situation to one in
Massinger's *Parliament of Love* is striking; but the plots take a different turn.

Webster, as observed below, seems to have been specially fond of
satirising the practitioners of the law.

[3] See *e. g.* a scene in which Compass learns his fate from two boys, of the
true river-breed, whom he meets on his return to 'sweet Blackwall.'

with Dekker. But the authority is worthless [1]; and the state-ment certainly derives but slight support from anything in the play itself. At the same time it may be noticed as a not unpleasing production. The romantic action, derived from the first story in Barnabe Rich's *Farewell to Militarie Profes-sion* (1581), and opening with a dumb show of unparalleled fulness [2], keeps up the reader's interest, and some homely humour of a genuine ring is supplied by honest Barnaby Bunch, who robustly sustains among Frenchmen the honour of 'England, where the poor may have a pot of ale for a penny, fresh ale, firm ale, nappy ale, nippitate ale, irregular, secular ale, courageous, contagious ale, alcumistical ale.' Neither in the humour nor in the pathos of this play is there anything which recalls Webster's manner ; in the former respect however it bears a certain resemblance to the handi-work of Dekker.

Plays by Webster only : The White Devil, or Vittoria Corombona (pr. 1612).

Of the two plays of Webster in which his tragic genius has produced its most potent effects, *The White Devil, or The Tragedy of Paulo Giordano Vrsini, Duke of Brachiano, with the Life and Death of Vittoria Corombona, the famous Venetian Curtizan*, first printed in 1612 and perhaps acted 1607-8 [3], is the earlier. Although I cannot agree with those who regard this tragedy as the masterpiece of its author, it is beyond all doubt a most remarkable work. Its plot as well as its characters appears to have been borrowed directly from an Italian source, inasmuch as the history of the Duke of Brachiano and his two wives, of whom the second bore the name of Vittoria Accorambuoni and was the widow of the nephew of Cardinal Montalto, afterwards Pope Sixtus V, does not appear to have been reproduced in any English or French version [4].

---

[1] See Dyce's Introduction, p. xvi, *note*.

[2] 'After an Alarum, enter, one way, the Duke of Burgundy; another way, the Duke of Anjou with his power ; they encounter: Burgundy is slain. Then enter the Duchess of Burgundy with young Frederick in her hand, who, being pursued by the French, leaps into a river, leaving the child upon the bank, who is presently found by the Duke of Brabant, who comes to aid Burgundy when it was too late.'

[3] See Fleay, *u.s.*, vol. ii. pp. 269-70.

[4] The story is told in 'Stendhal's' *Chroniques et Nouvelles* (Vittoria Accoram-buoni), Paris, 1855 ; and in J. A. Symond's delightful *Italian Byways* (1883),

This extraordinary tragedy, whose finest scenes and passages have, in the judgment of Mr. Swinburne, been never surpassed or equalled except by Shakspere ' in the crowning qualities of tragic or dramatic poetry,' must be described as at once highly elaborated and essentially imperfect. In the address *To the Reader* already referred to, Webster confesses with conscious pride that this play was the fruit of protracted labour; but his efforts appear to have been directed rather to accumulating and elaborating effective touches of detail than to producing a well-proportioned whole. The catastrophe seems to lag too far after the climax; and in spite of the mighty impression created by the genius of the author, it is difficult to resist a sense of weariness in the progress of the later part of the action. But a yet more serious defect appears to me to attach to *Vittoria Corombona*. The personages of this tragedy—above all that of the heroine—are conceived with the most striking original power and carried out with unerring consistency; but we crave—and crave in vain—some relief to the almost sickening combination of awe and loathing created by such characters and motives as this drama presents.

The character of Vittoria herself—the White Devil—is not easily to be put into words. Hot passion covering itself by an assumption of cool outward self-control and of contemptuous superiority to the ordinary fears or scruples of women,—this is a conception which we instinctively feel to be true to nature—to nature, that is, in one of her abnormal moods. In the first scene[1] in which Vittoria appears she reveals the deadliness of her passionate resolution, when relating to her paramour the dream which is to urge him on to the murder of his duchess and her own husband. The ghastliness of the imagery of the vision is indescribably effective, together with the horrible scornfulness of the closing phrase:

> ' When to my rescue there arose, methought,
> A whirlwind, which let fall a massy arm

whence it is reproduced in the same author's *Renaissance in Italy: The Catholic Reaction*, vol. i (1886), pp. 381 *seqq.*

[1] Act i. sc. 2.

> From that strong plant;
> And both were struck dead by that sacred yew,
> *In that base shallow grave that was their due.'*

The scene in which Vittoria is tried for the murder of her husband[1] has attracted the comment of several critics—among others of Charles Lamb, who strangely enough speaks of her ' innocence-resembling boldness.' Dyce demurs to this view[2], which appears to me utterly erroneous, and destructive of the consistency which the character throughout maintains.   Not ' sweetness ' and ' loveliness ' but a species of strange fascination, such as is only too often exercised by heartless pride, seems to pervade the figure and the speech of the defiant sinner who refuses to withdraw an inch from the position which she has assumed, and meets her judges with a front of withering scorn.   Almost equally effective are the burst of passion with which she turns upon the jealous Brachiano, and the gradual subsiding of her wrath, as of a fire, under his caresses[3].   The terrible energy of the last act is almost unparalleled ; but the character of Vittoria remains true to itself, except perhaps in the last—rather trivial—reflexion with which she dies[4].

The remaining characters of the tragedy are drawn with varying degrees of force ; but they all seem to stand forth as real human figures under the lurid glare of a storm-laden sky : nor is it easy to analyse the impression created by so dense a mixture of unwholesome humours, wild passions, and fearful sorrows.   The total effect is unspeakably ghastly—though in one of the most elaborately terrible

[1] Act iii. sc. 2.

[2] So, I am gratified to observe, does Mr. Gosse, who considers that ' Monticelso's altogether extravagant abuse has as much to do with the favour we feel for her as her own rather brazen confidence.'

[3] Act iv. sc. 2.

[4] How fine, on the other hand, is her preceding exclamation of horror :

> ' My soul, like to a ship in a black storm,
> Is driven, I know not whither.'

It is thus that this mysterious woman seems to pass away from us, rather than with her subsequent words :

> ' O, happy they that never saw the court,
> Nor ever knew great men but by report !'

scenes[1] the intention becomes too obvious, and 'several forms of distraction' exhibited by the mad Cornelia strike one as in some degree conventional, as they are to some extent plagiarised[2].

It must however be observed that in this play, as in *The Duchess of Malfi*, Webster creates some of his most powerful effects by single touches— flashes of genius which seem to light up of a sudden a wide horizon of emotions. It is in these flashes, so vivid as to illumine the dullest perception, so subtle as to search the closest heart, that Webster alone among our dramatists can be said at times to equal Shakspere[3].

The Duchess of Malfi[4] (first printed in 1623) bears to my mind the signs of a more matured workmanship than *The White Devil*. The action is indeed full of horrors, but not, so to speak, clogged with them ; the tragic effect is not less deep, but pity may claim an equal share in it with terror. The story (taken from a novel by Bandello which through Belleforest's French version found its way into Paynter's *Palace of Pleasure*[5]) is in itself simple and symmetrical,

The Duchess of Malfi (pr. 1623).

---

[1] Act v. sc. 1.

[2] This has even been asserted of the famous dirge ' Call for the robin-redbreast and the wren,' which Reed held to be in part derived from *Cymbeline*, act iv. sc. 2.

[3] Mr. Gosse has cited one of these passages, which, as he says, sums up the scope and destination of the play, viz. the tragically picturesque exclamation of Brachiano, when at last he sees clearly the tragedy of his ruined life (act iv. sc. 2) :

> 'Thou hast led me, like a heathen sacrifice,
>   With music and with fatal yokes of flowers,
>   To my eternal ruin.'

[4] The date of the performance of *The Duchess of Malfi* is unknown, but Mr. Fleay places it as early as 1612. According to a note in Mr. Rawdon Brown's *Translation of Diaries and Despatches of the Venetian Embassy* (reviewed in *Quarterly Review* for October, 1857), which I cite from *The Academy*, Basino, the Secretary of the Embassy, must have seen *The Duchess of Malfi* performed in 1618 ; for while complaining of the irreverence with which the Romish clergy are treated on the stage of Protestant countries, he gives an account of the part of a certain cardinal which cannot well refer to any play but this.

[5] In Robert Greene's *Gwydonius, the Carde of Fancie* (1584), mention is made among other instances of ' the rage of fancie ' of ' the duchess of *Malphey,* who chose for her husband her seruant *Vlrico.*'—Lope de Vega is stated to have founded on Bandello's novel (i. 26) his drama *El Mayordomo de la Duquesa de Amalfi* (1618). (Hazlitt ; cf. Klein, vol. x. p. 493.)

and the fifth act (though perhaps rather excessive in length [1])
seems a natural complement to the main action.   The death
of the unhappy Duchess, whose crime it was to marry her
steward from sheer love, is here avenged upon her brothers
and murderers by the instrument of their own cruelty.   In
the character of the Duchess there is little very specially
to attract ; but she is drawn with a simplicity not devoid of
power, and her artlessness is apparently designed to contrast
with the diabolical craft of her persecutors.   It is not however till the fourth act that the author has an opportunity
of putting forth his peculiar power.   He has here accumulated every element of horror of which the situation seems
to admit (indeed the dance of madmen is in every sense
superfluous) ; the preparations for the Duchess' death are
made in her presence ; her coffin is brought in, her dirge is
sung, then she is strangled, to revive only for a moment in
order to learn from her executioner, himself full of pity and
remorse, that her husband still lives.   This act abounds in
those marvellous touches of which Webster is master; the
most powerful of them all is the sudden thrill of pity in
the breast of the brother who has commanded her death, on
beholding his command fulfilled :

'*Bos.*   Do you not weep ?
         Other sins only speak ; murder shrieks out :
         The element of water moistens the earth,
         But blood flies upwards and bedews the heavens.
    Ferd. Cover her face ; mine eyes dazzle ; she died young.'

Although the character of Bosola in this tragedy displays a
composite kind of humour in which the author appears to
have taken a unique kind of pleasure [2], there is less variety in
the *dramatis personae* as a whole than in those of *The White
Devil*.   But the total impression left upon the mind by the
tragic action of *The Duchess of Malfi* is unsurpassed in
depth by anything else known to have been achieved by
Webster ; nor is the hope unreasonable that so masterly

---

[1] Possibly it was in part abbreviated in the performance, since the title-page
speaks of divers things having been printed ' that the length of the Play would
not beare in the Presentment.'

[2] Mr. Gosse, touching on the 'pungent bitterness and sombre railing' of
the speculative Bosola, shrewdly asks : 'Did the Clerk of St. Andrew's,
Holborn, talk so among his contemporaries, and mystify them, we wonder ?'

a work may permanently recover possession of the English stage[1].

The Devil's Law-Case, or, When Women go to Law, the Devil is full of Business (first printed in 1623, but probably acted some years earlier[2]), is a romantic comedy with a very complicated plot, the source of which seems uncertain[3]. Although quite in Webster's manner, and in the trial-scene[4] elaborating one of his favourite subjects, the management of a law-case, it is wholly inferior to the two tragedies briefly described above; and such interest as it possesses, apart from the excellence of particular passages[5], lies chiefly in the conduct of a story of many folds and with no very satisfactory ending.

The Devil's Law-Case (pr. 1623).

[1] I remember, not many years ago, seeing the Duchess of Malfi well acted by Miss Glyn; the effect which the tragedy produces on the stage is overpowering.—It had not to my knowledge been previously revived there; *The White Devil* is stated by Genest (vol. i. p. 346) to have been acted at the Theatre Royal in 1682, when the announcement on the stage of the election of a Pope may have met with a mingled reception.

[2] See Fleay, *English Drama*, vol. ii. p. 272, where it is pointed out that the allusion in act iv. sc. 2 cannot be, as Dyce supposed, to the massacre of Amboyna, which was not known in England till May, 1624 (Gardiner, vol. v. p. 242). I do not, however, know on what evidence Mr. Fleay holds that the play was performed by Queen Anne's company, which would date it before March, 1619. Mr. Fleay gives reasons for considering that it was written in 1610.

[3] Hazlitt could not find it in Goulart's *Histoires Admirables*, whence the *Biographia Dramatica* declares it to be taken. The incident of Contarino's being cured instead of killed by Romelio's dagger—

 'His steel has lighted in the former wound
 And made free passage for the congeal'd blood,' &c. (act iii. sc. 2)—

for which a parallel has been found in the 'miraculous' anecdote of Iason of Pherae, related by Valerius Maximus, i. 8, in some degree resembles one in Fletcher's *A Wife for a Month* (cf. *ante*, vol. ii. p. 711, *note*).

[4] Act iv. sc. 2.

[5] Some of these have been extracted by Charles Lamb. It is strange that he should not have included Leonora's speech to her waiting-woman (act iii. sc. 2), with its admirable tranquil satire:

  'Thou hast liv'd with me
 These forty years; we have grown old together,
 As many ladies and their women do,
 With talking nothing, and with doing less.
 We have spent our life in that which least concerns life,
 Only in putting on our clothes: and now I think on 't
 I have been a very courtly mistress to thee,
 I have given thee good words, but no deeds.'

He has not omitted the dirge in the funeral pageant (act v. sc. 5).

Appius
and
Virginia
(pr. 1654).

Finally, in *Appius and Virginia*, printed in 1654, probably after its author's death, we may consider ourselves justified in recognising a work of his later manhood, if not of his old age [1]. The theme is indeed one which might readily be supposed to have commended itself to Webster's love of the terrible; but he has treated it without adding fresh effects of his own invention to those which he found ready to his hand. Yet the play has genuine power; and were it not that the action seems to continue too long after the death of Virginia [2], this tragedy might be described as one of the most commendable efforts of its class. The evenness, however, of its execution, and the absence (except in the central situation) of any passages of a peculiarly striking or startling character, exclude *Appius and Virginia* from the brief list of Webster's most characteristic productions.

Of Roman history he seems to have had little knowledge; since, like the author of the old *Apius and Virginia* [3] before him, he derived the story of his play from Paynter's *Palace of Pleasure*, whither it had found its way from the *Pecorone* of Giovanni Fiorentino [4]. On the other hand, he has infused considerable life into the familiar tale, and has reproduced some of its characters, in particular the tyrant and his fawning henchman Marcus, with original distinctness. The scene at the tribunal [5], in which Appius contrives to cast the veil of fair and honourable dealing over his plot so success-

[1] Mr. Fleay, however, dates it *c.* 1609.   [2] Act iv. sc. 1.

[3] Cf. vol. i. p. 204. The Spanish poet Cueva produced a *Tragedia de Virginia y Apio Claudio* in 1580 (Klein, vol. ix. p. 219).—Webster's tragedy was adapted by Betterton under the title of *The Roman Father* (1679). John Dennis' play of *Appius and Virginia* (1709) will be mentioned below.

[4] Inconsistently with other passages in the play, and of course with history, Appius Claudius (act i. sc. 1) speaks of himself as 'so poor a plebeian.' Virginius, on the other hand, shows himself deserving of Appius' description of him as 'a proud Plebeian' by declaring his ancestors to 'have continued these eight hundred years' (act iv. sc. 1).

[5] Act iii. sc. 2. As to Samuel Crisp's *Virginia* (1754), for which Garrick wrote and spoke the Prologue, see *The Early Diary of Frances Burney*, ed. Ellis (1889), Preface, pp. xxxix, xlii. There were two other contemporary plays on the subject; one of them by John Moncreif was acted in 1755. (*Ib.*, vol. ii. p. 329.) Sheridan Knowles' declamatory *Virginius* was produced in 1820, in competition with another tragedy on the same perennial theme, and held the stage for many years.

fully that the honest Icilius can only exclaim bewildered,
'Sure all this is damn'd cunning,' is admirable; Webster,
as has been seen, excelled in scenes of this description.

Little needs to be added to the above in the way of
general comment on the characteristics of Webster's dramatic genius. The wonderful strength of these characteristics
displays itself with the utmost distinctness in *The White
Devil* and *The Duchess of Malfi*. Webster loves to accumulate the favourite furniture of theatrical terror—
murders and executions, the dagger and the pistol, the
cord and the coffin, together with skulls and ghosts, and
whatever horrors attend or are suggested by the central
horror of them all. Herein he is not exceptional among
the Elisabethans, of whom, from Kyd to Tourneur, so
many were alike addicted to the employment of the whole
apparatus of death. What is distinctive in Webster, is in
the first place the extraordinary intensity of his imagination
in this sphere of ideas, and again the elaborateness of his
workmanship, which enabled him to surpass—it may fairly
be said—all our old dramatists in a field which a large proportion were at all times ready to cultivate. As for later
endeavours in our literature to rival this familiarity with
death and its ghastly associations, they have rarely escaped
the danger of artificiality or succeeded in stimulating the
imaginative powers of any generation but their own. Among
all these poets of the grave and its terrors we meet with but
few whose very soul seems, like Webster's, a denizen of the
gloom by which their creations are overspread.

Webster's chief characteristics as a dramatist: The intensity of his imagination, and the elaborateness of his workmanship, in the sphere of the Terrible.

But Webster's most powerful plays and scenes are
characterised by something besides their effective appeal
to the emotion of terror. He has a true insight into
human nature, and is capable of exhibiting the operation of
powerful influences upon it with marvellous directness. He
is aware that men and women will lay open the inmost
recesses of their souls in moments of deep or sudden
agitation; he has learnt that on such occasions unexpected
contrasts—an impulse of genuine compassion in an assassin,
a movement of true dignity in a harlot—are wont to offer

His insight into human nature.

themselves to the surprised observer; he is acquainted with the fury and the bitterness, the goad and the after-sting of passion, and with the broken vocabulary of grief. All these he knows and understands, and is able to reproduce, not continually or wearisomely, but with that unerring recognition of supremely fitting occasions which is one of the highest, as it is beyond all doubt one of the rarest, gifts of true dramatic genius.

His humour.

It is impossible that a dramatist possessing this faculty should be without humour of a very remarkable order; and though we unfortunately possess but a single comedy which can be ascribed to Webster only, no doubt can exist as to his possession of the gift in question. Some of the comic characters in *The White Devil* (Flamineo and Camillo) are effectively drawn; the dry humour of Bosola's commentaries on life and its vicissitudes in *The Duchess of Malfi* has a quite original savour; and if Webster is to be held to have had any share in *A Cure for a Cuckold*, I cannot see why it should be thought self-evident that he was guiltless of any of its unrefined, but far from spiritless, fun. His satirical powers are great, as may be seen from the versatility with which he varies his attacks upon the favourite subject of his social satire—the law, its practice and its practitioners.

His poetic feeling.

It was equally out of the question that the characteristic powers of Webster's dramatic genius should have been unaccompanied by fine poetic feeling. Of this he occasionally gives evidence in passages of considerable beauty, though upon imagery he appears to have bestowed no very marked attention [1]. I am not aware that either

Webster and Shakspere.

in the respect of particular passages, or of entire scenes,

---

[1] In *The White Devil* occurs the original of the well-known thought—
> 'The good are better made by ill,
>   As odours crushed are sweeter still.'

See act i. sc. 1:
> 'Perfumes, the more they are chaf'd, the more they render
>   Their pleasing scents, and so affliction
>   Expresseth virtue fully, whether true,
>   Or else adulterate.'

The idea reappears elsewhere; and I see that Mr. Gosse has dwelt on the typical quality of the line in *The Duchess of Malfi*, act iii. sc. 5:
> 'Man, like to cassia, is proved best being bruised.'

Webster's debt to Shakspere is so large as it has been represented to be[1]; and I must confess my ignorance as to what support can (with the exception of Cornelia's madness) be found for Hazlitt's assertion[2] that Webster's two most famous tragedies are 'too like Shakespear, and often direct imitations of him, both in general conception and individual expression.' On the other hand, the same critic seems by no means to go too far in saying that this author's plays 'upon the whole perhaps come the nearest to Shakespear of anything we have on record.' What more requires to be said in acknowledgment of the true dramatic genius of which Webster was possessed?

But at the same time the meaning of the assertion should not be pressed beyond certain definite limits. In his power of revealing dramatically by truthful touches the secrets of human nature, Webster was like Shakspere. He was unlike him in but rarely combining with this power the art of exhibiting dramatically the developement of character under the influence of incident. The collapse of Bracciano's strength of will and of Appius' self-control under the influence of passion and of opportunity are forcibly brought home to us; but the White Devil herself, as her name is intended to imply, is an abnormal, though not impossible, being; while the Duchess of Malfi can hardly be said to have a character at all. What Webster in general reproduces with inimitable force, is a succession of situations of overpowering effect; in construction he is far from strong, and in characterisation he only exceptionally passes beyond the range of ordinary types. There seems little moral purpose at work in his most imposing efforts; and his imagination, instead of dwelling by preference on the associations of the law-court and the charnel-house, would have had to sustain itself on nutriment more diverse and more spiritual, in order to wing his mighty genius to freer and loftier flights.

Webster deficient in characterisation.

To this brief notice of a dramatic poet of high eminence

---

[1] Vittoria Corombona (if Mitford's emendation be correct) compares herself to Shakspere's Portia (act iii. sc. 2); but I can hardly think the emendation allowable, though it has been accepted by Dyce. See also *ante*, as to the dirge in the same play.

[2] *Lectures, &c.*, p. 124.

may be appended a few words concerning the two extant plays of a writer who was not indeed devoid of original force, but who might almost be said to have used whatever strength was in him for the purpose of throwing himself headlong over the precipice from which Webster's tragedy bids us look into the darkness beneath. Of the personal life of *Cyril* **CYRIL TOURNEUR**[1], or (as he writes himself on the title-*Tourneur* page of his chief non-dramatic poem) Turner, virtually *(fl. 1603–* nothing at all is known. His earliest acknowledged publica-*1613 c.).* tion, so far as we are aware, was a satire in the vein of Marston's efforts of the same description, but exaggerated in its mannerisms to an almost incredible extent, and quite unreadable. This production, printed in 1600, which bears the title of *The Transformed Metamorphosis*, is dedicated to Sir Christopher Heydon, a Norfolk gentleman who was knighted by Essex at Cadiz, and who, after being pardoned for suspected complicity in Essex' plot, seems to have largely given himself up to astrological learning[2]. No proof exists of Tourneur having been the author of a satirical prose tract, *Laugh and Lie Down, or The World's Folly* (1605), of which the dedication is signed ' C. T.,' or even of the anonymous *Funeral Poem on the Death of Sir Francis Vere* (1609); but he wrote one of a batch of three *Funeral Elegies* on the death of Henry Prince of Wales[3], printed in 1613, the other two being contributed by Webster and *His plays.* Thomas Heywood. Besides the two extant plays to be noticed immediately, a 'tragi-comedy' by him entitled *The*

[1] *The Plays and Poems of Cyril Tourneur*. Edited, with Critical Introduction and Notes, by John Churton Collins. Two vols., 1878. *The Revenger's Tragedy* is printed in *The Ancient British Drama*, vol. ii, and in Hazlitt's *Dodsley*, vol. x ; of *The Atheist's Tragedy* a reprint exists dated 1792. Of the plot of the latter an account will be found in Genest, vol. x. pp. 19-21.— Mr. Swinburne's essay in vol. xxi of *The Nineteenth Century* (1887) appears to me a very extravagant criticism.—For an earlier account of both the extant plays of Cyril Tourneur see *The Retrospective Review*, vol. vii. part ii.

[2] Cf. Collins' Introduction ; and see *The Dictionary of National Biography*, vol. xxvi (1891), where there is a list of Heydon's publications on this subject.—Among the mannerisms of the poem may be reckoned a quite extraordinary series of verbs formed with the termination *ize*: as *arterize, comfortize, Babellize.*

[3] Tourneur's effort was entitled *A Griefe on the Death of Prince Henrie, expressed in a Broken Elegie, according to the nature of such a Sorrow.*

Nobleman was entered on the Registers in 1612; but the
MS. of this play was one of those burnt by Warburton's
cook[1]. According to a letter stated to have been addressed
to Henslowe by the dramatist Robert Daborne, and dated
June 5, 1613, the latter entrusted the composition of an act
of a play on which he was engaged, called *The Arraignment
of London*, to Cyril Tourneur[2].

Of the two extant plays known as his, *The Atheist's
Tragedy, or The Honest Man's Revenge*, printed in 1611,
was unmistakeably the earlier. The crudity of its versification, which abounds in 'light endings' to the lines, and has
in fact a not very bearable kind of lilt, leaves no room for
doubt on this score. A passage in the play suggests that
it was written either during, or immediately after, the siege
of Ostend (1601–4)[3]. As a whole, it is a work of striking
originality; but this feature distinguishes rather the general
conception and manner of the play than particular passages
of high individual merit, of which but few remain to be
added to those extracted—with his usual felicity of choice—
by Charles Lamb[4]. The story, which was probably made
up from more sources than one, runs riot in some of its later

*The
Atheist's
Tragedy
(pr. 1611).*

---

[1] The authority is Collier's *The Alleyn Papers*, p. 58; cf. *ib.*, pp. 64 and 65.

[2] Mr. Fleay, *u. s.*, vol. ii. p. 331, expresses a strong disposition to assign,
on the evidence both of the diction and of the general conduct of the plot,
The Second Maiden's Tragedy to the author of *The Revenger's Tragedy*; but
(*ib.* p. 264) he considers Tourneur's authorship of the latter open to doubt.

[3] See act ii. sc. 1. I see that Mr. Fleay (*u. s.*, vol. ii. p. 263) also notices this.

[4] It is strange, however, that he should not have included in these either
the spirited lines in which Charlemont, in the first scene with his father, the
old Lord (act i. sc. 2), apologises for his 'affection to the war,' or the
second of the epitaphs in act iii. sc. 1. The latter is a brief elegy, in a
style of quaint but not unpleasing simplicity which one would have thought
foreign to Tourneur:

'*The Epitaph of Charlemont.*

'His body lies interr'd within this mould,
Who died a young man, yet departed old;
And all that strength of youth, that men can have,
Was ready still to drop into his grave.
Far ag'd in Virtue with a youthful eye,
He welcom'd it, being still prepar'd to die;
And living so, though young depriv'd of breath,
He did not suffer an untimely death.
But we may say of his brave bless'd decease:
He died in war, and yet he died in peace.'

turns, and is mixed up with a revolting underplot (turning on the amours of Levidulcia, which are represented with unspeakable grossness[1]). The author, incapable or reckless of distinguishing between the terrible and the grotesque, sought to cap the horror of the midnight murder in the gravel-pit by a churchyard scene full of real and sham ghosts[2]; and his atheist ends, when no longer master of his movements, by inflicting an accidental wound upon himself with the executioner's axe with which he was about to do to death the victims of his train of crimes. The exposition of the character of d'Amville, the ruthless villain of the play, is however impressive, and the connexion between his black emptiness of soul and the evil-doing to which he abandons himself is, though not very consecutively, kept in view down to his dying recantation[3]. Marlowe might have imagined such a hero, who, when thunder and lightning terrify the accomplice of his nocturnal crime, arrogantly philosophises on the origin of these phenomena[4]; —and who justifies incest by the general liberty allowed by nature to her creatures[5]. But the progress of the action fails to heighten the effect of the character; we have supped too full with horrors before the play is more than half done to have much stomach left for all that is to follow of lust and death; and the atheist's catastrophe —the overthrow of his reason by the death of his younger son and the consequent collapse of his schemes,—is not presented with overwhelming force[6]. Moreover, the moral

---

[1] An incident in this underplot is founded on a tale in the *Decamerone* (vii. 6).

[2] Old Montferrer's ghost, which as Genest notes appears not less than four times, on one of these occasions actually stands fire.

[3] At the outset D'Amville very succinctly explains his atheism to be due to the impression made upon his mind by the worldliness of his brother's Puritan chaplain:

'—But compare 's profession with his life;—
They so directly contradict themselves,
As if the end of his instructions were
But to divert the world from sinne, that hee
More easily might ingrosse it to himselfe.
By that I am confirm'd an Atheist.' (Act i. sc. 2.)

[4] Act ii. sc. 4.   [5] Act iv. sc. 3.

[6] Dramatic tact is, however, exhibited in the atheist's first revulsion

which this tragedy attempts to teach—that vengeance
should be left to Heaven—is hardly brought out as a principle of action, and the virtuous Charlemont and the
sorely-tried Castabella, even when re-united they lie down to
rest 'with either of them a Death's head for a pillow,' can
hardly be regarded as interesting in themselves.

If *The Atheist's Tragedy* seems to carry us back to the
period which gave rise to so many dramas on a theme
cognate to that of *Hamlet*, there can be no doubt but that
one of its most impressive passages[1] was suggested by *Hamlet*
itself.   But in truth ample evidence may be found elsewhere of its author's familiarity with Shakspere's ideas or
phraseology[2].

The Revenger's Tragedy, printed in 1607, had been uniformly assigned to Tourneur, until Mr. Fleay threw doubts
on the correctness of the assumption.   I cannot, however,
consider this scepticism warranted.   Undoubtedly, the
distance is considerable between the style of this play
and that of its predecessor ; and although the reflexion of
Shakspere is still constantly cast upon the troubled waters,
the writer has acquired a power of condensed expression
of his own which he owes to no example or model.   The
versification, again, differs essentially from that of *The
Atheist's Tragedy*; the structure of the verse is strong,
and its peculiar effect seems to me to gain from the frequent use of rime.   One can only conclude that the order
of sequence between the two plays according to the dates of
publication known to us must be reversed, and that *The
Revenger's Tragedy*, in its original form, was composed
several years before its successor.

*The
Revenger's
Tragedy
(pr.* 1607).

Unfortunately the plot of *The Revenger's Tragedy*, the
source of which is unknown, is in its sewer-like windings

towards belief in a higher power on the occasion of the death of his elder son.
See the dialogue with the Doctor, act v. sc. 1.

[1] See Charlemont's speech in the Churchyard—the time midnight, his
would-be assassin shadowing him in the background (act iv. sc. 3).

[2] See Castabella's appeal to Mercy as 'an attribute As high as Justice' (act iii.
sc. 4), and Sebastian's antithesis between the dictates of honour and those of
discretion (*ib.*, sc. 2).—Mr. Collins has marked some singularly faithful
echoes in this play of the ' ring, phrase and trick ' of Shakspere's style.

one of the blackest and most polluting devised by the perverted imagination of an age prone to feed on the worst
scandals of the Italian decadence. At the same time, an overpowering self-consistency pervades the picture of this name-
less Italian court,—its old Duke, the 'parched lascar'; his heir
Lussurioso, to whom every woman is a concubine at his beck
and call; his 'step-Duchess' ready for adultery with her
husband's bastard; her sons (a brood worse than Catharine
de' Medici's), Ambitioso, Supervacuo, and a third (the
perpetrator of the outrage that sets the action in motion)
who alone goes by a colourless name (Junior); his reckless
bastard Spurio; his obsequious judges, and his fawning
nobles. Vindici, the hero of the drama, a figure suggested
by *Hamlet* or *Hoffman*[1], and his brother Hippolito, come
near to realising the ideal of a tragedy of revenge which is
satirically propounded in a play of rather later date[2]. The
brothers do not indeed kill themselves, but they welcome
death as a fitting termination to their performance of their
self-appointed task. Horribly realistic in some of its effects,
which but too successfully express the 'quaintness of
malice' commended in Vindici by Hippolito, this play may
be described as wholly devoid of relief. While we feel
thankful that no comic effects are sought to be produced
in this stifling atmosphere, we are inspired with no human
sympathy even by the chaste Castiza, whose experiment
upon the better elements in her mother's nature excites in
us a pardonable fear that there is after all no difference between parent and child. The whole episode of the mother,
tempted by the pretended persuasions of her son to sinful
connivance with her daughter's shame, is against kind; and
the climax of Vindici's vengeance reaches the *non plus
ultra* of pruriency steeped in horrors[3]. It has been thought

---

[1] Cf. vol. i. p. 427. Chettle's tragedy opens with an expository soliloquy,
of which Tourneur might have invented the accessories.

[2] See La Writ's quotation in *The Little French Lawyer* (act iv. sc. 4):

> 'I love a dire revenge.
> Give me the man that will all others kill,
> And last himself.'

[3] He poisons the Duke by inducing him to kiss the skull of his victim,
Vindici's betrothed wife, dressed up as the face of a fresh victim for his senile

possible to find in such a play 'the noblest ardour of moral
emotion,' and 'the most fervent passion of eager and
indignant sympathy with all that is best and abhorrence
of all that is worst in women or in men.' Beyond dispute,
however, it contains evidence of high tragic power, and of
a gift of diction matching itself with extraordinary fitness
to demands such as few if any of our dramatists have ever
made upon their powers. Passages in this tragedy are illu-
minated by an imagery of singular distinctness as well as
intensity. And if, as we are not prepared to doubt, *The
Revenger's Tragedy* was Tourneur's work, it is with a sense
of amazement that we turn from this solitary monument of
his genius as a tragic poet of unmistakeable distinction.

In JOHN FORD [1] we are brought face to face with a very
noteworthy figure in the history of our later Elisabethan
drama, and with a writer who manifestly influenced its
progress, while helping to hasten its decay. He was born
April 17, 1586, at Ilsington in Devonshire, as the second son
of a gentleman of position ; his mother was a sister of Sir
John Popham, who became in turn Attorney-General and
Lord Chief Justice. It is probable that he was the John Ford
who matriculated at Exeter College, Oxford, early in 1601 ;
it is certain that he was towards the end of the following
year entered at the Middle Temple, while his cousin and
namesake (to whom he dedicated *The Lover's Melancholy*)
was a member of Gray's Inn. In 1606 Ford first came
before the world as an author, with an elegiac poem
entitled *Fame's Memorial*, in honour of the recently de-

*John Ford
(1586–
1640 c. or
post).*

---

lust, and then tramples upon him in triumph. This scene seems to have
been followed (at a distance) in later plays. (Cf. *ante*, p. 15, and *note* 1.)—The
final catastrophe of 'the young Duke' is managed by the more ordinary
expedient of a masque.

[1] *The Works of John Ford.* With Notes and Introduction by W. Gifford.
Two vols., 1827. This edition was republished in a revised form, with
a new Introduction, by Dyce, 3 vols., 1869. The *Fortnightly Review* for
July, 1871, contained a fine criticism of Ford by Mr. Swinburne. See also
Mr. Bullen's notice of Ford in vol. xix of *The Dictionary of National Biography*
(1889), and another by myself in the last edition of the *Encyclopaedia
Britannica.*—Concerning the sources of Ford's plays I have again had the
advantage of consulting Dr. E. Koeppel's *Quellen-Studien*, &c. (1897) ; but
their plots remain to an unusual extent untraceable.

ceased Charles Earl of Devonshire, to whose widow it is inscribed. The publication is to the credit of the young Templar's independence of spirit; for the Earl had died under the cloud of royal disfavour and public scandal, originating in his marriage with a lady well fitted to be the heroine of one of Ford's own dramas [1]; the tribute paid by the poet to her still more unfortunate brother—

> ' Renowned Devereux, whose awkward fate
> Was misconceited by foul envy's hate'—

was less likely to give offence to the authorities of the new *régime*. In this poem Ford alludes to his own love-troubles and their cause—'flint-hearted Lycia,' of whom nothing further remains on record. Indeed, notwithstanding his good social position, we hardly know more of his private life than of the personal careers of many of his fellow-dramatists who are wrapped in Bohemian obscurity. He seems at different times to have enjoyed the patronage or goodwill of several men of rank—among them of the well-known Earl (afterwards Duke) of Newcastle, himself a muse, and of the gallant Lord Craven, the faithful servant of Queen Elisabeth of Bohemia [2]. Other patrons of his were the Earls of Peterborough and Antrim. His tract or harangue on the ethics of chivalrous love, entitled *Honor Tryumphant, or The Peeres Challenge,* was composed on the occasion of the royal visit further celebrated by Ford in verses entitled *The Monarches Meeting. or The King of Denmarkes welcome into England* (1606) [3]. A book called *Sir Thomas Overburyes Ghost,* giving an account of that unfortunate man's life and death, was entered in the Stationers' Registers in 1615 as by Ford [4]; this cannot have been a play, since such a subject (as Mr. Bullen points out) could not possibly have been brought on the stage. In 1620 he

---

[1] The famous Penelope Rich—once thought to have been the Dark Lady of Shakspere's *Sonnets.* The poem seems to me above the average of such works; the closing stanza is particularly fine.

[2] His *Perkin Warbeck* and his *The Broken Heart* were dedicated to these noblemen respectively.

[3] *Honor Triumphant,* with the accompanying poems, was edited for the (Old) Shakespeare Society in 1843.

[4] Ford prefixed commendatory verses to Overbury's *The Wife.*

published another moral tract, entitled *A Line of Life*, which contains a passage or two of interest, but which ends with the most fulsome praise of King James I[1]. Towards the public Ford seems to have chosen to assume an attitude of independence[2] and self-consciousness[3]; the group of fellow-authors from whose pens tributes in his honour remain includes besides Shirley and Brome, Richard Crashaw, a true poet, whose delicate and in some respects morbid genius had certain points of contact with that of Ford. In his turn, he paid similar tributes to Massinger and Brome, as well as to Overbury, and perhaps to Barnabe Barnes, and was among those who honoured the memory of Jonson by a joint garland of verse[4]. The names of the contemporaries with whom he was associated as a dramatist included Dekker, Webster and William Rowley[5]. Yet in a poem published not many years after his death[6] he is ridiculed for a tendency to self-seclusion and melancholy; and according to Gifford, faint traditions survived in the neighbourhood of his birth-place, pointing to his having retired thither after he had brought to a close his labours as a dramatist, and perhaps his professional career as a lawyer or legal agent[7]. The expression 'he's far enough from home' in the *Prologue* to his *Fancies Chaste and Noble*, printed in 1638, and probably acted two years before that date, can hardly be thought to refer to his being out of the country[8]. In 1639 he published *The Lady's Trial*, first acted in 1637 or 1638; so that little more than a decade is spanned, according to their dates of publication, by the entire series of plays

---

[1] Reprinted with *Honour Triumphant, u s.*

[2] See the *Dedication* and *Prologue* of *The Lover's Melancholy*.

[3] See the fine *Prologue* and the *Epilogue* to *The Broken Heart*.

[4] Ford's contribution to *Jonsonus Virbius* is entitled *On the Best of English Poets, Ben Jonson, deceased.*

[5] See also Thomas Heywood's reference to him as 'Jacke Foorde,' *ante*, vol. i. p. 471.

[6] *Time-Poets*, in *Choice Drollery* (1656).

[7] He does not appear to have been called to the Bar; but I am not aware that any special knowledge of law-matters has been discovered in his plays, as it has been thought to show itself in a not very recondite allusion in Tourneur's *The Revenger's Tragedy* (act v. sc. i).

[8] Gifford abandoned this notion. See *Introduction*, p. xl.

of which he claimed the authorship. For the earliest of these, as will be seen, first appeared on the stage in 1628, and was printed in the following year. After 1639 all further traces of him are lost.

Joint plays by Ford and other dramatists.

The earliest performance, in 1628, of *The Lover's Melancholy*, described by the author as the first dramatic work of his 'that ever courted reader,' had undoubtedly been preceded by that of several plays in which he co-operated with other dramatists. Among these may first be

Ford, Dekker and William Rowley's The Witch of Edmonton (pr. 1658).

mentioned *The Witch of Edmonton, a Known True Story*, not printed till 1658, but probably produced in 1621, or not long afterwards[1]. This remarkable play, as noted above[2], was when first published attributed to the joint authorship of Dekker, Ford, Rowley, '&c.'—safety being evidently sought in numbers; but critical opinion has agreed in ascribing it in the main to Dekker and Ford. I confess at the same time that it is not obvious to me why the supposition should be excluded that William Rowley, whose literary identity seems to admit of so easy a treatment, had a substantial share in the play. In any case, there cannot be much likelihood of mistake in assuming Ford to have written at all events the earlier scenes, treating of the woes of Frank, Winnifrede and Susan. And assuredly the English drama includes very few domestic tragedies more harrowing than this play, of which its authors doubtless owed the immediate suggestion to a topic of the day, but which furnished Ford with an opportunity such as he would never have found by searching for it. For *The Witch*

---

[1] The evidence in favour of this date is presumptive only, but practically irresistible. Elisabeth Sawyer (who is the chief personage in the play) was executed in 1621 for witchcraft; and the interest excited by the incident could not have lasted very long. Dr. Gardiner (see his *History*, vol. vii. p. 323) recognises in this play a slight indication that the tide of the popular belief in witchcraft was beginning to turn, although 'even here the old woman was treated as being in actual possession of the powers which she claimed.'—The very rare tract (1621) of the Newgate Ordinary, Henry Goodcole, concerning the conviction and execution of Mother Sawyer, which had been seen neither by Gifford nor by Dyce, was printed in the re-issue of Dyce's edition by Messrs. Lawrence and Bullen, where Mr. Bullen points out how freely the dramatists availed themselves of this source.

[2] Cf. *ante*, vol. ii. p. 469.

of Edmonton differs from nearly all the rest of his extant plays by the perfect simplicity of its theme and the homely straightforwardness of the lesson conveyed by its action. The intensity of some of the scenes is, notwithstanding, undeniable, and a situation of overwhelming effectiveness is reached in the discovery by Frank's sister-in-law of his murder of his wife, as he lies sick in bed attended in disguise by the woman for whose sake he has been guilty of the crime. And in the delineation of these sisters, Ford—if it was he that drew these figures—has attained to a purity, as well as to a tenderness, unparalleled in any other of his plays. Probably the weird figure of the hunted hag was Dekker's invention, and to him is due, together with the buffoonery of the peasants who hunt her down and the tediousness which clogs these portions of the play, the enforcement of the salutary lesson that a human being may by persecution be turned into a witch.

The masque of *The Sun's Darling*, printed 1656, has likewise been already [1] described as probably a revision by Ford of an earlier production licensed under the title of *Phaeton*, 1597–98, as by Dekker, and never printed. The greater part of the masque as we have it, or at all events the last two acts, have been thought attributable to Ford; but the ground is unsafe, the more so as the partial inconsistency of the allegory [2] favours the notion of the work having been subjected to a revision. Much of the dialogue is very beautiful; the lyrics—in so far as they are original [3] —seem to me less excellent. The two dramatists likewise co-operated in another masque, not printed but licensed in 1624 under the title of *The Fairy Knight*, and in a play, licensed in the same year, called *The Bristowe Merchant*. This piece, non-extant like the other, was doubtless a domestic tragedy, possibly founded on an earlier play.

Other joint productions by Dekker and Ford.

[1] Cf. *ante*, vol. i. p. 470.
[2] In act v, the hero Raybright is of a sudden temporarily identified with the new sovereign—King Charles I, and his subjects are warned not to pretend to 'found rebellion upon conscience.'
[3] One of these (act ii. sc. 1) is taken from Lyly. A plagiarism from Jonson (*Epilogue* to *Every Man Out of his Humour*) is perhaps less excusable. (See Winter's speech, act v. sc. 1.)

Ford and
Webster's
A Murder
of a Son
upon a
Mother
(acted
1624).
A production of the same type must have been Ford and Webster's *A Murther of a Son upon a Mother*, licensed in the same year 1624, of which nothing further is known.

Plays
written by
Ford alone:
The Lover's
Melancholy
(acted
1628;
pr. 1629).
The Lover's Melancholy, acted in 1628 and printed in the following year, was, according to the author's own statement in the dedication addressed by him to the members of Gray's Inn, the first of his published plays; but he expresses himself in such a way as to indicate that it was not the earliest play produced by him on the stage. His mysterious hint that as this is his first dramatic publication, so it might prove his last, was doubtless taken by his legal friends for what it was worth.

An apocryphal anecdote attributes to Ben Jonson, whose *New Inn* had failed shortly after Ford's play had succeeded, the charge that the latter was stolen from Shakspere's papers. The story is a late and baseless invention [1]; nor can anything in the play itself be said to lend colour to it. The plot is indeed not without 'reminiscences' of Shakspere, in so far that the madness of the hero at times recalls Hamlet, while the gentle sweetness of the page Parthenophill cannot but bring to mind the loveliest and most pathetic of parallels. But Palladio's madness is the result of hopeless love; and the story of Eroclea is quite differently conducted from that of Viola [2]. From a famous non-dramatic work of the time, on the other hand, Ford, ' claiming a scholar's right [3],' borrowed the entire notion of an interlude on the subject of the several species of madness, as well as another passage

---

[1] According to Gifford it was raked up by Macklin, who revived *The Lover's Melancholy* in 1748 (see the Introduction to Jonson's *New Inn*). It had already been discredited by Malone in a dissertation, *Shakspeare, Ford and Ben Jonson*. Endymion Porter's epigram, on which Gifford expends his ire, has more point than truth; but it indicates that Ford was already known as a writer of plays when *The Lover's Melancholy* was produced:

'Quoth Ben to Tom : the Lover's stole ;
'Tis Shakspeare's every word ;
Indeed, says Tom, upon the whole,
'Tis much too good for Ford.'

[2] Certain resemblances are also noted in this play by Dr. Koeppel to Beaumont and Fletcher's *Philaster*; and Gifford has pointed out a similarity in part of the plot of *The Lover's Melancholy* to Massinger's *A Very Woman*. But see *ante*, p. 39, *note* 3. [3] See *Prologue*.

leading up to the exhibition[1]. To another source he
avowed himself indebted for the poetic narrative reproduced
in a beautiful passage in the early part of the play[2].

The physiological masque which Burton's work had
suggested to Ford might in truth have well been spared.
The merits of the play lie neither in this second-hand
effort of ingenuity, nor in the comic personages, which may
be a trifle more entertaining than is usual with Ford's characters of this description, but which the trenchant Gifford
is justified in branding as a 'despicable set of buffoons.'
These merits are to be found in the tender pathos of some
of the earlier parts of the play, and in the harmonious close
given to it by the justly-commended last scene, where
Meleander is gently restored from the gloomy madness of
despair to perfect happiness by the recovery of his daughter.
Upon the whole, however, though in passages of *The Lover's
Melancholy* the pathos seems to well up from the very
depths of human nature[3], and though its sentiment is
better guarded from the danger of passing into mere
sentimentality than might from the opening have seemed
likely, this work is to be regarded as one of high promise
rather than of matured excellence.

'Tis Pity She's a Whore was not published till 1633.
In the Dedication to the Earl of Peterborough the play is
described as 'the first-fruits' of the author's 'leisure'; but
the meaning of the term is not obvious, especially when
taken in connexion with Ford's acknowledgement of some
special employment with which he had been charged by
his patron; nor is there any certainty as to the date of its

*'Tis Pity
She's a
Whore
(pr.* 1633).

---

[1] In act iii. sc. 1.   The masque is in the following scene.

[2] See in act i. sc. 1 the famous version of the story of the nightingale's
death, taken from the Jesuit Strada's *Prolusiones Academicae* (1617).
(Certainly Parthenophill, if I may be pardoned for saying so, plays a rather
silly part in this narrative.) As to Strada and the two poetic versions of his
professorial exercise in imitation of Claudian by Ford and Crashaw see
E. W. Gosse, *Seventeenth-Century Studies*, pp. 159–161. A later version
was produced by Ambrose Philips in his Fifth Pastoral.

[3] So, in Thamasta's sudden cry 'Kala, O, Kala!' (act i. sc. 3), and
Palladio's deep-drawn lament (act iv. sc. 3):

'Parthenophill is lost, and I would see him;
For he is like to something I remember
A great while since, a long, long time ago.'

first performance [1].   It therefore seemed unnecessary to disturb the accepted order of sequence between this play and
The Lover's Melancholy, more especially since it cannot be
for a moment doubted which of the two plays exhibits
maturer dramatic powers.   But never has genius more miser-
ably misused its gifts.   If, as the title of *'Tis Pity She's a
Whore* implies, this tragedy be intended to awaken a feeling akin to sympathy, or bordering upon it, on behalf of the
heroine of its story of incest, the endeavour, so far as I can
judge, fails in achieving the purpose insinuated.   In truth,
the dramatist's desire is to leave an impression far other
and more perilous than that of a mere feeling of compassion
for a fair sinner ;—his purpose is to persuade us that passion
is irresistible.   But his efforts are vain, and so too is the
sophistry of those who seek to explain away their chief
force; for while recognising their charm, the soul revolts
against the fatalism which, in spite of the Friar's preaching
and Annabella's repentance, the sum-total of the action of
this drama implies.   The key-note to the conduct of
Giovanni lies in his words:

> ' All this I'll do, to free me from the rod
> Of vengeance; else I'll swear my fate's my god.'

Annabella, indeed, is brought to a recognition of her sin,
into which she has precipitately thrown herself, by warnings
of retribution ; but Giovanni, who, after long resistance, has
yielded to what he blasphemously calls his fate, meets death
with no other prayer than this:

> ' Where'er I go, let me enjoy this grace,
> Freely to view my Annabella's face [2].'

The poison of this poetic treatment of mortal sin is dissolved in a cup of sweetness, and the draught is offered by
a wary hand ; but self-delusion only can pretend to neglect
its ingredients, or to ignore its intention [3].

---

[1] Fleay, *u.s.*, vol. i. p. 233, says that it was acted by Queen Henrietta's
company at the Phœnix, *c.* 1626.

[2] This contrast between the bearing of the two characters is very
forcibly brought out by Mr. Swinburne.

[3] It seems to me necessary to speak without disguise on this subject,
instead of obscuring it by such criticisms as that of the late Mr. J. A.

The Broken Heart, with 'John Forde's' anagram '*Fide Honor,*' printed in 1633, is one of the plays by which Ford's gifts as a dramatist may be most fairly judged. The origin of the story on which it is founded is unknown ; but unless the Prologue's assertion that the plot is based on fact is to be taken literally, its source is probably some nearly contemporary novel.   Either Ford or the novelist from whom he borrowed made little account of historical probability in choosing Sparta as the scene of a love-tragedy which savours of mediaeval Italy.

The Broken Heart (pr. 1633).

The extraordinary plot of this tragedy, which as an instance of Ford's complicated but not obscure method of construction I have briefly sketched in a note below[1],

Symonds : 'English poets have given us the right key to the Italian temperament. . . . The love of Giovanni and Annabella is rightly depicted as more imaginative than sensual.' (*Renaissance in Italy,* vol. i. p. 412.) Even were this so, the scathing force of the following censure would hold good : ' The man who thus conceived the horrors of the Italian Renaissance in the spirit in which they were committed is Ford. In his great play he has caught the very tone of the Italian Renaissance : the abominableness of the play consisting not in the coarse slaughter scenes added merely to please the cockpit of an English theatre, but in the superficial innocence of tone, in its making evil lose the appearance of evil, even as it did to the men of the Renaissance.' (Vernon Lee, *Euphorion* (1884), vol. i. p. 99.)—From the point of view under which it seemed necessary to treat this play, the source of its revolting plot is of small importance. Ford might have become acquainted with a story to which an actual occurrence in Normandy is said to have given rise in 1603, and which had found its way into the collection of Pierre Matthieu (1606) and into that of François de Rosset (1619). He may also have heard of dark traditions nearer home, of which the memory has to this day not entirely died out. Or he may have been influenced by the example of Beaumont and Fletcher's *A King and No King* (1611) to follow their audacity in the choice, and to surpass it in the treatment, of his theme (cf. *ante,* vol. ii. p. 677).—It would appear that a French version of this play, by M. Maeterlinck, was performed not many years ago. (Koeppel, p. 182, *note.*)

[1] A youthful pair of lovers, Orgilus and Penthea, have been separated by the ambition of the lady's valorous brother, the Spartan general Ithocles. He has caused Penthea to marry Bassanes, a jealous dotard whose insane suspiciousness of itself suffices to drive the suffering Penthea to distraction. Ithocles bitterly repents his act; and the reader is at first led to suppose (see act iii. sc. 2) that Penthea's is the broken heart of which the play is to tell. Orgilus, in order to gain access to Penthea, has pretended a journey to Athens, while in reality remaining at Sparta in the disguise of a pupil of philosophy in the school of the wise Tecnicus. In an interview with Penthea, however, he learns that no hope is left for him—she loves him still, but will not stain her honour by breaking the loathsome bond to which she is

is in truth the story not of one, but of three broken hearts, and offers a surfeit of sadness. The characters are hardly worked out with adequate force, with the exception of

condemned. To take vengeance upon Ithocles, the original author of his and Penthea's misery, now becomes the object of the life of Orgilus. Ithocles is enamoured of the princess Calantha, whose hand her royal father wishes to bestow upon the prince of Argos; and in order to further his revenge, Orgilus urges on this desperate suit. Calantha returns the affections of Ithocles, having been sweetly moved thereto by Penthea (see the pathetic scene, act iii. sc. 5, where she recites her Will); and Orgilus resolves to prepare for them a misery like that to which he has been doomed himself.

Thus the situation is wrought up towards the climax. The death of the gentle Penthea, who has lost her reason, but with her dying breath bewails her lover's wretchedness and her brother's cruelty, determines Orgilus to accomplish his purpose. This he effects by a strangely realistic device (originally it would seem recorded by Pausanias, and introduced by Bandello into one of his novels (iv. 1), whence it also appears to have been borrowed by Barnaby Barnes into his *The Devil's Charter* (cf. *ante*, vol. ii. p. 626), and see Dyce's note *ad loc.*). In the presence of the wronged Penthea's corpse Ithocles is inveigled into a chair so contrived as to hold fast the sitter in an inextricable grasp; and then Orgilus stabs his victim, who dies without a groan. Meanwhile a festival is in progress at Court, over which the King being mortally sick has asked his daughter Calantha to preside. While she is leading the measure, the tidings are brought to her first of her father's death, then of Penthea's, then of that of her beloved Ithocles—the last message being whispered to her by the murderer himself. But in each case she orders the dance to proceed; and then calmly causing the intelligence to be repeated to her, bids the self-confessed assassin make himself ready for death, and orders her coronation—for she is now Queen—to be proceeded with. We are thus prepared for the final situation. In the last act, all are assembled for the solemnity, when Calantha, clad in her royal robes, proclaims her last will, making over her kingdom to the Argive prince and disposing of the great offices of State. She then declares that the oracle, sent from Delphos by Tecnicus, which had darkly foretold all the incidents of the catastrophe, is fulfilled down to its last clause that 'the Lifeless Trunk shall wed the Broken Heart';—and, placing a ring on the finger of the corpse of Ithocles, she sinks dead by his side. As she passes away, a dirge is heard—

> 'Glories, pleasures, pomps, delight and ease
>   Can but please
> Th' outward senses, when the mind
> Is or untroubled or by peace refin'd—
> Crowns may flourish and decay,
> Beauties shine, but fade away.
> Youth may revel, yet it must
> Lie down in a bed of dust.
> Earthly honours flow and waste,
> Time alone doth change and last.

Ithocles and Calantha, both of whom are nobly conceived. Nor is the progress in the mind of Orgilus from despair to the resolve of vengeance very subtly traced, though on the other hand a very striking effect is created by the momentary calm with which he lures his victim to his doom. The character of Penthea, deeply as we are affected by its pathos, cannot be described as wholly satisfactory; her sorrow, as Gifford has also taken occasion to point out, exhibits a trace of selfishness which interferes with the sympathy excited by her sufferings. In Bassanes, the jealous husband, doting folly is suddenly, and not very intelligibly, succeeded by conscientious repentance; and the remaining personages are more or less conventional.

What enchains our admiration in this play is, first, the skill of its construction, which to me at least seems very considerable; secondly and principally, the pathos of particular scenes[1]. In the last act Ford shows himself equal to the conduct of a situation of terrible intensity; in the scenes concerned with Penthea he is true to his most special gift, in seeming to lift the veil from the very depths of the grief of a woman doomed to hopeless suffering. Thus the play, though far from perfect, is typical of its author's powers as exerted to the utmost of their capability. It should be added that not only the concluding dirge, but also some other lyrics in this play, are distinguished by exquisite tenderness and grace.

Love's Sacrifice, also printed in 1633, with the statement that it was received 'generally well,' was probably acted

Love's Sacrifice (pr. 1633).

> Sorrows mingled with contents prepare
>   Rest for care;
> Love only reigns in death; though art
> Can find no comfort for a BROKEN HEART.'

Hazlitt (*Lectures on Dramatic Literature*, p. 184) pointed out the resemblance between the scene in which Calantha receives the news of the deaths during the dance, and the scene of the masque in Marston's *Malcontent* (act v, sc. 3); but the resemblance is only a very general one. (Cf. *ante*, p. 70, *note*, for the use of the same device in C. Tourneur's *The Revenger's Tragedy*.)

[1] Especially act ii. sc. 3; act iii. sc. 1; act iii. sc. 5; act iv. sc. 2; and act v. scenes 2 and 3.

about three years earlier[1]. This tragedy, though inferior in construction to *'Tis Pity*, is in some respects almost equally characteristic of its author[2]. Its theme is a tissue of passion and revenge, into which too many coarse threads are allowed to enter. The love of Bianca for Fernando, which arouses the jealousy of Bianca's husband and thus brings about the death of the whole trio, is represented as stopping short of actual guilt; the balance between virtue and crime thus remains as it were in suspense, and sympathy seems all but allowable. Never has the intensity of passion been more forcibly painted than in this very character of Bianca, who tempts and restrains, yields and overcomes, in the same moment. At last, when her secret has been betrayed, she bursts forth into wild declarations of her love, and recklessly defies her doom, at once boasting of her love and falsely accusing herself instead of her lover of the worst designs. Revolting as this harrowing picture is in one sense, it may undeniably be psychologically true; like certain other of Ford's female characters, Bianca resembles those conceptions of modern French romance in which temptation is represented as woman's doom. The dramatist has drawn so wavering a line between sin and self-restraint, guilt and innocence, that he may be suspected of having wished to leave unsettled the 'problem' which he proposes. If so, he stands from every point of view self-condemned. The bye-plot of the play is utterly revolting, and in the character of d'Avolos, and the passages in which he excites the jealousy of the Duke against Fernando, Ford has most

[1] Mr. Fleay, *u. s.* vol. i. p. 233, ingeniously suggests that the 'women-anticks' mentioned in act iii. sc. 2 refers to the French actresses who were hissed off the stage in 1629; the allusion is however not very palpable.— The dedication of this play, addressed to the author's kinsman and namesake, John Ford of Gray's Inn, contains an allusion to *Histrio-mastix* (1633).

[2] Crashaw's epigram on the two tragedies—

'Thou cheat'st us, Ford; mak'st one seem two by art:
What is Love's Sacrifice but the Broken Heart?'—

has of course a meaning consonant with the mystic theology of its author; but it is curious, though by no means surprising, to note the admiration of the religious for the dramatic poet. Mr. Gosse, *u. s.* p. 161, notes that this is the only reference made to any of the dramatists in Crashaw's writings.

palpably copied Iago[1]. A considerable proportion of *Love's Sacrifice* is in prose[2].

For *The Fancies Chaste and Noble* (printed 1638) Ford in the Prologue again claims the merit of originality, and this time without any reservation; but whether or not the plot be his own, it is difficult to imagine a worse-contrived one. At the risk of incurring suspicions of the worst kind, the Marquis of Siena has brought up his three nieces in absolute seclusion in his house; and at the close of the play he reveals the excellence of his intentions towards the three Fancies by bestowing their hands in marriage. In other words, every opportunity is afforded for pruriency; and we are then dismissed with the comfort that it was all an affair of the imagination. Combined with this hoax are two serious plots and an abundance of intolerable foolery. Touches of feeling are discoverable in the character of Flavia, and it may be admitted that the virtuous bearing of Castamela in the hour of her supposed danger introduces a refreshing change into the unpleasant atmosphere of the piece.

The Fancies Chaste and Noble (pr. 1638).

Of *The Lady's Trial* (acted 1638) little more need be said than that the main plot of this in parts finely-written comedy seems to me altogether feebly conceived and loosely constructed. From a moral point of view, it exposes itself to no such objections as those which must be made against other of Ford's plays. The suspicion cast on the fidelity of the heroine by the discovery of the importunities to which she has been subjected during her husband's absence, is on his return removed without much difficulty—indeed it seems doubtful whether he has ever allowed it to overcome his rooted belief in the virtues of his Spinella. Of the bye-plots, the one concerned with Benatzi is clumsily contrived; while that which brings before us the lisping Amoretta and her lovers must be set down as commonplace farce. Scarcely any merit is discoverable in this play beyond the even excellence of most of the diction and versification. In its plot a general

The Lady's Trial\acted 1638; pr. 1639).

---

[1] When d'Avolos is led off to his deserved death, he bids farewell to his judges in words not unlike those of Marinelli at the close of Lessing's *Emilia Galotti*.

[2] In act iii. sc. 4 a masque is once more introduced for facilitating a murder of revenge.

resemblance has been pointed out to that of Massinger's *The Fatal Dowry*, but the two plays differ entirely at the close [1].

Perkin Warbeck (pr. 1634).

The *Chronicle Historie of Perkin Warbeck* [2], as it is called on the title-page of the old quarto (printed 1634 with a dedication to the Earl of Newcastle), stands alone among Ford's works as an effort in the field of the historical drama. 'Studies of this nature' had, as the Prologue observes, been 'of late out of fashion' and 'unfollow'd'; and this historical drama carries us back, not indeed to the old Chronicle Histories themselves, whose crudities Ford could have no desire to revive, but to the Histories of Shakspere. In the series formed by these *Perkin Warbeck* may almost be said to supply a missing link; nor is its task unworthily accomplished, since in the whole of our dramatic literature no plays except Marlowe's *Edward II*, the anonymous *Edward III*, and this isolated effort by Ford, can prefer any claim to notice by the side of Shakspere's national historic dramas.

The subject of this tragedy is a most attractive one, which could not fail at various times to engage the attention of dramatic authors [3]. In the Tudor period, it would have required very delicate treatment; for the character of King Henry VII is not susceptible of being rendered interesting, except in a work written by a politician for politicians.

---

[1] See Koeppel, *u. s.*, pp. 185 *seqq.*—Of one of the most pleasing passages (Auria's speech, 'So resolute' &c., in act v. sc. 2) the main idea is apparently borrowed from *Othello.*—Pepys saw this play acted on March 3, 1689.

[2] An edition of this play has been published by Messrs. J. P. Pickburn and J. Le G. Brereton (Sydney, 1896).—No satisfactory evidence exists as to the date of the first performance of *Perkin Warbeck.*

[3] Ford's play (which had been reprinted on the occasion of a similar agitation of the public mind in 1714) was acted in London in the memorable year 1745, in which two other plays on the subject were hastily written, and one of them (by Macklin) was unsuccessfully produced.—A different interest attaches to the sketch of a drama *Warbeck* found among Schiller's posthumous papers (see *Werke*, 12mo. ed., vol. vii). Subtly conceived in its plot and as a study of character, it treats history with absolute freedom, and only carries the story up to the commencement of Warbeck's expedition. For Schiller's intentions with regard to the completion of the play see the ample collection of sketches and other material in vol. ii of Schiller's *Dramatischer Nachlass*, ed. G. Kettner (Weimar, 1895). Alfred Meissner's *Der Prätendent von York* was produced at Weimar in 1885. (*Geschichte meines Lebens*, 1884, vol. ii. pp. 332-4.)

Such a book was Bacon's *Life of Henry VII*, which he offered as a tribute to the statecraft of the master who had allowed him to be sacrificed to parliamentary indignation. On Bacon's book and on Thomas Gainsford's *True and Wonderful History of Perkin Warbeck, &c.* (1618)[1] Ford founded his play; but the dramatist is even more careful than the historian not to pass the bounds of suggestion in the shadows which he allows to fall over the character of the first Tudor King[2]. Yet the figure is skilfully drawn, and leaves an impression probably not far removed from historic truth. The impostor Warbeck is likewise treated with ability, although it cannot be said that the dramatist has made a real character out of his materials. But there is in him at least the suggestion of more than is visible on the surface. While no doubts are anywhere hinted as to the fact of his having been an impostor, he never betrays himself, and the key to the secret of both the man and his career is to be sought, not in King Henry's indignant remark that Perkin 'does but act,' but in his subsequent suggestion that

> ' The custom, sure, of being styl'd a King
> Hath fasten'd in his thought that he is such[3].'

Among the minor personages, the honest old Huntley, who is constrained by King James to give his daughter to the pretended Duke of York, is a character of admirably effective simplicity; and her lover, the faithful Dalyell (Dalzell), is likewise most pleasingly drawn. Even the adventurers who surround the impostor are spirited without being overdrawn sketches; and John-a-Water, the truism-loving mayor of Cork, is perhaps the only really humorous figure Ford ever brought upon the stage.

---

[1] See Koeppel, *u. s.* pp. 187 *seqq.*—Gainsford's narrative was reprinted in vol. xi of *The Harleian Miscellany.*—For the best and clearest modern historical examination of the story of Perkin Warbeck the reader will not fail to refer to the well-known essay by Mr. Gairdner, reprinted as an addition to his *History of the Life and Reign of Richard III* (1878).

[2] See particularly the close of act iii. sc. 3 (and Gifford and Dyce's note); and the admirable passage in act v. sc. 2 (where the King receives the news of the manner of Warbeck's capture).

[3] Act v. sc. 2.

The whole play, while rapid and interesting in action, is thus not inadequate to the dignity of the species which it essays, and to which it is to be regretted Ford should not have turned save in this solitary but successful effort.

Lost plays by Ford.

A tragedy by Ford named *Beauty in a Trance* was entered on the Stationers' Register in 1653, and three comedies, of which however his authorship remains as doubtful as the identity of the plays themselves [1], in 1660.

Ford's character- istics as a dramatist.

In Ford it needs but little power of judgment to discern an author who by the most striking features of his genius is entitled to an entirely distinct place among our most gifted dramatists. Some of his defects, indeed, he shares with others; but even here he may almost be said to make

His want of comic power.

comparison difficult. Of comic power he is on the whole signally devoid, and the gross under-plots by which he thinks it necessary to disfigure most of his works, and the utter brutality with which he is at the pains of investing the personages who figure in many of them, are unrelieved by any play of wit or humour. His low comedy is upon the whole the most contemptible of any in our pre-Restoration drama—certainly of any that was due to the invention of an author of mark; and his high comedy, or what is intended for it, must, notwithstanding his breeding, be

Exceptional merits of his single historical drama.

described as deficient in grace and lightness [2]. In but a single one of his dramas has he shown a certain power of comic characterisation; and from this point of view, as well as from others of more importance in his case, it is to be regretted that he should not have returned to, or sooner essayed, the historic drama, where he would have found most of his characters ready to his hand. The experience of this species would at the same time have accustomed him to a self-restraint

[1] See Fleay, *u. s.*, vol. i. p. 234.

[2] A passage in *The Fancies Chaste and Noble* seems epigrammatically to characterise a favourite dramatic type of which Massinger and Shirley were particularly fond: ' Modesty in pages
Shows not a virtue, boy, when it exceeds
Good manners.'

(Act iii. sc. 1.) But the reference is to greed rather than looseness of talk.

in choice of subjects, which might have prevented him from lamentable moral and artistic aberrations. As it was, Ford in *Perkin Warbeck* furnishes the only example of a History fitted in some measure to supply a gap in the Shaksperean series, though not to be brought into comparison with the works of which that series consists.

In the plays more peculiarly characteristic of this author, few readers will refuse to recognise a combination of varied excellences. As to that of form, indeed, Ford is surpassed by few if any of Shakspere's successors; for his art is always equal to its purpose, and rarely clogged or vitiated by affectation or mannerisms. His versification is distinguished by a fluency arguing no deficiency in strength; his verse is as sweet as Fletcher's, without having the same inclination towards looseness of texture and effeminacy of cadence. Though, for instance, Ford is fond of double-endings to his lines, his verse conveys no impression of excess in this or in any other particular; even 'love's measure' keeps the mean to which 'the smooth licentious poet' thought it a stranger [1]. His lyrical gift, as shown above all in *The Broken Heart*, is very great, although its exercise is not husbanded by him with sufficient care. In the construction of the plays for whose plots he seems to have largely depended on his own invention, he is on the whole hasty and reckless; in his *Broken Heart* he however shows himself capable of inventing and sustaining an action as perspicuous as it is complicated. *The Witch of Edmonton* too is excellently constructed in its main plot; but it is of course impossible to say whether the credit is in this instance to be given to Ford.

His versification.

His construction.

The strength of Ford's genius lies elsewhere. The intensity of his imagination enables him to reproduce situations of the most harrowing kind, and to reveal, with a vividness and suddenness wholly peculiar to himself, the depths of passion, sorrow, and despair which lie hidden in the hearts of men and women. The dark cloud which overshadowed the creative power of Webster,

His strength to be sought in the intensity of particular situations and passages.

---

[1] *'Tis Pity, &c.*, act ii. sc. 2. Ford's plays contain a large admixture of prose; but I am not aware that the quality of the prose in itself calls for remark.

had settled upon the imagination of Ford ; but to him it was given to make audible in the gloom the most secret throbbings of human anguish.   That he at times creates these effects by conceptions unutterably shocking to our consciousness of the immutable authority of moral laws, betrays an inherent weakness in his inventive power instead of enhancing our admiration of it.   The passion of Juliet is as intense, and the sympathy excited by her fate as irresistible, as are the guilty love of Annabella and the spasm of pity which her catastrophe excites in us ; and the horrible nature of the plot is therefore not of the essence of the emotions which the tragedy is intended to call forth. The character of Bianca is a subtle psychological study,—

Contrasts of passion and sweetness.

subtle as the analysis of a possible disease.   Of the irresistible eloquence of pure tenderness, such as that of Penthea's dying sufferings and Eroclea's devoted affection, Ford is likewise master ; yet it is not in these scenes, but in those where the ragings of passion alternate with sudden touches of thrilling sweetness, that his power is altogether exceptional.

Ford's tragedy fails to purify the emotions.

Ford was a dramatic poet of true genius; but his imagination moved at the best in a restricted sphere ; and few of our great English dramatists have more insidiously contributed to unsettle the true conception of the basis of true tragic effect.   The emotions are not purified by creations

> ' Sweeten'd in their mixture
> But tragical in issue '—

so long as the mixture remains unharmonised, and the mind continues to be perturbed by the spectacle of an unsolved conflict [1].   A dramatist who falls short of this, the highest end of tragedy, cannot lay claim to its greenest laurels.   The tragic power of Ford is therefore as incomplete in its total effect as it is fitful in its individual operations ; and

> ' It physics not the sickness of a mind
> Broken with griefs,'—

nor lends its aid to sustain that health of soul which seeks

---

[1] So that the spectator or reader is no wiser than the fool apostrophised by Ennius (Fr. *Phoenix, ap.* Ribbeck, *Römische Tragödie*, p. 192 :

' Stultus est qui [non] non cupienda cupiens cupienter cupit.'

one of its truest sustenances in perfect art. It excites; it
distresses; it astonishes; it entrances; but it fails to purify,
and by purifying to elevate and to strengthen. Let those
who may esteem these cavils futile turn from Ford to the
master-tragedians of all times, and they will acknowledge
that Aristotle's definition still remains a sufficient test of
the supreme adequacy of a tragic drama.

As to Ford's choice of themes, it condemns itself. There *His choice*
cannot be any question on this head as to the shifting criteria *of themes*
of times, localities and manners. All these a candid use of *at times as*
unsound as
the comparative method may be trusted to apply; but they *his treat-*
ment of
cannot reach the root of the matter. ' It was,' says Hazlitt [1], *them.*
' not the least of Shakespear's praise, that he never tampered
with unfair subjects. His genius was above it; his taste
kept aloof from it.' Ford's genius, on the contrary, was
attracted, as it were irresistibly, by the temptation to brush
with wings that should have borne it aloft into the liquid
air the fitful flickerings of an unholy flame. In his nature,
finely endowed as it was, there must have been something
unsound.

One further name remains, so far as I can judge, deserving
of a place on that roll of the later dramatists of genius
which closes a great chapter in the history of our literature.
The merits of Shirley—partly perhaps in deference to the *James*
reckless satire of Dryden and some of his contemporaries *Shirley*
(1596-
—have been usually treated with a negligence bordering *1666).*
on contempt; but an attentive perusal of his writings is,
I think, likely to modify the notion that his pretensions are
antiquated and that his doom is decay.

JAMES SHIRLEY [2], born September 18, 1596, in or near *His life.*
the parish of St. Mary Woolchurch, London, was educated

---

[1] *U. s.*, p. 179.

[2] *The Dramatic Works and Poems of James Shirley, with Notes by William
Gifford, and Additional Notes, and some Account of Shirley and his Writings.*
By Alexander Dyce, 6 vols., 1833. Cf. also Fleay, *English Drama.* vol. ii.
pp. 233-47, and my notice of Shirley in vol. lii of *The Dictionary of National
Biography* (1897). Dyce's edition, which is not likely to be superseded,
was welcomed by an interesting article in *The Quarterly Review* (vol. xlix)
for April 1833.—A selection of Shirley's plays, with an Introduction by
Mr. Edmund Gosse, has been published in the *Mermaid* series.

at Merchant Taylors' School, St. John's College, Oxford, and Catharine Hall, Cambridge, where the epigrammatist Thomas Bancroft[1] was his contemporary. He took his degrees in the latter University, and in 1618 and 1619 respectively published his earliest poem, *Eccho, or The Unfortunate Lovers*, supposed to be identical with his *Narcissus, or The Self-Lover*, printed in 1646, and contributed in MS. to the *Lacrymae Cantabrigienses* on the death of Queen Anne. Soon afterwards he took Orders, and is said by Wood to have become a minister at St. Albans. After, according to the same authority, being previously converted to the Church of Rome, he held the mastership of the St. Albans grammar-school from 1623 to 1625. Traces are observable in his plays of his cordial attachment to the beliefs and institutions of a faith to which he through life continued to adhere[2]. It is possible that an early marriage, which there are indications of his having contracted in or about 1623, may have added to his difficulties[3]. In or before 1625 he abandoned scholastic life, and settled in London, where, according to Wood, he 'lived in Gray's Inn, and set up for a play-maker.' Perhaps he had brought 'the first-fruits' of his dramatic Muse with him from Hertfordshire[4]. In the Prologue to his first play he protested against being supposed to set up as a regular purveyor for the theatre; but there can be no doubt that he speedily

---

[1] Bancroft's *Epigrams and Epitaphs* (1639) are interesting to us as celebrating a number of our great dramatists, including Shakspere.

[2] See the references to confession in *The Wedding* (act i. sc. 2 and act ii. sc. 1); to monastic vows and life in *The Grateful Servant* (act v. sc. 2); and cf. *ib.* act iii. sc. 3, the glorification of the Benedictine Order to which it is supposed that Shirley's confessor belonged. St. Albans was a Benedictine monastery, and a tragedy called *St. Albans* was entered in the Stationers' Register in 1639 under Shirley's name; but this has also been surmised (see Fleay, *u. s.*, vol. ii. p. 244) to have referred to the death of Hubert de Burgh, Earl of St. Albans and Clanrickard, which rumour connected with Wentworth (Strafford's) name; cf. Gardiner, *History*, &c., vol. vii. p. 185. See also the passage against sects in *The Gentleman of Venice*, act iii. sc. 1; and cf. *The Grateful Servant*, act iv. sc. 2, and *St. Patrick for Ireland* (*passim*).

[3] A Matthias Shirley, son of James Shirley, baptised in February 1624 at St. Giles', Cripplegate, is supposed to have been the dramatist's son.

[4] In his first play, *Love-Tricks*, the scene of 'The Complement-School' (act iii. sc. 5) suggests the schoolmaster.

found that he had chosen a sphere of work suitable to him. He remained faithful to it for a long series of years (1626–42), and during this period produced a very large number of plays, of which all but a few have been preserved to us, reaching a total not far short of forty. Although he declares that he never affected the ways of flattery[1], he gradually secured the patronage of many friends of the theatre, among whom King Charles I and his consort were the most conspicuous. The former is stated[2] to have furnished Shirley with the plot of *The Gamester*, which His Majesty afterwards declared to be 'the best play he had seen for seven years.' The dramatist's grateful attachment to Queen Henrietta Maria may have added zeal to the bitterness of his attack upon Prynne, whose *Histrio-mastix* had assailed the stage and, as was supposed, its royal patroness, and who was at the time awaiting his sentence in prison[3]. With the avowed intention of 'confuting' the diatribes of this censor of Interludes a most splendid masque was offered to the King and Queen early in 1634 by the members of the four Inns of Court; and this entertainment, called *The Triumph of Peace*, the cost of which is stated to have been upwards of £21,000, was composed by the loyal Shirley. He appears to have enjoyed the favour of other patrons. One of these, the Earl of Kildare[4], induced him in 1636 to pay a visit to Ireland, where a play by him was performed before the Lord Deputy, then Lord Wentworth, and whither he soon returned for a longer sojourn. The dates of his journeys to and from Ireland are not quite certain, but we know that four if not more of his plays[5] were produced in Dublin, and that he permanently resumed his life as a playwright in London in 1640. In the spring of this

---

[1] See the Prologue to *The Maid's Revenge*.

[2] By Sir Henry Herbert in his Office-book.

[3] See the Dedication of *The Bird in a Cage*, and cf. the lines prefixed by Shirley to Ford's *Love's Sacrifice*.

[4] See the Dedication of *The Royal Master*, the play referred to.

[5] In addition to the above-named, *St. Patrick for Ireland*; *The Constant Maid*; and *The Doubtful Heir*, produced at Dublin under the title of *Rosania, or Love's Victory*. Mr. Fleay would further add *The Gentleman of Venice* and *The Politician*.

year he addressed to Strafford congratulatory lines upon his
recovery from the illness which had become so serious
after the great minister's return from Ireland[1]. His active
labours for the stage came to an end with its temporary
suppression, and the rest of his life seems to have been
a more or less arduous struggle with necessity. After in
1641 he had brought out the tragedy of *The Cardinal*, which
he esteemed to be 'the best of his flock,' he produced in
the spring of 1642 the comedy of *The Sisters*; it is in the
Prologue to this play that he reveals the desolation that
had smitten the world for which he wrote, now that
'London had gone to York.' His next play, *The Court
Secret*, though ready for the stage, was never acted; for in
September of the same year all the theatres were closed by
Parliamentary Ordinance.

Leaving his wife and children behind him, Shirley
(according to Wood, to whom we owe virtually all that we
know concerning this dramatist's personal history) followed
to the wars his patron, the Earl (afterwards Duke) of Newcastle, and seems to have taken some sort of part[2] in his
campaigns, which came to an unsatisfactory end in the
summer of 1644. Not much other evidence is forthcoming
to support Wood's assertion that Shirley assisted Newcastle
in the 'composure' of certain plays, by the publication of
which his patron certainly increased neither his own fame nor
that of anybody else. On his return to London, Shirley
seems to have supported himself, partly by the liberality
of his friend, the accomplished scholar Thomas Stanley,
and partly by his pen. He published in 1646 a small
volume of *Poems*, including *Narcissus* and the dramatic
entertainment called *The Triumph of Beauty*; and the
address *To the Reader* prefixed to the first Folio of Beaumont and Fletcher's plays (1647) was from his hand.
Before long, however, he found it necessary to fall back
upon his old profession as a teacher; and to this he appears
to have adhered during the remainder of his days. His work

---

[1] He afterwards dedicated *The Court Secret* to Strafford's son and heir.

[2] This seems proved by the lines *To Odelia* (printed by Dyce, vol. vi.
p. 408).

as a schoolmaster led him to engage in publications directly
connected with his teaching, but in which he might put his
Pegasus to some sort of use in harness[1]. It is pleasing
to find that one of these works was hailed with commendatory verses by his literary friends and associates of other
days.   Although he likewise printed a number of his plays
—six of them, previously unpublished, in 1653, and others
in 1655 and 1659,—and although in 1653 his masque of
Cupid and Death was privately performed in the house
of the Portuguese ambassador, he seems gradually to have
made up his mind to abstain from all further dramatic
composition; and after once announcing his resolution[2],
he never broke it.   Unluckily, in his last years, he associated himself for literary purposes of a different sort with
John Ogilby, at whose theatre in Dublin one or more of
his plays had been performed, and who had now betaken
himself to classical translation, having been hospitably
taught a little Latin at Cambridge, and a little Greek by
David Whitford or Whitfield, at the time usher in the
school kept by Shirley.   Wood states that for this unsatisfactory associate Shirley drudged in his translations of both
Iliad and *Odyssey*, as well as of parts of Vergil; and though
Ogilby appears not to have acknowledged his assistance,
their names were bracketed together in a passage the reverse
of complimentary in one of Dryden's most popular satires[3].
In September 1666 (again according to Wood) the Great
Fire of London drove Shirley and his (second) wife from
their habitation in Whitefriars; and less than two months
afterwards they died—both 'within the compass of a natural
day'—'being in a manner overcome with affrightments, dis-

---

[1] The *Via ad Latinam linguam complanata* (1649) was accompanied by
rules for the manufacture of Latin and English verse, and the *Rudiments of
Grammar* (1656) by rules themselves versified.   The latter publication must
have had some repute, for it was reprinted in 1660 under the title of *Manductio*,
and long after Shirley's death, in 1726, under a more high-sounding title.

[2] See the *Preface* to *Honoria and Mammon* (1659).   The charge in *The
Session of the Poets* that he tried in vain to rival the performances of younger
writers is a palpable lie; as to the truth or falsehood of the companion statement that he 'owned' a play printed under the name of Edward Howard
nothing is known.

[3] 'Much Heywood, Shirley, Ogilby there lay.'   (*MacFlecknoe.*)

consolations, and other miseries occasion'd by that fire and their losses.' They were buried in the churchyard of St. Giles-in-the-Fields, in which suburban parish they had taken up their abode[1].

Shirley—perhaps partly by reason of that modesty which Langbaine[2] regretfully commends as shown in all his writings—seems to have been a favourite among his fellow-dramatists, to judge from the numerous commendatory verses, consistently cordial in tone, prefixed to his plays. Among the writers are Massinger and Ford, as well as Randolph, Habington, Stapylton, and May. With Fletcher[3], as well as with Chapman[4], he was—in one way or another—associated in the authorship of plays, and with the fame of the former it was his special pleasure to connect himself. Of Ben Jonson he speaks as 'our acknowledged master'—a tribute of feeling rather than of fact, so far as resemblance of style and manner is concerned[5]. His not unfrequent reminiscences of Shakspere are of course due to literary fealty only[6]. It seems strange that while echoes of the high opinion entertained of Shirley by his contemporaries are to be met with in the next generation, the satirical

---

[1] The evidence is doubtful on which John Shirley, a miscellaneous writer who flourished in the last twenty years of the century, and seems to have largely devoted himself to the abridgment of chivalrous romances, is supposed to have been a son of the dramatist. Henry Shirley, to whose plays a brief reference will be made below, was certainly no kinsman of James.

[2] P. 475.   [3] Cf. *ante*, vol. ii. p. 740, as to *The Night-Walker*.

[4] Cf. *ante*, p. 444, as to *The Ball* and *Chabot, Admiral of France*; but see below as to the former play.

[5] See the Dedication to *The Grateful Servant.* 'Dyce, while remarking on the difference of manner between Jonson and Shirley, points out Sir Solitary Plot in *The Example* as a direct imitation of the former by the latter. Gifford thinks that Puntarvolo in *Every Man Out of his Humour* furnished the hint for Jack Freshwater in *The Ball*; and notices plagiarisms from *The Alchemist* in *The Young Admiral* (act iv. sc. 1). *The Sad Shepherd* is quoted in *The Constant Maid* (act v. sc. 3).

[6] Shirley's quotations from or reminiscences of Shakspere are not unfrequent. Falstaff is quoted in *The Example* (act ii. sc. 1) and in *The Sisters* (act v. sc. 2); and there seems other reminiscences of *Henry IV* in *The Lady of Pleasure* (act ii. sc. 2) and *The Gamester* (act iv. sc. 1), as well as of *Henry V* in *The Cardinal* (act ii. sc. 1); of *Hamlet* in *The Duke's Mistress* (act v. sc. 1) and *The Politician* (act iv. sc. 3); of *Twelfth Night* in *The Grateful Servant*; of *Cymbeline* in *St. Patrick for Ireland* (act v. sc. 2); and of *A Midsummer Night's Dream* in *The Triumph of Beauty*. Shylock's pound of flesh is referred to in *The Bird in a Cage* (act ii. sc. 1).

tone of Dryden was immediately taken up by Oldham[1], and in a third satirist of the times, Robert Gould, became abuse[2]. Thanks, in the first instance, to the learning of Farmer, and above all to the insight of Charles Lamb, Shirley has gradually recovered his proper place in the list of our great Elisabethans—among whom he stands *extremus primorum.*

Shirley has left us a larger number of plays than any *His plays.* other dramatist except Shakspere and Fletcher. My notes must accordingly be brief; though hardly one of the thirty-three dramas here mentioned deserves to be passed by altogether.

Of Shirley's tragedies, *The Maid's Revenge* (licensed *Tragedies :* 1626) has been described by Dyce as the worst. Yet *The Maid's Revenge* the subject,—a fatal jealousy of sister against sister,—is *(acted 1626* dramatically so excellent that even a less powerful treat- *pr. 1639).* ment than Shirley's could hardly have left it ineffective. The plot, taken from a story in Reynolds' *God's Revenge against Murder*[3], is perspicuous ; while the diction, though hardly to be described as powerful, exhibits, especially in the striking last act, touches of genuine pathos. Castabella in her disguise might have graced a joint production of Beaumont and Fletcher ; while Diego, the pert page, is a specimen of a type which Massinger would not have cared to disown. The comic interlude of Dr. Sharkino and his wonderful cures is naturally introduced.

In *The Traitor*, licensed 1631, and printed in 1635, with *The Traitor* a Dedication to Newcastle, it is, on the other hand, easy to *(acted 1631 ; pr.* agree with Dyce, in recognising Shirley's best work of this *1635).* species, and indeed one of the finest of the romantic tragedies of this period. The plot is based on history; but the author has treated both the character and the fate of the principal personage of his drama with considerable freedom. The

---

[1] *Satire dissuading from Poetry* (Thompson's edn., vol. iii).

[2] He calls him 'the very D'Urfey of the age.'

[3] Bk. ii. hist. 7. According to Genest, vol. ii. pp. 73–4, Shirley's plot was copied by the very Robert Gould mentioned in the previous note as afterwards his assailant, in his tragedy of *The Rival Sisters, or The Violence of Love, c.* 1696).

real Lorenzino de' Medici seems to have been singularly heedless in his talk, although cautious in his designs ; and instead of, as in the play, falling an immediate victim to his own evil ambition, he survived his assassination of Duke Alessandro for eleven years, before vengeance, real or pretended, at last overtook him [1]. From a dramatic point of view—the only one with which we need here concern ourselves—it would be difficult to overrate the effectiveness of Shirley's tragedy. The supple windings of the arch-traitor Lorenzo are represented with consummate skill. For the furtherance of his schemes he cunningly avails himself of the vices of his kinsman the Duke as well as of the virtues of the noble Sciarrha, and with serpentine pliability evades the most imminent danger of discovery [2]. The weight of the tragic horrors accumulated in the catastrophe is overwhelming [3].

The authorship of this tragedy, which was repeatedly revived after the Restoration, was in 1692 claimed for the Jesuit Antony Rivers, but on no tenable grounds. In our own century its plot suggested that of a successful play by a man of versatile genius [4].

[1] See Roscoe's *Life of Lorenzo de' Medici*, chap. x.

[2] See particularly the admirably contrived passage (act iii. sc. 3), ' Whom talk'd he to,' &c.

[3] The terrible device of confronting the lustful Duke with the corpse of the object of his cruel passion recalls several variations (and some of an intolerable sort) on the same theme (cf. *ante*, pp. 15 and 70, and *notes*) ; but it forms a legitimate climax in Shirley's play. An admirable touch in the scene (act iii. sc. 2) where the masque fails of its effect upon the infatuated Duke —' Oh, the lethargy of princes'—recalls the closing words of Lessing's *Emilia Galotti*, a tragedy inspired by its author's enthusiastic appreciation of our old tragic drama.—After a fashion much affected by Shirley a comic episode is contrived by means of the timorous Depazzi, who makes his page Rogero rehearse with him a mock trial for treason (act iii. sc. 1).

[4] Pepys saw *The Traitor* performed not less than four times within the years 1660–7.—The claim set up in the dedication of the reprint of 1692 for Rivers was upheld by Motteux, but appears to have been purely fictitious.— Richard Lalor Sheil's *Evadne, or The Statue* owes to Shirley's tragedy the suggestion of the outline of its plot and the character of the traitorous favourite Ludovico. But Sheil's play, which was first performed in 1819 with an exceptionally powerful cast, is by no means a mere adaptation of Shirley's ; in the concluding situation a far milder theatrical effect is substituted for the appalling horrors of the last act of *The Traitor*; and the diction, which is very fluent and elegant, seems Sheil's own, though he occasionally borrows

To the same year belongs another tragedy—less ambi- *Love's*
tious in design, but hardly less powerful in character. *Cruelty*
The plot of *Love's Cruelty*, licensed 1631 and printed in *(1631, pr.*
1640, does not invite description [1] ; but the purpose of the *1640).*
play must be allowed to be genuinely moral, and its
spirit (notwithstanding some hazardously realistic scenes)
thoroughly healthy. It would be difficult to point to many
works of fiction which more forcibly bring home the truth
of the terrible facility with which, even in a noble nature,
moral weakness may be hurried into crime. The cruel
passion of Clariana, to which Hippolito falls a victim, is
depicted with an intensity approaching that which is characteristic of Ford.

Of Shirley's remaining tragedies, *The Duke's Mistress* *The Duke's*
(acted in 1636, before his first visit to Ireland, and printed *Mistress*
two years afterwards) may be passed by as relatively *(acted 1636,*
deficient in interest. It is, however, both in conception and *pr. 1638).*
in execution, far purer than the title might seem to imply ;
nor is there anything offensive about this piece except the
bye-plot concerned with the ill-favoured Fiametta and the
'gorgon' Scolopendra.

In *The Politician* (acted probably not later than 1639, but *The Politi-*
not printed till 1655 [2]) we have an effort of a very ambitious *cian (prob-*
kind ; some of its characters are cast in a tragic mould *ably by*
which they can hardly be said to fill. Among these are *1639).*
Gotharus the villainous 'politician' himself, his paramour
Queen Marpisa who in the end poisons him for having (by
mistake) caused the death of their son, Haraldus the unhappy but blameless offspring of sin, and Albina the

a flower from Shakspere.—The story of Lorenzo de' Medici forms the plot
of *Lorenzaccio*, the most ambitious, but hardly the most successful, of the
dramas of Alfred de Musset.

[1] Part of it is taken from one of the novels of the Queen of Navarre, or
from Cinthio's *Hecatommithi.*—This play was likewise revived after the
Restoration, and was seen by Pepys in 1667.

[2] Dyce supposed this play to be identical with *The Politique Father*,
licensed in 1641 ; but Mr. Fleay (*u. s.*, pp. 242 and '6) thinks that the latter
play was the same as *The Brothers*, and that *The Politician* was acted in
Dublin. The plot of this play is traced by Mr. Fleay to Bk. i of the famous
Countess of Montgomery's *Urania*, acted 1641, printed 1652, which has not
been accessible to me.

virtuous and devoted wife of the guilty Gotharus. The interest of the action is well sustained ; but the characters are designed without depth. In the personage of Haraldus a more genuine pathos is perhaps traceable than in that of Albina ; the impressive scene of his death, following upon an interview with his mother, vaguely recalls Hamlet's interview with Gertrude [1].

The Cardinal (acted 1641, pr. 1652).

The Cardinal, licensed 1641 and printed in 1652, was esteemed by the author himself his best tragic work [2], and brought him high commendations both before and after the Restoration [3]. The catastrophe of this tragedy is elaborated with a considerable expenditure of effort ; very possibly, as was suggested by Dyce, Webster's *Duchess of Malfi* exercised an influence upon its composition. A failure of artistic power is however observable in the treatment of the character of the Cardinal, who cannot be said to become its principal personage till towards the end of the play ; and the diction, as Dyce points out, has far less perspicuity than is usual with Shirley, so that the reader frequently finds himself in the situation of the Duchess when she tells the Cardinal :

> ' Your phrase has too much landscape, and I cannot
> Distinguish, at this distance you present,
> The figure perfect [4].'

[1] The device by which Haraldus' death is brought about is undignified. He is made drunk by two courtiers whom his father Gotharus has sent to cure him of his melancholy, and dies from the fever thus contracted. Shirley must have remembered *Hamlet* in writing this play ; possibly he also remembered Cassio in *Othello*.

[2] See *Dedication* and *Prologue*.

[3] Pepys saw it thrice—in 1662, '7 and '8.

[4] See act iv. sc. 2.—The scene of this play is laid at the Court of Navarre. The Prologue seems to indicate that no allusion is intended to another Court, where a Cardinal was at that time (1641) all-powerful. (The allusion in act ii. sc. 2 to the dangers which overbearing prelates might incur in England is extremely curious, especially from an old pupil of the Oxford College of which in his day Laud was President.) The Cardinal has induced the King to sanction the marriage of a beautiful young widow, the Duchess Rosaura, to the Cardinal's nephew, the proud and fiery Columbo. Rosaura's heart however belongs to the Count d'Alvarez ; and Columbo having been sent off in command of a military expedition, she entreats him by letter to release her from her engagement. He feigns assent, though at heart stung to fury by her breach of promise ; and on returning victorious from the wars

Of the rest of Shirley's plays the great majority may be *General*
described as romantic comedies, in which the element of *character of*
                                                          Shirley's
incident predominates.   Their scene is usually laid in *other plays.*
the favourite regions of the romantic drama, the lands of
the South ; and there is every reason for believing that the
instances are very few in which the author had derived the
materials of his plot from any previous narrative or dramatic
work.   These characteristics are not, however, common to *Plays of an*
all of Shirley's remaining dramas, and before noticing the *exceptional*
                                                            kind.
comedies falling under the most numerous division of his
plays, I may direct attention to a few of these which possess
more or less distinctive features of their own.

Among these the precedence belongs, by virtue at all *St. Patrick*
events of the dignity of subject, to *St. Patrick for Ireland.* *for Ireland*
                                                                 (pr. 1640).
This curious drama, printed in 1640[1], was produced two
or three years earlier, of course in Dublin, and does not

kills his innocent rival and casts his corpse before Rosaura's feet.   Under
the influence of the Cardinal, the King forgives Columbo this bloody deed,
and Rosaura resolves on private vengeance, for which a captain called
Hernando, who is smarting under an insult offered him by Columbo, presents
himself as a willing agent.

In the fifth act the plot, and with it the character of the Cardinal, take
a new turn.   Hitherto he has played no primary part in the action, and his
character has been that of a crafty but not wholly selfish schemer.   But
Columbo having been killed by Hernando, the Cardinal resolves on a double
crime—vengeance for his nephew's death is to follow the dishonour of the
Duchess whom he suspects to be its authoress.   Rosaura had feigned madness
in order to conceal her own intentions of revenge ; but the Cardinal pursues
his hideous design, which is only frustrated by Hernando's sword.   The King
appears on the scene ; and the Cardinal, believing himself on the point of
death from his wounds, pretends to have poisoned the Duchess, and feigning
repentance offers an antidote of which he drinks part.   But the antidote
itself proves to be poison ; and as his wounds were not really mortal he has
thus killed himself as well as his victim.

Thus in this extraordinary fifth act the character of the Cardinal changes
from politic ambition to villainy of the deepest dye.   It is this change which
seems to me to remain dramatically unaccounted for, and therefore inartistic.
The character of the terrible Columbo is drawn with a certain power ; but
the contrast of gentle modesty in his rival d'Alvarez is rather too strongly
marked ; the unhappy young man is almost insipid. The strength of the play
lies in the situations, especially those of the fifth act ; but even from this point
of view this tragedy hardly deserves to be ranked as high as *The Traitor.*

[1] On the title-page of the 1640 quarto of this play it is described as the
First Part, and the promise of a *Second Part* is held out in both the *Prologue*
and the *Epilogue* ; but none such is known to have been produced.—The play
was reprinted in 1751 at Dublin in Chetwood's *Select Collection of Old Plays.*

appear to have been licensed in England, where there was, more especially after the outbreak of the rebellion of 1641, no sympathy to spare for Ireland's national saint[1]. The nature of the reception accorded to this 'patron' play by the 'patrons' whom it found at Dublin[2] is unknown; but the mixture of religious sentiment and high spirits which it exhibits corresponds to the usages whereby St. Patrick was within recent memory annually honoured on his sacred mountain in Connemara. The Saint himself and his miracles—culminating in the inevitable expulsion of snakes from Ireland—can however hardly be said to constitute the principal interest of this drama, which centres rather in the strange doings of the pagans at King Leogarius' Court, especially of the chief priest Archimagus and his servant Rodomant (the clown of the piece), and of Prince Corybreus[3].

Although this play is evidently from the hand of a devout Catholic[4], and although it treats the figure of the Saint with genuine reverence, it cannot, as a whole, be said to exhibit any real enthusiasm or even elevation of tone. Shirley's crude attempt to combine the spirit of a miracle-play with the attractions of a drama of intrigue must be

[1] The London stage had recently been familiarised with the person of the Patron Saint of England in Kirke's play called *The Seven Champions of Christendom* (printed 1638), in which St. George took the leading part. This production is described by Genest (vol. x. p. 108), who considers it 'far from a bad play.'—Calderon's *Purgatorio de San Patricio* (Ticknor, vol. ii. p. 367) was founded on a popular book of devotion on the life of the Saint which, together with Calderon's drama itself, may have been known to Shirley; but the resemblances do not appear to be very close. For a translation of the Spanish play, and an account of the source from which its materials were drawn, see Mr. D. F. McCarthy's *Dramas of Calderon*, vol. ii.

[2]   'Give us your free votes, and let us style
         You patrons of the play, Him of the isle.' *Epilogue.*

[3] Corybreus visits the virtuous Emeria in the disguise of a god—an episode borrowed from Josephus or Bandello, which also recurs in Fletcher's *Mad Lover* (cf. *ante*, vol. ii. p. 701).

[4] St. Patrick is (like the heroine of Massinger's *Virgin Martyr*) watched over by an angelic guardian, named Victor. See also the passage (act v. sc. 2) in which St. Patrick consoles Emeria by foretelling that she will become the foundress of a religious order,—an expedient which (like that in Massinger's *Maid of Honour*, cf. *ante*, p. 20) would hardly have been adopted by a Protestant writer.

classed among the oddities of dramatic literature. In the absence of the promised Second Part the conversion of Ireland is left in a quite initiatory state.

While in *St. Patrick for Ireland* we have an element of the old miracle-play, Shirley's last dramatic work (if his own statement in the Dedication is to be accepted literally), *Honoria and Mammon* (published in 1659), announces itself as a 'Moral, dressed in dramatic ornament.' There is no proof that this production was ever intended for the stage, for which Shirley had probably long ceased to write. The work is an expansion of an earlier piece, called *A Contention for Honour and Riches*, an entertainment in the style of the old moralities (printed in 1633). In the later production typical characters are substituted for the partially abstract figures of the earlier ; but there is nothing in either to call for remark, although *Honoria and Mammon* is worth reading for some of the passages of satirical description contained in it[1]. Shirley has left some other entertainments of various kinds, which may be noticed at the foot of the page[2].

Honoria and Mammon (pr. 1659).

A Contention for Honour and Riches (pr. 1633).

---

[1] See especially the sketch of the habits of life of a young citizen (act v. sc. 1).

[2] *The Triumph of Peace*, the famous masque presented at Whitehall in 1633, is remarkable for its unusually large number of characters. Some of these are rather humorously conceived ; see especially the second anti-masque, introducing 'effects of peace' which may, as Opinion says, be more appropriately called 'corruption.' Among them are 'projectors' of various kinds—prototypes of the 'Gründer' too well known in Germany after the Peace of 1870. (For an account of the ostentatiously magnificent performance of this masque see Whitelocke's *Memorial of the English Affairs*, ed. 1853, vol. i. pp. 53–62 ; cf. Gardiner, *History, &c.*, vol. vii. p. 331). *The Triumph of Beauty* ('printed 1646, as performed 'at a private Recreation') treats the familiar myth which Peele had long ago made the subject of a play at Court in his *Arraignment of Paris* (cf. vol. i. p. 366), and introduces a company of shepherds headed by 'Bottle,' a very palpable imitation of Bottom the Weaver. The masque of *Cupid and Death* (performed in 1653 before the Portuguese ambassador, and printed in that year and again in 1659) reproduces the story of Cupid and Death exchanging their weapons ; and *The Contention of Ajax and Ulysses* (printed in 1659, as privately acted) treats with considerable fluency of rhetoric a well-known Ovidian episode, closing with the beautiful lyric *The glories of our birth and state*, supposed to have been suggested by the downfall, if not by the death, of Charles I, and said to have terrified the mind of Oliver Cromwell when recited to him. (See *Quarterly Review, u.s.*, p. 11. Gifford quotes a note of Oldys, according

*The
Arcadia
(before
1640).*

The Arcadia, which calls itself a 'Pastoral' (printed in 1640, after being acted some time previously—very probably as early as 1632 [1]), differs from the generality of Shirley's plays by the entire want of originality in its plot. It is, in fact, nothing but a dramatic version of the main argument, if it may so be called, of Sidney's famous romance. The action is drawn together with a certain degree of skill out of the loose network of that prolix work; but the story as thus condensed can hardly be said to wear any highly poetic aspect. As dramatised by Shirley, the adventures of Musidorus and Pamela are barely redeemed from dulness by the comic element of Mopsa's delusion; while an impression the reverse of pleasing is left by his treatment of the story—in itself not altogether attractive—of Pyrocles, who, disguised as an amazon, is beset by the admiration of both the parents of his beloved princess [2]. The Elisabethan Arcadia is itself sufficiently remote from the sweet simplicity of nature;—the Caroline Arcadia in its theatrical dress is even more absolutely artificial, though the version cannot be described as in substance untrue to its original [3].

Comedies :

The remainder of Shirley's comedies are in all essentials so closely akin to one another, that no purpose would be served by seeking to apply the epithet of romantic to a portion of them only, and to deny it to the rest, merely because of the locality in which their scenes respectively happen to lie. In a few instances this scene is England, in the greater number Italy—but no attempt is made by the

to which ' old Bowman used to sing' this song to King Charles himself.) It was afterwards printed as Butler's among his *Posthumous Works.*

[1] Mr. Fleay (p. 239) very ingeniously deduces from the references to 'the King's birth-day ' in act iii. sc. 1, taken together with certain other *data*, that Shirley's *Arcadia* was acted on the birthday of King Charles, November 19, in the year 1632. Thomas Heywood's *Love-Mistress*, also an Arcadian play (cf. *ante*, p. 583), was, he holds, presented on the same occasion in 1634.—It will be remembered with what ferocity Milton castigated the use of an 'Arcadian prayer'—Pamela's prayer—by the supposed author of *Eikon Basilike* in the time of his captivity.

[2] Cf. *ante*, p. 596, as to Day's *Isle of Gulls.*

[3] M'Namara Morgan's tragedy *Philoclea*, acted in 1753, about which time Shirley's play seems to have been printed, is of course founded on Sidney's romance, but seems to differ in treatment (see Genest, vol. iv. p. 395).

author to mark any distinction between the manners of these two countries; and it is needless to say in which of them Shirley found his personal models.

Thus, though the only indication of the scene of the earliest of Shirley's plays, *Love-Tricks, or The School of Complement* (licensed 1625, printed in 1631 under its second title and in subsequent editions), is an allusion to 'this our Fairy-isle,' the island in question is, as Gifford has pointed out, no other than England itself. The lover may be named Infortunio and a justice's clerk Ingeniolo, but they remain Englishmen almost as palpably as Jenkin remains a Welshman. This comedy, probably written while Shirley was still on the eve of adopting the profession of a playwright, has in it something of the freshness as well as of the lengthiness characteristic of juvenile works, and seems to have been very successful[1]. The plot is rather carelessly constructed[2], and the pastoral scenes are purely conventional; but some humour (though not of a very striking or novel kind) is infused into the scene of the 'Complement-School,' where the arts of politeness and eloquence are to be had ready-made on payment of a fee[3].

Love-Tricks (acted 1625, *pr.* 1631).

The Wedding (licensed 1626[4] and printed 1629) I am inclined to regard as a play of high merit;—without Langbaine's condescending qualification, 'considering the Time in which 'twas writ.' The plot is both interesting in itself and of great dramatic strength. It would be difficult to find a better constructed serious action; and the underplot which relieves it is full of life[5].

The Wedding (acted 1626, *pr.* 1629).

---

[1] It was revived after the Restoration, when Pepys saw it on August 5, 1667.

[2] There seems equally little reason why the heroine Selina should take a fancy to the old merchant Rufaldo, and why she should suddenly abandon him.

[3] See act iii. sc. 5.—Books of Polite Instruction were, as Gifford observes, very numerous in this age; and from these there were not many steps to such manuals of the art of success in the world as that earlier Chesterfield, Francis Osborne's, *Advice to a Son* (1656–8), which Pepys so assiduously studied. (See Judge Parry's *Introduction* to his delightful edition of this treatise, 1896.)

[4] See Mr. Fleay's (p. 236) obvious correction of a passage in act iii. sc. 2: 'in the second year of the reign of King Cupid.'—This seems to have been a very favourite piece; of the five sets of commendatory verses called forth by it one is by Ford.

[5] The action opens with the preparations for a wedding, which are inter-

The Brothers (acted 1626, pr. 1653).

The Brothers was licensed in 1626 and printed in 1653. For I am unable to adopt the contention of Mr. Fleay that the play published by Shirley himself under this title as one of the *Six New Plays* was a different one from that produced in 1626, and that this latter was the comedy called *Dick of Devonshire*, not known to have been printed till our own day[1]. The theme of *The Brothers* is one which both the sentimental and the comic drama of these latter days have reiterated with wearisome persistency; yet few tyrannical parents, either in real or in theatrical life, can have gone beyond the father of Felisarda, who is ordered by him to prefer suitor upon suitor according to their degrees of wealth. But there is an approach to genuine pathos in the mutual fidelity of the much-tried heroine and her lover Fernando; and a diverting element is supplied, at least in the earlier scenes, by the frank immorality of Luys.

The Witty Fair One (acted 1628, pr. 1633).

The Witty Fair One, licensed in 1628 and printed in 1633[2], is unpleasing in plot, but contains a considerable rupted in consequence of a dark suggestion as to the unfaithfulness of the bride, whispered to the bridegroom by his friend. A duel ensues, and in the moment of what seems to be his death the friend repeats his asseveration of the lady's guilt, of which he declares himself to have been the partner. But he recovers from his wound; and it finally proves that not the innocent Gratiana, but Lucibel (who appears in the play disguised as the page Millicent) had been his victim. The troubles of the falsely-accused bride, of the repentant sinner, of the desperate bridegroom who believes himself to have slain his friend, and of the injured but devoted Lucibel, are all at once terminated by a happy and natural *dénouement*.—The chief figures of the under-plot are Rawbone, a thin and thrifty citizen whom the doctor has told ' there's no way but one with him '—(*i. e.* he must die),—and ' that's not the way of all flesh,' says his interlocutor, and his fat rival Lodam, whose delectable duel is the most amusing scene of the play.

[1] Cf. *ante,* p. 583, *note.* Towards the close of *Dick of Devonshire* the Duke of Macada says :

> ' Letters shall forthwith fly into Madrid,
> To tell the King the storyes of Two Brothers,
> Worthy the Courtiers' reading.'

But this evidence is hardly sufficient in itself. While I agree with Mr. Fleay that Mr. Bullen has not made out a case for assigning *Dick of Devonshire* to Thomas Heywood, neither can I think that the authorship of this play has been brought home to Shirley. Mr. Fleay thinks that Shirley's original *The Brothers* was the play by him licensed as *The Politic Father* in 1641. But he gives no reason why Shirley should have ' determined not to publish ' this production.

[2] It was revived in 1667.

variety of characters. Among these the foolish knight
Sir Nicholas Treedle is the most amusing—particularly
in the scene where he submits to an examination and
lecture by his tutor[1]. The notion of the 'wild young
gentleman' Master Fowler being converted from the error
of his ways by means of a conspiracy to treat him as dead,
is perhaps better in the invention than in the execution;
but one of the epitaphs which he discovers to have been
written on him is meritorious [2].

The Grateful Servant, licensed in 1629 under the title of
The Faithful Servant, and printed in 1630 under the name
it afterwards retained, seems to me, so far as its main plot
is concerned, an extremely pleasing work. The theme of
the action is a noble one,—the unselfishness of true love [3];
and the play is undoubtedly distinguished by elevation of
sentiment, as well as by excellence of construction and
diction. It was worthy of being dedicated to Jonson (of
whose manner, however, it exhibits no traces) and of the
commendations bestowed on it by not less than nine fellow-
poets.

Changes, or Love in a Maze (licensed and printed 1632)
may be passed by as a comedy of inferior merit, hardly
successful in its treatment of an idea which might have been

*Changes, or
Love in a
Maze (acted
and printed
1632).*

---

[1] Act ii. sc. 1.

[2] 'How he died, some do suppose;
How he lived, the parish knows;
Whether he's gone to heaven or h—,
Ask not me, I cannot tell.'

[3] Foscari, the lover of Cleona, when he finds that the Duke is a suitor for
her hand, declares himself ready to renounce his aspirations to it. He has
given himself out for dead, having resolved to take the vows of a Benedictine monk, when a happier turn occurs in his fortunes. Leonora, the Duke's
former love, who has assumed the disguise of a page in order to escape from
another marriage, and has entered the service of Foscari, reveals her identity
to him. The relations between Foscari, Cleona, the Duke and Leonora-
Dulcino, recall *Twelfth Night* and its several analogues; but, notwithstanding
the difference, the resemblance to Shakspere's play cannot be regarded as
fortuitous, especially since one or two features of Malvolio reappear in
Cleona's 'foolish ambitious' steward Jacomo (otherwise a quite distinct
character).—The bye-plot of *The Grateful Servant* appears to be wholly
original; but though its intention may be good, the less said about it the
better.

made the basis of an excellent play [1]. Its popularity on its revival after the Restoration seems to have been unusual [2]. In the scene where Caperwit the poetaster discusses the importance of adjectives in poetry [3] we are reminded, as in *Love-Tricks*, of Shirley's scholastic experiences.

Hyde Park (acted 1632, *pr.* 1637). The action of *Love in a Maze* is laid in London, but the next two comedies in the list of Shirley's plays bring us into direct contact with the realities of contemporary life and manners. Only in so far as it is descriptive of these, can any special interest be said to attach to the comedy of *Hyde Park*, licensed 1632, acted in 1637, and revived with new realistic attractions after the Restoration [4]. Not much charm is to be found either in the supposed widow Bona-vent, or in the lively and capricious Mistress Carol, whose lover secures her affections by deluding her into a vow never to love him or desire his company. On the other hand, her chatter is full of entertaining allusions; and the scenes in the Park, with the races horse and foot, the gentlemen making their bets, and even the ladies venturing 'a pair of gloves,' furnish a gay and bustling picture of the idle life of the day.

[1] The situation of a man distracted by an equal passion for two sisters, both of whom are alike enamoured of him, is certainly an excellent starting-point for either a comic or a tragic complication, whether or not such a difficulty be in accordance with actual human experience. But Shirley has made little of it, and the comedy is uninteresting. The self-denying affection of Yongrave for Eugenia (act iv. sc. 1) repeats a motive already used by Shirley in *The Grateful Servant*.

[2] Pepys saw it not less than five times in the course of the years 1662-83, and Langbaine notes its successful revival in the following generation.—The felicitous title of *Love in a Maze*, which seems to have remained the stage-designation of Shirley's play, was borrowed by the late Mr. Dion Boucicault for a comedy of real literary merit.

[3] Act ii. sc. 2.

[4] According to Pepys, horses were brought on the stage in this piece (on its revival after the Restoration in 1668), the earliest record, according to Dyce, of 'a species of absurdity with which modern audiences are highly gratified.' The song in honour of the famous race-horses of the day (act iv. sc. 3) almost entitles *Hyde Park* to rank as the ancestor of a species which has since the days of Pepys been carried further than he would have thought possible, and which is known by the name of the 'sporting drama.'—The horse-races in *Hyde Park* are referred to in Glapthorne's *Wit in a Constable* (act ii. sc. 1).—The play was dedicated to the Earl of Holland (beheaded in 1649), who appears to have opened part of the Park to the public, and for whom Holland House was built.

The Ball, also licensed in 1632 and printed in 1639, is again chiefly noteworthy as a comedy of manners. This play was licensed as by Shirley; but on the title-page of the printed copy it is described as the joint composition of Shirley and Chapman. It would appear from a memorandum in Sir Henry Herbert's Office-book that in *The Ball* 'there were divers personated so naturally both of lords and others of the court' that the Master of the Revels would have forbidden the play, had he not been promised the omission of 'many things which he found faulte withal.' Mr. Fleay conjectures that for these passages in the play—which he supposes to have originally been entirely by Shirley—others of Chapman's writing were substituted. Chapman is *a priori* unlikely to have taken any share in the composition of comic scenes at so late a date as 1632, and it cannot be supposed that those in question were written at an earlier date[1]. If, as the title-page of the quarto asserted, he gave any assistance at all to Shirley in this play, it must have been of the slightest description[2]. The satire which remains in the play cannot upon the whole be said to be very biting, except in the case of the pretended traveller Jack Freshwater, of whom the notion was however more probably taken from a dramatic than from an actual original[3]. The main purpose of this comedy seems to have been to give the lie to the scandalous reports which had arisen in connexion with the first attempts at establishing Subscription Balls[4]. How far these early efforts in

Shirley (and Chapman)'s The Ball (1632).

---

[1] See Fleay, *English Drama*, vol. ii. pp. 238-9. The most important scene in the play (act v. sc. 1) speaks of the performance of ' a very pretty comedy call'd *Martheme* at the Bear-garden.' This might, as Mr. Fleay supposes, refer to the performance of *Bartholomew Fair* at the Hope in 1634 ; but two lines further the female actors of 1629 seem referred to, and there are other indications of a late date.

[2] This was Dyce's opinion, held in opposition to Gifford's.

[3] Viz., as Gifford suggests, from Puntarvolo in Jonson's *Every Man Out of his Humour*. Coryat, however, who is actually mentioned in act ii. sc. 1, and his Venetian experiences undoubtedly supplied many touches, though his travels were real enough. (See especially act v. sc. 1, where Jack Freshwater gives an astounding account of his grand tour from Gravesend, where it ultimately appears that he 'stay'd all this summer, expecting a wind.')

[4] These meetings, in which a golden ball is said to have been the badge of

support of what was to grow into one of the most respectable of British institutions had virtue on their side, it is perhaps impossible to ascertain. Shirley's comedy, seasoned as it was by unmistakeable personalities of dress, manner, or speech, doubtless stimulated curiosity while reproving captious tongues ; but whatever charm belonged to it has long since evaporated, and its intrinsic merits cannot be held to be considerable.

The Bird in a Cage (acted and pr. 1633).   *The Bird in a Cage*, as has been admirably conjectured by Mr. Fleay, seems to have been the same play as that originally licensed, in January 1633, under the title of *The Beauties*, and spitefully re-named before its publication later in the year, in order to point the reference to Prynne, then awaiting his sentence in prison[1].

The Young Admiral (acted 1633, pr. 1637).   In *The Young Admiral*, licensed in 1633 and printed in 1637, we meet with another of those romantic comedies which few of our dramatists can have produced with

the presiding lady (is this the ' device ' alluded to in act iv. sc. 3 ?), are by one of the characters charged with being attended by ' strange words ' and resulting in ' strange revels '; but the heroine Lucina (!) undertakes to prove their innocence to her lover. In act v the Ball is held—it consists in point of fact of the presentation of a masque—and the character of the amusement is vindicated.—I note in the *New English Dictionary, s. v.*, that no earlier instance than this is known of a precisely similar use of the term ' ball.' The word occurs in 1633 in the sense of a dance-measure or figure, in the phrase ' to dance a ball '—apparently a derived meaning only.

[1] See *English Drama*, vol. ii. pp. 239-40. The salient passage in the play is act iii. sc. 3, where the ladies of the Court of Mantua, called its ' beauties ' in the opening scene, resolve upon acting a play to ' please the princess.'—The Dedication of *The Bird in a Cage* is conceived in a spirit of almost savage sarcasm, which is only pardonable if the vital significance of the incident to both sides of the controversy is fairly taken into consideration. Prynne is apostrophised as an ' inimitable Mecenas,' and his captivity is adverted to as a ' happy retirement,' on which the writer professes to have ' had an early desire to congratulate ' him. ' No poem could tempt me with so fair a circumstance as this ' (Prynne's imprisonment) ' in the title ' (*The Bird in a Cage*). The patron's benevolent attention is particularly desired to the play personated by ladies introduced into the action. The allusion to love-locks (act i. sc. 1) is no doubt, as Gifford points out, pointed at Prynne's tract, *The Unloveliness of Love-locks*, mentioned in the Dedication. —The scene (act iv. sc. 1) in which Bonamico describes to the Duke the accomplishments and performances of the inhabitants of the cage is full of witty political allusions.—In act iii. sc. 1 there is a curious allusion to Shylock's bargain.—Altogether, the play would well repay editing as a curiosity. An adaptation of it, entitled *The Bird in a Cage, or Money works Wonders*, was performed in 1786. (Genest, vol. vi. p. 399.)

a facility exceeding Shirley's.   The ingeniously constructed
plot of this play skilfully prepares the double moral conflict
to be exhibited in the person of its hero.   Both the
tyrannous prince Cesario and his weak sire the King are
well drawn ; while a novel and highly effective incident
is furnished by the daring of Rosinda, who delivers herself
into the hands of the enemy and thus becomes a hostage
for Cesario's safety.   The comic episode of the trick played
upon the foolish Pazzarello by the sportive page Didimo,
who causes him to undergo a magic process warranted to
render him 'free from stick and shot,' is also, to the best of
my remembrance, original.   The Master of the Revels took
special notice in his Office-book of the circumstance that
this play might 'serve for a patterne to other poetts, not
only for the bettring of maners and language, but for the
improvement of the quality' (*i. e.* the actors) 'which hath
received some brushings of late[1].'   In view, however, of
the well-known personal connexion of King Charles I with
Shirley's next piece, it becomes difficult to suppose *The
Young Admiral* to have been selected as one of the King's
birthday plays because of its propriety of diction and
of action ; nor can this have been the chief reason why
the same play was in 1662 presented before King
Charles II on November 20 (the morrow of the anniversary
of his father's birthday)[2].

The celebrated comedy of *The Gamester* was licensed
1633 and printed in 1637.   The popularity which this play
long continued to enjoy in the several versions which successively appeared of it[3], must have had some other reason
than the royal origin of its plot[4] and the royal praise of its
execution.   It is probably to be accounted for in the first

*The Game-
ster (acted
1634, pr.
1637).*

---

[1] Cf. Collier, vol. i. p. 480, *note*.

[2] See Evelyn's *Diary, s. d.*

[3] Among these were Charles Johnson's *The Wife's Relief, or The Husband's
Cure* (1711), *The Gamesters*, by Garrick (1757 and 1772), and *The Wife's
Stratagem*, by Poole (1827).   Mrs. Centlivre's *The Gamester* (noticed below)
and Edward Moore's prose drama bearing the same title (1753) have no
connexion with Shirley's play.

[4] Part of the plot King Charles, or Shirley, seems to have found in one of
the *Two Hundred Novels* of Celio Malespini (ii. 96), or in the *Heptameron* of
the Queen of Navarre (i. 8).

instance by the ingenuity of the plot, of which the final
surprise—converting an apparently objectionable complication into a harmless stratagem—is cleverly kept secret till
quite the close of the play. Secondly, by the striking
vivacity of the action, in which the gambling scenes, the
follies of Barnacle the younger and their punishment,
and the pathetic loves of Beaumont and Violante[1], in
different ways relieve the progress of the main plot.
Thirdly, by the vigour of the composition ; for Shirley,
doubtless from a determination to do honour to a royal
command, was manifestly on his mettle when writing this
play.

It must however be remarked — more especially as
this play was in a widely-read essay by a justly popular
writer[2] treated as a typical work of a literary growth
which he sternly condemned—that few of Shirley's other
dramas are more obnoxious than *The Gamester* to the
charge of lasciviousness of diction and general grossness of
tone[3]. True, what is from this point of view so specially
offensive in the latter part of the play is mere pretence ;
but few spectators or readers are likely to possses sufficient
theatrical prescience to foresee the ultimate harmless issue
of the action. As a comedy of manners the play deserves
high praise, and the scenes in the Ordinary are full of life[4].
But notwithstanding such merits as these, it would in my
opinion be extremely unfair to Shirley to judge him as a
dramatist by this play, which cannot on the whole be said
to deserve its exceptional celebrity. The character of
Wilding is so ineffably contemptible that nothing can

---

[1] See particularly act iv. sc. 2.

[2] Charles Kingsley in his *Plays and Puritans* (republished 1873).

[3] Dr. Gardiner (*History, &c.*, vol. vii. p. 331), in his wish to insist
upon the essence of the immorality of this play, has surely treated it too
generously in saying that 'as far as words went it was innocent enough.
It contained no coarse jests or gross expressions.'

[4] In act iii. sc. 3 the three gamblers Sellaway, Acreless, and Littlestock
successively introduce a Lord, a Knight, and a Country-gentleman ; and the
descriptive dialogue has some historical interest. Young Barnacle follows,
reading astounding news in the New Coranto. 'Ancient Petarre,' as in
allusion to Ancient Pistol the impudent page is called, is an amusing picture
of the fashionable *gamin*.

retrieve it; Hazard is only tolerable by comparison; and though it would be hard not to credit this drama with a moral purpose, its merits are not such as to redeem the grossness which pervades the treatment, and indeed characterises the idea, of the main plot.

The Example, licensed 1634 and printed in 1637 [1], is a comedy strikingly original in its plot, and distinguished at the same time by the very direct and effective manner in which it enforces the moral of its story. The power of woman's virtue here receives a noble tribute at the hands of a dramatist whose elevation of sentiment is, generally speaking, one of his most honourable characteristics [2].

The Example (acted 1634, pr. 1637).

[1] Both this play and *The Opportunity* were revived after the Restoration. (See Genest, vol. i. pp. 339-40, where no precise dates are mentioned.)

[2] The chief personages of the action are Sir Walter Peregrine, who, being involved in debt, quits his country for a time in order to seek his fortunes in the Low Country wars; his wife; and a wild gallant Lord Fitzavarice (who by the bye is very inappropriately named; Shirley's names are usually happy, and in this play especially so, with the above exception). The current of Lord Fitzavarice's guilty passion for Lady Peregrine is broken by her fainting away, when in a pretended access of rage he has drawn his dagger upon her, and is changed into repentance when, on recovering from her swoon, she tells the trembling man how she has had

'a short but pleasing vision.
Methought, from a steep precipice as you were falling
Into the sea, an arm chain'd to a cloud
Caught hold, and drew you up to heaven'—

an image which is a kind of converse of a most striking one in Webster's *Vittoria Corombona* (cf. *ante*, p. 57). His thoughts are now entirely directed to proving his penitence and his reverence for the woman who has awakened his conscience; and he sends her as a gift, together with a rich necklace, a mortgage into which her husband had entered with him.

At this point—an admirable contrivance—the husband returns on a sudden visit to his wife, and rashly construes the gifts of gratitude into a proof of guilt. A duel is about to be fought between Peregrine and Fitzavarice, when a foolish gentleman who is anxious to escape from the office of second procures the serving of a writ upon Peregrine for another debt owing to Fitzavarice, and it is not till the latter has himself caused Peregrine's release that the truth begins to dawn upon the husband's mind. The duel is however fought, Lord Fitzavarice, who has revealed the story of his own wickedness and its overthrow, seeking death; but both the combatants are wounded, and honour being thus satisfied, all ends happily. Fitzavarice marries Lady Peregrine's sister Jacinta, whose treatment of a brace of foolish lovers has furnished the comic under-plot of the play.

It may be objected to the conduct of the plot that Sir Walter Peregrine might have rendered the latter part of the action unnecessary by hearing

The Oppor-
tunity
(acted 1634,
pr. 1640).

The Opportunity, licensed 1634 and printed 1640, is a comedy of 'errors.' Its whole action turns on the consequences of its hero (Aurelio) being mistaken for another person (Borgia). The plot therefore, as in all comedies of this description, labours under the disadvantage of resembling a pyramid standing on its apex; and in this instance the author has saved himself the trouble of accounting in any way for the marvellous 'consimility' which deceives a whole Court (including the real Borgia's father). But so much being taken for granted, the ingenuity is admirable with which, after the cup of good fortune has been raised to the hero's lips, it is dashed from them at the last moment by his not taking advantage of his *opportunity*; and the play is of its kind most entertaining, although not free either from licentiousness, or in one of its main situations from what is even worse [1].

Shirley's
(and Flet-
cher's ?)
The
Coronation
(acted 1635,
pr. 1640).

The Coronation, licensed in 1635 as by Shirley, was printed in 1640 as by Fletcher, who had died fifteen years previously. Shirley in 1652 claimed it as his own in the list of his plays appended by him to *The Cardinal*; but it was included in the Second Folio of Beaumont and Fletcher's works, printed in 1679, and in subsequent editions. Mr. Fleay has directed attention to the apparent reference in the first line of the *Prologue* (spoken by a woman) to an alteration in the original title. We might thus suppose, either that Fletcher's hand added an occasional touch to a first sketch

his wife out. For the rest, while the direct and emphatic tribute to virtue which the play offers merits recognition, it must be allowed that the repentant and generous Lord Fitzavarice seems to be treated by the author as an exception to the rule of society even more wonderful than the virtuous wife.

The comic characters in this play are not very striking. In the pretended wit, Confident Rapture, the high-flown phraseology of the fashionable lounger of the day is caricatured; and Dyce thinks Sir Solitary Plot a 'happy imitation' of Ben Jonson's characters of humour. I should be disposed to omit the epithet.

[1] The comic under-plot of the servant Pimponio, who is gulled by his masters, with the aid of an impudent page (little Ascanio, dressed for the purpose in the habit of a Switzer—'one of the lowest High Germans,' says Pimponio, 'that ever I look'd upon'), into fancying himself a prince, forms one of the 'drolls' in Kirkman's collection already frequently cited (*The Wits*, 1677).

of the work, or, which is under the circumstances more
probable, that Shirley inserted in it certain passages from
his master's hand which were in his possession.   But either
supposition is hazardous[1]; and if the particular passages[2]
in their sweetness, and to some extent in their rhythm,
suggest the presence of Fletcher's hand, it would nevertheless be unfair to deprive Shirley of the credit of any of the
unusually numerous beauties of detail to be found in this
play.   In any case the amount of his contributions must
be assumed to have been so slight as to leave Shirley's
claim to the sole authorship of the play virtually unimpaired.

The main intrigue of this comedy (in which there is
nothing historical beyond the sound of some of the names)
is that of the double discovery, at the time of a Queen's
coronation, that she has two brothers living who had been
supposed dead.   A love-story is interwoven with the main

---

[1] No trustworthy authority supports the tradition (if it deserve the name)
mentioned by R. Hitchcock in his *Historical View of the Irish Stage* (1788),
vol. i. p. 12, that Shirley possessed some 'sketches' of Beaumont and Fletcher,
'which, if true,' adds the annalist, 'in a great measure accounts for the
inequality so evident in all his pieces.'

[2] See the speech of Arcadius, act iii. sc. 2 :

> 'In my first state I had no enemies ;
> I was secure while I did grow beneath
> This expectation.   Humble valleys thrive with
> Their bosoms full of flowers, when the hills melt
> With lightning, and rough anger of the clouds ' ;

and the equally beautiful speech of Fortune in the Masque (act iv.
sc. 3) :

> ' *Fame.* This is the house of Love.
>   *Fort.*   It cannot be,
> This place has too much shade, and looks as if
> It had been quite forgotten of the spring
> And sun-beams.   Love affects society
> And heat ; here all is cold as the airs of winter ;
> No harmony to catch the busy ear
> Of passengers, no object of delight
> To take the wand'ring eyes ; no song, no groan
> Of lovers, no complaint of willow garlands :
> Love has a beacon on his palace-top
> Of flaming hearts, to call the weary pilgrim
> To rest, and dwell with him ; I see no fire
> To threaten, or to warm : can Love dwell here ? '

plot, with the result of bringing about a very complicated action.

The Lady of Pleasure (acted 1635, pr. 1637).

The Lady of Pleasure (licensed 1635 and printed 1637) brings us back from 'Epire' to more familiar ground. The idea of this play (which is chiefly valuable as a comedy of manners) is the attempt of a husband to cure his wife's rage for fashionable amusements and fashionable extravagance by pretending to adopt the same course of life himself, since he finds exhortation (which at the beginning of the piece he administers something after the fashion of Sir Peter Teazle) of no avail. He accordingly undertakes

'to dance, and play, and spend as fast as she does,'

and to make her jealous into the bargain, by enrolling himself among the admirers of a young widow (Celestina), who manages her several lovers with considerable skill as well as self-control. The variety of characters in this comedy is very remarkable[1], and must have rendered it extremely entertaining on the stage. The writing is, in part at least, excellent, though some passages are extremely gross.

The Constant Maid, or Love will find out the Way (pr. 1640).

The Constant Maid, or Love will find out the Way, printed under the first title only in 1640 with *St. Patrick for Ireland,* was in all probability like that play acted at Dublin in the course of the years 1636–9; it was reprinted in 1661 under the title of *Love will finde out the Way,* as by 'J. B.,' but again in 1667 with the double title as by 'J. S.' The scene of this comedy is laid in London; but it has little interest as a comedy of manners, and its main plot, though in part following familiar lines, cannot be said to be successfully constructed. Some pathetic power is however to be found in the scene[2] where the daughter upbraids the mother whom she believes to have stolen her love from her. The usurer Hornet promises well at the

---

[1] They include one of those representatives of the University man of the day who exemplify the very imperfect results upon manners and character which the dramatic teachers of the school of life attributed to that of the cloister; together with a series of frivolous coxcombs terminating in an ambitious barber of the name of Haircut. The character of the anonymous Lord is puzzling—was any personal reference here intended?

[2] Act iv. sc. 2.

opening[1]; but the extravagance of the trick played upon
him for the purpose of making him believe himself the
object of royal favour overshoots the mark[2].

The Royal Master, not licensed till 1638, in which year
it was also printed, had been previously acted in Dublin,
both in Ogilby's new theatre and before the Lord Deputy.
Thus an additional interest attaches to this play, which
seems to have attracted great favour, and is assuredly one
of the best comedies of intrigue of the dramatic period to
which it belongs ; and the *Epilogue*, a pleasing and elegant
lyric, appropriately links Shirley's name with Strafford's, to
whom it is addressed, and pays a tribute to the wife whom
we know the great statesman to have so tenderly loved[3].
The entanglement of the story of *The Royal Master* is most
ingeniously contrived, and the *dénouement* is at once effective
and pleasing.   The wiles of the King's favourite, Montalto,
are really subtle ; and the dramatist has created a poetic
figure of idyllic simplicity and sweetness in the character
of Domitilla, the girl of fifteen, who, having mistaken the
King's promise to provide her with a husband for a proof
of personal affection, fixes her love upon him.   The girlish
gaiety with which she rejects the eager courtesies of the
youthful Octavio[4], the sudden and mistaken fancy that a
fate 'too good and great for her' may after all be her

*The Royal
Master
(pr. 1638).*

----

[1] He says of himself :

> 'I always live obscurely, to avoid
> Taxations; I never pay the Church
> Her superstitious tithes.'   (Act ii. sc. 2.)

[2] The idea may have been borrowed from Fletcher's *The Noble Gentleman*
(cf. *ante*, vol. ii. p. 739); but in that play the delusion is appropriate to its
victim.

[3] Mr. Fleay, *u. s.*, p. 244, expresses his opinion that the address ' *To the
Irish gent . . .* ', printed in Dyce's edition, vol. vi. p. 491, and supposed by him
to be a prologue to a lost play called *The Irish Gentleman.* was written by
Shirley as a prologue to *The Royal Master*; but the internal evidence in
favour of the conjecture seems to be quite insufficient.—Not less than ten
commendatory tributes were printed with this play.—It appears to have
been reprinted in 1793.

[4] Act i. sc. 2.   She afterwards tells him (act iii. sc. 3)—with the ripe
wisdom of a young lady of fifteen—

> ' Men must not love till they be one-and twenty ;
> They will be mad before they come to age else.'

destiny, the pathos of her resignation[1], and the dignity of
her answer when the King at once tests her purity and
extinguishes her passion for him by feigning to make her
a dishonourable offer, are alike passages of charming freshness and truthfulness. And it is a most happily-conceived
close to this touching story, that the King succeeds in his
endeavour—

> 'to repair this pretty piece of innocence
> Whom I have brought into a waking dream
> Of passion.'

Octavio manfully braves the danger of the King's wrath,
and thus earns the right to win his love after all.

Judiciously edited, this play would be well fitted to grace
the stage, to which I hope it may be yet some day restored.
The diction is occasionally of very great beauty[2].

The Doubt-
ful Heir
(acted before
1640, pr.
1652).

The Doubtful Heir, originally produced at Dublin under
the title of *Rosania, or Love's Victory*, and licensed in 1640
under that name[3], was printed by Shirley in 1652. It is
a romantic comedy brimful of strange events, especially in
the last act, where the reader's breath is taken away by
a succession of two complete changes in the situation. The
chief attraction of the piece however lies in the pathos and

---

[1] 'And if he should despise me, as 'tis justice,
   Will heaven be angry, if I love him still?
   Or will the king call it a treason in me?
   If he do, I can willingly die for it,
   And with my last words, pray he may live happy.
   But why am I this trouble to your grace?
   My story is not worth one of your minutes.'
                                        (Act v. sc. 1.)

The story of Domitilla, which is taken from the *Decamerone*, is the same as
those of Alfred de Musset's charming play *Carmosine*, and of a very tender
little poem by George Eliot, *How Lisa loved the King*.

[2] See Montalto's speeches, act ii. sc. 1 and part of act iii. sc. 1.

[3] In the *Prologue at Dublin*, printed by Shirley among his *Poems* in 1646,
he refers to the circumstance that

> 'Such titles unto plays are now the mood,
> Aglaura, Claricilla,—names that may
> (Being ladies) grace, and bring guests to the play.'

Aglaura is the name of a tragi-comedy by Sir John Suckling (printed 1638);
Claricilla that of one by Thomas Killigrew (printed 1641). Shirley himself
seems to have been fertile, and as a rule happy, in the invention of
'romantic' female names, such as his age loved.

poetry of its love-passages [1], and in the general purity of tone characterising the conduct of the story. When this play was acted at the Globe the author, with a contempt for the body of his audience worthy of Ben Jonson, informed them in the *Prologue* [2] that he—

> ' did not calculate this play
> For this meridian '—

but for the smaller and more refined audience of the Black-friars. The humours of the Captain who presses his creditors into the military service and succeeds in educating them into fighting men, may have satisfied the requirements of a popular pit.

The Gentleman of Venice, licensed in 1639 (having, as Mr. Fleay thinks, been previously acted at Dublin), was printed in 1655. It is a romantic comedy of considerable spirit, and in parts written with much elegance. Of the two plots combined in its action the one is unendurable in conception, but carried out with a degree of self-restraint deserving acknowledgment [3]. The other turns on the more familiar notion of a supposed prince who proves to be the son of a gardener, and *vice versâ*. Touches are skilfully introduced which individualise the scene of the play, once more laid at Venice.

The Gentleman of Venice (acted 1639, pr. 1655).

The Imposture, which describes itself in the Prologue as the work of one who had ' been stranger long to the English scene,' was licensed in 1640, after Shirley's return to London, and printed in 1653. It labours under the disadvantage of a plot of personation too wildly improbable to beguile the reader into a belief in its reality [4]. But the

The Imposture (acted 1640, pr. 1653).

---

[1] See especially act ii. sc. 3 ; act iv. sc. 1 ; and the charming speech of Ferdinand at the close of act v. sc. 2.

[2] See the *Prologue at the Globe*. The play was printed by Shirley in 1654 ' as it was acted in the private House in Black-Friers.'

[3] Langbaine thought it traceable to a story in Edmund Gayton's *Pleasant (s. Festivons) Notes upon Don Quixot*; but this was not published till 1654, so that at the most a common source might be assumed.

[4] The villain of the piece is Flaviano, the Duke of Mantua's favourite. In order to prevent a marriage between the Duke of Ferrara's son, the brave Leonato, and the Duke of Mantua's daughter Fioretta, for whom Flaviano himself entertains a passion, he contrives that Juliana, an inmate of a nunnery whither she had retired after being ruined by Flaviano himself,

action is interesting, and proceeds with so much spirit that one can understand how the author should declare that this comedy may ' march in the first rank of his own compositions.'

The Sisters (acted 1642, pr. 1653).   The circumstances under which the comedy of *The Sisters* (licensed in April 1642 and printed in 1653) made its appearance on the stage have some interest ; for it was manifestly one of the last productions of the pre-Restoration drama[1]. In itself however the play is poor—being a variation on the old theme of the proud and the humble sister, of whom the former in the end proves to be supposititious. She has previously been fooled by the impudence of the captain of a band of robbers, who pretends first to be a ' Chaldean ' and then a prince. *The Sisters* seems rather hastily put together.

The Humorous Courtier (pr. 1640).   *The Humorous Courtier*, printed 1640, was probably acted some time previously, and has been supposed to be identical with *The Duke*, licensed with Shirley's name in 1631[2]. Though disfigured by intolerable grossness, this must be allowed to be a comedy singularly happy in the conception of its plot, which furnishes the opportunity for a varied developement of character on the basis of a single

shall pass herself off as the princess. (In the unaccountable conduct of the Duke in half falling in with this scheme lies the chief weakness of the plot.) In spite of the pretences of the false Fioretta, Leonato carries her off as his bride to his father's court. Here the imposture is in the end revealed by the arrival of the true Fioretta's brother Honorio and by that of Fioretta herself. All ends well except for Flaviano and Juliana, the latter of whom is sent into a house of penance. (The author seems to have felt that he is rather hard upon poor Juliana, for whom the reader too will conceive no very bitter dislike, and makes amends to her by means of an impudent little Epilogue, which ' Mrs. Ellen ' might have spoken with great effect.)—The comic bye-plot concerned with the coward Bertoldi may be described as wearisome. It is worth noting that the play contains (act i. sc. 2) a song of rejoicing for peace, possibly suggested by the cessation of arms recently concluded with the Scots, and certainly far superior to any other of the lyrics introduced by Shirley into his dramas.

[1] See the Prologue, which begins ' Does this look like a Term?' (*i. e.* as we should say like a ' season '). ' London is gone to York,' *i. e.* the King and Court had already moved thither. The play itself begins, as it were ominously, with the words ' I like not this last Proclamation.'

[2] See *English Drama*, vol. ii. p. 237, where *The Conceited Duke* (mentioned in 1639) is likewise concluded to be the same play.

action. Unfortunately, the play has come down to us in an extraordinary corrupt condition, and even Dyce's acumen has not invariably been able to restore a satisfactory text[1].

Finally, *The Court Secret* (not acted till after the Restoration; printed in 1653[2]) goes beyond all Shirley's other plays in the complexity of its plot, which turns on a double mistake as to the real identity of its youthful heroes Manuel and Carlo. The chivalrous courtesy of these noble rivals towards one another is a motive gracefully elaborated ; nor is the prison-scene between Manuel and Clara devoid of pathos; but it is difficult to be pleasurably affected by the progress of a play which requires so close an attention in order to keep the threads of its action together.

The Court Secret (pr. 1653).

Several plays by Shirley which are lost—unless in some cases they should be thought recognisable in later revisions bearing different titles—have been already incidentally mentioned.

---

[1] With the assistance of her lover Foscari Duke of Parma (whom she has pretended to dismiss from her court, but who returns to it in disguise), the Duchess of Mantua, by giving out that she intends to marry one of her own courtiers, exposes them to a trial of their honesty and good-will before which they all succumb. The ambitious Contarini, whose recent marriage might seem to have put him out of the question, endeavours to induce his wife either to commit suicide or to qualify herself for a divorce. The pretended misogynist Orseolo (the 'humorous courtier' who gives the play its name) reveals himself as the opposite of the character which he has professed. Together with these, the conceited Volterre, whose accomplishments consist in

> 'a little foreign vanity,
> Shewn in' [very] 'corrupted mixture
> Of foreign tongues,'

is at last undeceived and forgiven ; while the outrageously idiotic Depazzi, whose self-delusion endures to the last (after he has been offered the choice of 'four or five several deaths,' not one of which he can be ' got to accept '), is at last brought to saying 'I forgive your highness, I.' The idea of this comedy will accordingly be allowed to be an exceptionally felicitous one, though unfortunately there is too much 'hyperbolising' in its dialogue, according to Depazzi's conception of the meaning of the verb.

[2] It was dedicated to William Earl of Strafford, the son of the great statesman—which makes it strange that the author should have left standing the passage (act iv. sc. 3) :

> ' Some expire humbly
> I' the cradle, some dismiss'd upon a scaffold.'

—As to the performance of this play after the Restoration, see Genest, vol. i. p. 351.

A few plays of unknown or disputed authorship have been assigned to him, but in no instance, so far as I can judge, on tenable grounds. The tragedy of *Andromana, or The Merchant's Wife*, which was printed in 1640 with the initials 'J. S.', was attributed by Farmer to Shirley, but was unhesitatingly excluded from his works by Dyce[1]. This play, of which the plot is taken from the story of Plangus in Sidney's *Arcadia*, is certainly a wretched production, with which it is impossible to suppose that Shirley would have attempted to rival Fletcher's *Cupid's Revenge*, which treats the same theme. On the other hand, Dyce was inclined to approve Langbaine's supposition that Shirley was the author of the original version of *The Double Falsehood* which, apparently on the strength of its being similarly ascribed to 'Sh.,' Theobald published as Shakspere's; and this view is supported by the sagacious judgment of Genest[2]. The theme might have commended itself to Shirley, but we are hardly in a position to judge of the text of this much over-edited play, and in the absence of all external evidence of importance it would be unsafe to try to arrive at an opinion on the subject. Mr. A. H. Bullen is responsible for the suggestion, to which I cannot profess to accord a ready assent, that one of the plays said by Langbaine to have been left in MS. by Shirley was the comedy of *Captain Underwit*. This play, of which we owe our knowledge to Mr. Bullen himself[3], affects me like a parody on *The Woman Killed with Kindness*, although it contains passages aspiring to poetic effects which Heywood's play happily left unattempted. Underwit justifies his name by remaining a subsidiary character.

The fertility of Shirley as a dramatist, although in itself beyond doubt remarkable, has perhaps unduly impressed itself upon students of our literature as one of his chief literary characteristics. In respect of the mere quantity

---

[1] It was reprinted (with Shirley's name) in vol. iii of *The Ancient British Drama*, and is also included in vol. xiv of Mr. Hazlitt's *Dodsley*.

[2] Cf. *ante*, vol. i. p. 528, *note*; and vol. ii. p. 213.

[3] It is printed in vol. ii of his *Collection of Old English Plays*, with an *Introduction*, which brings home its date to 1639 or not long afterwards.

of his plays he cannot be brought into comparison with Thomas Heywood, and was possibly surpassed by some other of our writers. In any event, however, the thirty-two[1] dramatic works noticed above, in addition to three masques, and a certain number of plays of which Shirley was only joint author, constitute no mean or meagre legacy to our dramatic literature. Nor should it be overlooked that his achievements comprise successful endeavours in tragedy as well as in at least two distinct branches of comedy—the romantic comedy of incident and that of contemporary manners.

The originality of his plots. It is, however, in a different and more important sense that this writer challenges our admiration as one of the most productive writers of the illustrious band of which he completes the tale. In the invention of his plots Shirley is in a large proportion of instances all but incontestably original; and some of the most happily devised of his dramatic stories—such as those of *The Wedding, The Young Admiral, The Humorous Courtier, The Example*— appear to owe nothing to any invention but his own; while in such a tragedy as *The Traitor* the story is so completely re-cast by him that it may fairly be called his own[2].

Their unity. His general skilfulness in construction is on a par with his facility of invention. As a rule, he prefers to subordinate a less important (most frequently a comic) intrigue to the main plot of the piece, instead of adopting the always hazardous method of allowing two plots to run on as it were side by side with one another during a considerable part of the action. His plays thus generally possess the great merit of virtual if not actual unity. Already in his earlier works he shows a tendency towards concentrating the comic interest in a single scene[3]; but as he proceeded in

---

[1] Reckoning *Honoria and Mammon* and *A Contention for Honour and Riches* as one.

[2] Langbaine says of Shirley, that 'whatever he borrows from novels loses nothing in his hands.' No eye could surpass Fletcher's in swift readiness for recognising fine materials; but Shirley was more skilful—or perhaps more careful—in the use to which he put what he had appropriated.

[3] See *Love-Tricks* (act iii. sc. 5: The Complement-School); *The Maid's*

the practice of his art, he attained to a precision and effectiveness of construction such as we are apt to associate with the most artistic efforts of the modern French drama[1].

The variety of his themes. In his choice of themes Shirley's range is, if not absolutely wide, yet sufficiently varied to give to his plays a considerable multiplicity of interest. Religious heroism furnished him with the subject of one only—and that by no means the most successful—of his plays. But designing political ambition furnished a dramatic motive of which he made effective use, without, in his loyal acceptance of the existing order of things, troubling himself like Massinger with the insinuation of 'applications.' In the treatment of the passion of love he succeeds equally in depicting the cruelty of selfish and the pathos of self-sacrificing affection. While in representing the former he cannot attain to the white heat of Ford, and in finding words into which to translate the full sweetness of woman's love he leaves Fletcher unrivalled, he is in advance of both when illustrating the beauty of love's noblest fruit—self-abnegation.

His debts to others not such as to interfere with his independence as a dramatic poet. It was the fortune—good or bad—of Shirley to find open before him the entire volume, so to speak, of the best productions of our dramatic literature in its greatest age. He could not write without a consciousness of the creations which had preceded or were contemporary with his own; and this consciousness exhibits itself in an abundance of reminiscences. I have already touched on the abundance of those which reflect his familiarity with the works of the greatest of all his predecessors. With Fletcher he claimed literary connexion of special intimacy; analogies are traceable between his plays and Massinger's, and the powerful influence of Webster likewise makes itself perceived in one if not more of Shirley's tragedies. Yet, upon the whole, the independence of his workmanship is noteworthy in this respect also; and his knowledge of the bent of his own creative powers was too sure to allow him to imitate, except incidentally, writers not artistically con-

---

Revenge (act iii. sc. 2 : Sharkino's study) ; *The Wedding* (act iv. sc. 3 : the burlesque duel).

[1] See *The Cardinal* ; *The Royal Master.*

genial to himself. Aided no doubt by his knowledge of the theory of poetics, he seems to have acquired a very lucid insight into matters of style and versification[1]; but he was sufficiently master of these to avoid too close an adherence as a writer to any particular model.

His fertility and skill in the construction of plots, his manifest tact in suiting the taste of his public, and perhaps also in accommodating his plays to the gifts of the actors who were to perform them[2],—in a word, his talents as a writer for the theatre, should not be allowed to obscure qualities of another kind undoubtedly equally characteristic of him. In very few of our dramatists shall we meet with *His numerous passages of* so many passages of a poetic beauty, elaborate indeed, but *passages of* at the same time genuine, and finding its expression in *poetic and picturesque* imagery at once original and appropriate. Shirley was *beauty.* endowed with a sense of the picturesque, which would render many of these passages admirable themes for a painter who would allow them to linger in his mind; the hues and shades of the seasons of the year, and of the changes of day and night, and the world of flowers in particular, left their delicate impression upon the receptive fancy of this true poet. It may not be superfluous to direct the attention to some of these passages in a note[3]; for Shirley has on the whole been neglected as a writer; although in truth he was the last of our great dramatists to whom the Muses' hill remained a familiar haunt.

Shirley in my opinion excels less in comic than in *Shirley's comic* serious scenes and characters; but, besides a keen power *powers.*

---

[1] See the passage on the use and abuse of epithets in *Love in a Maze* (act ii. sc. 2), and the satire against word-painting in love-poetry in *The Sisters* (act iv. sc. 2). The latter may have suggested Newman's diatribe in Glapthorne's *Albertus Wallenstein* (act ii. sc. 2).

[2] It is curious to note how dramatic authors were beginning to pay respect to the actors. See the Dedication to *The Grateful Servant.*

[3] See, besides those already cited from *The Coronation, The Doubtful Heir,* &c., the following : *The Brothers* (act i. sc. 1 : 'Her eye did seem' &c., already noticed by Dr. Farmer) ; *The Witty Fair One* (act i. sc. 2 : 'So breaks the day' &c.) ; *The Wedding* (act ii. sc. 2 : 'Draw, imagine all' &c.); the truly grand speech of Montalto in *The Traitor* (act ii. sc. 2, beginning 'It will come') ; the speech of Corybreus in *St. Patrick for Ireland* (act ii. sc. 1, beginning 'Yes, and my rivals too') ; and Manuel's soliloquy in *The Court Secret* (act iv. sc. 2) ;—a by no means exhaustive list.

of observation which displays itself in many lifelike sketches of contemporary foibles and follies, he possessed a considerable amount of humour, and is not devoid of occasional

His comedy differs from that of the post-Restoration period. flashes of wit. In no respect, however, is the change from the pre- to the post-Restoration drama more marked than in the contrast observable between the dialogue of the comic dramatists who wrote in the reign of Charles II, and that of the last of the more eminent dramatic authors belonging to the previous generation. Passages might be quoted to show that, had Shirley after the Restoration cared to resume his labours for the stage, it would not have been difficult for him to train himself to the conversational brilliancy and the flash of repartee in which Congreve and his contemporaries excelled. But the traditions of a stronger and more masculine style of comedy are still perceptible in the last great writer of our old drama. Shirley, though not with uniform success, still sought to conceive comic characters standing on a broader and more solid basis, and to furnish types of human nature, not mere conventional representatives of the society which filled *Hyde Park*, or which flitted round the lady president of a fashionable *Ball*.

His morality likewise differs from that of his successors. And, as I have referred to the comparison which inevitably suggests itself between the last of our more eminent pre-Restoration dramatists and the successors whom we cannot call their equals, I may advert in conclusion to another point, of greater importance, though it may be dealt with in a very few words. It has been asked, What real difference is there between the morality of a Congreve and that of a Shirley? Is not sin equally rampant in the pages of both? Is there any necessity to draw nice distinctions between degrees of licentiousness, when the greater and the less degree (supposing a difference to exist) are equally intolerable? In answer to such questions, I can only say that Shirley seems to me less amenable than other and earlier writers to the charge of habitual grossness and licentiousness, and less prone to the exhibition of these qualities for the sake of the applause awaiting them. And above all, he differs from the comic dramatists of the post-Restoration period, or at least from some of the most prominent among them, in this all-important point, that his purpose is almost without exception moral. I can call to mind no play of his in which the victory of vice over virtue is represented in an attractive, or even in a ludicrous, light; he is no disciple of the social heresy that the pleasures of one class have a right to pollute the morals of another; he believes in the beauty of purity, and does homage to its inborn strength.   His plays are not fit reading for the young and inexperienced; neither are those of Massinger or Thomas Heywood, whose moral tendency few will be found to dispute; but, so far as I can judge, not one of our pre-Restoration dramatists, save Shakspere and again good Thomas Heywood, deserves less than Shirley to be singled out for condemnation as an offender against principles which in his generation and with his lights he sought to honour and uphold[1].

A considerable number of authors remain to be briefly *Minor* noticed as having contributed, each after his kind, to the *dramatists* dramatic literature of the reigns of James I and Charles I. *of this period.* To group these together on any strict principle of sequence is, except here and there, impossible; nor are the dramatic works of many among them of sufficient importance to make it worth while to engage in any such attempt. A large proportion of these dramatists belonged to the circle which acknowledged Ben Jonson as its chief; and among these the precedence may be given to one who, in spite of the well-known proverb, had the best reason for recognising the pre-eminence of his master.

Of RICHARD BROME (already mentioned[2] as joint author *Richard* with Thomas Heywood of *The Late Lancashire Witches,* *Brome (d.1652-3).*

---

[1] The following quotation from the lines addressed to Shirley by the dramatist and historian May, which I borrow from the *Quarterly* Reviewer, may seem to go further than is strictly warrantable; but it shows that the impression made by him upon his contemporaries was not very different from that which I have attempted to convey :

> ' All Muses are not guiltless; but such strains
> As thine deserve, if I may verdict give,
> In sober, chaste, and learned times to live.'

[2] *Ante,* vol. ii. p. 575.

we possess not less than fifteen independently written plays[1].   We know nothing about his life, except the significant fact that in his earlier days—at all events from 1614[2]—he was servant to Ben Jonson, and apparently remained so till his master's death in 1637.   In a eulogistic parody on the indignant *Ode* addressed by Jonson to himself on the failure of *The New Inn* in 1629, Randolph refers to 'what Brome swept from' the Master ; and in an edition of the Ode published three years after his death the reading 'Brome's sweepings' was introduced into its text. In some very characteristic, and not very refined, verses in commendation of Brome's first extant play, *The Northern Lass* (printed in 1632[3]), Jonson addresses the author as 'my faithful servant, and (by his continu'd virtue) my loving friend,' and, after explicitly referring to their domestic relation and Brome's faithful service, goes on to state that the applause bestowed on his play was just, inasmuch as it exhibits

> 'observation of those comick laws,
> Which I, your master, first did teach the age.
> You learnt it well, and for it serv'd your time,—
> A 'prenticeship, which few do now-a-days.'

John Hall, too, in his commendatory verses on Brome's last play[4], *The Jovial Crew*, says that Brome was 'by great Jonson once made free o' the Trade'; and Brome

---

[1] They have been republished, among Pearson's Reprints, in 3 vols., 1873. —Five of Richard Brome's plays were posthumously printed (in 1653) by Alexander Brome, others were printed by a 'stationer' Henry Brome ; but he was related to neither.—As to Richard Brome see also a careful dissertation by Dr. E. K. R. Faust (Halle, 1887), and a notice of him by me in vol. vi of *The Dictionary of National Biography* (1886).—An article on Brome's plays by the late J. A. Symonds was printed in *The Academy* for March 21, 1874.

[2] In the *Induction* to *Bartholomew Fair* the stage-keeper says : 'I am looking, lest the poet hear me, or his man, Master Brome.'

[3] A comedy called *A Fault in Friendship*, written by Brome in conjunction with Jonson's eldest son Benjamin, is stated to have been acted at the Curtain as early as 1623.

[4] He says in the Dedication that this play 'had the luck to tumble last of all in the epidemical ruin of the scene.'   Richard Brome therefore was active as a playwright up to the time of the closing of the theatres.

himself was naturally proud of the connexion. Of one of
his plays[1] he speaks, in the Prologue to it, as

> 'written, when
> It bore just judgment, and the seal of Ben';

and in the Epilogue to another[2] he appears again to refer
with veneration to the memory of his master. Brome
seems to have died in 1652 (in which year his last play
aforesaid was published with a Dedication from his own
hand) or early in 1653, when *Five New Playes* by him were
published by Alexander Brome, who informs the Readers
that their author is dead. For the rest, although he seems,
besides popular success, to have enjoyed the good-will of
several contemporary dramatists of note, including Fletcher,
Dekker, Ford and Shirley, he exhibits an amusing mixture
of modesty and self-consciousness as a dramatic writer.
He repeatedly begs his audience not to expect more than
they will find ; all he pretends to is ' but Mirth and Sense[3]';
he is content to term himself a 'Playmaker,' without
aspiring as yet to the names of 'Author, or Poet,' any more
than to the office of Laureate[4] ; 'a little wit, less learning,
no Poetry' is all he dare boast[5] ; but though he 'scarce
ever durst rank himself above the worst of Poets,' 'most
that he has writ has past the rest, And found good approbation of the best[6]' ; and though he only professes to help
to keep alive 'the weakest branch of the stage,' *i.e.* that
species of comedy which treats of 'low and home-bred
subjects,' he questions whether it is in truth the weakest,
or whether it be not

> 'as hard a labour for the Muse
> To move the Earth, as to dislodge a Star[7].'

Richard Brome appears to have deserved the success that

His modesty and his self-con- sciousness as a dramatist.

---

[1] *The City Wit.*   [2] *The Court Beggar.*
[3] Prologue to *The Novella.*
[4] Prologue to *The Damoiselle.*
[5] Prologue to *The Love-Sick Court.*—The passage in praise of poetry
in *The Sparagus Garden*, act iii. sc. 5, is noteworthy for its generous
fire.
[6] Prologue to *The Queen's Exchange.*
[7] Prologue to *The Antipodes.*

fell to his lot by two qualities deserving high respect in a literary man—a knowledge of his own powers and dili-

Brome's comedies of manners.

gence in training them. Of his plays the great majority are comedies, generally well-constructed and not deficient in a certain power of characterisation, dealing with themes from everyday life and illustrating its manners. The plots are rarely novel enough to be interesting ; and the characters are the familiar types of later Elisabethan comedy—decayed country-gentlemen, knights contemptible in various ways, gallants and gulls, city usurers, city wives and widows, and so forth. Plays of this ordinary and in the long run wearisome class are *A Mad Couple Well-Match'd* (printed 1653), *The Court Beggar* (printed 1653[1]), *The City Wit* (printed 1653[2]), *The Sparagus Garden* (acted 1635), *The Covent Garden Weeded* (printed 1659[3]), *The New Academy, or The New Exchange* (printed 1659). In *The Northern Lasse*, already mentioned as Brome's earliest and apparently one of his most popular plays, there is a pathetic character—that of the heroine, a deserted country-girl, who goes melancholy mad like the Jailor's Daughter in *The Two Noble Kinsmen*. The character seems to have struck the public as original ; but it possesses no exceptional merit. Similar touches of pathos occur in the ' poor wench' Phillis' reminiscences of her unhappy mother in *The Damoiselle, or The New Ordinary* (printed 1653), but the play is otherwise of a common type.

In others of his works Brome approaches a more ambitious species—that of romantic comedy of intrigue. Of *The*

[1] This is one of Brome's most amusing comedies. The old knight turned speculator, Sir Arthur Mendicant, is a happy attempt in Jonson's manner. The projectors are diverting, with the treasure of the Indies locked up—all in bullion—in their chests at home, and without so much as change for a shilling in their pockets. One of their schemes is a floating play-house. A masque is introduced into this play.

[2] In this may be noted the character of Sarpego, the pedant, as quite in Jonson's manner. Pyannet's question about the honesty of London tradesmen is curious: ' Why are your wares gumm'd; your shops dark ; your prices writ in strange characters? What, for honesty?' (Act ii.)

[3] These two plays are in parts extremely coarse. In *The Covent Garden Weeded* (act iii. sc. 1) will be found the items of a tavern bill of the period, which guests and drawer very realistically go through on the stage.

Novella (printed 1653), an early play, the scene is laid at *His*
Venice ; and the story is very unpleasant [1].   The elaborate   *romantic*
plot of *The English-Moor, or The Mock Marriage* (printed   *comedies*
1659) is ingeniously—though in one episode [2] most extravagantly—contrived ; and as an acting play this comedy
deserves praise, and a trace of ardour may be discerned in
some of the serious passages.   Still more ambitious in conception, and resembling some of Fletcher's or Massinger's
rather than Jonson's plays in manner, is the comedy of
The Love-Sick Court, or The Ambitious Politique (printed
1659), which opens admirably and altogether displays much
spirit [3].   *The Queen's Exchange* (printed 1657) and *The*   *and*
Queen and Concubine (printed 1659) are romantic dramas   *dramas of*
with a mainly serious interest.   The earlier of these two   *intrigue.*
plays has a most extraordinary plot, in which reminiscences
of *King Lear, Macbeth,* and of one or another early comedy
of 'Errors' seem to be mixed up ; but the action moves
briskly, and the author seems to have a hold on his audience
in both serious and comic scenes [4].   *The Queen and the*
Concubine strikes me as the best of Brome's efforts of its
sort ; the plot is well constructed and carried out ; a certain

---

[1] The character of a German ' Swatzenburgh,' who speaks a few words in
his native tongue, may be noticed.

[2] A husband paints his wife black in order to conceal her.—The servant
Buzzard in this play is evidently a relation of Jonson's Sir Amorous La-
Foole (cf. vol. ii. p. 366) : 'The Buzzards are all gentlemen.   We came in
with the Conqueror.   Our name (as the French has it) is Beau-desert ;
which signifies—Friends, what does it signify ?' (act iii. sc. 2.)

[3] The opening is a telling picture of a rebellion uncertain as to the precise
nature of its grievance.—This play contains two good comic figures, viz.
Garrula, who cannot tell her news for talking, and more especially the
pedantic tutor Geron, who is ' all for apopthegms,' and is ready for every
occasion with an illustration of something 'whilome' said or ' whilome ' done.

[4] See for resemblances to *King Lear,* act i. sc. 2, and *Macbeth,* act iii.   The
confusion between Anthynus and King Osriick is of the ' Error' type ; but
I do not mean in this latter instance to suggest any specific reminiscence.—
Jeffery in this play is a very good Fool ; see *e.g.* his reception of the news
of the King's illness in the midst of the preparations for rejoicings : ' The
King is sick.'   *J.* ' Then let us drink his health.'   ' He is sick exceedingly.'
J. ' Then let us drink exceedingly,' &c. (act ii. sc. 2.)—The Genius who
appears in this play (act iv) to encourage Anthynus (and help on the action
by presenting a dumb-show) may have been suggested by Massinger's
Virgin Martyr.   I have noted in Brome more than one possible reminiscence
of Massinger.

force is shown in the character of the brave Sforza and a certain tenderness in that of the ill-used Queen Eulalia, for whom again Shaksperean prototypes might be discoverable.

Brome's A Joviall Crew (1641). Originality was by no means the note of honest 'Dick Brome'; and even in his comedy of *A Joviall Crew, or The Merry Beggars* (acted 1641 ; printed 1652) he was possibly only availing himself of an idea suggested to him by Fletcher's *The Beggars' Bush*[1] or, less directly, by more than one of Jonson's productions. The notion of presenting on the stage a picture of the manners of a society of professional beggars is here wedded to a sufficiently improbable plot ; and the scenes illustrating the title of the play contain little that to a modern reader will be otherwise than repulsive. Yet the work had a long life on the stage—in later times perhaps partly because of the extraordinary popularity of *The Beggar's Opera*[2]. Lastly,

The Antipodes (1630). a more genuine effort in the direction of originality was Brome's comedy of *The Antipodes* (acted 1630; printed 1640), which partakes of the character of a moral masque. In order to cure the madness of a youthful traveller, his physician presents to him, as a play within the play, the picture of a Utopia, or world turned upside down. It would be interesting to know whence Brome derived this fantastic notion ; perhaps he had been looking into Bacon's *New Atlantis* (published 1627), or he may have derived a general hint from Jonson's masque of *The World in the Moon* (1620). To the so-called *Travels of Sir John Mandeville* the play itself repeatedly refers[3].

Richard Brome a type of the skilful playwright The above-mentioned plays comprise the dramatic remains of an author whose manifest and confessed lack of poetic gifts enables us to make a shrewd guess as to the course which the later history of the Elisabethan drama

---

[1] Cf. *ante*, vol. ii. pp. 725 *seqq.*

[2] *The Beggar's Opera* was produced in 1728; and Brome's play was itself revived, adapted as an 'Opera,' in 1731, in which shape it seems to have been performed as late as 1791.

[3] See act i. sc. 3, *et al.*—The *New Atlantis* is referred to in Cartwright's *Ordinary* (act ii. sc. 3). Brome's comedy contains some curious observations on the progress of the actor's art on the English stage (see act ii. sc. 2). Among the Antipodes ' all their poets are Puritanes.'

might have taken, had it been left to depend on the labours *without original genius.* of skilled and trained workmen devoid of literary genius. In common fairness, however, Richard Brome should not be set down as a mere imitator of his master Ben Jonson. Doubtless, the author of *Bartholomew Fair* and *The Alchemist* guided his apprentice's hand to its most successful achievements ; and in his choice as well as execution of comic types Brome was obviously under the direct influence of his master.   But under different circumstances he might very possibly have with equal success imitated what was imitable in Fletcher or Massinger or Shirley; and it was in all probability a mere accident that he was too preoccupied by Jonsonian models to turn his thoughts except occasionally towards the serious romantic drama.   From this point of view the perusal of the works of a writer of Brome's calibre is not wholly unprofitable.   Few of our playwrights have known their craft better than he ; and the preferences of the times are more safely to be gauged from such a series of plays as his, than from a study of works exhibiting anything like originality of mind.

THOMAS RANDOLPH[1] during his short life gave evidence *Thomas Randolph (1605–1635).* of great literary talent, and as an author attained to a quite exceptional popularity among his contemporaries.   Born in 1605, at Newnham-cum-Badby in Northamptonshire, as the son of the steward to Edward Lord Zouch (in his younger days the associate and patron of Sir Henry Wotton), he was educated at Westminster and at Trinity College, Cambridge, where he was elected to a fellowship and seems to have ordinarily resided till 1632.   Before, however, coming in that year to reside in London, he had already acquired some familiarity with the literary life of the capital, and had been accepted as a 'son' by Ben Jonson.   It is stated—and there seems no reason for doubting the truth of the statement—that Randolph's convivial

---

[1] *Poetical and Dramatic Works of Thomas Randolph.* Edited by W. Carew Hazlitt, 2 vols., 1875. Cf. Mr. Sidney Lee's notice of Randolph in vol. xlvii of *The Dictionary of National Biography* (1896), and Mr. Fleay's notes in *English Drama,* vol. ii. pp. 164 *seqq.*

indulgences hastened his end.   After withdrawing into the country, in order to escape from his creditors and to recruit his health, he died at Blatherwick in March 1635.   His publications had in the main been more or less connected with the incidents of the University life of which he was himself so animating an element ; three years after his death a volume of Poems, including *The Muses' Looking-Glass* and *Amyntas*, were published, probably by his brother Robert.

Among our seventeenth-century poets Randolph holds, if not a conspicuous, at least a unique position ; and in the literary records of Cambridge he will always hold his place as one of the representative wits of his University.   He was prolific alike of English and of Latin verse ; and as a matter of course provided apt material for the dramatic performances upon which, as has been seen, the minds of residents were then so largely intent.   We have it, indeed, on his own authority [1] that when he

> ' contented liv'd by Cham's fair streams,
>   Without desire to see the prouder Thames,'

his favourite occupation was to repeat the ' deep and learned lays ' of ' the shepherd of Stagira.'   His first publication, however, was concerned with *Aristippus, or The Joviall Philosopher. Presented in a private Shew. To which is added The Conceited Pedler* (1630).   It is a mere academical *jeu d'esprit*, of which the immediate purpose is to extol the virtues of sack and to decry its rival, ale, whose praises Randolph has, by way of compensation, sung in another of his poems [2].   This amusing little interlude—for it is nothing more—includes a burlesque of a lecture on philosophy, together with a triumphant cantata by Simplicius in honour of his tutor and in obloquy of the schoolmen :—

> ' Aristippus is better in every letter
>   Than Faber Parisiensis ;
>   Than Scotus, Socinus and Thomas Aquinas,
>   Or Gregory Gandavensis,' &c.

[1] See the passage in *An Eclogue to Master Jonson*, cited by Mr. Hazlitt and by Mr. Lee.

[2] *The high and mighty Commendation of the Virtue of a Pot of Good Ale.—* John Gilbert Cooper's *Epistles from Aristippus in Retirement* (1757–8), which

The Conceited Pedler is an even less ambitious University 'show,' consisting simply of a monologue delivered by a pedlar who has brought with him from his travels ' for the benefit of this Royal University' a collection of wares which he exhibits and comments upon. They comprise 'half-a-dozen of incomparable points'—including a 'point of good manners' ('this point is almost found in our college, and, I thank the heavens for't, it begins to be tagged with Latin '), and ' a point of false doctrine' ('made of a dangerous stubborn leather tagged at one end with self-conceit, at the other with wilful opinion ')—a looking-glass, a whetstone, night-caps, and a lady in alabaster, whom the pedlar apostrophises in a quasi-parody on a famous passage in Marlowe's *Doctor Faustus*.

With the comedy of *The Jealous Lovers*, acted at Trinity in 1632 before King Charles I and Queen Henrietta Maria, Randolph achieved a literary success, to which abundant testimony is borne by the English and Latin commendatory verses [1] from various sources, prefixed to the published play. The blank-verse in which it is written has a dignified flow, and the style is chastely decorated with classical ornament. But although the play contains a large number of characters (for the most part of the regular Plautine type), and shows considerable spirit in its general execution, the *dilettante* author betrays himself in the utter artificiality of the plot, which ends with an altogether inadmissible surprise. The main motive of the comedy lies in the jealousy, rising almost to the height of madness, with which the faithful Evadne is persecuted by her lover Tyndarus, and with which an equally faithful lover Pamphilus is in turn persecuted by his mistress Techmessa. In order to try the constancy of the objects of their love and suspicion, Tyndarus and Techmessa go to the length of feigning death, and of causing themselves to be carried in coffins into the churchyard. This test having unexpectedly demonstrated the fidelity of

The Jealous Lovers (acted and printed 1632).

were satirised by John Byrom, represent a curious attempt to domesticate in English literature the easy style of verse of Chapelle and Chaulieu, La Farre and Gresset.

[1] They are preceded by a number of dedications—an unusual practice surely, for which the author apologises to the reader.

Evadne and Pamphilus [1], the virtue of each is about to be
rewarded by marriage—when Hymen by a manifestation
of his ill-will forbids the banns.   The jealousy of the lovers
proves to have been the result of a divinely-inspired instinct;
for Tyndarus is the brother of Evadne, and Techmessa
the sister of Pamphilus!   This species of solution—which
savours of an ineptitude not unfamiliar to the pastoral
drama—as a matter of course stultifies the entire dramatic
interest of the plot.   The comic characters are likewise
artificial, though less conspicuously so; and admirable as
is the writing of the play, one guesses that the renowned
University wit had not quite mastered the secret of the 'low
vein' to which he had condescended [2].

The Muses'
Looking-
Glass
(*acted by*
1635:
pr. 1638).
Of Randolph's two remaining plays the more remarkable
seems to me *The Muses' Looking-Glasse,* which Sir Aston
Cokayne in some commendatory verses calls *The Entertain-*
ment, and which was, no doubt, acted at Cambridge.
This justly celebrated production [3] furnishes an interesting
illustration of the effect exercised upon literary minds of
quick apprehension by the theories and examples which
they found in Jonson's comedy of character.   *The Muses'*
Looking Glass is modestly described by the personage who
acts as a kind of presenter to the piece as—

'a mere Olla Podrida,
A medley of ill-plac'd, and worse-penn'd humours'—

and the author's intention is announced to be to show, in
a succession of scenes,

'How comedy presents each single vice
Ridiculous.'

These vices are introduced in pairs, according to the

---

[1] It furnished at the same time an opportunity for a clever imitation, or
expansion, of the humours of the grave-diggers' scene in *Hamlet.* See
act iv. sc. 3.

[2] See the Dedication to Sir Christopher Hatton (afterwards Viscount
Hatton, who erected a monument to Randolph's memory in Blatherwick
Church).

[3] *The Muses' Looking-Glass* long remained popular. Jeremy Collier is
stated by Mr. Lee to have written a preface for the new edition which
appeared in 1706. Some scenes from the play were performed in 1748
and 1749 (Genest, vol. iv. pp. 250-1); and in 1756 it was adapted under the
name of *The Mirror* (*ib.,* vol. x. p. 178).

Aristotelian theory, as the opposite extremes of each other, with a virtue holding the mean. In other words, the play is a satire in dramatic form, whose secondary object is to vindicate the moral power of comedy. Humorously enough, the 'masque' of the several characters, concluding with the glorification of 'golden Mediocrity' as the 'mother of Virtues[1],' is exhibited by a player, Roscius, before two Puritan spectators, Bird the featherman and Mrs. Flowerdew, a haberdasher of small wares, who are thus led to recognise the value of comedy as the inheritress of the virtue of the glass sent by Apollo. Admirable as a literary composition, this dramatic satire exhibits the influence of Jonson's example upon his pupil; but it should be observed that the scholarly Randolph differs from his master in so far that he dispenses with the element of action, and therefore neither produces, nor intends to produce, a drama. *Amyntas, or The Impossible Dowry* (acted before the King and Queen at Whitehall, and first printed in 1638) is a pastoral play of the Italian type. Though on the whole deficient in poetic touch, it is by no means devoid of freshness, and even of occasional vigour of style. The play and its *dramatis personae* are made up of the materials which Guarini and Tasso had stereotyped for this species of production; but the plot owes nothing to the *Aminta* of the latter poet. The wrath of Ceres and a couple of obscure oracles[2] form the pivots of the action, which ingeniously enough combines its more or less artificial elements into a well-connected whole. The chief representatives of sentiment are an outlawed father, a mad

Amyntas (pr. 1638).

---

[1] All the Virtues joining in a dance, seem to Mrs. Flowerdew 'the Family of Love' (cf. *ante*, vol. ii. p. 517). The first scene, which leaves the Puritans still wholly unconverted, is an amusing satire on the prejudice cherished against the drama even by tradesmen drawing an income out of it; at the close they acknowledge themselves convinced that 'comedies are good exercises,' and rejoice that they have escaped 'going to hell the narrow way.'

[2] One of these explains the second title of the play. Amyntas loses his wits in trying to interpret an oracle which makes his marriage conditional on his paying as a dowry 'that which he has not, may not, cannot have.' Answer (as revealed by Echo, in a scene repeating a device familiar to both pastoral literature and the drama) : a husband.

lover, and three shepherdesses severally described as 'sad,' 'distressed,' and 'wavering'; while the comic personages form a vivacious crew who carry on amongst themselves a practical joke unmistakeably akin to the imposition practised upon Falstaff in the last act of *The Merry Wives*[1]. But the dialogue is in general brisk almost to a fault; and the production as a whole is certainly not obnoxious to the imputation that it remains on the level of the commonplace. On the contrary, it gives proof of a strong dramatic capacity, unluckily applied to an utterly artificial species, which had not yet been freed from trammels such as in truth might have been ignored without much loss to literature.

Plays ascribed to Randolph on unsatisfactory evidence. The very curious play published in 1651 as 'translated out of Aristophanes his Plutus by Thomas Randolph,' with the superscription of 'Πλουτοφθαλμία Πλουτογαμία, *a pleasant comedie entituled Hey for Honesty, Down with Knavery*,' further purports on its title-page to be 'augmented' by its publisher 'F. J.' As a matter of fact, the date of 1651 fits it so much better than any date before 1635, that inasmuch as it was never included in any authoritative edition of Randolph's writings, no sufficient reason seems to exist for ascribing it to him[2].

A Latin comedy entitled *Cornelianum Dolum*, which was entered in the Stationers' Register as by 'T. R.,' with

---

[1] This scene (act iii. sc. 4) is printed in Halliwell-Phillipps' *Illustrations of the Fairy Mythology of a Midsummer Night's Dream* (*Shakespeare Society's Publications*, 1845). The sham fairies recite some creditable rimed Latin verse.—The mad Amyntas' delusion (act iii. sc. 3) that Mopsus is a dog (with a fine classical pedigree) was doubtless suggested by a well-known passage in *King Lear*.

[2] This was effectively shown in a criticism of Mr. Hazlitt's edition which appeared in *The Saturday Review*, August 21, 1875.—The play is in itself worthy of notice. The simple plot of the *Plutus* is expanded by divers additions. Poverty ('Penia Poverty, or Penia Penniless') engages in an attempt at armed resistance; and the action, after being in other ways varied, concludes with the marriage of the god of Wealth with Mistress Honesty, 'an honest scrivener's daughter.' The locality of the comedy is, in order to invest it with the force of a satire applicable to the times, transplanted to London; and Plutus becomes the son and heir of Pinchback Truepenny. The social, political and literary foibles of the age are so vividly touched, that this comedy possesses an interest independent of its literary merits. Among the more broadly comic scenes one (act iii. sc. 1) will be noticed, where Poverty marshals her forces, led by Higgen (cf.

a complimentary description well suited to him, has been thought assignable to more than one other writer of the age[1], but may be passed by here. Whether or not this play is to be added to his achievements, it is clear that Randolph was a genuine classical scholar of the lighter type, whose love for our national dramatic literature, apparent from the allusions to Shakspere and other English dramatists scattered through his pages, might have helped to secure to him a position of importance in a period in which he was not to survive to play a part.

Another 'son' of Ben Jonson's was WILLIAM CART- WRIGHT, a prominent member of the Fantastic School of poets, who flourished in the first two Stuart reigns, and author of a few dramatic works that have come down to us. Cartwright, who enjoyed great celebrity as, according to Wood, 'the most florid and seraphical preacher in the University' of Oxford, was an enthusiastic adherent of the royal cause, and after suffering a brief imprisonment as a member of the Council of War, died at Oxford of the so-called camp disease, on November 29, 1643, in the thirty-third year of his age. The poetical works of this writer, who seems to have enjoyed an unusual measure of favour with his literary contemporaries[2], are chiefly valuable

William Cartwright (1611– 1643).

Fletcher's *The Beggars' Bush, ante*, vol. ii. p. 725), by Brun, 'a worthy Scot of gallant race' who left one of his two arms behind him at Chevy Chase, by 'Caradoc, true lord of Wales,' and by
        'brave Redshank too, Termock by name,
    Wonder of Redshanks and Hibernia's fame'—
an 'all-round' representative body, or 'Falstaff's regiment,' as their com- mander calls them. In the last scene of all, the Pope, whose authority has come to an end under the new *régime*, in vain seeks to recover it by a free use of the Spiritual Treasure at his command, and finishes with a ribald doggrel, Aristophanic at all events in its impudence. The rhythm of the equally indecorous *Threttanelo* in act ii. sc. 1 is genuinely spirited. If Randolph was innocent of all this, he had an imitator of cognate *verve.*— (The *Plutus* of Aristophanes was performed in the original Greek at Zurich in 1531, on which occasion Zwingli, being experienced in music, 'modos fecit.' See a notice of a pamphlet on the subject by Arnold Hug (Zurich, 1874), in *Sybel's Historische Zeitschrift*, vol. xxxv. (1876), p. 474).
  [1] See Fleay, and Lee, *u. s.*
  [2] No inconsiderable part of the volume containing Cartwright's *Comedies, Tragi-Comedies, with other Poems* (1651) is filled by memorial and commen-

to us as examples of the extreme developement of pane-
gyrical poetry—a species apt at times to soar to the dizziest
heights in order to drop into bathos.   Cartwright's pen
devoted itself with special willingness to the praises of the
King, the Queen, and all the Royal Family [1]—as well as of
great noblemen, bishops, and peeresses, and here and there
a man of letters.   The extravagant conceits with which
he intersperses his poetry are signally characteristic of the
school to which he belongs, and though he translated parts
of both Horace and Martial, he learnt from them neither
the grace nor the force which are to be found in simplicity.

His 'tragi-
comedies.'

This radical defect is apparent in the three 'tragi-
comedies' which remain from the hand of this author.
They are one and all thoroughly fantastic in both subject
and treatment; and a fatal artificiality deprives them of

The Royal
Slave acted
1636).

any real interest.   The story of *The Royal Slave* (performed, with music by Henry Lawes, before the King and
Queen at Christ Church in 1636, when it gave so much
delight to the Queen that it was in the same year acted by
the King's company at Hampton Court) tells the adventures
of an Ephesian, who, when a prisoner at the Persian Court,
is 'adorned with all the Robes of Majesty' and invested
with 'all Privileges for three full days, that he may do
what he will, and then certainly be led to death.'   Within

datory verses, among them contributions by Henry Lawes (who set some
of Cartwright's songs to music) and Izaak Walton.   The remainder are
largely by Oxonians and Templars; and although it must be conceded that
the poets of this age, especially those who were 'sworn of the tribe of Ben,'
were adepts in the art of 'mutual congratulation,' the *consensus* is particularly striking in Cartwright's case.   Ben Jonson himself said of him, in
his own venerable way: 'My son Cartwright writes all like a man.'   Bishop
Fell of Oxford declared that 'Cartwright was the utmost man could come
to.'   King Charles I wore mourning on the day of his burial in Christ
Church Cathedral.   Cartwright's hatred of the Puritans is sufficiently
apparent from *The Ordinary*; see especially the conclusion, with its
reference to the migrations to New England, where a ready reception is
promised to such as will nose

'a little treason 'gainst the King,
Bark something at the bishops.'

[1] His *November, or Signal Dayes observed in that Month in relation to the*
Crown and Royal Family, was published posthumously in 1671.   See
Mr. Bullen's notice of him in vol. ix of *The Dictionary of National Biography*
(1887).

these three days his heroic courage and magnanimity converts King Arsamnes into an admiring friend and ally. The plot of *The Lady-Errant* (first printed 1651) is even more fanciful; it is in part a reproduction of the fancy of a women's commonwealth already made familiar to the stage by Fletcher's *The Sea Voyage*[1]; but the character of the Lady-Errant herself is not very intelligible, and the conduct of the whole action by no means dramatically effective.   Finally, *The Siege, or Love's Convert* (first printed 1651) borrows part of its plot from a not very impressive anecdote related of Pausanias by Plutarch in his *Life of Cimon*[2].   According to the adaptation of the story given in the play, Leucasia, a virgin of Byzantium, is sent as a sacrifice to the tyrant Misander, whom her father has persuaded her to kill in his slumbers, but on suddenly awaking he stabs her while she is withdrawing irresolute.   There is nothing dramatic in this; and the remainder of the play is occupied in the conversion of the tyrant into a virtuous lover by means of Leucasia's eloquence.

All these plays are thoroughly rhetorical in manner. The serious dialogue is elevated in sentiment, and occasionally graceful in form ; but we miss any real play of passion or depth of pathos springing from a truly dramatic imagination.   The comic scenes are almost wholly conventional; for of comic power Cartwright seems to have been devoid.   More or less absorbed in the life of his university, though under aspects more important than those which occupied Randolph, Cartwright must have been without the wider experience of men and manners which in a comic dramatist so often serves as a substitute for originality. In his comedy of *The Ordinary* (first printed 1651) he undertook to essay a picture of real life in Jonson's manner ; but he confesses in the Prologue that he has only obtained

The Lady Errant (pr. 1651).

The Siege (pr. 1651).

The Ordinary (pr. 1651).

---

[1] Cf. *ante*, vol. ii. p. 728.

[2] Cap. 6.   Mr. Fleay says that the story is reproduced in the *Decamerone*, but I cannot identify his reference.—It has been treated by a modern German dramatist, Heinrich Kruse, in the tragedy, *Das Mädchen von Byzanz* (Leipzig, 1877).

his materials at second-hand [1].   The result is that this
play is one of the least enjoyable productions of its kind.
A flimsy plot serves as the opportunity for depicting the
ways of life of a gang of rascals, ruffians, and tricksters,
the scum of London society, who use as the centre of their
operations a dining-club at a tavern,—the 'Ordinary' which
gives its name to the play.   Jonson was the model whom
Cartwright followed in passages as well as in the general
conception of this comedy [2]; but the phase of manners
which is depicted in part of it might have been suggested
by numerous passages in other dramatists.   As a matter
of course the play abounds in satire against the Puritans.
Cartwright's comic and serious styles are equally fluent;
but he has no power of original characterisation, and no
native spring of humour [3].   In occasional grossness this
eminent Oxford divine was capable of equalling most of
the dramatists contemporary with himself.

*Jasper
Mayne
(1604–
1672).*

JASPER MAYNE (1604–1672), Archdeacon of Chichester
and translator of Lucian, was a friend and admirer of
Cartwright and of Cartwright's literary chief, Ben Jonson [4];
and both of the plays preserved from his hand belong in
date of composition to the period before the outbreak of
the Civil War.   For in 1639 he accepted a College living,
and though he is said by Wood to have cherished till a late
date a liking for 'acting students,' the remainder of his life,
which ended at Christ Church, Oxford, in 1672, was spent

---

[1]   'His conversation will not yet supply
      Follies enough to make a comedy ;
      .   .   .   .   .   nor act we here
      Scenes, which perhaps you should see liv'd elsewhere.'

[2]   See Gifford's note to Jonson's *Alchemist* (act i. sc. 1 ; vol. iv. p. 32); and
cf., as having suggested the elaborate description of a 'military dinner' in
The Ordinary (act ii. sc. 1), the speech of the Cook in Jonson's masque of
Neptune's Triumph.—See also the gambling scene in an Ordinary in
Middleton's *Michaelmas Term* (*ante,* vol. ii. p. 514), and cf. Dekker's *The
Whore of Babylon* (vol. ii. p. 212 in *Works*).

[3]   The antiquary Moth, who indulges in what is meant for Chaucerian
English, is not a felicitous effort.—Cartwright overflowed with wit as dis-
tinguished from humour ; see for instance his *A New Year's Gift to Brian
Lord Bishop of Sarum, upon the Author's entering into Holy Orders.*

[4]   See the extravagantly encomiastic lines by him prefixed to Cartwright's
Poems, and his contribution to *Jonsonus Virbius.*

apart from such pursuits. His comedy *The City-Match*[1], The City-
which was acted before the King and the Queen at Match (pr.
Whitehall, was printed at Oxford in 1639. Mayne depre- 1639).
cates the application of severe criticism to this comedy, and
it has in truth little to commend it but a certain fluency of
style[2]. The action is in part extravagantly farcical[3], and
the course taken by it is morally unsatisfactory. So trifling
a production should not be broken on a wheel ; but Mayne
was in Orders when he wrote this play, though not as yet
celebrated as 'theologus accurate doctus et annunciator
evangelii disertus.'

Mayne's second play, *The Amorous War*, a tragi-comedy
printed in 1648, has a plot of extravagant absurdity. The
Thracian princess Roxane, with whom King Archidamus
of Bithynia had run away, is taken prisoner with her ladies
in a war of retaliation waged against the Bithynians by her
brother King Eurymedon. But they escape and come into
the Bithynian camp, to offer their assistance in the war, and
otherwise to place themselves at the disposal of their unsus-
pecting husbands. The faithfulness of King Archidamus,
which is not imitated by his lords, may be intended as a
compliment to the conjugal virtues of Charles I ; for the
writer is at no pains to disguise his political sentiments[4].

---

[1] Printed in vol. xiii of Hazlitt's *Dodsley*.

[2] With this low opinion of *The City-Match* that of Pepys is in accord,
who saw it on September 28, 1668, and thought it ' but a silly play.' In
1755 it was performed under the title of *The Schemers, or The City Match*,
with some additions to the fourth act by William Bromfield (see Genest,
vol. iv. p. 409) ; and in 1828 J. R. Planché produced a comedy called
The Merchant's Wedding, or London Frolics in 1638, principally taken from
The City-Match, but also in part founded upon Cooke's *Greene's Tu Quoque*
and Chapman's *The Widow's Tears* (*ib.* vol. x. p. 429).

[3] The funny scene in which the drunken Timothy is exhibited as a talking
fish recalls the mummy in Gay, Pope and Arbuthnot's farce of *Three Hours
after Marriage*. Seathrift says that he hates his son ' worse than a *privy-
seal*.' (We are in the reign of Charles I.)

[4] See act v. sc. 3 :
        ' If it were reall, I expect
    That passages so fit for History,
    Shall not scape *Mercuries* or *Scout-Gazettes* ;
    But shortly be recorded with the Deedes
    Of *Democraticke John*, or the *Red-nos'd Burgesse*,
    Who enacts *Ordinances* in *Sacke* ; or with
    The Life and Death of *preaching Nol, and Rowland*.'

A great deal of licentiousness is to be found in some of the scenes of this play, to which a certain merit of brightness and animation is not to be denied. It contains an extremely pretty lyric, beginning 'Time is a feather'd thing [1].'

Thomas May (1595-1650).

THOMAS MAY (1595-1650) is best known by his History of the Long Parliament. As a dramatist he is hardly likely to be criticised with the degree of *animus* that led his early associate Clarendon to describe him as one who in his later days 'seemed to all men to have lost his wits when he left his honesty; and so shortly after died miserable and neglected.' May had no reason for rejoicing in his early intimacy with Clarendon, whose portrait of him is more enduring than brass; but no very different impression is left by a summary of his character and career from the pen of a living historian unsurpassed in his knowledge of the Revolutionary period [2]. May's dramatic efforts constituted his first essays in literature, to which he turned as the diligent son of a prodigal father, being prevented by an impediment in his speech from trying his fortunes in professional life.

The Heir (acted 1620; pr. 1622).

His first piece was *The Heir*, acted in 1620 [3]; a comedy, which, notwithstanding the objectionable nature of its under-plot, is in many respects deserving of praise. Its main-plot is both ingenious and interesting [4]; the action progresses

---

[1] This was pointed out to me by the late Mr. F. T. Palgrave.—The song is printed in the late Professor Henry Morley's *The King and the Commons* (1868).

[2] Compare with the character of May in Part I of Clarendon's *Life* (edn. 1827, vol. i. p. 39) the notice of him by Mr. C. H. Firth in vol. xxxvii of *The Dictionary of National Biography* (1894). See also Marvell's *Tom May's Death* in his *Works*, ed. Grosart (Fuller Worthies Series), vol. i. p. 237.— Whatever may be the truth as to the circumstances of May's death, he was buried in Westminster Abbey at the expense of the Council of State; and the subsequent treatment of his remains and monument are not very much to the purpose.

[3] Reprinted in vol. xi of Hazlitt's *Dodsley.*—*The Heir* was altered in 1702 by Mrs. Carroll, under the title of *The Stolen Heiress, or The Salamanca Doctor Out-plotted.* Genest (vol. ii. p. 264) says that this play is 'wretchedly inferior' to its original.

[4] It turns principally on the design of a cruel father, by giving out his absent son as dead, to attract a wealthy suitor to his daughter and 'heir';

with great spirit; and several passages of the play are notable both for an element of genuine pathos, and for considerable beauty of diction. *The Old Couple* [1] (possibly, as Mr. Fleay surmises [2], written before *The Heir*) is a rhetorical comedy in verse, not devoid of fluency or occasional grace, but undistinguished by dramatic merits [3]. *The Old Couple (pr. 1658).*

May's remaining plays are tragedies on classical subjects. *The Tragedy of Antigone, the Theban Princess*, printed in 1631, is introduced by a dedication to Endymion Porter, a liberal patron to many poets, and a preface on the nature of tragedy and comedy. *The Tragedy of Cleopatra, Queen of Ægypt*, acted in 1626 and printed in 1639, covers much the same historical ground as Shakspere's play; and was followed by *The Tragedy of Julia Agrippina, Empress of Rome*, acted in 1628 and also printed in 1639 [4]. He also wrote a Latin play entitled *Julius Caesar*. *His tragedies on classical subjects.*

Mr. Fleay, on grounds which appear to me insufficient for such an assumption, is disposed to ascribe to May the authorship of the fine old tragedy of *Nero*, printed in 1624 [5]. Before accepting this supposition, it would be necessary to trace a close resemblance in the style of this play to that of May's acknowledged tragedies and some degree of continuity between it and *Agrippina*. *Nero* is, however, manifestly the work of a highly accomplished scholar, such as May undoubtedly was, and the theme must have had special interest for the translator and continuer of Lucan. It is, moreover, the work of a dramatic poet capable of writing admirable blank verse of the stronger sort, and *May's (?) Nero (pr. 1624).*

---

the device is frustrated by the re-appearance of the son and the Juliet-like constancy of Leucothoë to the offspring of her father's enemy.

[1] Reprinted in vol. xii of Hazlitt's *Dodsley*.

[2] *English Drama*, vol. ii. p. 83.

[3] It is curious that May should have imitated a well-known passage in *Macbeth* (act v. sc. 5: 'The time has been, &c.') in both these plays; see *The Heir*, act iii. sc. 2 and *The Old Couple*, act ii. A scene in *The Heir* (act iv. sc. 1) adds another to the several examples already quoted (*ante*, vol. ii. p. 134) of imitations of Dogberry's address to the Watch in *Much Ado about Nothing*.—One of the characters in *The Old Couple* is, for no obvious reason, named Euphues.

[4] For an account of the last two, see Genest, vol. x. pp. 49–50.

[5] Reprinted in vol. i of Mr. Bullen's *Collection of Old English Plays* (1882); and in a volume of the *Mermaid Series*.

often pithy in the substance of his diction. The canvas is crowded with characters, but they are graphically distinguished, and the whole picture of the feather-brained despot and his strangely-assorted surroundings is, without any slavish dependence on Tacitus and the other classical authorities, skilful in the choice and disposition of its details as well as striking in its total effect.

Sir John Suckling (1609–1641 or 1642).

Among the dramatists of this period SIR JOHN SUCK-LING (1609–1641 or 1642[1]), largely by reason of his active personality, holds a somewhat prominent place. He was the son of a courtier of James I, and himself a favourite of society, a traveller and a campaigner;—in 1639 he raised a troop of horse, at a cost which their services by no means repaid, for King Charles against the Scotch. ' Good, easy Suckling' (as one of Steele's heroines calls him) seems to have addressed himself to authorship with the buoyancy which sustained him in his other enterprises[2]. Both his verse and his prose, though not extensive in quantity, are so full of vivacity that he holds a place of his own among the Cavalier poets of his times. None of his writings are more sparkling and pleasing than passages in his odd comedy of *The Goblins* (printed in 1646), a production which defies—and as a drama hardly deserves—analysis. The conduct of its plot is at once dragging and breathless. The 'goblins,' it may be expedient to note, are no real goblins, but thieves who under their chief Tamoren frighten the kingdom of 'Francelia' by their devils' pranks, and deal out a rough kind of justice in the fashion of Robin Hood and his merry men; and their chief is in reality not a king of thieves at all, but the surviving head of a fallen noble family. The course of the action in this Bohemian Arcadia is utterly bewildering; but opportunity is found for much pretty writing—especially in the love-scenes of the innocent little Reginella—and for some smart touches of literary and

The Goblins (pr. 1646).

----

[1] *The Poems, Plays and other Remains of Sir John Suckling.* With Life, &c. By W. C. Hazlitt, 2 vols., 1874.

[2] See his pamphlet of advice to the King, noted in *State Papers, Domestic, Charles I*, 1640–1, p. 521. This volume contains other references to Suckling.

social criticism. One finds some little difficulty in understanding how this sprightly fancy could have stood the test
of stage-performance; but the rapid succession of scenes
and the intermixture of lively dialogue with music, songs,
and a superabundance of action may have taken away the
breath of the spectators, and carried them on with victorious
speed to the rather calmer close of the piece [1].

    Suckling's tragedy of *Aglaura* (acted by 1638, perhaps
even before *The Goblins* [2], and printed 1646) is in many
of its passages almost equally characteristic of its author,
whose wit and lyric power create their own opportunities [3]
for themselves in the midst of a sombre and sanguinary
plot. This play is further distinguished among the tragedies of this period by a rapidity of action which seems to
have been a necessity to the writer; and by some touches
of genuine passion. In the last act (where the heroine by
a fatal error kills her husband instead of the lascivious King)
the horrors are piled up so unsparingly that for the reproduction of the play at the Court the author was fain to
compose another conclusion, in which both the King and
Aglaura are kept alive [4]. *The Sad One* (printed 1658),

*Aglaura
(acted by
1638;
pr. 1646).*

*The
Sad One
(pr. 1658).*

---

  [1] Dryden, in the Preface to *The Tempest*, declares that Suckling's Reginella
is ‘an open imitation of Shakspere's Miranda,’ and that ‘his spirits, though
counterfeit, yet are copies from Ariel.’

  [2] See Fleay, *u. s.*, vol. ii. p. 255. The initial cost of this play was great;
and Suckling, with ‘unheard-of prodigality, gave eight or ten new suits of
clothes to the players.’ The Folio edition of *Aglaura* was ridiculed for its
size and amount of margin in some rather sprightly lines by Richard Brome
(see *Works*, vol. ii), who ought to have lived in the days of duodecimos:
‘Give me,’ he says,
‘the sociable Pocket-books.
These empty Folios only please the Cooks.’

  [3] The former partly in the wit-combat between the ‘platonique’ Semanthe
(who is ‘of the new religion in love,’ preached by Fletcher's Faithful Shepherdess and by Lovel in Jonson's *The New Inn*) and two young Lords ‘anti-
platoniques’; the latter in two well-known songs, ‘Why so pale and wan,
fond Lover,’ and ‘No, no, fair Heretic’ (act iv. sc. 1)—which are also
printed among Suckling's miscellaneous poems.

    [4] ‘Tis strange perchance (you'll think) that she that died
      At Christmas, should at Easter be a bride.’
Prologue to the Court.

Flecknoe, in his *Short Discourse on the English Stage* (cited by Genest,
vol. x. p. 250), mentions a witty saying with respect to *Aglaura*, ‘that

which is in a fragmentary condition, bears a general resemblance to *Aglaura*, and contains one or two of those vigorous and pleasing descriptive touches in which the author of *The Wedding* excelled.

Brennoralt (pr. 1646). The tragedy of *Brennoralt* (printed 1646) is a less effective play than *Aglaura*, inasmuch as the plot lacks real concentration of interest. The relation between Almerius and Iphigene, which at first seems to show a certain resemblance to the friendship of the Two Noble Kinsmen in Fletcher's tragedy, proves to have been simply one of mutual attraction between a man and a disguised woman; and the character of the hero proper of the drama, the noble-minded 'discontent' Brennoralt, savours of rhetorical effort. The play is, however, curious as containing some very palpable allusions to the political situation of the times—for there is little difficulty in identifying the 'Lithuanians' with the Scotch. 'Religion' is referred to as one of the causes of the rebellion which seeks to secure the support of Brennoralt; and the 'Lithuanians' (the scene of the play is laid in Poland) are derisively informed, in the spirit of Churchill's satire, that they 'had of all least reason' to rebel—

> 'For would the King be unjust to you, he cannot:
> Where there's so little to be had.'

Shackerley Marmion (1603–1639). Suckling, who in his *Session of the Poets* showed himself the most reckless of free-lances, belonged to no particular group or school of dramatists; but in his companion in arms, SHACKERLEY MARMION (1603–1639)[1], we have another of the humbler followers of Ben Jonson. He was, like May, the son of a country gentleman who had been obliged to sell his estate; his life in London seems to have been animated by the wish to hasten the ruin of his branch of an ancient family. In 1638 he took service in Sir John Suckling's troop of horse, but after the winter expedition was invalided at York and returned to London,

'twas full of fine flowers, but they seemed rather stuck, than growing there.'

[1] *The Dramatic Works of Shackerley Marmion.* With Prefatory Memoir, Introduction, and Notes. (By James Maidment and W. H. Logan. Edinburgh, 1875.)

where he died in January 1639. He was author of an elaborate ' moral ' (i. e. psychological) poem entitled *Cupid and Psyche* (1637), which he presented to Charles Lewis, the prudent eldest son of the Queen of Bohemia ; but his plays are distinguished rather by the accomplishments of a scholar (Marmion had been educated at Wadham College, Oxford) than by dramatic power. Indeed, *Holland's Leaguer* (acted and printed 1632) may almost be said to resemble an attempt to bring on the stage a few chapters of Theophrastus or one of his later imitators. The main plot—which turns on the rescue of Philautus'[1] nobler self from the fatuity of his conceit by a virtuous lady who in the end proves to be his sister—is moral in intention, but undramatic in execution; the second plot, concerned with the siege of the infamous locality indicated by the title of the play[2], is full of grossness unredeemed by humour. *A Fine Companion* (acted by 1633, and printed in the same year) is a comedy of a very similar kind. Although the Prologue, which borrows part of its phraseology from Persius, raises a hope of better things, the plot of the play proves to be of a quite ordinary type, being designed to set forth how—

Holland's Leaguer (acted and pr. 1632).

A Fine Companion (acted by 1633, and pr. 1633).

'Wealth shall be put back, when wit shall thrive';

and how scheming and doting old age are alike impotent against the passionate determination of youth[3]. The more sustained passages of this comedy are, as a rule, well written, but the characters (including a variety of the Bobadil species) and the situations are alike devoid of originality. The title of the play would appear to have been derived from that of a popular song[4].

The Antiquary[5], acted by 1636 and printed in 1641, is

---

[1] Another name from *Euphues*.

[2] A pamphlet which bears the same title, but has little or no connexion with the play, was printed in the same year ; and other evidence exists of the notoriety of the place.

[3] The Prologue takes a very high tone, but sensibly deprecates written appeals against the popular verdict by means of Commendatory Epistles. See Fleay, *u. s.*, vol. ii. pp. 66-7, for suggested explanations of the allusions in this Prologue, and of theatrical allusions in *Holland's Leaguer*

[4] See act iv. sc. 1.

[5] Printed in vol. iii of *The Ancient British Drama*, and in vol. xiii of Hazlitt's *Dodsley*.

The Anti-
quary
(acted by
1636;
pr. 1641).

a third comedy *eiusdem farinae.* It is written with a certain elegance of manner; but the personage from whom the play takes its title, the antiquary Veterano, is the mere outline of an individuality; and his foible, which has been treated with such excellent effect in literature, cannot, as here exhibited, be said to rise even to the dignity of a 'humour.' In other words, the character is well imagined, but not put to any use such as true comic genius would have found for it [1].

Sir John
Denham
(1615-
1688).

The Sophy
(acted
1641;
pr. 1642).

SIR JOHN DENHAM (1615-1688), the author of *Cooper's Hill,* a poem memorable in the history of our literature by reason both of its theme and of the form of its verse, seems only to have composed a single play [2]. *The Sophy,* acted at Blackfriars in 1641, and printed in the following year, was written after its author had already paraphrased in English verse the second book of the *Æneid* (not printed till many years afterwards), and when he must have been engaged upon his celebrated descriptive poem, of which the first edition likewise appeared in 1642. In obedience to the advice of King Charles, Denham abstained from writing verse while engaged in the active political service of the Crown, of which he deserved so well; in his old age he was himself involved in one of the most repulsive of the tragic catastrophes which diversified the merry times of Charles II. *The Sophy* on its production met with extraordinary praise [3]. Its celebrity is no doubt attributable in part to the impressive character of its versification. Denham's 'majesty' and 'strength' are acknowledged by Dryden and by Pope; and in these respects *The Sophy* is

[1] A play called *The Crafty Merchant, or The Souldier'd Citizen* was attributed to Marmion in Warburton's list; but Mr. Fleay is inclined to assign it to William Bonen, observing that 'Marmion took care not to leave his plays unpublished.' (*English Drama,* vol. i. p. 32.)

[2] He also came forward to complete 'the Matchless Orinda's' translation of Corneille's *Pompée,* of which she had left the fifth act unwritten at the time of her death (1664

[3] Waller said of its author, that 'he broke out like the Irish rebellion' threescore thousand strong, when nobody was aware, or in the least suspected it.—*The Sophy* is, in a very exceptional way, referred to by name in the contemporary play of *Andromana* (cf. *ante,* p. 120), act iii. sc. 5.

worthy of the poet of *Cooper's Hill*. But the more immediate success of this tragedy must have been chiefly due to
the management of the action, which Denham had derived
from the *Travels of Sir Thomas Herbert* (1634)[1]. The
central situation of the plot is extremely pathetic in
character. The machinations of Haly, the villainous
favourite of Abbas, King of Persia, induce that monarch
to imprison his noble son Merza, and to have his eyes put
out. Half-maddened by his injuries, the Prince is about to
revenge himself on his father by taking the life of his own
little daughter, Fatyma, when he is recalled to his better
self by the child's appeal to the love of her mother, his
faithful wife, Erythaea. The Prince is poisoned by the
intriguer, at the moment when deliverance is at hand, and
the King dies haunted by the memory of his many crimes
—while the task of wreaking vengeance upon the villainous
Haly is left to the youthful Sophy, Prince Merza's son.

The style of this production is rhetorical, but sustained;
its value was overrated by Denham's contemporaries, but it
is certainly one of the best tragedies of its time, and had
doubtless been produced under the inspiration of worthy
models[2]. In the political wisdom which it teaches in one
of its most striking scenes, something nobler than party
spirit reveals itself; and a lesson is enforced deserving the
attention both of kings and of rebels who misuse religion
as an instrument or as a pretext[3].

WILLIAM HABINGTON (1605–1654), the author of *William
Castara*, and also distinguished as a historian, has left us *Habington
(1605–
1654).*

---

[1] Robert Baron's tragedy *Mirza* was printed about 1647. It was founded
on the same story as Denham's, but Baron in his prefatory address states
that he had finished three acts of *Mirza* before he knew that Denham had
written a play on the same subject. See for an account of Baron's play,
Genest, vol. x. pp. 119 *seqq.*, and cf. *infra.* Genest says that Denham's
play wants incident, and that Baron avoids this fault by introducing
additional characters. In act iv, Mirza ' takes Fatima by the neck, breaks it,
and swings her about '; he then ' endeavours to get hold of Soffie, but is
prevented.'

[2] There is some similitude between the plot of *The Sophy* and that of
Chapman's *Revenge for Honour* (*ante*, vol. ii. p. 431); and a certain likeness
between the two dramatists in the moral gravity of their political thought.

[3] See act iv. sc. 1.

a 'tragi-comedy,' *The Queene of Arragon*[1] (1640). This
work shows its author to have been a man of a refinement
of tone and elevation of sentiment not common among
contemporary dramatists. The play, which is a romantic
drama in Shirley's manner, cannot, however, be commended
either for neatness of construction or for vigour of action;
in a word, the merits which it possesses are not dramatic.
Perhaps the most interesting feature of this play is to
be found in certain passages which seem to show that
Habington was capable of thinking for himself on political
and social questions, instead of falling in with the extravagant worship of existing institutions usual to the stage-poets
of his times. The facts recorded of his life agree with the
internal evidence of the passages in question[2].

[1] Printed in vol. xiii of Hazlitt's *Dodsley.* It was originally given to the
press, against the author's consent, by Philip Earl of Pembroke and Montgomery, who had as Lord Chamberlain caused it to be acted at Court. where
it was well received. (See also Collier, ii. 98.) It was revived after the
Restoration, with a Prologue and Epilogue by the author of *Hudibras.* This
Prologue touches rather wittily on critics (of a kind not absolutely extinct),
who
        'decrying all of all that write,
    Think to erect a Trade of judging by 't.
    Small Poetry, like other Heresies,
    By being persecuted multiplies.' :

[2] See the speeches of Ascanio in act iii. sc. 1 :
                'The stars shoot
    An equal influence on the open cottage
    Where the poor shepherd's child is rudely nurs'd,
    And on the cradle where the prince is rock'd
    With care and whisper.
Quen.   And what hence infer you!
Asc.   That no distinction is 'tween man and man,
    But as his virtues add to him a glory,
    Or vices cloud him';

and that of Decastro in act v. sc. 1 ('The acts of princes,' &c.); and cf. the
striking episode between Sanmartino and the Soldier in act ii.sc. 1, where there
is a genuine burst of democratic spirit.—Habington, the son of a gentleman
who narrowly escaped death in the days of the discovery of the Gunpowder
Plot, and who received part of his education at St. Omer, withstood the
influences to which he was thus exposed. He seems at one time to have
enjoyed the goodwill of Charles I, who is said to have encouraged him to
publish his *History of Edward IV*; and later in life to have inclined to good
relations with Oliver Cromwell. Independence of mind, perhaps fortified
by his historical studies, must accordingly in some measure have separated
him from the tendencies which according to his birth, education, and position
he might have expected to adopt. Such phenomena are always worth

Of HENRY GLAPTHORNE[1] a sufficient number of plays
has been preserved to enable us to judge of his powers as
a dramatist ; which it is, however, impossible to rate very
highly.   The most pleasing of his dramatic works is the
pastoral tragedy of *Argalus and Parthenia* (printed 1639),
which is founded upon a charming episode in the Third
Book of Sidney's *Arcadia* already previously versified by
Quarles.   It cannot, however, be said that Glapthorne has
succeeded in reproducing the delicate touches of pathos
characterising this part of Sidney's romance ; or that the
comic element added by him can be accounted a gain.
The diction of the serious passages, though florid in its
imagery, is not devoid of vigour ; and in the scene of the
duel between Argalus and Amphialus there is a touch of
dramatic truthfulness which appears to me singularly
effective[2].

The romantic comedy of *The Ladies' Priviledge* (printed
1640) has received high praise ; but its merits are almost
entirely confined to the fluency, and occasional eloquence,
of its diction.   The plot is not only extravagant, but its
point is, so to speak, broken off[3] ; and what pathos some

*Henry
Glapthorne
(temp.
Charles I).*

*His plays :
Argalus
and
Parthenia
(pr. 1639).*

*The Ladies'
Privilege
(pr. 1640).*

noting. Furthermore, he appears to have looked with dislike upon the
vicious habits of Court life ; he celebrated his mistress and wife under the name
of *Castara* ; and a passage in *The Queene of Arragon* (act iv. sc. 1) seems to
testify to the same spirit.—The play, by the bye, contains a parody on Pistol's
famous maxim in this form : ' Base is the wight that thinks.' (Act ii. sc. 1.)

[1] *The Plays and Poems of Henry Glapthorne, now first collected, with
Illustrative Notes and a Memoir of the Author.* 2 vols., 1874. (One of
Mr. Pearson's reprints. The Memoir, which, in the absence of any trustworthy biographical information, is swelled by some documentary evidence
as to the profane language indulged in by *George* Glapthorne, whom the
editor on no grounds whatever conjectures to have been the dramatist's
brother, cites a critical article on Henry Glapthorne from *The Retrospective
Review*, vol. x.)

[2] I refer to Argalus' death-swoon :

> ' Ha ! Methinks I tread
> On slippery glass, my unsupporting feet
> Dance measures on light waves, and I am sinking
> Into the watery bosoms, there to rest
> For all eternity.'

(Act iv).—The dirge sung at the close of this play is an adaptation of the
Elegie upon the death of his Sister, Mrs. Priscilla Glapthorne, published in the
same year.

[3] The 'Ladies' Privilege' is a peculiar right supposed to have obtained

of the situations possess, lies in their intention rather than
their execution.

*Albertus
Wallen-
stein
(pr.* 1639). Far inferior in style to both these plays, though possessing a special interest on account of its subject, is
Glapthorne's only extant attempt at historical tragedy.
This term is, however, in truth a misnomer in the case of
Albertus Wallenstein, first printed in 1639, five years after
the event which it commemorates. The death of Wallenstein was too extraordinary and mysterious an event
to fail of attracting public attention in England; and in
this play we have the more or less distant echo of some
version of the transaction furnished to London *quidnuncs*
by some Staple of News office of the day [1]. For the love-
intrigue and the double murder consequent upon it Glapthorne's invention may fairly be held responsible [2]. The
scene of this far from admirable play lies alternately at
'Egers' and at the Emperor's Court. Wallenstein is here
an ambitious ruffian who murders his son Albertus for
engaging in an amour with one of the Duchess' women, and

by usage at Genoa (a state with a highly complicated constitution), where
the scene of the play is laid. By inducing a condemned prisoner to marry her,
a maiden may secure to him his life and liberty. In order to test his affection
for her, Chrisea calls upon her betrothed, the victorious general Doria, to
resign her hand and obtain for her that of his friend Vitelli, who is in love
with her sister. Doria supposes himself to have killed the latter in a quarrel
with Chrisea's kinsman Bonivet, and is condemned to death. Chrisea refuses
to exert her privilege, in order to prolong the trial to which she has put
Doria; and the claim is made by another lady. Doria reluctantly accepts
her hand; and though everything ends happily, inasmuch as the lady proves
to be Doria's faithful page Sabelli in disguise, the contrast between his loyal
fidelity and Chrisea's haughtiness thus fails to be carried to any real
dramatic climax.

[1] It can hardly be supposed to have been written immediately after the
assassination of Wallenstein, an event of which the significance must have
been obscure. Mr. Fleay points out that a passage in act v. sc. 1—

'Are you the man
Have swayed the Roman empire four-and-twenty years,'—

would be truer both to metre and to fact—but it would not be quite true to the
latter—if the emendation 'fourteen years' were accepted, since Ferdinand II
succeeded as emperor in 1612. He thinks that the alteration was made to
avoid any supposition of allusion to Charles I, who also became King in
1625. (See *English Drama*, vol. i. p. 246.)

[2] Wallenstein's sons are purely fictitious. No trace of any such personages
exists in history.

causes her to be hanged on the stage, in *Spanish Tragedy*
fashion. His other son is married at 'Egers' to Emilia,
daughter of 'Saxon Waymar.' Wallenstein — here we
come upon a fortuitous resemblance to Schiller—is haunted
by anticipations of his fate, and vainly seeks the repose of
sleep before the murder, being haunted by the ghosts of
the murdered 'Albertus and his lovely Bride.' 'Newman'
(Schiller's Neumann) is a comic character of a gross cast.
The play contains no mention of Wallenstein's astrological
pursuits, unless an allusion to them be sought in his
declaration that he will not fall like a comet 'by his own
fire consumed.' The whole play is a crude and feeble
attempt, which altogether misses its effect by representing
Wallenstein as a vulgar domestic monster, who exclaims as
he falls :

> 'I die,
> Not for my ambition, but my cruelty[1].'

Glapthorne's comedies of modern life are of no mark.
The Hollander (written in 1635, published in 1640) is
a coarse production, though remarkable in some of its
passages for the copious flow of imagery usual in its author.
The play is curious for the expression which it gives to the
prevalent hatred of the Dutch. *Wit in a Constable* (written
in 1639, and printed in the following year) may perhaps find
more favour as a picture of manners. The reader will not
fail to notice the caricature of the University man who
has made an indifferent use of his library, together with
a palpable imitation—one among many—of a famous scene
in *Much Ado about Nothing* in Constable Busie's address
to his watchmen [2].

*His come-
dies : The
Hollander
(written
1635;
pr.* 1640).

*Wit in a
Constable
(written
1639;
pr.* 1640).

The Duchess of Fernandina, a tragedy entered in 1660
as by Glapthorne, was burnt, together with *The Vestal*, by
Warburton's cook; a tragedy entered in 1653 as Glapthorne's under the title of *The Paraside, a Revenge for*

---

[1] It is hardly necessary to observe that neither Schiller nor Coleridge
appears to have been aware of the existence of Glapthorne's tragedy.
A contemporary French play on the subject by Sarrasin, and an Italian, are
mentioned by Elze in the Introduction to his edition of Chapman's *Alphonsus*,
p. 24.

[2] Act v. sc. 1.

Honor, has been supposed to be identical with *The Revenge for Honour,* doubtfully attributed to Chapman; perhaps it was a revision by Glapthorne of some older play. More confidently the comedy of *The Lady Mother,* licensed in 1635 with certain 'reformations,' has been attributed to Glapthorne [1]. I am not disposed to think the test of apparent repetition (or anticipation) of passages occurring in plays undoubtedly Glapthorne's decisive; but there is nothing improbable in the supposition [2]. The plot of this play turns on the unpleasant theme of the amorous jealousy of a mother against her own daughters, which brings her to the pass of having to confess herself before the judge guilty of subornation of murder. At last, all comes right, including the fatuous delusion of the Lady's Steward, a shameless copy of Malvolio. Unpleasing as the subject of the play is, it must be allowed to be rather superior than inferior in style to most of Glapthorne's dramatic writing.

Glap-thorne's (?) The Lady Mother (acted 1635).

This dramatist, as has been pointed out by a previous writer [3], resembles Shirley in style,—more especially in his love for poetic imagery. Glapthorne's metaphors taken from the world of flowers and from natural phenomena in general [4] pleasingly relieve the commonplace character of his ideas. In no other respect is he worthy of being singled out from the crowd of contemporary dramatists. He was also productive as an erotic and elegiac poet. Of his life, as observed, practically nothing is known, except that he was clearly a devoted adherent of the Court party. One of his plays [5] is dedicated to Wentworth (Strafford); some of his poems are addressed to royal or noble personages; and

Glap-thorne's fondness for poetic imagery.

His con-nexion with the Court party.

---

[1] Both by Mr. Bullen, who has reprinted the play in vol. ii of his *Collection, &c.* (1883), and by Mr. Fleay, who thinks it was probably the same play as *The Noble Trial,* entered in 1660 and burnt by Warburton's cook.

[2] In act ii. sc. 1 there is a reference to 'Papenham's' 'overthrow at Maestricht,' i. e. his repulse from that town in August, 1632. Could the play have been written before the news had arrived of Pappenheim's death at Lützen on November 16?

[3] Cf. *Memoir,* p. viii.

[4] See particularly *Argalus and Parthenia, The Hollander,* and *The Ladies' Privilege.*

[5] *Wit in a Constable.*

he wrote—in the fatal year 1642—a mournful lament on the empty palace of Whitehall, dedicated to his 'noble Friend and Gossip, Captaine Richard Lovelace[1].' The cause of his imprisonment, to which he refers in an earlier poem, is unknown. The publication of *Whitehall, and other Poems* in 1643 is the last trace we have of him. Two of his plays are known to have been acted after the Restoration.

No enlargement seems necessary of this list of noteworthy dramatists belonging to the early Stuart period who either died before the outbreak of the Civil War, or were of no further literary service to the stage after its re-opening. Obviously, a few plays worth remembering may have been submerged, and the name of a less fortunate dramatist or two may have been overlooked by literary historians, who are not as a rule under the sway of traditions quite so tenacious as those of the pit and the green-room. Without, therefore, pretending in any sense to completeness, I subjoin a few brief references to authors whom, for one reason or another, it might seem inequitable to omit from any attempt to exhibit the progress, up to indicated limits, of our dramatic literature. *Other dramatists of the first two Stuart reigns.*

No further reference seems necessary to ROBERT DABORNE (d. 1628), whose reputation as a dramatist is merged in that of the writers of enduring fame with whom he co-operated[2]. He died as Dean of Lismore, having, at all events during the last decade of his life, devoted his chief energies to the service of the Church in Ireland. His only extant plays, composed so far as is known independently, are a tragedy on a familiar theme, *The Christian turn'd Turk, or The Tragicall Lives and Deaths of the two famous Pyrates, Ward and Danseker* (printed 1612), and a tragi-comedy, *The Poor Man's Comfort*, apparently acted about the same time as the preceding, near the close of the first decade of the century. *Robert Daborne (d. 1628).*

Within the same years LEWIS MACHIN, of whom personally nothing is known, joined GERVASE MARKHAM *Lewis Machin and Gervase Markham.*

---

[1] Glapthorne's poetic mistress is Lucinda, as Lovelace's is Lucasta.

[2] Cf. *ante*, p. 4 *et al.*

(1568–c. 1637) in the composition of a 'historicall comedy,'
The Dumb Knight[1], which was first printed in 1608, with
an address by Machin 'to the Understanding Reader.'
Mr. Fleay is probably near the truth in supposing the
meaning of this address to be that Markham kept himself
out of the way of apologising for those satirical—or libellous
—portions of the play of which he was the author.   To the
modern reader this comedy seems by no means devoid either
of spirit or of feeling, although he may resent the quotations
from '*The Maid's Philosophy, or Venus and Adonis*[2]' as
representing a phase of Shakspere-criticism resembling that
of Part I of *The Return from Parnassus*[3].   It cannot for
a moment be supposed that the scene in the last act, where
the Queen and Philocles are watched by the jealous King
while they are engaged in a game at cards, and where the
several interlocutors equivocate, consciously or unconsciously, upon the technical terms used in playing the game,
was otherwise than copied from a celebrated passsage in
Thomas Heywood's *A Woman Killed with Kindness*, which
was certainly on the stage in 1603[4].   But the construction
of the play, though its story is interesting and almost
containing matter enough for more than one action—quite
apart from the vulgar under-plot—is rather rude ; and two
ordeals of combat[5] seem rather excessive for a single play.
The figure of the *Dumb Knight* is heroic—but the *afflatus*
is wanting which *The Two Noble Kinsmen* caught from its
epical original.   Gervase Markham, an early example of
the book-maker extraordinary, whose multitudinous literary
adventures cannot be chronicled here, and whose hostility
to Shakspere has been supposed to have passed beyond
the sphere of literary criticism[6], was also joint author, with
WILLIAM SAMPSON, of a tragedy, *Herod and Antipater,
with the Death af Fair Mariam*[7] (printed 1622).

[1] Printed in vol. x of Hazlitt's *Dodsley*.
[2] See act iv.   [3] Cf. *ante*, vol. ii. p. 639.
[4] See act v; and cf. *ante*, vol. ii. p. 564, *note*. The pun on the name of
the game *Saint* (i. e. *Cent* or *cientos* = hundred) occurs in Heywood, but the
whole notion of the scene is manifestly taken from him.
[5] See acts i and v.   [6] Cf. Fleay, *u. s.*, vol. ii. pp. 58–9.
[7] As to Lady Elizabeth Carew's *Mariam*, see *ante*, p. 15.

In the earlier part of the period covered by this chapter, *Robert Tailor.* ROBERT TAILOR (otherwise unknown) wrote a play called *The Hog hath lost his Pearl*[1], an odd farrago of extravagant romance and equally extravagant farce, which obtained notoriety, by being, in 1613, acted at Whitefriars by sixteen London apprentices, who were stopped by the sheriffs before the end of the piece, 'some six or seven of them' being 'carried to perform the last act at Bridewell[2].'

LODOWICK BARRY was the author of *Ram-Alley, or Merry-Tricks*[3] (printed in 1611), a comedy which appears *Lodowick Barry.* to have earned much popularity by the extreme grossness of its fun; but he appears not to have lived to fulfil his contingent promise of mending his manners as a playwright[4].

HENRY SHIRLEY, who was killed in a quarrel in 1627, *Henry Shirley.* can have been no relation of the celebrated dramatist; of his own plays none has been preserved except *The Martyr'd Souldier*[5], a kind of latter-day miracle-play, whose action is placed in the times of Belisarius and Genseric. It conveys the impression of a hand imperfectly trained to dramatic work; yet four other plays were entered as Henry Shirley's in the Stationers' Registers.

ROBERT DAVENPORT, also known as a writer of didactic *Robert Davenport.* verse, seems to have gained considerable reputation as

---

[1] Printed in vol. iii of *The Ancient British Drama*, and in vol. xi of Hazlitt's *Dodsley*.

[2] See a letter from Sir Henry Wotton to Sir Edmund Bacon, printed in *Reliquiae Wottonianae*. Wotton facetiously reports that the 'prentices had invited to their performance 'rather their Mistresses than their Masters.'— The serious plot of this piece is concerned with a crime against friendship very compendiously atoned for by remorse; the comic intrigue has the air of a parody on Shylock and Jessica.—The everlasting echo-device is also repeated in this worthless play.

[3] Printed in vol. x of Hazlitt's *Dodsley*.

[4] In the Prologue he promises that if his 'home-bred mirth' finds favour, he will labour till he produces something which the Puritans themselves may witness without taking offence.—A famous line from *Othello* is rather amusingly parodied in this play.—*Ram Alley* was revived in 1723 or 1724, with Pinkethman as old Justice Tutchin, apparently one of his last parts. (See Genest, vol. iii. pp. 135-6.)

[5] Reprinted in vol. i of Mr. A. H. Bullen's *Old English Plays* (1882).

a dramatist, which may help to account for the strange entry in the Stationers' Registers, September, 1653, of a work entitled *Henry I and Henry II* as by Shakspere and Davenport[1]. This appears to be the lost play of *Henry I*, licensed in 1624[2], another of the plays burnt by the too famous cook. Davenport wrote another tragedy, *King John and Matilda*, which was printed in 1655[3], and two comedies, *A New Trick to cheat the Divell*, and *The City Nightcap*, the latter of which was licensed in 1624, though not printed till the year after the Restoration[4]. The extremely unpleasant plot of this play, which, as one of the personages observes at the opening, centres in

> 'an old point, and wondrous frequent
> In most of our Italian comedies[5],'

is, so to speak, burlesqued in the under-plot. Davenport was also associated as a playwright with THOMAS DRUE, from whose hand no independently written work has been preserved.

Thomas Goffe.

THOMAS GOFFE (1591–1629) was famed as a preacher not less than as a dramatist, and his three tragedies, though not published till after his death, were acted by the students of Christ Church while he was a resident at Oxford. They should accordingly be judged with lenience, more especially as the author wished them to be regarded as his *nugae*, and in one instance seems to have hesitated whether to make an end of his muse's progeny in the flames[6]. But it is difficult to bear with such rant as that of *The Raging Turk, or Bajazet the Second*, in the course of which the Emperor might well come to doubt whether he had not

---

[1] Cf. *ante*, vol. ii. p. 213.

[2] See Collier, vol. i. p. 425; and cf. Fleay, *u. s.*, vol. i. p. 104.

[3] According to Genest, vol. i. p. 235, this tragedy, which was printed in 1655, was to a considerable extent borrowed from Chettle and Munday's *The Death of Robert Earl of Huntington* (cf. *ante*, vol. i. p. 433).

[4] Printed in vol. iii of *The Ancient British Drama* and in vol. xiii of Hazlitt's *Dodsley*.

[5] It is in point of fact, as Mr. Fleay points out, made up from Boccaccio and Cervantes.

[6] See Meighen's dedication of *The Raging Turk*, and his lines to the author on transcribing (*not* translating) *The Courageous Turk*.

> ' crackt the vital thread
> Of all his Bassaes ';

and with the still more repulsive bombast of *The Courageous Turk, or Amurath the First*, who is converted by a sham ghost from the designs of a ravishing Tarquin into the murderous heroism of the imperial lover of Hiren the Fair Greek. Nothing of a nature to redeem these excesses is to be found in these plays or in *The Tragedie of Orestes*; and much might be said in excuse of a reader who should erroneously associate them with an earlier period of our drama than that to which they actually belong[1]. These plays contain a good deal of rime. They were collected into a volume in 1656 by Goffe's admiring friend, Richard Meighen.

WILLIAM BOWYER seems to have been the author of a play called *The Valiant Scot* (printed 1637), which in the Dedication signed by him under that name he offers to the Marquis of Hamilton as 'one amongst his meanest followers in his Lordship's practicall life of a Souldier';— ' What he has he bestows upon him.' Yet in the title-page the play announces itself as ' by J. W., Gent.' Hamilton's ' practical life' as a volunteer auxiliary of Gustavus Adolphus had come to an unsuccessful end in 1634, and it was not till 1638 that he began to play an important part at home in Scotland in the King's service; so that the combination of theme and date in this play, taken together with the fact of its dedication to Hamilton, is less noteworthy than might at first sight appear. The subject of the play is the career and catastrophe of Sir William Wallace, dealt with in the artless fashion of a Chronicle History, but with the addition of a romantic effect or two suggested by later theatrical reminiscences[2]. If the author of this rather crude com-

William Bowyer (?).

---

[1] Goffe was absurdly credited with the authorship of Part I of *The Tragedy and Reign of Selimus* (cf. *ante*, vol. i. p. 405).

[2] See the scenes in act iii leading up to and including the death of Selby, and Wallace's magnanimous proposals for burying his slain enemy, stolen from the well-known passage in *Cymbeline*, act iv. sc. 2. At the close Wallace has, before meeting his doom, to undergo the visitation of a series of ghosts, Peggy's, talking her impossible Scotch, among the number. Thereupon Bruce is crowned, swears fealty to Edward, stabs Comyn, and concludes a league of perfect love with England, all in a trice.

position was a Scotchman, he had a very strange notion of Scottish dialect, for the language which he puts into the mouth of the beauteous Peggie resembles no known form of Lowland speech. For that matter, however, neither does any other contemporary specimen of stage Scotch [1].

Lodowick Carlell.

Of LODOWICK CARLELL, who as a courtier for many years served Charles I, and Henrietta Maria both before and after the King's death, not less than eight plays are preserved, several of which seem to have been favourites at Whitehall. Nor is this preference discreditable either to patrons or to purveyor. Carlell's plays, in so far as I am acquainted with them, show few traces of poetical inspiration; and in fact, if the printed copies in any degree reproduce the original text, it cannot be described as much more than inflated prose, occasionally striving after metre and even lapsing into rime. Yet at the same time he is distinguished by a certain refinement of feeling which compensates for many deficiencies. *The Deserving Favourite*, printed in 1629, is a production of undeniable merit. The title of the play is justified by the magnanimity of 'the Duke,' whose character is drawn with a determined effort to realise an ideal of chivalry in high places; and the plot, which provides the Duke's rival in the affections of the heroine Clarinda—when she proves to be his sister—with a refuge in the love of the royal huntress Cleonarda, is not contrived without originality and skill. I confess to having derived pleasure from this play, artificial though much of it is in sentiment. In *The Fool would be a Favourit, or The Discreet Lover* (printed in 1657), the serious interest is fainter, and has to be diversified with the aid of the comic character of Young Gudgen, a rustic aspirant after Court honours. *Osmond the Great Turk, or The Noble Servant* (printed with the last-named play), seems to go a long way towards deserting the dramatic method for that of the romances which were coming into favour; and this tendency is even more overpowering in *Arviragus and Philicia*, a tragi-comedy in two parts (printed 1639), of which the scene is laid in Ancient Britain, and of

[1] See, for instance, John Tatham's *The Scots' Figaries* (1652).

which the plot manifestly follows the line of some forgotten romance. Of the other extant plays of Carlell I can give no account at first hand ; but *The Passionate Lovers*, also in two parts (printed in 1655), seems to be of a romantic type resembling *The Deserving Favourite*. A reprint of Carlell's plays, which have been very diversely judged, would be welcome[1].

To the latter part of the period belongs THOMAS RAWLINS, who was engraver at the Mint under both Charles I and Charles II, the author of a tragedy called *The Rebellion*, printed 1640, but probably performed three years earlier. It contains one quite novel 'motive,' but is otherwise unmarked by originality[2]. *Thomas Rawlins.*

WILLIAM HEMINGE, an Oxford graduate said to have been a son of Shakspere's fellow-player, wrote a tragedy called *The Fatal Contrast*, based on a French chronicle, which was acted before the closing of the theatres, and having been printed in 1653, was revived and reprinted *William Heminge.*

---

[1] In the Prologue to *The Deserving Favourite* this author happily expresses the limits of his powers, and perhaps also the romantic inspiration which animated his best work :

> 'Doe not expect strong Lines, nor Mirth, though they
> Justly the Towne wits and the Vulgar sway :
> What hope have we, then, that our Play can please
> This more judicious Presence, wanting these ?
> We have a hope (the Author sayes) this Night
> Love in our weaknesse shall expresse his might.'—

For an account of some of Carlell's plays see Genest, vol. x. pp. 24 *seqq.*—According to the same authority, vol. i. p. 73, the *Heraclius* (such is the title of one of his plays, printed in 1664), which Pepys saw on February 4, 1667, ' was not Carlell's, but another translation from Corneille.' (Pepys had previously seen *Heraclius* on March 8, 1664.)

[2] Printed in vol. iii of *The Ancient British Drama*, and vol. xiv of Hazlitt's *Dodsley*.—To judge from the commendatory verses, *The Rebellion* would seem to have enjoyed great favour, doubtless on account of the novelty referred to in the text. The hero makes love and gains glory under the disguise of a tailor ; and this brilliant fancy furnishes the occasion for some scenes which recall Dekker's glorification of another handicraft. (Cf. *ante*, vol. ii. p. 456.) The villain of the play bears the time-honoured name of ' Machvile.' (Cf. vol. i. p. 339, *note*.) For the rest, *The Rebellion* is a concoction as full of incident as any play applauded by the 'Prentices a generation or so earlier.

after the Restoration under new titles [1]. Another play by
him, *The Jews' Tragedy*, on the capture of Jerusalem by
Titus, was printed in 1652, some years after the author's
death.

Nathaniel Richards.

From the pen of NATHANIEL RICHARDS, a graduate of
Caius College, who also wrote *Sacred and Satirical Poems*,
a single dramatic work only remains—*The Tragedy of
Messallina the Roman Emperesse*, printed in 1640, as divers
times acted. The play is based on Tacitus and Juvenal;
but while the author shows a certain freedom in his use of his
historical materials, he is pedantic enough to introduce a
long quotation from the *Sixth Satire* in the original Latin [2].

Joseph Rutter.

JOSEPH RUTTER, who is said to have at one time lived in
the house of Sir Kenelm Digby, is credited with the authorship of the 'pastoral tragi-comedy,' *The Shepherd's Holy-day*,
which was printed with his initials in 1635, as performed
before the King and Queen at Whitehall. This production
was warmly praised by Ben Jonson, who saluted 'his Joseph'
as his 'dear son and right learned friend [3].' It is dedicated
to Digby, and its plot is supposed to have some reference to
a love-intrigue in which he was concerned. In itself,
although well written, this is not a specially interesting
sample of the species to which it belongs.

Lewis Sharpe.

LEWIS SHARPE wrote a play called *The Noble Stranger*,
printed in 1640, of which Langbaine with cautious commendation remarks that if it be 'look'd upon with mild Eyes,
it will weigh against some Plays writ' in his own time. He
refers, however, not to the main plot, which very clearly
unfolds the simple romantic tale of a noble stranger who,
after being banished for venturing to woo the Princess of
Naples, returns to claim her as the Prince of Portingall;
but to a scene of act iv, which contains some of the usual
criticisms of contemporary drama, including a diverting
allusion to Ben Jonson.

[1] *Love and Revenge,* and *The Eunuch.*
[2] Richards seems about this time to have been a schoolmaster.
[3] See *Underwoods,* xxii. Rutter afterwards contributed to *Jonsonus Virbius.*—*The Shepherd's Holiday* is printed in vol. xii of Hazlitt's *Dodsley.*

HENRY KILLIGREW (1613–1700), the youngest brother *Henry* of Sir William and the elder Thomas Killigrew, and father *Killigrew.* of the Anne Killigrew immortalised by Dryden, who at the outbreak of the Civil War became Chaplain to the King's army, and after the Restoration was appointed Master of the Savoy; but his dramatic effort, *The Conspiracy*, was 'juvenile' in every sense of the word[1]. This play, published in 1638, was to have been produced on the occasion of the marriage of Buckingham's only daughter, and was afterwards publicly performed. It was reprinted, in a revised form, in 1653 under the title of *Pallantus and Eudora*.

SIR WILLIAM BERKELEY, who died in 1677, after holding *Sir* a place at Court under Charles I, and subsequently the *William* *Berkeley.* governorship of the colony of Virginia, in 1638 published a play called *The Lost Lady*, which I cannot agree with Mr. Fleay in considering worthless[2]. The heroine of this 'tragi-comedy' assumes a male disguise in order to escape from the power of her uncle, who rather than permit her union with her lover Lysides has sought to compass her death; and then barely escapes being poisoned by her lover himself. The somewhat complicated plot leading up to this situation is cleverly managed, and the writing is effective in the serious as well as in the comic parts of the action. Berkeley understands how to sustain and heighten in its progress the interest of a dramatic argument intrinsically ingenious and perspicuous; and he is at the same time not altogether devoid of a certain subtlety of thought and vivacity of wit[3]. Possibly, a lost play called *Cornelia*,

[1] See *ap.* Langbaine, p. 310, the anecdote of Lord Falkland's apology for 'the Indecorum that appear'd in the part of Cleander, who being represented as a Person of seventeen years old, is made to speak words, that would better sute with the Age of Thirty.' 'Sir, 'tis not altogether so monstrous and impossible for One of Seventeen Years to speak at such a rate, when He that made him speak in that Manner, and writ the whole Play, was Himself no Older.'—Mr. Fleay, vol. ii. p. 23, says that this was the first play publicly performed with scenery.—According to Mr. Aitkin, in vol. xxxi of *The Dictionary of National Biography* (1892), Sir Charles Sedley's *The Tyrant King of Crete* was an adaptation of Henry Killigrew's play. (See below.)

[2] It is printed in vol. xii of Hazlitt's *Dodsley*.

[3] See, for an example of the former, Lysides' soliloquy on suicide in act v;

by 'Sir William Bartley,' was likewise by the author of *The Lost Lady*.

Richard Lovelace.

Unfortunately, or perhaps not altogether so for his literary fame, which actually rests on the rare charm of a few songs from his hand, we possess neither of the two plays of RICHARD LOVELACE (1618–1658), who has himself become part of the poetry of Cavalier tradition. *The Scholar*, of which the Prologue and Epilogue were included in *Lucasta* (printed 1649), was a comedy written by him for performance, in 1636, at Gloucester Hall, Oxford, of which he was a member, and afterwards performed at Whitehall. *The Soldier*—as if to mark an antithesis in the poet's career—was a tragedy written by him in 1639, when he had obtained a commission in the army which advanced against the Scots as far as Berwick, and remained unacted.

Dramatists who wrote both before and after the Civil War and Commonwealth periods.

Finally, several of the dramatists of the period beginning with the Restoration had already produced plays in that preceding the Great Revolution. The list of these includes, besides Abraham Cowley [1], whose literary fame, however, connects itself more intimately with a later age than that now under review, Sir Robert Stapylton, John Tatham, Thomas Killigrew the elder (as a play-writer the most prolific of his family), and Sir William D'Avenant. The activity of

and, for the latter, the frolicsome Irene's advice, act i. sc. 2, to censurers of 'minor poets' : 'Let me counsel you : lay them aside till they have contracted an inch of dust ; then with your finger write their epitaph, expressing the mutual quiet they gave men, and received from them.'—A very attractive reminiscence of *The Lost Lady* occurs in the delightful *Letters of Dorothy Osborne to Sir William Temple* (1652–4), edited by E. A. Parry (ed. 1888), p. 294 : 'They will have me at my part in a play ; *The Lost Lady* it is, and I am she.'

[1] Among Cowley's dramatic works, the pastoral comedy of *Love's Riddle*, and the comedy of *The Guardian*, were, together with the Latin academical comedy *Naufragium Joculare* (to be noticed immediately), written before the Restoration. *The Guardian*, acted at Trinity before Prince Charles in 1641, was, as will be seen, afterwards reproduced in an altered form and with a different name. *Love's Riddle*, written by Cowley when a King's Scholar at Westminster, and published in 1638, is a pastoral drama which, notwithstanding the elaborateness of its plot, need be credited with no greater gravity of purpose than that suggested by Alupis' refrain—

"'tis but a folly
To be melancholy.'

the last two of these writers, the rival managers of the two
new playhouses for which a royal patent was granted immediately after the Restoration, divides itself nearly equally
between two different epochs in the history of our dramatic
literature. A few remarks concerning each of them seem
accordingly called for both in this place, and at a rather
later point.

THOMAS KILLIGREW[1] (1612–1683), known as the elder   *Thomas*
by way of distinction from his son and namesake[2], was   *Killigrew*
a favourite companion of King Charles II in both evil and   *(1612–*
fortunate times. As to the gifts by which he gained his   1683).
traditional—or, as it was affirmed, actual[3]—office of 'the
King's Jester,' we must trust the evidence of a few anec-
dotes ; but even supposing the wit which they certainly
attest to have been characteristic of all his sayings, it may
be doubted whether 'Tom' Killigrew ever said a better
thing of any of the objects of his satire (including King
Charles himself) than was written concerning him by the
grave Denham—

> 'Had Cowley ne'er spoke, Killigrew ne'er writ,
>   Combined in one, they'd made a matchless wit[4].'

In justice to him, however, it should be remembered that,
unlike his four earlier plays, the seven later, which will be
mentioned below, were, at least primarily, written by the
author purely as a literary diversion during his travels in
the service of the exiled Charles II. His earlier four plays
seem likewise to have been written abroad, when between
the years 1635 and 1642 he sojourned in France, Italy, and
Switzerland ; but at least three of these were acted on the
public stage before the outbreak of the Civil War. The four
plays in question are the tragi-comedies of *The Prisoners,*

---

[1] *Comedies and Tragedies.* Written by Thomas Killigrew. Fol. 1664.

[2] Thomas Killigrew the younger, who was gentleman of the bedchamber
to the Prince of Wales, afterwards King George II, wrote a comedy called
Chit Chat, the date of which (1719) falls outside the range of this book.

[3] Pepys writes under Feb. 13, 1668 : 'Mr. Brisband tells me in discourse
that Tom Killigrew hath a fee out of the Wardrobe for cap and bells, under
the title of the King's Foole or Jester ; and may revile or jeere any body,
the greatest person, without offence, by the privilege of his place.'

[4] Cited by Genest, vol. i. p. 391.

Claracilla (acted *c.* 1636 [1]), of which the scene is laid in
Sicily, and *The Princesse, or Love at First Sight*, in which
the satire against soldiers and their self-government may seem
worthy of notice, together with the comedy of the *The
Parson's Wedding* [2], acted in 1640. The last-named, which
like *Claracilla* was revived after the Restoration, is a play
of the utmost coarseness ; in point of fact, the satirical
ribaldry which accompanies the working out of its congenial
theme—the over-reaching of a parson by a soldier—is most
properly described by the word blackguardly. The tag-
epilogue in this play is singularly modern in manner.

Sir Wil-
liam d'Ave-
nant (1606-
1668).

His life.

SIR WILLIAM D'AVENANT [3], the author of *Gondibert*
and of a large number of plays, of which a sufficiently large
number have been preserved to enable us to estimate for
ourselves the dramatic powers of a writer extremely popular
in his own age though forgotten by posterity, was born
at Oxford early in 1606. The scandalous story as to his
birth need not be again mentioned here [4], whether or not
it be true that he was himself 'contented enough' to find
it meet with credit. Early in life D'Avenant became page to
a great Court lady, from whose service he afterwards passed
into that of Sir Fulke Greville, Lord Brooke, whose love of
letters may have encouraged similar tastes in his follower.
The death of Lord Brooke in 1628 left D'Avenant to provide for himself ; and in 1629 he produced his first play,
Albovine. He rapidly rose to reputation as a writer of

---

[1] Fleay, *u. s.*, vol. ii. p. 25.

[2] Printed in vol. ii of *The Ancient British Drama* and in vol. xiv of
Hazlitt's *Dodsley*. Its plot has been traced back by Dibdin (vol. iv. p. 94) to
Calderon's *Dama Duende*, and its chief incident was found by Langbaine's
vigilant eye in Lodowick Barry's *Ram-Alley*, Shackerley Marmion's *The
Antiquary*, and other plays, 'but in none so well manag'd as in this.'

[3] *The Dramatic Works of Sir William D'Avenant, with Prefatory Memoir
and Notes.* (By James Maidment and W. H. Logan.) (5 vols., 1872-4.)
See also Mr. Joseph Knight's notice of D'Avenant in vol. xiv of *The
Dictionary of National Biography* (1888).—Dr. Karl Elze has contributed an
essay on D'Avenant to the *Shakespeare Jahrbuch*, vol. iv. (1869).

[4] Cf. *ante*, vol. ii. p. 41.—This tradition or rumour was made the subject of a short sentimental play, *Davenant*, by J. Aicard, performed by
the Comédie Française on the occasion of their visit to London in 1879.
The chief part in the piece had originally been designed for Mlle. Sarah
Bernhardt.

plays, masques, and other poems; and after the death of
Ben Jonson was, in 1638, appointed to the Poet-Laureateship,
which he held under both Charles I and Charles II. In
1639 he obtained a royal patent for the erection of a theatre
(the project of course remained unexecuted); and in the
same year he was made governor of the King's and Queen's
company of players. In 1641 he was involved in a royalist
conspiracy, and saved himself from arrest by flight to
France. During the Civil War he returned to England
with military stores sent by the Queen; served with so
much distinction at the siege of Gloucester in 1643 that he
received the honour of knighthood; was after another
absence in France (where he became a Catholic) employed
on a confidential mission from the Queen to the King when
at Newcastle in 1646, in which, according to Clarendon,
he failed to distinguish himself; and was afterwards, when
on his way to Virginia as her agent, arrested off the French
coast and imprisoned in Cowes Castle [1]. Soon after his
release he published his poem of *Gondibert* (1651), and
then, after undergoing a further imprisonment for debt,
from 1657 onwards engaged in those attempts at reviving,
or keeping alive, the drama which, together with the chief
data of his career in connexion with the theatre after the
Restoration, will be briefly adverted to below. He died
in 1668 and was buried in Westminster Abbey, where
a stone was placed on his tomb with the inscription 'O rare
Sr. Will. Davenant.'

The career of Charles I's second laureate was thus a *His ideas*
typical one; and the same epithet may be applied to those of *on dra-*
matic com-
his plays which he produced before the Restoration. Devoid *position.*
of all higher original genius, D'Avenant applied himself, in
no vulgar spirit nor without taking full advantage of such
lights as were vouchsafed to him, to the task of satisfying
what to him was the supreme criterion of merit, viz. the most
cultivated taste (or what appeared to him such) of his age.
From this point of view the Preface to *Gondibert*—his most
ambitious work, although it remained a fragment—well

---

[1] For his petition for a full release, see *State Papers, Domestic,* 1654, p. 107;
cf. *ib.,* Preface, p. xxxii.

deserves study, more especially since it contains some interesting observations on the relations between dramatic and
epic poetry [1]. The epic itself proves its author to have
been under the influence of one of the most finished of
conceptions in the poetic drama, of which he was to
survive to show his imperfect apprehension in a revision
of notorious ineptitude [1].

[1] Setting forth with the assumption that the common crowd is not to be
taught by poetry, D'Avenant seeks to justify his choice of theme as Christian
(this for the benefit of Hobbes, to whom the Preface was addressed, and who
replied to it), and as heroic. From the material of his ' new building' he
passes to the form, and it is here that his discourse begins to have a special
interest for us. He says—and the declaration gains in interest from the
fact that it was made when the theatres were closed, and after the great
age of our drama had passed away for ever—that, so far as he is aware, no
nation 'hath in repres018?ment of great actions (either by *Heroicks* or
Dramaticks) digested story into so pleasant and instructive a method as the
English by their *Drama*.' And he offers to the form which he loves best
and esteems highest, the homage of the sincerest kind of flattery—imitation,
at all events in theory or intention. He has, he says, constructed his heroic
poem of *Gondibert* on the model of a regular drama : 'in which I did not
only observe the Symmetry (proportioning five *Books* to five *Acts*), and
Canto's to *Scenes* (the *Scenes* having their number ever govern'd by occasion),
but all the shadowing, happy strokes, secret graces, and even the Drapery
(which together make the second beauty) I have (I hope) exactly follow'd ;
and those compositions of second beauty I observe in the *Drama* to be the
under-walks, interweaving, or correspondence of lesser design in *Scenes*, not
the great motion of the main-plot, and coherence of its *Acts*.' There
follows an extremely ingenious skeleton scheme of the progress of a
dramatic action through its five normal stages, which though too long for
quotation here, is quite worth notice ; 'to these Meanders of the English
Stage I have cut out the Walks of my Poem.' Unfortunately, D'Avenant
left his experiment in a very incomplete condition. His poem never reaches
the point at and beyond which the most important tests become applicable
to dramatic construction ; and the excessive amplitude of the descriptive
method used by him in introducing the chief personages of his story is
essentially undramatic. For the rest, D'Avenant's design of building up an
epic poem on a dramatic model received the ready approval of Hobbes, who
appears to have expended but few pipes of tobacco upon the consideration
of his friend's theory. He opines that 'the figure of an Epique Poem, and of
a Tragedy, ought to be the same ; for they differ no more but in that they
are pronounced by one, or many, Persons.' They differ, if in nothing else,
in that the epos and the corresponding forms of prose fiction are not, like
the drama, under a binding law requiring its action to be complete in itself.
Where this necessity is absent, the entire scheme of acts with crisis (or
counter-turn) and catastrophe (or unbinding) becomes more or less superfluous.—I pass by some remarks contained in this Preface on metre, though
they are not without significance for the history of dramatic versification.

[2] See below as to his invention of the scheme of Dryden's *The Tempest, or*

In his pre-Revolution plays he succeeded in reproducing, *Character* *of his earlier* *plays.* more faithfully than a greater writer could have done, not only the tastes and sentiments, but as it were the very temper of mind and tone of morality of his age, so far as they were within his view. The enthusiasm which he dedicated to such a patron as Endymion Porter expressed his sympathy with a whole phase of social and artistic feeling of which 'his Endymion[1]' was no unworthy representative. As a dramatist, D'Avenant may, in the earlier series of his plays, be described as a limb of Fletcher, whom he resembled in his audacious choice of subjects, in his roving rather than soaring flights of fancy, and in his love of warm descriptive colouring. On occasion, he reveals some traces of the tenderness and even of the poetic feeling of his predecessor; but of the humour in which Fletcher abounded D'Avenant seems to me to possess little or nothing. He is not incapable of passion; but he is in general so unmeasured in expression as to make it difficult to distinguish between his passion and his rant. Burying his characters beneath accumulations of incident, he seems to lose sight of them in the process; and although a certain advance is observable in the successive plays belonging to this earlier group, hardly one of them seems to possess an intrinsic title to special remembrance. The subject of *The Tragedy of Albovine, King of the Lombards*, *Albovine* printed 1622[2] and dedicated to Somerset (many years *(pr. 1629)*. after his fall), is the well-known story of Alboin and Rosamund, probably taken by D'Avenant from Beueforest's

---

The Enchanted Island.—In the epic, the wounded Gondibert finds his way to the abode of the great magician Astragon, who cures him of his wounds. While under his care, Gondibert falls in love with Birtha, the sweet guileless daughter of the sage ; and thus opens an episode which we might agree with Hobbes in calling an 'incomparable description of Love,' were it not, in its earliest passages at all events, obviously modelled on the scenes between Prospero, Miranda and Ferdinand. Yet, even so, and with the best intentions, D'Avenant could not avoid introducing a cynical touch into his adopted fancy.

[1] See his address *To the Lady Olivia Porter*, cited *ap.* Maidment and Logan, vol. ii. p. 113.

[2] The version in the folio edition of D'Avenant's *Works* (1673) is a prose alteration, mainly in the way of abridgment.

translation[1] of one of Bandello's tales. The author revels
in the mixture of blood and lust which his plot supplies;
and he has apparently himself introduced some of its
most revolting elements. Two of the characters in *Albovine*
are named Gondibert and Rhodolinda. The dramatist's
workmanship is coarse; both in the management of his
action and in details of treatment and expression the spirit of
licence seems to run riot in this play. Nor is anything very

The Cruel Brother (pr. 1630). different to be said concerning *The Cruel Brother* (printed
1630), where again we have a King's 'boy' or favourite
—a character which could hardly have been brought on
the stage after this fashion in the preceding reign. The
plot is a commonplace story of cruel lust; but the scene
in which the heroine is put to death on the stage shows
that D'Avenant was eager to emulate Webster and Ford
in their refinements of the horrible. Into this play is
introduced an apparent caricature of George Wither, the
author of *Abuses Stript and Whipt*[2], whom Jonson also
introduced into one of his masques[3]. The figure of Cas-
truccio is a disgraceful libel on an honourable, if not always

The Just Italian (pr. 1630). consistent, man. D'Avenant's third extant play, *The Just
Italian* (printed 1630), is equally offensive in the character
of its plot, to which occasional poetic touches will fail to
reconcile the reader[4].

The Platonic Lovers (pr. 1636). In *The Platonick Lovers* (printed 1636) D'Avenant essayed
the field of high comedy; nor was the subject ill-chosen,
or ill-dictated. The author says in the Prologue, referring
either to this play or to his masque of *The Temple of Love*,
that he

> 'had command
> T' interpret what he scarce doth understand'—

an assertion for which every credit will be given him; but
to throw gentle ridicule on a fashionable fancy either very
silly or very dangerous[5] was in itself an excellent comic

---

[1] *Histoires Tragiques,* iv. 19.
[2] See especially act ii.
[3] *Time Vindicated, &c.* Cf. *ante,* vol. ii. p. 396, *note.*
[4] This play is compared by the recent editors of D'Avenant to Fletcher's
Rule a Wife and Have a Wife (acted 1624).
[5] The whim of so-called 'Platonic love'—as to which one of the characters

idea. But some delicacy of feeling, if not propriety of treatment, was indispensable; and since he neither possessed the one nor attempted the other, D'Avenant has only produced a play which may be said to be not altogether unpleasing and upon the whole healthy in tone. In the scenes between the two Platonic lovers Eurithea and Theander (before Theander's conversion) there is, moreover, considerable beauty of poetic expression. The comedy of *The Wits* (printed 1636), on the other hand, though of a *The Wits* type less exacting, seems to me to have been greatly *(pr. 1636).*

in D'Avenant's play says with perfect truth, though with a ribald intention, that

> ' they father on him ' [*i. e.* Plato] ' a fantastic love
> He never knew, poor gentleman '—

came into fashion at Court about 1634. (See a quotation from Howell's *Letters* in Maidment and Logan's *D'Avenant,* vol. ii. p. 3.) The idea was that of meeting with the intentions, or at least on the terms, of

> ' Lovers of a pure
> Celestial kind, such as some style Platonical,
> A new Court epithet scarce understood ;
> But all they woo, Sir, is the spirit, face,
> And heart; therefore their conversation is
> More safe to fame.' (Act i.)

The notion, about which there is nothing in the least original, while its claim of ' safety' admits of two interpretations, is also referred to in D'Avenant's masque of *The Temple of Love* and in Suckling's *Aglaura* (act ii). Jonson in his *New Inn* (act iii. sc. 2), where Lovel defends 'Platonic' love, as usual shows that he knows what he is talking about, though the passage is cold. *The New Inn* was produced in 1629. The ' Platonic love,' fashionable at the Court of King Charles I, was a fancy imported from France, whither it had come from Italy. In the Augustan age the term ' a Platonic ' seems to have become an accepted piece of slang. See Arbuthnot's *History of John Bull,* ch. viii : ' Very pretty indeed ! a wife must never go abroad with a Platonic to see a play or a ball ; she must never stir without her husband, &c.' The *Grand Cyrus* of Mlle. de Scudéry glorifies Platonic love, and her *Clélie*— with its famous *carte du pays de Tendre,* intended as a harmless jest— developes the fancy into artificial exaggeration. See V. Cousin, *La Sociéte Française au 17me Siècle, &c.,* vol. ii. pp. 302 *seqq.*—As to the mediaeval conceptions of ' Platonic love,' and the developement of the combination between these and the ideas of chivalry into the new science of *galanterie,* see St. Marc-Girardin, *Cours de Littérature Dramatique,* vol. ii. sect. xxxvi, and vol. iii. sect. xxxvii.—This fancy, or fashion, forms the subject of the curious comedy of *Lady Alimony* (printed in vol. xiv of Hazlitt's *Dodsley*), which was published in 1659, professing—of course ironically—to be ' duly Authorised, daily Acted, and frequently Followed.' The personages of this dramatic satire consist mainly of the six ' alimony ladies,' their ' cashiered overvalued[1]. King Charles I, no very rigorous judge on the morality of stage-plays, is said to have disliked its plot, although, moved by D'Avenant through the mediation of Endymion Porter, he obliged the Licenser to restore passages of the text which had seemed to Sir Henry Herbert to require expurgation[2]. *The Wits* certainly contains one comic situation of a breadth which would have suited the most frolic pages of Boccaccio; but as a whole the play seems to me tedious, perhaps because I fail to perceive the essence of the difference suggested in it between rural ambition desirous of living on its 'wits' in town, and the claims of town gallantry to a monopoly of the art.

Love and Honour (1634; pr. 1649).

Love and Honour (licensed 1634; printed 1649), which was revived with extreme success after the Restoration, is noticeable on account of its plot, which would be very effective were it not overburdened by an excess of ingenuity; indeed, in the last act our breath is almost taken away by the conflict of generosity and the rapid succession of discoveries. The diction is full of similes, but none of them strike me as altogether novel.

The Unfortunate Lovers (acted 1638; pr. 1643).

The Unfortunate Lovers (licensed 1638; printed 1643) has two heroines (Amaranta and Arthiopa); and it must be allowed that the heroic magnanimity of Amaranta contains the germ of a highly dramatic character; her death, which has a touch of Fletcher when at his best, is genuinely pathetic[3].

consorts,' and their 'Platonic confidants.' (It also contains a 'Constable and Watch' scene, act iii. sc. 3.) This play is by Wood most absurdly attributed to Lodge and Greene.

[1] It was revived after the Restoration, and Pepys repeatedly went to see it. (Reprinted in the two earlier editions of *Dodsley*.)

[2] See as to this amusing incident Collier, vol. i. pp. 483-4. Herbert noted: 'The King is pleased to take faith, death, 'slight,' [the restored words] 'for asseverations and no oaths, to which I do humbly submit as my master's judgment; but under favour conceive them to be oaths, and enter them here to declare my opinion and submission.'

[3]   '*Am.* Go, tell Arthiopa she needs not fear
              Her rival now; my bridal bed is in
              The earth.
    Alt.   Oh stay! there may be help!
    Am.   When you
        Come near my grave, if any flower can grow
        On such unlucky ground, pray water't with
        A single tear, that's all I ask. Mercy, Heaven. [*She dies.*'
(Act iv, *ad fin.*)

The above comprise the extant dramas produced by D'Avenant before the Revolution. Concerning a few other plays from his hand we only know that they were licensed before that date, though they were not printed till the folio of 1673. Whether or not they were all written before the outbreak of the Civil War, it must be allowed that they exhibit a moderation to which D'Avenant's previous plays are strangers, and which may possibly have been due in part to *Histriomastix*. They possess no other claim to consideration. The tragi-comedy called in the Folio *The Siege* is supposed to be the same play as *The Colonel*, licensed in 1629. *News from Plymouth* (licensed 1635) is a bustling comedy of manners, but, notwithstanding the dangerous choice of its scene, no gross example of its class. *The Fair Favourite* (licensed 1638) is a tolerably effective romantic drama, in which a trying situation is treated with a certain delicacy and elevation of sentiment. *The Distresses,* thought to have been the same as *The Spanish Lovers,* licensed 1639, is another drama of intrigue, not very perspicuous in the conduct of the plot, which I should surmise to be taken from some Spanish source.

The Siege (lic. 1629?).

News from Plymouth (lic. 1635).

The Fair Favourite (lic. 1638).

The Distresses (lic. 1639).

Of D'Avenant's masques belonging to this period, *The Temple of Love* (of which the subject is the new-fashioned 'cold northerly opinion' of 'Platonic Love') was acted by the Queen and her ladies on Shrove-Tuesday, 1634 ; *The Prince d'Amour* [1] by the members of the Middle Temple, in 1635, for the entertainment of the Palatine Princes Charles Lewis and Rupert ; *Britannia Triumphans* (a loyal masque in honour of the great deeds of 'Britanocles, the glory of the western world,' and containing a passage reflecting on the Puritans) on Twelfth-Night, 1637, and *Salmacida Spolia* in January, 1639, both at Whitehall. The last contains an obvious reference to the rebellious tendencies of the times ; the title signifies the victories of royal Wisdom over the devices of Discord.

D'Avenant's masques.

---

[1] 'The Prince d'Amour' was the festive title given by the members of the Middle Temple to the leader of their Christmas revels. See Dudley Carleton to J. Chamberlain in *Calendar of State Papers, Domestic Series, Elisabeth*, p. 136 (December 29, 1601).

Academical plays.

During this period the academical drama continued to pursue its course, which, as has been seen, occasionally landed it at Court or on the popular stage. Doubtless the instances were more numerous, when the players would not treat with the scholars who came up from Oxford and Cambridge 'with dorsers full of lamentable tragedies and ridiculous comedies[1]'; and a good market without money stood open to them *in nativo solo*.

J. Tomkis' (?) Lingua (pr. 1607).

The earliest example of this class of drama must belong to the very commencement of the reign of James I, and indeed it may be questioned whether this play was not produced before the death of Elisabeth. The first of the many editions of *Lingua, or The Combat of the Tongue and the Five Senses for Superiority*[2], was printed in 1607; but even should the expressions occurring in the play, 'our gracious sovereign Psyche' and 'for our queen or for our country,' not be held decisive, another passage shows it to have been written before the year 1602 was far off[3]. That this comedy was written for an academical audience is clear from its whole character, as well as from at least one incidental allusion, which would have fallen flat except before hearers accustomed to the humours of undergraduates[4]. The authorship of *Lingua* was long attributed to Antony Brewer, a dramatic writer whom it would be unsafe to set down as the writer of more than one extant play, *The Love-*

[1] See Shirley's *The Witty Fair One* (act iv. sc. 2).

[2] Printed in vol. ix of Hazlitt's *Dodsley*.

[3] See act iv. sc. 7. Mr. Fleay, *u.s.*, vol. ii. pp. 261, where he gives an extract from an article published by him in *Shakespeariana* for March, 1885, makes light of the expressions cited, and remarks that Queen Elisabeth would have resented a play reflecting so strongly on the female sex; but I remain convinced. Mr. Fleay points out, as indicating a date soon after the Queen's death, a passage in act v. sc. 3 (where, by the way, 'our dread queen Psyche' also occurs): 'I remember about the year 1602 many used this skew kind of language.' This would suit either 1602 or 1603. He even goes so far as to conjecture that the play was performed at Hinchinbrook, when the heads of the University of Cambridge came to meet the King on his journey to London, in April, 1603; and, as will be seen, he has accommodated to this supposition the story that Oliver Cromwell took part in the performance.

[4] See act iv. sc. 2: 'I should judge this action' (*i.e.* gesture) 'most absurd, unless we should come to a comedy, as gentlemen to the Commencement, only to see men speak.' 'To *see* men speak' is good.

sick King[1]. The supposition that he wrote *Lingua* is founded on a mere blunder. A very plausible claim, on the other hand, has recently been preferred on behalf of the author of *Albumazar*, whose name is written 'Tomkis' in the MS. of that play, but who seems identifiable with John Tomkins, known to have been a scholar of Trinity in 1594, and to have graduated B.A. from that college four years afterwards. *Lingua* and *Albumazar* alike show their author to have been familiar with Italian, besides exhibiting other mutual internal resemblances[2].

Lingua, which is exceedingly well written, holds the mean between the moralities of the later type and the masques of the period of its production. It is of great length, and though it has a kind of plot and plenty of action, must have proved attractive chiefly through the excellence of its rhetorical and descriptive passages[3]. 'All the senses,'—so one of the characters summarises the preceding action[4],—'fell out about a crown fallen from heaven, and pitch'd a field for it; but Vicegerent Common Sense hearing of it, took upon him to umpire the contention, in which regard he hath appointed them (their arms dismissed) to appear before him, charging every one to bring as it were in a show, their proper objects, that by them he may determine of their several excellences.' Memory, as 'Master Register,' is called upon to read the charges brought by the Five Senses against Lingua, who aspires to be ranked as a sixth and to obtain the prize. Memory having forgotten her spectacles ('I left them in the 349th page of Hall's

[1] This '*Tragical History, with the Life and Death of Cartesmunda, the Fair Nun of Winchester*,' which in the historical part of its plot treats of the Danish occupation of the reigns of Ethelred and Alfred, was printed in 1655. Antony Brewer has been also supposed to have been author of the comedy of *The Country Girl*, designated on its title-page under the initials 'T. B.' This might have been 'Tony' Brewer; it might also have been Thomas Brewer, author of a prose tract, *The Life and Death of the Merry Devil of Edmonton* (printed in 1631, and probably the same as a book entered on the Registers under that title in 1608).

[2] See Fleay, *u. s.*; where it is further stated that Dr. Furnivall, in April 1890, discovered definite evidence as to Tomkis' authorship.

[3] Attention should be directed to Anamnestes' speech on the difference between Comedy and Tragedy, and the hints which follow on the old and new style of actors' delivery (act iv. sc. 2).

[4] Act iii. sc. 2.

Chronicles '), the indictment is read by her page Ana-mnestes ; a long disputation, full of flowing rhetoric, is conducted by the Senses and their assistants—thus Auditus is accompanied by Tragedus and Comedus, and Olfactus by Tobacco, who talks in an Indian tongue not yet classified by comparative philologists, and whose virtues are summarised by his master in a passage of much eloquence [1]. Finally, Communis Sensus delivers a rather witty decision on the issue. Lingua is judged to ' be no Sense simply : only thus much we from henceforth pronounce, that all women for your sake shall have six Senses, that is, seeing, hearing, tasting, smelling, touching, and the last and feminine sense, the sense of speaking.' This concludes the real plot of the play ; the fifth act being occupied with the evil results consequent upon all the Senses attending a banquet given by Gustus.

Such is the substance of an exceedingly well written academical entertainment, the enduring popularity of which is attested by its numerous editions. According to a legend which seems traceable as far back as 1657, but into the foundations of which it is superfluous to enquire, the part of Tactus (Touch) in this comedy was taken by ' the late Usurper Cromwell.' This fiction inevitably suggested the further fable, that the mock contention in the play for the crown swelled Oliver's ambition so high ' that afterwards he contended for it in earnest [2].'

B. Holy-
day's Tech-
nogamia
(acted and
pr. 1618).

Technogamia, or The Marriage of the Arts, acted in Christ Church Hall on February 13, 1618, and repeated before King James I at Woodstock in 1621, but printed

---

[1] 'Genius of all swaggerers, profess'd enemy to physicians, sweet ointment for sour teeth, firm knot of good fellowship, adamant of company, swift wind to spread the wings of time, *hated of none but those that know him not, and of so great deserts, that whoso is acquainted with him can hardly forsake him.'* (Act iv. sc. 5.) Charles Lamb's *Ode* alone has excelled the pathos of this eulogium ; Charles Kingsley has matched its dignity in a famous passage of *Westward Ho.*

[2] As Cromwell was not admitted at Cambridge till 1616, he would in 1603 have been somewhat young to take part in such a performance ; but Mr. Fleay, never to be beaten, suggests that he may have been made use of by his uncle at Hinchinbrook to perform the part of the 'small, thin, fellow ' in act iv. sc. 5, who in reply to a query from *Appetitus* announces himself as ' Beer, forsooth : Beer, forsooth '—*i. e.* as Small-Beer.

already in the year of its first performance, seems to have been the only dramatic production of its author, Barton Holyday, a learned divine who was created Archdeacon of Oxford early in the reign of Charles I. He was born in 1593, the son of an Oxford tradesman, and in 1618, the year in which *Technogamia* was acted in his college, accompanied Sir Francis Stewart to Spain, where he won the favourable consideration of Gondomar. He died in 1661, leaving behind him translations of Juvenal, Persius, and the Odes of Horace, and a poetic *Survey of the World* in ten books.

This comedy, or morality as it might be more appropriately called, is of great length and complicated in plot. The leading idea seems to be the confusion which is created by unsuitable *liaisons* between arts and sciences not well suited to one another, by their estrangement from those with which they should naturally be united, and by their unhappy flirtations with pseudo-sciences such as Magic and Astrology. In the end ' Polites, a Magistrate' who avows himself the ' Deputie only' of 'our aged and retired Prince *Metaphysicus* (... from whom, as from our Soueraigne, wee hold all wee haue'), arranges a series of appropriate marriages. Astronomia (daughter to Physica) is united to Geographus; while her other lover Geometres is assigned to Arithmetica, who trusts ' we two shall be alwaies euen.' Poeta, who throughout the play has distinguished himself by his capacity for getting into scrapes and has cherished a foolish passion for Astronomia, is married to his proper mate Historia, promising that his love shall more inseparably follow her ' then the *Hexameter* the *Pentameter* ; or the *Adonicke* the *Sapphicke.*' The remaining characters are likewise provided for, Logicus being left unmarried, to his own content : ' I care not for marrying; I see no good Foundation for any such Relation.' Magus and Astrologia are bidden ' depart the Common-Wealth for euer,' while Medicus and Causidicus are, on promise of amendment, pardoned their corrupt practices.

Doubtless many curious illustrations could be derived from this play for the history of studies in the University;

but such researches are not of interest to everybody.   King
James is said to have found the play very tedious, and it is
certainly long [1].   The author probably need not have been
at the pains of excusing himself in his *Epilogue* for the
farcical elements introduced by him into his comedy

> ' to satisfie the Weake
> Shee-Academickes ' ;

with whom not a few of the other sex may have sympathised.
Several of the personified arts and sciences are provided
with servants—Phantastes is the servant of Geographus ;
Melancholico is Poeta's man ; Choler acts as usher under the
schoolmaster Grammaticus, and Phlegmatico, who is in-
ordinately addicted to tobacco [2], is the attendant of Logicus,
while Sanguis very appropriately waits upon Medicus [3].
Physiognomus and Cheiromantes are two fortune-tellers
who talk gipsy cant and add to the vivacity of the action,
which is at times more striking than its perspicuity.   Yet it
is abundantly evident that the author of this odd production
was a good scholar, a shrewd critic, and a fair wit [4].

[1] Indeed it seems to have, doubtless unjustly, acquired the reputation of
being the longest play in the English language.

[2] See his song,   ' Tobacco 's a Musician
> And in a Pipe delighteth,' &c.,

(act ii. sc. 3).   The lyrics in this play are remarkably lively.

[3] The costume of Sanguis is ' a red suite ; on the brest whereof was
a man with his nose bleeding ; on the backe, one let bloud in the arme ; in
a red hat, red band, stockings, red pumps,' &c. (act i. sc. 9) ; the costumes
are very minutely described in this play, particular attention being throughout given to the colour of the ' pumps '). Elsewhere Polites eulogises
Sanguis as ' an honest servant, and more faithfull to the whole Bodie of
the Common-wealth, than any one Corrupt Member ' (act v. sc. 6).   It may
perhaps be noted that Harvey's discovery had been first brought forward
three years before the publication of *Technogamia.*

[4] See *e. g.* Polites' remarks on the defects of ' your common geographers '
(act iv. sc. 1) ; Historia's irreverent criticism of ' one *Lucretius,* a Romane
Gentleman . . . that fell in love with *Physica,* shee from whom *Physica* the
mother of *Astronomia* deriues now both her name and linage, which Gentleman, in the passion of his loue, writ books in the praise of her beauty ; but
what wrinkle-fac'd Verses they are, let the present age judge ; and if her
beautie was like his lines, sure she was past her three-score. when hee fell in
loue with her ; but alas, there was neuer any of that family that euer came
neere the *Historias* for beauty ' (act iv. sc. 2) ; Magus' conjecture, on Poeta's
reciting some English hexameter and pentameter verses when the worse for
wine, that ' in some such humour this kind of Verses was first made amongst
vs ' (act iii. sc. 6) ; and Grammaticus' pun against law-cases, which ' are Datiue
cases to the Lawyers ; but Ablatiue to the Clients ' (act iv. sc. 6).

The comedy of *Albumazar*[1], performed before King
James I by the members of Trinity College on the occasion of his celebrated visit to Cambridge in March, 1615[2],
was printed in the following year, and again in 1634 without the author's name.   In a MS. account of the proceedings
at Cambridge in the middle of last century, preserved in
the library of Sir Edward Deering, which is confirmed in
several respects by contemporary evidence[3], the authorship of *Albumazar* is attributed to Mr. Tomkis of Trinity,
who has with fair conclusiveness been identified with JOHN
TOMKINS, a scholar of that college who graduated there in
1598, and was the son of the organist of the Chapel Royal.
Nothing further is known of its author, to whom, as has been
seen, the play of *Lingua*, performed some ten years before
Albumazar, has been recently with some probability likewise attributed.   *Albumazar* seems to have enjoyed a certain
celebrity down to the time of the Restoration ; and in 1668
it was revived, with a Prologue, by Dryden, in which he quite
erroneously declares Jonson's *Alchemist* to have been founded
on this academical drama.   Inasmuch as the *Alchemist* was
produced in 1610, this assertion would seem on the face
of it absurd ; but *Albumazar* had been in certain quarters
erroneously dated 1603, perhaps in order to remove one
difficulty out of the way of the ridiculous conjecture attributing the authorship of it to Shakspere[4].   Garrick again
revived *Albumazar* on two successive occasions, in 1747 and
in 1773[5].   At the time of its original presentation before
King James on his visit to Cambridge, when the wits of
several colleges were seeking to outvie one another with

J. Tomkis'
Albumazar
(acted 1614;
pr. 1615).

---

[1] Printed in vol. xi of Hazlitt's *Dodsley*, and in vol. ii. of *The Ancient
British Drama.*

[2] See below as to Ruggle's *Ignoramus.*

[3] A letter from Chamberlain to Carleton, dated March 16, 1614.

[4] See Dryden's *Works*, vol. x ; and cf. note to the late Mr. W. D. Christie's
Globe edition of *Dryden*, p. 401.   The *First Report of the Historical MSS. Commission* (1874), p. x, contains the following curious statement : 'Mr. Henry
Ingall, in the belief that he had discovered in a drama entitled *Albumazar*
(attributed by him to Shakespeare) some marginal notes, which he supposes
to be in the handwriting of Shakespeare, laid the play, with other interesting
papers, before the Commissioners.'

[5] On the latter occasion with some immaterial alterations of his own.
(See Genest, vol. v. p. 394.)

their productions, Trinity College claimed this comedy as alike of its own 'invention' and 'action'; but it was in truth an imitation of *L'Astrologo*, an Italian comedy by G.-B. della Porta, printed at Venice in 1606 [1]—and so close an imitation, even in its most amusing scene [2], that it cannot be said to possess any claim to originality. *Albumazar* is academical in its lengthiness, but written with considerable fluency and occasional felicity of expression [3].

Phineas Fletcher's Sicelides (acted 1615; *pr.* 1631). A word may here be added as to yet a third play prepared for the entertainment of the royal visitor to Cambridge in March, 1615, although this was not actually performed until after the sun of the King's presence had ceased to shine. PHINEAS FLETCHER (1582–1650), the elder of the two brothers, first cousins of the famous dramatist, shows himself in his later poetical productions, and above all in the allegory of *The Purple Island*, a follower of Spenser in treatment as well as in form; indeed, he may without injustice to his brother Giles be said to be the most distinguished Spenserian in our seventeenth-century literature. Although he had already for several years previously been known in the University as a writer of verse, the special characteristics of his poetic style are less marked in the pastoral drama which he composed for the occasion of the King's visit; but abundant opportunity is found there for the display of qualities which lend a charm to all Phineas Fletcher's poetry —a sincere love of nature and a power, which his love of allegorical detail itself could not obscure, of occasionally reflecting his thoughts in language of simple and almost transparent beauty. *Sicelides, a Piscatory* [4], which was

[1] For an account of this, see Klein, vol. v. pp. 661 *seqq.*

[2] Act iii. sc. 7.

[3] The Astrologer's introductory lecture on the Art of Cheating is doubtless taken from its counterpart in the Italian original; but the following, whether original or not, is to the point, besides fitting well into the history of this particular play :

> '*Har.* And yet he steals : one author from another.
>   This poet is that poet's plagiary,
>   And he a third's, till they all end in Homer.
> *Alb.* And Homer filch'd all from an Egyptian priestess.
>   The world's a theatre of theft.' (Act i. sc. 1.)

[4] See vol. iii of Dr. Grosart's edition of *The Poems of Phineas Fletcher, D.D.*, in his invaluable *Fuller Worthies Series* (4 vols., 1869).

printed in 1631, either surreptitiously or at least without the
supervision of the author, has a plot of greater interest than
is usual in a pastoral drama (for the difference between
fishermen and shepherds is of course without any real importance, while giving opportunities for much effective poetic
ornament). The opening, which in the second scene of the
play prepares us for the sacrifice of the lovely Olinda to an
Andromeda-like doom[1], is followed by a not less interesting
rescue, and through the five acts of the drama, with the aid
of enchantments and 'desamours,' the succession of surprises
continues, interrupted only by an unconscionably large admixture of that least palatable among the ingredients of
modern pastoral poetry, which is intended to suggest distinct
colour and simultaneously to furnish comic relief. Of
characterisation this pastoral contains as little as other
examples of the species; the charm of its diction, however,
is not only great, but remarkably varied. A poem is
assuredly worth study, which is made beautiful by descriptive passages of the sweetest simplicity[2], and of a rare
contemplative stillness[3]; by a dialogue at times instinct
with the fire and the dolours of the passion of love[4]; by
truly dramatic narratives[5]; by bursts of lyric emotion[6];

---

[1] The episode, as already Langbaine pointed out, is imitated from Bk. iv
of the *Metamorphoses*, just as Armillus' story (in sc. 4 of the same act) of
Glaucus, Scylla and Circe is taken from Bk. xiv of Ovid's poem. In each case
Fletcher may have likewise had recourse to well-known modern versions.
The 'orke' comes straight from Ariosto; and much learning might be
accumulated on the subject of this 'marine animal.'

[2] See in act i. sc. 3 the charming passage beginning:

> 'Thou know'st by Neptune's temple close there growes
> A sacred garden, where every flower blowes,
> Here blushing roses, there the lillies white,
> Here hyacinth, and there narcissus bright' &c.

[3] See in act iii. sc. 6 the evening harmony:

> 'The oxe now feeles no yoke, all labour sleepes;
> The soule, unbent, this as her play-time keepes,
> And sportes itselfe in fancie's winding streames,
> Bathing his thoughts in thousand wingèd dreames,' &c.

[4] See act iii. sc. 2, and the admirable opening of act iv. sc. 1.

[5] See the narrative of Nomicus the priest, act v. sc. 5.

[6] See the Chorus, 'Love is the sire' (not the 'fire,' as *ap*. Grosart), at the
close of act iii. sc. 6.

as well as by single lines or couplets of pregnant force[1] or enshrining figures of irresistible charm[2].

J. Fisher's Fuimus Troes (pr. 1633).

The rhetorical drama of *Fuimus Troes, the True Trojans*, printed in 1633 [3], may likewise receive a passing notice among the productions of the Academical Muse. Its author, Dr. JASPER FISHER, who at the time of its composition appears to have been rector of Wilsden in Bedfordshire, held, or had held, the position of Divinity or Philosophy Reader at Magdalen College, Oxford, where this play was performed by the students. It treats of Julius Caesar's two invasions of Britain, and is to a large extent based on Geoffrey of Monmouth. The style of this composition is both fluent and florid; and the classical learning of the Briton kings and princes is as amazing as are the metaphysical and prophetical acquirements of the Druids. The ghosts of Brennus and Camillus are conducted by Mercury to their functions in Induction and Epilogue; the final purpose of the author apparently being to signify that Romans and Britons by their deeds equally justified their Trojan descent. The play abounds in lyrics, one of which, for no ostensible purpose, attempts the Scottish dialect—or what the author supposes to be such [4].

P. Strode's The Floating Island (pr. 1655).

Another University play was the tragi-comedy of *The Floating Island*, by Dr. PHILIP STRODE, Public Orator at Oxford and afterwards Canon of Christ Church, performed at his college before King Charles I, with music by Henry Lawes, August 29, 1636. It was printed in 1655, when royalists had become less fastidious than Lord Carnarvon had shown himself on the occasion of its performance before royalty, when, notwithstanding, or because of its deadly anti-Puritanical allusions, he declared it to be 'the worst that ever he saw, but one that he saw at Cambridge [5].'

---

[1] See the opening line of act ii. sc. 2; 'Love not back reflected,' act i. sc. 4; 'Beauty when most uncloth'd,' act ii. sc. 4; 'After a child, a friend,' act v. sc. 3.

[2] Act v. sc. 5:   'The guilty sea
          With soft embraces wrapt his limbs.'
(Cf. *Le Pêcheur d'Islande.*)

[3] Reprinted in vol. xii of Hazlitt's *Dodsley*.

[4] See '2d Song,' act iii. sc. 9.

[5] Cf. Gardiner, *History*, &c., vol. viii. p. 150.

Another University play belonging to the latter part of this period was *The Sophister*, printed in 1638.

In humble, or at least secondary, sequence to these products of higher education mention may be accorded to *Apollo Shrouing*, an English play 'composed for the scholars of the Free School of Hadleigh in Suffolk, and acted by them on Shrove Tuesday, being the 6th of February, 1626.' This production, while devoid of distinctive merit, and by no means abundantly seasoned with wit, is curious as an illustration of the enduring manner of the later moralities. The idea of the action, such as it is, consists in the conflict between the claims of Learning and the wiles of Queen *Hedone*, practised by the agency of her messenger, the sea-nymph *Siren*.

No account, however summary, of the progress of the academical drama in its connexion with our literature, can pass by the two most conspicuous examples of this particular kind of product because they were written in a language as living as their own to the hearers for whom these efforts of wit were primarily intended. *Ignoramus* in especial, first acted in 1614 and first printed in 1630, is in its way a classic; nor has the echo of the laughter to which it excited the Solomon of English kings yet died out in the field of dramatic literature in which it holds an acknowledged primacy[1]. Its author, GEORGE RUGGLE, born in 1575 at Lavenham in Suffolk, was successively a member of St. John's and Trinity, and in 1598 was elected to a fellowship at Clare Hall, Cambridge. His reputation for learning is described as very great—in fact, great enough to entitle him to rank

The Sophister (pr. 1638).

Apollo's Shrouing (acted 1626).

George Ruggle's Ignoramus (acted 1614; pr. 1630).

---

[1] The standard edition of *Ignoramus* is that by J. S. Hawkins, 1787, which is accompanied by a Memoir, Glossary, and apparatus of Introduction and Commentaries of a completeness rarely equalled. For this very reason, a modern edition of this edition has become a *desideratum* of our times. The best connected account of the significance of this comedy and its performance for the history of University life will be found in a standard work of learning on every part of its subject, Mr. J. Bass Mullinger's *University of Cambridge from the Injunctions of 1535 to the Accession of Charles I* (1884), pp. 529 *seqq.*, where the circumstances under which the play was produced, and its plot, are described with equal lucidity. The biographical notice of Ruggle in vol. xlix of *The Dictionary of National Biography* (1897) is by Mr. Sidney Lee.

with the most eminent men of the day in the several faculties
of the University who were the chosen associates of Nicholas
Ferrar[1].   His fame, however, rests on the authorship of
a literary effort of the same flavour as the *Epistolae
Obscurorum Virorum*, but unlike these devoid of any
historical or literary significance.   Besides a comedy called
Re Vera, or Verily, of unknown date, Ruggle had, as has
been already mentioned, in 1597 composed the comedy of
Club-Law for performance at Clare Hall, under conditions
which could not fail to heighten the existing ill-will between
town and gown.   The question of precedence between the
Mayor and the Vice-Chancellor was repeatedly raised in
a provocative fashion by the townsmen; and in these proceedings the leading part was taken by Francis Brackyn,
who as Deputy-Recorder of Cambridge had already been
satirised in Part II of *The Return from Parnassus*[2].   He
it was whom, for the delectation of King James on an
expected royal visit to Cambridge, the ingenious Ruggle
resolved to make the hero of a Latin comedy.

The royal visit, which was designed to do honour to the
Earl of Suffolk, the new Vice-Chancellor of the University,
actually took place in March, 1615, when, among a variety
of dramatic entertainments offered to the King and Charles
Prince of Wales, *Ignoramus*, a comedy presented by members of Clare Hall with the aid of a few actors from other
colleges, was performed in the hall of Trinity.   Other plays
acted there during the King's stay were a Latin comedy,
Aemilia, by 'Cecill' of St. John's, *Albumazar*[3], a Latin
pastoral, and *Melanthe*, by S. Brookes of Trinity; the royal
party had left Cambridge before the performance at King's
of an English comedy by Phineas Fletcher of that college[4].
The success of *Ignoramus* was so great, and the King was
so pleased with the wit and the fun of the play, that it cast
a rosy light over his entire visit to the University; he visited

---

[1] See Jebb's *Life* in *Nicholas Ferrar, Two Lives, &c.*, edited by J. E. B.
Mayor (Cambridge, 1853), p. 171.

[2] Cf. *ante*, vol. ii. p. 639, *note*.   [3] Cf. *ante*, p. 179.

[4] See an account of the visit by Chamberlain to Carleton, cited in *Court and
Times of James I*, vol. i. pp. 303 *seqq.*, and cf. Sir Edward Deering's MS.
cited *ante*, p. 179.—As to *Sicelides*, see *ante*, pp. 180 *seqq.*

all the colleges, except two or three, and 'commended them
above Oxford.'   And in the following May he came again,
and *Ignoramus* had to be repeated with a new Prologue
and other additions ; and of this *Prologus Posterior* the chief
feature consists of a burlesque trial and condemnation of
Gaspar Scioppius, the eminent but foul-mouthed Latinist
who had recklessly covered the King with literary mud of
every description.   The Aristophanic sentence passed on
his assailant is said to have moved James I to irrepressible
demonstrations of joy ; and the comedy had thus become
part of the history of a controversy with which Europe
rang [1].

The reputation of *Ignoramus* was thus thoroughly established, and although attempts were made by members of
the legal profession to retort upon the satire of the play—
the wits of the Inns of Court not being accustomed to hear
the foibles of their profession ridiculed by members of the
Universities—they failed to bring the laugh over to their
side [2].   Long remembered 'where the studious lawyers
have their bowers,' *Ignoramus*, which had been translated
into English by R. C. (supposed to be Robert Codrington)
in 1662, was in 1678 adapted by Edward Ravenscroft, and
in this form appeared on the stage.   In the original Latin,
the comedy was acted by the Westminster Scholars in 1712
and on several subsequent occasions in the course of the
century [3]; it was also acted at Bury St. Edmunds School
in 1731, and at Merchant Taylors' in 1763.   Ruggle
died in 1622, two years after he had vacated his fellowship ; the work which has made him famous was printed

[1] Of the King's second visit, Mr. Mullinger, pp. 544 *seqq.*, cites the account
by the University Registrary, James Tabor.—As to Scioppius and King
James, see Mr. J. Crossley's note in *Diary and Correspondence of Dr. Worth-
ington* (*Chetham Society's Publications*), vol. i. p. 128, and, more fully, vol. ii.
of Nisard's *Gladiateurs de la République des Lettres*, &c. (Paris, 1860), and
Bayle's *Dictionnaire*.   By my distinguished friend Mr. R. C. Christie's kindness I was enabled to give some account of these matters in my essay on
Sir Henry Wotton (1898).

[2] See Genest, vol. i. p. 389.—Mr. Mullinger refers, without attaching credit
to it, to the story that Selden wrote his *History of Tithes* from resentment at
the way in which the profession to which he belonged had been assailed.

[3] A new fifth act, for use at Westminster School, is stated to have been
added to the editions of 1713 and 1787.

posthumously (in 1630), and against what seems to have been his desire [1].

The plot of *Ignoramus* is taken from the Italian comedy of *La Trappolaria* by G.-B. Porta, which in its turn was based upon the *Pseudolus* of Plautus, though mixed with modern elements after the fashion of the Italian comedy of this period [2]. But the originality of Ruggle's play consists in the substitution for the characters of a captain and his servants of those of the lawyer and his clerks; and in these personages, notably of course in the part of Ignoramus himself, lay at once the personal satire and the fun of the play. Though the whole of it is written with great spirit —partly in Plautine iambics, partly in a medley of Latin and English prose—attention is designedly concentrated on the main personage. Ignoramus is intended as a satire on the barbarous ignorance and equally barbarous phraseology of a pettifogger who can talk neither Latin, nor French, nor good King's English, but only a vile professional jargon of his own, which goes far to justify an attempt in the course of the play to exorcise him as possessed by evil spirits. He hates the University and all its ways [3], and is intended as a living example of barbarous Philistinism. His speech is accordingly made up of the terms of his profession, which he introduces with extraordinary promptitude to garnish his horrible Latin; 'lingua mea,' he says, 'vadit ad verba accustomata: Puto me placitare jam [4].' The characteristics satirised in Ignoramus are not, however, confined to such comparatively harmless peculiarities of his profession as a barbarous phraseology; for his principles are on a level with

---

[1] The Latin play of *Loiola*, written against the Jesuits and performed before King James at Cambridge in 1622, was not by Ruggle, but by John Hacket of Trinity College (afterwards Bishop of Coventry and Lichfield). A copy of it is in the Chatsworth Library.

[2] Cf. Klein, vol. v. p. 663.

[3] 'Sunt magni idiotae, et clerici nihilorum, isti Universitantes: miror quomodo spendisti tuum tempus inter eos.' *Mus.*: 'Ut plurimum versatus sum in *Logica.*' *Igr.* '*Logica?* Quae villa, quod burgum est *Logica?*' *Mus.*: 'Est una artium liberalium.' *Igr.* 'Liberalium? Sic putabam. In nomine Dei, stude artes parcas et lucrosas: non est mundus pro artibus liberalibus jam.'

[4] These terms Ruggle derived from various sources, among others from a work which acquired a most signal notoriety in the political history of this reign—Cowell's *Interpreter* (suppressed by proclamation in 1610).

his style of speech, and his great desire is 'capere in manum' whomsoever he can, so that a poetic justice is exercised upon him by his finding himself all but 'murderatus,' before in the epilogue he finally takes his departure 'bootatus et spurratus' for London.

The famous *Naufragium Joculare* of Abraham Cowley, whose later contributions to our dramatic literature will be noticed below, is another diverting specimen—apparently innocent of any purpose but diversion—of the same kind of production. Acted at Trinity in 1638, it obtained celebrity through the boisterous fun of a scene in the first act of the play. This scene, in which a drunken company are deluded into the belief that they are suffering shipwreck, till their request to be led 'in inferiora navis' is very summarily complied with, was doubtless taken by Cowley from Plautus, although he might have traced the idea to an earlier source, or have found it in a recently printed English play [1]. The Latinity of this amusing comedy ('Scena Dunkerka') is not always strictly classical; but it abounds in quotations bespeaking the learning as well as the ready wit of its youthful author; and shows that he and his contemporaries at Cambridge well understood the *ars jocandi*, of which Aemylio shows himself so accomplished a professor [2].

Abraham Cowley's Naufragium Joculare (acted 1638).

It would serve no purpose to attempt to exhaust the list of other Oxford or Cambridge men who during this period produced Latin plays. The ingenious *Bellum Grammaticale sive Nominum Verborumque Discordia Civilis*, which was printed at Oxford in 1635, may have been revived on the academic stage at that date, but had been performed before Queen Elisabeth in the Hall of Christ Church as far back as 1592 [3]. On the other hand, Peter Hausted's *Senile*

Other Academical plays in Latin.

[1] Cf. *ante*, vol. ii. p. 566 and *note*; and add a reference to Athenaeus' story, and the house called the Trireme in the city of Akragas, in Freeman's *History of Sicily*, vol. ii. (1891), p. 392 and *note*.

[2] See act iii. sc. 2. The comedy is printed in vol. iii of the three vol. edition of Cowley's *Works* (1711).—Charles Johnson's *Fortune in her Wits* (1706), which was not acted, is said by Dibdin, vol. v. p. 50, to be a bad translation of Cowley's *Naufragium Joculare*.

[3] The name of the author of this play was Spense. It is a very happy and—if the necessary allowance be made—not excessively long drawn-out *jeu d'esprit* of a sort which one age thinks captivating, and another

Odium, performed at Queens' College, Cambridge, of which the author was a member, and printed in 1633, is a Latin comedy of intrigue, in half-Terentian, half-Italian, style, that appears to call for no special remark [1]. Its author likewise produced an English play, entitled *The Rival Friends*, which was acted by the members of his college before King Charles I and his Queen on their visit to Cambridge in March 1633.

Masque writers of the reigns of James I and Charles I.   Finally, but few among the writers of masques, pageants, and similar entertainments during the reigns of James I and Charles I appear to be entitled by their literary remains to specific mention in a summary, however brief, of the progress of English dramatic literature. Ben Jonson long held an undisputed pre-eminence among the poets who devoted part of their energies to this class of productions, and was no doubt gratified during his sojourn in Scotland by the news communicated by a friendly pen, 'that the late Masque,' composed by some writer unknown to us, 'was not so approved of by the King, as in former times, and that ' his 'absence was regretted [2].' Jonson's quarrel with Inigo Jones for a time interfered with his activity as literary partner in the provision of court entertainments, and sickness must likewise have stayed his hand ; but though he had enemies, his pre-eminence as a writer of masques remained virtually unchallenged. Among the other dramatists whose

pedantic. The plot turns on a conflict between the King of Nouns (*Poeta*) and the King of Verbs (*Amo*), which sets the entire province of Grammar at odds, lets loose the Grammaticae Pestes, Solecismus, Barbarismus, Traulismus and Cacatonus to range at their own sweet will, and is finally settled by the intervention of the judges of Grammar, Priscianus, Linacrus, Despanterius, and Lillius. The application of grammatical definitions, rules and maxims to the supposed action is very clever, though parallels might be easily adduced from contemporary dramatic, and probably other, literature. The doubtful position of Duke *Participium*, who owes a kind of double allegiance, is specially happy. The sentences ultimately pronounced by the judges quibble after the same delectable fashion.—I owe my acquaintance with this play, as well as with the *Senile Odium* and *Apollo Shrouing*, to a volume kindly lent me by Professor Dowden.

[1] A copy of Latin iambics was prefixed to it on publication, by Edward King, the friend whom Milton afterwards mourned in *Lycidas*. (Masson's *Life of Milton*, vol. i. p. 649.)

[2] Drummond to Jonson, in a letter cited from Gifford by Collier, vol. i. p. 401.

productions have been surveyed in the preceding chapters, Daniel, Chapman, Marston, and Beaumont have been mentioned as authors of entertainments designed for the Court and nobility; while Dekker, Middleton, and Anthony Munday were busy in doing similar service to their patrons of the City, in the reign of James I[1]. Among writers of masques not known as dramatists proper, the most successful seems to have been THOMAS CAMPION[2], a lyrical poet of rare endowment and a most accomplished classical scholar. It seems probable that he at some time studied at Cambridge; but no record exists as to where he took his degree of Doctor of Medicine. Before this he had temporarily been a member of Gray's Inn. He is mentioned as a poet as early as 1593, in the *Prologue* to Peele's *Honour of the Garter*[3], although he had published nothing previously to that date; and in Meres' *Palladis Tamia* (1598) he is praised for his Latin verse. His songs, many of which by their very opening lines announce themselves as destined to live on the lips of lovers, are instinct with grace and charm, while avoiding that redundancy of phrase which tempted other lyrical writers

Thomas Campion (d. 1619– 20).

---

[1] As Jonson sneered at Munday, and Marston (see *The Insatiate Countess*, act ii *ad in.*) at City shows in general, so Glapthorne rather happily satirises the City poets of his day (see *Wit in a Constable*, act i. sc. 1):

> ' perchance
> You may arrive to be the City Poet,
> And send the little moisture of your brain
> To grace a Lord Mayor's festival with shows,
> Alluding to his trade, or to the company
> Of which he 's free.'

Per contra, Sir John Harington's account (*Nugae Antiquae*, vol. i. pp. 349–51) of the failure of the masque representing the advent of the Queen of Sheba, devised by the Earl of Salisbury and others for the meeting of James I and his Danish brother-in-law at Theobald's in 1606—and of the causes of that failure—may be noted as a painfully graphic picture of low manners in high places.

[2] *The Works of Thomas Campion.* Edited by A. H. Bullen (with an Introduction), 1889.—See also Nichols' *Progresses, &c., of James I*, vol. ii. pp. 104, 553.

[3] —'Why go'st not thou,
> That richly cloth'st conceit with well-made words,
> Campion.'

No connexion is known to exist between him and the Jesuit Edmund Campion. One of his *Divine and Moral Songs* is in honour of the Fifth of November, and his rejoicing in the Palatinate marriage is particularly cordial.

of this age into tediousness.   Although he half apologises
for the apparent unfitness—

> ' That holy hymns with lovers' cases are knit
> Both in one quire [1] '—

his secular verse largely exceeds his sacred in amount.
In truth, however, both are so pure and sweet that no
objection need be taken to their intermixture; while it is
difficult to repress a doubt whether the genius of Campion
fitted him for loftier strains of religious poetry [2].   His
Songs of Mourning on the death of Prince Henry, though
they ingeniously vary the treatment of their theme as
addressing themselves in turn to the various members of
the royal family, to the country, and to the world at large,
cannot be said to rise to the heights of elegiac poetry; his
copious Latin verse is, as might have been expected, largely
imitative in style ; and his chief effort in prose possesses
an accidental rather than an intrinsic interest [3].   On the
whole, although the lyrical passages in his masques exhibit
the delightful qualities which have given a just celebrity
to his *Books of Airs*,—including a notable freedom in the
choice of metres and a rare elegance of diction—they cannot,
unless here and there, be numbered among the choicest pro-
His ductions of his poetical genius.   The *Description* of a masque
masques. presented before the King at Whitehall on Twelfth Night,
1607, on the occasion of the marriage of Lord Hay (after-

---

[1] *To the Reader.* (*Second Book of Airs, containing Light Conceits of Lovers.*)

[2] He certainly falls short of success in paraphrase (see ' As by the streams
of Babylon '), nor can many of the *Divine and Morall Songs* lay claim to the
exquisite beauty of that beginning ' Never weather-beaten sail more willing
beat to shore.'

[3] Campion's *Observations in the Art of English Poesie* appeared in 1602,
with a Dedication to Thomas Sackville, Lord Buckhurst and Earl of
Dorset, whose name holds so memorable a place in the history of our
literature, and in that of the drama in particular. (Cf. *ante*, vol. i. p. 199.)
In this Dedication the author declares the intention of his treatise to have
been the introduction of a true form of versifying into the English language,
in lieu of ' the vulgar and artificial custom of riming'; the chapter devoted
to the exposure of the 'unapteness of rime in poesy' gave rise to Daniel's
Defence of Rhyme. (Cf. *ante*, vol. ii. p. 617.) The treatise itself rather unfairly enlivens its 'illustrations' by a personality or two—among them an
epigram, directed as it would seem against Barnabe Barnes (cf. *ante*, vol. ii.
p. 626), whom Campion assails elsewhere both in English and in Latin.—He
also wrote a treatise on Counterpoint, which Mr. Bullen has not reprinted.

wards Viscount Doncaster and Earl of Carlisle), invites
notice, in view of the later public career of the popular
nobleman in whose honour it was performed [1]. If the
unavoidable incense be condoned that is here offered to
that ' Phoebus '—

> 'Which in this happy Western Isle is placed
> As he in heaven, one lamp enlight'ning all
> That under his benign,'—

the text of this masque, and more especially Flora's
opening song, will be allowed to possess the charm of a
very sweet simplicity. The *Relation* of an entertainment
offered to Queen Anne [2] by Lord Knollys at Caversham
House, Reading, April, 1613, is naturally slight in texture;
it introduces the character of a Cynic, who is soon driven
out of his attempt to maintain the attitude of Diogenes
towards society. Very elaborate, on the other hand—more
like a play, according to a contemporary report—is Campion's contribution to the festivities on the occasion of the
wedding of Princess Elisabeth, in February, 1613, in the
shape of *The Lords' Masque*, which presses into its service
a variety of mythological abstractions, including the well-
imagined symbolism of a contention of Orpheus against
Mania for the freedom of Entheus, and ending with Latin
prophecies by ' Old Sibylla, reverend dame [3].' This masque,
unlike the two entertainments previously mentioned, contains a dance of Antics, or as they are in this instance
called, Frantics; a similar device is also introduced into the
masque presented in celebration of the marriage of the
Earl of Somerset and Lady Frances Howard, in December,

---

[1] This was the Doncaster—celebrated for his good dinners and for his
general attractiveness as a member of society—upon whom, soon after the
outbreak of the (Thirty Years') War, James I imposed the task of pacifying
Europe in his name, and who was sagacious enough to recognise the
futility of his mission.

[2] ' Paradise were meeter far
To entertain so bright a star.
But why errs my folly so?
Paradise is where you are,
Heav'n above, and heav'n below.'

[3] The Sibyl salutes Elisabeth with unconscious truthfulness, as
'*parens
Regum, imperatorum.*'

1613. Campion's effort on this ill-omened occasion has perhaps less literary value than can be claimed for most of his productions. From a dramatic point of view none of them possesses much importance, chiefly because Campion's inventive powers are by no means conspicuous [1].

For the same unhallowed festival the gentlemen of Gray's Inn produced *The Masque of Flowers*, which comprised an anti-masque intended for the personal address of the King [2].

Other masque-writers of the period. A *unicum* in its way is a masque, written by ROBERT WHITE, and performed in 1617 before the Queen at Deptford by a college of young ladies on the appropriate subject of *Cupid's Banishment* [3].

Charles I appears to have begun with a less lavish expenditure upon such matters than that in which his father had indulged himself in the earlier part of his reign, when in seven years he had spent more than £4,000 on masques [4]. But the taste was by no means extinct as yet, and continued to be met by the efforts of Ben Jonson, THOMAS CAREW, and others. Carew was one of the lightest of the poets of the Fantastic School, and the masque *Coelum Britannicum*, in which the King's Majesty moved as the central sun, and which contained not less than eight anti-masques, was by far his most elaborate effort. It was performed at Whitehall in 1634, with music by Henry Lawes [5].

AURELIAN TOWNSHEND is mentioned as the author of two masques, *Albin's Triumph* and *Temple Restored*, performed in 1632. Inigo Jones was at that time incensed

---

[1] Three of his masques are printed by Nichols.

[2] See Nichols, *u. s.*, vol. iii. p. 735. The anti-masque consists of the trial of a challenge sent from Silenus to Kawasha, 'that Wine is more woorthy than Tobacco, and cheereth man's spirit more, the same to be tried at two severall Weapons, Song and Dance.'

[3] Nichols, *u. s.*, pp. 283 *seqq.*

[4] Collier, vol. i. p. 349 and *note*, where a very considerable part of this sum is said to have been expended on the production of Jonson's *Masque of Blackness* and the revels of 1604-5.

[5] See Masson's *Life of Milton*, vol. i. p. 587. Lord Brackley and Mr. Thomas Egerton, who acted the Brothers in *Comus*, were among the performers of Carew's masque. (See the list *ap.* Fleay, *English Drama*, vol. i. p. 45.) Cf. also Dibdin, *History of the Stage*, vol. iv. p. 231.

against Jonson—and in the next year the expenditure on masques may have, together with the Queen's performance in a pastoral, contributed to rouse the ire of the Puritan censor of the stage[1]. But Prynne's invectives produced no immediate result so far as the production of masques was concerned[2], and the species seemed more likely to decline in consequence of internal inanition than because of external attacks. Shirley, whose literary judgment was keen, lays much stress on the decay of the masque as a form of literary composition[3]; so that it becomes quite unnecessary to speculate how far the shortcomings observable in later dramatic entertainments of this class may have been due to secondary causes, such as the growing financial difficulties of the King. Indeed, it would almost seem as if these drawbacks had more immediately affected the regular stage than the amusements of the Court. During the years preceding the outbreak of the troubles, the presentation of masques, for which William D'Avenant[4] seems to have become the principal poetical purveyor, continued ; SIR ASTON COKAYNE (who is not known to have produced

---

[1] Cf. *infra*.

[2] At Lincoln's Inn (see the Dedication of *Histriomastix*) the practice of masques at Christmas had been discontinued before the publication of Prynne's diatribe. The other Inns of Court, however, kept up the usage, especially the Middle Temple, where the old custom of electing a 'Prince d'Amour' to preside over the Christmas revels prevailed both in James' and in Charles' reign. (Cf. *ante* as to D'Avenant's masque of that name.)

[3] The passage is worth quoting as giving a very faithful account of the masque, when it is unredeemed by poetic genius :

'Things go not now
By learning ; I have read, 'tis but to bring
Some pretty impossibilities, for anti-masques,
A little sense and wit disposed with thrift,
With here and there monsters to make them laugh
For the grand business, to have Mercury
Or Venus' dandiprat, to usher in
Some of the gods, that are good fellows, dancing,
Or goddesses ; and now and then a song,
To fill a gap :—a thousand crowns, perhaps,
For him that made it, and there's all the wit.'

The Royal Master, act ii. sc. 1.

The ordinary masque-writer was certainly little anxious to secure much beyond the 'mere entertainment' which Sarpego in Chapman's *Gentleman Usher* (act iii) seeks to distinguish from the 'Morality' of a masque.

[4] See *ante*, p. 173, and cf. Fleay, *History of the Stage*, pp. 351-2.

any plays before the Restoration) was in this reign author of at least one slight masque[1]; others were, in its later years, composed by THOMAS NABBES, a meritorious author who wrote dramatic works of various kinds, as well as other verse and historical prose[2]. One of the masques of which he was the author possesses a certain interest as having, so far as is known, been the first dramatic composi-

---

[1] The *Masque presented at Brethie* in Derbyshire on Twelfth Night, 1639, before Philip Earl of Chesterfield. (Printed in Cokayne's *Dramatic Works*, 1874.) This production is not redeemed from commonplace by a feature in the scheme which recalls part of the plot of *Comus*. Two sons of the Earl (acted by the boys themselves) appear in the anti-masque, having fallen into the rude hands of Satyrs. 'What would you have?' the Lar Familiaris of the house asks them.

> '*1st Boy.* I would go to my father.
> *2nd Boy.* And I unto my mother.
> *Lar.* Who is your father?
> *1st Boy.* The ever-honour'd Earl of Chesterfield,' &c.

[2] Nabbes' works were privately printed by Mr. Bullen in his new collection of *Old English Plays*; but this edition has not been accessible to me. Through Mr. C. H. Firth's kindness, however, I have been enabled to make acquaintance with Nabbes' tragedy of *The Unfortunate Mother* and with his comedy of *Tottenham Court*. The former play, printed in 1640, was not acted, having been refused by the players; Mr. Fleay (*u. s.*, p. 121) ingeniously concludes from a passage in the *Proem* ('No Politician tells his plots unto Those in the Pit') that it was written in rivalry to Shirley's *The Politician*, acted in 1639. A comparison between this and a very different play, Cyril Tourneur's *The Revenger's Tragedy*, which it resembles in the nomenclature of its *dramatis personae*, would illustrate the gap, or gulf, which separates dramatised passion from the free use by ordinary stage-craft of the most extraordinary motives. Corvino, the villainous schemer of the play, before his evil designs are revealed, has the satisfaction of accomplishing much more than he could have imagined it to be within his power to bring about.— 'Fortune,' he rather finely says, has been 'his Machiavel'; but neither he nor his victims, the unfortunate Duchess and her two high-spirited bastard sons, nor any of the other characters of the play, rise above the level of the ordinary figures of the tragedy of this period. The diction, if it never rises to the accents of true passion, at least avoids bombast. —*Tottenham Court*, printed in 1638, opens with a decidedly striking scene. Two runaway lovers are separated from one another on the stage by the bewildering darkness of the night, while in the distance are heard the cries of the lady's enraged uncle, who is following with his tenants in pursuit. The remainder of this comedy, which chiefly plays at a favourite pleasure-resort of the London tradesmen of the day, is not so vulgar as might have been expected. For a description of some of Nabbes' other plays, see Genest, vol. x. pp. 57 *seqq.*, and cf. Fleay, *English Drama*, vol. ii. p. 118. Mr. Lee has written a notice of Nabbes in vol. xl of *The Dictionary of National Biography* (1894); he appears to have been of humble origin, but to have resided for some time at Exeter College, Oxford.

tion of the kind ever exhibited on a public stage [1]. This is
the elaborate piece entitled *Microcosmus* (printed in 1637) [2].
Albeit, in accordance with its ambitious title, furnished
forth with a bewildering multitude of *dramatis personae*,
including the Four Elements, the Four Complexions, and
the Five Senses, this ' moral masque ' is in point of fact but
one more version of the old contention between Sensuality
and Virtuous Love.   The hero, Physander, who represents
the ' little world ' of man [3], is guided through conflict and
error to ultimate re-union with his celestial wife Bellanima,
who ' signifies the soul.'

His Micro-
cosmus
(pr. 1637).

In the belated effort of Nabbes there was nothing really
new or important ; nor is it in the way of contrast with his
respectable endeavour to combine morality and masquerade
that I proceed to touch on an early masterpiece from the
hand of one of the greatest of our poets.   Through *Comus*,
the most purely poetical of all his literary creations, the
name of Milton connects itself, as it were accidentally, with
the half-forgotten names which have filled the preceding
pages ; and a few words concerning this work, and the
tragedy of Milton's old age, may not unfitly conclude this
survey of English dramatic literature previously to the outbreak of the great Puritan Revolution.

---

[1] According to Malone, quoted *ap*. Dodsley, ' a masque for dancers of
the ropes ' was allowed at the Fortune Theatre in 1624 ; but this (as is there
observed) was probably mere dumb-show and dancing.

[2] Printed in vol. ix of Dodsley's *Old Plays* (1827).

[3] ' The perfect analogy between the world and man ' here indicated, was
no novel idea with writers of this class of production.   See the explanatory
address *To the Reader*, prefixed to Ford and Dekker's *The Sun's Darling* ;
and cf. Dyce's note *ad loc.*, where Nabbes' masque is described as ' written
with better effect, and on a plan far more ingeniously constructed, than Ford
and Dekker's.'—Another late attempt on the lines of the old moralities is
*Pathomachia, or Love's Loadstone, or the Battle of the Affections shadowed by
a feigned Siege of the City of Pathopolis*, an allegorical drama in prose, printed
in 1630.   This piece contains allusions to the Gunpowder Plot, Ravaillac's
murder, and so forth ; besides a scene in which Justice makes short
work of Curiosity and Jealousy—the former being a kind of mixture
between Puritan and Latitudinarian, who inspired the Mar-Prelate
pamphlets, loves no Rochets, and ' would have Fellows in Colledges to
have Wives.'   Yet it is devoid of force, and accordingly without general
interest.

John Milton (1608-1674).

In 1632—the twenty-fifth year of his age—Milton had completed his University career. He left Cambridge, where his life had been blameless, and where, by unbroken application, he had acquired a store of learning sufficient to make even a laborious student of modern days blush. Not only was he beyond a doubt one of the most accomplished Latinists of the University; not only had he attained to a competent knowledge of Greek and Hebrew, and passed through the inevitable courses of Logic and Philosophy; but in modern literature, English, Latin, French, and Italian, he had become master of various sources which were afterwards, though not at all in the same measure, to feed by their contributions the mighty stream of his creative genius.

His life in the period 1632-1638.

This course of studies he continued and developed in the rural retirement of his father's home at Horton in Buckinghamshire, where he spent the years from 1632 to 1638. It can hardly be doubted that the chief motive of this retirement had been the change which had gradually come over Milton's mind with regard to his original intention of taking Orders in the Church of England. The primary causes of this change are no doubt to be sought in the condition of that Church itself, and in the rapid growth within it, during the early years of the new reign, of ideas and tendencies which seemed to triumph in Laud's elevation to the Primacy in 1633—the year after that in which Milton quitted Cambridge[1]. His thoughts were therefore now turned towards a literary life; and to this purpose he henceforth remained devoted, until changes of which he could never have dreamt stirred in him an active interest in public affairs, and ultimately brought him for a short space of time into personal contact with the administration of the Commonwealth. To the student at Horton the literary world of the neighbouring capital could offer few attractions. Here Ben Jonson still reigned supreme; and Milton was ready to acknowledge him as the leader of what still remained the most popular branch of literature—the dramatic[2]. But the haunts of the veteran and his 'sons' were not such as a youth of Milton's

[1] See chap. v of Masson's *Life of Milton*.

[2] See the well-known parallel passages in the *Allegro* and the *Penseroso*, probably written before *Comus*.

disposition was likely to frequent; his visits to London were rare, and if he became personally known to any of the dramatic writers, this was most probably brought about by the musicians William and Henry Lawes, with the latter of whom he was on terms of friendship. Under the occasional influence of such acquaintances and of others, chiefly scientific men[1], but generally among his Greek, Latin, Italian, and English books, and amidst the surroundings of rural scenery, Milton spent the years in which he produced the group of works to which *Comus* and its predecessor *Arcades* belong.

The *Arcades* was probably produced in the same year, 1634, as its more famous successor, and is mainly interesting as a preliminary attempt. It was probably written at the instigation of Henry Lawes, who composed the music for its performance at Harefield House, as part of an entertainment presented to the Dowager Countess of Derby, a daughter of Sir John Spencer of Althorpe, and the Amarillis of Spenser's *Colin Clout's Come Home Again*. Her grandchildren performed this masque, which is slight in construction, and differs but little from the Jonsonian type[2]. The graceful flow of its verse rises to eloquence in the passage in praise of Music—the art to which the place of honour is given at the conclusion of both *L'Allegro* and *Il Penseroso*—the art which after being the joy of Milton's youth became one of the consolations of his blind old age[3].

His Arcades (acted probably 1633–4; printed 1645).

But the *Arcades* was only a brief essay in a field where, very soon afterwards, Milton's genius produced an immortal masterpiece. *Comus* was written, doubtless also at the invita-

His Comus (1634; pr. 1637).

---

[1] Masson, *u. s.*, p. 566. He visited London to take lessons in music and mathematics.—Professor Masson suggests that Milton may have taken an interest in the performance of Shirley's masque of *The Triumph of Peace* (Feb. 1634) as a 'musical opportunity,' especially as his brother Christopher was then a student of the Inner Temple.

[2] Cf. especially Jonson's *Part of the King's Entertainment* (1603), where, as was, greatly to Gifford's indignation, observed by Warton, 'the Genius speaks somewhat in Milton's manner.'

[3] 'What a pity,' exclaims Edward Fitzgerald, 'Handel could not have written music to some great masque, such as Ben Jonson or Milton would have written, if they had known of such a musician to write for.' (*Letters and Literary Remains*, 1889, vol. i. p. 131.) Undoubtedly, musical as was this age in England, it may be said to have missed the opportunity of raising the masque to a higher level by the inspiration of poetry's favourite sister art.

tion of Lawes (who composed the music and undertook the general management [1]), for performance at Ludlow Castle in Shropshire, the official residence of the Earl of Bridgewater (the step-son of the lady honoured in the *Arcades*) as Lord President of Wales. He had rather tardily arrived at Ludlow late in 1633, and the festivities on the occasion continued over the greater part of the following year. In this connexion the entertainment devised by Milton and his friend was produced on Michaelmas-night, September 29th, 1634. The principal parts were performed by the Earl's youthful sons and daughter, who represented the two Brothers and the Lady of the Masque; Lawes filled the part of the Attendant Spirit; the names of the remaining performers have not been preserved.

It is well known that a story was current at a comparatively late date [2] to the effect that this masque—which neither in the first nor in the second edition of Milton's poems bore its distinctive title of *Comus*—was founded on a real incident. According to this tale, the two brothers and their sister, being on their way to Ludlow from the house of some relatives in Herefordshire, were benighted in Haywood Forest; and this adventure was said to have been narrated by Lawes to Milton, and to have been used by him as the foundation of his plot—if plot it can be called.

After what has been observed in previous passages of this book [3] on the nature of the species to which Milton's *Comus* belongs, it may seem superfluous to point out why the severest strictures which have been passed on this production—those of Johnson in his *Life of Milton*—miss the mark. He criticises the action of *Comus* as improbable even in those parts in which it is merely human. What the poet undertakes to present is, however, not the semblance of a real action, but the allegorical reproduction of a thought already presumed to be uppermost in the minds of a particular audience. The masque is of its nature an occasional

---

[1] Masson, *u.s.*, p. 610.

[2] Oldys (who lived about a century afterwards) is believed to be the earliest known authority for this 'legend.'

[3] Vol. i. pp. 150 *seqq.*; vol. ii. pp. 387 *seqq.*

piece, and its literary value is quite independent of its
dramatic effectiveness [1]. Glaring improbabilities it may as
a matter of good taste be advisable to avoid ; but the improbability which Johnson half-contemptuously stigmatises
in *Comus* will hardly be admitted to fall under the above
category. So, again, when he reprehends as 'contrary to
the nature of dramatic representation' the circumstance
that 'the prologue spoken in the wild wood by the Attendant Spirit is addressed to the audience,' he forgets that
the laws, internal as well as external, of dramatic representation are here altogether out of question. In truth, his
entire commentary on his text, that 'as a drama *Comus* is
deficient,' proceeds on a false assumption. The masque
depends for its effect on a combination of poetic, decorative,
and musical elements ; and the danger lies in the likelihood
of the first of these being overpowered by the others. But the
effect of every particular masque is intended to suit its own
occasion ; this effect cannot in performance be reproduced
at will; as a permanent work, therefore, *Comus*, like any other
masque, should be judged by qualities quite independent of
its merits or demerits as an occasional dramatic spectacle.

By the power of his genius, which—perhaps unconsciously
—carried him far beyond the occasion of his task, Milton
elevated a species of composition, usually employed as
a mere vehicle of compliment, to the level of a poetic
tribute, not to an individual, but to Virtue itself. To Henry
Lawes he may have been indebted for the happy choice of
the basis on which he reared a superstructure of incomparable
nobility. It cannot be doubted that he was further indebted
to other—literary—sources for the choice of the main
figures and the use of some of the incidents which support
the slight fable of his poem [2]. In details of diction he

---

[1] *Comus, e.g.*, is quite unsuitable for performance on the stage, though it
has frequently made its appearance there. It was first acted at Drury Lane
in 1738, as altered by John Dalton, with musical accompaniments by
Dr. Arne. This adaptation, frequently printed, is stated to have been
banished from the stage by George Coleman about 1772. *Comus* has since
been from time to time revived, notably by Macready. My own experience of a more recent revival leads me to think such attempts
mistakes.

[2] It has already been pointed out (vol. i. p. 373) that Milton, who was a

here, as elsewhere, wove into the rich robe of his poetic diction many flowers derived from other poets[1]. But both in conception and in execution the poem remains, in the highest sense of the word, original. The concluding lines of the Spirit's epilogue[2]—lines which Milton afterwards inscribed as his motto in the album of an Italian admirer— express in brief the main idea of *Comus*. The sublimity of Milton's genius—the quality which, in the literature of his own country at all events, so pre-eminently distinguishes him as a poet—shines forth with marvellous fulness in this glorious work of his youth. The execution falls but little short of the conception. The lyric portions, although perhaps Macaulay goes too far in describing them as completely overshadowing the dramatic, are among the poet's noblest verse; and the dialogue, though its versification is less stately and its diction less ample than that of *Paradise Lost*, which indeed almost precludes dramatic declamation, rises at the climax of the moral interest—in the argument between Comus and the Lady—to almost matchless beauty[3]. Indeed there may be those who cannot suppress a wish that Milton had always adhered to this earlier and easier treatment of his favourite metre—easier I mean to hands under which language passed into combinations 'musical, as is Apollo's lute.'

Finally, it should be pointed out that it is impossible not to recognise in *Comus* a twofold allegory. If in the

reader of Peele, was indebted to *The Old Wives' Tale* for the suggestion of the figures which in his hands became Comus, the Lady, her Brothers, and the Attendant Spirit. Instead (as might otherwise have seemed a natural process) of taking directly from the myth of Circe the idea of the central figure of the magician and the associations surrounding it, he may have used a Latin poem *Comus* (by Puteanus of Louvain), republished at Oxford in this very year 1634. He may have been acquainted with Ben Jonson's masque of *Pleasure Reconciled to Virtue* (1619), in which Comus is one of the characters. And beyond all doubt he had been a reader of Fletcher's *Faithful Shepherdess* (revived at Court and at the theatres in 1633-4). Cf. vol. ii. pp. 396, *note*, 663; and see Masson, *u. s.*, p. 622.

[1] For instances I may refer the reader to the notes on *Comus* in Mr. R. C. Browne's edition of Milton's *English Poems* (Clarendon Press Series, 1870).

[2] 'Mortals, that would follow me,' &c.

[3] Johnson, forgetting that the dialogue here represents as it were the summary of the case of Virtue against Vice before the tribunal of humanity, desiderates 'a brisker reciprocation of objections and replies.'

Allegro and the *Penseroso* the poet still holds the balance
between the two temperaments and tendencies of mind
which lay at the root of the division of the nation, and
describes the nobler aspects of either, while already indicating his preference for the one,—in *Comus* we have before
us an unmistakeable allegory of the conflict between the
two. The Revel-god is thus not only the representative of
Incontinence ; he is also a type of those whom the poet
regarded as the actual votaries of the view of life which
he abhorred. While *Comus* never falls from the height
of poetic allegory to that lower level of satire which
even *Lycidas* cannot be said wholly to avoid, yet the
secondary intention of the poem seems to me too clearly
marked to admit of being disputed by any candid
student.

Such were the relations, as revealed in this immortal *His drama-*
masque, between the great poet of the Revolution epoch *tic designs.*
and the age from which he still 'dwelt apart,' and which
mirrored itself only too faithfully in so much of its dramatic
literature. Independently of the character of his own poetic
gifts, it was hardly possible that Milton should have connected himself directly with the drama in these the days
of its gradual, but certain, moral as well as literary decay.
His fertile intellect indeed busied itself on more than one
occasion with thoughts of the dramatic form of composition.
But such schemings were not inspired by any dramatic performances which he may occasionally have witnessed on the
London stage, or by the remembrance of the academical
comedies which he boasted of having hissed in his student-
days at Cambridge[1]. His design of treating the subject
of *Paradise Lost* in the form of a mystery may be passed
by[2]; the other dramatic projects formed by him were
doubtless intended to follow the lines of ancient classical
tragedy. He is stated to have left behind him a list of not less

---

[1] See the passage from the *Apology for Smectymnuus* quoted in Masson,
p. 224.

[2] As to Milton's several drafts of this subject, ' as meditated for dramatic
treatment,' see Mr. Masson's new edition of Milton's *Poetical Works*, vol. i.
p. 45.

than one hundred and two dramatic subjects, of which sixty were Scriptural, thirty-three from British, and five from Scottish history [1]. On these schemes it is unnecessary to dwell: I mention one of them, because the suggestion of it was probably due to a contemporary publication by an English poet of literary merit. Milton seems to have jotted down the subject of the *Christus Patiens* as suitable for a dramatic poem in 1640–1, and it was in 1640 that George Sandys had published, with a dedication to Charles I, his English version of the *Christus Patiens* of Hugo Grotius (1617) [2]. Milton designed that his tragedy should centre in the scene of the Agony in the Garden; it is noticeable that several other themes from the life of Christ were about the same time noted by him for dramatic treatment [3]. Besides these schemes and titles, Milton, as is known, has left to posterity only one other completed work directly connecting

[1] See Masson's edition of Milton's *Poetical Works* (1874), vol. i. p. 44. Among the Scottish subjects was *Macbeth*. 'Milton's intention,' according to Steevens, whose note I cite from Mr. Howard Furness' *Variorum* edition of *Macbeth*, p. 299, 'was to have begun with the arrival of Malcolm at Macduff's castle. "The matter of Duncan," says he, "may be expressed by the appearing of his ghost." '

[2] As to the Χριστὸς Πάσχων and Hugo Grotius' tragedy, see *ante*, vol. i. pp. 4–5 and *note*.—George Sandys' (1578–1644) English version of the latter bore the title *Christ's Passion, a Tragedie, with Annotations*. In the Dedication he speaks of himself as 'in the shadow of the King's absence, dismissed from arms by an act of Time'—an expression supposed to refer to his own advanced age. Falkland's *Lines to the Author*, prefixed to Sandys' version in accordance with the custom of the age, sound the praises of both author and translator—and indeed both were deserving of celebration. As already noticed, Hugo Grotius' treatment of his theme is, within obvious limits, such as no writer on a Gospel theme, least of all on the central one, will outstep except at his peril. Jesus in person prologises to the first act, and St. Peter to the second; there is a chorus of Jewish women, and another of Roman soldiers. The Latinity of the work exhibits a vigorous handling of the language such as perhaps no other modern age has rivalled. Sandys' English translation is not unworthy of an author whose skill obtained for him the praise of Dryden, while we may presume that it was the earnestness of his tone which rendered him 'savoury' to Richard Baxter. The decasyllabic couplet, it will be remembered, still awaited perfection ; on the other hand, rimed couplets of four-foot verse are used by Sandys in lyrical passages with something of the combination of grace and dignity familiar to students of other better-known Caroline poets.

[3] See Masson's edition of *Poetical Works*, vol. ii. p. 5 (Introduction to *Paradise Regained*).

itself with our dramatic literature. Of this, though belonging in date to a much later year, I may here briefly speak in
conclusion, before asking the reader to return to a period
of our national life and literature in which the struggle
reviewed by the author of *Samson Agonistes* was still
in a preparatory stage.

Milton's masque of *Comus* reflects the moral indignation
with which the representative of Puritanism under its
loftiest aspect, when its hopes were high and its strength was
on the eve of self-assertion, regarded the representatives
of moral and social decay. The one poetic creation, on the
other hand, to which he gave a regular dramatic form was
the fruit of different times and different conditions, though
the spirit of the writer remained the same. *Samson Agonistes,*
printed in the same volume as *Paradise Regained* (1671),
is the utterance of the faithful upholder of an oppressed
and persecuted cause ; but it is no cry of doubt or despair.
Milton had not suffered outwardly in any serious way from
the powers of the Restoration ; his escape from their
vengeance in its first heat had been marvellous ; then, after
the passing of the Indemnity Bill, he had undergone
temporary restraint.   But these were the least of his
griefs.   The cause to which he had consecrated the labours
of his manhood had been trampled in the dust ; many of
its champions had been led to death or driven into exile,
and the cause itself had become a by-word in the mouths
of 'antics, mummers, mimics,' as well as in the high places
of Church and State.   For himself there remained nothing
to hope, and but little to fear ;—his work had been done,
and death ' who sets all free ' would speedily pay ' his
ransom now and full discharge ' from the moral bondage
of life in a servile age and self-dishonoured nation.   But for
the cause which to him was that of truth and virtue as
well as of his country, hope was not dead in his breast—
could not be dead till life itself was extinct, even as the
light had long been quenched in his eyes amid ' the blaze
of noon' that enveloped him.

Such was the spirit in which the blind poet composed
this tragedy of *Samson Agonistes*, the historical and bio-

*His
Samson
Agonistes
(pr.* 1671).

graphical interest of which is therefore extremely great.
And to this circumstance is doubtless to be attributed the
favour, it might perhaps be said the reverence, with which
this poem has been regarded by posterity.   For who
could contemplate without sympathy the last utterance
of so lofty a political and religious faith, or without
emotion the blind poet's creation of the blind hero?
On passages such as that in which a fiery indignation
brands with lofty wrath

> 'nations grown corrupt
> And by their vices brought to servitude,'

who

> 'love bondage more than liberty,
> Bondage with ease than strenuous liberty,'—

or that where, in strains of the deepest pathos and of
the most thrilling directness, the blind Samson laments
his last and least endurable loss—the loss of sight [1]—
it is impossible to dwell without feelings of reverence and
awe.   Nor are other touches of a different character wanting
to remind the reader, how much Milton has revealed in this
poem of the bitterest private as well as public experiences
of his life [2].

From a purely literary point of view the tragedy of
Samson Agonistes, which, as the Preface needlessly states,
was 'never intended to the stage,' cannot be said to possess
merits commensurate with its historical and biographical
value [3].   That it has escaped representation under conditions
wholly uncongenial to it, may be due not only to the sacred

---

[1] 'O first created beam, and thou great Word,' &c.

[2] I refer to the passage on 'wedlock-treachery,' and to the whole tone of
the scene between Samson and Dalila, without going the length of Phillips
in supposing Milton to have in Samson's rejection of Dalila intended a direct
personal reminiscence.   Cf. Masson's *Life of Milton*, vol. iii. p. 441.   See
also *ib.* vol. v. pp. 674–5 as to the chorus after Dalila's departure, the greater
part of which is almost literally excerpted from the Divorce pamphlets.   As
to the form and the prefatory observations in general, see *ib.* vol. vi. pp. 661
seqq.

[3] The English stage appears not to have been wholly unfamiliar with the
subject of this tragedy.   See *Diary of the Duke of Stettin's Journey* (*Transactions of Royal Historical Society, New Series*, vol. vi, 1892, p. 6): On
September 15, 1602, was acted in the afternoon '*eine tragica comoedia von
Samsone und dem halben Stamm Benjamin.*'

character of the source of the subject, but also to the
circumstance that by composing music to it as an oratorio
Handel has removed it for ever from possible contact with
the play-house[1].   Into a criticism of Milton's rather perfunctory prefatory remarks *On that sort of dramatic poem
which is called Tragedy* it seems unnecessary to enter ; the
array of examples by which he supports the dignity of
tragedy reminds one of the old defences of the drama in the
Elisabethan tracts; and the appeal to the examples of
Greek and Italian tragedy was merely a necessary preface
to the method followed in the drama itself.   *Samson
Agonistes* is alike conceived in the spirit of Attic tragedy and
modelled on its outward form.   A great scholar[2] has recorded his opinion, that few plays afford a finer specimen of
tragic irony, and that from this point of view Milton's work
merits comparison with Ajax and the second Oedipus.   Like
the Attic tragedies, *Samson Agonistes* is not divided into acts
and scenes ; the catastrophe is announced by a Messenger ;
and a Chorus accompanies with reflexions and lyrical outbursts the developement of the action, which at first proceeds
rather slowly.   The character of Samson is finely and
consistently conceived, and there is dramatic life—alas !—in
the shifting wiles of Dalila.

Passages of this poem, which in details as well as in the
whole nature of its construction exhibits Milton's familiarity
with Greek tragedy, reveal all the condensed vigour and
lofty enthusiasm of their author's genius ; elsewhere he exhibits, not less characteristically, his favourite mannerisms of
style, his classical inversions and his sesquipedalian words[3].
The metre of the lyrical passages is, as he himself says, ' of
all sorts '; and though these passages are in part full of
exquisite rhythmical beauty, the licence of now using now
eschewing rime, and the doubtful felicity of some of the
rimes themselves, tend to disturb the general harmony of
the effect.   In the narrative of the Messenger, the force

[1] Handel's *Samson* was first performed in 1743.

[2] See Bishop Thirlwall, *On the Irony of Sophocles* (in *Philological Museum*,
vol. ii. p. 536).

[3] See *e. g.* the passage beginning ' My griefs not only pain me.'

of which is heightened by the previous broken announcement, the epical genius of Milton unfolds its full strength.

Review of the period from Shakspere to the Civil War.

Limits of the influence of Shakspere and the greatest of his fellow-dramatists.

In literary, as in all other, history it is generally difficult to say where growth passes into decline, and where in the midst of exuberant life the first signs announce themselves of the beginning of the end. Shakspere is justly regarded as the Sophocles, and as something more than the Sophocles, of the English drama; but neither the Greek nor the English poet can by his greatness cause us to forget that the works of no one man—however pre-eminent among his fellows or for all time—convey a complete expression of even a single side of a nation's literary life in any given age. The death of Sophocles, in whose works we are rightly taught to admire the very flower of the Attic drama, was actually preceded by that of Euripides, the representative of incipient decay; and Phaedra had sobbed forth her sinful sorrows to the accompaniment of Carian flutings a generation before the *Oedipus Coloneus* once more recalled to the Athenians the lofty dignity of Sophoclean tragedy. While Shakspere's creative power was still, to all intents and purposes, at its height, English comedy in the hands of Jonson, and English tragedy in those of Beaumont and Fletcher, had already begun to pass into what may be called their transnormal period. The course of individual genius sways and at times directs the progress of a whole chapter of literary life, but without ever either absorbing it or singly and absolutely determining it even for a time.

The entire growth of English dramatic literature in the period contemporary with Shakspere's manhood and in that following upon his death exhibits the unmistakeable traces of his influence. In a less degree, other dramatists of genius, above all Jonson and Fletcher, impressed the mark of their individualities upon the drama of their own and of the succeeding generations. But had another Fletcher, another Jonson, even another Shakspere appeared, they could only have delayed and modified, they could not have permanently arrested or diverted, the main current of our dramatic literature. For as an integral part of the nation's life the history of our drama was subject to the influences determining the history of the nation itself; and only by becoming a literary drama pure and simple—such, for instance, as that of the German Romanticists had to content itself with remaining in the days of Tieck and his fellows—could it have lived an artificial life on its own conditions, and forced its blossoms in its own hothouse.

Many of the features marking the period of our dramatic literature which may be described as the period of its gradual decline therefore remain unintelligible without some knowledge of the general course of our national history in the earlier half of the seventeenth century.   Nor is it likely that without such a knowledge many readers would care to engage in the study of the chapter of our literature now under review, in which shadow so largely alternates with light.   Here it may perhaps be possible, without appealing directly to any other sources besides the dramatic works noticed in the preceding pages, to recall some of those signs of the times which announced the close of one period in our national history, and the approach of its successor. And with regard to these two periods it will be specially remembered that the one which was passing away had found in the drama an agent and an exponent of many of its determining forces; while towards the symptoms premonitory of change the drama could not assume any but a hostile attitude. *Historical aspects of the period.*

Doubtless, even in the instance of so tangible a movement as the Puritan Revolution, no hard and fast line breaks the continuity of our national life.   That Revolution was itself an historical growth; its roots lay as deep in the national past as the origin of many of the ideas which it combated, and of the institutions which it temporarily overthrew or permanently modified.   We can now dispassionately trace the genesis of the forces which contributed to it, and estimate the results to which it led. We can recognise a conservative element in much of its political action, and a logical sequence in the gradual unfolding of its religious ideas.   But we need not, like so many of our ancestors over whose lives it still cast its shadow, shut *Approach of the Great Revolution.*

our eyes to the fact, that the victory of the Puritan
movement assured to it a power which outlasted its extravagances and the tyranny of the reaction in part produced by them ; and that the informing spirit of Puritanism
—the belief in the obligatory character of a moral law
revealed to man, and interpreted to him by his individual
conscience—entered into the very heart and soul of the
nation, and established an enduring hold upon it.

A struggle, in principle defensive, for political rights
which had fallen into abeyance, or which were now first
looked upon as a distinct portion of the national inheritance,
came to be combined with a desire for religious liberty which
the Tudor Reformation had ignored or to all appearance
The nation effectually repressed. The nation only began definitively to
gradually divide itself into two camps, when an institution of real
divided into historical significance and of at least fancied historical
two parties. continuity seemed to be in danger from the new movement.
King James' undignified cry of 'No bishops no King'
expressed the fear which finally consolidated the Cavalier
The party party. But from the very first, those whom traditions,
chosen by interests, and associations attached to existing forms in
the drama- Church and State, those who clung to these forms as the
tists. visible expressions of the national past, and those who
cherished them as the best guarantees of a continuance of
the existing settlement, naturally showed no hesitation in
their attitude of resistance. The Court and its surroundings,
the Church, the Universities, and the Legal Corporations,
were conservative by instinct, whatever elements of agitation might here and there have introduced themselves into
these spheres of society. The national literature had
given occasional signs of a desire to shake off the control
of the influences which had predominated over its growth ;
but its main tenor was still determined by the ideas
and sentiments of those classes of society to which it
chiefly addressed itself. On the theatre had fallen some
of the earliest blasts of an atmosphere laden with storms of
a still unsuspected power. Personal ill-will and a natural
desire for self-preservation accordingly helped to heighten
the political preferences of our dramatists ; but it was in

any case almost inevitable that they and their patrons should abhor the prospect of the national life being diverted in its course from what seemed the traditions of the great Elisabethan age.

But in truth, the nation had begun to pass into another phase of its history, before Elisabeth had followed the arch-foe of Elisabethan England to the grave. The memory of the great days of the Virgin Queen had already become a mere sentiment in those of her successor ;—a sentiment which only another period of effort for a noble cause could convert into a really effective spring of action. Had England under James I, or even under Charles I, taken a resolute part in the great European struggle, the traditions of a great national epoch must have counted for much in the decision of that war of wars, and the effect of their influence would have been felt at home as well as abroad. The days of Queen Elisabeth served as a popular phrase even in the mouth of Charles I when he first addressed the Parliament which was to overthrow his authority ; they would not have seemed at an end had Ralegh been allowed to hurl defiance at Spain,—had the bold counsels of Bacon found favour with his Sovereign,— had even an English army worthy of the name been sent to save the Palatinate, with the battle-cry which had been heard from the decks of the Great Armada. As it was, the would-be pacific policy of James and the more ex-cusable uncertainty in the counsels of Charles doomed England to virtual inaction in the midst of a tremendous European crisis ; and the ancient glories rusted in the national consciousness. This result is accurately reflected in the drama, which addressed itself to London, the sole focus of national aspirations in favour of a policy of active intervention in the affairs of the world—except of such as still lingered in the seaports of the southern coasts.

The feebleness of the foreign policy of the age

reflected in the drama.

The reminiscences of the great Elisabethan struggle observable in the extant plays of the entire half-century are but few and feeble. To the greatness of Henry VIII's truest daughter, Shakspere—if it was he—paid as it were a parting tribute. Not long afterwards Chapman proved

Elisabethan reminiscences.

that reverence for her greatness as a sovereign had survived the last opportunities of personal flattery[1]. Dekker, in a production reflecting more credit upon his patriotism than upon his art, attempts a picture of her worst dangers and her most glorious triumph[2]. Thomas Heywood recalls the early difficulties of her life which laid the foundation of the position afterwards approved by her, whether she would or not, as the champion of the Protestant cause[3]. But these are only the last echoes of a loyalty which had been a living sentiment in those from whom they proceeded. In the dramatic literature of the next two generations Queen Elisabeth and the glories with which her name was identified seem all but forgotten[4].

Isolated references to important transactions of contemporary European history.

The reigns of James and Charles brought no national achievements to serve as substitutes for these ancient glories; and the great events which filled the theatre of European history, and of which as a nation England remained little more than a spectator, are left all but unnoticed by references or allusions in our contemporary dramatic literature. Here and there an exceptionally striking incident or character is, so to speak, made free of the stage; the siege of Ostend (which ended two days after our peace had been signed with Spain) is frequently used as an illustration by our dramatists[5]; and a generation afterwards the 'ghost of Tilly' points a joke in a comedy[6], and the death of Wallenstein is re-enacted on the London boards in a gross caricature of the historical

The drama not allowed free comment on such topics.

drama[7]. But the mighty struggles of the times, which Englishmen were breathlessly following in the narratives of *Mercurius Gallobelgicus* and the flying sheets of the *New Coranto,* and of which they were greedily absorbing such

---

[1] *Byron's Conspiracy,* act iii, and *passim.*   [2] *The Whore of Babylon.*
[3] *If You Know not Me, You Know Nobody.*
[4] It seems hardly worth while to refer, by way of exception, to the faint echoes of the old national sentiment audible in Massinger, and in one or two other dramatists.
[5] See *e. g.* Fletcher's *The Woman's Prize* (act i. sc. 3), and especially his *Love's Cure* (act i. sc. 1).
[6] Shirley's *The Example* (act iii. sc. 1).
[7] Cf. *ante,* p. 152, as to Glapthorne's *Albertus Wallenstein.* The same writer in *The Lady Mother* refers to Pappenheim ; cf. *ante,* p. 154.

veracious versions as could be obtained from sources like the 'Staple of News Office,' were left aside as unfit themes for treatment or even for mention by an unemancipated drama; the deeds and the sufferings of foreign peoples were almost as sacred from theatrical comment as the persons of foreign sovereigns [1]—just as the affairs of Europe were as a rule left aside as having no concern with the sympathies or antipathies of our insular people, and as appropriately reserved for consideration among the King's mysteries of State. If now and then public feeling, excited by the apparent collapse of a policy contravening the plainest traditions of the national sentiment, broke bounds and encouraged a daring playwright to unmuzzle himself along with it [2], prompt measures of repression were at hand to deal with so exceptional an audacity, and soon all was outwardly calm again. Offences, as Envy says in *Muce-dorus* [3], speedily brought 'danger, or at least restraint' upon their authors; the tragic drama contented itself with veiled allusions which to this day remain open to speculation as to their precise meaning [4]; and if Thalia was schooled with rather more difficulty than her more sober sister, she too learnt the necessity of caution, and was content to substitute harmless generalities for more palpable expressions of opinion.

The generalities in question are not, however, devoid of instructiveness. Our dramatic literature in this period furnishes but few clues as to what Englishmen thought or liked to hear about the foreign policy of their government; on the other hand, it reveals with tolerable distinctness what they thought and liked to hear about the nations with whom that policy had to deal. National loves and hatreds are not wont to die in a day; and though travel and peaceful intercourse had accustomed Englishmen to greater tolerance of foreigners in general—till the satirical could even describe our people as 'famous for dejecting our own

General public feeling, as reflected in the drama, towards particular foreign nations:

---

[1] Cf. *ante*, vol. ii. pp. 422 and 496, and *infra*.

[2] Cf. *ib.*, pp. 524, *seqq.*, as to Middleton's *A Game at Chess*, and *ante*, p. 9, note, as to *The Spanish Viceroy*.

[3] *ad fin.* As to the restrictions on the liberty of the theatres in such matters, and the principal recorded occasions on which offence was given and taken, *vide infra*.   [4] Cf. *ante*, p. 32 *et al.*

countrymen' by contrast [1]—yet the old antipathies proved
Germany; as long-lived as the old sympathies [2]. The intimate relations established between England and Germany in the
Reformation period were doubtless drawn still closer by
the large number of Germans who were settled in London [3].
The course of political events increased the good-will felt
by Englishmen towards their Protestant kinsmen ; and the
marriage of the Princess Elisabeth, which several of our
dramatists helped to celebrate in loyal masques, was the
the Dutch; most popular act of the policy of King James [4]. Dutchmen
would have been even more uniformly subjected to good-
humoured comment from the single point of view of their
supposed favourite national propensity, had not habits and
customs much more offensive to the theatre than drinking-
bouts been identified in their most pronounced forms with
Amsterdam [5]. An isolated act of Dutch colonial violence—
in which Englishmen were the sufferers—was allowed to
pass almost as unheeded by the stage as it remained un-
the Danes; avenged by the Government [6]. The incarnation of the

---

[1] So says Freshwater in Shirley's *The Ball* (act iii. sc. 3). And cf. the
Tutor's advice in Shirley's *The Witty Fair One* (act ii. sc. 1).

[2] Not many Englishmen would have cared to confess with the author of
the *Religio Medici* : ' Those National repugnances do not touch me.' (Part
ii. sec. 1 ; see also the wise remarks in sec. 4.)

[3] Elze (see Introduction to Chapman's *Alphonsus*, p. 9) concludes that of
the 10,000 foreigners living in London in 1621 a great part were Germans.—
No doubt a fair proportion of these were ' poor Palatines,' though not quite of
the same sort as their compatriots of a later age. (As to the general and special
antipathies of the Londoners of this period against foreigners—including
Scotchmen—see M. Pattison, *Isaac Casaubon*, pp. 430-1.)

[4] In addition to these masques (by Campion, Chapman, and Beaumont)
may be noticed the production, soon after the marriage, of a historical drama,
Hector of Germany, or The Palsgrave, Prince Elector. It is described by
Genest, vol. x. p. 95.

[5] The word ' drunk,' says Brains in Shirley's *The Witty Fair One* (vol. ii.
p. 2), ' is good English now : it was Dutch.' Cf. also the character of Vandunk
(*alias* Vandrunk) in Fletcher and Massinger's *The Beggar's Bush* (*ante*, vol. ii.
p. 726 *note*), and the phrases ' upsee Dutch ' or ' upsee Freeze.' But a class of
words and ideas very different from those which English soldiers were supposed to have imported from the Low Countries, were brought over by sectaries
such as those whom Middleton rudely satirises in *The Family of Love*.

[6] The massacre at Amboyna (see below as to Dryden's play on the subject)
is referred to in passing in Fletcher's *The Fair Maid of the Inn* (act iv. sc. 2).
It is pointedly denounced in Shirley's *Honoria and Mammon* (act i. sc. 2),
but this was printed in 1659, and probably not designed for the stage.

Danish people in the eyes of Englishmen was King James'
brother-in-law, Christian IV; and it is not wonderful that
the memory of a certain ' heavy-headed revel ' which had
consecrated the alliance between the two monarchs, should
have survived in allusions to a national habit of which the
royal visit had supplied so notorious an illustration [1].   But
these are mere surface hits.   Towards France and French-   *France;*
men public feeling in England could not but be in the
main friendly so long as Henry of Navarre sat on its
neighbouring throne ; yet it may be doubted whether his
reign was long enough to allow the feelings of national
good-will between the two countries to attain to any great
degree of warmth, though the charms of his personal
character seem to have been well known to Englishmen [2].
After his death such hopes as might have been founded
upon the designs, real or supposed, of his European policy
passed away; and in spite of the efforts of Buckingham,
the French marriage of Charles I was looked upon by the
nation chiefly in a spirit of suspicion against the dangers
of a Catholic connexion.   But the dramatists were of course
too much in sympathy with the Court, and too greatly
dependent upon its favours, to give expression to any such
fears ; and in the end they had particular occasion to identify
the interests of the theatre with loyalty to the person of
Queen Henrietta Maria [3].   Traffic and intercourse with
France must, however, have steadily increased both before
and after Buckingham's unfortunate war ; and nothing is
more common in the dramas of this period than a display
of some knowledge of the French tongue.

The deep-seated national antipathy against Spain and   *Spain and Spaniards;*

---

[1] See Beaumont and Fletcher's *The Knight of Malta* (act v. sc. 1), and
Fletcher's *The Captain* (act iii. sc. 2).

[2] Cf. Chapman's *Byron's Conspiracy* and *Byron's Tragedy.*—In so late
a play as D'Avenant's *The Cruel Brother* (act ii) may be observed a pointedly
unfriendly characterisation of the French.   I notice that in his monograph
on *Queen Elisabeth* (*Twelve English Statesmen Series*), Professor Beesly
expresses an opinion, that in the Queen's time the nation at large was
inveterately hostile to the French, and rather admired the formal Spaniards.

[3] *Vide infra* as to Prynne's *Histriomastix.*   Both Shirley and Massinger
were specially devoted to the Queen, the latter apparently in some measure
for party reasons.

everything Spanish was little if at all abated by James'
treaty of peace, or by the policy of conciliation, and of
deference to Spanish advice, which it ushered in. The
schemes of Spain continued to be the bugbear of the popular
political imagination even after their real nature had long
ceased to justify any such apprehensions; while the arrogance of Spanish manners was as constantly as ever a subject
of resentment and a theme of satire[1]. It seemed worth
while to discuss at some length the expression which this
antipathy found on a particular occasion, when it concentrated itself in an attack upon the particular statesman
who to English eyes necessarily seemed the embodiment
of Spanish policy[2]. But the ill-will which the stage
loved to manifest against Spaniards in general had a
deeper source than fear of the intrigues of Gondomar, or
abhorrence of the scheme of the Spanish Marriage. The
nation had not yet unlearnt its belief that Spain was the
natural enemy of England, and the Spaniard the born
opposite of the Englishman. An ineradicable suspicion of
Spain formed an integral element in the national patriotism
of a Bacon as well as in that of the popular talkers and
writers whom by the King's orders he sought to suppress.
As contrasted with Spain, France seemed worthy of 'praise
and love'; and there is perhaps nothing more significant
of the intensity of the feeling, than that a cultivated English
poet should be found not less blind to the brilliant achievements of contemporary Spanish literature, than he is keen-
sighted in recalling one of the most enduring social defects

Italy.   of the Spanish character[3]. Italy still exercised its potent
charm over the minds of Englishmen; but it must not be

---

[1] In Earle's *Microcosmography* (1628) a tobacco-seller's shop is 'the place
only where Spain is commended and preferred before England itself.' The
popular dislike of Spanish manners lasted into the days of the Civil War,
when 'Castilian' was a term of reproach *vice* 'Cavalier' disused. (*Memoirs
of Col. Hutchinson*, ed. 1885, vol. ii. p. 45.)—The nickname 'Don Diego'
is applied to a person with a very formal air as late as 1711. (*Wentworth
Papers*, p. 195.)   [2] Cf. *ante*, vol. ii. pp. 524 *seqq.*
[3] See Ford's *Love's Sacrifice* (act i. sc. 1), where Spain is described with
bold untruthfulness as
                                        'a climate
                      Too hot to nourish arts '—

forgotten that—with the exception perhaps of some realistic sketches from Venetian and other Italian life, and of some close reproductions of actual episodes of intrigue or crime [1] —the Italy of our dramatists is in most cases a purely conventional scene. Thus, the Italian who intrigues and declaims in a hundred plays of this period is not so much a representative of his own nation, as the usual citizen of the world of dramatic fiction in general.

Turning our glance homewards, we shall not be sur- *Faint re-* prised to observe how faint a reflexion the political *flexion in* struggle in progress during the whole of this period finds *of the* in its dramatic literature. It is easier to account for so *political* singular a phenomenon in literary history, than to indicate *home.* a parallel to it. The familiar themes of domestic political controversy at the most call forth a casual allusion; as when an accidental reference in a dramatist of no eminence reminds us that he was writing in days darkened by the activity of the Star-Chamber and the High-Commission Court [2]. Still less do we expect anything like invective or satire against the system of government which two reigns sought in vain to make permanent; and we are almost surprised when we find a warm supporter of the cause of Charles I satirically expounding a 'thorough' method of managing affairs of State as commending itself to unscrupulous ambition [3]. The venerable grievance of monopolies alone seems to command as by prescriptive right a fair measure of satire, even from the most loyal lips [4]. Their 'abolition' might almost claim to be an article

while the Spanish nation is appropriately enough characterised as
'proud
And in [its] pride unsociable.'

[1] Vernon Lee in *Euphorion* (1884), vol. i. pp. 70 *seqq.*, shows how in this respect the English dramatists laid bare certain aspects of the Renascence age in Italy which Italian Renascence literature itself preferred to ignore. (Cf. *ante* as to Ford.)

[2] Brome's *The English-Moor* (act i. sc. 1).

[3] Shirley's *The Constant Maid* (act iii. sc. 1); but not more than one or two touches in Playfair's speech admit of the supposition that they were suggested by actual observation; and I am far from wishing to insinuate that any political significance was intended even in these. Cf. also as to Massinger, *The Bondman* and *The Emperor of the East* (*ante*, pp. 17 and 30).

[4] See D'Avenant's *The Cruel Brother* (act i), and *Love and Honour* (act ii).

of royalist belief. For the rest, even had the dramatists of this period at heart sympathised with the efforts of its Eliots and Pyms, they would have been restrained by their knowledge of the dangers awaiting those who ventured, even in spheres less subject to restraint than the theatre, to 'speak their minds freely of the prince and *Absolutist* State[1].' But in truth their writings rarely offer any indica-
sentiments
of the tion of conceptions of government out of harmony with the
dramatists. patriarchal ideals of James I and his favourite political philosophers. They generally express themselves, and may be fairly concluded to have thought, as if a good king, or a king who would be good enough to be good, were still the utmost possibility of State-life. The duty of the sovereign is recognised as freely as it was by James himself; but the duty of the citizen is simply to obey his master. In such men as Chapman, Massinger, and Denham, traces are observable of a manlier view of civic responsibilities, duties, and claims[2]; but the majority of these dramatists— Fletcher may be taken as their type—seem quite unaware of any principle of government but the right divine, of any political system but absolute monarchy, or of any corrective of the excesses of kings but the dagger and the bowl[3]. Towards the close of the period we recognise a special purpose in the conventional expressions in praise of loyalty and in condemnation of sedition[4]; and, as is well known, more than one of the Caroline dramatists were to give personal proofs of their fidelity to the cause of the Crown. But it would be futile to seek for any signs of an insight into the great political questions of the times in the drama of the age which preceded and prepared that of our Great Revolution.

The drama It must not be forgotten that in this period the English,
and the
royal or in other words, the London stage addressed itself, even
family more exclusively than before, to particular classes of the population; that it considered itself bound by tradition to the

[1] See Massinger's *The Roman Actor* (act i. sc. 1).
[2] In justice to Ford, the spirited passage which opens act iii. sc. 4 of *The Broken Heart* should be cited as deserving the same commendation.
[3] See Beaumont and Fletcher's *The Maid's Tragedy*.
[4] See *e. g.* Suckling's *Brennoralt*.

Court and the royal family, to the service of whose principal members the theatrical companies were nominally attached ; and that though it likewise appealed to popular favour and support, its authors courted the patronage of Whitehall as the highest acknowledgment of their efforts. Much therefore in the tone and spirit of our dramatic literature depended on the nature of the personal influence traceable to the throne and its immediate surroundings. King James I had *under* been a friend to the drama in days when to favour it was to *James I* assert his own royal independence in Scotland ; and in England he proved himself consistently well-disposed towards the stage. But, apart from the fact that his literary tastes gradually became absorbed in theological controversy [1], it was out of the question that our dramatic literature should have been inspired either by his person, his character, or his acts, to an enthusiasm capable of becoming, like that aroused by the Virgin Queen, a really productive influence. In James' consort there was, in the expressive words of his episcopal biographer, 'little to make him uxorious,' and little to animate poets who were not officially called upon to celebrate the virtues of ' Bel-Anna.' It is true that, crypto-convert as she was, the only serious part of her life lay in her pleasures, and both as patroness and as performer she enduringly associated her name with the history of the English masque [2]. But how could any but a surface impression be left upon any form of art by so essentially frivolous a nature ? Of the royal princes the eldest died before the promise of his youth could have ripened into fulfilment ; and his sister, the fairest flower of the Court, was transplanted, amidst the sympathetic hopes of the nation, to a foreign soil, before life could have schooled her gaiety and high-spirit into the fortitude of self-devotion. Among James' favourites none attracted the good-will of the nation, until towards the close of the reign Buckingham

[1] Cf. M. Pattison, *Isaac Casaubon* (1875), pp. 321 *seqq.*

[2] She was also fond of plays ; and when in the *Hatfield Papers* (as cited by Dr. Brewer) we find Burbage in 1604 stating that ' there is no new play that the Queen hath not seen,' we account it creditable to her that on his advice *Love's Labour's Lost* was revived for her entertainment at the Earl of Southampton's house.

by venturing upon a new line of foreign policy acquired a fleeting popularity, which his far from ignoble personality seemed fitted for sustaining. The Court of this King could have little influence in the direction of strengthening or renewing that sentiment of loyalty which had constituted so important an element in the feelings, it may be said in the moral life, of the preceding age. It was necessary to seek for inspiring examples in a wider range; but among the great nobles of this age we meet with few examples of that genial grandeur which commands the admiration and good-will of a whole generation, and exercises so beneficent an influence upon the spirit of its literature. Exceptions become less rare as the life of the sections of society in immediate contact with the Court begins to rise from the depths to which it had sunk in the dark days of the ascendancy *and* of Somerset. The accession and (after its early difficulties *Charles I.* had been overcome) the marriage of Charles I in this respect brought about a more marked change for the better. Only a short-sighted judgment will dispute the effect attributable —especially in such a period as this—to the personal examples of virtuous lives led on thrones; and it would be idle to set down the devotion with which so many fortunes and lives were sacrificed in the cause of King Charles I as *The loyalty* the result of an abstract principle only. The genuine love *of the* *dramatists.* of art and letters which both Queen Henrietta Maria and her husband cherished and manifoldly displayed, no doubt contributed to the growth of a personal loyalty which would have been impossible in the previous reign; and the Queen's patronage of the stage went in some points beyond that of her predecessors[1]. But the diatribes of embittered contemporary partisanship will not induce us to ignore the great influence of the personally virtuous lives of King Charles and his Queen upon the moral consciousness of large sections of society. This influence is cordially

[1] See Fleay, *History of the Stage*, pp. 313-4. Henrietta Maria, who had taken over the Queen of Bohemia's players, openly attended their performances at the private theatres. The great Elisabeth had displayed her dancing at Court, and Anne had appeared in Masques by Jonson and Daniel. But Henrietta Maria, by performing in a Pastoral Play, directly challenged the censure of the Puritan adversaries of the stage.

acknowledged by a dramatic poet, the natural nobility of whose principles seems to me recognisable beneath a facile and yielding disposition [1].

But loyalty, and those impulses of personal attachment which are cognate to it, are, except in the hour of supreme conflict, incapable of absorbing in themselves even the moral sentiment of a nation, or even that of a class. In the period under review, the life of English society, more especially in those spheres with which the stage was more immediately associated, needed some more universal and more enduring principle for the strengthening and sweetening of its current. Very manifestly, religion had been on the one hand so persistently mixed up with the designs and the conflicts of political life, and on the other so obstinately identified with theological dogma and the disputations of the Churches, that it had inevitably come to be regarded by many men and women as a thing outside their inner life. In England the religious belief of the nation had been nominally fixed by authority; the forms of religious worship had been ordered by rules for which, though confessedly human in origin, it was sought to establish an immutable fixity; and the authoritative maintenance of this system in its entirety was an abomination in the eyes of those who conscientiously struggled against a part of its ordinances. At the same time, many highly-cultivated minds were no doubt to be found, more particularly in the regions of clerical and academical life and of seclusion from the glare of the world, who derived a deep as well as eager religious inspiration from hopes and endeavours pointing towards the nobler, more refined, and more spiritual Anglicanism of the future. In the front, however, or on the surface of the life of society with which the theatre was in contact, those men and women were most observable upon whom the ecclesiastical disputes and conflicts of the times can have exercised little other effect beyond that of deadening the inner significance

The drama and the national religion.

---

[1] See Shirley's *The Lady of Pleasure* (act iv. sc. 3):

> 'Truth, and your love of innocence, which shine
> So bright in the two royal luminaries
> At court.'

of the religious forms handed down to them. I cannot dwell here upon this the most important aspect of the age ; but it is clear that in those regions of society where life was most rapid and diverse a strange oscillation was common between indifference and unthinking superstition.

Unbelief and super- stition. In times when we may well credit the dramatist's assertion that unbelief was fashionable[1], an eager acceptance of delusions as to supernatural agencies and forces obtained even among enlightened thinkers and reckless men of the world. Much of this was no doubt due to the slow advance of the light of science ; but it is obvious that the light of higher and kindlier influences had necessarily become obscured in so turbid a moral atmosphere as that which hung over so many European countries in this period of civil and religious wars. Our dramatic literature only too faithfully reproduces that void in the religious life of many to whom it addressed itself which a helpless credulity sought in vain to fill ; nor is it possible to ignore the melancholy fact that but few of its writers expose, while others pander to, or at least alternately satirise and encourage [2], the prevalent superstitions connected with the belief in magic and witchcraft, and in cognate monstrous creations of fear and ignorance. But it is perhaps well not to carry too far generalisations for which it is impossible here to exhibit the basis ; while as a matter of fact no such basis exists for a serious discussion as to how much and how little those among our dramatists [3] who had sought a refuge in the Church of Rome owed to this step in the general system of their morality, or in its particular impulses.

Social vices of the Court of Too frequently ignoring the most powerful influences towards a great and noble activity, and unwilling to show

---

[1]   ' To be of no religion
Argues a subtle moral understanding,
And it is often cherished.'
                    Fletcher, *The Elder Brother* (act v. sc. i).

[2] Of the former two categories no examples need be quoted; but the recklessness of the times in such matters is illustrated by the circumstance that Fletcher draws Peter Vecchio in *The Chances* as a self-avowed impostor, while Sulpitia in his *Custom of the Country* is a witch of real, though not irresistible, power.

[3] Massinger and Shirley—not to mention Jonson's temporary conversion.

that deference to the inner law which implies moral self- *James I*
control, the society whose life is largely reflected in the drama *and its*
of this period sank into a turbid depth of intrigue and of *ings.*
secret vice and crime.   It may reasonably be questioned
whether the life of those classes which are most exposed to
the temptations of opportunity, wealth, and pleasure, has in
any age of English history been more deeply polluted than
in that of James I ; and much of this corruption survived
into the days of his successor.   The Court of James and its
immediate surroundings were a hot-bed of social iniquities ;
the story of its foul secrets is like the touch of the poisoned
glove or handkerchief—the symbols if not the actual instruments of some of its darkest crimes.   Mutual suspicion
became in these spheres of life a necessary condition of
social intercourse [1] ; every one was plotting, in company or
on his own account ; and where several combined, one
was usually found ready to betray the rest.

Happily for the social life of this country, the capital has *The grow-*
never—even in the days of its most rapid and most *ing import-*
astonishing growth—actually succeeded in absorbing all *arrogance*
the best forces of the nation.   For good or for evil, London *of London*
has never become to England what ancient Rome and
modern Paris have been to the empires or republics of
which they have formed the centres.   In the period of
which I am speaking may, however, be noticed signs of an
unhealthy tendency towards a consummation which later
ages have combated with imperfect success.   In the reigns
of Elisabeth and James I London increased on a scale
which appears for divers reasons to have seriously alarmed
the governments of both these sovereigns ; the advance
of luxury and splendour in the life of the wealthier classes
continued to enhance the attractions of their place of abode
or frequent resort ; and the practice of spending part of
the year—the Season as we call it—in London grew more
general with those who came in search of the excitement

---

[1] ' Every man in this age,' says Dion in Beaumont and Fletcher's *Philaster*
(act i. sc. 1), ' hath not a soul of crystal, for all men to read their actions
through : men's hearts and faces are so far asunder, that they hold no
intelligence.'

and pleasure, as well as with those who came for the business, of Michaelmas Term[1]. The frequent progresses of Elisabeth and James I, however burdensome they may have proved to those who had the honour of providing for the royal entertainment, must have tended in some measure to decentralise the luxury of social life; still, London became more and more the seat of pleasure, magnificence, and display, the chosen home of art and literature, and likewise the resort of idleness and the haunt of dissipation. Charles I's intelligent love of architecture, sculpture, and painting did much to increase the importance of the capital, while he sought in vain to counteract by legislation the growing tendency to non-residence on the part of country-gentlemen. The sense of contrast between town and country therefore begins to be a characteristic sign of *reflected in* the times. Nowhere could it be expected to exhibit itself *the drama.* more prominently than in the drama. Its pictures of manners came more and more to confine themselves to reproductions of London life, or of country life as it presented itself to the eyes of a Londoner. Those refreshing glimpses of the greenwoods and the meadows, the homesteads and the orchards of old England, which charm us in an earlier dramatist like Greene and in Shakspere, a true child of the Midlands, become rarer and rarer in his successors; and the rural life of the stage approaches that conventional fiction into which it afterwards altogether hardened. The country and its charms are growing as unfamiliar to the town-wits as they are to the citizens' wives in Beaumont and Fletcher's comedy who sentimentally marvel 'how fine the fields be! what sweet living 'tis in the country!' and charitably conclude as to their rural fellow-creatures, 'Poor souls, God help 'em, they live as contentedly as one of us[2].'

Its fa- From much the same point of view the social types of *vourite* the drama of this period seem to succeed one another with *social types.* constant iteration. From the country come the long family

---

[1] See Middleton's comedy of that name.
[2] *A King and No King* (act ii. sc. 2). And cf. D'Avenant's *The Wits* (act ii. sc. 1).

of gulls who foolishly flutter towards their own destruction; in the country dwell the broken-down gentlemen whose estates are falling into the hands of successful city merchants or grasping city usurers.   The decay of country-gentlemen is the frequent theme of invective or lament [1]; and Master Plenty who 'eats his venison with his neighbours in the country,' instead of presenting his game to the usurer [2], or Master Aimwell who 'keeps a warm house i' the country amongst his tenants' and takes no pride in travelling to London with a footman and a page [3], are almost exceptional types.   Town life seems to be regarded as the normal state of existence, or at least as one compared with which all others are dull and tame.   Again and again attention has been directed in the preceding pages to the contemptuous scorn with which our comic dramatists [4] refer to the crude fruits of University breeding; the only school of knowledge which they recognise is the school of life in town.   Here the true centre of society is the Court; next to it comes that profession in which alone money can be made in a gentlemanly way [5]; an Inns-of-Court-man is almost the equal of a courtier in the eyes of the admiring world [6], and the stage and he are mutually indispensable to one another [7].   The physician's profession is beginning to come into honour [8]; but he, like the clergyman, only holds a subordinate rank.   Trade is still shut out from society; and the endeavour of citizens to make their sons gentlemen

---

[1] So in Massinger and Brome.

[2] Massinger's *The City Madam* (act i. sc. 2).

[3] Shirley's *The Witty Fair One* (act i. sc. 2).

[4] Middleton especially. Yet oddly enough the tone among undergraduates seems to have struck a foreign observer such as the Duke of Pomerania-Stettin (see his *Diary, u.s.*), as that of would-be men of the world. He visited Cambridge in 1602, and considered that the students kept more dogs and hounds than books.

[5] 'There is no virtue,' says Quintiliano in Chapman's *May-Day* (act i`, 'can scape the account of baseness if it get money, but gaming and law.' At the Inns of Court (*vide infra*) money was to be got in both ways.

[6] 'A fashion,' says Liladam in Massinger's *The Fatal Dowry* (act v. sc. 1), 'which any courtier or inns-of-court-man would follow willingly.'

[7] 'Your Inns of Court men,' we read in Earle's *Microcosmography* (1628), 'were undone but for him' (the player); 'he is their chief guest and employment, and the sole business that makes them afternoon's men.'

[8] See Massinger's *A Very Woman*.

is the surest mark of an envious inferiority[1]. In this gentlemen's world noble birth still enjoys an undisputed prerogative ; and no measure is observed in pouring contempt on the mushroom growths of yesterday, the knights of recent creation[2].

Prominent features in the manners of the times.

Exclusiveness and refinement are by no means not synonymous terms ; and the outward features of the habits and manners of town society in this period ill correspond to its tendency to self-glorification. The extravagant fantasticality of the Elisabethan age survives in some of the usages of its successor ; but no feature of its social life is more long-lived than its coarseness. The English love of drinking was as yet by no means on the decline[3] ; and the grossness of the national idea of a good dinner was still such as to require many a generation for its gradual refinement[4]. The vice of gaming defied the regulations by which the attempt was

[1]   'We that had
   Our breeding from a trade, cits, as you call us,
   Though we hate gentlemen ourselves, yet are
   Ambitious to make all our children gentlemen.'
                     Shirley's *The Gamester* (act i. sc. 1).

[2] This familiar topic might be illustrated from an endless number of passages ; some have been collected by Collier in a note to Field's *A Woman is a Weathercocke* (act iii. sc. 3).—The old and the new kinds of knights are very succinctly contrasted by Middleton in his *A Mad World, my Masters* (act i. sc. 1) : 'My grandsire, Sir Bounteous Progress, is a knight of thousands, and therefore no knight since one thousand six hundred.' The name Progress is in itself excellently chosen, though from a different point of view it would have well suited some of the knights of King James I.—Altogether, there was hardly ever a less correct statement of its kind than that of Sparkish in Wycherley's *The Country Wife* (act iv. sc. 1), where the habit of making knights the favourite fools of the stage is reprehended as an innovation.

[3] Illustrations are here again too numerous to need citation ; but see *e. g.* Piso's answer to the question 'Are the Englishmen such stubborn drinkers ?' in Fletcher's *The Captain* (act iii. sc. 2), or Adorni's assertion (imitated from *Othello*) :   'Your English
   .   .   .   .   .   .   to say truth
   Out drinks the Dutch, as is the common proverb :
   The Dutchman drinks his buttons off, the English
   Doublet and all away'—
in Glapthorne's *The Ladies' Privilege* (act iii).

[4] Holdfast's description in Massinger's *The City Madam* (act ii. sc. 1) is hardly a caricature. 'The pheasants drench'd with ambergris' may be cited as a typical delicacy of the age. That criticism was beginning to exert itself on the important subject of dinners may, however, be gathered from Beaumont and Fletcher's *The Woman-Hater* (act i. sc. 2).

made to repress it in its favourite haunts[1], and assumed
a new form in connexion with a national sport which
became one of the amusements of the gay world, under
conditions not highly conducive to refinement[2].   The
passion for dress raged with unabated vigour in both sexes,
and gave full employment to the artists devoted to the
invention of 'strange and exquisite new fashions[3].'   From
the 'neat historical shirts[4]' and 'religious petticoats[5]'
whose fresco-embroideries must have recalled the robes of
Queen Elisabeth in all her glory, and from the Spanish and
Danish and Italian novelties of James' reign, the mode went
on to that elegant artificiality of costume which is so well
known to us from the portraits by Vandyke.   The future
had in store audacities and absurdities far less bearable;
but to the Puritanism which even in such externals
was intent upon a change to graver and simpler ways,
the love-locks which enraged Prynne[6] might seem to
typify the height of effeminacy in male fashions, and the
patches of taffety which graced the cheeks of the ladies[7] of
Henrietta Maria's Court, to mark the final banishment of
female modesty.   More noteworthy in the same connexion
is the ardour with which Englishmen in this period sought
to excel in the most frivolous and least manly of accomplishments[8], and the eagerness with which they welcomed

*Extrava-
gance,
artificiality,
and effemi-
nacy in
dress.*

---

[1] *Viz.* the Inns of Court.   See the note in Dodsley (vol. vii, 1825) on a
passage in W. Rowley's *A Match at Midnight* (act i. sc. 1).

[2] See Shirley's *Hyde Park.*

[3] See the Tailor in Fletcher's *The Fair Maid of the Inn* (act iv. sc. 2).

[4] Fletcher's *The Custom of the Country* (act ii. sc. 3).

[5] Mayne's *The City-Match* (act ii. sc. 2).

[6] Cf. Shirley's *The Bird in a Cage* (act i. sc. 1).—The long hair worn by
men in the previous generation is satirised by one of the dramatists themselves.   'I know many young gentlemen wear longer hair than their
mistresses.'   Middleton's *More Dissemblers besides Women* (act i. sc. 4).

[7] Cf. Glapthorne's *The Ladies' Privilege* (act iii, *ad in.*).   'Pretty!' says
the Queen in Suckling's *Aglaura* (act i. sc. 1), looking upon a flower in one
of her ladies' hands; 'is it the child of nature, or of some fair hand?'   ''Tis
as the beauty,' is the reply, 'of some faces, *art's issue only.*'

[8] See Fletcher's *The Island Princess* (act i. sc. 1), where the 'Portugals'
and Spaniards are said to seek to excel in riding, the French in courtship,
and 'the dancing English in carrying a fair presence.'   And cf. Massinger's
The Emperor of the East (act i. sc. 2) for a description of the effeminate life
of a 'young courtier.'

*Importa-
tion of
foreign
fashions.*
the foreign fashions, introduced by the travelled gallants.
The knowledge brought home from abroad was, we may
guess, often little better worth the bringing than that with
which Onos returned to Corinth, after putting a girdle about
Europe [1].   Forks and toothpicks [2], and cognate inventions
of foreign ingenuity, were the trophies of travels which in
the Tudor days had enriched the English world with very
different novelties from beyond the sea.

*Partial
advance of
refinement
in man-
ners.*
The amusements of life were at the same time to some
degree refined and civilised by contact with foreign usages
and manners ; and more especially, though the world was
ready to suspect what was harmless [3], it can hardly be doubted
that in the days of Henrietta Maria English society learnt
something of innocent gaiety as well as of doubtful lightness
from France.   A certain abatement of fierceness is moreover perceptible in the conduct of social life, which is by no
means to be confounded with the tendency, noted above, to
effeminacy of manners.   If it was complained that men had
begun to wear poniards instead of swords [4], there was good
reason for this besides the imitation of foreign fashions.
The practice of duelling, after being reduced to an elaborate
system of procedure, was gradually, if not falling into disuse,
more or less accommodating itself to respect for the law ; and
even on the stage it was beginning to be denounced as
a social enormity [5].

[1] See Fletcher's *The Queen of Corinth* (act ii. sc. 4).
[2] Cf. Fletcher's *The Chances* (act i. sc. 2); Shirley's *The Ball* (act i. sc. 1).
[3] See Shirley's *The Ball.*
[4] Fletcher's *The Custom of the Country* (act ii. sc. 3).
[5] The subject is a rather complicated one. The practice of duelling is
visited with censure in Fletcher's *The Queen of Corinth* (act iv. sc. 4 ; see
Conon's speech), and in his *The Little French Lawyer* (act i. sc. 1 ; see
Cleremont's speech ; cf. however *ante*, vol. ii. p. 721, *note*), but from Glapthorne's *The Ladies' Privilege* (act iii, Adorni it would seem that the ' Land's
laws ' were contemned when this play was written (by 1640). In
Massinger's *The Guardian* (act ii. sc. 1 the practice is vehemently deplored,
and in D'Avenant's *The Just Italian* (act iv, *ad fin.*) spoken of as unreasonable. From Webster and W. Rowley's *A Cure for a Cuckold* (*temp.* Charles I)
it would appear that duels between Englishmen had to be fought out of the
country—on Calais sands. (Cf. Earle's *Microcosmography*, No. xlii, *A Surgeon* ;
and see the curious reference to the folly of interposing between duellists, *ib.*
No. xlvi, *A Sceptic in Religion*).   In Thomas Heywood and William
Rowley's *Fortune by Land and Sea* formal arrangements are made for a

Of the two influences, indeed, which contribute most *Imperfect* directly to refine and soften the manners of an age, we find *educational culture.* evidence enough in this period among the classes of society whose condition I am more especially seeking to illustrate. But the social value set upon the higher culture which education supplies must have greatly varied even in those classes to which it was most readily accessible. When Shirley's Bombo describes ignorance as 'every day coming into fashion [1],' he is merely hazarding a joke against bad writing; but the passage may be taken as indicating deficiencies of a glaring character, if not of general occurrence. Letters had been encouraged by a long line of English sovereigns; but it is the spread of education rather than the example of patronage which makes a love of good literature a national sentiment. Probably even a more select public than that addressed by the sham pedlars in Fletcher and Shirley's *The Night-Walker* [2] would have preferred their literary wares to more nutritious food; and Calipso in Massinger's *The Guardian* [3] echoed the preferences of her betters in her commendation of antique romances. A nobler conception, in fine, of the relations *Unsatis-* between the two sexes, such as was in many individual *factory* instances brought into relief by the troubles and the trials *relations between* of the great conflict (Charles and his Queen, the Earl and *the sexes.* the Countess of Strafford, the Duke and the Duchess of Newcastle), would, if more universally prevalent, have largely contributed to purify and elevate the society of the preceding period. But we cannot shut our eyes to the

duel on Hounslow Heath; but this play was probably at last sketched under Queen Elisabeth. (A curious account of a contemporary series of Court duels, about the year 1633, will be found in Sir Henry Wotton's *Letters to Sir Edmund Bacon.*) The allusions to the systematic regulation of the art of quarrelling and duelling (which could not but lead to its gradual discontinuance), to the famous handbook of Coranza, and to professional swordsmen are very frequent; see *e. g.* Beaumont and Fletcher's *A King and No King* (act iv. sc. 3); Fletcher's *Love's Cure* (Priorato *passim*); Fletcher and Shirley's *Love's Pilgrimage* (act v. sc. 4); Massinger's *The Unnatural Combat* (act ii. sc. 2); and D'Avenant's play just cited (act iv).

[1] Shirley's *The Royal Master* (act iii. sc. 3). Cf. a similar sally (of a much earlier date) in Chapman; *ante*, vol. ii. p. 435, *note* 5.

[2] Act iii. sc. 3.

[3] Act i. sc. 2.

The women of the period. opposite influences, on which our dramatic literature furnishes only too copious a commentary. On this topic it will suffice to remark that there must have been much in the training of women to produce the effects so persistently illustrated by the dramatists. Undoubtedly, the education of women of the highest social class had signally advanced under Elisabeth and James; of this convincing proofs are to be found in the letters of the great Queen herself, and of several of the ladies whose names were prominent in Court circles about the beginning of the century—admirable examples both of handwriting and of composition. But it is manifest that the education of the large majority of women beneath the highest class was generally at the best confined to the hurried teaching of a few superficial accomplishments[1]; and the excessive demureness which was evidently demanded from girls and women of all classes, and of which the 'mannerly forsooth[2]' is the typical expression, points to an artificial system of training such as could not but be frequently productive of most disastrous results. The fetters were clasped so tightly that when cast off they were flung to the winds, frivolity, folly, and vice imposing in their place

[1] 'You've many daughters so well brought up, they speak French naturally at fifteen, and they are turned to the Spanish and Italian half a year after.' Middleton, *More Dissemblers besides Women* (act i. sc. 4). It may be observed that during the whole of the sixteenth and seventeenth centuries the instances are comparatively rare in England—and in Northern countries in general—of that type of the highly educated woman which was one of the most beautiful products of the Italian Renascence. This contrast has been pointed out by Gregorovius in his biography of *Lucrezia Borgia*; the exceptions to it are familiar, so far as England is concerned, to every student of the life and literature of the Tudor and Stuart periods, and would form one of the most delightful series in an ideal national gallery of portraits.

[2] Holyday's *Technogamia* (act i. sc. 2); and cf. Fletcher's *Love's Cure* (act iii. sc. 4), where however Clara is not precisely a type of maiden demureness. 'Forsooth' afterwards came to be regarded as a *bourgeois* phrase; see Sir R. Howard's *The Committee* (act i. sc. 1), and Mrs. Centlivre's *The Platonic Lady* (act iii. sc. 1). For the manners of fashionable ladies see Shirley's *Hyde Park*, if a direct kind of portraiture be desired. But I may remark that I have in the above illustrations thought myself justified in adopting Dyce's view that 'Shirley and his contemporaries, wherever their Scene is laid, generally make their characters think, and speak, and act like those that were moving around them.' (Note to *Dramatis Personae* of *Love Tricks*.)

the bonds of a new servitude. Under happier circumstances Queen Henrietta Maria might perhaps have proved better able to introduce together with more liberal manners more liberal principles of social intercourse ; but the age was too suspicious to welcome her efforts in this direction, and if (as seems probable) she sanctioned the foolish fashion of ' Platonic love [1],' not all of these efforts were distinguished by prudence. But if, with reference to the years during which she shared her husband's throne, we rightly despise the scandal that aspersed her fame, we may likewise refuse to accept as true the picture drawn by so many dramatists of the standard of female virtue prevailing in humbler spheres. And in any case, we shall prefer to refrain from hastily drawing invidious conclusions as to this or any other aspect of a past age. Our dramatists, we may well rest assured, might have found many noble models of female purity and virtue to inspire their creations, and we can only regret that they should have made so partial a use of the opportunities they possessed.

From these notes on the age and society in which the dramatists of this period lived and which their works illustrate, it is time to pass to the more special conditions attaching to the production, and in a certain measure affecting the character, of those works themselves.

The history of the theatre in the reigns of James I and Charles I is a subject on which it forms no part of my purpose to touch, except in so far as may be necessary in order to render more intelligible in some of its features the progress of our dramatic literature in this period. The stage of these times had no quarrel with the authority of the Crown, on which the regulation of its conditions of existence depended, although it incessantly waged a sort of petty warfare, which hardly ever came near assuming important proportions, against restrictions imposed on it in the name of the respect due to the Crown and its allies, and to good manners and morals in general. The existence

The stage under James I and Charles I.

---

[1] See on this subject the observations *ante* on D'Avenant's comedy of *The Platonic Lovers*.

of such restrictions, or the necessity of a recognition of the principle on which they were enforced, was not in itself regarded as a grievance ; nor could there be any mistake as to the benevolence of the despotism of such a Master of the Revels as Sir Henry Herbert [1], who looked upon himself as responsible for all the public amusements of the kingdom,— and in whom a little pedantry was hardly to be thought out of place.   The theatre of these times, in truth, had but one hostile power to dread, unless the Plague, which so frequently closed its doors [2], be regarded as a second.   But the enmity of Puritanism was inveterate and irreconcileable, and in the end to all intents and purposes destroyed for a time the activity of the stage.

Its relations with the King and the Royal Family.   From the Court the stage in the first two Stuart reigns received nothing but goodwill ; and it must be remembered that in this period, more absolutely than even under the last of the Tudors, the Court constituted the centre of the life of the upper classes in London.   Even under the great Queen, who had inherited the whole of the traditions of the Tudors, the remnant of the old nobility, and the after-growth of the new, had been something more than the dependants of the royal favour and of those whom it distinguished.   In the first and second years of James I's reign the principal companies of players, hitherto nominally attached to the service of great officers of State or noble-men of high distinction, were by virtue of royal patents taken into the service of the King, the Queen, and other members of the royal family respectively ; and the same was the case with the companies of children performers. The Lord Chamberlain's company (of which Shakspere and Richard Burbage were members) were, on May 19, 1603, patented as the King's Servants, which title had been already two years previously conferred on them during their visit to Scotland [3].   The Earl of Worcester's players were

---

[1] He administered his office from the beginning of 1622 till the outbreak of the Civil War.

[2] The theatres were closed on account of the Plague for at least five months in each year from 1606–10 ; and in 1608–9 for seventeen months consecutively.   (Fleay, *History of the Stage*, p. 167.)

[3] Fleay's *History of the Stage*, p. 188; cf. for the Privy Seal which pre-

in the same year taken into the service of Queen Anne[1],
and the Earl of Nottingham's, in 1607, into that of Henry
Prince of Wales[2].   On Prince Henry's death in 1612 the
services of his company were transferred to the young
Elector Palatine[3].   They continued to go by his name long
after his patronage could have been of any service to them
in return, until in 1632 they were provided with a new
protector, the infant Prince of Wales (afterwards King
Charles II)[4].   In 1610 and 1611 respectively Prince Charles
and the Princess Elisabeth likewise took players into their
service[5].   Of the two children's companies the Children of the
Chapel, whose title had soon after the opening of the new
reign been changed into that of the Children of Her Majesty's
Revels, were ultimately merged into the company known as
the Lady (Princess) Elisabeth's, and afterwards as the Queen
of Bohemia's servants; and the Children of Paul's seem to
have been superseded by a company afterwards merged in
Prince Charles' (the Duke of York's), and after the death of
his elder brother known as the Prince's Servants[6].   Thus,
before the middle of the reign of James I, five companies,
all officially connected with the royal family, had come to
constitute the chief bodies, or practically one subdivided
body, of actors in London ; and the same arrangement was
continued in principle under his successor, one of whose
first acts was to renew the royal licence to the King's
company of comedians, while Queen Henrietta Maria took

ceded the Patent by two days, Collier, vol. i. p. 334, and Hazlitt, *The English
Drama and Stage*, &c., p. 38.

[1] Fleay, *u. s.*, p. 191, where see the criticisms on the document *ap.* Collier,
u. s., pp. 336-7.   The Queen's Players attended her funeral in 1618, on
which occasion an allowance was made to each of four yards of black cloth.
(*Ib.*, p. 397.)

[2] Fleay, *u. s.*, p. 200 ; Collier, *u. s.*, p. 337, who quotes Gilbert Dugdale's
Time Triumphant (1604), for which see Nichols' *Progresses of James I*, vol. i.
pp. 408 *seqq.*

[3] Fleay, *u. s.*, p. 168 ; Collier, *u. s.*, p. 337 ; Hazlitt, *u. s.*, p. 44.

[4] Fleay, p. 312.   In 1629 King Charles I took them into his own service
as a second company, under the designation of the Company of the King's
Revels.

[5] Fleay, p. 168.

[6] Fleay, p. 165 ; and cf. pp. 184-8.   See also Collier, p. 339 ; and Hazlitt,
p. 40.

over that which had nominally served the Queen of Bohemia [1]. Already in 1603 the right had been withdrawn from members of the nobility of authorising the performance of plays in any part of the country [2]; and in 1615 a transitory attempt was made to licence, under the name of 'Her Majesty's Servants, of her Royal Chamber in Bristol,' a travelling company of players, who were prohibited from remaining in any one place more than fourteen days [3]. Thus, the general result of the establishment of an exclusive connexion between the stage and the royal family was a centralisation of control and influence, which in a very marked way affected the general character of our dramatic literature. The royal favour, which in times of difficulty might even be depended upon for bounties towards meeting the most ordinary professional requirements [4], was the first condition of prosperity, if not of existence; and the authority of the Crown could more directly and systematically than ever assume the control of the stage [5].

[1] Fleay, p. 312; cf. Collier, vol. i. p. 435; Hazlitt, p. 57.

[2] This is implied by the statute of that year, which repealed the Elisabethan statutes freeing from the penalties of vagrancy actors travelling in the country with a nobleman's licence. See Collier, vol. i. pp. 345–6.

[3] Collier, vol. i. p. 395. This was the company of which Samuel Daniel was appointed licenser; cf. *ante*, vol. ii. p. 618.—The ordinary companies must have often travelled in the country to eke out a subsistence, when the Plague was in London.

[4] Thus, in 1625, the King granted 100 marks to his players for 'apparel.' Collier, vol. i. p. 439; Hazlitt, p. 42.

[5] I have not thought it desirable to enter into a discussion as to the theatres actually open in London at different times during the period treated of in this chapter. No other English writer has examined this subject with so much care as Mr. Fleay, for whose conclusions I must refer the reader to the sections 'D' (Theatres) concerning the periods 1603–1614, 1614–1625, and 1625–1636 respectively, in his *History of the Stage*, pp. 201 *seqq.* The number of London theatres in occupation by performing companies seems to have generally varied from five to six; and of these the Globe (except during the period of its rebuilding after the fire of 1613) and the Blackfriars, from about 1610 onwards, were continually in the occupation of the King's men. The Red Bull, at the upper end of St. John's Street, Clerkenwell, is first definitely mentioned as a regular theatre in 1609. The Curtain, occupied by a succession of companies under King James, was closed in 1623; in 1629 its place was taken by the new theatre in Salisbury Court, which stood on the site of the Whitefriars theatre, closed in 1613, and was, like it, a private house. Thus, with the Fortune and the Cockpit (in Drury Lane), there were at the close of the period six houses; or, as Prynne says (see one of

Upon the whole, however, the exercise of this authority, *Legislation* whether founded on Parliamentary Statutes or on Orders in *and official* Council, and whether making itself felt through the regular *the stage.* official channel of the Master of the Revels or by direct personal interference on the part of the King, appears to have been sparing and judicious. In 1606 a general statute, directed against the 'jesting and profane' use of sacred names on the stage, imposed a distinct but perfectly legitimate restraint in a particular direction upon the licence of dramatists or actors[1]. To an examination from this point of view of plays for which a licence was asked for performance on the stage, and to a supervision of their actual performance, the attention of the Master of the Revels was therefore consistently directed; and the elastic authority of the High-Commission Court more than once interfered to stop what it regarded as instances of excess[2]. A more delicate task was that of preventing the theatre from trenching on the dangerous ground of political references or allusions. We cannot be surprised that in the reign of James I, who instructed his son to appreciate a King's obligation to Heaven 'for making him a little God to sit on his throne[3],' an ordinance should have been passed against ' representing any modern Christian King' in plays on the stage[4]. The date and the occasion of this Order is unknown ;

the Dedications of his *Histrio-Mastix*, 1633), ' all the ancient Divells Chappels are five in number,' to which, he complains, a sixth has ' now' been added.

[1] Collier, vol. i. p. 356; Hazlitt, p. 42. This act inflicted a penalty of £10 on every person who should 'jestingly and profanely' use the name of the Trinity, or of any of its persons, in any stage-play or other entertainment.

[2] The introduction by the actors of offensive oaths into Jonson's *The Magnetic Lady* (1633) subjected them to censure from the High-Commission Court (cf. *ante*, vol. ii. p. 377, *note*). Sir Henry Herbert, as already mentioned, entered with conscientious assiduity upon the task of expurgatory supervision, which seems to have commended itself to the punctilious temper of his mind. It has been seen how well pleased he was to approve of Shirley's *The Young Admiral* (1634), in contrast with other plays with which ' as performed of late ' he had been obliged to find fault (*ante*, vol. ii. p. 109). King Charles I's interference with his Bowdlerisation, in the same year, of D'Avenant's comedy of *The Wits* has already been noted; see *ante*, p. 172 *note*).

[3] *Religio Regis*.

[4] See Secretary Conway's letter of August 12, 1624, complaining of the

but it furnished a convenient safeguard against the most objectionable kind of theatrical personality. Offences were occasionally committed against it, and led to more or less prompt measures of interference [1]. Unwelcome political or personal allusions in particular passages required a nicer judgment; and we have incidentally noted occasions which show some latitude of liberty to have been allowed, as well as others which led to unpleasant consequences for authors or actors [2]. In general, the theatre could hardly

representation of the King of Spain, Gondomar, &c., in *A Game at Chess* (cf. *ante*, vol. ii. p. 527, *note*, and see Collier, vol. i. p. 428). Since Conway writes that 'His Majesty remembers well, there was a commandment and restraint given,' &c., the ordinance may be assumed to have been issued in the reign of James.

[1] The most noteworthy case is that just referred to, *viz.* Middleton's *Game at Chess* (1624), which had passed the eye of the Master of the Revels before it was interfered with. Either this Order, or more general considerations of propriety, led to other interpositions of authority. In 1604 a tragedy, not extant, on the subject of the conspiracy of Gowry, after being twice performed, was in danger of being prohibited; perhaps this play occasioned the Order in question. (See Chamberlain's letter to Winwood, *ap.* Collier, vol. i. p. 344, and Fleay, *English Drama*, vol. ii. p. 329.) In 1608, a scene in Chapman's *Byron's Conspiracy*, where the Queen of France was unbecomingly introduced, gave offence, and perhaps also the introduction of Queen Elisabeth into the play. (Cf. *ante*, vol. ii. p. 422.) In 1617 an attempt to bring upon the stage a representation of the death of the Marshal d'Ancre was nipped in the bud by the vigilance of the Privy Council. As the responsibility of the Marshal's death was assumed by the young King Lewis XIII (cf. Schmidt, *Geschichte Frankreichs*, iii. 440), this proceeding was directed by obvious political caution.

[2] Among the latter, the case of *Eastward Ho* in 1605 will be especially remembered (cf. *ante*, vol. ii. p. 311).—In 1631 Sir H. Herbert refused to license a play by Massinger, because of its introduction of 'dangerous matter, as the deposing of Sebastian King of Portugal.' This play has now been discovered in Massinger's *Believe as You List* (*ante*, pp. 8—where see as to a supposed previous indiscretion by Massinger—and 31).—On the production of Shirley and Chapman's *The Ball* (1632; cf. *ante*, p. 107) the Master of the Revels objected to the manner in which 'divers lords and others of the Court' were personated in it, but was satisfied by promises of omissions and not 'suffering it to be done by the poet any more.'—A peculiar case s that of a play called *The Spanish Viceroy* (attributed without evidence to Massinger), which is supposed to have contained allusions to Gondomar. and which the players in 1624 ventured to act without licence, whereupon they were forced to make a humble apology and promise not to venture on any other such offence. (Cf. vol. ii. p. 530, *note*, and *ante.* p. 9, *note.*)—The summary interference of civic authority with Tailor's *The Hog hath lost his Pearl* (Collier, vol. i. p. 369; cf. *ante*, p. 157) can hardly be regarded as anything but a special proceeding against an offence committed under exceptional

expect to be allowed a liberty of speech concerning matters of State which the government of James denied to the public at large [1]; and if such a dramatist as Massinger ventured upon occasional political criticism, he took care to leave it voiceless to any but understanding ears. Charles I's goodwill to the stage did not, however, prevent him in one instance at least from personally assuming the functions of censor towards a play of this very writer [2]; and when soon afterwards he again complained of an indiscreet political reference in a play, we meet with almost the only recorded instance of insubordination on the part of the players—a remarkable illustration in little of the signature of the times at large [3].

circumstances, and which had no political or religious party significance.— A more serious apprentices' riot occurred in March 1617, when the Cockpit theatre was attacked and damaged. (See Collier, vol. i. pp. 384 *seqq.*)

[1] See the Proclamation against excess of lavish speech of matters of State (probably drawn up by Bacon himself) in Spedding's *Letters and Life of Bacon*, vii. 156.

[2] In 1639 Charles I ordered a passage in a play by Massinger called *The King and the Subject*, which contained a dangerous expression about an intention to   ' raise supplies what ways we please
                    And force you to subscribe to blanks '—
to be changed as ' too insolent.' (Cf. *ante*, p. 9.)

[3] At the time when Charles I was projecting a second expedition against the Scotch in 1640, he took occasion personally to complain to the Master of the Revels of a play acted at the Cockpit which ' had relation to the passages of the King's journey to the North.' The actors failed to comply with the prohibition which ensued ; but do not appear to have been treated with severity (Collier, vol. ii. pp. 30-1).—In general the hand of the royal authority cannot be said to have rested heavily on the poor player in the first two Stuart reigns, and considering the conditions of the times, the Crown must be held to have exacted no greater deference than in self-respect it was bound to demand. That it could not altogether prevail, like-wise lay in the nature of the case.—(From Bazin's *Théâtre Chinois, Introduction*, p. xxx, we learn that the Chinese Penal Code prohibits the introduction on the stage of an emperor or empress, or of any famous prince, minister, or general of the past. But the scenes in which such personages appear are said to be among the favourites of Chinese audiences, and the prohibition is regarded as to all intents and purposes obsolete.—In illustration of the fact that neither Stuart nor other kings are necessarily the worst despots in matters theatrical, the reader may be referred to the account of the changes and suppressions ordered by authority in plays represented at Paris during the (old) Commune, in Th. Muret's *L'Histoire par le Théâtre*, vol. i. pp. 88 *seqq.*—at a time when the theatrical censorship had been abolished.—When at a later date the French armies overran Europe, they carried with them the sensitiveness of all French *régimes* as to the influence of the stage. During the French occupation of Hamburg in 1807, Lessing's *Minna von*

For the rest, so far as legislative or Crown action was
concerned, the theatre was, until the time of its suppression,
protected by the royal goodwill against the growth of
the Puritan hostility to which it was exposed. That it was
protected to good purpose would seem proved, if by no
other evidence, by the growing numbers of those who
adopted the actor's profession[1], as well as by the fortunes
gained by its leading representatives[2]. The authorities of
the City had ceased to assert themselves after the fashion
in which, no further back than 1589 or 1590, they had
silenced the Children of St. Paul's, because of performances
in which ridicule had been cast upon ideas or opinions
commanding the sympathy of early Puritanism[3]. In the
reign of James I, indeed, the City is on one occasion—in 1617
—said to have been successful in preventing the establishment of a new theatre; but neither the efforts of the
Corporation nor the turbulence of the apprentices succeeded
during the next few years in diminishing the number

*Slightness
of its effect
on admi-
nistration
or legisla-
tion.*

of those already in existence[4]. The complaints of the
inhabitants of Blackfriars, renewed in 1631 and 1633,
and their prayers for a removal of the playhouse as
interfering with traffic and religious worship, fell on deaf
ears[5]. Although in the famous declaration of the year
1618 concerning Lawful Sports to be used on Sundays, and
on the occasion of its still more famous revival in 1633, stage-
plays were excluded from the entertainments authorised
for that day[6], this omission cannot be viewed in the light

Barnhelm had to be performed with the part of Riccaut de la Morlinière
left out. See F. L. Schmidt's *Denkwürdigkeiten*, vol. i. p. 212; and cf. *ib.*,
vol. ii. pp. 12 *seqq.* for similar instances.

[1] Cf. Collier, vol. i. pp. 375-6, and Richard Nichols' epigram *In Fuscum*
there cited.

[2] Shakspere died as a man of substance in the country; but it is clear
that Richard Burbage was accounted rich in London.

[3] Cf. Collier, vol. i. p. 272, and the passage in Heywood's *Apology for Actors*
cited there.

[4] Collier, vol. i. pp. 380 *seqq.*, has a document purporting to establish the
intervention of the corporation; as to the riots, see Fleay, *History of the
Stage*, p. 310.

[5] Collier, vol. i. pp. 455 (where the petition of the inhabitants to Laud as
Bishop of London is given) and 476; cf. Fleay, *u.s.*, pp. 344 and 346.

[6] Collier, vol. i. pp. 396, 476.

of a concession to Puritan opinion. The first statute passed after the accession of Charles I had enforced the same prohibition of interludes and common plays, while permitting other lawful sports and pastimes, on Sundays[1]. In the same year, 1625, the Lord Mayor and Aldermen took occasion from a visitation of the plague to represent to the Privy Council the desirableness of the entire suppression of the playhouses in the vicinity of the City[2]; but with the cessation of the pestilence the actors returned to London as usual. In the country, where their visits were by no means always welcome when they came from a plague-stricken city, they were doubtless at times exposed to rough treatment, and on one occasion—in 1633—the Mayor of Puritan Banbury is found committing six unlucky players to prison as 'wandering rogues[3].'

The hostility of the Puritans to the theatre, however, found many other ways of expressing itself. The institution was 'a very great beam, an exceeding great beam[4]' in their eyes; and if it was 'a necessity' and a fashion with them 'to rail against plays' among one another[5], it was a duty of conscience to seek to convert words into action. Compared with the theatre, such minor 'profane exercises' as 'playing at barley-break, moulding of cockle-bread[6],' and even baiting of bears, might seem to sink into insignificance. And an uneasy feeling must at all times have prevailed in the neighbourhood of Blackfriars and elsewhere in London, that perverts might be made in the way exemplified in *The Muse's Looking-Glass*[7]. The strong draughts administered to the apprentices of the City by Thomas Heywood

Its intensity and bitterness.

---

[1] Collier, vol. i. p. 434; Hazlitt, p. 59.
[2] Collier, vol. i. p. 438.   [3] *Ib.* pp. 473–4.
[4] Jonson's *Bartholomew Fair*, act v. sc. 3.—How bitterly even highly-cultivated Puritans resented the attitude taken up against them by the stage may be seen from such a passage as that in Mrs. Hutchinson's *Memoirs of Colonel Hutchinson* (ed. 1885, vol. i. p. 115), where she says that they were 'not only the sport of the pulpit, which was become but a more solemn sort of stage, but every stage, and every fable, and every puppet-play, belched forth profane scoffs upon them . . . and all fiddlers and mimics learnt to abuse them, as finding it the most graceful way of fooling.'
[5] Jonson's *The Alchemist* (act iii. sc. 2).
[6] Brome's *Covent Garden Weeded* (act iv).   [7] *Ante*, p. 135.

and his fellow playwrights could hardly fail to leave behind them cravings which would refuse to be satisfied by the spectacle of the Lord Mayor's pageant on its annual progress through Cheapside. And, though doubtless the dramatists loved to paint in too glaring colours the opposition of City dames to the principles as well as to the domestic comfort of City fathers and husbands, the spirit of ambition or of curiosity may have stirred many a female heart to sigh for a good place out of the common throng at a Court masque, or even ' in a private box ta'en up at a new play [1] '; since it seemed almost against kind that a lady should not have ' leave to see the theatre twice a week [2].'

Its short-sightedness. The motives which prompted the Puritan hatred of the theatre were not ignoble ; the spirit which had produced that hatred was in its origin a lofty spirit ; but the manner in which it manifested itself was shortsighted, and the result to which it tended was one which not unfrequently awaits a policy of total abstinence. The Puritans were in earnest in their desire to cleanse and elevate the life and the morality of their age, but they failed to recognise the true answer to the question whether it was well to banish from society the operation, under its own natural conditions, of a form of literature well adapted if ' well used' to ' instruct to good life, inform manners,' and 'no less persuade and lead' society, than they sought to ' threaten and compel it [3].' To such a question the Puritans would probably have replied, that dramatic literature, as it presented itself on the stage, could not be with advantage used, because of the evil admixture contained in it. But it was precisely herein that their error lay. They made no attempt to reform the stage ; what they desired was to annihilate it.

Its powers and its prospects. As a matter of course, this endeavour could not for a long time be carried on except in a tentative way. How could the action of the legislature be expected to suppress an institution enjoying the constant favour of the Crown and

---

[1] Massinger's *The City Madam* (act ii. sc. 2).

[2] Massinger's *The Guardian* (act i. sc. 2).

[3] I borrow the noble language of Jonson, in a passage of a more general and in part different bearing, in his *Discoveries.*

the nobility,—though, as Gifford says, actors and spectators little knew that they were 'sporting on the verge of a precipice,' when the gossips in one of Jonson's later comedies hopefully appealed to the possibilities of Parliaments—if Parliaments there were to be—in the future [1]. And the temper of the House of Commons was gradually growing such, that its ear might well lend itself to supplications to which it would have refused to listen in the days of Elisabeth. What could be done, was mainly that the civic authorities in London should be on the alert in using every opportunity of narrowing and reducing the range of activity enjoyed by the theatre, and that country mayors and magistrates, animated by a similar spirit, should let no opportunity pass of letting vagrant actors feel their power. What could be said and written, and could thus contribute to influence the public mind in the direction of the suppression of stage-plays, belonged to a wider sphere of effort, and to one more largely open to the adversaries of the detested institution.

An examination of publications directed against the stage is fortunately not indispensable in a sketch of the history of our dramatic literature ; and I may therefore, with a single exception, content myself with a mere reference to the works of this description preserved from the period under notice. The mantle of Gosson and Stubbes and of their fellow-publicists [2] descended to a series of successors. In 1616, the year of Shakspere's death, the author of a treatise apparently written in the favourite Theophrastic manner of the times, undertakes to prove the assertion that 'player is now a name of contempt'; and furnishes an odd compound of attacks upon the profession and its irreligious practices, and of remarks on the art of acting which betray some experience of it on one or the other side of the curtain [3]. In

Anti-theatrical literature, 1616–1625.

---

[1] 'Well, they talk we shall have no more parliaments, God bless us! but an we have, I hope Zeal-of-the-land Busy and my gossip Rabbi Troubletruth will start up, and see we shall have painful good ministers to keep school and catechise our youth, and not teach them to speak plays and act fables of false news in this manner, to the super-vexation of town and country.' *The Staple of News* (act iii *ad fin.*).

[2] Cf. vol. i. pp. 458 *seqq.*

[3] See Hazlitt, p. 228 *seqq.* The title of the whole publication is *The Rich*

1625, *A Short Treatise of Stage Playes* was presented to the first Parliament of Charles I, with a request that upon view of the treatise the matter of stage-plays might be once more taken into consideration, and that 'by some few words added to the former Statutes' plays might be 'restreyned for euer hereafter[1].' Parliament, however, was contented with the act already noticed prohibiting the performance of plays on Sundays; and it is not till some years later that we come across the next, and the most famous, literary effort of Puritan hostility against the stage in the famous *Histrio-Mastix, the Players Scourge, or Actor's Tragaedie*, by William Prynne (published in 1632, though dated 1633).

Prynne's Histrio-mastix (1632).

This *magnum opus* of Puritan enthusiasm and learning—for it exhibits both qualities in a very extraordinary degree—appears to have been the fruit of seven years' labour. Its author, a young barrister of Lincoln's Inn, whose first published treatise is dated 1627, but who seems to have begun his book against stage-plays some three years earlier, may have been encouraged in his undertaking by the current of opinion in that Society[2]. Unlike their brethren in the Temple and at Gray's Inn, the Benchers of Lincoln's Inn had prohibited the 'disorderly Bacchanalian Grand-Christmasses' which it was customary to celebrate by dramatic or quasi-dramatic entertainments. To them therefore in the first instance, to the students of the Inns of Court, too long

---

Cabinet Furnished with Varietie of Descriptions, by T. G. — Gainsford perhaps, according to Mr. Hazlitt's conjectural query.

[1] See Hazlitt, p. 231 *seqq.* This pamphlet, which is extremely learned, developes seven 'reasons which proue Stage playes to be unlawfull': their heathen origin. their impious or abominable subjects, the vices of players (of which the assumption by men of women's apparel is first, as offending against Deut. xxii. 5), the participation in sin of which spectators are guilty, the evil effects of plays, the censures passed upon them by ' all orthodoxall Protestantz of all ages and times which maintayned the generall doctrine of the Catholike Church,' as well as by Papists, Parliament, the Civil Law and eminent heathens, and finally the judgments inflicted by God upon players and beholders, from the death of King Philip of Macedonia to fatalities which attended the fall of a playhouse at London in 1583, and a Jesuit performance at Lyons in 1607.

[2] He is said to have been influenced in his theological opinions by the well-known Puritan divine Dr. John Preston, who held the preachership at Lincoln's Inn from 1622 to his death in 1628.

known as the patrons of stage-plays, in the second, and
finally to the Christian Reader in general, he dedicates his
work. It is no light shaft which he directs against the object
of his wrath ; for the book consists of more than a thousand
closely-printed small quarto pages—as why should it not,
when the play-books which it denounces are occasionally
growing 'from Quarto into Folio,' and 'Shackspeers Plaies
are printed in the best Crowne paper, far better than most
Bibles.' Prynne's treatise is accordingly as solid as it is
elaborate,—the work of an indefatigable reader who never
fails to give chapter and verse for every one of the thousands
of quotations constituting the bulk of his materials, who
disposes his arguments in regularly arranged groups (grimly
distributed into Parts, Acts, and Scenes), and who puts each
argument forward in regular syllogistic form. Occasionally
a 'Chorus' of reflexions is introduced, and a 'Catastrophe,'
with a long quotation from the Jesuit Mariana and a short
passage from St. Augustine, concludes the whole. The tone
of the work is in general dry and calm ; but the author is
capable of rising to eloquence, as in the final exhortation in
act v of the Second Part. In the choice of the arguments
themselves, as will be seen from the brief sketch of the book
appended below the text [1], there is nothing new ; but they

---

[1] The following is the course of the argument of *Part I*:

Stage-plays had their original from the Devil (act i. sc. 1) ; were invented
and practised by his instruments ('Idolatrous Infidels and the deboisest
Pagans'), (sc. 2) ; are therefore necessarily sinful and unlawful unto Christians (act ii) ; they are the pomps and vanities of this wicked world which
Christians renounce in baptism (*Chorus*). They are unlawful, because their
style and subject-matter are scurrilous and obscene (act iii. sc. 1), bloody
and tyrannical (sc. 2), heathenish and profane (in the oaths which they
introduce and the vices and villanies which they represent), (sc. 3), false
and fabulous (sc. 4), often impious, sacrilegious, and blasphemous (in their
misuse of the Sacred Name especially), (sc. 5), most satirically invective
against persons and offices, especially against religion and religious Christians (here the objection is waived aside that it is not against persons but
against their vices that plays direct their satire), (sc. 6), idle, frothy, superfluous and unprofitable, 'as vaine as vanity it selfe' (sc. 7). They are sinful
and utterly unlawful to Christians, in respect both of their actors (witness
the Fathers, Marcus Aurelius, &c., and 'two penitent reclaimed Play-
Poets,' *viz.* the author of *The Third Blast of Retrait from Playes and Theatres*,
1588, and Stephen Gosson), (act iv. sc. 1), and of their spectators (no argument to be drawn *per contra* from the circumstance that 'perchance some

are nowhere else developed with anything like the same fulness; and for the historian of the drama Prynne's treatise

few exorbitant histrionicall (but far from good) Divines, at leastwise from good Christians, may sometimes attend Theaters,' or that 'some puny un-converted Christian Novices may be occasionally drawne unto Stage-playes'), (sc. 2). They are likewise so in respect of their concomitants, *viz.* hypocrisy (all acting is dissimulation), (act v. sc. 1), obscenity and lasciviousness (sc. 2), gross effeminacy (sc. 3), extreme vanity, &c. (sc. 4), the nature of the characters acted (heathen gods, devils, &c.), (sc. 5), the ordinary apparel of the performers, which is womanish (sc. 6), and costly and lewd (sc. 7), the lascivious dancing (sc. 8) and songs (sc. 9) and music (sc. 10) introduced into them, and the profuse lascivious laughter which they provoke (sc. 11). They are so moreover from their pernicious effects, *viz.* the 'prodigall mis-pence of much precious time' (act vi. sc. 1), the 'prodigall vaine expence of money or estate' (from 2*d.* to sometimes 4 or 5*s.* day by day, 'if Coach-hire, Boate-hire, Tobacco, Wine, Beere and suchlike vaine expences be cast into the reckoning'), (sc. 2); besides which they foment divers sinful lusts (sc. 3), actual sin (sc. 4), corrupt the minds and vitiate the manners of both actors and spectators (sc. 5), produce sloth and idleness (sc. 6), luxury and drunken-ness (sc. 7), banish modesty and shamefacedness (sc. 8), teach treachery, cozenage and deceit (sc. 9), 'cruelty, fiercenesse, brawles, seditions, tumults, murthers and the like' (sc. 10), 'idle, frothie, scurrilous, lewde, prophane discourse' (sc. 11), indispose men to religious duties and thus render in-effectual religious ordinances (sc. 12), call forth antipathy to the practical power of grace and holiness (sc. 13); 'inamor' men with sin and vanity and harden them in their sins (sc. 14), 'effeminate' actors and spectators (sc. 15), 'incorporate' men into 'lewde, deboist, ungodly company' (sc. 16), draw them on to atheism, heathenism, and gross idolatry and profaneness (sc. 17), cause a manifest breach of all God's Commandments (sc. 18), draw God's fearful judgments upon their composers, actors, and spectators and upon 'those Republicks that tolerate or approve them' (sc. 19), and 'eternally damne men's soules' ('a fruit, a consequent with a witnesse, which should cause all Players, all Play-poets, all Play-haunters to looke about them'), (sc. 20). Act vii contains the authorities against stage-plays 'marshalled in seven distinct squadrons,' *viz.* Canonical and Apocryphal Scripture (sc. 1), 'the whole primitive Church both before and under the Law and Gospel' (sc. 2), Councils, Synods, and Canonical Constitutions (sc. 3, which fills 113 pages by itself), ancient Fathers of the Church (sc. 4), modern Christian writers (including Petrarch, Wicliffe, Æneas Sylvius, Mr. John Calvin, Martin Bucer, Peter Martyr, Matthew Parker, Bellarmine, and Dr. Thomas Beard in his *Theatre of God's Judgment* (second edition, 1631)—110 being nominally mentioned, and the whole array estimated at 'above 150 moderne Protestant and Popish authors of all sortes'), (sc. 5), heathen writers and philosophers (including Plautus), (sc. 6), and Pagan and Christian States and Magistrates (sc. 7). The *Chorus* points out how the two champions of Stage-plays, Lodge and Heywood, 'cannot withstand these all-conquering troopes.' However, in Act viii the author proceeds to the refutation of apologetic objections, *viz.* that plays are not prohibited, but rather approved and commended by Scripture (sc. 1), that they were tolerated and applauded as innocent, pleasant, and honest recreation by furnishes an ample repository of much useful learning. It is to be observed that his acquaintance with the stage-plays of his own times was obviously of the most limited description. He states that on his first arrival in London he had 'heard and seene foure severall Playes, to which the importunity of some ill acquaintance drew me whiles I was yet a novice'; and in one passage he refers to a reflexion upon Puritan attacks against the stage made in a play produced at the opening of the new theatre (at Whitefriars). But he never quotes, or otherwise appeals to, illustrations from the English drama of his own or any other period. As to 'professed printed Play-Champions,' he observes that he only knows of two, both 'scribbling hackney Players'— *viz.* Lodge in his *Play of Playes* and (Thomas) Heywood in his *Apology for Actors*; and to the arguments of the latter he addresses himself at length. The treatise is intended to make good a conclusion—and nothing short of it—in favour of the total suppression of stage-plays; and from this point of view the whole of the argument is conducted.

Prynne's treatise, as is well known, led to his being summoned before the High-Commission Court and Star- *Its consequences to the author.*

Greeks and Romans (Heywood), (sc. 2), that they are not only commendable, but necessary in a commonwealth for solemnities and for the recreation of the people (Heywood), (sc. 3), that they are lawful as ancient and 'frequented by many, yea most' (Heywood), (sc. 4), that they contain much good history, counsel, poetry, wit, and learning (sc. 5), that they are as good as sermons and that many learn as much good at a play as at a sermon ('Oh blasphemy intollerable,' as already previous authors have exclaimed), (sc. 6), that (as was scurrilously observed at the Whitefriars) nobody but Puritans objects to them (this section includes the vindication of Puritanism referred to in the text and is the most interesting passage of the book).— The comparatively brief *Part II* draws the Conclusions which result from the above (here there is a *lacuna* in the Cambridge University Library copy) : the writing of stage-plays is unlawful to Christians (act ii. sc. 1), the profession of actors is infamous (the distinction made in favour of academical plays is untenable), (sc. 2), and unlawful (sc. 3) ; likewise the beholding of plays (act iii). Act iv refutes various objections, *viz.* why should a play not be written, acted, and seen acted if it may be read ; plays have their educational uses ; they explain and impress upon the mind 'dark histories'; as men go to see a play without evil purpose, what harm can there be in it? practically plays do no harm to many. Act v concludes the whole with an exhortation couched in terms of earnest, almost passionate eloquence, terminating with the discourse of Mariana and the passage from St. Augustine noted in the text as the 'catastrophe' of this 'tragedy.'

Chamber, which condemned his book to be burnt, and the author to be expelled from the Bar and his Inn, to be deprived of his Oxford degree, to stand in the pillory, to lose both his ears, to pay a fine of £5,000 to the King, and to be perpetually imprisoned. It is not quite clear on what grounds this sentence (which was renewed three years later) was passed—but there can be little doubt of the special reason which determined it. This appears to have been found, not in passages admitting of a very direct application to the existing Government and to the authorised ritual of the Church, but in a reflexion added to the Table of Contents. The reflexion in question, which accompanied the heading as to the practice of women-actors (mentioned in the text as 'lately introduced in a Play personated in Blacke-friers Play-house'), seemed intolerable to official and to loyal eyes. For, about the time when the book was published— according to one account on the day before, according to another but shortly afterwards—the Queen and her ladies had themselves acted in a Pastoral at Whitehall [1]. There is no reason for supposing Prynne to have intended any personal reference ; and no credit need be attached to the assertion of Whitelocke, that Laud (whom Prynne certainly regarded as the chief author of the proceedings against him) represented the passage in this light to the King. But the coincidence was one which could not fail to attract public attention ; nor can any doubt remain as to the correctness of the contemporary statement which attributed to it both the enquiry and the rigorous sentence which followed [2].

[1] This pastoral appears to be that mentioned in a letter from John Pory to Sir Thomas Puckering of September 20, 1632, as one ' penned by Mr. Walter Montague, wherein her Majesty is pleased to act a part, as well for her recreation as for the exercise of her English.' Its title was *The Shepherd's Paradise*, and Sir John Suckling described it as perfectly unintelligible. See Maidment and Logan's *The Dramatic Works of Sir Wm. D'Avenant*, i. 283, 285.

[2] See Collier, vol. i. pp. 465 *seqq.* and Mr. C. H. Firth's notice of Prynne in vol. xlvi of *The Dictionary of National Biography* (1896) ; and cf. *Documents relating to the proceedings against William Prynne in* 1634 *and* 1637, edited by S. R. Gardiner for the Camden Society, 1877.—Whitelocke's statement that the Queen's pastoral was performed six weeks before *Histrio-Mastix* was published, cannot be said to be in itself absolutely conclusive.

Prynne was not placed in the pillory till May, 1634; but the excitement caused by his offence and its treatment found a loud echo in contemporary dramatic literature already during his twelve months' imprisonment before sentence, as well as later, both before and after his second pillorying[1]. In the theatrical world it would seem as if Prynne's attack had produced a feeling of anger not unaccompanied by consolations, in addition to that derived from the punishment of the offender. For the honour of the Queen had, so to speak, been identified with the cause of the theatre, and the hand of authority had fallen heavily upon the representative Puritan who was regarded as the assailant of both[2]. During the brief period, however, which remained for the stage before its existence was suppressed by the outbreak of the Revolution, the plays produced upon it show an unmistakeable improvement in tone—an advance which may doubtless in part at least be attributed to Prynne's invective[3].

Its effect upon the theatre.

But the evil fortune which the adversaries of the stage desired for it was soon to avenge the sufferings of their

The stage overwhelmed by the Revolution.

[1] See the Dedications to Heywood's *The English Traveller*, and his *A Maidenhead well Lost*, and the Prologue to their Sacred Majesties at Hampton Court (Pearson, vol. vi. p. 342); Jonson's *The Magnetic Lady* (act i. sc. 1 and act iii. sc. 4) and *The Sad Shepherd* (act i. sc. 2); Fletcher and Shirley's *The Night-Walker* (act iii. sc. 4); the mock Dedication of Shirley's *A Bird in a Cage;* the Dedication of Ford's *Love's Sacrifice;* and a passage in Mayne's *City-Match.*—So late as 1649 an unscrupulous wit attempted to revenge the stage upon its now powerful enemy by publishing a mock *Retractation* by the author of *Histriomastix,* which the latter had to declare ' a mere Forgery and imposture ' by means of a public ' vindication.' Both *Mr. William Prynn his Defence of Stage-Plays, or a Retractation of a former Book of his called Histrio-Mastix,* and Prynne's denial, are printed in Hazlitt, *u. s.—The Theatrum Triumphans . . . an Answer to Mr. Prins Histrio-Mastix,* said to have been written by Sir Richard Baker, was published in 1670.

[2] See above, p. 91, as to the splendid masque, *The Triumph of Peace* (written by Shirley', offered by the Inns of Court to the King and Queen in 1634 as a demonstration against Prynne's publication.

[3] Cf. *ante,* p. 173, as to some of D'Avenant's later pre-Restoration plays. Other plays of this period are beyond cavil on the score of impropriety— above all Denham's *The Sophy,* which was unusually successful. Cf. *ante,* p. 148.—In 1639 a personal attack upon an alderman of the City of London in a play performed at the Red Bull, according to Collier, vol. ii. p. 26, led to an Order in Council against the actors.

champion. In 1639 the Scottish rebellion had in reality triumphed over the King; in 1640 he had once more—after eleven years of non-parliamentary government—summoned a Parliament and dismissed it less than a month after its meeting ; in the summer of that year a cessation of arms had been agreed upon with the Scots[1]; and in the month of October the High-Commission Court had held its last sitting at St. Paul's, and the people had torn up the benches to the cry of ' No Bishops! no High-Commission !' By November the Parliament—the Long Parliament—had met; and Prynne, after his triumphant return to London from his Jersey prison, was preferring a complaint to it concerning his treatment, and collecting evidence against Archbishop Laud. Well might the insignificant recipients of the royal favour, the members of a despised but hated profession, feel that their day also had come ! ' Monopolers are downe,' says one of the two actors who in a mock Dialogue published in 1641 [2] lament their ' sad and solitary conditions' (great sickness, and in some quarters the plague, had broken out in London[3], and the play-houses must have been temporarily closed), ' Projectors are downe, the High Commission Court is downe, the Starre-Chambre is down, and (some think) Bishops will downe, and why should we then that are farre inferior to any of those not justly feare, least we should be downe too.' This gloomy forecast was to be speedily verified. At Christmas 1641–2 only a single play was acted at Court, and both the King and the Queen were absent from the performance[4]. On the last day of February Charles I left the neighbourhood of London ; and soon afterwards, in the Prologue to a play licensed in April—Shirley's *The Sisters*[5]—we hear that

[1] As to the temporary stoppage of the performances of Beeston's Company at the Cockpit, in May, 1640, for performing a play which had not been licensed, and which contained allusions to the King's projected Scottish expedition, see Collier, vol. ii. p. 30.

[2] *The Stage-Players Complaint*, printed in Hazlitt, pp. 253 *seqq.*

[3] Forster, *The Grand Remonstrance*, p. 184.

[4] See Fleay, *History of the Stage*, p. 351. The play was Beaumont and Fletcher's *The Scornful Lady.*

[5] Cf. *ante*, p. 118. The Dedication of this play contains a striking picture of the desolation which soon befell the drama and its patrons.

'Our poet thinks the whole town is not well
.   .   .   .
London is gone to York.'

The Register of the Master of the Revels closes in June with the ominous entry of a play called *The Irish Rebellion*, and 'here,' he adds, 'ended my allowance of plays, for the war began in August, 1642[1].' So far as the stage was concerned, the catastrophe came rapidly enough; for on September 2 was published the Ordinance of the Lords and Commons, which after a brief and solemn preamble commanded 'that while these sad causes and set-times of humiliation do continue, public stage-plays shall cease and be forborne[2].'

Theatres closed Sept. 2, 1642.

Of the broken remnants of life preserved by the theatre in the dark days which now ensued I shall speak very briefly at the beginning of my next chapter. Here it may be well to add a few words as to the condition in which our dramatic literature stood when overtaken by this eclipse, and as to some of the internal causes which had helped to bring its fate upon it.

In justice to the dramatists and to the stage of this period, it should be remembered that their difficulties were by no means confined to the task of attracting the public on which their prosperity depended, while seeking to conciliate the official authorities and to withstand a swelling tide of powerful hostility. A national theatre and drama have at all times to contend against influences not the less dangerous because they are to some extent themselves dramatic in origin. Among these standing hindrances is to be reckoned the competition of entertainments which borrow from the drama all the elements in it most directly attractive to the hungriest of organs, the eye—of others which pride themselves on their aristocratic or fashionable exclusiveness—and of yet others which revel unabashed in the frank breadth of their popularity. From the Masques

Circum-stances affecting dramatic produc-tivity in this period.

Competi-tion of other enter-tainments.

[1] Collier, vol. ii. p. 36.
[2] *Ib.*; Hazlitt, p. 63; Gardiner, *History of the Great Civil War*, vol. i (1886), p. 17.

and Triumphs at Court and at the great houses of the
nobility, with their Olympuses and Parnassuses built by
Inigo Jones and filled with goddesses and nymphs in the
gold-spangled vestments designed by his all-inventive
brain, to the City pageants and the fire-works and sea-
fights on patient Thames,—from the jousts and barriers at
Whitehall and Hampton Court to the allegorical devices at
the Inns of Court and the Latin plays at the Universities,—
down even to the brief but thrilling theatrical excitements
of Bartholomew Fair and the ' Ninevitical motions [1]' of the
inanimate drama,—rivals innumerable tempted away the
public of these times from the true Thalia and Melpomene.

*and of
foreign
actors and
actresses.*
And as the period under review approached its close, the
English theatre had even to compete with the more
legitimate rivalry of foreign performers. The unfavourable
reception in 1629 of the French *actresses* filled the author of
Histrio-Mastix with pious gladness ; but a second French
company (which has been supposed to have consisted of
men only) was in 1635 established for a time in the very
precincts of the palace. These French competitors were
immediately afterwards followed by Spanish ; and though
the notices of their presence happen to be contemporaneous
with others of payments made by the King's orders to
English actors, these payments were in part very tardy
settlements of his obligations [2].

*Progress of
the art of
acting.*
Over such permanent or temporary rivals the English
drama was indeed certain to prevail, so long as it maintained itself as a living branch of the national literature,
and so long as competent interpreters brought its products

---

[1] Middleton's *Blurt, Master Constable* (act i. sc. 1).

[2] For details as to the visits of French actors, unsuccessful in 1629, but in
1635 settled for a time in the royal ' manage-house' as a theatre, see Collier,
vol. i. p. 451, and vol. ii. pp. 2 *seqq.* As to a performance by Spanish actors
in December 1635, see *ib.* p. 4.—The *filles Françaises de la Reine* who acted
at Whitehall in the same month (cf. Fleay, *History of the Stage*, p. 319) are
no doubt correctly concluded by Collier to have been French ladies in
attendance upon the Queen.—In this year the King appears to have settled
some debts to various companies of English players—one debt among them
of from nine to eleven years' standing.—The jealousy of the English stage
against the French players may perhaps have given rise to a curious passage
in ridicule of French acting in Glapthorne's *The Ladies' Privilege*, printed
1640 (act ii).

freshly home to the public at large. The noble art which, if true to its best ends, stands by the side of dramatic poetry as Automedon stood in the chariot by the side of Achilles, had in the great days of our drama animated its mightiest and sweetest creations. 'In this time,' says a dramatist of the next period, 'were poets and actors in their greatest flourish; Jonson and Shakespeare, with Beaumont and Fletcher, their poets, and Field and Burbadge, their actors [1].'   And other evidence, which need not be held to be invalidated by the perennial tendency of mankind to extol the past at the expense of the present, shows that in the period 'before the wars' the art of acting at least maintained itself on the level to which it had been brought by Shakspere's associates and contemporaries, 'Burbadge, Heminge, and others of the older sort [2].' Gradually, however, the profession of the actor had become to a greater extent than formerly dissociated from that of dramatic authorship, though they were still (as in the instance of Field) occasionally combined ; but this tendency towards a division of labour was, as in the case of most highly-developed pursuits, inevitable and in many respects advantageous. In the dramatists of this period—from Jonson *e. g.* at one end of the series to Shirley at the other —we find signs of a discriminating appreciation of artistic merit in actors. And the 'quality' itself was doubtless encouraged by the interest which it excited [3], by the esteem which the conduct of some of its most prominent members secured [4], and by the profitable returns which its pursuit

[1] R. Flecknoe, in his *Short Discourse of the English Stage,* printed 1664, quoted by Collier in his *Memoirs of the Principal Actors in the Plays of Shakespeare* (Shakesp. Soc. Publ., 1846), p. 211.

[2] See James Wright's *Historia Histrionica,* an interesting tract in the form of a dialogue on the history of the stage, printed in vol. xii of Dodsley's *Old Plays* (1780), and in vol. i of Mr. R. W. Lowe's edition of Colley Cibber's *Apology* (1889).

[3] Thus it was customary, already in the days of Alleyn and Kemp, for money to be staked in wagers on particular actors, 'that is the opinion of certain judges they would exceed particular rivals.' Collier, *Memoirs of Actors,* p. 42.

[4] 'All these companies,' says Trueman in *Historia Histrionica,* after enumerating the principal houses of the period before the wars—the Blackfriars and the Globe (the King's), the Cockpit or Phoenix in Drury Lane (the

might under now well-established conditions ensure[1], to set that high value on itself which often helps to create and maintain the prosperity of a profession. Few could hope to end as munificent benefactors of the nation, like Edward Alleyn ; but unless troublous times arrived, none were condemned to the oppressive fear that it would be their lot to live or to die without a fair measure of esteem from those whose esteem they prized. And when the troubles actually came, most of the actors whom their years permitted, instead of slinking into Alsatia, 'went into the King's army, and, like good men and true, served their old master' in a different capacity ; and more than one of them fell on the field of honour[2].

The progress of the actor's art, as there is every reason to believe, kept pace with the esteem in which its members were personally held. Actors learnt to value their own dignity, and to pay a corresponding respect to the works which it was their task to interpret. Plays no longer suffered at their hands for the benefit of the groundlings; and the stage was purged from the 'barbarism' which in the days of Tarleton, and even in those of Kemp, had permitted popular favourites, instead of 'speaking to their co-actors in the scene,' to 'hold interlocutions with the audience[3].'

Queen's), the Private House in Salisbury Street (the Prince's Servants), the Fortune near Whitecross Street, and the Red Bull at the upper end of St. John's Street—'(the two last mostly frequented by citizens, and the meaner sort of people), got money, and lived in reputation, especially those of the Blackfriars, *who were men of grave and sober behaviour.*'

[1] Already in *The Returne from Pernassus*, Part ii. act iv. sc. 3, Kemp tells the two Cambridge students who seek instruction from him and Burbage, 'you have happened upon the most excellent vocation in the world for money.' The system of shares gave a fixed proportion of profits, according to agreement, to all the players except the hired men ; and was carefully observed in matters of detail. See Webster and Dekker's *A Cure for a Cuckold*, act ii. sc. 3, and Mr. Hazlitt's note. In Massinger's *The Picture* (act ii. sc. 1) the purchase of a share is treated as a step necessary to any one becoming an actor.

[2] *Historia Histrionica.*—The esteem in which the actor's art, when worthily exercised, was held by thoughtful men, is illustrated by Sir Thomas Overbury's *Character* of *An Excellent Actor* (*temp.* James I).

[3] See the curious passage in Brome's *The Antipodes*, act ii. sc. 2. There is, it must be allowed, a certain force in the excuse which Letoy there advances on behalf of the old favourites of the populace, that they—

One very peculiar usage of the English stage, to which *Women's*
parts acted
by boys. this period still adhered like its predecessors, cannot be passed by in the present connexion. Nothing leaves so strange an impression on the reader of a large number of the plays of this time—including in particular those of Beaumont and Fletcher, and many that have been dealt with in the present chapter—as the remembrance of the fact that the women's parts in them were still invariably filled by boys. The general history of the drama cannot be said to furnish any complete analogy to this practice, and it was foreign to that modern national drama—the Spanish—with which it is in this period most interesting to compare our own[1]. No doubt, little Solomon Pavy, Stephen Hammerton[2], young Field, and others, drew tears as readily as any actress has called them forth in later days ; and in juvenile

> ' Spent their wits, because
> The Poets were wise enough to save their own
> For profitabler uses.'

[1] It is quite unnecessary to go back to the practice of Eastern varieties of the drama ; but their divergence on this head is curious. On the ancient Indian stage women were ordinarily represented by women ; but it appears not to have been uncommon for men or lads to personate female characters, especially of a grave cast. (Wilson, *Theatre of the Hindus, Introduction,* p. lxviii.) Women have not been permitted to appear on the Chinese stage since the Emperor Khien-long admitted an actress among his inferior wives or concubines. (Bazin, *Théâtre Chinois, Introduction,* p. xlv.)—Grillparzer dwells on the essential difference between the Spanish and the contemporary English theatre—a difference redounding very materially to the advantage of the former—lying in the fact that in Spain the women's parts were played by women. They here even acted the parts of young men and boys (*e. g.* in *Las mocedades de Roland*). He observes, that the acting of female parts by men on the Greek and Roman stage furnished no analogy, inasmuch as the relations between the sexes were never the subject of the action. (This remark of course requires qualification, even with regard to Attic tragedy ; but the real difference consists in the conditions of the Greek theatre, the distance between spectators and stage, the use of masks, &c.) When Grillparzer goes on to observe that the performance of Shakspere's Juliet by a male actor is to be regarded as the depth of bad taste, while the effect of a double disguise of sex (as in the case of Viola) is quite inconceivable, he is in harmony with modern feeling, which prefers the conceptions of Shakspere's imagination to the usage of Shakspere's theatre. Some fine observations in this sense will be found in Lady Martin (Miss Helen Faucit)'s book *On some of Shakspere's Female Characters*, where she characteristically states that the one passage in *As You Like It* against which her feelings revolted was the epilogue (spoken by Rosalind as a woman, but unpoetical in tone).

[2] *Historia Histrionica.*

characters better critics than the citizen's wife in Beaumont and Fletcher's burlesque may have found reason for appreciating the delightful freshness of 'Master Moncaster's scholars[1],' and other performers of tender age. Moreover, habit counts for much in matters of this kind ; and in point of fact it was hardly more absurd for a boy to pour forth the sorrows of the Faithful Shepherdess, than it is for a female Orsino to sing the secret of men's enjoyment of life. And if it justly revolts us to find so much passion and so much wantonness proceeding from mouths which the freshness of youth, and the reverence due to it, should have kept undefiled, we should on the other hand remember that the moral objections to be urged against many of the plays of this period are diminished by the circumstance that up to a late date no women had a share in performing them.

Earliest appear- ances of actresses in England.   The Puritans objected to the acting of female characters on grounds all their own ; for they deemed it a plain offence against Scripture that one sex should don the apparel of the other[2]. Of course this was very far from implying any approval on their part of the performance of female characters by women. When, as already noted, in 1629 actresses made their first public appearance in England in the persons of certain Frenchwomen who, according to what had long been the custom of their country, formed part of a company that visited London in that year and acted a farce at the Blackfriars, they were very ill received[3], notwithstanding

---

[1] *I. e.* the Merchant Taylors' boys (see *The Knight of the Burning Pestle,* act i. sc. 1). So in Chapman's *The Gentleman-Usher* (act ii) Sarpego apprises the spectators of his masque :

> 'Women will ensue,
> Which, I must tell you true,
> No women are indeed,
> But Pages made for need
> To fill up women's places
> By virtue of their faces
> And other hidden graces.

It may be worth noting that a standard of age, low according to our notions, must have been usual for the heroines of seventeenth century love-plots.

[2] See the *Shorte Treatise against Stage-Playes* (1625) cited above.

[3] According to a letter which Collier says he discovered in the Archbishop's Library at Lambeth, and which he conjectured to have been addressed to Laud, they were 'hissed, hooted, and pippin-pelted from the stage.' (Vol. i. p. 452.)

which they reappeared a fortnight later at the Red Bull.
Prynne, in a marginal note to his *Histrio-Mastix*, denounced
them as ' monsters,' and their attempt as ' impudent, shame-
ful, unwomanish, graceless,' &c., &c.   The next French
company appears to have comprised no actresses [1]; and the
innovation was probably not repeated on the public stage
in England before the Restoration [2].   It is clear that the
expediency of the change was considered open to grave
doubts even by warm friends of the theatre [3], while for
some time after it had become familiar to the stage it
was condemned as an indignity even by liberal-minded
observers.   Perhaps the indifferent reputation of the agents
by whom it was carried out may have contributed to this
dislike of it; although it should at the same time be borne
in mind that in the masques at Court ladies had constantly
taken part as performers, and that there was no very broad
distinction to be drawn between Queen Anne's appearance
in such entertainments and Queen Henrietta Maria's and
her ladies' unlucky participation in a pastoral play—so

---

[1] Cf. *ante*, p. 248.

[2] That actresses were not unknown to the stage during the reign of
Charles I would appear from a passage in Brome's *The Court-Beggar*,
act v. sc. 2, cited by Professor Henry Morley in his *First Sketch*, p. 636.
This would contravene the supposition adopted by Dyce and approved by
Mr. Lowe (*Thomas Betterton*, p. 81), that Mrs. Hughes, Prince Rupert's
mistress, was the actress who performed the part of Desdemona on December 8,
1660, and thus (according to Thomas Jordan's *Prologue*) the first woman
that appeared on the English public stage.   Colley Cibber, in his *Apology*,
p. 76, roundly asserts that ' before the Restoration no Actresses had ever
been seen upon the English stage,' and the author of the *Historia Histrionica*
seems to imply the same thing.   According to a note of Messrs. Maidment
and Logan in their edition of D'Avenant's *Dramatic Works*, vol. iii. pp. 278-9,
' when *The Siege of Rhodes* was first presented to the public at Rutland
House in 1656, Mrs. Coleman, wife of Mr. Edward Coleman, performed the
part of Ianthe, which stamps her as the first female who appeared on
a public stage in this country.'—The repugnance which continued to be felt
against the practice after the Restoration is exemplified by Evelyn's note
(*Diary*, October, 18, 1666), in which he records that he ' now (and never
till now),' saw ' foule and undecent' women acting, and descants on the evil
results of such a practice.—The woman who speaks the Prologue to Shirley's
The Coronation must have been presented by an actor.   ' A French Prologue'
even in this sense is designated as a ' new trick ' in the Prologue to Randolph's
Amyntas (1640) ; female Epilogues had the precedent of *As You Like It*.

[3] See a curious passage in the mock *Mr. William Prynn His Defence of
Stage-Plays* (1649 , mentioned above, p. 270.

that, everything considered, the tardiness with which the practice was domesticated on the public stage in London remains surprising.

Scenery and costume. With reference, finally, to the outward aids of scenery and costume, a progress is again noticeable in the usages of this period as compared with those of the Elisabethan theatre. The history of the use of scenery on the English stage is in its earlier phases involved in a certain obscurity; but it seems established that by the close of the period under discussion plays had come to be performed in scenery more or less appropriate to the place of action, and that, as the scenery was moveable, actual changes of scene had begun to supersede the more primitive methods of indicating locality, and were at times resorted to with considerable frequency[1]. The possibility of an occasional change of scene was on the whole not calculated to increase the tendency of our English drama to break up each act into a large number of scenes, but rather to incline playwrights to take thought of accommodating the construction of their plays to the measure of the theatrical facilities at their disposal. On the whole, the entire system of stage-arrangements, which lent itself to a rapid and easy succession of scenes devoid of any real connexion with one another, must have remained essentially the same as in Shakspere's times, as might easily be shown by a survey from this point of view of the acting drama of the next generation[2].

[1] Collier, vol. iii. p. 175, states himself to be inclined to think that Malone was right, when he said that 'the first notice of anything like moveable scenes being used in England is in the narrative of the entertainment given to King James at Oxford in 1605, when three plays were performed in the hall at Christ Church.' With Collier's general notes on the subject should be compared Dyce's note to Fletcher's *Nice Valour*, act iv. sc. 1. Suckling's *Aglaura* (printed 1646) has been described as 'the first play acted in England with scenes, such decorations having been previously confined to masques.' (See Hazlitt's *Introduction* to Suckling's *Works*, p. xxxvii.) See also above as to Henry Killigrew's *Conspiracy.*— Sir Samuel Tuke's *The Adventures of Five Hours* (produced soon after the Restoration, and printed 1662) displays indubitable evidence of changes of scenery.

[2] It might prove quite worth while to pursue this topic, which is by no means devoid of significance, in its details. In a very suggestive paper by the late Julian Schmidt in the *Preussische Jahrbücher* for September, 1874, it is pointed out how the arrangement of the Shaksperean stage, in contrast to that of Corneille, made possible a succession of scenes unconnected with

The machinery of the stage no doubt borrowed some of the devices by which the masque-writers eked out the more imaginative part of their task; but, after all, there was not much of novelty made upon them in this respect [1]. In the matter of costume, again, the public theatre of this period cannot but have desired, so far as possible, to follow the example set by the entertainments that found favour at Court. Already in the Elisabethan age we have examples of an extravagant outlay upon theatrical dress; but appropriateness, together with effectiveness, was now beginning to be kept in view in the choice of it. Inigo Jones, whose vigorous sketches enable us to form some conception of the fantastic figures which dazzled and diverted Whitehall, has left us at least two illustrations of the costume of dramatic characters at a time falling, 'if not during the lifetime, very shortly after the decease of Shakespeare [2]'; and there is every reason for concluding that the stage of this period was fully alive to all that is really requisite in this often over-indulged branch of its economy.

Enough has been said to illustrate the nature of the outward conditions under which the dramatists of this period worked, and of the age for which they laboured and of which they formed part. Something might be added concerning the means which they employed for recommending

The drama-tists as appealing to their patrons.

one another, by the use of purely formal expedients. Socrates, after finishing his communication to his confidential friend, exclaims : 'But I see Critias coming ; let us depart' ; whereupon, 'enter Critias.' No doubt, a connexion of this sort is, as the eminent critic observes, only nominally 'organic.' It is, in fact, the result of an attempt to maintain that unity of place which, when combined with an observance of Corneille's rule of '*la liaison des scènes*,' seemed so commendable to Dryden. (See his *Essay on Dramatic Poesy*.)

[1] Ste-Beuve, in his *Port-Royal* (vol. ii. pp. 9-10, ed. 1867), gives an account of the extraordinary decorative inventions which in the winter of 1640-1 amused the French Court. But the chief mechanical device, of 'le Ciel ouvert, d'où Jupiter, ayant paru dans son trône, descendit sur la terre,' cannot after all have differed very greatly from the chairs in which Venus and other divinities descended on the early English stage, or ascended from it.

[2] See the plates accompaning Cunningham's *Life of Inigo Jones*, with Planché's remarks. (Old *Shakespeare Society's Publications*, 1848.) The sketches in question comprise Romeo in the Pilgrim's dress (act i. sc. 5) and the Jack Cade of the *Second Part* of *Henry VI*.

*Dedica-
tions.*
themselves to the favour of individual patrons and to that of
their chief patron the public.   But little would be gained by
scanning the tone and temper of Dedications, often of course
inspired by sentiments of gratitude, admiration, or friendship, but as often written for the customary fee [1] ; or by
*Prologues
and Epi-
logues.*
enquiring into the variations attempted in the Prologues and
Epilogues from the customary appeal to the goodwill of
the audience, accompanied by an assurance of the un-
objectionable character of the play.   A desire is manifest
in not a few of the Prologues and Epilogues of this period
to take a fuller advantage of the opportunity offered ; but
for one reason or another it is generally left unused.   Here
and there a mistaken comment is deprecated, or a charge of
plagiarism is warded off.   Few, however, of these dramatists
were so unwise in their generation as to attempt to ' rail '
their public ' into approbation ' like Ben Jonson, or modest
enough to furnish it with a candid estimate of their powers
like Jonson's faithful servant Brome.   It was not till the
next period of the drama that, especially in Dryden's hands,
the use of the Prologue was to be materially expanded and
intensified, and even that of the Epilogue rendered more
palatable or stimulating, by the introduction of elements of
not purely conventional rhetoric and wit.   A certain amount
of effort in this direction is already observable [2] ; but it fails
as yet to reach any generally notable height.   These aids
to success must not as a rule be taken for more than they
are worth—like those Commendatory Verses which were

---

[1] It appears from the mock Dedication of Field's *A Woman is a Weathercocke* that the ordinary fee for these complimentary efforts was 40*s*.

[2] Shirley refers to it in the Prologue to his *The Imposture* (1640) :
    ' Since that poetic schism possess'd the age,
      A prologue must have more wit than the play.'
Mayne in his *The City Match* (1639 ; act v. sc. 2) ridicules the
    ' buskin'd prologue, in
      A stately, high, majestic motion, bare ' ;
and Fletcher, in the Epilogue to *The Custom of the Country*, roundly declares :
    ' Why there should be an epilogue to a play,
      I know no cause.'
See for some valuable hints on the character of our Prologues and Epilogues
before, in, and after Dryden, and for much curious information as to stage-
usages derived from them, *A Study of the Prologue and Epilogue in English
Literature*, by G. S. B. (1884).

a pleasing fashion of contemporary, and especially dramatic authorship, but which in many cases have to be counted rather than weighed in order to determine their value [1].

An attempt will be made in the concluding chapter of this book to vindicate part of a position which in the present place it may be held permissible to assume. In the period following upon the Restoration, the signs of decline exhibited by our dramatic literature in the previous period were exchanged for signs of decay; and in still later periods this decay was succeeded by a not indeed unbroken, but to all appearance immoveable, stillness resembling that of death. This is therefore the point in my narrative, where it seems most fitting to cast a retrospective glance over the course which had been run and the results which had been accomplished by our dramatic literature in the period closing with the outbreak of the Great Civil War. All literary growths, it should never be forgotten, are continuous; and even such an event as the closing of the theatres during a decade and a half was unable to prevent the drama, so soon as they had re-opened, from linking its new course with that of its past. To be sure, like the Cavaliers who on their return in the days of King Charles II often found it to be no easy matter to recover possession of their estates, so the dramatic authors of the Restoration age were met by many new conditions which there was no ignoring or refusing. But it is one thing to shut one's eyes to the differences between a Shirley and a Wycherley, a Fletcher and a Congreve, a Massinger and an Otway,—and another to acknowledge that the influences and tendencies which resulted in decay were in many respects a consistent developement of those which had led to decline.

But in truth none but a narrow method of criticism could, in reviewing as a whole the history of the drama of Elisabeth's later years and of the reigns of James I and Charles I, remain contented with tracing the causes of its impending

Summary of the literary history of the drama in this period.

Nature of the change in the next period.

Obvious errors traceable in the course of our

---

[1] Chapman, in his *Byron's Conspiracy* (act iii), has a very striking passage, too long for quotation, on the inanity of commendatory tributes of this description.

*dramatic
literature
in the
period
under
review.*
downfall to the errors recognisable in its course. These
are written too clearly on the surface to need a lengthy
exposition. With a body of writers devoted to any particular branch of literary effort, as with an individual author,
excess of activity in any one sphere of production must inevitably lead to exhaustion. The soil will refuse to bear
an endless succession of good crops,—in time it will either
have to lie fallow, or it must continue to produce at its
*Its exces-
sive pro-
ductivity
in the
national
dramatic
forms.* peril. Our dramatic poets, instead of husbanding their
resources with ordinary prudence, expended them with
reckless prodigality. Every dramatic form commending
itself to the national genius and to the national sympathy
was essayed. None was left aside except those which
had virtually become impossible in our literature after the
Reformation, and those which had from the first been
purely artificial importations, favoured by the special aspirations or affectations of the Renascence. The mystery could
not in this country, as in Spain, give birth to the *auto*, and
the boundary-lines of the religious drama were only crossed
on a single occasion by Massinger [1]; for Shirley's attempt
of the same kind [2] hardly deserves serious attention. The
direct imitations of the Classical drama become few and
feeble ; Chapman, who naturally enough had a liking for its
forms [3], made no serious attempt to reproduce its essentials;
experiments like those of Daniel and Stirling at the close of
the Elisabethan age, and that of Milton in the evening
of his life, are but the diversions or the consolations of the
student or the recluse—mere isolated efforts of independent
and single-minded scholarship. The light and festive gaiety
of Italian and French farce, which connects the earliest self-
disportings of French comic genius directly with the first
literary labours of Molière, was never likely to establish itself
on English soil without the support of more solid adjuncts ;
nor could the French fashions and tastes of the days
of Henrietta Maria, any more than those of the days of
Charles II, effectively teach our English dramatists the art

---

[1] *The Virgin Martyr.*   [2] *St. Patrick for Ireland.*
[3] The *Nuntius e.g.*, who appears in several of his plays (*The Blinde
Beggar ; Bussy d'Ambois ; Caesar and Pompey*).

to trifle[1].   The forms which the drama of the period under
review left for its successors to essay were either bastard
imitations of uncongenial foreign growths, or loose and
fragmentary innovations.   With the exception of the opera,
the modern pantomime, and the modern farce—and a few
more ephemeral extravagances—the pre-Restoration drama
included every dramatic form which has proved capable of
domesticating itself in the national literature and on the
national stage ; and in many of these forms it exhausted its
strength by an excess of productivity.

But its choice of forms was not throughout directed by
a clear insight into the special capabilities of our national
dramatic literature.   Thus, in the former half of the seventeenth century our dramatists failed steadily to develope
that species which, if it had continued to be assiduously
cultivated, might have kept their art in full and vital connexion with the main tide of the national life.   Under
influences partly no doubt beyond their control, they
abandoned creative effort in the field of the national
historical drama, after Shakspere's immortal achievements
in it had indeed made rivalry difficult, but had not closed
the field itself against his successors.   They left this noble
province of their art—with few exceptions, such as Ford's
Perkin Warbeck—empty and deserted.   Only those who,
like Thomas Heywood or Samuel Rowley, at times purposely addressed themselves to the boisterous sympathies
of imperfectly cultivated audiences, resorted to the subjects
as well as to the forms of the old Chronicle History,—and
being by design old-fashioned were in effect retrogressive[2].

Certain national species neglected. The national historical drama.

---

[1] Thomas Heywood, certainly one of the most typically English among
the later Elisabethan dramatists, amusingly insists upon the solidity of the
English drama as one of its distinctive characteristics :

> 'Those [dramas] that frequent are
> In Italy and France, even in these days,
> Compar'd with ours, are rather jigs than Plays :
> Like of the Spanish may be said, and Dutch,—
> None versed in language but confess them such.
> They do not build their projects on that ground,
> Nor have their phrases half the weight and sound
> Our laboured Scenes have had.'
> Prologue to *A Challenge for Beauty* (printed 1636).

[2] Already Chapman in *A Humorous Day's Mirth* (printed 1599) is found

The higher kind of historical drama in general. Of the remainder, some ventured upon efforts akin to the endeavours of the national historical drama, in treating themes derived from the history of nations in moral or intellectual sympathy with our own, or connected with it by more than transitory ties of sentiment or opinion. But even here the mantle of the author of *Bussy d'Ambois* and *Byron* remained almost unclaimed, except now and then by Fletcher and Massinger; while the learning displayed by Jonson in his Roman tragedies lay like an incubus upon his successors. They preferred to feed their imaginations, now and then with the grave narratives of De Thou or Tacitus, but as a rule with the thinner material of romantic *Impoverishment of the tragic drama.* fiction. Italian, Spanish, and French intrigues, Byzantine and Persian court-plots, British legend tinged with the less sombre hues of French romance, supplied our tragic poets with a range of themes seemingly endless in their abundance, but really moving within limits the reverse of wide. The historical drama proper was dead; and tragedy was gradually passing towards the artificialities of the heroic plays of the Restoration and the dead calm of the pseudo-classical efforts of a still later period.

Comedy of character gives way to comedy of manners. In comedy the contact remained closer between the national drama and the national life. Here again Shakspere, though he had accomplished so much, had by no means closed the door against further progress. He, the unrivalled master of comic as of tragic characterisation, had only begun the work of creating an English comedy of character[1]. It was in this direction that the genius of Jonson achieved its greatest victories; but his consciousness of his aims interfered with his freedom of workmanship, and he lacked, especially in his later productions, the serenity, the buoyancy, the gaiety of mind which Thalia

ridiculing the ʻ old-fashioned plays,' in which the king sits ʻ having his wife, his counsel, his children, and his fool about him, to whom he will sit and point very learnedly as followeth :

> ʻ My counsel grave, and you my noble peers,
> My tender wife and you, my children dear,
> And thou my fool.'
>
> (Act i *ad in.*)

[1] Cf. vol. ii. pp. 272 *seqq.*

bestows as enduring gifts upon her chosen favourites. His
contemporaries and successors were less consistently intent
upon that study of men fortified by the study of books—
that comparative review, in a word, of interesting or mirthful human types—which alone can suggest new and true
varieties of dramatic character. With all their inventiveness,
and their advantages, in many cases superior to their predecessors' in the way of experience in particular spheres of
life, they were too prone to devote themselves to the invention of ingenious plots and diverting situations, rather than
to the exploration of the workings of human nature. Their
observation confined itself to the surface instead of pene-
trating to the substance ; and while assiduously depicting
numerous varieties of manners, they reproduced, with what
to us may well seem wearisome reiteration, a limited series
of types—to which only here and there Dekker, Chapman,
Middleton, or Massinger added one that might claim to be
called new. This series is indeed considerably wider than
that of the new Attic, and its heirs Latin and Italian
comedy, but it is far from inexhaustible, and its constant
self-repetitions must at times have produced the effect of
sameness even upon the generation whose tastes it sought
to satisfy [1].

The enormous fertility of our dramatic literature within
the range of the species to which it confined itself—a
fertility which increased with the progress of time and at
last attained to almost incredible proportions [2]—could not
but lead to a deterioration of style, or at all events, tend in
the direction of a rapidity of production with which excellence of style is rarely compatible. This is one of the
reasons, though by no means the only one, accounting for
the rhetorical note which is so characteristic of the tragic

*Tendency
to rhe-
torical
superfici-
ality*

---

[1]   ' Such a citizen
        As the plays flout still [*i. e.* constantly], and is made the subject
        Of all the stages.'
                Field, *A Woman is a Weathercocke* (act ii. sc. 1).

[2] According to *Histrio-mastix*, who appeals to information received from
' Stationers,' above forty thousand play-books had been printed within the
two years preceding the composition of the treatise. (See the *Epistle
Dedicatory to the Benchers of Lincoln's Inn*.)

as well as the comic drama of this period. Declamation for declamation's sake in serious passages, and railing for railing's sake[1] in comic, constantly take the place of attempts to stir profounder depths of emotion, or to probe more latent sources of anger or contempt; and the ease that attends the conditions of production revenges itself by a growing artificiality of manner—one of the surest signs *and con-* of decline. If, on the other hand, in those creations which *ventional* seem more directly inspired by the breath of poetic fancy, *artificiality* *in style.* we miss the airy lightness and the upward impulse of Shakspere's most enchanting creations—if even in their happiest moments the wings of their imaginative genius seem unable wholly to lift a Fletcher or a Shirley away from the surroundings of a less translucent atmosphere— this is not to be exclusively ascribed either to the restricted measure of their own powers or to the untoward force of circumstances. The curse of conventionality rested more especially on direct endeavours to rescue for the regular drama part of the domain occupied by purely artificial growths, such as the masque and the pastoral drama; the features of the same small selection of models reappear in a succession of works to which a world of originals was, so to speak, open for portraiture; and fancy seems never less free than when she is seeking to escape from the world of the real.

Degenera- Finally, a degeneracy far from uniform in degree, but *tion in* unmistakeably characteristic of the dramatic literature of this *moral tone.* period as a whole, is noticeable in the moral tone of its productions. Some critics hold that this element has no concern whatever with the value of works of art as such. But whoever will reflect on the progress of any nation's artistic life side by side with that of its general history, will, I am convinced, arrive at a contrary result. Not less surely than in the history of Greek sculpture (which it is possible to survey with a certain relative completeness) a succession

---

[1] Already Chapman makes his Claudio say in *All Fools* (act ii),

> ''Faith, that same vein of railing is become
> Now most applausive; your best Poet is
> He that rails grossest.'

of experiences in the general history of Greek society reflect
themselves with unmistakeable distinctness, the history of
our drama from the days of the early Elisabethans to those
of the contemporaries of the Restoration reveals the ascendancy and the decline of moral influences in the same
succession as that exhibited by the general course of our
national life. To assert that the drama of the reigns of
James and Charles reflects a social life devoid of ideals
of virtue either public or private, would be as futile as to
ignore the wide difference in moral tone or note traceable
between Massinger and Fletcher, or between Shirley and
Ford respectively. But the growing apathy observable in
particular spheres of society in this period towards some of
the most important restraining forces that operate in public
and in private relations, marks the dramatic literature of these
times as distinctly as it marks the times themselves. Personally, Marlowe must have been more impatient of any kind of
restraint than Ford; but the earlier writer was very far from
entertaining—or pretending to entertain—that contempt for
the power of moral forces which in the later shocks us far
more than his representation of unbridled passion. Shakspere
himself had not, so far as we know, ever realised the highest
ideal of free civic virtue ; his Brutus, intended to embody
some such conception, is enveloped in a half-rhetorical, half-
elegiac haze ; but neither he nor his times would have
thought it possible to sink to the level of Fletcher and the
age for which Fletcher and his later associates wrote—an
age in which it seems impossible for a man to draw his
breath freely, or to think of a prince otherwise than as
a despot, benevolent or malevolent, but a master in either
case of the souls and the bodies of his subjects.

Yet the dramatic literature of this age (and the rest of
its literature furnishes grounds for the same conclusion)
had not yet reached that extreme of moral weakness which
belongs only to a generation which, like a population among
which the Plague has declared its irresistible mastery, has
cast away fear and hope, and is drifting without either cross
or anchor. A few signs, but only a very few, are as yet
perceptible of a tendency to take conscious delight in the

This decline of moral sentiment not hopeless.

absence of lofty ideals, to glory in the inversion of right
and wrong, to sneer at the impotence of virtue, and to exult
in the supremacy of vice. Indeed, far from displaying so
deadly a progress of decay, our dramatic literature, like the
society of which it exhibits the reflexion, shows in the later
part of this period certain signs of recovery in the moral
tone of its productions; and, under influences which
cannot even be glanced at here, this reaction might have
assumed even more unmistakeable proportions, had it not
been seemingly overwhelmed by the waves of a far mightier
movement.

Influence of foreign dramatic literatures slight as a whole: What our drama in this period achieved, is not wholly
to be ascribed to the self-determining and self-renewing
powers of a representative growth of the national life. Its
general course, as well as the creative activity of its individual
authors, was also in some measure affected, in this as in
all other periods, by the influence of foreign examples.
How far this influence extended is a question to which
different answers will be given, and which others are better
qualified to decide than myself. But I remain convinced
that, except in the case of merely subsidiary and secondary
growths—such as above all the pastoral drama, of which I am
not at present speaking—no foreign dramatic literature in
this period exercised any really vital influence upon the
progress of our own. Far too much importance has, as it
seems to me, been attached to the coincidence in subject,
and even in particulars of treatment, between individual
Italian;   English and foreign plays. Thus, it need not be denied
that, now as formerly, Italian tragedy occasionally supplied
at first hand plots and even characters to English dramatists,
while of course both they and their Italian contemporaries
constantly resorted for their materials to Italian prose
fiction in its native or translated form. But Italian tragedy,
partly under the influence of the new growths just referred
to, partly because of its timid adherence to classical models,
sank into decline more rapidly than the English sister-
growth, though, unlike the latter, it was in another century
to experience a new birth. Italian comedy, while actively
influencing the theatre of other Western nations by the

living examples of its loose popular form—the *commedia dell' arte*—had in its professedly literary branch—the *commedia erudita*—gradually emancipated itself from the rules of classical examples, without, notwithstanding its assiduity, producing in its turn any works of high comic genius[1]. The most direct traces of its influence upon the English drama of this period are probably to be sought for in the academical plays, which addressed themselves to audiences comparable from some points of view to the literary societies that formed the real home and birth-place of the Italian comedies of this age.   French tragedy clung yet more con- *French;* sistently than Italian to the traditions of classical form, even when, as in the remarkable political dramas which accompanied the great civil struggles of the close of the sixteenth century, it sought to enter into direct relations with the times.   The struggle between classical tragedy, which had already become an established part of French national literature, and the romantic drama was still in progress ; but, in spite of the access of vitality derived by the latter from the influences of the Italian pastoral and the vigorous growth of the Spanish drama, the victory of classicism in French tragedy was already to all intents and purposes assured[2].   French comedy was better able to retain its essentially national character.   But neither the classicising school of French tragedy, whose sway was soon to be definitively established by Corneille, nor the long-lived growth of French farce, could directly influence our own dramatic literature, with which they could no longer find points of contact.   It was only at a later period, when the English drama was turning aside from the traditions of its own past, that French examples could immediately and powerfully affect its progress.

The really predominating dramatic literature of the *Spanish.* earlier half of the seventeenth century on the continent of Europe was, however, neither the Italian nor the French, but the Spanish.   This, as it would not be difficult to show, was partly the result of causes extending far beyond the

---

[1] Cf. Sismondi, *Lit. of the South of Europe*, chap. xv.
[2] Cf. Ebert, *Entwicklungsgeschichte der französischen Tragödie*, pp. 176 *seqq.*

range of mere literary influences. From Spain proceeded in the sixteenth century—though the close of the fifteenth was its real seed-time—that great spiritual and intellectual movement which is but imperfectly designated under the name of the Catholic Reaction. For something more than a mere revulsion against the Protestant Reformation lay at the root of a movement which, from another point of view, might be more appropriately termed a revival; which mastered the anti-religious self-assurance of the Italian Renascence; and which, if it ended by becoming the servant of Rome, had in the first instance transformed the spirit of Rome herself[1]. But these considerations lie beyond my present subject. The great age of the Spanish drama was one of the last births of this mighty movement, so far as it affected the peninsula, and accompanied the concluding period of its activity like a luminous after-glow. Herein lies one of the causes that help to explain the artificiality of the Spanish drama, a feature so marked that no brilliancy of colouring is capable of concealing it. Thus—strange as it may seem—the higher and more important national impulses to which the flower of Spanish dramatic literature owed its origin, and the operation of which it so unmistakeably reveals, were not those which—speaking generally—it communicated to other European literatures; and while it furnished numberless suggestions to these in matters of detail, no drama has ever remained so exclusively national as the Spanish, and no other of the same importance has accordingly to so small an extent vitally influenced foreign dramatic growths.

It is necessary for me to speak on this subject with diffidence, inasmuch as my own acquaintance with Spanish dramatic literature is in substance derived through translations only, or at second-hand. Yet, even so, I have little hesitation in asserting that the connexion between the Spanish and the English drama in this period, which is sometimes assumed to have been extremely intimate, will, the more the subject is enquired into, be found to reduce

[1] See an exposition of this view in Maurenbrecher's *Studien und Skizzen zu der Reformationszeit.*

itself to a narrow range of indebtedness on the part of our writers. A narrow range—but at the same time one that covers a long series of details bearing a more or less close resemblance to one another. To the English, as also to the French and Italian drama of the seventeenth and even of the eighteenth century, the prolific Spanish dramatists of the close of the sixteenth and the seventeenth supplied a whole arsenal of 'plots, incidents, and situations[1].' Several instances of this description have been noted in the preceding pages, particularly in the case of works by Beaumont and Fletcher, and of others by Middleton and Webster. More could no doubt be added by students of the less as well as the better known of Lope de Vega's Spanish contemporaries. A few characters too may have been taken by our English dramatists directly from Spanish originals. But—apart from the fact that in many instances a Spanish novel[2], and not a drama, has been ascertained to have been the original source of the plot of an English play, and that in many other instances the story may not have been borrowed directly from the Spanish play to which it is ultimately traceable—the conclusion seems unavoidable, that among the elements peculiar to the Spanish drama none can be shown to have been taken over by our own and assimilated to its growth. So long as this position remains unshaken—so long as the contention must be regarded as preposterous, that our drama would have been cast in different forms from those which it actually assumed, had no dramatic work of Cervantes or Lope or Calderon ever reached our shores—so long as no specifically Spanish origin can be ascribed to any important comic type, to any prominent tragic character, to any variety of comic or tragic form in the English drama of this period, —its claims to originality remain unimpaired by any

[1] Cf. Lewes, *The Spanish Drama*, chap. i. See also Sismondi, chap. xxxv, and Ticknor, chap. xxvi.

[2] Dryden, in the Preface to his *An Evening's Love* (founded on a play by Calderon), where he enumerates instances of borrowed plots, says that 'Beaumont and Fletcher had most of theirs from Spanish novels,' and mentions several examples. This seems to imply that Dryden did not suppose Beaumont and Fletcher to have largely borrowed directly from Spanish *plays*.

suggestion as to its indebtedness to Spanish prototypes. In other words—borrowed from a critic already quoted—the obligations with respect to incident and intrigue on the part of our dramatists towards their Spanish contemporaries and predecessors no more detract from the merits of the English poets 'than Shakspere's occasional adoption of plots from the Italian novelists diminishes our admiration for his wondrous inventive genius[1].' At all events, the *onus probandi* lies with those who have as yet failed to show cause for a supposition intrinsically improbable. A drama at once so national and so artificial as the Spanish could hardly be expected materially to influence another dramatic growth, which in its turn was less exclusively, but not less genuinely, national.

Mutual indebtedness of the English dramatists in non-essentials.

If our dramatists unhesitatingly borrowed their plots, or parts of their plots, from foreign sources, they were equally unscrupulous in their use of materials readier of access. In fact, they recognised no right on the part of any one author to elements which he might or might not have himself derived from sources open to all alike; and though herein they may at times have exceeded the liberty which if rightly understood every author is entitled to claim, they appear to have at no time seriously begrudged one another the right of borrowing what are after all mere accidents in a dramatic work[2]. The constant co-operation of two or more authors in the composition of single plays, of which it is needless again to cite examples, must frequently have rendered the identification of 'property in ideas' of this description extremely difficult; and doubtless modern

---

[1] Lewes, p. 8. The debts to the Spaniards of our dramatists in the period after the Restoration will be briefly considered in my next chapter.

[2] The practice is alluded to, not very wrathfully, by Middleton (himself variously supposed to have either perpetrated or suffered from a 'reminiscence' of a less wholesale kind) in *The Spanish Gipsy* (act ii. sc. 2):

'*San.* We'll invoke together, so you will not steal my plot.
Rod. 'Tis not my fashion.
San. But now-a-days 'tis all the fashion.'—

According to Professor Wilson (*Hindu Theatre*, vol. ii. p. 258) the practice of plagiarism was not unknown to the later Indian drama. Kálidása was borrowed from by the author of *Ratnévali* (*The Necklace*), A. D. 1120 c., and he in his turn was plagiarised by a later writer (cf. *ib.*, p. 391).

commentators have often wasted their labour—and at times their indignation—upon the detection of 'reminiscences' or 'plagiarisms' to which the original authors of the passages in question would themselves have been supremely indifferent.

It remains to cast one concluding glance upon the achievements of our national English drama in the period from the close of Elisabeth's reign to the outbreak of the Great Revolution. Its annals in this age include, together with numerous names relatively insignificant, many that will never lose their lustre in the history of our poetic literature. Nothing would be more futile than an attempt to range these in order of merit, after the childish fashion in which Byron amused himself by constructing pyramidal lists of his poetic contemporaries. Moreover, the note of original genius is its distinctiveness; and no comparison of this kind could weigh in opposite scales the brilliancy of Fletcher and the intensity of Webster, the pleasant gaiety of Middleton and the seductive sweetness of Ford. The later Elisabethan dramatists and their after-growth of the next age could not indeed themselves fail to look up to a few names as holding an undisputed pre-eminence. Thus Webster, in a passage already cited [1], singles out the 'full and heightened style' of Chapman, the 'laboured and understanding works' of Jonson, and the 'no less worthy composures' of Beaumont and Fletcher as the first objects of his admiration, but in naming after these Shakspere and Dekker and Heywood, he guards himself against any imputation of a desire to detract from the deserts of the latter in their turn. If in this passage, written in or before the year 1612, we cannot pretend to find either a complete or a wholly judicious appreciation of contemporary merit, it proves at least a desire on the part of one dramatist, himself distinguished by singular excellence in a limited range of creations, to render justice to various kinds of poetic genius. While, therefore, Webster's blindness to the pre-eminence of the greatest of his fellow-dramatists, whom he simply classes *inter pares*, may fill us with amazement, yet the

Summary of the achievements of our dramatic literature in this period.

Acknowledged pre-eminence of a few great writers.

[1] From the address *To the Reader* prefixed to *Vittoria Corombona*.

general spirit of his tribute remains deserving of imitation. Among Shakspere's contemporaries and successors there is but one who by the energy of his genius not less than by the circumstances of his literary career stands in a position of indisputable primacy among his fellows. Jonson, to whom a whole generation of younger dramatists readily did homage as their veteran chief, was alone in sober truth the founder of a school or family—in the old Greek artists' acceptation of the idea—of dramatists. But his influence in this direction was due in the first instance to the earnest consciousness with which through life he addressed himself to the cultivation of his art; so that there was truth as well as humour in the self-assertion put into his mouth by one of the youngest and most talented of his followers, who represents him as 'plainly telling' the assembled poets of the age how

> 'he deserv'd the Bays,
> For his were called Works, where others were but Plays[1].'

Yet, whatever his followers may have thought, Jonson's pre-eminence was not one which extended to both branches of the regular drama, although it is true that he essayed

them both with equally indomitable determination. But his achievements in tragedy—the branch of our dramatic literature in this period on which I will first touch—fell short of the highest success. Such as they are, his tragic efforts, together with those of Chapman and an isolated work by Ford, stand virtually alone in this period as examples of sustained effort in the field of historic tragedy proper, to which none of Fletcher's or Massinger's plays can justly be described as belonging. But the merits of these creations, varied and severally interesting as they are, failed to secure vitality to one of the noblest of English dramatic growths. The excursions made by Thomas Heywood and others into the still popular domain of the Chronicle History were made in the teeth of the law of artistic progress[2].

---

[1] See Suckling's *A Sessions of the Poets*.

[2] I have not thought it necessary to refer again to the quite exceptional instances of plays treating themes of recent or contemporary foreign history (see under *Massinger* and *Glapthorne*).—In September, 1602, the afore-

With the great body of the dramatists of this and the next *Historic* period tragedy had passed into a phase where its interest *tragedy neglected* depends mainly upon its situations, where novelty is there- *for ro-* fore a necessary ingredient in the plot, and where the *mantic* primary task of the dramatist lies in the skilful and effective *and 'tragi-* use of incident. The romantic tragedies and so-called *comedy.* tragi-comedies [1] which crowd our literature from Dekker to Fletcher, and from Webster to Shirley, together constitute a growth so exuberant as at first sight to fill us with astonishment. The sources from which their subjects were *Variety of* derived had constantly increased in number and variety. *subjects;* Besides Italian, French, and Spanish fiction, original or translated—a storehouse comprehensive enough to include a variety of writers ranging from Cervantes to Honoré d'Urfé—and in addition to such native literary sources as Sidney's *Arcadia*, the contemporary foreign drama, and the Spanish in particular, offered occasional opportunities for resort. And, over and above these, a new series of materials was at hand, since our dramatists had begun to regard events and episodes of English domestic life as fit subjects for tragic treatment. Domestic tragedy of this description was indeed no novelty on the English stage ; Shakspere himself may not improbably have touched with his master-hand more than one effort of the kind ; but Thomas Heywood may be regarded as the first who achieved any work of considerable literary value in this field, in which he was followed by Middleton and many others. Yet in contrast to this wide variety of sources, and *and com-* consequent apparent variety of themes, the number of *parative* *paucity of* motives of which—at least as a rule—the tragic drama of *motives.* this period made use was comparatively small and limited. Hence, notwithstanding the diversity of subjects to be found

mentioned Duke of Stettin saw on a London stage a 'comedy' on the capture of Stuhlweissenburg by the Turks, and its recovery by the Christians (*Diary*, p. 6).

[1] The sense in which this term is generally used in literary criticism is that of plays freely mingling tragic and comic scenes, characters and interest; but the narrower sense in which it is generally employed by the dramatists of this period is that of a play serious in its main interest but ending happily.

in the tragic dramas of such writers as Marston, Webster, Fletcher, Ford, and Shirley, an impression of sameness is undeniably left upon us by a continuous perusal of their works. This impression is largely, though not wholly, attributable to the constant recurrence of the same motives —such as politic ambition, conjugal jealousy, absolute female devotion, unbridled masculine passion—in plays of which the time and locality are so infinitely various. Another

Excess of passion. cause leading to the same result is the want of moderation which these dramatists and their contemporaries habitually exhibit in the treatment of the passions employed by them as favourite motives in the conduct of their tragic actions. A distinguished critic[1] has remarked with incontestable truth—although it is obvious how easily the observation lends itself to dangerous misinterpretation—that ' passions only vary and differ from one another when they are moderated ; it is then that each has its own language and gesture ; it is then that they interest by their diversity. When they are excessive, they become uniform ; and exaggeration, which is supposed to be a way of bringing a passion into greater relief, in fact effaces and destroys it.' Not all the tragic poets of this period are in the same measure amenable to this charge ; and in Webster, and in Ford more especially, the sameness of exaggerated passion is broken by those marvellously sudden and subtle touches through which their tragic genius creates its most striking effects. Nor will the tendency to excess of passion which Beaumont and Fletcher undoubtedly exhibit be confounded with their distinctive power of sustaining tenderly pathetic characters and situations, in a degree unequalled by the creations of any of their contemporaries. Massinger's dignity of sentiment and Shirley's gift of poetic illustration come less into question here, since these qualities, though respectively among the most salient characteristics of these writers, bear less directly upon their general conception of the purposes and effects of

Distinctive merits and defects tragic art. The features common to the generality of the romantic tragedies of this period (as we may fairly call them

[1] See the chapter *De l'Émotion Dramatique* in St.-Marc Girardin's *Cours de Littérature Dramatique*, vol. i. p. 8.

in a body) are, on the one hand, ingenuity in the choice and *common* facility in the construction of plots, a command of incident *to the* *romantic* which our earlier drama had never approached, a flow of *tragedies of* impassioned diction capable of sustaining actions both long *this period.* and full—but, on the other, a certain poverty in the choice of motives (such as cannot be gainsaid on a comparison from this point of view of Shakspere's successors with Shakspere himself), a monotony of pitch in the treatment of different kinds of passions, and—it must be added—a sameness in the constant use of particular devices in the conduct of dramatic plots[1].

In comedy, the genius and the insight of Jonson had *Examples* pointed the way to a steady and legitimate advance. His *of Jonson* *and Shak-* theory of 'humours,' translated into the language of dra- *spere in* matic art, signified a recognition of the paramount impor- *comedy.* tance attaching in the comic drama to the production of distinctive human types. If appeal is made to the experience of the comic drama and of comic fiction in the history of the world at large, the sources open to such an exercise of the creative power may fairly be held inexhaustible. Jonson— and Shakspere—had therefore, while showing the way, by no means simultaneously closed the gate in this field of art upon their contemporaries and successors. Yet in this, the most interesting field of the comic dramatist's labours, Jonson's fellows or followers only now and then produced individual dramatic figures rivalling those invented by him, while in copiousness and variety his gallery of types as a whole remained unapproached. In return, the favourite *Comic types* types of Jonsonian comedy, to which Dekker, Marston and *of character* *elaborated,* Chapman had indisputably, though in no large measure, *and new* added others of their own, were elaborated with incessant *types occa-* *sionally* zeal and remarkable effect by their contemporaries and *added.* successors. After a very different fashion from that in

---

[1] In comedy Chapman had (see his *May-Day*) at an early point in this period (1611) condemned 'transformances' as 'the stale refuge of miserable Poets'; but there was one transformance—by means of doublet and hose— of which neither English tragedy nor English comedy ever tired, and which they left to future generations of dramatists as a heritage of doubtful value, notwithstanding the consecration which it had received from its use by Shakspere and in an early master-piece of Beaumont and Fletcher.

which the Roman comedians reiterated the ordinary types of the New Comedy, the inexhaustible *verve* of Middleton, the fresh naturalness of Heywood, the gay facility of Fletcher, the observant humour of Field, and the ready versatility of Shirley—to cite no further names—mirrored in innumerable pictures of contemporary life the undying foibles and follies of mankind. As comedians of manners more than one of these surpassed the old master, not indeed in conscientiousness and correctness of detail, but in lightness accompanied by sureness of touch ; while in the construction of plots the access of abundant new materials, and the superior elasticity in treatment which inevitably accompanies an artistic growth commending itself so easily to the enjoyment of its patrons, likewise enabled these writers to maintain what may I think be described as an uninterrupted advance. Thus, without any wish to lose sight of the vices and defects which the comedy of this period left to be aggravated by its successor, our comic drama from Jonson to Shirley may be asserted to remain unsurpassed as a comedy of manners, while as a comedy of character it at least defies comparison with any other preceding or contemporaneous growth of our national literature. Its weaknesses, like those of every literary movement which suffers from fulness of blood, are most grievously apparent in the main body of its inferior writers, who but rarely schooled themselves with care, like honest Brome, into a judicious knowledge of their own capacities ; but whatever examples may be chosen purposely or at haphazard to illustrate the continuous decline of our comic drama, it cannot, even within the limits which it had failed materially to enlarge, be justly said to have exhausted its vitality before the catastrophe of the Revolution.

The Pastoral Drama and the Masque.

To the subsidiary developement of the Pastoral Drama and to the hybrid growth of the Masque I need not here return. In both of these species, many of our dramatists found special opportunities for the exercise of those lyrical gifts, which in the regular drama likewise occasionally

Verse

shine forth with a brilliant or a softly subdued light. On the general subject of the progress of English dramatic

versification in this period much light has been thrown by
recent research ; but the time has perhaps hardly arrived
for a comparative survey which should attempt to cover the
whole field of the earlier Stuart drama. Yet it would
probably be difficult to point to any other feature of our
dramatic literature in which the individuality of particular
writers so distinctly asserts itself, even under the controlling
influence of generally prevalent usages and tendencies. We
can hardly, *e.g.* conceive of Fletcher adopting any form of
blank-verse except that which he made his own, and which
seems almost as truly a part of him as his fluid morality ;
or of Massinger modifying the versification of Fletcher
in any other way than that which actually commended
itself to his practice, and which harmonises so well with the
sententious disposition of his mind. In the later dramatists
of this period less mannerism of versification is perceptible
than in some of the earlier ; but it is not too much to say
that precisely in those writers who like Shirley show the
fullest sense of the value of their art, may be found the most
abundant evidence of care for its outward form. The
inferior dramatists of the close of Charles I's reign incline
to a looseness of versification which shows how easily familiarity passes into contempt, and how want of character
is apt to reflect itself even in the mere externals of artistic
composition. Prose had been conquered for the drama in *and prose*
an earlier period ; nothing was needed on this head but to *in the*
dramatic
maintain an established right ; and this was not likely *literature of*
to be relinquished by comedy. Obvious causes prevented *this period.*
dramatic prose from adopting the peculiar structure and
colouring which characterise so large a proportion of the
political and religious writing and oratory of the period.
On the other hand, the condensed and pregnant phraseology
of the stage, as specially developed under the influence of
Jonsonian comedy of character, had a close affinity with
the sentementious style that dignifies the essay—and character—literature of the age of Overbury, Earle, and Bacon,
causing much of it to fall upon our ears like reminiscences
of the Elisabethan drama.

One word may be permitted in conclusion, as we take *Conclusion.*

leave of the cluster of names, great and small, which the annals of our dramatic literature have preserved to us as those of Shakspere's contemporaries and more immediate successors. With him, these men shared the effects of the electrical contact between mind and mind—often between genius and genius—and the impulse begotten of it towards creative activity. Like him, and like his predecessors, they were subject to the influence of their times, while many of them could not but be affected by the examples of those who were their masters as well as their fellows. They cannot therefore be fully understood or duly valued as writers, unless account is taken of their connexion with one another, with their contemporaries and predecessors, and with Shakspere himself; and to become familiar with them individually is but part of the task of such as desire to estimate them justly. But the conscientious study of individual genius is the beginning, as the sympathetic appreciation of it is the end, of literary criticism. 'We wish,' Lessing makes his epigrams say on behalf of himself and his fellow-poets, 'to be less praised and more diligently read.' The meed of popular fame may safely be left to adjust itself; the task of the student of literature is to examine with his own eyes, and to have trust in the light which, all in good time, will make clear to him the difference between genius and its accidents.

CHAPTER IX.

THE LATER STUART DRAMA.

THE fatal Ordinance of the Lords and Commons, bearing date September 2, 1642, had, as has been seen [1], proclaimed the absolute cessation of all stage-plays during the continuance of 'these sad causes and set-times of humiliation.' Once more bishops and players were fellows [2], as in the old Mar-prelate days; but this time Martin had the upper hand. Many actors and playwrights followed the fortunes of the royal cause in the field, where one of them at least sacrificed his life [3]. A single actor alone is known to have chosen the side of the Parliament, professed himself a Presbyterian, and settled as a tradesman in the City, 'within the territory of Father Calamy [4].' Some of the players whose occupation at home was gone may have tried their fortunes abroad [5];

---

[1] *Ante*, p. 247.

[2] 'But Times are chang'd; and it is worth our note,
    Bishops and Players both suffer'd in one vote.'
Alexander Brome, *Upon the Ingenious Comedies of Mr. Richard Brome.* (R. Brome's *Works*, vol. i. p. viii.)

[3] See Hugh Peters' report to the House of Commons of the death at the taking of Basing House (October 14, 1645) of 'Robinson, the player, who, a little before the storm, was known to be mocking and scorning the Parliament.' (Collier, vol. iii. p. 479, where this personage is identified with William Robins or Robinson, who had been a member of Queen Anne's Company in 1619).—A tract published at Christmas, 1642-3, and cited by Collier, vol. ii. p. 39, observes that 'if either the Court play-writers be commanded to read the Scriptures, or the City Scripture readers be commanded to write plays—this, as it would much advantage our part, so would it much disadvantage the King's; for, as by it we should gain a new place of edifying, so Captain Trigg, and the rest of the players which are now in service, would doubtlessly return to their callings, and much lessen the King's army.'

[4] Wright's *Historia Histrionica.*

[5] The probability that some English actors during this period attempted

upon those who lingered on in the familiar London haunts
the hand of power, and often no doubt the pressure of want,
lay heavy[1]; and if their voices were not altogether mute,
their complaints could be addressed to an imaginary tribunal
only[2].   The Parliamentary Ordinance of September 2, 1642,
continued in force till, in 1647, the war was considered virtually at an end; but the spirit of reprobation of theatrical
entertainments survived it, and on July 17, 1647, the Houses
of Parliament renewed the Ordinance, fixing January 1 following as the date of its expiration[3].   It is uncertain
whether this renewal had been in part provoked by occasional attempts at dramatic entertainments of one kind or
another ; the only infraction of it of which we have distinct
notice was a performance of Beaumont and Fletcher's
A King and No King, at Salisbury Court, which was
promptly stopped by the sheriffs, who arrested one of the
players—apparently some time in 1647[4].   Parliament, however, had neglected to provide for a second renewal of the
Ordinance, when January, 1648, came round; and several
theatres promptly opened their doors to large audiences.   At
one of these houses—the Fortune—not less than one hundred
and twenty coaches set down visitors on a single day; at
another—the Red Bull—Beaumont and Fletcher's *Wit*

to earn a living by performances on the Continent, is supported by the
circumstance that an English comedian is mentioned at Vienna in 1654.
See Karajan, *Abraham a Sancta Clara*, p. 113, *note*.

[1] John Lowin, who had been a member of the King's Company with
Shakspere, is said in the *Historia Histrionica* to have 'in his latter days kept
an inn (the Three Pigeons) at Brentford, where he dyed very old . . . and
his poverty was as great as his age.'   The date of his death appears to have
been 1659.

[2] See *The Actors' Remonstrance* of January, 1643 (printed *ap.* Hazlitt,
u.s., pp. 259 *seqq.*), where a complaint is preferred to 'great Phoebus' and
the 'Sacred Sisters,' that stage-plays are prohibited, while 'the exercise at
the Beares Colledge and the motions of the Puppets' are 'still in force and
vigour.'

[3] Gardiner, *History of the Great Civil War*, vol. iii. p. 307.

[4] See Fleay, *History of the Stage*, p. 365.   Collier, as is there pointed out,
gives two dates for this occurrence, 1664 (vol. ii. p. 37) and 1647 (*ib.* p. 40).
Mr. Fleay thinks it 'must have been a performance, in 1647, by a scratch company made up of those members of the King's men and Beeston's boys who
were in that year co-operating in the publication of the folio Beaumont and
Fletcher.'

without Money was performed [1]; at a third—the Cockpit—
the representation of Fletcher's *The Bloody Brother* was
interrupted by the arrival of a party of soldiers, and the
actors were temporarily imprisoned [2]. The wrath of Parliament having been thus thoroughly aroused, a final Ordinance was passed by it on February 11, authorising the
Lord Mayor, Justices of the Peace, and Sheriffs to pull
down all stage-galleries, seats and boxes, and publicly to
flog all actors and compel them to enter into recognisances
'never to act or play any plays or interludes any more, on
pain of being dealt with as incorrigible rogues.' All the
moneys collected at surreptitious performances were appropriated to the benefit of the poor, and a fine of five shillings
imposed upon every one found present as a spectator on such
an occasion [3]. One or two interventions of force were still
required in order to suppress the incorrigible vitality of
the theatre; even after September 18 of the same year a
Provost-Marshal had been appointed to seize ballad-singers
and suppress stage-plays [4]. But upon the whole the policy
of complete repression proved for a time effective.

But the enemies of the drama had not calculated upon an
elasticity, which it had exhibited under worse oppression
than theirs. Dancing had been prohibited by no Parliamentary Ordinance; and where, in those spheres of society
which had favoured masques at least as much as plays,
the slighter dramatic form was still in occasional request,
a taste for the more substantial was unlikely to have been
entirely lost [5]. Upon the lower orders the drama contrived
to retain a hold by means of the performance, under various
pretexts, of comic scenes or episodes derived—since of

---

[1] Gardiner, *u. s.*, p. 308.   [2] *Historia Histrionica.*
[3] Gardiner, *u. s.*,; cf. Collier, vol. ii. p. 43; Hazlitt, p. 66.
[4] Collier, pp. 45–7. The dates of the interrupted performances in question
were December 29, 1648, at Salisbury Court, and December 20, 1649, at
the Red Bull.
[5] The Inns of Court had long been among the homes of the drama. In
November, 1651, a masque was presented at the Middle Temple; the proceedings being opened with the Hundredth Psalm, sung by the Benchers in
the Hall; after which, having drunk a cup of hypocras, they retired to their
chambers, and—to speak profanely—the fun began. (Gardiner, *History of
the Commonwealth and Protectorate*, vol. ii. pp. 11, 12.)

adaptation there could not be much question—from extant plays. These representations are said to have occasionally taken place at the Red Bull theatre, but must for the most part have been confined to extemporised stages at fairs in town or country. Many of these farces or 'drolls' or 'droll-humours,' as they were called, seem to have been contrived by an actor of the name of Robert Cox, who was likewise a principal performer in them ; but others were no doubt described with sufficient accuracy by the publisher of a numerous collection of them as 'written' (*i.e.* conveyed) 'I know not when, by several Persons, I know not who [1].'

and the Protecto-rate. In Oliver's time a certain relaxation of the rigid rules prohibiting any kind of dramatic performance could hardly fail to ensue, when the Protector became desirous of

[1] See Dyce, Beaumont and Fletcher's *Works*, vol. i. p. 200 ; and Mr. J. W. Ebsworth's *Introduction* to *Westminster Drolleries* (1671 and 1672).—Of one of these, entitled *Merry Conceits of Bottom the Weaver*, printed in 1646, a reprint was edited in 1860 by Mr. Halliwell-Phillipps, who also printed in 1859 a collection of *Shakespearian Drolls*, from a volume published near the end of the seventeenth century. Eleven drolls prepared by Robert Cox were published in 1672. But the standard collection of these Drolls is the bookseller Francis Kirkman's publication, which appeared in 1672 under the title of *The Wits, or Sport upon Sport*; and to which repeated reference has previously been made in the present work. It professes to contain a series of drolls and farces, printed as they were acted 'in Publique and Private, in London at Bartholomew, and in the Country at other Faires, in Halls and Taverns, on several Mountebancks Stages at Charing Cross, Lincolns Inn Fields, and other places, by several Stroleing Players, Fools and Fidlers, and the Mountebancks Zanies, with Loud Laughter and great Applause.' The Preface, which is signed by the readers' 'old Servant,' H. Marsh, describes these drolls as 'Rump Drolls,' *i. e.* as acted in the time of the Rump Parliament ; and from a passage in Ludlow's *Memoirs*, the reference to which I have mislaid, I conclude that in the Puritan age the word 'to droll' was used as a synonym for 'to act.' (For the earlier use of 'droll' and 'drollery' as equivalent to 'puppet' and 'puppet-show,' see Nares, *s. v.*)—Kirkman's collection includes several scenes from Beaumont and Fletcher's plays, one from *Hamlet* ('The Grave-Makers'), one from *The Alchemist*, one from Shirley's *Love Tricks*, &c. ; the choice being manifestly determined by the thought of what would be likely to please an audience of the least refined sort. Others (the series comprising *Simpleton the Smith, Bumpkin, Simpkin, Hobbinat*, and *Swabber*) appear to have owed their origin to the inventive powers of Robert Cox, who is said to have been irresistible when he appeared as Young Simpleton 'with a great piece of Bread and Butter,' complaining that a man cannot be left undisturbed to 'eat a little bit for his After-noon's Lunchin.'

attracting the goodwill of the moderate party ; nor was it in any case possible for the vigilance of authority to control the enterprise of the vagrant drama in every part of the country [1]. While the village green or the hall of the country mansion thus, as in the days of the old minstrels, continued to offer an occasional welcome to the players, they once more—about the middle of the Protectorate period—began to raise their heads in London.

In 1656 Sir William D'Avenant, through his influence with the Lord Keeper, Sir Bulstrode Whitelocke, who a few years previously had obtained the poet's release from the Tower, received permission to produce, at 'the back part of Rutland House' in Aldersgate Street, an entertainment of declamation and music 'after the manner of the ancients'; and the performance actually took place there on May 21. This curious substitute for the real thing—which only in its concluding words ventured to hint at the desirability of the real thing itself [2]—was succeeded in the same year, and at the same place, by the same author's

D'Ave-nant's devices.

---

[1] The Dyce Library contains a pamphlet entitled ' *Tragi-Comoedia.* Being a Brief Relation of the Strange and Wonderfull hand of God discovered at Witny' [Witney in Oxfordshire] 'in the Comedy Acted there February the Third, where there were some slaine, many hurt, with severall other Remarkable Passages. Together with what was preached in three Sermons on that occasion . . . by John Rowe of Corpus Christi College in Oxford, Lecturer in the Town of Witny. Oxford, 1653.' This refers to an accident which occurred during the performance of the play of *Mucedorus* (cf. Collier, vol. ii. p. 47), which had been previously presented at several other country places.—In the Council Order Book, on the margin of the copy of a letter prohibiting horse-races and similar pretexts for the meetings of disaffected persons in the North of England, Mrs. Everett Green found the following mysterious note: ' Old Noll's rules to put down interludes (?) of the 99 ; then to govern the 100th.—J. C.' See *Calendar of State Papers, Domestic,* 1654, *Preface,* p. xxi and p. 246, *note.*

[2] The entertainment (printed in D'Avenant's *Dramatic Works,* vol. iii) began with a 'concert of instrumental music.' Next follows an argumentative dialogue between 'Diogenes, the cynic' and 'Aristophanes the poet' sitting 'in two gilded rostras' on the subject of public amusements—especially the diversions of music and scenery. The curtains having been closed, more instrumental and vocal music ensued. To this succeeds a Dialogue between a Parisian and a Londoner, clad 'in the livery-robes of both cities,' concerning the pre-eminence of Paris or London. The Londoner's harangue was prefaced by 'a concert of music, imitating the waits of London.' This Dialogue, which possesses some antiquarian interest, closes with a song, of which the first verse runs as follows :

Siege of Rhodes, 'made a Representation by the Art of Prospective in Scenes, and the Story sung in Recitative Musick,' which was published, apparently on September 29, 1656, with a Preface dated on the previous August 17, but without a dedication. It had been communicated by the author 'hot from the press' to Sir Bulstrode Whitelocke, whom D'Avenant declares to be his 'supreme judge,' although he does 'not despair to have the honour of inviting him to be a spectator[1].' The production may be described as an epitome of the *First Part* of the Opera performed and printed after the Restoration[2]. Two years later—apparently towards the close of 1658, some little time after Richard Cromwell had succeeded to the Protectorship—D'Avenant ventured to produce at a public theatre, the Cockpit in Drury Lane, an entertainment similar to *The Siege of Rhodes*, entitled *The Cruelties of the Spaniards in Peru*. The subject was chosen with felicitous audacity, inasmuch as the country was in the midst of a war against Spain ; and when, on December 23, instructions were issued for an official examination of the poet and the actors, so as to ascertain the nature of the work, and by what authority it had been exhibited in public,

> 'London is smother'd with sulph'rous fires ;
>   Still she wears a black hood and cloak
>   Of sea-coal smoke,
>   As if she mourned for brewers and dyers.
> *Chorus.* But she is cool'd and cleans'd by streams
>   Of flowing and of ebbing Thames.'

The Epilogue in its concluding lines seems, as already observed, to go to the root of the intention of the entertainment :

> 'Perhaps, some were so cozen'd as to come
> To see us weave in the dramatic loom
>   .   .   .   .   .
> These were your plays, *but get them if you can.*'

Part of the music for this entertainment was written by Henry Lawes, and part by Captain Henry Cook, originally one of the Children of the King's Chapel, afterwards (in the Civil War) a captain in the royal service, and Master of the Chapel under King Charles II. Cook was one of the original performers in D'Avenant's *Siege of Rhodes*. He died in 1672.

[1] See D'Avenant's letter which Whitelocke inserted in his *Memorials* under date of September 3, 1656.

[2] *Vide infra* ; where see as to the significance attached by Dryden to the circumstances under which D'Avenant's first opera was produced.

a general report on the subject of the acting of stage-plays
was at the same time ordered by the Council of State [1].
The tone of this Order suggests its intention, and in 1659
D'Avenant followed up his production with yet another of
the same kind, *The History of Sir Francis Drake*, which
he published in the course of the same year [2]. Thus with
the aid of a sister-art, whose co-operation was not always
to prove beneficial to it, the English drama had boldly
anticipated the political Restoration, and was no longer
hiding its head when that much-desired transaction was
finally accomplished. D'Avenant seems, still at the Cockpit,   *The re-*
in Drury Lane, to have progressed without let or hindrance   *opening*
                                                                 of the
to the performance of regular plays of his own composi-   *theatres.*
tion [3]; and very soon after Monk had entered London, in
February, 1660, a licence was obtained from the General for
the opening of this enterprising house as a regular theatre
by John Rhodes, a bookseller at Charing Cross, said to have
been formerly wardrobe-keeper to the King's Company at
Blackfriars, who had doubtless for some time been collecting
a company of old actors there [4]. Another gathering of old
actors soon formed themselves into a company at the Red
Bull, from which it had proved so difficult to oust the drama
in the worst days of oppression; and a third began to act
at Salisbury Court, in Whitefriars [5]. On August 21 King   *Theatrical*
                                                                 companies
Charles II issued a patent, granting to Thomas Killigrew [6]   *after the*
and Sir William D'Avenant the right of 'creating' two   *Restora-*
                                                                 tion.
companies of players. A vehement protest ensued on the

[1] See R. W. Lowe, *Thomas Betterton*, p. 10.

[2] Both of these pieces were afterwards included by D'Avenant in his
comic entertainment, *The Playhouse to be Let.*

[3] See the *Prefatory Memoir* to D'Avenant's *Dramatic Works*, p. li. The
plays were *The Fair Favourite* (cf. *ante*, p. 173); *The Law against Lovers*
(founded on *Measure for Measure* and *Much Ado about Nothing*, and reproduced in 1662); *The Siege* (to be briefly described below), and *The Distresses*
(cf. *ante, ib.*).

[4] Genest, vol. i. p. 30, and cf. Lowe, *Betterton*, pp. 58–9.

[5] See the Order from Sir Henry Herbert, dated August 20, and addressed
to the actors of these three playhouses, cited by Mr. Lowe, p. 63. This was
on the day before the issue of the royal patent.

[6] Dibdin, *Complete History of the Stage*, vol. iv. p. 23, states the grant to
have been made to Thomas Killigrew's younger brother, Dr. Henry
Killigrew.

part of the Master of the Revels ; the Salisbury Court company appears not to have immediately stopped its performances; and disputes and difficulties followed which appear in October, 1660, to have resulted in the formation of a single King's Company, consisting of members of both the Red Bull and the Cockpit Companies [1]. In November, however, the two patentees agreed upon a distinct and definite division of the actors between the two companies [2], which came to be known as the King's (Killigrew's) and the Duke of York's (D'Avenant's) respectively. The Duke of York's Company, from 1661, acted at a house built for them in Lincoln's Inn Fields (Portugal Row), and from 1673 in the magnificent theatre (erected some years after D'Avenant's death) in Salisbury Court, Fleet Street, on a site known as Dorset Garden. The King's, from 1663, occupied the Theatre Royal, in Drury Lane, although the house was not yet called by that historic name. The further changes which occurred during the remainder of the period treated of in these volumes I cannot here pursue [3]. In reference, however, to the extraordinary activity of the English stage, and to the corresponding fertility of

---

[1] Dibdin, *u. s.*, p. 68.   [2] *Ib.* p. 72.

[3] It may, however, be convenient to state in a note that the companies were afterwards, by agreement, amalgamated (from 1682) ; and that, in consequence of a movement among the actors which had the sympathy of the public, against the selfish policy of the patentees, a royal licence was in 1695 with characteristic good sense granted by William III to the Company which henceforth performed at the Tennis Court in Lincoln's Inn Fields. The theatre in the Haymarket was built by Sir John Vanbrugh in 1705 ; and the Lincoln's Inn Company migrated to a new house in Covent Garden in 1733. A theatre in Goodman's Fields—afterwards rendered famous by the first appearance of Garrick—seems to have led a fitful existence from 1729 or 1732 ; and the number of London theatres might have further increased even then—for there is no limit to human hopefulness in this branch of speculation—had not the famous Act of 1737 deprived the Crown of the power of licensing any further theatres. In my text I have largely availed myself of the admirable account by Mr. Lowe, who has corrected Genest's mistaken interpretation of certain passages in Pepys. Pepys' *Diary*, from which the data as to plays have been extracted by Mr. Wheatley in the volume already repeatedly cited, remains of course the standard authority as to the history of the Restoration stage ; for details as to the concluding part of the period here treated the reader may resort to Genest, vols. i and ii, Dibdin, vol. iv, the Introduction to Baker's *Biographia Dramatica*, and the amusing and often instructive narrative of Colley Cibber in his *Apology*.

our dramatic literature in the period immediately ensuing
upon the Restoration, it may be worth while to note the
circumstance that it was a rule with the rival companies
that neither should ever attempt a play acted by the other[1].
Thus a sentiment superior to that of direct personal rivalry *Flourish-*
came to animate the efforts of the brilliant talents which at *ing con-*
dition of
this time illustrated the English stage ; for though old play- *the art of*
goers remained to uphold the memories of the past[2], there *acting.*
can be little doubt that the actor's art had never previously
flourished in England as it did in the days of Betterton and
his contemporaries.   The sunshine neither of royal nor of
popular favour was now wanting to the players ; and if they
basked in it rather too consciously, a profession which had
suffered so cruelly might be held to possess a claim to some
measure of indulgence[3].   It should not be forgotten, that from
the Restoration onwards women's parts were invariably acted
by women—an innovation which in this period led to consequences for the social history of the stage on which it is
unnecessary to dwell, but which from an artistic point of
view gave an important fresh impulse to the efforts of the
theatre[4].

But to return for a moment to the period of the suppression of the theatres.   The love of the drama had been to

[1] Cibber's *Apology*, p. 77 (second edition).

[2] See the comparison of the old and the Restoration actors in Wright's
Historia Histrionica.

[3] As early as February 23, 1661, Pepys remarks : ' I see the gallants do
begin to be tyred with the vanity and pride of the theatre actors, who are
indeed grown very proud and rich.'

[4] So Cibber very justly observes in his *Apology*, p. 76.—Not a few of the
actresses of this period—Mrs. Bracegirdle, Mrs. Barry and others—were
unmistakeably distinguished artists as well as beautiful women.—The innovation of women acting female parts was soon followed by the introduction of the utterly vicious practice—from which it is to be feared the
stage will never wholly rid itself—of their occasionally performing male
characters. See Dryden's Prologue to *The Tempest.* In 1672 (probably) the
male characters in Dryden's *The Maiden Queen* seem to have been performed
by women.   Other plays, among them Thomas Killigrew's *The Parson's
Wedding*, are stated in the *Historia Histrionica* to have in this period been
acted ' all by women.'—As to the date of the first introduction of actresses
on the English stage cf. *ante*, pp. 248, 252.—It may be added that the ' lady-
actors' at the Court of Charles II probably surpassed their predecessors both
in enthusiasm and in talent.   See Waller's *Prologue for the Lady-Actors*
(Bell's edition of Waller's *Poems*, p. 221).

some extent kept alive by means more legitimate than the surreptitious performance of mutilated plays, and appealing more forcibly to the sympathies of those classes upon which the prospects of a future revival of our dramatic literature in *Plays pub-* the main depended.   In the darkest days of the drama and *lished in* its patrons—'in this tragical age, where the theatre hath *the Com-* been so much out-acted'—one of the most gifted of the *monwealth* pre-Restoration dramatists besought the public to turn to *period by* *Shirley,* the pages of the most popular among his predecessors, whose works were now—in 1647—first brought before the reader in a collected form [1].   Shirley, moreover, published several of his own plays during the period of the suppres- *Francis* sion of the theatres [2].   A poet widely different in tone and *Quarles* talent, but whose name is preserved from oblivion by a touch *(1592–* *1644),* of originality in his most characteristic productions [3], was FRANCIS QUARLES, who after accompanying the Princess Elisabeth to Heidelberg in 1613, and in the period of the Civil War sturdily upholding the royal cause till his death in 1644, left behind him a comedy, *The Virgin Widow*, privately acted at Chelsea and published in 1649.   This effort, termed by Langbaine an innocent, inoffensive play, appears to have been both his first and his only contribution to the drama.   Several dramatists of the younger generation *Sir* likewise showed signs of not despairing of their art.   The in- *William* *D'Avenant* defatigable and irrepressible D'Avenant—to whom much *and the* should be forgiven for his valiant adherence to an apparently *Killigrews.* hopeless cause—in 1643 and 1649 published two of his plays (significantly enough, without the usual commen- datory verses) which had already been acted, but not

---

[1] See Shirley's Preface to the Folio (1647) edition of Beaumont and Fletcher.

[2] Cf. *ante*, pp. 92–3 ; and Dyce's *Shirley*, vol. i, *Introduction*, p. li.

[3] Quarles connects himself by his famous *Emblems* with a curious element in our older dramatic literature (cf. *ante*, vol. ii. p. 285). By the post-Restora- tion dramatists this volume seems to have been regarded as the type of an old- fashioned book of sober diversion ; see Southerne's *The Maid's Last Prayer* (act iii. sc. 1), and I think I have met with a similar passage in one of Steele's comedies. But Quarles' *Virgin Widow* cannot have been forgotten in the Restoration period ; since one of the most famous passages in *The Rehearsal* (the soliloquy of Volscius with one boot on and the other off) appears to have been written partly in ridicule of a passage in Quarles' play.

printed [1]. Thomas Killigrew [2] and his brother Henry's [3] juvenile play, *The Conspiracy*, was republished in 1653 under the title of *Pallantus and Eudora* [4].

Towards the close of the Protectorate SIR ASTON COKAYNE [5] (to allow him the title of his disputed baronetcy) published two plays, one of which, although by no means original, is not devoid of merit. Few men in his age made greater sacrifices for the cause to which on political and on religious grounds he stedfastly adhered; yet after the Restoration he had to sell both his Derbyshire and his Warwickshire estates, and died a ruined man in lodgings at Derby. The vanity which led Sir Aston Cokayne to boast of his intimacy with Jonson, Massinger, and other of the poets of Jonson's later days, will therefore not be visited on him severely. His own productions included, besides the translation of an Italian prose romance, *Dianea*, by the Venetian Giovanni Francisco Loredano (1654), a collection of *Small Poems* (1658), among which a place was found for a *Masque presented at Brethie* in Derbyshire before the author's kinsman, the first Earl of Chesterfield [6], re-printed as *A Chain of Golden Poems* (1659) with the author's two comedies. Of these *The Obstinate Lady* had previously (1659) appeared in a surreptitious impression; it is a romantic comedy in the style of the pre-Revolution period, written like most of the contemporary pieces of the same class,

Sir Aston Cokayne (1608–1684).

---

[1] *The Unfortunate Lovers* and *Love and Honour* (cf. *ante*, p. 172).

[2] Cf. *ante*, p. 165.

[3] Dr. Henry Killigrew, afterwards Master of the Savoy, who died in 1700.

[4] This play was afterwards adapted by Sir Charles Sedley under the title of *The Tyrant King of Crete*.

[5] *The Dramatic Works of Sir Aston Cokain.* With Prefatory Memoir and Notes by J. Maidment and W. H. Logan, 1874.—(Cf. *ante*, p. 193.)—From the *Cockayne Memoranda* (privately printed) in the British Museum, it appears that the male line of the Cokaynes of Derbyshire ended in the poet.

[6] The two excellent youths, who lose their way into the Anti-masque of Satyrs, were obviously suggested by the Two Brothers in *Comus*. But the imitation does not go much further than the following:

> '*1st Boy.* I would go to my father.
> *2nd Boy.* And I unto my mother.
> *Lar.* Who is your father?
> *1st Boy.* The ever-honour'd Earl of Chesterfield,' &c.

with much fluency, but devoid of poetic or dramatic merit. The main plot is a vulgarised version of the idea, in itself not very pleasing, of Massinger's *A Very Woman*[1]. The second of these plays, *Trappolin Creduto Principe, or Trappolin Supposed a Prince*, announces itself as an ' Italian Tragi-Comedy'; but the author protests that ' it is no translation[2].' The laughable plot of this piece, which had a prolonged vitality in various forms, is a new version of the story of *Olde Fortunatus*[3]. The comedy as a whole is not unentertaining, although occasionally very coarse; it is written partly in prose, partly in blank-verse, and includes a masque in rime in the middle of the piece. In 1662 Cokayne re-issued his Poems and Comedies, together with *The Tragedy of Ovid*, an odd farrago of very doubtful learning and highly sensational tragic effects. These latter are evolved out of the main plot, which treats of the jealousy of Bassanes, a young lord of Tomos, who kills his chaste wife's lover, and then binds her in a chair, after forcing into her hand the heart of her supposed paramour[4]. Ovid is put to death with the rest of the chief personages; he has played a quite perfunctory part throughout, and expires on receiving the news that his last hopes of a recall to Rome are at an end. The comic scenes introduce a further series of highly-seasoned effects[5], and the play also includes

---

[1] Cf. *ante*, p. 38. Lorece's nonsensical account of his travels unmistakeably recalls Jack Freshwater's in Shirley's *The Ball* (cf. *ante*, p. 107).

[2] See *Prologue:*   ' It is no translation, for he ne'er
　　　　　　　　　　But twice in Venice did it ever hear.'

Several adaptations of Cokayne's *Trappolin* were produced after the Restoration; one of these by Allan Ramsay, with additional songs set to Scotch airs, was published in 1733. A comic ' barletta ' founded on *Trappolin*, and entitled *The Duke and the Devil*, had a run at Covent Garden in 1833.— It may be worth mentioning (cf. *ante*, vol. i. p. 339, *note*) that in Cokayne's piece the Duke of Florence, during whose absence the sham Duke plays his pranks, leaves behind him as one of his lieutenants ' the Lord Machavil,' ' one of those that doth in Florence nourish vice.'—Cokayne had been a traveller, and his knowledge of Italy is illustrated by the catalogue of Italian towns in *Trappolin*, act ii. sc. 3.

[3] Cf. *ante*, vol. ii. p. 457.

[4] Cf. *ante*, p. 79, *note*, as to the last scene of Ford's *Broken Heart*, of which this might almost be supposed to be a parody.

[5] Hannibal, a banished Italian captain, invites a skeleton on a gibbet to supper; the skeleton avails himself of the invitation; and Hannibal in return

a long masque. Altogether, Cokayne's quickness in the appropriation of other dramatist's ideas is undeniable, and, together with his fluency, makes up the sum of his merits as a playwright.

Another royalist who took an active part in the Civil War, though a physician by profession, WILLIAM CHAM-BERLAYNE[1] (born 1619; died 1689), the author of the 'heroic poem' *Pharonnida*, avowedly composed his only extant play for reading while 'the mourning stage was silent.' This is the tragi-comedy printed in 1658 under the title of *Love's Victory*; and altered for the stage in 1678 as *Wits Led by the Nose, or a Poet's Revenge*. The author inveighs against the blind age when

'in a cell
The scholar stews his catholic brains for food';

but the product is in this instance a mixture or 'meander' of romantic and comic scenes, of which fluency of composition and a tendency to operatic effects are the most notable characteristics. Praise has been given to the management of the West-country dialect in which some of the personages talk; Chamberlayne lived all his life at Shaftesbury in Dorsetshire. The metre is still blank-verse.

William Chamberlayne (1619–1689).

Among other plays published in the period of the suppression of the theatres was ROBERT BARON'S *Mirza*, 'a Tragedie really acted in Persia, in the last Age, illustrated with historicall annotations.' As already mentioned[2], the story of this play, which, inasmuch as it was dedicated

Robert Baron.

---

dines with the spectre, and is duly carried off by devils. This device, which Cokayne is supposed to have borrowed from the Italian *Il Ateista Fulminato*, resembles the famous situation (borrowed from a Spanish play) in Molière's *Le Festin de Pierre*, afterwards copied by Shadwell in *The Libertine* (see below).

[1] *Pharonnida* (*and Love's Victory*). By William Chamberlayne. 3 vols. 1820. *Pharonnida*, which was originally published in 1659, is a romantic poem of great length, in rimed heroics, in which Southey took great delight. In 1683 it was, in accordance with the fashion of the times, turned into a prose-novel under the title of *Eromena, or The Noble Stranger.*—*Love's Victory* forms the subject of a paper in *The Retrospective Review*, vol. i. part ii. —See also in Mr. E. W. Gosse's *From Shakespeare to Pope* (1885), pp. 197–203, an interesting account of Chamberlayne and his *Pharonnida*.

[2] *Ante*, p. 149, *note*.

to the King, can hardly have been published later than
1648, is the same as that of Sir John Denham's *Sophy*
(1642); but Baron declares that he had finished three acts
of his tragedy before he cast eyes on Denham's.   He
was, however, so unscrupulous a plagiarist—this very
play, as Langbaine points out[1], contains unmistakeable
reminiscences of Jonson's *Catiline*—that his assertion is unlikely to be considered decisive.   Several old plays were, as
Langbaine further shows, ascribed by Edward Phillips and
Winstanley to Baron in pure mistake; it seems uncertain
whether they were justified in assigning to him a comedy,
not known to have been printed, entitled *The History of
Donquixot, or the Knight of the ill-formed face.*

Sir William Lower (d. 1662). . SIR WILLIAM LOWER, whose services had been conspicuous in the Civil War[2], about 1655 found his way to
Holland, where he held some post in the household of
Mary Princess of Holland, and beguiled his leisure by
the translation of French plays.   In earlier days (1639)
he had published a tragedy, entitled *The Phoenix in her
Flames*, which must be allowed to possess a certain dignity
of style, to some extent justifying its lofty pretensions
in scheme and nomenclature.   The heroine, Phoenicia,
daughter of the King of Arabia, expires in self-kindled
aromatic flames, on learning the death of Prince Amandus
of Damascus, brought about by the passionate fury of her
kinsman Alecto.   The blank-verse of the play, in which
prose scenes are interspersed, is at least equal to that of
Sir William Lower's translations from Corneille, *Polyeuctes
the Martyr* (1655) and *Horatius* (1656).   After his return to
England Sir William Lower published, in 1661, *Three so-*

---

[1] *An Account of the Dramatick Poets*, p. 12. Baron was author of *The
Cyprian Academy* and of other verse in which whole passages were taken
from Milton's *Minor Poems*.   See Mr. Joseph Knight's notice of Baron in
vol. iii of *The Dictionary of National Biography* (1885).—As to the evidence
showing such a play to have existed (which Langbaine doubts), see Halliwell-
Phillipps' *Dictionary of Old English Plays*, p. 77.

[2] In 1644 he carried off the Mayor of Reading in order to extract a con-
tribution from the Corporation; early in 1646 he was taken prisoner himself.
See Mr. Thomas Secombe's notice of him in vol. xxxiv of *The Dictionary of
National Biography* (1893).

called New Playes, among which *The Enchanted Lovers*
(previously printed at the Hague) seems to have been
original, while *The Amorous Fantasme* (dedicated to the
Queen of Bohemia) was taken from Quinault.

Who would care to speculate as to what might have
been the course of our dramatic literature, had no civil
conflict broken out to cause the temporary closing of the
theatres, or had that conflict terminated with a Restoration
honestly endeavouring to do justice to all the main elements
in the combination to which the King actually owed his
recall? As it was, the dramatic branch of our literature
was more than any other subjected to a rush of impulses
and influences which nothing short of the power of genius,
conscious of its purposes and relying upon its own independent strength, could have withstood and overcome.
At such epochs a great personality may in literary, as in
political or religious life, do much to arrest the flood and to
control the storm, even though they may not entirely or
absolutely submit to his behests. But, most unhappily, the
foremost writer of the Restoration period lent himself, with
a facility without a parallel in the history of our literature,
to the reflexion or satisfaction of demands sanctioned by
no more authoritative stamp than that of the fashion of
the day, and with the same buoyancy with which as a
partisan he threw himself into the breach against the
defenders of opposite principles in politics or religion, stood
forward as a champion of defiance against morality.
Dryden's genius, incapable of 'dwelling apart' like Milton's,
seemed doomed to serve. In the eager haste of political
and religious strife,—under the pressure of a necessity with
which he could not pause to hold parley,—under the garish
light of a royal favour and a party patronage which he
chose to regard as indispensable conditions of existence,—in
the hot air of controversy and factions which he had accustomed himself to breathe as if it had been vitally
necessary to him,—he plied his pen in panegyric and invective, in rhetoric and satire, in confessions, apologies,
declarations, recantations. Thus he was, in his own in-

*The effects
of the
Restoration
period upon
a dramatic
literature
uncon-
trolled by
the power
of indi-
vidual
genius.*

comparable phrase, 'hurried down' his age instead of helping to guide it ; and where he failed to stand, no less gifted representative of letters was for many a long day found ready to take arms against the current.

The political results of the Restoration   The political results of the Restoration need not be touched upon here, except from one or two special points of view.   The return of a Stuart King by no means undid the work of the Civil Conflict, in so far as that work was in itself restorative and conservative ; and when the selfish corruptness of Charles II and the headstrong perversity of James II had ended by bringing about another Revolution, a fresh combination of parties re-established on a still safer *as viewed by the Court party* basis the securities won in the days of Charles I.   But the Court party proper—to which it would be a monstrous error to apply the name of conservative—still lived in the traditions, and clung to the formulae, of absolute government ; their politics consisted in a clamorous deference to the manifest wishes of the Sovereign, and in a denunciation of the opponents of his policy at home and abroad as undistinguish-*and the great body of the dramatists of the age.* able from the enemies of the national throne.   The great majority of the dramatists unhesitatingly fell in with this convenient method of argument.   The many are unfit to govern, one is called upon to rule—such is the burden of their *The political and* political wisdom and of their political satire, from the worthy Lord Orrery and the trenchant Sir Robert Howard onwards.   In the hands of Dryden and others, the tragedy of the Restoration lends itself to diatribes against limited monarchy[1] and to exaltation of the right divine.   The wit of comedy in the same period directs itself either against the memories of republican government[2], or against the

---

[1] Such as the (not ineffective) passage in Dryden's *The Conquest of Granada*, Part II, act i. sc. 2.—It may perhaps be noted that the old rule against the introduction of 'modern Christian Kings' on the stage (cf. *ante*, vol. ii. p. 422) is violated by Sir Robert Howard in *The Duke of Lerma*, where Philip IV, who had only recently died, appears.   Later, in 1701, Mrs. Pix brought Peter the Great on the stage in *The Czar of Muscovy* (Dibdin, vol. iv. p. 344) ; but perhaps he was considered 'no Lord's Anointed, but a Russian Bear.'

[2] Tatham's *The Rump, or The Mirrour of the late Times* was acted immediately after the Restoration, and printed in 1661.—In the *Unfortunate Usurper*, printed 1663, a tragedy of which the plot is founded on the story

adversaries of the policy of the Crown. The stage was made a vehicle of political partisanship, more particularly in the days of the Exclusion Bill, and of the consequent political troubles, which lasted more or less till 1684. In this period the allusions in Prologues and Epilogues become far too numerous to mention, and Shaftesbury as the head and front of the Opposition is attacked and caricatured in every way that ingenuity can devise[1]. Religious partisanship as a matter of course intermingled with political—for, as the very lucid madman says in Congreve[2], 'religion and politics are a couple of topics no more like one another than oil and vinegar ; and yet these two, beaten together by a state-cook, make sauce for the whole nation.' Thus in uncompromising intensity of partisanship the majority of the Restoration dramatists go far beyond their predecessors ; and in their personal abuse of the enemies, real or supposed, of the cause with which they have identified themselves, add a new element—than which none could be more deplorable—to the literature of the theatre.

religious partisanship of the dramatists, encouraged by the Restoration ;

No voice—except that of Milton prophesying in his days of darkness—was heard to protest against this servility of sentiment, although at least one poet of unimpeachable loyalty bravely resolved to pour ridicule upon the evil

of Andronicus Comnenus, 'old Nol and his son Dick,' as well as the Rump Parliament, are stated to be vilified.—Sir Robert Howard in 1665 produced *The Committee* ; Crowne in 1673 *City Politics* ; Mrs. Behn in 1682 *The Round-heads*. Other plays of this description are mentioned by Dibdin : Sheppard's *The Committee-Man Curried* seems to have been written as early as 1647 (Genest, vol. x. p. 121) ; Needham's *The Levellers Levelled* was an 'interlude' of the same year (*ib.* vol. viii. p. 329). Henry Neville's *Shuffling, Cutting and Dealing in a Game of Picquet, being acted from 1653 by O. P. and others with Great Applause* (printed 1659), is a brief pasquinade on republican parties and politicians, with which dramatic literature has no concern. (Reprinted in *Harleian Miscellany* (edn. 1810), vol. vii.

[1] See below as to Dryden and Lee's *The Duke of Guise* (1682). Shaftesbury was also personally satirised or attacked in Nevil Payne's *The Siege of Constantinople* (1675 ; see Genest, vol. i. p. 167) ; in Mrs. Behn's *The City Heiress* (1681 ; see *ib.* p. 319) ; in Southerne's *The Loyal Brother, or The Persian Prince* (1682 ; see *ib.* p. 323) ; in Otway's *Venice Preserved* (1682) ; in Dryden's *Albion and Albanius* (1685) ; in Crowne's *City Politics* (1683) ; and doubtless in many other plays. Otway's *Caius Marius* (1680) is seasoned with allusions to the troublous times in which it was produced, and Rochester adapted Fletcher's *Valentinian* (1684 or 1685) to the doctrine of non-resistance in its most advanced stage. [2] *Love for Love*, act iv. sc. 10.

intensified in the latter part of the reign of Charles II; excrescences of his own party[1]. The discovery that the stage might be employed as an auxiliary in political and religious partisanship, it should in common fairness be added, had been utilised by the opponents as well as by the supporters of the policy of the Court ; the ' Popish Plot ' excitement had for a time obliged the Court itself to swim with the current of Protestant prejudice ; Settle raked up the scandalous legend of *Pope Joan* ; and Shadwell stood forth as the representative of the public horror of the bugbears of Roman and of Anglican priestcraft[2]. These efforts are, however, impersonal in their character as compared with those which were protected by the aegis of Court favour. Of the Revolution of 1688 no immediate reflexion is perceptible in our dramatic literature, though a few pamphlets in a dramatic shape appear to have hailed the downfall of King James[3]. The Revolution brought to the throne a prince,

---

[1] See below as to Cowley's *Cutter of Coleman Street.*

[2] See *The Lancashire Witches* and *Teague O'Dively the Irish Priest* (1681). Carpenter's *The Pragmatical Jesuit New-Leavened* (cf. Dibdin, vol. iv. p. 140; Genest, vol. x. p. 142) seems to belong to the same period.

[3] Of the plays mentioned by Genest, vol. i. p. 468, as published in 1690, I have read the first, *The Abdicated Prince, or The Adventures of Four Years.* The scene of this tragi-comedy is said to lie at ' Alba Regalis'; and the whole piece transparently allegorises the transactions of the reign of James II, who appears under the coarsely satiric name of Cullydada, king of Hungaria Nova, and in accordance with a well-known popular scandal confesses to having caused the death of his brother, Charles II. Queen Mary of Modena is made the victim of the grossest ribaldry ; she carries on a low intrigue with Count Dudamore, the special favourite of the Mufti (the Pope); and the deception widely believed to have been practised as to the birth of a Prince of Wales is enacted at length. Other characters in this disgraceful production, which is unredeemed by a touch either of feeling or of wit, are Pietro (Father Petre), Philodemus Duke of Monumora (Monmouth), Barbarossa (Jeffreys), &c., &c. The honest Remanquo acts throughout as a kind of eavesdropper and chorus.—It cannot be supposed that this contemptible stuff was ever intended for the stage. *The Bloody Duke, or The Adventures for a Crown,* likewise plays at 'Alba Regalis,' and seems to turn on the story of the Popish Plot ; it was written by the author of *The Abdicated Prince. The Banished Duke, or The Tragedy of Infortunatus,* was acted at the Theatre Royal, and printed 1690; the scene is said by Halliwell-Phillipps to lie in a village in Belgium ; Monmouth appears under the name of Infortunatus, and James II and Queen Mary of Modena under those of Romanus and Papissa. *The Royal Flight, or the Conquest of Ireland,* is said by the same authority to be a farce designed to ridicule the conduct of James in connexion with his 'abdication.' A tragi-comedy entitled *The Royal*

whose marriage with the Princess Royal had been hailed as a well-omened event by at least one dramatic writer [1]. In England, William III never showed the slightest sympathy with any of the excesses of religious or political partisanship, and, having at no time cared much for any amusement but hunting, never darkened the door of a theatre. Of course such manifestations of feeling as the dramatists now indulged in had to accommodate themselves to the principles of the new *régime*. Shadwell was laureate, and he at least could honestly proclaim opinions which had always been his; while for the former adherents of the Stuart monarchy nothing remained but to despond with Dryden [2], or to acquiesce with Crowne [3]. The stage had a kindly patroness in the good Queen Mary, whom one of the funeral sermons preached after her lamented death praised for her love of play-going and other gentle amusements [4]. But neither the personal character of her consort nor the system of rule which his judgment and self-control preserved from collapse was of a nature to fire dramatic enthusiasm; it was easier to suppress what seemed provocative of hostile criticism [5], than, except at seasons of special excitement, to call forth demonstrations of loyal sympathy [6]. The personal unpopularity of William has probably been on

moderated after the Revolution of 1688;

Flight, or the Irish Expedition (acted and printed in 1690), ends with the arrival of King William at Carrickfergus (June 14).

[1] Edward Cooke's tragedy, *Love's Triumph, or The Royal Union* (1678), which was dedicated to the Princess of Orange, must—although its scene was laid in Babylon, the story being taken from the romance of *Cassandra*—have been designed as a complimentary tribute with reference to the wedding of November, 1677. It does not appear to have been intended for the stage.

[2] See the closing lines of his *King Arthur* (1691).

[3] See his *The English Friar* (1689).

[4] E. Gosse, *Congreve* (in *Great Writers Series*, 1888), p. 59; and cf. H. Barton Baker, *The London Stage* (1889), vol. i. pp. 61-2. In her youth the Princess Mary had performed at Court the character of Calisto in Crowne's play of that name, her sister the Princess Anne taking the part of Nyphe. See Crowne's *Dramatic Works*, vol. i. p. 248; and cf. Evelyn's *Life of Mrs. Godolphin*, and *Diary*, December 15, 1674.

[5] The Master of the Revels is said to have cut out act i from *Richard III*, lest the distresses of King Henry VI might too vividly recall those of the royal exile in France.

[6] Thus after the discovery of the Assassination Plot in 1696, John Dennis in 1697 produced his *A Plot and No Plot, or Jacobite Cruelty*.—Rowe professed to have intended the personages of Tamerlane and Bajazet in his

the whole exaggerated ; but his government was in general little loved even by those who most sincerely detested the proceedings of the rule which he had ousted ; and although anti-Jacobites contended against Jacobites, the 'Williamites' were (unless near the close of the King's

subsides in the reign of Queen Anne. reign) hardly to be accounted a national party. The effect created by Jeremy Collier's judicious exposure of the immorality of the contemporary stage had not passed away when Queen Anne came to the throne, or during the early years of her reign. A Royal Order conceived in the sense of his strictures was issued in January, 1704 ; but though the House of Lords went out of its way to thank the Queen for her effort, it had to be repeated a few months afterwards [1]. Queen Anne herself was devoid of love for the drama, and neither encouraged the public stage nor, unless exceptionally, allowed performances at Court. The main national interest of her reign was the great war in which the flag of Great Britain was borne aloft beyond the rivalry of the nations ; and to such an interest as this it was impossible that a dramatic literature trained to a pettier range of associations should so much as attempt to do justice. Moreover, although the issues of the war had in the eyes of part of the nation distanced the conflicting pretensions of the two contending factions—although a popular dramatist of the age could even venture to assert that 'faction' itself ' slept ' [2]—the strife of parties still occupied the centre of the arena. When the war closed, one of the two great parties, to whose game there seemed no ending, claimed the half-intercepted glories of the struggle, and the other the more solid honour of having conducted it to a satisfactory close. The stage, or rather on this occasion the audience, was content to make use of the really colourless background of Addison's *Cato* for a demonstration of this rivalry.

Tamerlane (1702) as poetic parallels of William III and Lewis XIV respectively. The likenesses were certainly vague enough to need pointing out.

[1] For the original Order, see Genest, vol. ii. p. 296, and cf. as to the Order of March, 1704, and as to another of 1711, prohibiting the abuses of standing on the stage or going behind the scenes, Ashton, *Social Life in the Reign of Queen Anne* (edn. 1883), p. 256.

[2] See the Prologue to Farquhar's *The Beaux' Stratagem* (1707).

Another aspect of the political results of the Restoration and the Revolution may be noted as reflecting its weak hues in the dramatic literature of this period. The reign of Charles II was not wholly destitute of warlike glories; but the challenge to the Dutch was really due to dynastic inspirations, nor had the mercantile rivalry of which they availed themselves risen to the height of a national enthusiasm. The foreign policy of the Protectorate had been far more perplexing than inspiring, and had failed except incidentally to command the sympathies of a people ignorant of its varying purposes and preoccupied with domestic questions and difficulties. In the beginning of the Restoration age it is instructive to observe in our dramatic literature the continued evident aversion to soldiers and soldiering[1], due to the oppressive remembrance of the military era of the Civil War and the Commonwealth. Such attempts as Dryden's to excite popular animosity against the Dutch[2] must be reprobated as among the unworthiest efforts by which he ever degraded his pen. Of the long struggle against French preponderance in the affairs of Europe which King William induced England to maintain only occasional echoes seem audible on the contemporary stage[3]. He left its inheritance to the great general who served a popular English Queen, and who carried the military glory of the nation to an unprecedented height. In such times the note of a patriotic spirit could not but again make itself heard; and in the comedies of Farquhar, and still more in those of Steele, we are occasionally reminded that England had engaged in a mighty contest, and that she had sympathy as well as admiration to bestow upon the brave soldiers, whose valour was helping to raise her to the foremost rank among European nations.

The Restoration, however, signifies not only a political

Drawbacks to a patriotic enthusiasm for war.

---

[1] See *e. g.* Thomas Killigrew's *The Princess;* D'Avenant's *The Siege.*

[2] See *The Massacre of Amboyna;* and cf. *The State of Innocence.*

[3] In 1690 appeared a tragi-comedy, *The Siege and Surrender of Mons,* in which the author states it to be his intention to expose the villainy of the priests, and the intrigues of the French; in 1691 a tragi-comedy, *The Siege of Derry;* and in 1698 a 'droll' called *The Siege of Namur* was acted at Bartholomew Fair.

Social effects of the Restoration limited in their range. change, but also a social reaction. The backward movement was indeed probably neither so deep nor so broad as has frequently been assumed. On the part of the nation at large the reaction was not against the essence of Puritanism. The Restoration, indeed, and the movements which had preceded it, implied a revulsion and a protest against the domination of an extreme and extravagant minority; but it would be to mistake the historical character of the English nation, were we to suppose the great body of it to have been hurried into the opposite extreme, and to have exchanged a fanatical observance of an unnatural code for an equally irrational lawlessness. With the extreme developements of the Revolution which had momentarily triumphed in the victory of the army over the Parliament, which Oliver Cromwell had with difficulty held in check, and which after his death again sought to thrust themselves forward, the nation at large had never sympathised; and it was as a liberation from the fear of their ultimate victory that men who had by no means shared in the sentimental loyalty of the Cavaliers—even the sober-minded Presbyterians of the great towns—welcomed the return of the Stuarts. Charles II brought with him what these men, as parties to the contract, had not designed to include in it; but the licence and wantonness of his Court, and the literature which that Court affected, and of which it accordingly soon found a supply equal to the demand, were not the manners and the literature of the nation. Thus—for I leave aside other illustrations from the literature of the period [1]— the Restoration stage failed either to revive the old national

Literature and the stage no longer national.

----

[1] *Hudibras*, by far the most popular book of the age, and published almost immediately after the Restoration, is after all only an attack upon the outside of the Puritan movement,—upon its formulae and figures rather than upon its inner sense and spirit—and merely repeated with humorous variations the comments which during the rule of Puritanism men had been making 'under the rose,' and which after its overthrow they found it a natural relief to make aloud. *Hudibras* went little further than this; and the popularity of Butler's burlesque can hardly be said to prove that the inner spirit of Puritanism was extinct in the English people.—How differently the social reaction affected different spheres even of London society—connected though they were in their several ways with Court or Government—might be easily shown by a comparison from this point of view of the *Memoirs* of Grammont with the *Diary* of Pepys, and of both with the *Diary* of Evelyn.

drama, or to substitute in its place a new genuinely national growth.   The theatres were regarded by large sections even of the inhabitants of London in no other light than that of centres of idleness and mischief; and although the classes which composed their public were probably even more restricted than they had been in the Elisabethan days, it was the tastes of these classes only which the dramatists of the Restoration were anxious to gratify.

The literature of the stage was not only out of sympathy with the opinions and sentiments of the people at large, but was in part both intended and received as an insult to them. The moral philosophy which, however distantly, reflected itself in much of this literature was not an edifying one ; and after passing through this medium, the teachings of Hobbes presented themselves as the naked conclusion that a conscience or a moral sense, or any essential distinctions between Right and Wrong, might alike be dismissed as non-existent.   While Parliament was seeking to rivet a hard-and-fast ecclesiastical system upon the nation, the ministers of religion were treated with undisguised dislike or contempt by the dramatists, with whatever Church they might themselves happen to be individually connected [1].

The moral tone of the stage not in sympathy with that of the people at large.

Thus the drama, living by the breath of fashion and by the favour of a class, helped to divorce the literary activity of the nation from its other energies.   In Charles II's and James II's age the leaders of polite literature were the hangers-on of the Court, while the capital was still small enough to find a real as well as nominal centre of social fashions in a palace.   In the next-ensuing reigns, those sections of society which were most conspicuously associated with political party-life

The drama loses its full connexion with the national life.

---

[1] This hatred of priests as such—to which Jeremy Collier had good reason to advert in his *Short View,* though his charges were not based on altogether tenable grounds—is a very significant note of the tragedy as well as the comedy of the Restoration age.   For examples see Dryden's *The Indian Emperor* (act i. sc. 2); *The Spanish Friar, passim*; and the Mufti in *Don Sebastian,* written after the author's conversion to the Church of Rome. A similar spirit is discernible in Lee (see his *Lucius Junius Brutus*) and in Crowne (see his *Thyestes,* act iv. sc. 2, and Epilogue).   Even Rowe has characters such as Magas (in *The Ambitious Stepmother*) and the Dervise (in *Tamerlane*).

and with the literary and artistic diversions of the capital were only beginning to recover a fuller sympathy with the moral, intellectual, and social life of wider classes of the population. Literature already in the reigns of William and of Anne contributed to this desirable result, but it was the literature of prose essays and the beginnings of prose fiction, not that of the stage. Not the drama, but the writings of De Foe, Steele, and Addison, and of their successors the great novelists of the eighteenth century, restored to our popular literature its genuinely national character. There is, then, nothing paradoxical in the assertion that the later Stuart drama—from the Restoration to the close of the reign of Anne—is not essentially a national growth. It stands under the special influence of classes whose opinions and sentiments, and whose manners and morals, are often very far from reflecting those of the nation at large.

The influence of the Court of Charles II upon the drama—in what sense beneficial, The direct influence of the Court and of its central figure the King is made a boast by the drama of the Restoration age. That this influence was altogether pernicious it would probably be an error to suppose. Dryden's assertion[1] that the refinement of conversation, due to the Court 'and particularly to the King, whose example gives a law to it,' benefited the language of the stage, doubtless contained an element of truth, although the term 'refinement' unsatisfactorily expresses the combination of ease, lightness, and wit which—but little beyond which—was to be derived from the source in question. Comedy, however, in so far as it addressed itself to the representation of manners, could not but profit from so direct a contact with those social spheres which must always give the law to many of its forms. 'The greatest pleasure,' says a dramatist of this age[2], that King Charles 'had from the stage was in comedy, and he often commanded me to write it.' The comic drama of the Restoration period has its faults as well as its vices; but in ease of manner and freedom of movement—the prerogatives, whatever they are worth, of the

---

[1] *Defence of the Epilogue* (to Part II of *The Conquest of Granada*, 1672).
[2] Crowne, in the Dedication of *Sir Courtly Nice*.

world of high life—its superiority to Elisabethan comedy on the one hand, and to the comedy of the Georgian period, taken as a whole, on the other, is incontestable. Yet this advantage was far outweighed by the damage which, as Dryden was to live to declare[1], was done to the stage by the low standard of morality which the Court communicated to the theatre. It became in sober truth a 'house of scandal' behind as well as in front of the curtain; and there is no need to show how conscious the dramatists themselves were of the fact. The responsibility of these aberrations cannot be shifted from the dramatists to their patrons; but a different Court would at all events have made possible a different stage. From the good-will of a Charles II or the fitful patronage of a Rochester[2] no efforts of a higher kind could derive a real or a lasting encouragement. *and in what sense pernicious.*

The influence of King and Court, however, also helped very materially to augment, and in particular directions to create, a tendency which rarely stands in need of encouragement in any dramatic literature. Lord Orrery[3] and Dryden[4] ascribe to the direct influence of the royal taste the earliest examples and the subsequent popularity of those 'Heroic Plays' of which more will have to be said in this chapter, and which from the first stood under the direct influence of foreign literary growths[5]. But inasmuch as this particular instance is merely the most striking example of its kind observable in the history of the later Stuart drama, it may be well to consider *seriatim* the foreign *The influence of foreign dramatic literatures upon our own encouraged.*

---

[1] Epilogue to *The Pilgrim* (1700).

[2] Rochester (to whom, under the name of Rosidore, Lee pays an admiring tribute in *The Princess of Cleves*, act i) is the very type of that species of patron which is the curse of literary men. In order to oust Dryden from the eminence which he was on the eve of securing, Rochester fostered the feeble dramatic talent of Settle; to reduce Settle to his level, and to spite Dryden, he encouraged the efforts of Crowne; and to leave Crowne in no doubt as to the source of fashionable success, he bestowed his fickle favours upon the youthful Otway, whom he likewise afterwards abandoned.

See the Preface to his *Plays.*

See the Dedication to his *The Indian Emperor.*

[5] See Dryden's *Essay of Heroic Plays, ad in.* I shall return to this subject below.

literary influences to which, partly with the aid of fashion, it became more or less subject.

Isolated followers of the ancients.

Of the dramatic literatures which had hitherto *directly* influenced our own, those of classical antiquity need hardly be taken into account in connexion with the later Stuart period. Milton's *Samson Agonistes* was an experiment which will at all times find followers in those who venture to treat the art of dramatic sculpture as one not altogether lost; but the Attic drama can only be imitated, it cannot be brought back, whether the name of the modern poet be Milton, or Mason, or Matthew Arnold. Even in the early days of our dramatic literature Seneca, not Sophocles, had served as a model to our tragic poets, as well as to their Italian and French predecessors and contemporaries. And again, it had been the narrower range of the New Comedy in its Latin reproduction, not the glorious freedom of the Old, from which the authors of our first English comedies had borrowed plots, or subjects, or characters. In the Restoration and next-following periods it would be an error to seek in an occasional *Œdipus* or *Thyestes* any proof of personal study of classical tragedy[1], or to suppose that Plautus and Terence were habitually resorted to except through such mediation as that of Molière. Here and there a classical scholar essayed his skill in translating Greek or Latin plays[2], but mere exercises of the study have no connexion with a living dramatic literature.

Nature of contact with the Italian drama.

The Italian drama, as well as Italian fiction, doubtless still continued occasionally to supply English playwrights with plots[3]; and the remains of the extraordinary popu-

[1] These tragedies, by Dryden and Lee, and by Crowne, will be noticed below. Charles D'Avenant's *Circe* (1677), which I have not seen, is stated to have been founded on the *Iphigenia in Tauride* of Euripides. Charles Gildon's *Phaeton, or The Fatal Divorce* (1698) is said to have been founded in plot, and in many particular passages, upon the *Medea*.

[2] Dibdin (vol. iv. pp. 137–40) mentions a translation of Sophocles' *Electra* by Wase, and of Aristophanes' *Clouds* by Stanley (not, it would seem, the learned Thomas Stanley), and the translation by Charles Hoole of all the comedies of Terence. The date of publication of the last-named was 1676.

[3] See *e. g.* Wilson's *Belphegor* and Cokayne's *Trappolin Creduto Principe.*— In Farquhar's *The Twin Rivals* (1702) a poet in want of a plot is still recommended to 'read the Italian' as well as the 'Spanish plays' (act iii. sc. 1).

larity once enjoyed by the master-pieces of the Italian pastoral drama still produced occasional translations of the *Pastor Fido* and the *Aminta*[1]. But the chief contact between the Italian and the English theatre in this period arose in connexion with the introduction of a new dramatic species, the opera—as to which a few words will suffice below.

Unlike Italian dramatic literature, that of Spain was in the latter half of the seventeenth century still a vigorous growth. Ruiz de Alarcon, in whose comedies, as contrasted with those of Lope, literary historians have recognised the distinctive element of a moral purpose[2], had died shortly after the most brilliant of Spanish dramatists. Tirso de Molina, whose comic genius seems to have been of a more light-hearted type, but who is praised for the extraordinary grace and ease of his Castilian dialogue, and for an ingenuity in the construction of plots, in which however he at times resorted to the most improbable expedients[3], survived till 1648. The date is unknown of the death of Francisco de Rojas Zorilla (born 1607), who was largely plundered by the French dramatists of the latter half of the century[4]; but he appears to have flourished for some time after the English Restoration. The Spanish dramatist, however, whose manner seems to come nearest to that of the masterpieces of French and later English comedy of

Influence of later Spanish dramatists.

---

[1] The former was translated by both Sir R. Fanshawe and Elkanah Settle, the latter (1671) by John Dancer, an Irish dramatist, who also translated French tragedies.

[2] Klein, vol. xi. part i. p. 5, where a remark to the same effect is quoted from Hartzenbusch, and other Spanish authorities are appealed to in support of it. Alarcon died in 1639, Lope de Vega in 1635.—On a play by Alarcon, as is noted below, Corneille founded *Le Menteur*, which was translated into English, and furnished the subject of comedies by Steele and Foote.

[3] *Ib.* p. 114 *seqq.* On Tirso's *El Burlador de Sevilla y Convivad de Piedra* (which borrowed its own story from the *Chronicle of Seville*), or on an Italian adaptation of it, Molière founded his *Le Festin de Pierre* (cf. Ticknor, ii. 324, and Klein, *u. s.*, p. 161 *seqq.*). Tirso has been highly praised by M. du Viel-Castel.—As to Shadwell's *The Libertine*, see below.—Goldoni (see his *Memoirs*, English translation, vol. i. pp. 260 *seqq.*), who says that the examples of Molière and Thomas Corneille induced him (in his *Don Juan Tenorio*) to 'give a similar treat to his countrymen, that he might be on somewhat decent terms with the devil,' speaks of the original Spanish piece as a wretched play.—The title of Molière's *Le Festin de Pierre*, as has been pointed out, involves a mistranslation.

[4] Klein, p. 186.

character, and to whom the former directly, the latter indirectly, must have been in no inconsiderable degree indebted, was Agustin Moreto[1], who died in 1669. Finally, the great poet Calderon de la Barca continued his extraordinary productivity to the close of a long life in 1681. In him the religious and national enthusiasm and the artificiality of the Spanish drama alike reached their highest point; but, while our English dramatists found an occasional resource[2] in his highly-wrought plots, the singular brilliancy of his tragic style could not be transmitted to a foreign literature without a tender delicacy of treatment such as was to be applied to it in later times and under very different conditions.

English followers of the Spanish dramatists.   The attention of English authors had long been directed to the Spanish drama; and the tastes of King Charles II, however much he might in literary as in other matters be inclined to allow France the *jus praecedendi*, well accorded with the manner and matter of the more recent developements of Spanish dramatic literature. Particularly, therefore, in the earlier part of this reign our dramatists are found continuing to avail themselves of Spanish originals,

---

[1] Moreto's masterpiece, *El Desden con el Desden*, is familiar to the German stage, under the title of *Donna Diana*, and was introduced to the English in 1864 by a version from the hand of Mr. Westland Marston. See H. Morley, *The Journal of a London Playgoer*, p. 321. For an exposition of Moreto's dramatic developement see Klein, *u. s.*, pp. 258-446. Upon *El Desden con el Desden* were founded Molière's *Princesse d'Elide* and Gozzi's *Principessa Filomena*. (See the Preface to C. A. West's very readable German version.) I am not aware of any English play having been founded upon Moreto except Crowne's *Sir Courtly Nice*; but his style of comedy seems to present many points of resemblance to that which was popular on the English stage in the latter half of the seventeenth century. His *El lindo Don Diego* ('pretty Don Diego') is described by Klein (p. 296) as the first of the species known in the Spanish drama as the *comedia de figuron*, 'whose hero is no stereotyped character-mask, but a comic mock-figure reflected on to the stage as a picture of the age and its manners from the fool's world of actual social life'—in fact a character of *affectation*, to borrow an expression of Congreve's. He is at the same time the Spanish fop, corresponding to the English fops of Etherege, Vanbrugh, and Colley Cibber. As a whole the comedy of Moreto seems to admit of being described as social comedy, simpler in plot and more vigorous in the drawing of character than that of his Spanish predecessors.

[2] Cf. *ante*, vol. ii. p. 736, as to a possible debt on the part of Fletcher; and see below.

or to use Spanish sources, like some of their predecessors
before the Restoration. Thus, GEORGE DIGBY, EARL OF *G. Digby,*
BRISTOL (died 1676), who played so prominent and inter- *Earl of Bristol*
esting a part in the political history of the times, and in *(1612–*
the earlier part his career exerted himself so actively as *1676),*
King James' ambassador at Madrid, besides 'making out
of Spanish,' *i.e.* Calderon, two comedies which have been
lost [1], adapted a third play by the same poet (*No Siempre lo
Peor es Cierto*) under the title of *Elvira, or The Worse not
always True* (printed 1667) [2]. We have here a long and
interesting intrigue ending with the vindication of suspected
fidelity, and the action, especially at the close, is abundant.
The style is formal, both in the serious parts and even in the
protracted humours of the servants Chichon and Francisca;
and apart from the circumstance that the dialogue is too
lengthy for English taste, the play reads too palpably like
a translation.   Lord Bristol is likewise said to have joined
SIR SAMUEL TUKE (a gentleman who had served the *Sir Samuel*
King in the Civil War, and who died in 1673) in his *Tuke (d. 1673).*
adaptation, made by the advice of King Charles II, of
Calderon's *Los Empeños de Seis Horas*, under the title of
The Adventures of Five Hours [3] (printed 1662). This is
a genuine Spanish comedy of intrigue, bustling and amusing
in its English dress, and here and there seasoned with allusions (such as those directed against the Dutch) evidently
added by English hands.   But the decency of the dialogue
would of itself suffice to show that it is no English comedy.

---

[1] '*Tis Better than It Was* and *Worse and Worse*, taken, as Ticknor (vol. ii.
p. 392, *note*) thinks there can be little doubt, from Calderon's *Mejor Está que
Estaba* and *Peor Está que Estaba* respectively.

[2] Printed in Hazlitt's *Dodsley*, vol. xv, and in *The Ancient British Drama*, vol. iii.

[3] *Ib.*—Mr. Gosse, *Seventeenth Century Studies*, p. 224. says that 'in 1662–3
this very successful play . . . was awakening delusive hopes of a new great
dramatist'; and in 1666 (August 15 and 16) Pepys arrived at the conclusion
that 'when all is done, it is the best play that ever I read in my life,' and
(August 20) on reading *Othello*, which he had 'ever heretofore esteemed
a mighty good play,' could not, having so lately read *The Adventures of Five
Hours*, esteem *The Moor of Venice* other than 'a mean thing.'—Sir Samuel
Tuke should be distinguished from Richard Tuke, who in 1672 published
a moral drama entitled *The Soul's Warfare*, but afterwards re-named *The
Divine Comedian, or The Right Use of Plays*. It was dedicated to the good
Lady Warwick, who died in this year.

Sir Richard Fanshawe (1607–1666).   SIR RICHARD FANSHAWE (1607–1666), who represented both Charles I and Charles II at Madrid, translated two plays of Antonio de Mendoza[1]; and among the works of more than one English dramatist of the reign of Charles II we shall notice plays of indubitably Spanish extraction[2]. Now and then an older Spanish play or story[3] may have been similarly turned to account.

The French drama under Lewis XIV.   But by far the most important influence exercised upon the English drama of this period by any foreign literature proceeded from that of France. At the time of the Restoration French literature in its various branches had as yet by no means definitively settled into those forms in which it for so long a period exercised a potent sway over the literatures of other European countries. Till within a few years of the return of the Stuarts France had been agitated by the wars of the Fronde—a revolt carried on by a strange combination of heterogeneous forces against the Cardinal-Minister, Mazarin. Nor was it till the year 1661 that Lewis XIV, round whose person the whole literary movement as well as the political system of his age was to revolve, began to govern on his own account. Of the political expediency—indeed of the political necessity—of the attitude assumed by the French monarchy during the earlier years of his rule there can be no doubt, nor of

[1] *Querer per solo querer* (printed 1671) and the *Fiestas de Aranjuez* (1670). As to the great injustice inflicted upon Sir Richard Fanshawe by his recall from Madrid, where his place was wanted for the unlucky Lord Sandwich, see Mr. Wheatley's note to Pepys' *Diary*, under December 8, 1664.

[2] Dryden's *The Wild Gallant* and *The Rival Ladies*, and doubtless also Lord Orrery's *Guzman*, were from Spanish sources; Thomas Killigrew's *The Parson's Wedding* (acted 1664) was taken from Calderon's *Dama Duende*; of Crowne's *Sir Courtly Nice* the plot (already, as it proved, used by a previous author) had been suggested to him by King Charles II from Moreto's *No Puede Ser*; Wycherley owed the most amusing scenes of his *The Gentleman Dancing-Master* to Calderon's *El Maestro de Danzar*; Dryden's *An Evening's Love* came only indirectly from Calderon through Thomas Corneille; Steele's *The Lying Lover* similarly from Alarcon; Mrs. Centlivre took her *The Perplex'd Lovers*, and probably also one or two other of her comedies, from a Spanish source; Colley Cibber's *She Would and She Would Not* derived its plot from *The Counterfeits*, a play 'of Spanish extraction,' by a dramatist named Leanard (Dibdin, vol. iv. p. 144).

[3] As in Crowne's *The Curious Impertinent* from *Don Quixote*, or in D'Urfey's dramatic version of that novel, so severely handled by Jeremy Collier.

the generous and lofty ideas which animated him and his counsellors. This spirit communicated itself to the master-minds of French literature, to whose efforts in this its greatest period prejudice alone can deny the credit due to true nobility of sentiment. But neither a nation nor its literature can be transformed at once ; and in manner as in matter the French men of letters trained under the influences of the second quarter of the seventeenth century differ from those whose youth belongs to the third, as again the writers of the earlier are to be distinguished from those of the later part of Lewis XIV's reign. His greatness, and that of the literature which adorned it, alike had their period of rise, their meridian, and their decline. My present purpose, however, is only to dwell upon the transformation to which I have referred, in so far as it affected two branches of French literature, both of which materially influenced the progress of our English drama. These were naturally and necessarily the branches which commended themselves to the favour of the classes in French society with whom and with whose tastes the patrons and the authors of English dramatic works could alone be brought into a more than passing contact.

The troubles and terrors of the great civil and religious *Reaction* wars of the sixteenth century had—in accordance with *towards refinement* a law of human nature which reflects itself repeatedly in *in higher* the history of literature—called forth in certain spheres of *French society and* French social life a reaction towards culture and refinement. *literature.* The people, according to its wont, solaced or distracted its weariness of political and social troubles by listening to the ministers of that gaiety, seasoned with something of cynicism, which has always flourished in the darkest hours of French popular life[1]. But in other regions of society, the influence of the same reaction is observable even in the midst of the evil days which succeeded the death of Henry IV. In the very year of the king's assassination Honoré d'Urfé

[1] These were the days of the *Tabarinades*, of which M. C. Louandre in his *Chefs-d'œuvre des Conteurs Français au XVIIme Siècle* (1873-4) has re-published some specimens more diverting than edifying. A summary of parts of this publication by the editor will be found in the *Revue des deux Mondes*, March 1, 1874.

published the first volume of his pastoral romance *L'Astrée*, which turned courtiers into shepherds and shepherds into heroes of fiction. Soon afterwards Camus produced his devotional romances, and Lourdelot his narrative of the triumphs of 'perfect love.' To the cultivation of delicacy of sentiment was added a desire for correctness and elegance of diction, since Malherbe had appeared as the scholarly reformer of the native tongue, and since Richelieu had established the Academy as a literary Areopagus. D'Urfé had after all only sought to domesticate in France a literary growth—that of the pastoral romance—already familiar to Italy and Spain, and to England likewise; and to substitute for the moribund romance of chivalry the romance of gallantry in a pastoral dress[1]. The form introduced by him was developed by subsequent writers, and Gomberville (born 1609) forms a kind of link between the pastoral romance of platonic chivalry and the elaborations of a completed system or code of neo-romantic gallantry by Calprenède and the Scudérys[2]. In these authors, together perhaps with one or two others of less prominence, we have the typical representatives of that group of romance-writers which was to exercise so marked an influence upon the English drama of the latter half of the seventeenth century.

The salons of the Précieuses. Nowhere was the determination to take refuge in an imaginary world, and through this medium to view the actual, more likely to assert itself than in those circles where women of taste and accomplishments were conspicuous as the patronesses of literature and the leaders of fashion ; and in the capital, at all events, ladies of a less elevated rank were certain to follow in the footsteps of their social superiors. From this period, as is well known, date the glories of those earliest of French *salons*, which exercised so notable an influence upon the literature as well as the social life of their age. The ridicule which more especially through Molière's comedy descended upon the

---

[1] See St. Marc-Girardin, *u. s.*, vol. iii. sect. xxxviii, where the progressive scale in the treatment of the regard due to women, and of the love and honour due to them, in the representative romances of three several periods —the *Amadis*, the *Astrée*, and the *Clélie*—is admirably brought out.

[2] Cf. Dunlop, *History of Fiction*, chap. x.

pretenders to authority in the world of sentiment and taste, had no doubt not been originally designed as a reflexion upon its real leaders; and the last days of the Hôtel Rambouillet had already passed away when the *Précieuses Ridicules* invited the laughter of the Parisian world. But the tempest of recrimination which the dramatic satire excited would hardly have raged as it did, had it been thought solely and entirely applicable to provincial exaggerations[1].

The typical romances of the species in question are, as observed, primarily those of de la Calprenède (who died in 1663), and those of Madeleine de Scudéry (1607–1701), which appeared under the name of her brother Georges (1601–1667). (Calprenède, like Georges de Scudéry, was also known as a dramatist.) Calprenède's famous productions of this kind are *Cléopâtre*, *Cassandre*, and *Pharamond*. Mlle. de Scudéry wrote *Artamène, ou Le Grand Cyrus*, followed by *Clélie* and *Almahide, ou L'Esclave Reine*. The scene of her last romance, *Mathilde d'Aguilar*, lay, like that of *Almahide*, in part among the conflicts of the Christians with the Moors. Gomberville (1600–1674) may, more especially by virtue of his *Polexandre*, be classed with these writers. Madame de la Fayette's (1634–1693) *La Princesse de Clèves* differs from their most celebrated romances in so far as it bears some sort of relation to historical fact. The popular works of the Abbé de St. Réal (1639–1692) belong rather to the category of romantic history than to that of historical romance[2].

Chief French romances of this age.

---

[1] Victor Cousin, in *La Société Française au XVIIme Siècle d'après le Grand Cyrus de Mlle. de Scudéry* (1858), vol. ii. pp. 185 and 297 and *note*, points out that the satire of *Les Précieuses Ridicules* and *Les Femmes Savantes* was by no means directed against the mistress and frequenters of the Hôtel Rambouillet, or even against Mlle. de Scudéry and her circle in the Rue de Beauce. The same may doubtless be asserted of the satire of the novel *La Précieuse ou Le Mystère de la Ruelle* by the Abbé Pure, reproduced on the stage under the title of *Les Fausses Précieuses*, which Molière was accused of having copied. See the very instructive remarks on the whole of this subject, which I cannot further pursue here, in M. V. Fournel's article on Molière in vol. xxxv of the *Nouvelle Biographie Générale* (1865).

[2] The following are doubtless only a few instances out of many in which the English dramatists derived the subjects of their plays directly from these romances. On Calprenède's *Cléopâtre* Mrs. Behn founded *The Young King* (1679) and Lee his *Gloriana, or The Court of Augustus*; from his *Pharamond*

The chief characteristics of the most celebrated of these romances are generally supposed to be fairly reproduced in Boileau's satirical dialogue (*Les Héros de Roman*), which though described by himself as 'the least frivolous work which has yet proceeded from my pen,' he was well-bred enough not to publish till after the death of Mlle. de Scudéry. Yet this Lucianic dialogue, of which the good sense and the gay humour are alike remarkable, in point of fact only directs its ridicule against particular features in these romances and in the dramas of a cognate type— above all against their practice of confining the business of heroic life to love-making, and reducing the heroes of anti- quity and history to the level of gentlemen entirely given up to this particular pursuit[1]. These are certainly features

Lee took the plot of his *Theodosius, or The Force of Love.* From *Mustapha et Zéangir* Lord Orrery took the story of his *Mustapha*, and from *L'Illustre Bassa* was also taken Settle's *Ibrahim.* Calprenède's *Cassandre* supplied Banks with the story of his *The Rival Kings* (1677), and probably Lee with part of that of *The Rival Queens.* Part of Dryden's *Secret Love, or The Maiden Queen*, and of his *Marriage à la Mode*, and a scene of his *Aureng- zebe*, came from *Le Grand Cyrus*; as of course did *Cyrus the Great, or The Tragedy of Love* (1696) by John Banks. Dryden's *Conquest of Granada* was founded on *Almahide*, though for the character of Almanzor he was partly indebted to Calprenède. *Clélie* furnished Lee with part of the plot of his *Lucius Junius Brutus*, and *The Princess of Clèves* with that of his tragedy of the same name. Otway borrowed the stories of both his *Don Carlos* and his *Venice Preserved* from the Abbé de St. Réal.—Among the translations proper of these romances were one of *Pharamond*, and one of *Almahide* by Milton's nephew, John Phillips, both published in 1677.

[1] The following passage is worthy of quotation, as containing the gist of a criticism which must be passed on a whole series of 'heroic plays' :

'*Pluton.* Et sont-ce des Héros ?

Diogène. Comment, si ce sont des Héros ! Ce sont eux qui ont toujours le haut bout dans les Livres, et qui battent infailliblement les autres.

Pluton. Nomme m'en par plaisir quelques-uns.

Diogène. Volontiers. Orondate, Spitridate, Alcamène, Mélinte, Britomare, Merindor, Artaxandre, &c.

Pluton. Et tous ces Héros-là, ont-ils fait vœu comme les autres de ne jamais s'entretenir que d'Amour ?

Diogène. Cela serait beau qu'ils ne l'eussent pas fait. Et de quel droit se disaient-ils Héros, s'ils n'étaient point amoureux ? *N'est-ce pas l'Amour qui fait aujourd'hui la Vertu héroïque ?* '

M. de St. Marc-Girardin, *u.s.*, cites from Mlle. de Scudéry's *Clélie* the follow- ing short statement of the duty of heroes by Amilcar, one of the chief person- ages of the romance : 'Quand on est longtemps avec les femmes, il faut de nécessité leur parler, ou de l'amour qu'elles nous donnent, ou de celui qu'elles ont donné, ou de celui qu'elles peuvent donner.'

which our dramatists faithfully reproduced, when taking
their plots from Calprenède's or Mlle. de Scudéry's endless
volumes. The heroes of more than one drama by Dryden
or Lee inspire the feeling of wonder expressed by Boileau's
Pluto when he declares it 'difficult to suppose that the
Cyruses and Alexanders have suddenly, as I am informed
they have, become Celadons and Thyrsises'; and lend point
to the French poet's direct warning against 'giving a French
air to ancient Italy' by turning Cato into a fashionable lover
and Brutus into a fop. In judging of the reasons which
account for the popularity of these romances, it should however be remembered that to their age they were not insipid
as they are to us—inasmuch as many of the figures which
we find devoid of interest were intended and accepted as
portraits of living personages[1]. This gave a semblance of
reality to the Romans and Orientals of Mlle. de Scudéry
which cannot be claimed for those of Lee or Dryden; nor
should it be overlooked that the conditions of the drama
render indispensable, in the case of scenes and characters
intended for the stage, a measure of historic as well as of
local propriety that may be dispensed with in narrative.
For the rest, the morality of these romances is consistently
pure and honourable; and the ethical problems treated in
them are not unreal like the pomp and paraphernalia of
their manner and style. Moreover, these problems are often
such as could have suggested themselves to none but refined
minds, and their solutions are never out of harmony with
a conscientious view of life and its responsibilities. The
romances themselves are, to be sure, tedious enough with their
men of honour, their heroic love, and their nice expositions
of true gallantry;—but their men of honour are chivalrous
gentlemen who, though wearing the dress of ancient Romans
or Turkish viziers or Frankish kings, and using the language
of the Court of Versailles, are true to the principles that
lie at the root of modern Christian society; their heroic
love is a pure and virtuous sentiment; and their gallantry

---

[1] Victor Cousin, with the help of a Key bearing date 1687, which he was
fortunate enough to discover in the library of the Arsenal, is able to furnish
a complete identification of all the personages in *The Grand Cyrus.*

is after all but one form of that tribute of respect to woman and her influence which, when commanding the assent of an age, never fails to soften its manners and purify its morals. Nor is it unworthy of notice, that the approval of admirable women was not denied to a conception of their part in life which appealed to the noblest elements in their natures[1].

Relations between the French romances and the English drama. It might have been well had our dramatists taken over into their plays more of the moral tendencies, and less of the mere externals, of these romances. They copied the interesting stories, the grand historic names, and the enchantingly distant scenes; they borrowed the high-sounding terms and phrases of heroic virtue and heroic love; they appropriated deeds of valour achieved on the grand scale of Artamenes, who exterminates a hundred-thousand men with his own hand in the course of a single novel[2]; and they revelled in descriptions as detailed as that which in Boileau's Dialogue the voluble Sappho gives of 'the illustrious maiden'—Mlle. de Scudéry herself. They were well content to seize upon plots, to transplant characters, and to copy phrases; but their views of morality and society were at best superficially coloured so as to agree with their models; in a word—with exceptions on which it is here unnecessary to dwell—they took over what was extravagant and artificial because of its extravagance and artificiality, and cared little for applying it to any purpose but that of creating brilliant or striking effects. The novelists themselves are not to be judged by the use which

---

[1] Mme. de Sévigné in 1698 was reminded of her 'chers romans' by the exiled royal family at St. Germains, and by their chivalrous resolve to accept nothing more than what was necessary from the munificent hands of their generous Protectors. (*Lettres*, ed. Mommerqué, vol. viii. p. 434, Paris, 1862.)— Dorothy Osborne (see her *Letters to Sir William Temple*) largely depended on the mental *pabulum* of such romances as the *Grand Cyrus* and *Cléopâtre*. I do not know whether she ever read the *Princesse de Clèves*, of whom St. Marc-Girardin so well writes: 'Elle meurt comme une sainte, après avoir témoigné par sa vie l'ascendant de l'honneur, sans que l'honneur ait besoin de s'appuyer sur un sentiment surhumain.'—In the third volume of the *Cours de Littérature Dramatique* will be found an analysis of the central idea of this story, and an instructive elucidation of the general moral standpoint of this school of writers.

[2] The computation is Sir Walter Scott's. See his Introduction to Dryden's *The Conquest of Granada.*

was made of them [1]. In so far, however, as resort to these romances relieved our tragic dramatists from the temptation to seek for their plots in stories of loathsome intrigue or unnatural crime, the use which they made of the *romans de longue haleine* of Mlle. de Scudéry and her contemporaries amounted to a distinct benefit; and even in the midst of the tremendous situations, appropriately accompanied by the 'heroic' bombast, of Dryden or Lee, we seem to breathe more freely than among the psychological or physiological problems imagined by Webster or Ford.

Of still greater significance for the history of our dramatic literature than this fashionable school of French romance, however, is the developement of the French drama itself in the middle and the later part of the seventeenth century. Much of that drama in this age is indeed of essentially the same kind as the romance-literature to which I have just adverted, and as such fell under the censures of the same satirist. Calprenède, Georges de Scudéry, and those Obscure Ones whose memory survives in the Satires of Boileau, composed plays in which detailed enquiry might doubtless discover the originals of more that one English heroic play of the Restoration age. But it seems needless to press this point further. In this respect at least the age of Lewis XIV in France resembles the Periclean age of Athens, that in the drama it found not only the most brilliant but the most faithful representative of its higher general culture. The classicism of Corneille and Racine is but pseudo-classical, and the supremacy claimed for their works among the masterpieces of modern dramatic art has long since been overthrown by a sounder criticism. But most assuredly their art could not have been what it was, or have exercised the influence which may unhesitatingly be ascribed to it, had it not been in true sympathy with the best life of the nation and the age which it adorned. In the progress of the dramatic genius of Corneille is traceable

The French drama of this period.

Its relation to French national life.

---

[1] The use made by the English dramatists of these romances of course only added to the popularity which they enjoyed as works of fiction—in which shape they must have long continued to be 'épuisés' by fashionable ladies like Melantha in Dryden's *Marriage à la Mode* (see act iii. sc. 1).

the progress of the French nation from a period of struggles to one of monarchical order and grandeur; while Racine reflects the serene calm, satisfied with the acceptance of fixed forms and pervaded by the spirit of religiosity, which characterises settled periods of a national history. But though the sphere of ideas within which these dramatic poets move is thus not unreal, it is so limited as to exclude much that was at work in the hearts and minds of the people. The French tragedy of this period seems to 'sweep by,' rather than to absorb into itself, a national life of great variety and richness; and though the great master of contemporary French comedy, Molière, contrives to assimilate elements of truly popular origin, together with the products of foreign literary growths, in him too we seem to miss the full freedom of an art, happiest when not bound to regulate the use of its creative energies by the approval or disapproval of kings.

Its exotic elements.   Viewed from without, the masterpieces of the French drama of this period accordingly commended themselves for imitation by those qualities and features which were imitable, not by those which were organically connected with the history and character of the nation whence it sprang. French tragedy borrowed its forms from classical antiquity, and laid down for itself a code of rules, for most of which it claimed the incontrovertible sanction of classical authority. As a matter of fact, the theories which in his Essays on Dramatic Poetry—especially in that on *The Three Unities*—Corneille put forth as paramount, were published by him in his old age, when his creative powers had diminished and his greatest tragedies had long been before the world [1]. The use of rime in tragedy was first authoritatively commended by Italian criticism [2], which still enjoyed a paramount authority, although it was the example of the rimed Alexandrines of Corneille and the other French poets, in both tragedy and comedy, which impressed the practice upon the notice of English dramatists. In comedy

---

[1] They belong to the year 1659; *The Cid* had been produced in 1636, and followed by *Horace* (1639), *Cinna* (1639), and *Polyeucte* (1640).

[2] *Viz.* in the prefatory discourse to Cardinal Sforza Pallavicini's *Erminigilda* (1655). See H. Morley, *First Sketch, &c.*, p. 634.

Molière borrowed from the Spaniards and the Italians much
else that thus reached our English literature at second-hand;
and his debts to Latin comedy have probably been under-
rather than over-rated.

In estimating the influence of the French dramatic litera- *Influence*
ture of the seventeenth century upon our own, it is not *of the*
French
sufficient to attempt the task—in itself almost endless— *upon the*
of tracing particular English plays to particular French *English*
drama.
originals. A few data, designed to illustrate rather than
exhaust this branch of the subject, are appended in a
note [1]. But while neither translations nor adaptations

---

[1] The chief French dramatists of the seventeenth century who come into
question are Pierre Corneille (1606-1684); Philippe Quinault (1637-1688);
Jean Racine (1639-1699); Thomas Corneille (1625-1709), and Jean François
Regnard (1665-1709). Among the plays of these authors translated or
reproduced by English dramatists within, or shortly before, this period were,
in the case of Pierre Corneille, besides *Le Menteur*, of which an anonymous
version appeared as early as 1661, *Le Cid*, translated by Joseph Rutter;
Pompée and *Horace*, translated by 'Orinda's matchless Muse,' Mrs. Catharine
Philips, as to whom see Mr. E. W. Gosse's essay in his *Seventeenth Century
Studies*, where an interesting account is given of the translation of *Pompée*, and
of its production on the stage in 1663 through the good offices of Lord Orrery;
of *Horace* she only lived to finish four acts; Crowne wrote a Prologue to it in
1668-9; *Horace*, translated by Charles Cotton and previously translated by
Sir William Lower; *Pompée*, translated by certain 'persons of honour,' *viz.*
Waller, who contributed act i, Sir Edward Filmore, Sir Charles Sedley,
and the future Earls of Dorset and Middlesex; cf. Dryden's *Essay of
Dramatic Poesy*, where this translation is described as a powerful 'argument'
in favour of verse. *Héraclius*, a play of which the plot, according to Gibbon
(*Decline and Fall*, ch. xlvi, *note*), 'requires more than one representation to
be understood clearly, and, after an interval of some years, is said to have
puzzled the author himself,' was translated by Lodowick Carlell; *Nicomède*
by Cotton, and by John Dancer. Quinault's *Agrippa* was likewise translated
by Dancer; and his *L'Amour Indiscret* helped to supply the materials of
(Newcastle and) Dryden's *Sir Martin Marall*. Racine's *Bérénice* was used
by Otway for his *Titus and Berenice*; his *Iphigénie* was translated by Boyer
under the title of *Achilles, or Iphigenia in Aulis* (1699), and republished
(1714) under the title of *The Victim, or Achilles and Iphigenia in Aulis*,
on the appearance (1714) of Charles Johnson's *The Victim*, another version
of *Iphigénie*. Racine's *Andromaque* is the original of Ambrose Philips' *The
Distrest Mother* (1712); and on his *Phèdre* Edmund Smith appears to have
modelled his *Phaedra and Hippolytus* (1707), for which Addison wrote the
Prologue, and Prior the Epilogue. From his *Les Plaideurs* Wycherley in
The Plain Dealer borrowed the famous character of the Widow Blackacre.
Of Molière's plays (taking them in chronological order) I have noted the
following translations or reproductions: *L'Etourdi* furnished the chief source
of *Sir Martin Marall*; *Le Dépit Amoureux* contributed a scene to Dryden's

could reproduce in the English language the outward form
of the masterpieces of French tragedy and comedy, it was
possible to borrow subjects, plots and characters, but not
to transplant the spirit of either the serious or the comic
drama of contemporary France.

*Rime in
French and
in English
tragedy.*
In form, as will be seen, French tragedy suggested the
substitution of rime for blank-verse to Lord Orrery, 'the
matchless Orinda,' and others, above all to Dryden, whose
master-hand alone could have ensured even temporary
success to so hopeless an experiment. For a time, with
the support of the personal taste of King Charles II, the

An Evening's Love and parts of the plots of Ravenscroft's *The Wrangling
Lovers* and of Vanbrugh's *The Mistake*; *Les Précieuses Ridicules* suggested
a leading character in Shadwell's *Bury Fair*, and part of Dryden's *An Evening's Love*; a translation (in broken English) of *Sganarelle* constitutes act ii of
Sir W. D'Avenant's *The Playhouse to be Let*; and the same play, besides
being used for a comedy called *Tom Essence, or The Modish Wife* (1676), was
translated by Vanbrugh; on *L'École des Maris* was partly founded Sir Charles
Sedley's *The Mulberry Garden*; it was also used, together with *L'École des
Femmes*, by Wycherley for his *The Country Wife*; to *Les Fâcheux* Shadwell
was indebted for his *The Sullen Lovers, or The Impertinents*; *L'École des
Femmes* was translated in 1671 by Pope's friend Caryl under the title of
Sir Solomon; *La Critique de l'École des Femmes* furnished a scene to
Wycherley's *The Plain Dealer*; *Le Mariage Forcé* supplied the greater part of
Ravenscroft's *Scaramouch, &c.* (1677) and part of Mrs. Centlivre's *Love's
Contrivance*, which was also indebted to *Le Médecin malgré lui*; *Don Juan, ou
Le Festin de Pierre* (itself not original), suggested the general design of Shad-
well's *The Libertine*; without *Le Misanthrope* Wycherley would hardly have
imagined his *The Plain Dealer*; *Le Sicilien, ou L'Amour Peintre* furnished an
episode in the plot of Crowne's *The Country Wit*; *Le Tartuffe, ou L'Im-
posteur*, after being translated by Medbourne in 1670, suggested *The English
Friar* of Crowne, besides more famous comedies of a date beyond the range
of the present work; *Amphitryon* was known to Dryden, when writing his
play of the same name; *L'Avare* suggested *The Miser* of Shadwell; *George
Dandin, ou le Mari Confondu* was adapted by Betterton under the title of
The Amorous Widow; *Monsieur de Pourceaugnac* (afterwards translated by
Vanbrugh as *Squire Trelooby*) and *Le Bourgeois Gentilhomme* (under the title
of *The Citizen turned Gentleman*) were reproduced by Ravenscroft in 1671
and 1672; *Les Fourberies de Scapin* was reproduced by Otway as *The Cheats
of Scapin*; *Psyché* was, though only very partially, used by Shadwell in his
play of the same name; and *Le Malade Imaginaire*, together with *Monsieur
de Pourceaugnac*, helped Mrs. Behn in the composition of her comedy of
Sir Patient Fancy. To these may be added (besides two of Scarron's (1610–
1660) plays which served D'Avenant for the composition of *The Man's the
Master*) Corneille's *Le Menteur*, from which Steele took his *The Lying Lover*;
Thomas Corneille's *Le Feint Astrologue* (from Calderon), which Dryden
adapted as *An Evening's Love, or The Mock Astrologer*; and Regnard's *Le
Joueur*, from which Mrs. Centlivre took her *The Gamester*.

innovation maintained itself; when Dryden announced his intention to abandon it [1], the practice was doomed; and even before this we find it treated with undisguised ridicule by a leading comic dramatist [2]. There is no necessity in this place to refer to the arguments urged for and against it, which will be briefly noticed below. It proved impossible permanently to domesticate in English tragedy a form differing from that which had become proper to it, which it had adopted as its own, and the attempt to introduce rimed couplets into English comedy was even more transitory [3]. But in truth these couplets in the hands of Dryden and his followers are something very different from the Alexandrines of Corneille, Racine, and Molière. The latter merely dignify and refine the style of polite conversation and courtly speech; the former not only modify expression, but may without exaggeration be said to change the tone of thought. It would not be easy to find any satisfactory reason for this difference in the nature of 'heroic' verse itself; for it was of course not antecedently necessary that this English metre should stereotype itself into the form elaborated in succession by Waller, Dryden, and Pope. But a poetic form, like a poetic species, cannot do violence to its history; and the English heroic couplet, when it came to be used by Dryden for the drama, had already grown radically unsuitable for such an application.

While imitating the form of the masterpieces of French tragedy the English dramatists showed little disposition to transfer the spirit of these works to their own. Already Corneille lives in a world of sentiment appropriate to the society in and for which he wrote; the chivalrous pride and the passionate resolution of his earlier heroes and heroines yield to the necessities of the public welfare, and the sanctity of authority in Church and State is the Destiny which rules

The spirit of French tragedy not communicated to English.

---

[1] In 1678. For details see the remarks on Dryden below.

[2] In Wycherley's *The Plain Dealer* (act ii. sc. 1), produced in 1674, Novel says that he counselled the author of *The Country Wife* (*i. e.* Wycherley himself) ' to put his play into rhyme; for rhyme, you know, often makes mystical nonsense pass with the critics for wit, and a double-meaning saying with the ladies for soft, tender and moving passion.'

[3] See below as to Etherege.

his tragic ends [1].   Racine is the representative of an age in which a glorious rule of Order seems to have been established, and in which men and women feel able to give themselves up to the study of the emotions of the heart. The reaction of which I spoke above [2] has reached its climax, and the tenderest of human feelings has become the absorbing theme of tragic poetry.   At the same time Racine represents in their full influence the refinement and the dignity of manner cherished in the social region in which he moved, and the reverential attitude towards religious and monarchical authority which was its primary law.   The tragic poets of the English Restoration period are in general strangers alike to the tone, the taste, and the moral spirit of Racine.   Heroic virtue and heroic love are their themes as well as his ; but, unlike him, they have little thought of investing the one with courtly dignity and representing the other as at once delicate and pure.   They as it were by instinct lower the passion which like him they are content to make the prevailing motive of their conceptions, and in seeking to give their pictures of it an impressive force, they take refuge in an expedient to which he never condescends—*viz.* in bombast.   So little of what is essential in the spirit and manner of French tragedy is really assimilated by our English writers, that the resemblance of subjects and the acceptance of rules which concern the construction and conduct of dramatic actions become unimportant in comparison.

The spirit and manner of Molière imperfectly communicated to   In the case of comedy, the difference is not so absolute, but it is equally noticeable.   Molière was copied by our English dramatists more unscrupulously than probably any other writer has been copied before or since ; but to his copyists neither his spirit nor his manner descended.   It

---

[1] See a striking passage in Hettner, *Literaturgeschichte des* 18. *Jahrhunderts*, ii. 10.—If we may trust a letter from Voltaire to the Second Earl of Stair (see *The Stair Annals*, vol. ii. p. 129), a proposal was made about 1719 to remodel French versification in accordance with English practice by ' banishing rime from poetry.'   Voltaire received the proposal with natural hesitation as to a reply.   In this case, however, it is not dramatic versification which is specially in question.

[2] *Ante*, p. 307.

must indeed be allowed that these vary considerably in his *English* several works. He was the inheritor of the traditions of the *comedy.* New Greek comedy and of those of French farce; he was both a satirist and a humourist; at times he displays the sentiments of a loyal courtier, at others that gay spirit of Opposition which in France has at all times been held is indispensable in a popular wit. His comedies range from elaborate and subtle pictures of human character in its enduring types to lively sketches of social follies and literary extravagances, and broad appeals to the traditional sources of vulgar merriment. Under the general control of sure artistic taste, his style suits itself in turn to every one of these species. And his morality, it must be allowed, is not less flexible when it comes into contact with the chief social weakness of his age. Molière may with equal success be shown to be an advocate and a satirist of the sanctity of the institution of marriage; and if he defends it directly, he also indirectly helps to make it ridiculous.

The English comedy of this period, which, in spite of the pleasing illusions to the contrary in which genial critics have indulged, is almost entirely a comedy of actualities, gained both strength and buoyancy from what it owed to Molière. Without the help of his light and perspicuous plots our comic dramatists would probably have continued to resort more largely to those Spanish models in which attention is absorbed by the conduct of a complicated intrigue. Had they refrained from taking advantage of the suggestive variety and human truthfulness of some of his most powerful characters, they might have continued to ring the changes on a more restricted number of types, or have altogether abandoned the endeavour to draw character in favour of the easier and naturally more attractive practice of copying or caricaturing the follies and the foibles, the manners and the men, of their own age. While, in accordance with the genius of the nation to which they belonged, they imparted a stronger and more realistic colouring to the characters which they took over from Molière, these dramatists too generally substituted for the often reckless gaiety of Molière's dialogue a much grosser salt—at times a mere pretence of salt—of their own[1].   The brilliant style of Congreve and his contemporaries belongs to a later period, and cannot be said to be founded on that of Molière[2].   Of his morality our later comedy in general only borrowed what suited it and its public—*viz.* the loosest moods.   But it would be monstrous to hold him responsible for the sins of which on this head our comic drama made itself guilty.

In addition to these literary influences, certain other artistic tastes and fashions affected the progress of our drama in this period, which had also been imported from abroad, but which easily commended themselves to a public only too ready in such matters to be guided by its neighbours.

The Opera.   The history of the Opera is interesting to the student of English dramatic literature from two points of view only. Few English dramatic works possessing any literary importance are included among the contributions to this hybrid species ; and those which rather contain operatic elements, than constitute operas properly so called, are in general likewise productions of little permanent literary value.   On the other hand, the Opera usurped so large a share of fashionable favour that the progress of the English drama could not fail to suffer from the success of this foreign importation on the boards of English theatres ; and the complaints of our dramatists are both loud and deep as to the difficulty which they experienced in maintaining a struggle against it [3].

---

[1] By way of illustration, *Le Dépit Amoureux*, act iv. sc. 3, may be compared with the scene borrowed from it in Dryden's *An Evening's Love* (also act iv. sc. 3).

[2] Perhaps, however, the example of Molière and French dramatic literature in general may have encouraged a tendency to greater length of dialogue than was usual in our earlier writers.   Already D'Avenant (*The Play-House to be Let*, act i) makes the Player say :

'The French convey their arguments too much
In dialogue : their speeches are too long,'

and contrast this feature with the narrowness of French plots.

[3] I have much pleasure in referring the reader, if interested in the subject, to the pleasant rejoinder made to the above remarks in my first edition by Mr. H. Sutherland Edwards in his book *The Lyrical Drama* (1881), vol. ii. pp. 122 *seqq.*

Italian tragedy seems from the first to have followed the *Italian Opera* example of the ancient classical stage in admitting a musical element. But this remained nothing more than an accessory, until towards the close of the sixteenth century the experiment was first made of producing a dramatic work written throughout with a view to its being sung[1]. The lyrical passages were connected with one another by speeches and dialogues in what was called the *stilo recitativo*; and aided by the splendour of decorations and machinery, the new species flourished in Italy throughout the seventeenth century, and has, with modifications of no essential importance, endured to our own days.

Italian Opera proper came to England at a relatively late *in England.* date—about the beginning of the eighteenth century—and in such a form that the whole force of fashion was needed in order to ensure it a welcome. But our 'tramontane taste,' to borrow Colley Cibber's phrase [2], tolerated its introduction ' in a lame hobbling Translation into our own Language, with false Quantities, or Metre out of Measure, to its original Notes, sung by our own unskilful Voices, with Graces misapply'd to almost every Sentiment, and with Action, lifeless and unmeaning, through every character.' Soon it became usual to allow Italian singers, 'qualified for the Opera' or otherwise, to sing in their native tongue, and the rage for these entertainments, fostered by judicious management, increased. The genius of a great German musician was employed to compose operas, generally written in English and translated into Italian; and in spite of the protestations of some English dramatists [3], and with the aid of

---

[1] The *Daphne* of Ottavio Rinuccini, with whom co-operated three musicians, Peri, Giacopo Corsi, and Caccini, is regarded by Sismondi (*Literature of the South of Europe*, vol. i. p. 469) as the first Italian opera. Its date is 1594 or 1597. For a fuller account of Rinuccini's efforts see Klein, vol. v. pp. 523 *seqq.*

[2] *Apology*, p. 262.

[3] These are far too numerous to cite; but mention may be made of one of the most elaborate among them, John Dennis' *Essay on the Operas after the Italian Manner, which are about to be establish'd on the English Stage. With some Reflections on the Damage which they may bring to the Publick* (1706). In his Preface Dennis declares his strictures to be directed only against those Operas which are entirely Musical, ' for those which are Dramatical may be

others [1], a species, which from the nature of the case as a literary variety eludes criticism, continued to flourish at the close of the period now under survey.

French Opera.

But before Italian Opera thus came into competition with the English drama in its own domain, that drama had indirectly been largely influenced by the species. Opera established its popularity in France in the latter half of the seventeenth century, particularly under the influence of the Italian musician Lulli [2] (1633-1687) and the French dramatist Quinault (1637-1688). The favour obtained by the entertainments produced by them caused French dramatists of the highest mark—the elder as well as the younger Corneille and Molière—to essay the same kind of composition ; and under the influence of these examples it found its way into English dramatic literature. The invasion was hastened by the accidental circumstance that, during the period immediately preceding the Restoration, the ingenuity of D'Avenant was in search of some kind of entertainment which, while containing dramatic elements,

English Opera.

might call itself by some other name than 'stage-play.' And the eagerness with which on the re-opening of the theatres English composers of great talent welcomed the opportunity of applying their art to the illustration of dramatic compositions, made the transition easy from the drama em-

---

partly defended by the Example of the Antients.' He argues that Operas have everywhere driven out poetry—so in Italy and in France. Music, he says, is 'not subservient to Reason.' Operatic entertainments infuse no generous sentiments or thoughts—if an opera is to do this, it must be 'writ with Force.' But this is incompatible with music, 'especially in so masculine a language as ours.' He goes on to argue with much vigour that in itself 'an Opera after the Italian fashion is monstrous . . . in Italy however 'tis a beautiful harmonious Monster, but here in England 'tis an ugly howling one. . . . England may produce the greatest Tragick poets in Europe, but there is scarce one Nation in the Christian world, but is qualified to surpass us in Operas. The very nations from whom we have taken the Opera will despise us in consequence.'

[1] *e. g.* Vanbrugh and Congreve opened the Haymarket Theatre with Owen McSwiney's *Camilla*, a translated Italian Opera, in 1706 ; Aaron Hill wrote *Rinaldo* (1711), for which Handel composed the music.

[2]   'Tous ces lieux communs de Morale lubrique,
      Que Lulli réchauffa des sons de sa Musique.'
                              Boileau, *Satire X.*

bellished with musical passages to the drama intended to
be either altogether sung, or to resemble the opera in the
manner and style even of the general dialogue. The
varieties of 'English opera' in this period are accordingly
numerous, and it is hardly worth while to attempt an
accurate distinction between them. Thus, Purcell wrote
music for Lee's *Theodosius* and for adaptations of Fletcher's
The Prophetess and of Shakspere's *A Midsummer Night's
Dream*. Lock similarly illustrated D'Avenant's adaptation
of *Macbeth*. Of the opera in a stricter sense Dryden's
Albion and Albanius (1685) may be regarded as an example;
and in the Preface to this production Dryden attempts
a definition of the species. He there characterises an opera
as 'a poetical tale, or fiction, represented by vocal and
instrumental music, adorned with scenes, machines, and
dances,' and adds that 'the persons of this musical drama
are generally supernatural.' On the other hand, George
Granville (Lord Lansdowne) in the Preface to his *The
British Enchanters, or No Magick like Love* [1] (1706), which
is described as 'a Dramatick Poem with Scenes, Machines,
Musick and Decorations,' &c., recommends that 'the Dialogue, which in the French and Italian is set to notes, and
sung,' should be 'pronounced; if the numbers are of themselves harmonious, there will be no need of Musick to set
them off.' Such influence as the opera exercised upon the
character of our dramatic literature—especially upon those
branches of it which contained an imaginative element—
could only be in one direction. Combining the artificialities

---

[1] This opera is generally agreeable in versification (it contains by-the-by
a passage which is a reminiscence of Dryden's *Song for St. Cecilia's Day*, and
two to which Pope can hardly have been a stranger), but the treatment of
the story (which introduces a good enchanter and a bad enchantress—
Urganda—and Amadis of Gaul to boot) is commonplace.—Among later
operas, Addison's *Rosamond* (1707) may be mentioned for the sake of its
author's name, to which, however, it adds little lustre, and because of its unfortunate prominence in the history of the first endeavour (made by its
composer Thomas Clayton) to establish English opera on the national stage.
It appears to have been intended as a kind of protest against the librettos
of operas written to suit the English performers, who helped out the arias
and duets sung by the Italians in their native tongue. But its short
lines render it unpleasing as a literary effort, and the music to which it was
set is stated to have been singularly poor.

of the masque and the pastoral with conventional impossibilities of its own, and trusting for effect to the adjuncts of
action and poetry rather than to action and poetry themselves, the opera furnished an evil example to those
dramatists who, while seeking their effects beyond the
domain of the actual, simultaneously cast to the winds
all considerations of dramatic probability and propriety.
Reckless as usual, Dryden yielded to this temptation with
a readiness not so excusable in him as it was in his
less gifted contemporaries; although his genius made it
impossible for him even to err without splendour. In
general, the tendencies encouraged by the example of the
opera could not possibly prove anything but pernicious
to the general progress of those departments of our dramatic
literature which were affected by it; and hardly any of
them escaped these tendencies altogether [1].

The Ballet.   The above quotations illustrate one other innovation of
this period to which it is necessary to advert. Music was by
no means the only adjunct which the drama of this period
called in to its aid. Together with the opera, the ballet
had become a favourite entertainment of the French
Court, having been likewise introduced from Italy, the
true home of pantomimic dance. It commended itself
very speedily [2] to the tastes of the English Court and of

---

[1] It may be incidentally noticed that the practice of introducing occasional
lyrics into plays continued to find favour after the Restoration. These
songs were collected both before and after the re-opening of the theatres
under the generic title of *Drolleries*. See the Introduction to Mr. Ebsworth's
edition of the *Westminster Drolleries* of 1671 and 1672—a characteristic collection, prefaced by a very genial Introduction, of what I fear is for the most
part worthless verse.—Professor Saintsbury (Additions and Corrections to
Dryden's *Works*, vol. xviii. p. 299) is inclined to doubt the supposition that
Dryden (unless it were exceptionally) reproduced French songs in the
lyrics introduced into his plays.

[2] Already in 1663 Dryden says (act iii. sc. 1):

'The poetry of the foot takes most of late';

and in *The Play-House to be Let* D'Avenant (act i) makes the Dancing-
Master distinguish from historical dancing—

'down-right plain history
Exprest in figures on the floor, a kind
Of morals in dumb-shows by men and beasts'—

the public which sought its inspirations in this region—and
soon became a favourite expedient for enhancing the effects
of operatic or quasi-operatic dramas, as well as for furnishing
to comedies an agreeable *intermezzo* or exhilarating finish.
Indeed, we hardly come across a comic drama without
finding 'the dancers' introduced into it, as a rule unconnected with the action save by some formal expedient.
Finally, the practice of employing regular scenes [1], and the *Scenes,*
developement of theatrical machinery of all kinds, together *machinery,*
and
with an increasing taste for brilliancy and magnificence in *costume.*
the externals of dress, contributed to suggest new opportunities to dramatic composition. From the age of the
Restoration [2] dates the doubtful practice of 'revivals' of
plays—in other words, of representations of them intended
to furnish stage attractions or variations, of one sort or
another, beyond those of an ordinary reproduction. At *Adapta-*
the same time, 'revivals' of the Restoration age serve to *tions of*
earlier
remind us that the dramatic literature of this period, like *English*
the theatre itself, was quite unable to dissociate itself *plays.*
from the previous history of our national drama. The
dramatists of the later Stuart reigns, as will be seen, succeeded but imperfectly in reconciling the influences of
foreign literatures and the tendencies of their own age
with the traditions of Elisabethan and early Stuart
dramatic literature. Yet, though in their original form,
the masterpieces of that literature were frequently decried
as more or less obsolete [3], the adaptations of old English

---

from what the player facetiously calls 'high history upon ropes.' The representative of this form of art, Jacob Hall, is one of the best-known figures in
Grammont's gallery of contemporary portraits.

[1] See below as to D'Avenant's *The Siege of Rhodes*. In his essay *Of Heroic
Plays*, Dryden says that D'Avenant derived the use of scenes from the Italian
operas of the day.

[2] The taste for magnificence of dress was of course in part due to the fact
that there were now actresses as well as actors on the stage.

[3] See Dryden's *Defence of the Epilogue* (*An Essay on the Dramatic Poetry of
the Last Age*), and cf., together with the various expressions of opinion by
Pepys, the passage in Evelyn's *Diary*, November 26, 1661, cited by Sir Walter
Scott in his *Essay on the Drama* : 'I saw *Hamlet, Prince of Denmark*, played,
but now the old plays began to disgust this refined age, since his Majesty's
being so long abroad.'

tragedies and comedies constitute no inconsiderable proportion of the dramatic productions of the age. Several
such versions of Shaksperean dramas have been already
noticed [1]; but Chapman [2], Beaumont and Fletcher [3], Webster [4], and others [5] were likewise either adapted or otherwise
turned to account. That such was the case, is of course the
reverse of surprising ; but the fact is worth insisting on, even
in a preliminary summary of the various influences at work
in this period of intermingled change and return.

Dramatists who wrote both before the Revolution and after the Restoration.

Milton.

Few of the writers who had contributed to our dramatic
literature before the outbreak of the Civil War survived
the restoration of the Stuart monarchy, and fewer still were
found ready to resume their old labours in the new times.
Mention has already been made of the solemn poetic protest,
full of both indignation and pathos, sent forth from his soli-
tude by MILTON against the victory of the Philistines [6]. As
a remonstrance *Samson Agonistes* necessarily passed unheeded, and least of all was the age disposed to take into
account the note of hopefulness discernible in the great poet's
submission to the Uncontrollable Will. In the dramatic
literature of the Restoration there was no place for Milton's

[1] Cf. vol. i. pp. 513 *seqq.* Besides the adaptations there noticed, may be
mentioned D'Avenant's *Macbeth*; Shadwell's *Timon of Athens*; Otway's
Caius Marius (a barefaced theft from *Romeo and Juliet*); James Howard's
Romeo and Juliet (in which the lovers are kept alive) ; Ravenscroft's *Titus
Andronicus* (1678) ; Tate's *King Lear* (1681) ; Betterton's *Henry IV* (1700).

[2] Tate's *Cuckolds' Haven* (1685) is from *Eastward Ho*.

[3] D'Avenant's *The Rivals* is taken from *The Two Noble Kinsmen*, and the
bye-plot of his *The Siege* from *The Humorous Lieutenant*; Waller altered *The
Maid's Tragedy* (1682), Betterton *The Prophetess* (1690), Vanbrugh *The
Pilgrim* (1700), D'Urfey *The Sea Voyage* (1685), Tate *The Island Princess*
(1687) ; *The Wild-Goose-Chase* is the original of Farquhar's *The Inconstant*.

[4] Betterton adapted *Appius and Virginia* as *The Roman Virgin* (1669).

[5] John Leanerd worked on materials from Brewer and Middleton (*Poetical
Register*, p. 160 ; Dibdin, iv. 144) ; Ravenscroft produced parts of a comedy by
Davenport (*ib.* 131), whose *The City Night-Cap* was adapted by Mrs. Behn in
The Amorous Prince (1671). Of older plays she adapted *Lust's Dominion* as
Abdelazar (1671), Wilkins' *The Miseries of Enforced Marriage* as *The Town
Fop* (1677), and Middleton's *A Mad World, my Masters* as *The City Heiress*
(1682).—The subject of Marlowe's tragedy served the unfortunate William
Mountfort for his *Doctor Faustus* (acted between 1684 and 1688, printed 1697),
of which the remainder was harlequinade. (See O. Francke's edition,
Heilbronn, 1886.)   [6] *Ante*, pp. 203, *seqq.*

tragedy. Another great name—not towering in an eminence like Milton's, but rising far above the level of the ordinary literary adherents of the royal cause—was to acquire fresh lustre in the years succeeding the Restoration. As a drama- *Cowley.* tist, however, COWLEY only produced one work in his later years, and even this was merely a new version of a piece written by him in those jovial Cambridge days to which we owe the humorous Latin play already described[1]. *The Guardian*, after being acted at Cambridge in 1641–2, had been published in 1650, and, according to the author's own account, was several times acted in private during the troubles. *His Cutter of Coleman Street* (1661). Much of it, however, must have been re-written, in order to suit the time in which the action of *Cutter of Coleman Street*[2] (as the new version was called) was laid, and the special significance with which its chief comic characters, Cutter and Worm, were invested. The comedy, as acted in 1661, seems to have subjected Cowley to censure as having been intended for abuse and satire of the Royalists, besides being guilty of profaneness. In his Preface, which is well worth reading, he accordingly defends himself with effective indignation against both charges—and this he could upon the whole well afford to do. What enraged these injudicious assailants, proves to us the moral courage of the poet. As a tried friend of the monarchy he rendered a real service to its cause, and to that of social order at large, by thus boldly and bravely satirising the scum of the loyal party at the very time when its ignobler elements were actively striving to remain at the top; and for the sake of the spirit of manliness which pervades this comedy we may readily pardon its occasional coarseness and the farcical improbabilities of its plot[3].

---

[1] See *ante*, p. 187, as to *Naufragium Joculare*.

[2] Printed in vol. ii of *The Works of Mr. Abraham Cowley* (3 vols. 1710–1). 'Cutter' signifies swaggering bully. (See *How a Man may Choose a Good Wife from a Bad*, act v. sc. 1: 'Sir, do you not pink doublets?... I took you for a Cutter, you are of a great kindred.'—Roger North, in his *Lives of the Norths*, vol. ii. p. 57 (ed. 1826), says of Laurence Hyde Earl of Rochester (the 'Lory' of Dryden's *The Young Statesmen*), that one of his infirmities was 'passion, in which he would swear like a cutter.'—Coleman Street had an ancient notoriety. In Dekker's *Seven Deadly Sins of London* (1606), Lying 'musters together all the *Hackneymen* and *Horse-coursers* in and about *Coleman-streete.*'

[3] The freshness and indeed boisterousness of the writing of this comedy,

Sir William D'Ave- nant's later plays.

Among writers of lesser note who composed plays both before and after the Restoration SIR WILLIAM D'AVENANT must here receive final mention.   The works produced by him after the stage for which he had laboured with so much courage and zeal had been once more restored to honour need not, however, detain us long.   *The Siege of Rhodes*, which had been brought out as an entertainment of scenery and music in 1656, was now elaborated in form ; a Second Part (divided, unlike the first, into acts and scenes) was added, and both were performed in 1662, and printed in the following year.   The interest attaching to this production is historical only; but while *The Siege of Rhodes* deserves lasting recognition on account of the swift courage and versatile ingenuity displayed in its original production, the interest attaching to it as the first attempt at English opera has but little concern with literature.   An enquiry into the nature of the scenery employed in it must be left to theatrical antiquarians [1] ; with regard to its literary characteristics, it too closely resembled the many modern opera-texts, towards which it stands in an indistinct relation of parentage, to call for closer criticism.   The dialogue is partly in heroic couplets, partly in short rimed lines ; the latter only can be supposed to have been given

The Siege of Rhodes (1656 and 1662).

not less than the extravagance of its plot, betray its early origin. But in the chief characters there is considerable humour. Cutter and Worm are two swaggerers who conceal their vagabond characters under cover of their devotion to the good cause. To further their purposes, they are quite ready to ruin one another or to perpetrate any deed of horror. Cutter even marries the daughter of a saint and soap-boiler, betokening his transitory conversion to a Puritan frame of mind by announcing a series of visions, of which the most striking is the 'return' of himself and Tabitha on a Purple Dromedary. Colonel Jolly too, though his manners are little better than his morals, and his facetious daughter Aurelia, are drawn fresh from life. The sentimental characters, Young Truman and Lucia, exhibit touches of pathos from which an inferior and less self-confident hand would perhaps have shrunk.

[1] So far as one can gather, this 'scenery' appears to have consisted of great single backgrounds painted panorama-wise, and frequently changed. Thus we have represented 'the true prospect of the city of Rhodes,' 'the prospect of Mount Philermus,' with Solyman's army in the plain below,' &c., &c. This species of back-scene stereotyped itself for so long a period as to have exercised a distinct influence upon the progress of landscape-paint- ing, and to have given rise to some very interesting efforts of the art quite unconsciously adapted to a purpose for which they were never intended.

recitativo [1]. *Part II*, which appears to have missed success on the stage, contains however some vigorous lines, and has a good Epilogue [2]. Together with this, the ingenuity of the author in introducing some patriotic flourishes into the play, seems to call for some sort of acknowledgement [3].

From this opera must be distinguished another of D'Ave- nant's plays, which was not printed before its inclusion in the folio of 1673, but which is supposed to have been acted under the Protectorate, before the re-opening of the theatres. There seems, however, no sufficient reason for concluding that *The Siege*, any more than one or two other of D'Avenant's plays, previously noticed as first printed in the Folio [4], was actually performed after the outbreak of the troubles. It has in any case little to distinguish it from these, being a romantic drama, very much to the purpose, and therefore impressive in the conduct of its main plot, and telling the story of a brave maiden who, by refusing to sanction the treason committed for her sake by her lover, incites him to the heroism of despair [5]. The bye-plot, although not wholly original, is carried out with a certain humour [6]. After the

The Siege
(*pr.* 1673).

---

[1] Speaking (and very wittily) in defence of rimed verse, Dryden (in the dedication of *The Rival Ladies*) says that 'if we owe the invention of it to Mr. Waller, we are acknowledging for the noblest use of it to Sir William D'Avenant, who at once brought it upon the stage, and made it perfect in *The Siege of Rhodes*.'

[2] Pepys set to music the song, 'Beauty, retire,' &c. in act iv. sc. 2 of *Part II*; and his composition is stated by Mr. Wheatley (*s. d.* December 6, 1665) to be preserved in the Pepysian Library at Cambridge.

[3] Thus, the lines—

'For what will not the valiant English do,
When beauty is distress'd and virtue too?' (*Part I*)

seem almost to deserve being acknowledged as its motto by the British 'nautical drama.'

[4] See *ante*, p. 173, as to *News from Plymouth*, &c.

[5] This obviously suggested the plot of John Hughes' *The Siege of Damascus* (1720), in which the poet is blamed by Gibbon (ch. ii, *note*) for having 'produced a frigid catastrophe' by 'softening the guilt of the hero and the despair of the heroine.'

[6] It is in part borrowed from Fletcher's *The Humorous Lieutenant* (*ante*, vol. ii. p. 702). Though the notion might have advantageously been left unrepeated, the scenes in which the vainglory of the volunteers is exposed are not unamusing. The caricature of a duel in act iv is worthy of notice ; and altogether it is clear that this play was written at a time when the shady sides of soldiering had come to be tolerably well understood.

Restoration D'Avenant seems to have become inclined to sink the author in the manager, and to have contented himself in the main with dressing up old productions of his own, or adapting to dominant tastes the labours of others.

The Play-house to be Let (1663 circ.)

His *The Playhouse to be Let* (acted probably about 1663) is a comic entertainment composed of a series of more or less heterogeneous materials—'four plays in one,' as they would have been called in the days of Beaumont and Fletcher [1]—tied together by a device familiar enough to the modern stage [2]. The opening and the closing act alone were both new and—after their fashion—original. *The Man's the Master* (acted 1668, printed 1669), a lively comedy chiefly in prose, appears to be in subject, and partly in language, borrowed from two French comedies [3].

Adaptations of old plays.

The rest of D'Avenant's productions are mere alterations of masterpieces of the English drama ; *The Rivals* (acted and printed 1668) being a free adaptation of *The Two Noble Kinsmen* [4]; and *Macbeth* (printed 1673) an adulteration of Shakspere, for which Lock composed the music [5]. Finally,

---

[1] Cf. *ante*, vol. ii. p. 666.

[2] A series of competitors for a vacant theatre present in turn their several performances. Two of the entertainments in question (which occupy acts ii and iv) were operas already produced by D'Avenant at the Cockpit before the Restoration (cf. *ante*, p. 262). Act ii is a translation (in broken English) of Molière's *Sganarelle* (*le Cocu Imaginaire*). Act v is a burlesque on the loves of Antony and Cleopatra which is quite equal in the broad vulgarity of its buffoonery to the efforts of later competitors. I quote a specimen by way of illustrating the permanency of the style of humour affected by one branch of the modern English drama :—

'*Cleopatra* : I'll not be scar'd, though he look ne'er so hideous ;
He may go snick-up, if he hates Nymphidius.'

[3] Scarron's *Jodelet, ou le Maistre Valet*, and the same author's *L'Héritier ridicule*.

[4] The 'parcel-gilt' entertainment of the huntsmen in act iv is an original insertion by D'Avenant. This was the play in which 'Moll Davis' is said to have enchanted King Charles II by singing, as the shepherdess Celania, the song, 'My lodging's on the cold ground.'

[5] Cf. *ante*, vol. ii. p. 173.—I learn on excellent authority, that the music to *Macbeth* by Lock was different from that popularly called by his name, and is not known to exist —D'Avenant's (or presumably his) *Macbeth* delighted the soul of Pepys, who describes it as 'a most excellent play in all respects, but especially in divertissement, though it be a deep tragedy ; which is a strange perfection in a tragedy, it being most proper here, and suitable.' *Diary*, January 7, 1667. On December 10, 1663, Pepys looked forward with guileless joy, to 'a rare play to be acted this week of Sir William

it was D'Avenant who invented, though it was Dryden who carried out, the idea of 'the counterpart of Shakspere's plot' in *The Tempest, or The Enchanted Island* (acted 1667 and printed 1674), already noticed [1], and to be enumerated below among Dryden's dramatic works.

Soon after the production of this strange monument of perverted ingenuity, D'Avenant died—in the year 1668. Although, in taking leave of him, it is impossible to echo the particular tribute to his 'quick and piercing imagination' with which Dryden commended their joint production to his readers, yet we may in some degree share the 'gratitude' professed by the younger and greater writer in commemorating the elder. Dryden's praise of D'Avenant cannot be acknowledged as true, that 'he borrowed not of any other; and his imaginations were such as could not easily enter into any other man [2].' But, with all his shortcomings and excesses, D'Avenant must retain in the annals of our drama the historical position which he secured by his opportune energy and courage—of forming the chief connecting link between two periods of our dramatic literature. Both of these had, like himself, their faults and vices; but the later period derived the best and truest part of its vitality from the earlier, of whose traditions he contrived to carry something across the gap. Thus it would be not less unjust than ungenerous to ignore his services to a cause which he had loyally at heart, and which but for him might have sunk into still more abject hopelessness, and have recovered itself under conditions even less favourable to its national character. The English drama owes to D'Avenant more than one doubtful gift; but it also owes to him in some degree the endurance, under however perverted a form, of a love for its great masters, and the maintenance of such historic continuity as it was able to preserve [3].

*D'Ave-
nant's
position in
our drama-
tic litera-
ture.*

D'Avenant's. The story of Henry the Eighth with all his wives'; but it seems uncertain whether the *Henry VIII* which was performed at different times in this reign was actually an adaptation by D'Avenant.

   [1] Vol. ii. p. 200.

   [2] See the Preface to *The Tempest* in Dryden's *Works*.

   [3] Sir William D'Avenant's son Charles wrote one 'tragedy,' *Circe* (1677),

*Other
dramatists
who wrote
both before
and after
the Restora-
tion.*

*The Duke
of New-
castle
(1592–
1676);*

*and the
Duchess
(d. 1676).*

Certain other names—so far as the vitality of their dramatic writings is concerned, little more than names—serve
to connect together the dramatic literature of the pre- and
the post-Restoration periods.   The DUKE OF NEWCASTLE
(William Cavendish, 1592–1676), who in the history of
the Civil Troubles played a conspicuous rather than an
important part, is best remembered by the biographical
tribute paid to his virtues and accomplishments by the
effusive piety of his consort.   Nor has any work of the
DUCHESS OF NEWCASTLE (Margaret, daughter of Sir
Thomas Lucas, died 1676) proved so enduring a monument of her extraordinary if not always most discreetly
invested talents, as (more especially if note is taken of
the autobiographical sketch of her own youth included
in it) her memorial of her consort.   Although not her
intellectual equal, he was with all his shortcomings not
unworthy of her devotion[1].   As writers of plays this
celebrated couple in some measure blended their creative
impulses[2].   But while it would be quite unfair to the
Duchess to suppose that she claimed for herself any of
the praise which she lavished upon her husband's efforts as
a dramatist[3], it is quite evident that her own productions
in this capacity were especially due to the genius of the

of which I can furnish no account.   It is described by Genest (vol. i. p. 209)
as more properly an opera, and founded on the *Iphigenia in Tauris* of
Euripides.

[1] See *The Life of William Cavendish Duke of Newcastle ; to which is added
The Life of Margaret Duchess of Newcastle.*   Edited by C. H. Firth, 1886 ; and
cf. an essay on them by M. Émile Montégut, and Mr. Edward Jenkins' sketch
The Cavalier and his Lady.   An article on the Duchess appeared in *The
Retrospective Review*, vol. i (1853).

[2] The Duke contributed songs to the plays of the Duchess as well as to his
own : and is stated to have written five scenes of her play, *The Lady Contemplation.*   On the other hand, Pepys (see *Diary*, March 30, 1667) designates
the play *The Humorous Lovers*, which was published as the Duke's, as ' my
Lady Newcastle's ' ; and excuses his determination of seeing a play which
he describes as 'the most silly thing that ever came upon a stage,' and
one that made him ' sick to see it,' by his desire 'the better' to 'understand her.'

[3] ' I may justly call him the best lyric and dramatic poet of his age.   His
Comedies do sufficiently show his great observation and judgment ; for
they are composed of these three ingredients, *viz.* wit, humour, and satire ;
and his chief desire in them is to divulge and laugh at the follies of mankind ;
to persecute vice, and to encourage virtue.'

authoress of *Nature's Pictures drawn by Fancie's Pencil*, and contained only occasional contributions from her husband's pen. Of the Duke's own four comedies none attained to an enduring celebrity, like his treatise (published in both French and English) on horsemanship. Two of these comedies, printed in 1649, appear to have been acted before the closing of the theatres—*The Country Captaine*, which, according to Pepys' computation, was performed about 1636[1], probably dated from a rather later period, when the taste for military titles and manners which it ridicules had more generally set in. For the rest, the contempt expressed for this play by Pepys is not stronger than what it deserves; nor is the companion comedy, *The Variety*, which is stated to have been acted at the Blackfriars, much superior, though it proved popular enough for one of its scenes, turning on the humours of Monsieur Galliard, a French dancing-master of the usual consuming ambition, to be afterwards made into a droll[2]. The Duke's two remaining comedies, *The Humorous Lovers*, and *The Triumphant Widow, or The Medley of Humours*[3], both of which were acted after the Restoration, and printed in 1677, furnish rather better reading. In the former, Master Furres, a kind of *Malade Imaginaire*, and Sir Anthony Altalk, a coxcomb 'pretending to poetry,' are personages not much out of the common, but Mistress Hood, an old school-mistress who has become the instructress of young maids in the ways of the town, is drawn with a certain power of satire. The *Triumphant Widow* opens well with a scene between four rogues and their Footpad captain, in Beggar's Opera style and with a song in Beggar's Opera metre[4], and with the help of Shaksperean reminiscences[5] sustains a certain kind of interest in its pro-

---

[1] He saw it on October 26, 1661—'the first time it hath been acted this twenty-five years'—and pronounced it ' so silly a play as in all my life I never saw, and the first that ever I was weary of in my life.'

[2] It is included in Kirkman's collection, *The Wits*.

[3] Of this, as Halliwell-Phillipps points out, Shadwell transferred a great part into his *Bury Fair* (1689), the best character in which is, however, taken from Molière.

[4] 'Since ev'ry Profession's become a lewd cheat,' &c.

[5] Footpad reappears as a kind of Autolycus ; Lady Haughty, the widow, with her maid Nan reviews her suitors, including the soldier whose talk is all

gress. He also, as will be seen below, translated Molière's *L'Étourdi*, which Dryden adapted for the English stage under the title of *Sir Martin Mar-All*, but which, after being performed in 1697, was entered under this name in the Stationers' Register. Inasmuch as Ben Jonson wrote two masques on the occasion of royal visits to the Earl of Newcastle (which half ruined him [1]), while Shirley dedicated to him his finest tragedy, the patronage of this magnificent noble was fortunate enough to include the leading spirits of not less than three periods of our dramatic literature.

The Duchess, although persistently flattered by both great writers and small, has a lasting claim to be remembered on her own account; but numerous as her plays were, they cannot be said to have proportionately contributed to her fame. Twenty-one of them were published in a folio volume in 1662, and a supplementary folio, containing five more, followed in 1668. Langbaine, who gives the titles of nearly all of them, also cites the modest boast of the Duchess's 'General Prologue,' that her dramatic compositions differ from those of Jonson, Shakspere, and Beaumont and Fletcher—and from those of Jonson more especially because he could read the Greek and Latin poets, and she could not:

> 'All my Plays and Plots, my own poor Brain did make;
> From Plutarch's story I nere took a Plot,
> Nor from Romances, nor from Don Quixot,
> As others have, for to assist their Wit;
> But I upon mine own Foundation writ.'

Her 'own foundation' consisted partly of metaphysical conceptions and partly of her own personal experiences, mixed up together in dramatic allegories. The long-winded abstractions, who do duty as characters, are left as free as possible from technical restraint, frequently even from that of a division of the play into acts. In truth, the fertility of her invention in the way of bits of character and flashes of dialogue was such as to overflow all considerations of

of Naseby, Edgehill, the first and second Newbury, Marston Moor, and the rest, &c.

[1] *Love's Welcome at Welbeck* and *Love's Welcome at Bolsover*. Cf. *ante*, vol. ii. p. 393, *note*.

time and space ; so that her works include a whole series of scenes for which she could not find room in the piece of which they had been originally intended to form part[1], together with a fragment of a play which she had at first meant to insert in another, in a parenthetic fashion particularly to her taste [2]. Her predilection was for extravaganza, where she could give the rein to her imagination, without losing sight of the realities of life for which she had a quick satiric eye. Now and then, her fancy suggests a dramatic scheme such as with care might have been worked out to some purpose ; thus *The Convent of Pleasure*—a women's ' cloister of freedom ' for the perennial enjoyment of the true pleasures of life—recalls nobler elaborations of similar Utopian dreams [3]. More frequently, however, she quite loses herself in unrefined fun, and at times falls into a licence of coarse dialogue, resembling, I regret to say, that in which the comedies of her contemporary, Mrs. Aphra Behn, abound [4]. Of anything like a rational plot few traces are observable in those of her comedies which I have attempted to peruse ; on the other hand, they overflow with clever talk in dialogue or quasi-monologue, which she strives to animate by an *afflatus* of philosophic thought as well as of facetious observation. All these ' ingredients,' to quote herself, she ' mixes together, and puts them into a Mystical pot,' which she entitles *Youth's Glory and Death's Bouquet*, or *The Blazing World, or The Comical Hash*. Some of her plays are understood to contain attempts at direct self-portraiture [5].

HENRY VISCOUNT FALKLAND, the son of the illustrious victim, if we may so call him, of the outbreak of that Civil War into which he entered heart-broken and with no policy but a determination to die, appears to have inherited his father's and his grandmother's love of learning, and to have been likewise a man of public spirit [6]. He left behind him

Lord Falkland.

---

[1] *The Presence.* [2] *The Blazing World.*

[3] Here again we have a play within the play.

[4] See *The Bridals*, and *The Female Wits.*

[5] Lady Contemplation in the comedy so called (in two Parts), and Lady Chastity in *The Matrimonial Trouble*, a tragi-comedy (likewise in two Parts).

[6] In the short biographical notices of him discoverable, there seem traces of confusion between father and son. Thus, although the latter may be the

a single play, *The Marriage Night*, printed in 1664[1];
whether it was ever acted seems uncertain. This production is interesting by virtue of a certain general dramatic
power observable in it. accompanied by occasional flashes of
highly effective expression ; but also because of the evidence
which it furnishes of its author's familiarity with the pre-
Revolution drama. Of this the scene imitating the first
dialogue between Brutus and Cassius [2], and the one following
upon it, between 'three Townsmen as the Watch,' may not
be regarded as exceptional instances ; but I much mistake
unless the lurid colouring of the action, together with certain suggestions in the plot, notwithstanding the difference
in issue, is partly due to reminiscences of *The Revenger's
Tragedy* of Cyril Tourneur [3]. In any case, the play is one of
the most notable aftergrowths of later Elisabethan tragedy.

*Sir Robert
Stapylton.*

Another loyal adherent of the royal cause (though he had
abandoned the Roman Catholic faith in which he had been
trained), SIR ROBERT STAPYLTON, after the Restoration,
when he was appointed gentleman-usher by King Charles II,
produced a comedy *The Slighted Maid* (1663), a tragi-
comedy *The Step-mother* (1664), and a tragedy *Hero and
Leander* (1669). The last of these plays possesses a certain
interest as an attempt to treat dramatically an immortal
epical theme. Langbaine says that wherever Musaeus and
Juvenal are in esteem Stapylton's fame will survive [4] ; but
his tragedy fails to preserve the dignity of a subject consecrated by English as well as Greek literature and art. In
the Prologue to the play, he protests against the puppets
that have played 'mock Hero and Leander'; but his own
overcrowding of the theme with a concomitant intrigue and
the business of a *Romeo and Juliet* nurse is hardly less

author of the Epilogue to Rochester's adaptation of *Valentinian*, it must have
been his father who wrote the commendatory verses to Sandys' *Christ's
Passion* (1640). The son was Lord-Lieutenant of Oxfordshire.
   [1] Reprinted in vol. xv of Hazlitt's *Dodsley*.
   [2] Avowedly ; for Dessandro tells his brother that his words were 'spoken
with the soul of Cassius ' (act iii. sc. 1).   [3] *Ante*, p. 69.
   [4] He translated both these authors 'and Strada too' into English verse,
as well as modern French works into prose. As to his version of Juvenal,
see the *Essay on Satire*, prefixed by Dryden to his own translations from
Juvenal, in vol. xiii of the *Works*.

objectionable, while the climax of Hero's reception of her prize swimmer, habited in ' vest and night-cap ' and oiled for his record exploit, comes perilously near to bathos—such as under the circumstances ought specially to have been avoided.   The diction of the play, while hardly ever rising into poetry, rarely swells into rant.

Sir Samuel Tuke, Sir Richard Fanshawe, and George Digby Earl of Bristol have been already mentioned as adapters or translators of Spanish plays [1]; none of these came before the public as original English dramatists.   It may therefore suffice, before passing to writers less intimately connecting themselves with pre-Restoration phases of our drama, to notice one whose plays, though in no instance published before the date of the Restoration, should assuredly be characterised as an aftergrowth of an earlier school.   Had the spirit of Jonson revisited his ancient haunts in the Restoration period, none among its dramatists—except perhaps Shadwell—could so justly have claimed to be 'sworn of the tribe of Ben,' as JOHN WILSON [2], whose name deserves to be remembered by the admirers of ripe wit, accompanied by dramatic force.

John Wilson (d. 1696).

From a contemporary doggrel it would appear that Wilson was a Scotchman; and there are one or two indications in his plays of a connexion with Scotland.   He is known to have been called to the bar from Lincoln's Inn in 1646; and is supposed afterwards to have become secretary in Ireland to the Duke of York, through whose influence he was, shortly before the death of Charles II, appointed Recorder of Londonderry.   After the famous siege he appears to have moved to Dublin, where he resided for some years.   In 1696 he died in London.   He composed some legal and political works, and translated the *Encomium Moriae* of Erasmus.   Of his intimate acquaintance with legal phraseology he gives amusing evidence in one of his plays [3]; and his wit, like Jonson's own, is generally impregnated with his learning.

[1] *Ante*, pp. 305-6.

[2] *The Dramatic Works of John Wilson.* With *Memoir*, &c. (by James Maidment and W. H. Logan), 1874.   [3] *The Cheats.*

His comedies.

In his two comedies, *The Cheats* (written 1662) and *The Projectors* (printed 1664), Wilson shows himself a follower of Jonson; indeed the latter play contains evident reminiscences of *The Devil is an Ass,* which his *Belphegor* likewise to a certain extent resembles in plot. Wilson has much of the learning, the wit, and the power of clear and vigorous characterisation, which belonged to the great master; but he has also some of Jonson's lengthiness and excessive copiousness of prose diction; and perhaps these two plays are more enjoyable in reading than they might prove on the stage.

The Cheats (1662).

The Cheats however was very popular. The plot of neither comedy is worthy of praise; the strength of both lies in the characters, some of which are excellent: thus in *The Cheats* the astrological quack Mopus, and more especially the dissenting minister Scruple,—a caricature which in his preface the author vigorously defends as being directed only against the ' abuse of the venerable name' of religion[1].

The Projectors (*pr.* 1644`.

In *The Projectors,* where the fun is not quite so broad, we meet with a bevy of adventurers, who work upon the folly of Sir Gudgeon Credulous, and a usurer Suckdry, whose love and fear for his gold and whose treatment of his unhappy servant Leanchops are however borrowed features[2]. In any case Wilson deserves the credit of having introduced on the English stage an admirable addition to Jonson's character-types of the Miser. He has further added a burlesque woman's rights' meeting, which is very ludicrous, and was doubtless suggested by Aristophanes.

[1] Scruple is certainly as diverting and vigorous a piece of satire as any branch of our literature has produced on this familiar theme, and specially reminds us that we are in the days of *Hudibras.* His favourite resting-place is among the admiring women of his congregation, where he is found solacing, not himself, but ' the creature' from a 'scandalous' bowl which 'looketh like a wassail.' He consents to conform for a living of £300 a year, but is induced to come back to his flock for £400 (' Let a man strive never so much against it, natural affection will return upon him '), whereupon he sells the good-will of his living (not the living itself—for ' I remember me, the Casuists make a notable difference ').

[2] They are of course borrowed from the *Aulularia.* I see no reason to suppose that Wilson was acquainted with Molière's *L'Avare* (not actually *known* to have been performed before 1668); but the near coincidence of date is certainly suspicious. Had Wilson borrowed from Molière, he would surely have made more of the scene (act ii. sc. 1) where Suckdry believes himself to have lost his gold.

Besides these two admirable comedies, Wilson wrote a *His Andro-*
tragedy, *Andronicus Comnenius* (printed 1664), and a tragi- *nicus Com-*
comedy, *Belphegor, or The Marriage of the Devil* (printed *nenius (pr.*
1691). The former, felicitous in choice of subject, is written *1664).*
with great vigour and spirit ; and though in one scene the
author is guilty of very gross plagiarism, the scenes among
the citizens, the characters of Philo, Andreas' zany (who
acts as jackal to the lion, and resembles the Moor in
Schiller's *Fiesco*), and of Manuel, the usurper's virtuous son,
are as original as they are striking[1]. *Belphegor* is the least *His Belphe-*
interesting of Wilson's plays, though likewise closely con- *gor, or The*
necting itself with our earlier drama (it is in fact nothing but *the Devil*
a more elaborate—and very well written—version of a theme *(pr. 1691).*
with which we are already familiar from earlier plays[2]).
Wilson however, as he tells us, took the story from Macchiavelli. He has given some relief to this fantastically
humorous fiction by the nobly-conceived characters of
Montalto and his wife Portia.

Wilson seems to have made little pretension to the title *Wilson's*
of a dramatist[3]; but he had both the necessary gifts and *sterling*
the necessary application ; and of him too Ben Jonson *merits as a*
might have said that he 'writes all like a man.' He shows *dramatist.*
originality even where he borrows his themes ; he draws
character with clearness and strength ; and the manliness

---

[1] 'The genuine adventures' of Andronicus Comnenius, says Gibbon
(ch. xlviii), ' might form the subject of a very singular romance.' The theme
seems to have been treated (in 1661) by another dramatist before Wilson.
The latter confines himself to the second part of this strange story, which
bears a remarkable likeness to that of Richard III, whom Andronicus certainly
resembled both in his ruthless ambition and in his capacity for government.
An imitation of Shakspere was therefore not easily to be avoided ; but,
except in the scene where Andronicus makes love to Anna, the widow of his
victim, Wilson cannot be said to have resorted to imitation.—The political
allusions in this play the author seems to have had no desire to conceal (see
the Dedication) ; those in act iv. sc. 5 are of interest, as manifestly pointed
at the hole-and-corner 'constituent assembly' mania of the period just
preceding the Restoration.

[2] Cf. *ante*, vol. ii. p. 606 as to Haughton's *The Devil and his Dame* ; and *ib.*
pp. 372 and 465 as to *The Devil is an Ass*, and *If it be not good, the Devil is in
it*. As to Macchiavelli's *novella*, see Herford, *u. s.*, pp. 308 *seqq.* Wilson
leaves the question open whether the original author was Macchiavelli or
Straparola.

[3] See Dedication to *Andronicus Comnenius*.

of his serious as well as of his comic writing refreshes and invigorates the student of the literary period in which, unfortunately perhaps for his literary reputation, it was this writer's lot to live. Of poetic ornament he is bare ; but he is equally free from meretricious glitter and artificiality. Had he been born a generation earlier, when his activity might have fallen in with the strong current of a dramatically creative age, he could hardly have failed to gain a distinguished place among our dramatists.

Roger Boyle, Earl of Orrery (1621– 1679), the father of English heroic plays.

One further name will be more conveniently mentioned before than after that of the foremost literary genius of the Restoration age. To Roger Boyle, EARL OF ORRERY[1] (1621–1679), has been ascribed the introduction on the English stage of the habit of writing plays in rimed verse ; and though none of his dramatic productions is known to have been acted before 1664, some of them would seem to have been in Dryden's hands when in dedicating his *Rival Ladies* to Orrery he recommended the fashion which in that play he had quite incidentally attempted to exemplify[2]. And Orrery himself speaks of himself as if he had been the originator of the new fashion, when describing his tragedy of *The Black Prince* (not acted till 1667)[3] as 'wrote in a new way'—'in the French Manner, because I heard the King declare himself more in favour of their Way of Writing than ours. My poor Attempt,' he continues, 'cannot please his Majesty, but my Example may incite others who can.' As a matter of fact, there seems no reason for depriving Dryden of the doubtful honour of having to all intents and purposes originated the

[1] *The Dramatic Works of Roger Boyle, Earl of Orrery.* 2 vols. 1739.

[2] The Dedication (printed 1664) of *The Rival Ladies* (acted 1663) is as careless a piece of writing as any of which Dryden was ever guilty. He here asserts that the ' new way,' by which he must mean rimed verse on the stage, is not so much a new way as an old way revived ; for it was, he states, ' many years before Shakspeare's plays,' introduced in the tragedy of *Queen Gorboduc.* Blank verse, he proceeds to inform Lord Orrery, was invented by Shakspere. But, with equally characteristic generosity, he attributes the revival of the rimed couplet to Waller, and its re-introduction on the stage to D'Avenant, ' who at once brought it ' there, ' and made it perfect,' in *The Siege of Rhodes* (cf. *ante*, p. 282).

[3] See Pepys' *Diary*, October 19, 1667 ; ' the first time it was acted.'

usage to which his authority alone gave stability, and which
his abandonment of it doomed to quick extinction.

Lord Orrery's biography is full of interest; as Lord
Broghill he played a part of very high importance in public
affairs; and if at the Restoration he secured Ireland to the
King, it may be doubted whether, ten years before, that
island would without him not have been lost to the Commonwealth.   But his plays may notwithstanding be treated
with great brevity.   Sir Walter Scott says of him that 'he
deserved Dryden's panegyric in every respect except as
a poet'; and Dryden himself compliments him by the
assertion[1]: 'the muses have seldom employed your thoughts,
but when some violent fit of the gout has snatched you from
affairs of state; and, like the priestess of Apollo, you never
come to deliver his oracles, but unwillingly, and in torment.'
It must not be forgotten that, in addition to his plays, he
wrote what is perhaps the most notable English attempt in
the style of Calprenède and the Scudérys, the romance of
Parthenissa, of which he published the first part (in six
volumes) in 1654, the year when he became a member of
the Protector's first parliament, and which appeared in a
complete form in 1665.   In Orrery's plays the monarchist *Character-
tendencies of his mind (it was largely at his instigation that *istics of
his plays.*
Oliver's second parliament offered to him the title of King)
are illustrated by repeated references to the great danger of
managing affairs through the agency of a council instead
of by the will of a single man; but he was too clear-sighted
a statesman and too thorough a soldier to incline to political
declamation, and his sentiments are not as a rule displayed
after a very demonstrative fashion.   It may, however, be
noted as significant of the romantic side both of his
personal character and of the literary style which he
affected, that more than once in his plays he applies
to unheroic conduct the epithet 'low'—as if the force of
invective could not well go further[2].   But the chief interest

---

[1] In the *Dedication* already cited.
[2] Thus in *Henry V*:
> 'He who resigns his Love, though for a King,
> Does, as he is a Lover, a low thing.'

which these productions possess after all attaches to their form, and to their exemplification of the use of the heroic couplet, in which they are throughout written. The uncertainty as to the dates of composition of most of these plays makes it difficult to estimate the progress of their author as a writer of verse ; and while the general frigidity of *Mustapha, the Son of Solyman the Magnificent* (acted in 1665) seems occasionally to catch a spark of fire, in *The Black Prince* (acted in 1667) congelation appears again to have set in. Altogether, Lord Orrery shows himself capable of using his metre with considerable effect in dialogue, though not unfrequently he lapses into prosaic turns.

The sentiment of these dramas is on the whole at least as monotonous as their form. In the world of the dramatic imagination of this writer, whose own experiences of life had a very different kind of story to tell, everything revolves round the sentiment of love. *The History of Henry the Fifth*, acted in 1664[1] and printed in 1667, excites a faint curiosity as to the measure of the failure of Heroic Tragedy when essaying, in the period of its own infancy, competition with Shakspere. Lord Orrery may be allowed a certain amount of credit for the persistency with which he maintains the originality of his dramatic treatment of his theme[2] ; to what extent, if to any, he was indebted for it to an earlier narrative poem on the subject[3] I have not been able to ascertain. The general effectiveness of the dramatic idea of Owen Tudor's generous renunciation of his passion for

The History of Henry V (1664).

[1] Pepys records seeing it acted on August 13, 1664, calling it 'the new play.' He praises it as 'the most full of height and raptures of wit and sense' that he ever heard, but criticises one or two points not inaptly.

[2] The only scene in which he seems to have had Shakspere in his mind is act iv. sc. 1, when the French and English lords debate the Salic Law; and here it must be allowed that Lord Orrery displays some dialectic skill. Princess Catharine's argument on the side of Reason *v.* Love is altogether to her credit ; but her conduct towards Tudor is hardly more pleasing than is her reproof of him cited in a previous note.

[3] Hugh Holland's *Pancharis: the First Books.* Containing *The Preparation of the Love between Owen Tudyr and the Queene.* The late Mr. Collier issued a reprint of this poem, which was published in 1603, with a Dedication to King James and a statement that the author had long intended to dedicate it to Queen Elisabeth—to whom (he was a convert to Rome) he had not invariably shown himself respectful.

Princess Catharine in favour of the Sovereign in whose
name he has come to woo her is evident from the repeated
use made of it in our drama[1] ; but it needed bolder treatment than was bestowed upon it by the author of this
heroic play.   In *Mustapha, the Son of Solyman the Magni-*   *Mustapha*
ficent (acted 1665, and repeated at Court in the presence of   (1665).
the King and Queen in the following year[2]) Lord Orrery
probably reached the highest point to which as a dramatic
poet it was given to him to attain.   Pure in sentiment
and chaste in expression, like all the rest of his plays,
Mustapha shows that not only had he caught from French
examples something of that dignity of style which reconciles us even to a dialogue typyically conventional, but that
he was also capable of drawing character with spirit[3].
The not altogether faultless plot, taken from an episode
entitled *Mustapha et Zéangir* in Georges de Scudéry's
romance of *L'Illustre Bassa*, is, however, a love-intrigue
pure and simple[4] ; and, although Solyman the Magnificent's
speeches are not entirely free from rant, the general tone
of his Turks is gently amorous[5].   The heroine of *The*   *The Black*
Black Prince (acted 1667) is a widow with four lovers   *Prince*
(1667).
—the Kings of England and of France, the Black Prince,
and Lord Delawar ; but not one of them, nor the fair
countess whom they adore, succeeds in arousing our sympathy.   This play is stated to have been ill received,

---

[1] Cf. *ante*, vol. i. p. 398, *note* 2.

[2] See Evelyn's *Diary*, s. d. October 18. (Lord Broghill was shortly afterwards created Earl of Orrery.)   The passage is a notable one, for Evelyn in
it gives very plain reasons why as a respectable man he had given up going,
except very rarely, to public theatres. Lord Broghill's tragedy he considered
extremely well written, ' tho' in my mind I did not approve of any such
pastime in a time of such judgments and calamities.' (A General Fast had
been ordered for October 10, on account of Fire, Plague and War.)

[3] *Viz.* that of Roxolana.   See her first scene, where she protects the
Hungarian infant-King, and the last act.

[4] The two sons of Solyman, Mustapha and Zéangir, form a pair of noble
kinsmen ready for any act of self-sacrifice ; the fault of the plot lies in the
absence of any sufficient reason that might induce us to pardon Roxolana for
plotting her stepson's ruin, in the interest of her own offspring.

[5] Lord Orrery's *Mustapha* may be compared with Lord Brooke's tragedy
of the same name (*ante*, vol. ii. p. 616).—The subject has also been treated
by several French dramatists. (See La Harpe, *Cours de Littérature*, vol. xvi.
p. 136, and vol. xxi. pp. i. *seqq.*)

though apparently not because of any intrinsic demerit[1].

Tryphon (1668). The tragedy of *Tryphon* (acted 1668), of which the subject is from Syriac history[2], was more successful; but it is impossible to deceive oneself as to its personages being

Herod the Great (pr. 1694). more than lay-figures. Two tragedies by Lord Orrery were printed after his death, viz. *Herod the Great* in 1694, and *Altemira* in 1702. The former treats a theme with which we have already met in our dramatic literature, and which reappeared more than once in its subsequent course[3]. It is, perhaps, the most striking of its author's plays, so far at least as variety of action is concerned; it contains ghosts enough and to spare, and an accumulation of crimes such as we are accustomed to in Webster or Tourneur. The

Altemira (pr. 1702). tragedy of *Altemira* is of a much inferior cast. The author has here essayed a comic character, called Filladen; but the scene in which he and the other lords review the ladies of the Court is as devoid of wit as the lyrics interspersed are of charm[4].

---

[1] Pepys, who saw the play when performed for the first time on October 19, records its being nearly hissed off the stage because of the reading of a very long letter. There is force in his criticism, that in this play ' the contrivance, and all that was witty, which indeed was much, and very witty, was almost the same that had been in ' the author's two former plays, ' and the same points and turns of wit in both, and in this very same play often repeated, but in excellent language.'

[2] See Book i of *The Maccabees*, chapters xii–xiii.

[3] Cf. *ante*, pp. 15 and 156. A *Herod and Mariamne*, written by Samuel Pordage, was brought on the stage by Settle in 1674. Fenton's *Mariamne* appeared in 1723; Voltaire's in 1724. Calderon's *El Mayor Monstruo los Zelos* likewise treats the story of Mariamne and the jealous tetrarch (see Ticknor, vol. ii. p. 383). Tristan's (F. L'Hermite) *La Mariamne* (1636), imitated from Calderon, is said to have drawn tears from Cardinal Richelieu, by whose emotion the performer of Herod was in his turn all but overcome. To Hebbel's fine tragedy, *Herodes und Mariamne*, reference has already been made.

[4] In the Epilogue written for this play by Lord Orrery's grandson Charles Boyle, afterwards third Earl, occur three lines which so succinctly (though not very politely) sum up the canons of criticism applied to comedy by the audiences of his age that I cannot help quoting them :

> ' This Play, I 'm horribly afraid, can't last;
> Allow it pretty, 'tis confounded chaste,
> And contradicts too much the present taste.'

The third Earl of Orrery was himself the author of a comedy, *As You Find It* (printed 1703, and republished with his grandfather's plays in the edition mentioned above), which is a rather lively play in the style of Colley Cibber's earlier works. A husband is reclaimed (rather late in the play) by a not very

Besides this tragedy, Lord Orrery left behind him, likewise unfinished, an uninteresting comedy, *Guzman* (printed 1693), the plot and style of which—it contains a mock astrologer and a foolish cowardly coxcomb given to ridiculous pedantical oaths—point to some Spanish source.

Guzman (*pr.* 1693).

The tragi-comedy called *The General*, which was performed in 1664, and is described by Pepys [1] as altogether inferior to *Henry V*, although brought out in Orrery's name, was never acknowledged by him. It must have been a different play from that which Shirley wrote a prologue for its performance at Dublin [2].

To Orrery has also been ascribed a play called *Master Antony* [3]. *The Tragedy of King Saul*, printed in 1703 and said to be written by a peer, was conjectured to be his by Horace Walpole [4].

Whether our dramatic literature would in the main continue in the paths marked out by its preceding history, or become a follower of foreign developements, or, pursuing a middle course, seek to find in a combination of national and foreign elements the conditions of a new life of its own, was a question admitting of solution by the exertions of no single writer, however gifted and however fertile. Yet the example set by such a writer, if a man of exceptional genius and extraordinary creative vigour, could not but exercise the most important influence upon the ultimate settlement of the problem. Thus, as a matter of fact, the future of our drama as a literary growth came to depend in a signally large measure upon the views formed concerning the theory of dramatic composition, and upon the actual contributions made to dramatic literature, by the leading writer of his age—Dryden.

---

commendable stratagem on the part of his wife. The description of a 'Chocolate-House' in act iii. sc. 1 of this comedy might be worth extracting.

[1] *Diary*, September 28, 1664.

[2] See Dyce, Shirley's *Works*, vol. vi. p. 495. This play, according to Halliwell-Phillipps, was published in 1853, from a MS. in private hands.

[3] (Curll's) *Poetical Register, &c.* (1719), p. 22, and Halliwell-Phillipps.

[4] Horace Walpole to the Rev. Henry Zouch (*Letters*, ed. Cunningham, vol. iii. p. 187. Cunningham seems to approve the conjecture).

*John Dry-
den* (1631–
1700). JOHN DRYDEN[1] (1631–1700) first came before the public as a dramatic writer early in the year 1663. He was at that time, though already known and recognised as a person of some position in the world of letters and science (as is shown by his election as a member of the Royal Society in 1662), in more or less straitened circumstances, and had apparently resolved to trust to his literary labours for the advancement of his fortunes in life. He lodged at a book-seller's, and associated with men connected with the Court party, such as Sir Robert Howard, whose sister he was about to marry. Two theatrical companies were now regularly performing; and it was thus inevitable that a young writer with his talents and in his surroundings should become a writer for the theatre. In the course of the year 1662 he wrote the first play of his that was produced on the stage[2].

*His The
Wild Gal-
lant* (1663). *The Wild Gallant* (acted February 1663) proved a failure; it was written, as the author confesses, 'while he was yet unfledged and wanted knowledge,' and from the Second Epilogue (written for the revival of the comedy) in 1669 he would seem to have been half ashamed of 'this motley garniture of fool and farce.' According to the prevailing fashion, he 'endangered' himself, to use his own expression, with 'a Spanish plot'—which is in parts utterly extravagant, while the coarseness of the execution is extreme. The most humorous passage of the play is, moreover, stolen from Ben Jonson[3].

[1] For Dryden's dramas and essays the reader is referred to Sir Walter Scott's edition of Dryden's *Works*, 18 vols., revised and corrected by Professor Saintsbury (1882–93). The Life prefixed to this edition was based on the labours of Malone; the generous and sympathetic tone of criticism is characteristic of Sir Walter Scott. The critical matter in the successive shorter biographies of Dryden which have been published from Johnson to Messrs. W. D. Christie and Saintsbury, is too large and varied in amount to admit of specification. *The Retrospective Review*, vol. i. part i, contains an essay on *Dryden's Dramatic Works*, with numerous extracts. Dryden's Heroic Plays have been made the subject of a separate enquiry by P. Holz-hausen in *Englische Studien*, vols. xiii, xv and xvi (1890–2); see also A. Tüchert, *Dryden als Dramatiker in seinen Beziehungen zu M. de Scudéry's Romandichtung* (Zweibrücken, 1885).

[2] He is said to have already in 1660 meditated a play on the fate of the Duke of Guise, of which he used one scene for the tragedy of 1682.

[3] *Viz.* the incident of Trice's solitary duel with a couple of dice-boxes (act i. sc. 3); cf. Carlo and his cups in *Every Man Out of his Humour* (act v.

For the plot of Dryden's second acted drama, *The Rival Ladies* (brought on the stage in 1664), he again had recourse to a Spanish original.   In this complicated love-intrigue two rivals are concerned, who have alike disguised themselves as pages in order to serve the master of their affections, while he is enamoured of a third lady.   The treatment of this action cannot be praised for its refinement[1]; but any insinuation of deliberate grossness seems out of place as applied to this early play of Dryden's, which may be concluded to have been successful[2].   On the other hand, it is manifest that the author of this comedy was already feeling his way in something besides the matter of versification, important as he knew this to be for the effect of his plays.   As Mr. Saintsbury has hinted, this early play of Dryden's contains the first example of 'the amatory battledore-and-shuttlecock,' which may be described as a Senecan tradition run to seed, and which was to give rise to most excellent ridicule[3].   At the same time, nothing is so noteworthy in this play as the tentative, but already bold and effective, introduction of the use of rime into two of its principal scenes[4].   In the Dedication of this play to Lord Orrery, already repeatedly cited, Dryden appeals to 'his lordship's example' as a writer of rimed verse—possibly in one or more dramas known by private circulation—and defends the usage chiefly because it 'bounds and circumscribes' and 'most regulates the fancy[5].'   *A priori*, if the

sc. 4).—Bibber the Tailor (of 'fiery facias') is imitated in *The Rehearsal*. Readers of *The Pirate* will remember how, according to Claud Halcro, Timothy Thimblethwaite 'was thought to be the original of little Tom Bibber, in glorious John's comedy of *The Wild Gallant.*'

[1] The two pages fight a duel for Gonsalvo (one of them having proposed that they should 'scratch for him'); and a mutual discovery results.   In the end, after some hairbreadth 'scapes, all ends well, one of the rivals receiving the gift of Gonsalvo's heart ('not worn out but polished by the wearing' of his previous passion), the other being otherwise provided for.

[2] Pepys, who saw it on August 4, 1664, more than six months after its first appearance on the stage, thought it 'a very innocent and most pretty witty play.'

[3] See act iv. sc. 1; and see *The Rehearsal* and *Repartees between Cat and Puss at a Caterwauling (in a Modern Heroic Way)* in the *Poems of Samuel Butler.*

[4] Act iii. sc. 1 and Act iv. sc. 1.

[5] Dryden's assertion that the French term 'prose mesurée' covers, and

history of the earlier Stuart drama is dispassionately considered, an effect of this sort, had it necessarily flowed from
the use of the rimed couplet in dramatic compositions,
would have deserved to be extolled as something more
than salutary.

Dryden and Sir R. Howard's The Indian Queen (1664).
The extent to which Dryden assisted his friend—now his
brother-in-law—Sir Robert Howard, in the tragedy of *The
Indian Queen*—acted 1664, printed as Howard's among
his *Four New Plays* (1665), and not included as Dryden's
even in the folio edition of his *Dramatic Works*, published
in 1701—must remain undecided, at all events till a verse-
test shall have been perfected for application to our Restoration dramatists. Its preparation will in the present instance
be rendered easier by Howard's frank confession, that in the
way of rimed couplets in dramatic works, none wrote better
than Dryden, and none worse than himself[1]. Dryden manifestly seized the opportunity of being invited to assist in the
composition of his friend's play, which was put on the stage
with an unusual expenditure on externals[2], to carry out the
principles of versification which he had adopted. The
whole of this tragedy except the charm and songs in act iii.
sc. 2 and act v. sc. 1 (which are in shorter rimed metres) is
written in heroic couplets ; and in so far as Dryden was its
author, it may be designated as the first of his Heroic
Plays. As might be expected from the fact of the joint
authorship, the versification is unequal; it seems to improve
in the latter half of the play, and of a few passages (such
as one towards the close of act ii, and Zempoalla's cynical
definition of virtue and honour in act iii. sc. 1) it may be

suits even better than the term 'blank verse,' the 'kind of writing' which he
supposes Shakspere to have 'invented,' would argue him devoid of critical
insight, were it not manifestly mere recklessness. It is worthy of observation that he declines to adduce French examples of tragedy in rime, because,
as he says, 'it is the fate of our countrymen to admit little of theirs among
us, but the basest of their men, the extravagancies of their fashions, and the
frippery of their merchandise.' (The imitation of the French drama was only
beginning, and the use of other French materials never amounted to anything
so exceptional as to startle a public which, according to Dryden's quotation
from Barclay, was in the habit of despising foreigners and all their ways).

[1] See Scott's quotation, in his remarks prefixed to *The Indian Queen*, from
Howard's *Introduction to the Great Favourite, or The Duke of Lerma.*

[2] See Pepys' *Diary*, January 27, and Evelyn's, February 10, 1664.

safely asserted that Howard could never have written them. As for the play itself, though the Epilogue takes credit for the novelty of the choice of the New World as the scene of the action, it also remarks with self-condemnatory justice that

> 'Shows may be found that never yet were seen;
> 'Tis hard to find such wit as ne'er has been.'—

For the action itself is thoroughly commonplace, and the personages are Peruvians and Mexicans neither more nor less than the characters in Fletcher's *Princess* are islanders of the East Indian Archipelago.

The success of *The Indian Queen* encouraged Dryden to produce (in 1665) a 'sequel' under the title of *The Indian Emperor, or The Conquest of Mexico by the Spaniards*, which was brought out with the same scenery and dresses, and received with equal, or even greater, favour. *The Indian Emperor* may be said to have permanently established its author's reputation as a dramatist. The plot of this tragedy is 'original'; it is a tissue of conflicting loves contrived and carried on after a fashion which became typical for the heroic plays of the age[1]. In a word, the chief attraction of the play doubtless consisted neither in the cleverness and spirit of particular passages in the dialogue, nor even in the effectiveness or strong sensationalism of particular situations[2], but in the uniformly pleasing flow of the versification, and in the supernatural business introduced. For us, however, the main interest of this production lies in the fact that the form of versification which Dryden desired to establish in the English serious drama was here for the first time fairly on its trial; and that, without proving

Dryden's The Indian Emperor (1665.

---

[1] Cortez falls in love with Montezuma's daughter Cydaria; Montezuma is in love with Almeria; Almeria with Cortez; both Montezuma's sons with Almeria's sister Alibech; Almeria's brother Orbellan with their sister Cydaria.—For a complete analysis of the action of this play, viewed as a type of the heroic drama, pervaded by the motives of heroic honour and love, see P. Holzhausen, *u. s.*, vol. xv. pp. 19 *seqq.*

[2] For examples, see the ingenious introduction of the question of the Papal Supremacy act i. sc. 2), the theological disputation between Montezuma and the Christian Priest, before the former and his High Priest are racked on the stage (act v. sc. 2), and the magnanimity of Cortez to his would-be assassin and their duel by moonlight (act iii. scs. 2 and 3).

throughout adequate to the demands imposed upon its new-fledged strength (see *e.g.* the important first scene of act iv), it achieved a success which on the whole cannot be described as other than brilliant although it manifestly lacked the elements of permanence [1].

His Secret Love, or The Maiden Queen (1667).

That Dryden still remained in doubt as to the possibility of enduringly establishing the results of this experiment, is shown by the fact that his next play, the tragi-comedy of *Secret Love, or The Maiden Queen* (acted early in 1667, before the publication of the *Essay of Dramatic Poesy*), again exhibits a mixture of rime, blank-verse, and prose [2]. This play, of which the serious or 'heroic' portion is founded on a narrative included in one of Mlle. de Scudéry's romances, supposed to be based on history [3], is a very spirited production, and justifies the predilection which King Charles II displayed for it [4]. The serious portion, though not devoid of merit, has a blemish of which the author was well aware [5]; but the chief merit of the play

---

[1] It may be pointed out that *A Defence of an Essay of Dramatic Poesy*, published in 1667 with the second edition of *The Indian Emperor*, has no special connexion with that play.

[2] In the first *Prologue* to this play the author is said to have attempted

'a mingled chime
Of Jonson's humour with Corneille's rime.'

[3] The story of Philocles and the Queen of Corinth in *Artamène, ou le Grand Cyrus*. In the character of the Queen, as Dryden states in his Preface to the play, 'that of the famous Christina, Queen of Sweden,' was supposed to be represented. Scandal was extremely busy with the life and adventures of Gustavus Adolphus' daughter and successor (who resigned her throne in 1654, and died as a convert to the Catholic faith in 1689). But though few more eccentric figures are to be found in history, Queen Christina was probably, as the Swedish historian Geijer puts it, 'better than her reputation.' The circumstances under which she refused the hand of her kinsman Charles Gustavus the Count Palatine, but caused him to be appointed her successor, bear a superficial resemblance to the conduct of the Queen in Dryden's play towards Lysimantes 'first Prince of the Blood'; Philocles, whose original in the romance is called Myrinthe, seems to be meant for Count Magnus Gabriel de la Gardie, the earliest of Queen Christina's favourites, whom she actually married to Charles Gustavus's sister, just as in the play Philocles is married to Candiope the sister of Lysimantes. Cf. V. Cousin, *u. s.*, vol. i. pp. 211-212. De la Gardie was an even more contemptible character than Philocles.

[4] 'It has been owned in so particular a manner by his majesty, that he has graced it with the title of his play.' (*Preface.*)

[5] *Viz.* the weakness of the character of Philocles, which Dryden accordingly

lies in the comic passages between the unstable Celadon
and his mistress Florimel—who marry one another with
their eyes perfectly open, though the lady was first courted
as a ' miss in a mask [1].' If a licence in both situation and
sentiment which it would not be easy to defend be frankly
condoned, the fresh and enjoyable gaiety of these figures
will be readily acknowledged ; Florimel (to whose mirthful
ways full justice was no doubt done by Nell Gwynn) is a
lively and delightful type evidently drawn from real life [2].

In the same year 1667 were probably acted two plays,
of neither of which the credit—such as it is—belongs
wholly to Dryden. The comedy of *Sir Martin Mar-All,*
or The Feigned Innocence (printed 1668) was an adaptation
by Dryden for the English stage of the Duke of Newcastle's translation of Molière's earliest comedy *L'Étourdi*
(first acted 1653), and was not published by Dryden with
his own name till 1697.   Scott, who notes that Quinault's
L'Amour Indiscret was likewise put under contribution [3],
has shown in what respects Dryden's comedy varies from
Molière's ; but he has I think overstated the case in observing
that, with the necessary allowances, the French play is
followed in the English ' with considerable exactness.' The
merits, however, of *Sir Martin Mar-All* (which was very
successful) lie in the humour, novel so far as I know to the
English drama, of the chief character [4], and in the ease of
the dialogue ; the episode foisted into Molière's plot by
Dryden forms a gratuitous addition of grossness [5].   Unlike

Sir Martin
Mar-All
(1667).

seeks to defend in the *Preface*; but the objection to it is to be sought, not as
Dryden supposes it to have been, in the fact that Philocles is an imperfect
character, but in his being an ignoble one.   The character of the Queen,
which Dryden declares himself to have intended as exhibiting ' one
great and absolute pattern of honour ' in his play, seems to me well-
sustained and effective.

[1] See act ii. sc. 1.   This has, I believe, been stated to be the first known
instance of the use of the disagreeable abbreviation ' Miss.'

[2] An unimportant situation in this play is borrowed from Shirley's *Love in
a Maze* (see Dyce's Introduction to that play in Shirley's *Works*, ii. 270).

[3] The first suggestion of both Molière's and Quinault's ' Headless Man '
has been sought in *L'Inavvertito* of N. Barbieri (1630).

[4] Dryden's translation of the title is excellent.   An *étourdi* is a blunderer
who never does the right thing at the right moment, and always does the
wrong thing instead.

[5] M. F. Sarcey, in his *La Comédie Française à Londres*, 1879 (*ap.* G. D.

its French original, Dryden's comedy is in prose. The other and better-known adaptation, probably produced in this year (though not printed till 1670), is mainly in blank-verse and prose, but rimed passages are interspersed. This is Dryden's execution of D'Avenant's design upon Shakspere under *The Tempest, or The Enchanted Island* the title of *The Tempest, or The Enchanted Island*[1]. I need not dwell again on this deplorable aberration, of *Island* which already the Prologue seems to convey a premonition; (1667). for it begins with some justly celebrated lines in praise of Shakspere, and ends with some frank ribaldry *àpropos* of the performance of a boy-character (doubtless Ariel) by a woman. Dryden must bear his share of the responsibility for this act of sacrilege, more especially as he went out of his way to confess that the main addition made to Shakspere's plot by D'Avenant[2], and his invitation to co-operation on this basis, pleased him so much that he ' never writ anything with more delight.' It is however clear, both from his own generously-meant account of D'Avenant's share in the work, and from the nature of the versification, which is of a kind to which Dryden would at this time hardly have returned in a play substantially his own, that Dryden's share in this perversion of Shakspere was very small so far as actual composition was concerned, and was chiefly confined to arrangement for the stage.

An Evening's Love, or The Mock Astrologer (1668).
Another adaptation was soon afterwards produced by Dryden in the prose comedy of *An Evening's Love, or The Mock Astrologer* (acted and printed 1668), which he acknowledges to be taken in part from the younger Corneille's *Le Feint Astrologue*, a version of Calderon's *El Astrologo Fingido*. But Dryden seems to claim credit for the addition of the two ' chief persons ' in the play, Wild-

Heylli in his *C. F. à L.*, 1871–9), mentions that the great, and to him surprising, success of *L'Étourdi* when played at London in that year by the famous Parisian company, was stated to be partly accounted for by the fact that the English public was familiar with *Les Bévues de M. Martin*, a 'pièce très célèbre et presque populaire' by Dryden.

[1] Cf. *ante*, vol. i. p. 513 and vol. ii. p. 200.—Shadwell, in 1673, went a step further than D'Avenant and Dryden had gone, and turned *The Tempest* into an opera.

[2] The invention of the character of Hippolito, the man who had never seen a woman, as a counterpart to Miranda. (See *Preface*)

blood and Jacinta, omitting to mention what Scott has pointed out, that the greater part of the quarrelling scene between the pair is copied (not, however, as Scott says, 'literally') from *Le Dépit Amoureux* of Molière[1]. The comedy is very vivacious, and Dryden moves quite at his ease in the dialogue; but I am unable to subscribe to Scott's preference of Jacinta and Wildblood to Florimel and Celadon[2].

About this time, or rather earlier (1667), Dryden had become virtually a partner in the King's Company, by which he was regularly retained as a writer[3]. Thus a recognised position, as well as a proved and acknowledged power to please, was lending more and more of authority to the pronouncements which he was accustoming himself to send forth as to the theory and practice of dramatic composition. Considerable interest attaches to the first of these noteworthy critical essays and supplements, which as a whole, notwithstanding the variations in their views and the unsoundness of some at least of their contentions, possess a permanent interest for the student of dramatic literature. The immediate occasion of the *Essay of Dramatic Poesy*, written in 1665, but not given to the world till early in 1668, or at the close of the preceding year[4], hardly accounts

Dryden's Essay of Dramatic Poesy (1667 or 1668).

---

[1] Act iv. sc. 3 in both plays. Dryden could have afforded to be candid. For in the *Epilogue* he boldly boasts of himself that as to the French
    'He did not steal their plots, but made them prize';
and in the *Preface* he defends himself not infelicitously against the charge of stealing part of his plays; declaring that he will continue to do so, so long as he makes what he appropriates his own, by 'heightening it for our theatre (which is incomparably more curious in all the ornaments of dramatic poesy than the French or Spanish).'

[2] Pepys, who mentions *An Evening's Love*, is the sole authority for attributing to Dryden a non-extant play, translated by him 'out of French,' which (see *Diary*, September 15, 1668) he calls *The Ladies à la Mode*, but of which no trace has been discovered, unless it be identified with *Damoiselles à la Mode* by Richard Flecknoe (1667) or *The Mall, or The Modish Lovers* (printed 1674, with a Preface by ' J. D.')

[3] See Christie's *Memoir*, Globe Edition, p. xxix. Dryden bound himself to produce three plays a year, but actually only produced ten in as many years (end of 1667 to beginning of 1678).

[4] See the subsequent note as to Sir Robert Howard's *Preface*.—Dryden republished the *Essay* in a revised form in 1684, with a *Dedication* to the Earl of Dorset (Lord Buckhurst). In this *Dedication* he professes to

for the breadth of its range of argument.   Possibly, the
publication, in 1664, of Richard Flecknoe's *A Short Discourse of the English Stage* had suggested to Dryden the
thought of an essay which should transcend the limits of
a purely prefatory discourse [1] ; but there can hardly be
any doubt that the fortunate design of discussing some
of the principles of dramatic poetry in their application
to contemporary literature was fostered in him and in his
English literary associates or antagonists by French example.
Corneille, the first great representative of French tragedy in
the seventeenth century, by his *Examens* also gave a new
and important impulse to the higher criticism of dramatic
compositions, and the personal influence of such a born critic
as St. Evremont sustained the impulse in the country of
his adoption [2].   The *Essay of Dramatic Poesy*, on whose
general significance in the history of English prose composition and style I cannot here dilate, is most agreeably
and stimulatively written in the form of a dialogue between
four literary friends [3].   It may be briefly described as a
defence of the double position, that English dramatists are
justified in maintaining the superior freedom of the modern
as compared with the ancient, and of the English as compared with the French, drama ; and that it would be to
the advantage to the effect of their art should they agree
upon adopting the innovation of rimed verse.   The earlier
portions of the argument are maintained with notable skill

have laid aside the practice of ' verse ' in dramatic composition, because he
found it ' troublesome and slow ' ; but asserts that he is ' in no ways altered
from his opinion of it, at least with any reasons that have opposed it.'

[1] This is the supposition of Genest, vol. x. p. 252. Flecknoe's discourse,
which was printed with his pastoral tragi-comedy of *Love's Kingdom*
(described *ib.*, p. 248), will be found in Mr. Hazlitt's *The English Drama and
Stage*. It certainly contains some good things, and increases the difficulty
in accounting for Dryden's association of Flecknoe with Shadwell in his
immortal satire, except on the supposition that he intended to annoy the
' True Blue Protestant Poet ' by proclaiming him successor to an Irish
Catholic Priest—which Flecknoe appears to have been.

[2] See Saintsbury's *Dryden (English Men of Letters* series), pp. 124-5.

[3] ' Neander ' and ' Lisideius ' are anagrammatical names for Dryden and
Sidley (Sir Charles Sedley) ; Crites is Sir Robert Howard ; Eugenius (as
Prior informs us) Buckhurst (Dorset). The *Essay* is printed in vol. xv of
Scott and Saintsbury's *Dryden*.

and force, and constitute the most enduring claim of the *Essay* to remembrance in the history of criticism. Many of the observations are both keen and just, and worthy of the brilliant inheritor of great national literary traditions. Dryden, in the person of Neander, arrives at conclusions anticipatory of those formed by later critics, with whom he might seem to have had little in common ; he asserts that the English drama includes many plays 'as regular' as 'any of the French,' and distinguished, moreover, by a greater variety of plot and characters ; and he declares ' secondly, that in most of the irregular plays of Shakespeare or Fletcher (for Jonson's are for the most part regular) there is a more masculine fancy, and greater spirit in the writing, than there is in any of the French.' Clearly, then, it was not with French comedy or tragedy, but with our own national drama, that Dryden, at this early stage of his own productivity as a dramatist, desired to connect the further progress of our dramatic literature. At the same time he was anxious to maintain the innovation of rimed verse, to a discussion of which the latter part of the dialogue is devoted. In opposition to the opinion of Crites (Howard[1]), Neander maintains that in serious plays (for he excludes comedy) rime is ' more effectual ' than blank-verse. In the hands of a good poet, rime, if duly placed, is not unnatural ; and if it can be made natural in itself, there is no reason why it should become unnatural in a play. If there are thoughts which are little and mean in rime, such are

Its preference of the English to the French drama.

Its plea for rime.

[1] This opinion had been put forth by Howard in the Preface to *Four New Plays* (1665), (reprinted in the third edition of Howard's *Dramatic Works*, 1722), and had furnished the immediate occasion for Dryden's *Essay*. Howard argues that what is appropriate in a poem, ' being a premeditated Form of Thoughts upon design'd Occasions,' need not be appropriate in a drama, ' which is presented as the present effect of Accidents.' He adds, with some point, that an unnatural effect is produced ' when a Piece of Verse is made up by one that knew not what the other meant to say, and the former Verse answered as perfectly in Sound as the last is supplied in Measure ; so that the Smartness of a Reply, which has its Beauty by coming from sudden Thoughts, seems lost by that which rather looks like a Design of two, than the Answer of one.' (It is odd, by the bye, that in *The Duke of Lerma*, which is not generally in rime, Howard should employ it in at least two passages where the situation demands the expression of strong natural emotion.)

necessarily likewise to be found in blank-verse. And the judgment of a poet is assisted rather than impeded by a form which regulates and restricts the movement of an overflowing fancy.

Sir Robert Howard's reply.

To this *Essay* Sir Robert Howard, who had been throughout treated with the greatest courtesy by his brother-in-law [1], replied in a Preface to a play (*The Duke of Lerma*) published by him in 1668. He here comments on Dryden's defence of rime, and on the futility of the attempt made in the *Essay* to lay down general rules for plays as to Time and Place. The tone of this reply is not ill-humoured [2], and the author pays a very modestly-conceived compliment to the talents of his antagonist. Dryden answered in *A Defence of an Essay of Dramatic Poesy*, prefixed to the second edition of *The Indian Emperor* (1668), which is full of vivacity and banter, and must have annoyed Dryden's 'noble opponent' both where it illustrated his knowledge of Latin, and where it commented on the peculiarities of his logic [3]. The arguments at issue are, however, not materially advanced; Dryden maintains his view that 'Prose though the rightful prince, yet is by common consent deposed, as too weak for the government of serious plays'; that 'Blank Verse is blemished with the weakness of his predecessor'; and that Rime, though he 'has somewhat of the usurper in him,' 'is brave, and generous, and his dominion pleasing.' As for the unities of time and place, he contents himself with demanding so much self-restraint as is reconcileable with a reasonable latitude.

Dryden's A Defence of an Essay of Dramatic Poesy (1668).

---

[1] Dryden had married Sir Robert Howard's sister in December, 1663.

[2] It is, I think, unfairly represented by Scott, vol. i. p. 84 ; and by Christie, p. xxvii. That a personal quarrel was the result of this controversy seems to be a conclusion from the lampoons of Dryden's enemies, Shadwell in particular. See Christie, and Morley, *First Sketch*, p. 655. If there was such a quarrel, it was made up some years before Howard's death in 1698.

[3] The very amusing passage concerning the Unity of Place (where the truth that 'the stage being one place cannot be two' is said to be 'as great a secret as that we are all mortal') is held to allude to the speech of Sir Positive Atall in Shadwell's *The Sullen Lovers* : 'Betwixt you and I, let me tell you, we are all mortal,' and simultaneously to glance at a poem by Howard *On the Fear of Death*. In his first comedy Shadwell had caricatured Howard as the positive knight, and in the *Preface* had attacked Dryden's *Essay of Dramatic Poesy*.

And in this position the question for the present remained. Without wholly renouncing their freedom as to
the management of time and place, Dryden and the contemporary writers of the serious drama endeavoured to
approximate their practice to the spirit of laws of which
they acknowledged the general advantages. As to rime,
they continued to employ it so long as it pleased—in
other words, so long as Dryden himself chose to employ it.
The further developement of Dryden's general theories on
the fittest course to be pursued by the English serious drama
will be duly noted; but his defence of rime as an appropriate and desirable part of English tragic form has been
definitively rejected in theory as well as abandoned in
practice. As a matter of fact, already in Dryden's day
rimed couplets had for English ears acquired a different
sound from that which they possessed and possess for
French [1], partly because of the peculiar uses to which the
practice of our dramatists (with variations indeed, but with
a general steady tendency in the same direction) come to
restrict them, partly from their constant employment in
branches of poetry in which their effect was adverse to the
semblance of continuity which is indispensable in dramatic
dialogue. In the ears of English audiences, however much
a passing fashion might endeavour to conceal the fact, they
could not but constitute an impediment, instead of an aid,
to dramatic illusion. The use of rime was therefore at
variance with that definition of a play which Lisideius,
with the approval of his interlocutors, gives in the *Essay*,
and which requires it to be 'a just and lively image of
human nature.' Moreover, even if the possibility of rimed
verse proving itself a suitable metre for serious English plays
might still be considered an open question, the task of carrying the demonstration to a successful issue was one before

Dryden's views as to rime in the English drama in-admissible.

---

[1] See on this head the excellent remarks of M. Taine, *Histoire de la Littérature Anglaise*, ed. 1866, vol. iii. p. 187; and cf. *ante*, p. 317.—It has been
already noted, that in 1655 Sforza Pallavicino (afterwards Cardinal) published his tragedy *Erminigildo*, with a Preface defending the use of rime.
But the innovation, notwithstanding the rimed tragedies of Martelli,
found but little favour. See Walker, *Historical Memoir on Italian Tragedy*,
p. 194.

which even the elastic genius of Dryden was likely in the end to succumb. He afterwards confessed, that though he adhered to his theories on the subject, he found the continuation of the effort ' too troublesome,' and that he had grown weary of ' his long-lov'd mistress.' For the present, however, according to his wont, he revelled in *Dryden's Tyrannic Love, or The Royal Martyr (1668 or 1669).* the prodigal power of his genius. His next dramatic composition, the tragedy of *Tyrannic Love, or The Royal Martyr* (printed 1670; acted probably 1669 or towards the end of 1668), is one of the most characteristic, as it is in some respects one of the most successful, of his Heroic Plays Written entirely in rimed verse, it contains passages which would almost warrant a belief that *si sic omnia dixisset* he might have succeeded in vindicating the new form in the eyes of posterity as well as of his contemporaries[1]. Yet even from this play it would not be difficult to quote other passages, in which the form either remains inadequate, or helps to create an effect far more rhetorical than seems appropriate to the occasion. The expedient of broken lines, moreover, which Dryden extolled so highly as a useful relief, is obviously as a rule unsuited to rimed verse—indeed, the way in which it is employed by some contemporary dramatists is at times almost ludicrous[2]; while a few stray Alexandrines likewise come upon us as unwelcome intruders.

In this tragedy, a historical theme treated freely (and in part, as Dryden acknowledges, incorrectly), *viz.* the persecutions of the Christians by Maximin, is connected with the

---

[1] See *e. g.* Maximin's opening lines in act iii. sc. 1 ; his speech ('I'll find that power o'er wills') act iv. sc. 1 ; and his speech act v. sc. 1 ('What had the Gods to do with me or mine'), which last I cannot follow Scott in condemning.

[2] I am not aware, however, that any of them has in this respect gone beyond a passage of *The Conquest of Granada* (Part II, act iv. sc. 3), where Almanzor says to his Mother's Ghost :

' Well mayst thou make thy boast whoe'er thou art !
Thou art the first e'er made Almanzor start.
My legs
Shall bear me to thee in their own despite,' &c.

But it must be conceded that in other passages of this play, in which the broken lines are very frequent, they have a surprising rhythmical effectiveness.

legend of the martyrdom of St. Catharine [1]. The general flow of the action is full of that kind of animation which few poets have possessed Dryden's power of imparting to the work of their hands; but while the character of Maximin is sustained with genuine vigour, St. Catharine, on the other hand, is hardly to be called a dramatic personage [2]. As to the miracle on the stage, wrought by the guardian angel Amariel with the aid of operatic machinery, one can only wonder at an audience capable of enjoying in succession, first the episode in question, and then the notorious farcical Epilogue to this Heroic Tragedy *in excelsis* [3].

Tyrannic Love was succeeded (late in 1669 or early in 1670) by a yet more celebrated tragedy, in two Parts [4]. Independently of the various theatrical and literary consequences of its production, *Almanzor and Almahide, or* *Almanzor and Alma-hide, or*

[1] The comparison with Massinger and Dekker's *The Virgin Martyr* (*ante*, p. 12) naturally suggests itself; but Dryden's tragedy, though similar in some points of the action as well as in the general character of the argument, is written independently of Massinger's. In the latter the heroine is attended by one angelic guide—in Dryden's, hosts of good and of evil spirits contend over her couch. This not very effective interlude (which was duly burlesqued in *The Rehearsal*, act v) was probably intended to gratify the tastes of the Duchess of Monmouth, to whose husband the play is dedicated.—Dryden expressly denies having taken anything of importance out of two French plays on the subject, *L'Amour Tyrannique* and *Sainte Catherine*. The latter, by Desfontaines, was found by M. Beljame in a *Recueil de Tragédies Saintes*, published at Paris in 1666; and Professor Saintsbury, to whom the discovery was communicated, has traced a few slight resemblances to this play in Dryden's.—In *Tyrannic Love* (act v. sc. 1) occurs a famous passage:
    'Here we stand shivering on the bank, and cry,
        When we should plunge into eternity.'
[2] Her argument with the priest (act ii. sc. 1) ends rather abruptly with his conversion; to give him his due, he had not argued badly up to her final speech. In the *Parallel of Poetry and Painting*, prefixed by Dryden to his *Translation* of Du Fresnoy (Scott and Saintsbury's *Dryden*, vol. xvii. p. 301), he characteristically pleads guilty to having in St. Catharine created a character unsuited to the stage, as the entire perfection of a saint, if sought to be represented there, produces 'impious thoughts in the beholding,' and incline them to 'accuse the heavens of injustice.'
[3] The *Epilogue* was spoken by Nell Gwynn, who had acted Valeria. After at the outset apostrophising in terms of startling downrightness the person who was to 'carry her off dead,' the speaker proceeds to announce herself to her friends in front as 'the ghost of poor departed Nelly.'
[4] This writing of plays in parts, though no novelty on the stage, is ridiculed in *The Rehearsal*. 'Whereas,' says Bayes, act iv. sc. 1, 'every one makes five Acts to one Play, what do I but make five Plays to one Plot?'

The Con-
quest of
Granada
(1669 or
1670).

The Conquest of Granada by the Spaniards has been generally, and justly, regarded as the most prominent type of the 'heroic plays' of this age. Its historical background and part of its plot were borrowed by Dryden from Madeleine de Scudéry's romance of *Almahide*; but besides deriving certain turns in action and dialogue from the Spanish work on which the French authoress founded her story, he has interwoven with it, as already Langbaine pointed out, portions of the stories of *Le Grand Cyrus* and of *Ibrahim ou L'Illustre Bassa*[1]. Furthermore, Dryden confesses in his lofty way, that of the chief character of the play, Almanzor, he had derived 'the first image from the Achilles of Homer, the next from Tasso's Rinaldo (who was a copy of the former), and the third from the Artaban of Monsieur Calpranède[2], who had imitated both. He is,' the English poet complacently adds, 'on a grand scale (not like the heroes of French romance[3])'—and in truth, one ventures to think, would have created no wholly pleasant sensation in the *salons* where those romances were indigenous. Without pretending to decide the question whether 'the most probable of the actions' of this hero are not impossible, we shall readily allow that the spirit of the dialogue of this play is from first to last nothing short of amazing. If a vast quantity of rant is requisite to give expression to the 'over-boiling[4]' courage of Almanzor, and if the conception of his pride and valour are alike hyper-Achillean—so that altogether he was a fit model for the caricature of Drawcansir in *The Rehearsal*[5]—yet many of the turns of diction are extraordinarily vigorous, and the

---

[1] Cf. A. Tüchert, *u. s.*, p. 26. From the *Grand Cyrus* comes the story of Lyndaraxa, her lovers and her brothers; from *Ibrahim* that of the loves of Ozmyn and Benzayda. The full argument of *The Conquest of Granada* is given by Mr. Saintsbury in his *Dryden* (*English Men of Letters* series), pp. 46 *seqq.*

[2] In his *Cléopâtre*.

[3] *Essay on Heroic Plays.*

[4] 'I have formed a hero, I confess, not absolutely perfect, but of an excessive and over-boiling courage; but Homer and Tasso are my predecessors.' *Dedication.*

[5] ' Who is that Drawcansir?

' *Bayes.* Why, Sir, a fierce Hero that fights his Mistriss, snubs up Kings, baffles Armies, and does what he will, without regard to good manners, justice, or numbers.' *The Rehearsal* (act iv. sc. 1).

force of the impetus which enables the author to sustain
the character through ten acts is simply without a parallel.
The extravagance of the conception is, however, such as to
render the entire character at times almost grotesque, while
the bombast of particular passages renders them ludicrous
so soon as we pause to examine into their meaning.   Of
the other characters the best is Almahide—a picture
of real female dignity, against which the passion of love
contends in vain.   The ambitious Lyndaxara, on the other
hand, seems to me drawn without power.   The remaining
personages are in themselves uninteresting; but the entire
play is written with such marvellous spirit that, hurried
along by its resistless current, the reader has no breath left
with which to protest his weariness.

Something of Almanzor's arrogance of spirit must have
communicated itself to the poet when in the *Epilogue* to
this play he ventured to boast that he and his fellows
had left the old poets—even Jonson—behind, because their
age had been altogether distanced by the new generation:

> ' Our ladies and our men now speak more wit
>   In conversation, than those poets writ.'

This arrogance having justly given offence, and Rochester, *The De-*
who in a fit of spleen at the success of *The Conquest of* *fence of the*
Epilogue,
Granada was about to divert from Dryden the fickle sun- *&c.* (1672).
shine of his favour, having hurled at him a coarse denial of
the major in his proposition[1], the poet, put on his mettle,
published by way of a postscript to his play (in 1672) a
*Defence of the Epilogue, or an Essay on the Dramatic
Poetry of the Last Age.*   In this short Essay he sought to
maintain the assertion that language had become correcter
since the days of Shakspere, Fletcher and Jonson, and wit
both correcter and more courtly.   This result he boldly
ascribes to the Court, and particularly to the King, who
was certainly devoid neither of literary discernment nor of
goodwill towards the stage, but who is as likely as not to
have received the compliment with one of those favourite

---

[1] Asking him, in fact, whether he was so sure of his being a wit
and a poet himself? The lines are quoted *ap.* Scott and Saintsbury,
vol. iv. p. 244.

expletives which were his best-known contributions to the
formation of a Caroline style[1].

But before Dryden published his masterpiece in the
'heroic' drama, accompanied both by the Essay just mentioned and by another of greater importance in which he
endeavoured to defend the entire species so brilliantly
exemplified in this play, those shafts which success has most
to fear—the shafts of ridicule—had clattered down upon
his gorgeous armour, and had found more than one hole in it.
It should be stated at once that the effect of *The Rehearsal*
has been much exaggerated[2]; for it left 'heroic plays'
very much where it found them; and they continued to
be produced and applauded so long as Dryden chose to
expend the efforts of his genius upon them[3]. Indeed,
it is questionable whether this lively *jeu d'esprit* can properly be said to have been directed essentially against
'rimed heroic plays'; and, in any case, it would have been
more effective as a literary effort, and would have better
deserved the renown which it has commanded, had it not
mixed up odds and ends from so many kinds of plays in
the cauldron of its ridicule, and had it concentrated its
attack upon the one English dramatist of his age, the scale
of whose extravagances dwarfed the efforts of all his
competitors for public applause, as the powers of his genius
eclipsed their talents. But the authors of this burlesque,
among whom besides the principal author, George Villiers,

---

[1] The argument of this *Essay* is carried on chiefly by means of petty criticisms of passages in the old writers. We, on the contrary, Dryden maintains,
have refined the language by adding new words and phrases (but with his
usual sound sense, he blames those who corrupt English by mixing it too
much with French), and by applying words to new significations. We have
better opportunities, for 'greatness' is now easier of access than it then
was; and 'as the excellency of' the King's 'nature forgave the rebellion,
so the excellency of his manners reformed the barbarisms of his subjects.' In
all this there is just enough truth to show that there are two sides to every
question.

[2] So *e. g.* by Hettner, in his chapter on Dryden (admirable in the main) in
his *Litteraturgeschichte des 18. Jahrhunderts*, vol. i. p. 90, where, after speaking of *The Rehearsal*, he says that 'rimed heroic tragedy was now lost for
ever,' though noting that it was still occasionally performed.

[3] This was already pointed out by R. Bell in *The Life of Dryden* prefixed
to his useful popular edition.

DUKE OF BUCKINGHAM, were said to have been Samuel
Butler (the author of *Hudibras*), Martin Clifford (Master
of the Charterhouse), and Dr. Thomas Sprat[1] (Bishop of
Rochester and Dean of Westminster), can have had no intention beyond that of ridiculing what they thought either
deserving of laughter or likely to excite it; and were so far
from intending a crushing attack upon Dryden as a dramatist,
that it seems as if first Sir William D'Avenant, and then Sir
Robert Howard (under the name of Bilboa), had been chosen
as the hero of the burlesque. D'Avenant however died in
time to escape the honour (in 1668); and Dryden's appointment to the poet-laureateship (in 1669), together with the
success of his *Conquest of Granada*, clearly entitled him to
the preference over his brother-in-law. Thus this elaborate
trifle, which is said to have been begun in 1663 and to have
been ready for representation in 1665 (when the Plague
intervened), was, in a modified form, at last produced on
December 7, 1671. The success of *The Rehearsal* is too
well known to need description; it went through five editions
in Buckingham's life-time, and is stated to have gone through
sixteen more since; it was the parent of a long if not
altogether illustrious line of descendants, among which
Sheridan's *Critic* has alone rivalled it in popularity[2]; it
supplied an eminent writer with the title of a celebrated
satire[3], and many small writers with an infinity of small
jokes, and it affixed to Dryden, who was caricatured in its
hero Bayes, a nickname which clung to him through life[4].

[1] In *The Session of the Poets* 'malicious Matt. Clifford and spiritual S—t'
are said to have joined with Buckingham (who was the patron of both) in
a 'Play Tripartite.'

[2] D'Urfey in 1721 published a 'sequel' to *The Rehearsal*, entitled *The Two
Queens of Brentford, or Bayes no Poetaster, a Musical Farce or Comical Opera*.

[3] Marvell's *The Rehearsal Transprosed.*—Fielding's excellent *The Life and
Death of Tom Thumb the Great* (1731) shows how *The Rehearsal* had failed
to exhaust the capabilities of its subject. Dryden's plays themselves furnish
Fielding with many opportunities for ridicule.

[4] The only mention of *The Rehearsal* made by Dryden in verse is the contemptuous statement in Epistle ix, *Letter to Sir George Etherege* (*Works*,
vol. xi):
> 'His grace of Bucks has made a farce
> And you, whose comic wit is terse all
> Can hardly fall below Rehearsal,'

together with the subsequent allusion to the 'ten years' which it took the

Nature and
objects of
its satire.
More than this, however, it did not effect ; and there
seems accordingly no necessity for dwelling upon it at
any further length, more especially as much of its wit has
inevitably grown as musty as the large majority of the
plays held up to ridicule in it by means of quoted passages
and parodied phrases or situations. The larger proportion
of these plays would have died a natural death without this
friendly assistance. The ridicule showered on ' Bayes '—
besides personalities which have long lost such savour as
they ever possessed—turns upon his supposed mechanical
manufacture of plots, plays, and passages with the help of
a book of ' Drama Commonplaces ' (act i. sc. 1). The idea
is droll in itself, but quite pointless as applied to Dryden.
He is further ridiculed for his Prologues, and—in what
strikes me as the wittiest passage in the whole satire—
for the defectiveness of his plots[1]. Among his plays

Duke to carry out his dramatic idea. In his *Vindication of the Duke of
Guise* (*Works*, vol. ii) he contemptuously apprises an assailant who had
spoken of him under ' the noble name of Bayes,' with which he was now
constantly assailed, that Bayes was the brat of his own father, and could be
mistaken for nobody else—not a particularly happy retort, but one which he
repeated in the *Essay on Satire* prefixed to his *Translations of Juvenal* (*ib.*
vol. xiii), where he adds that he had another reason for not answering *The
Rehearsal, viz.* that he knew ' his betters ' to be more concerned in that
satire than himself. In the *Epilogue* to *All for Love* he seems to disclaim
identification with Mr. Bayes ; and it is amusing to find him turning the
burlesque simile of the ' Two Kings of Brentford ' against the two heroes of
Corneille's *Œdipe* (see Preface to *Œdipus*) ; and quoting another facetious
scene in the play with good-humour as an illustration in his *Life of Plutarch*
(*Works*, vol. xvii. p. 74). The sarcastic reference to ' the great Duke of B.'
in Dryden's letter to Rochester, dated 1673 (*ib.* vol. xviii. p. 93), is hardly
worth citing.

According to a note in *The Early Diary of Frances Burney*, edited by
R. A. Ellis (1889), vol. i. p. 153, Horace Walpole was of opinion that
Cibber's Bayes was far superior to Garrick's famous impersonation, which
involved him in a duel and other discomforts. ' Old Cibber preserved the
solemn coxcomb, and was the caricature of a great poet, as the part was
meant to be, not what Garrick made Bayes, a garreteer bard.' Lord Chesterfield entertained the same objection to Garrick's way of playing Bayes,
which he asserted to be ' a serious, solemn character.'

[1] The passage occurs in the *Epilogue* :

> ' The Play is at an end, but where's the Plot ?
> That circumstance our Poet Bayes forgot ;
> And we can boast, though 'tis a plotting Age,
> No place is freer from it than the Stage.'

The Wild Gallant with its deservedly satirised repartees,
Tyrannic Love, *The Conquest of Granada* with Drawcansir's
bombast [1], and others are impartially ridiculed. Among
better-known authors besides Dryden, Sir William D'Avenant, Fanshawe [2], Quarles [3], Stapylton [4], and Mrs. Aphra
Behn supply materials and opportunities; the ridicule of
the Opera and Ballet is most legitimate ; what particular
play, if any, suggested the famous Two Kings of Brentford,
remains, so far as I know, undiscovered. The fun of this
farrago of prose, blank-verse, song and dance—which fun
need not for a moment be denied—is not of a nature to
require further illustration [5].

Dryden, whose disposition was framed in a large mould,
suffered this loose attack upon his general position as a
dramatist neither to interfere with his activity nor to crush
his spirit. In the following year (1672) he published with his
Conquest of Granada an Essay *Of Heroic Plays*, which though
slight and probably not the fruit of protracted thought, at
all events proves that he had not as yet relinquished the
ambition of further successes in the same direction. He no
longer admits the use of heroic couplets in serious plays to
be a question open to dispute. Repeating his former arguments in favour of rime, he traces the history of heroic plays
on the English stage to Sir William D'Avenant's operas,
which lacked certain elements since supplied. ' An heroic
play,' he continues, ' ought to be an imitation, in little, of

*Dryden's
Essay of
Heroic
Plays
(1672).*

---

[1] ' He that dares drink, and for that drink dares die,
     And, knowing this, dares yet drink on, am I.' (Act iv. sc. 1.)

[2] As to Sir Richard Fanshawe, the translator of two Spanish plays and of
the *Pastor Fido* of Guarini (1640), cf. *ante*, p. 306.

[3] Cf. *ante*, p. 286.

[4] As to Sir Robert Stapylton, whose comedy of *The Slighted Maid* (pr. 1663)
figures in *The Rehearsal*, cf. *ante*, p. 336, where see as to his *Tragedie of Hero
and Leander* (1668).

[5] The necessary details and explanations, so far as they are obtainable,
will be found in the Introduction and illustrations to Professor Arber's
Reprint of *The Rehearsal* (*English Reprints*, 1869), from which I have borrowed some information. The *Key to the Rehearsal* in vol. ii of *The
Miscellaneous Works of Buckingham* (' collected and prepar'd for the Press
by the Late Ingenious Mr. Thomas Brown ') pretends to be by the Duke, but
is neither genuine nor (as a cursory examination will suffice to show)
complete.

an heroic poem, and consequently, love and valour ought to be the subject of it.' He claims for 'an heroic poet' exemption from the necessity of a bare representation of 'what is true or exceeding probable'; and thus seeks to justify the introduction of supernatural agency. He upholds, as familiar to the stage and as necessary to raise the imagination of the audience, resort to the noise and paraphernalia of war. And defending his typical character of Almanzor, he declares that he will 'never subject his characters to the French standard, where love and honour are to be weighed by drams and scruples.'

In the first instance, however, having vindicated his position by taking up this defiant attitude, Dryden hereupon turned to a species of dramatic writing for which, as he more than once declared, he felt less qualified by nature, but which, as best suited his personal circumstances, could be produced at the most rapid rate. Of the two comedies *The Assignation, or Love in a Nunnery* (acted 1672), and *Marriage à-la-Mode* (acted 1673), the latter appears to have been very well, and the former ill, received[1]. In both cases the public, I think, judged rightly. *The Assignation*, though written with great ease and containing one rather humorous character (the bungling Benito[2]), is a worthless play, which cannot be said to rise above the level of the comic dramatist (Sir Charles Sedley) to whom it was dedicated, and to whom Dryden professed himself ignorant whether as a 'poet' he would be preferred[3]. *Marriage à-la-Mode*, on the other hand, is thoroughly amusing in its comic action, which, though occasionally as Melantha would say *risquée* to a considerable degree, is yet (as the author with some pride points out in the Epilogue) kept within

His The Assignation, or Love in a Nunnery (1672).

Marriage à-la-Mode (1673).

[1] The unfavourable reception of *The Assignation* was accentuated by the satisfaction which it afforded to Edward Ravenscroft, whose *Citizen Turned Gentleman* (imitated from Molière) Dryden had treated with derision in his *Prologue*.

[2] 'All things,' he says (act v. sc. 2), 'go cross to men of sense: would I had been born with the brains of a shopkeeper, that I might have thriven without knowing why I did so.'

[3] In the *Epilogue* Dryden deprecates the supposition that he intended any scandal against nuns; but Hippolyte is hardly a specimen at the selection of which a devout Catholic could have rejoiced.

certain bounds. The character of the 'fair impertinent' Melantha herself, a fashionable lady and 'one of those who run mad in new French words[1],' is excellent; Congreve has hardly surpassed it; and we are already near to the height of the Restoration comedy of manners[2]. The play is partly in prose, partly in blank-verse.

In the same year (1673) Dryden produced—with a far more regrettable rapidity—a tragedy which Scott justly describes as 'beneath criticism,' and which may be dismissed accordingly. *Amboyna, or The Cruelties of the Dutch to the English Merchants,* was (see Dedication) 'contrived or written in a month'—practically, therefore, to order. It is an attempt to inflame popular feeling against the Dutch, war with whom had been declared in the previous year, by reviving the memory of an atrocity committed just fifty years before, and condoned by the feeble Government of James I[3]. The play might be described as one of the most ordinary 'sensational' kind, were it not that even here the 'heroic' sentiment finds occasion for venting itself, the whole crime being traced to a guilty love-passion. The 'patriotic' invective fills a moderately sensitive historic conscience with shame instead of sym-

Amboyna (1673).

---

[1] '*Philotis* ... You have so drained all the French plays and romances, that they are not able to supply you with words for your daily expense. *Melantha.* Drained? What a word's there! *Épuisée*, you sot you.' (Act iii. sc. 1.)

[2] The sudden *peripeteia* in *Marriage à-la-Mode* is ridiculed in *The Rehearsal*—another proof of the readiness with which the authors of that dramatic satire caught at any excess or defect in any known play of the time, whether the play itself might be deserving of praise or of censure.

[3] The murder (on the pretence of a plot having been formed by them) of the English merchants at Amboyna (one of the Molucca islands) could not fail to create 'some little excitement; but this quickly died away,' and the deed, though deeply resented by King James, was in the end left unavenged. See Gardiner, *History of England*, &c., vol. v. pp. 242 *et post*; and vol. vi. pp. 188 *et post*, and cf. as to the attempt of Charles I to obtain compensation on the occasion of marriage-negotiations with the House of Orange in 1654, *Ib.* vol. ii. p. 125. A narrative of the Amboyna outrages was appended to a treatise of the inflammatory-patriotic kind, published in 1673 under the title of *A Further Justification of the Present War against the Netherlands*, by Henry Stubbs, 'a lover of the Honour and Welfare of old England.' The event is referred to by at least two pre-Restoration dramatists, *viz*. Fletcher, *The Fair Maid of the Inn*, act iv. sc. 2, and Shirley, *Honoria and Mammon*, act i. sc. 2.

pathy[1], while the horrors perpetrated on the stage, or all but on it, inspire as much disgust as compassion[2].

A stray spark of this half-artificial patriotic fire finds its way[3] into Dryden's next dramatic work—if it deserve that name. The 'opera' of *The State of Innocence and Fall of Man*, though never intended for representation, is a more extraordinary though a less deplorable aberration from good taste than *Amboyna*. This would-be dramatic version of *Paradise Lost* was first published in 1674, shortly after Milton's death. It seems to have been intended, partly as a seasonable tribute to the genius of a poet whose greatness Dryden in *The Author's Apology for Heroic Poetry and Poetic Licence*, prefixed to his 'opera,' acknowledges with characteristic straightforwardness[4], but more especially as a proof that this rare masterpiece admitted of the addition of yet another charm of which the secret happened to be denied to its author. Obviously, the question cannot be discussed here, whether a dramatic treatment of Milton's theme, such as it had received before *Paradise Lost* was written and such as may perhaps have contributed to inspire one of the greatest of the world's epical poems, was in the highest and fullest sense appropriate

The State of Innocence and Fall of Man (printed 1674).

---

[1] It is a well-known but instructive fact that the tone of the patriotic war-party of the day was to hold the Dutch up to ridicule as a nation of *shop-keepers.* Cf. act ii. sc. 1 of this play. The 'Let Caesar live, and Carthage be subdued' echoes the 'Delenda est Carthago' of Shaftesbury—who was to live to seek a refuge among the people he had sought to ruin.—In *Amboyna*, by-the-bye, occurs the long-lived rollicking lyric,

> 'Who ever saw a noble sight
> That never viewed a brave sea-fight,' &c. (Act iii. sc. 3.)

[2] See, for instance, the torturing on the stage of the English—one of whom is 'led with matches tied to his hands.' (Act v. sc. 1.)

[3] In *The State of Innocence* (act i. sc. 1) Lucifer addresses the infernal powers as

> 'Most *high and mighty* lords, who better fell
> From heaven, to rise *states-general* of hell.'

(Doubtless anything but a reminiscence of Vondel's identification of Lucifer with the founder of the Dutch Republic.)

[4] 'The original' of his version he describes as 'undoubtedly one of the greatest, most noble and most sublime poems which either this age or nation has produced.' Under the circumstances, this tribute weighs heavier than the passing compliment to 'your Ariosto' in the Dedication to the young Duchess of York (Mary of Modena).

to it [1].   Dryden addressed himself, not to the subject itself,
but to the epical treatment which it had received at Milton's
hands, and deliberately ran an uncalled-for risk, in spite of
the warnings addressed to his too facile contemporaries
by a fellow-poet, whose appreciation of Milton and his
masterpiece was the result of something more than literary
insight [2].   There can be no doubt, but that Dryden's
dominant motive, in attempting an experiment so hazardous
that even his splendid audacity could not altogether
ignore its perils, was his belief in his mastery of the
particular form of verse—the rimed couplet—with which
he had chosen for the time to identify his literary reputation.
He seems to have caused his intention to become known to
Milton, if the well-known anecdote be true that the latter
replied to this communication : 'Aye, you may *tag* my
verses, if you will.'   And at a much later date (1693) he
certainly persisted in asserting that Milton's ' own particular
reason' for objecting to rime was that it was 'not his talent;
he had neither the ease of doing it, nor the graces of it';
and in support of this assertion appealed to the ' constrained
and forced' character of the rime in Milton's juvenile poems [3].
Dryden's daring attempt resulted in a *tour de force*, which in
any hands but his own could not have failed to be a pitiable
failure.   As it is, the '*poetic license,*' claimed for heroic

---

[1] Hayley's opinion is well known that Milton's imagination originally
caught fire from Giovanni-Battista Andreino's *Adamo*, an early seventeenth-
century Italian *rappresentazione* of the mystery-type, as well as the fact that
Milton himself at one time thought of treating the theme of *Paradise Lost* in
a dramatic form.   Professor Masson has exhaustively discussed the whole
subject in his *Life of Milton*, and in vol. i of his edition of *The Poetical
Works*.

[2] See Marvell, *On Paradise Lost*:

> ' Or, if a Work so infinite be spanned,
> Jealous I was, that some less skilful hand,
> Such as disquiet always what is well,
> And by ill imitating would excel,
> Might hence presume the whole creation's day
> *To change in scenes, and show it in a play.*'

These admirable lines are cited by Scott.   They appeared originally in the
1674 edition of *Paradise Lost*.

[3] See *Essay on Satire*, prefixed to Dryden's *Translations from Juvenal*
(*Works*, vol. xiii).

poetry in the *Preface*, of 'speaking things in verse which are beyond the severity of prose' is here put to very strange uses. The first sensations of Eve on her birth into Paradise as here depicted, perilously resemble a young beauty's impressions of her first ball :

> ' Sure, I am something which they wish to be,
> And cannot ; I myself am proud of me[1].'

At a later stage of her experiences, she consoles herself for the catastrophe of her primitive happiness by a more than optimistic philosophy, on beholding a vision of Heaven full of Angels and blessed Spirits :

> ' Ravished with joy, I can but half repent
> The sin, which Heaven makes happy in the event[2].'

Aureng-Zebe (1676). In the tragedy of *Aureng-Zebe*, acted and printed 1676, Dryden once more, and for the last time, produced a rimed heroic play. In the *Dedication* to Mulgrave (Buckinghamshire), he professes himself weary of low comedy, to which, as has been seen, motives of convenience had induced him to return, and desirous, if he ' must be condemned to rhyme,' of ' some ease in his change of punishment.' He wishes to be ' no more the Sisyphus of the stage'; in other words, he at that time entertained the thought (which he failed to carry into execution[3]) of composing an epic poem. And in the justly celebrated *Prologue* to this play, he gives frank expression to his weariness ' of his long-loved mistress, Rhyme'; as it were throws up his weapon in confessing that

> ' Passion 's too fierce to be in fetters bound,
> And nature flies him like enchanted ground';

and, while protesting that his present is his most successful effort in the ' correct' style, avows, with a sincerity which all but atones, not only for this boast, but for the unbecoming arrogance of the *Epilogue* to *The Conquest of Granada*, that

> ' Spite of all his pride, a secret shame
> Invades his breast at Shakespeare's sacred name :

---

[1] Act ii. sc. 2.   [2] Act v. sc. 1.

[3] He appears to have contemplated the subjects of *The Black Prince* and *King Arthur*. The period of his Satires did not begin till 1681.

> Awed when he hears his god-like Romans rage,
> He, in a just despair, would quit the stage ;
> And to an age less polished, more unskilled,
> Does, with disdain, the foremost honours yield.'

The magnanimity which lies at the root of such a confession is one of the rarest, as it is one of the most delightful, of qualities in an eminent man of letters ; nor has there ever been an English author of whom this quality is more characteristic than it is of Dryden, in whose case it may well be allowed to cover a multitude of errors. The tragedy *Aureng-Zebe* has been diversely judged [1]; on the whole, however, it must be held both for better and for worse to fall short of Dryden's supreme achievement among his heroic plays, *The Conquest of Granada*. If the diction of the later play has less of vehement force [2], it is on the other hand varied by passages more subtly impressive ; and the verse itself is less monotonously true to the self-established pattern [3]. The historical theme is treated with considerable freedom, for Aureng-Zebe (Great Mogul from 1660 to 1707) was a living prince [4]; but although the master of India was not altogether unacquainted with the course of English affairs, and came into very direct contact with English enter-

---

[1] Charles II, who altered an incident in the play, pronounced it to be the best of all Dryden's tragedies.

[2] At the close, however, the author compensates himself by Nourmahal's madness for his previous comparative moderation.

[3] Cf. Saintsbury, *u. s.*, p. 57, as to the tendency in *Aureng-Zebe* to *enjambement*.

[4] In Narcissus Luttrell's *Brief Relation* (vol. ii. p. 629) occurs under date December 1, 1692, the announcement that 'Aurenzeb, the great mogul, died lately in the 99 year of his age.' But on January 11, 1696, the Earl of Middleton writes to Colonel Sackville : 'The General of Batavia sent an ambassador to the Mogul, who, among other things, told him that they had drove away the English King, and sent a servant of theirs to rule that people; to which old Aurungzebe replied that he was glad of it ; that the English had wickedly defrauded his subjects of what was due to them, and against the public faith had plundered them at sea; and now that they had subdued them, he expected they should make him serious reparation. Depend upon it, the story is seriously true.'—The most easily accessible account of *Aurungzib*, 'the great Puritan Emperor of India' as he has been called, is to be found in Dr. Stanley Lane Poole's monograph in *The Rulers of India Series* (1893). His name became more widely known to western readers through the *Voyages* of Tavernier (of which an English translation appeared in 1678) and of Bernier, both of which have been recently reprinted.

prise in his own latitudes, his name can scarcely have come home more closely to Englishmen at large than that of Mithridates, the subject of a tragedy by Racine, to which the author of *Aureng-Zebe* was assuredly no stranger. (A single scene in this play was borrowed by Dryden from the *Grand Cyrus*.) The absence of all supernatural machinery is noticeable as a further indication of the change which was preparing itself in the author's theories of dramatic composition and effect.

All for Love, or The World Well Lost (1678).

When two years later (1678), without having accomplished his epical design, Dryden, encouraged perhaps by an addition to his pension which may have been due to Mulgrave's influence[1], returned once more to dramatic composition, a curious but characteristic mixture of self-consciousness with generous admiration for the greatness of 'the divine Shakespeare' prompted him to a unique effort in the history of his career as a dramatic poet. In the *Preface* to the tragedy of *All for Love, or The World Well Lost* he takes credit for a more exact observance of the unities of time, place, and action 'than perhaps the English theatre requires.' But he boldly rejects the models of the Ancients as 'too little for English tragedy'; and freely declares that he has not observed 'the nicety of manners of the French,' 'who want the genius which animates our stage.' He has taken Shakspere as his model for his style, and, in order to follow this model the more freely, he has, without renouncing his theories on the subject, 'disencumbered' himself 'from rhyme.' As to the result, he hopes he may affirm that by imitating Shakspere he has 'excelled himself throughout the play,' particularly in the first scene between Antony and Ventidius.

Dryden abandons the use of rime in tragedy.

All for Love and Antony and Cleopatra.

All for Love may be almost described as a trial of strength not only against Shakspere, upon whose *Antony and Cleopatra* Dryden's tragedy may be fairly said to be to some extent based, but against many of the chief wits of the nation before and after Shakspere. Dryden's complacency in the result is not wholly unjustified. In a sense, his tragedy is original; the character of Antony is drawn

[1] See the opening of the *Dedication* of *Aureng-Zebe*.

with considerable skill; the dominion which passion is capable of acquiring over a human being is, I think, exhibited quite as effectively as it is in Shakspere—but Dryden's Antony lacks elevation. His Cleopatra is comparatively uninteresting. The writing maintains a high level throughout; and the scene to which, as just noted, the author directs special attention is undoubtedly admirable. The construction of the play is close and effective; and its general tone is sufficiently moderated, without becoming open to the charge of tameness. Within certain limits, there assuredly never was a more flexible genius than Dryden's. The tasks which he set himself, without actually failing in their performance, are many and extraordinary; in the present instance he cannot be said to rival Shakspere on his own ground, but he follows him on it without making himself guilty of servile imitation or breaking down from lack of original force. *All for Love* has been not unjustly designated by an eminent critic [1] as 'Dryden's finest play.'

Passing by the outrageous comedy of *Limberham, or The Kind Keeper* (acted 1678), the dramatic merits of which wholly fail to redeem its outrageous indecency, while its professed moral intention is entirely lost in its shameless personal purpose [2], we come to a play in which Dryden, contrary to his custom and that of his age, co-operated with another author. The tragedy of *Œdipus* (acted late in 1678) was the joint composition of Dryden and Lee, the former having arranged the plan of the whole and contributed the first and third acts [3]. This tragedy,

Limber-
ham
(1678).

Dryden
and Lee's
Œdipus
(1678).

---

[1] Mr. Leslie Stephen.—As to Sir Charles Sedley's would-be parallel venture (1677), see below.

[2] The character of Limberham was generally applied to Lauderdale; probably it was also intended to convey reminiscences of Shaftesbury; and in this sense only may the asseveration of the *Preface*, that in this play 'no one character has been drawn from any single man,' be accepted. *Limberham*, after having been acted thrice, was stopped; apparently because of its social satire quite as much as because of its personal allusiveness.—The name 'Limberham' survived for some time as a term of suggestive opprobrium (see Southerne's *The Maid's Last Prayer* (1693), act iii. sc. 3.

[3] Act ii clearly betrays an inferior hand; Lee's rant (for there is a distinction of style even in rant) is different from Dryden's.

which should be compared not only with Corneille's but
also with Sophocles' and Seneca's treatment of the same
theme, is constructed with no ordinary skill, as well as
written with undeniable power[1].   How, then, is the fact to
be explained that its horrors remain as intolerable to the
reader, as on an attempted revival of the play they appear
to have proved to the spectators[2]?   Dryden, I think, failed
to perceive the real nature of the Greek trilogy, which
provides the opportunity of a harmonious solution for even
the most terrible situations.   Thus, we are reconciled with
the awful events of the *Œdipus Tyrannus* by the peaceful
termination which they find in the *Œdipus Coloneus*[3].   But
a tragedy such as this English *Œdipus* sickens the mind
like a banquet of horrors, which no apparatus of outward
ornament can enable us to endure.

Dryden's   Dryden's adaptation of *Troilus and Cressida* (printed in
Truth
Found   1679[4]) with the additional title of *Truth Found Too Late*
Too Late   was accompanied by an *Epistle Dedicatory*[5], and a *Preface*,

[1] Dryden has upon the whole adhered to the Greek myth, though (notwithstanding his opinion—see *Preface*—that the ancient method which
dispenses with an under-plot, as it is the easiest, is perhaps also the most
natural and the best) he has thought it necessary to invent an under-plot.
This (dealing with Eurydice and Adrastus) is at all events noble in conception, though the method of interweaving it with the main action (observe
the suddenness of Creon's change in act ii. sc. 1) is rather audacious.   The
examination of Phorbas (act iv. sc. 1) seems to me one of the most effective
situations with which I am acquainted in the modern drama.

[2] Scott states that, when the play was revived about 1778 (there is no
notice of this occasion in Genest), the audience were unable to support the
play to an end, and the boxes were all emptied before the Third Act was
concluded.

[3] Cf. Schneidewin, *Einleitung zum Œdipus auf Kolonos*, p. 31, where the
close of the *Philoctetes* is compared.—*Mutatis mutandis*, a not dissimilar contrast might possibly be with propriety drawn between the *Prometheus Vinctus*
of Æschylus and the *Prometheus Unbound* of Shelley.   In the latter the
conflict is only *stated*; in the former (even without the help of Droysen's
attractive endeavour to expound the probable character of the entire Prome-
thean trilogy, *Des Aischylos Werke übersetzt*, second edition, 1841) we seem
to perceive the solution as well as the problem.

[4] Cf. vol. i. p. 513, and *note*.   To what has there been said it need only be
added that Dryden has redeemed Cressid's character by making her kill
herself.   Chaucer was sorry for her; Dryden thinks that this mixture of
pity and reproach will not suffice, and thus ventures entirely to alter the
traditional character of the catastrophe.

[5] It is here that Dryden broached his notion of an Academy of the English

which were conceived in much the same spirit, and of *and its Preface: The Grounds of Criticism in Tragedy* (1679). which the latter holds a noteworthy place among his critical essays. After dwelling on the alterations introduced by him into Shakspere's play, he proceeds to a consideration of *The Grounds of Criticism in Tragedy*. Having examined the Aristotelian definition of tragedy, he proceeds to expound the proper nature of a tragic action. It must be *one* (here he refers to the innovation of a double action, introduced by Terence and adopted by the modern drama); it must exhibit order; it must be great; it must be probable (though not necessarily historically true). He next passes to a consideration of the chief *desiderata* in dramatic plots, manners and characters, dwelling on the imperfections, on the first head, of Shakspere and Fletcher, and, on the second, of the French (the manners in whose plays are invariably French). On the th'rd head, he extols Shakspere for the distinctness of his characters, as implying his insight into the passions he depicts—while Fletcher, who excelled 'in the softer' as Shakspere did 'in the more manly passions,' is, 'to conclude all,' described as 'a limb of Shakespeare.'

Manifestly, then, Dryden's views of the serious drama *Dryden's change of stand-point in his views of tragedy.* had by this time undergone a gradual, but very important, revolution. The author of *The Grounds of Criticism in Tragedy* was no longer enamoured of the irregularity of the Elisabethans, but desired unity and closeness of form in tragic action, while the element which he commended for imitation in Shakspere (and concomitantly in Fletcher) was their art of characterisation. Undoubtedly, Dryden had now attained to a truer perception of what was worthiest of admiration, and worthiest of imitation, in the great masters of our national drama. Undoubtedly, too, when

Language—a scheme which we have agreed to dismiss as visionary, even since Parliament has ceased to hold itself charged with the custodianship of the national vocabulary and diction.—As a curious parallel to Dryden's complaints, it may be noticed that when Goethe was turning his attention to opera and learning Italian, he complained warmly of the 'barbarous' character of his native tongue. (Düntzer, *Charlotte von Stein*, vol. i. p. 251.) Such complaints made by two poets, each of whom was master of his own language, are striking, on whatever foundations they may respectively be held to have rested.

he indited such criticism, he was in his own mind sealing the doom of that false and meretricious style of tragedy which his authority had transitorily domesticated on the English stage and in English literature. But while he had the wisdom to perceive, and the candour to proclaim, much that was true concerning the essence and the methods of the tragic art, he lacked—perhaps at all times, certainly at this advanced stage of his career—the creative power that might have enabled him fixedly to exemplify the doctrines which he now professed [1].

The Spanish Friar (1681).

For that branch of the drama indeed, which he held in inferior regard, his brilliant literary endowment still more than sufficed. The comic portion of the tragi-comedy of *The Spanish Friar, or The Double Discovery* (acted 1681) is generally acknowledged to be one of Dryden's happiest dramatic efforts. Of the two well-combined [2] plots the comic one bears a partial resemblance to that of Fletcher's *The Spanish Curate* [3]; the Friar himself, however, is by no means a copy of the Curate, but rather a fat rascal of incontestable originality. This part of the action is carried on with extraordinary spirit, and its central figure is one

---

[1] See on this Essay Hettner's remarks, *u. s.*, pp. 92–93.

[2] Perhaps Johnson, and Scott after him, have (though on different grounds) unnecessarily extolled Dryden's skill in making the serious and the comic plots in this play tally with one another. I confess myself unable to see anything altogether out of the common in the construction of *The Spanish Friar*, though certainly the two plots are here combined with greater ease than in many other instances. Much the same view is, I find, taken by the critic of *The Retrospective Review, u. s.*

[3] Professor Wilson (*Theatre of the Hindus*, vol. i. p. 181) compares the interweaving of the two plots in the Indian drama of *The Toy-cart*, to its advantage, with the celebrated Western example of this sort of combination in *The Spanish Friar*. In the Indian play, however, as Professor Wilson himself points out, though the deposition of Palaka brings about a happy consummation in the loves of the Brahma and the Courtesan, it never competes with this part of the action in the interest of the audience.—The general subject of the combination of plots in the modern, and more especially the Elisabethan and later English, drama (as contrasted with the single fable of ancient tragedy) is illustrated by C. Hense's interesting article, *Polymythie in dramatischen Dichtungen Shakespeares*, in *Jahrbuch*, vol. xi (1876).—In his *Parallel of Poetry and Painting*, cited in a previous note, Dryden censures 'our English tragi-comedy,' and its mixture of mirth and gravity, as 'wholly Gothic,' and includes in this condemnation his *Spanish Friar*, 'fond as he otherwise is of' the play.

of the most humorous creations of our later drama, which
may be enjoyed without a discussion of its bearing upon
the biographical question of Dryden's religious opinions or
sentiments[1]. As for the serious plot, though interesting
and not ineffective, it has the great blemish of representing
the heroine (Leonora) as morally guilty of a crime and
thus unworthy of sympathy[2]. The writing of this play
in both its serious and comic portions is throughout admirable. Dryden was by this time master of an easy but
dignified movement in his blank-verse ; and the merits of
his comic prose dialogue, as exemplified by this play, have
not to my knowledge been at any time surpassed[3].

The political atmosphere, of which the signs are always *Lee and*
legible in the productions of a writer like Dryden, had *Dryden's*
The Duke
become far more heavily laden when (in December, 1682) *of Guise*
he in conjunction with Lee produced the tragedy of *The* (1682).
Duke of Guise. Dryden had already at an earlier period
composed some scenes on the subject, of which he now

---

[1] Dryden, as incidentally remarked in a previous note (*ante*, p. 299),
entertained a genuine hatred of priests, like many of his contemporaries
addicted to the world and the stage. Moreover, though he became a convert, his nature was without bitterness and his religious sentiment without
depth. He could rise to lyric religious emotion, as has been superabundantly
proved by the Hymns which, owing to the investigations of Mr. Orby
Shipley, have in part at least been virtually brought home to Dryden (cf.
Appendix B in vol. xviii of Scott and Saintsbury's edition) ; and he was
never wanting as a clever controversialist and a thorough-going partisan.
But he was not the man to force himself into sympathy with the Inquisition
(see a striking passage in his *Life of Lucian, ib.* p. 66), or into sacerdotal
affections of any sort. (Cf. below as to *Don Sebastian.*)—On the other hand,
it would be absurd to suppose any evidence of special bitterness against the
Church of Rome to be discoverable in *The Spanish Friar.* The *Epilogue,*
which draws a moral in that direction, is not by Dryden. At the same
time, it was only too much in consonance with his general readiness to adapt
himself to the times for which he wrote, that in 1678, when there was
a general belief in the supposed recent discovery of a Popish plot, he should
have gone further in anti-priestly satire than he would probably have done
under other circumstances.

[2] Torrismond should have erroneously supposed Leonora to have sanctioned the order for his father's death, instead of her actually sanctioning it.

[3] In *The Spanish Friar* occurs a statement which Dr. Johnson appears to
have plagiarised in his famous political aphorism as to the real founder of
the Whig party: 'That's a stale cheat ;
    The primitive rebel, Lucifer, first used it,
    And was the first reformer of the skies.'

made use ; Lee contributed the remainder, which he supplemented by some scenes and passages from a play which
he too had lying by him on the theme, familiar to
the English drama, of *The Massacre of Paris* [1]. Whatever
credit may be given to the *Vindication* afterwards published
by Dryden, it is not denied even there that the tragedy
of *The Duke of Guise* was produced with a political intention. ' Our play's a parallel '—says the Prologue; and
the same idea was soon afterwards (in 1684) elaborated by
Dryden in his Dedication to the King of a translation of
part of a French prose-work on the *History of the League* [2].
It is of little moment that Dryden afterwards insisted that
the parallel was one ' not of the men, but of the times.'
The *Epilogue*, which is designed as an onslaught upon the
' Trimmers,' disputes the justice of the theory that ' Whigs
must talk and Tories hold their tongue'; and by means of
this tragedy two Tories had certainly endeavoured to swell
the clamour of the popular contention. The Lord Chamberlain (Arlington) however perceived that the parallel might
be carried too far by the spectators ; and *The Duke of Guise*
was not allowed to be acted till the height of the popular
excitement was over, though the strife was soon to revive in
another form [3].

[1] Cf. vol. i. p. 354. Lee's *Massacre of Paris* was produced in 1690
(cf. *infra*).

[2] Maimbourg's. (See Scott and Saintsbury, vol. xvii. pp. 81 *seqq.* The
' Specimen ' reaches to the death of Guise.)

[3] The situation of the national affairs seemed to have arrived at its crisis
during the ' times' to which this play furnishes a parallel. The return of
Monmouth to London in 1679 (cf. in the play the appearance of Guise at
Paris), the continued Popish Plot prosecutions 1678–9, and the removal
of Shaftesbury from office (1679) had provided the Opposition with a hero,
a pretext, and a leader. The Exclusion Bill agitation of 1680 had brought
the Whigs (as about this time they began to be called) into direct conflict
with the Court. In 1681, notwithstanding a petition to the contrary of
sixteen Whig peers (cf. in the play act i. sc. 1, the Council of Sixteen), the
famous Parliament was held at Oxford (cf. in the play the States-General at
Blois). In November, 1681, the bill of indictment against Shaftesbury was
presented to the Middlesex Grand Jury, and the documentary evidence
relied upon by the Crown consisted (see Christie's *Life of Shaftesbury*,
vol. ii. p. 423) in ' a project of association' found among his papers, though
unsigned and not in his handwriting, 'for Defence of the Protestant religion
and of the King and Parliament, and for the prevention of the Duke of
York's accession' (cf. the League in the play, and see also *Prologue*). In

In days when, to borrow Scott's expression, the stage
'absolutely foamed with politics[1],' when Settle derided the
Church of Rome by exhibiting the history of a female
Pope, and Shadwell held up both Roman Catholics and
High Churchmen to reprobation and contempt, it is not
to be wondered that the author of *Absalom and Achitophel*
(1681) and *The Medal* (1682) should have also mingled in
the fray in his capacity as a dramatist. When the 'Protestant
flail' was at work in the theatre as well as in the streets, it
was natural that Dryden's glittering foil should have once
more flashed forth in support of an associate's onslaught
upon their common adversaries.   But in truth Dryden
seems to have contributed relatively little[2] to a play which
arouses no interest corresponding to the occasion which
produced it ; nor is this self-restraint to be regretted, considering that in a play allowed to be performed on the

December, 1682, Shaftesbury was a refugee abroad, and Monmouth under
arrest.—In the *Vindication of the Duke of Guise* (1683) against attacks by
Shadwell and others, Dryden, after asserting that he undertook the play in
1660, that the scene of Guise's return was taken almost *verbatim* from
Davila's work *Delle Guerre Civili di Francia*, upon which other passages
were likewise founded, and that he had asked the Lord Chamberlain to
satisfy his scruples by a comparison, points out at length how a parallel
between Henry III and Charles II would be monstrous, &c., how he had
no intention of attacking Monmouth, &c., and how the whole charge against
himself was a mere party-trick.   It must therefore be left for the reader to
determine for himself how much and how little of the parallel has a special
application—whether *e. g.* the fair Marmoutière in the play was really
meant for the Duchess of Monmouth.   One 'parallel,' which cannot have
been designed, is singularly infelicitous, though it was hardly to be avoided ;
for Navarre, the rightful heir, corresponds to James Duke of York ! See
the King's speech in act v. sc. 1, where under the name of his 'royal brother
of Navarre' he draws an easily recognisable portrait of one—

'Brave, but not rash, successful, but not proud.'
The Archbishop adds—
'Some say, revengeful';
and the King retorts :
'Some then libel him.'

[1] Cf. as to the political and party use made of the stage in this period, *ante*,
pp. 292 *seqq.* and *notes*.

[2] Dryden wrote the opening scene, the whole of act iv (where occurs the
supposed parallel between Guise and Monmouth, and where the citizens
are ridiculed), and the first part of act v (where he makes himself in a
measure responsible for the vindication of the assassination of the hero, and
where, in sc. 2, he places himself in competition with Marlowe, in the
tremendous last scene of *Doctor Faustus*).

public stage he could not possibly have approached the direct force of his great political poem—even were satirical allegory more compatible with dramatic action than it has usually proved to be [1]. The parts written by Lee are to be commended for the absence of rant [2].

Dryden's Albion and Albanius (1685).

The taste for political allegory to which we owe Dryden's literary masterpiece was still strong in him, when he conceived the notion of composing an operatic entertainment, allegorically representing the chief events of King Charles II's reign, as 'a prologue to a play of the nature of *The Tempest* [3]'—in other words, to the 'dramatic opera' of *King Arthur* afterwards actually produced by him. The history of *Albion and Albanius* was however doubly unfortunate. The cycle of its allegory, like the triumph of the Reaction which it celebrated, seemed complete, when Fate intervened with her own catastrophe. The courtly poet had summoned up before the eyes of his spectators the city Augusta (London), in the days when Democracy and Zelota held sway over it and the land. They had been shown by him how Archon (Monk) had charmed the Revolution to sleep, and how the royal brothers Albion (Charles II) and Albanius (James Duke of York) had thereupon returned to a rejoicing people. In implacable wrath the fiends had resorted to the expedient of forging a plot (the 'Popish Plot'), of which 'the basest, blackest of the Stygian band' (Titus Oates [4]) was appointed the denouncer.

---

[1] The most notable example of this combination is Vondel's *Lucifer* (1654), which unmistakeably allegorises the revolt of the Netherlands and the part played in it by William of Orange, without subordinating its dramatic action to its allegorical meaning.—A political significance has been traced by Michelet in Racine's *Esther* and *Athalie.*—The comedies of Aristophanes are really extravaganzas, and to be judged from a distinct point of view.

[2] The same remark is made by Scott. The odd story of Malicorne is said to be from a French source ; the infernal agency is very much out of place here, though the demagogic tricks of the devil Melanax are effective (see act iv. sc. 2 and act iv. sc. 4, where Melanax appears among the citizens in a 'fanatic habit,' to address to them 'a word of godly exhortation' to sedition. Was this meant for the 'Protestant joiner,' Stephen College, executed in 1681 ?)

[3] See Preface to *Albion and Albanius.*

[4] This character is drawn with a gusto showing that even Corah had not exhausted the author's powers of giving expression to his loathing. In the

For a time faction had triumphed, and the good Albanius was driven into exile. But sedition was divided among itself—and quarrels had arisen between the White Boys (Monmouth's adherents) and the Sectaries armed with 'Protestant flails.' Then, a real plot (the Rye-House Plot), with a one-eyed archer (Rumbold) for its chief instrument, had been formed and revealed ; the eyes of the nation had been opened, and the good Albanius had returned.

So far the opera seemed complete, and it was actually in rehearsal, when the original of Albion died—under circumstances which once more spread a deep depression over the nation. However, discouragement is not allowed to penetrate into the atmosphere of Courts. An apotheosis of Albion and a glorification of the accession had to be promptly added; and a new royal virtue, not very prominent in the days of good King Albion, having now shone forth upon the nation, the *Epilogue* celebrates 'Plain Dealing' as constituting for the first time 'the jewel of a crown.'

But the misfortunes of this unlucky opera were not yet over. It had only been performed for the sixth time (on June 13, 1685, having been produced on the 3rd of the same month) when the news of Monmouth's landing reached London. The opera was never acted again ; nor was the loss of any moment to the stage, since the piece has all the extravagance and all the artificiality characteristic of compositions of its class. Further criticism is therefore needless ; while it is likewise needless to add that Dryden's lyric talent enabled him, even in a composition bearing every mark of haste, to produce verse very superior to that of such early examples of 'English opera' as *The Siege of Rhodes*. All the same, the jingle of the short lines in *Albion and Albanius* is hardly to be endured [1].

opera he is represented as a personage who had gone through a metempsychosis of villains from Cain downwards, till at last he had

'gained a body fit for sin,
Where all his crimes
Of former times
Lie crowded in a skin.' (Act ii. sc. 1.)

[1] The music, composed by Charles II's French band-master Grabu, was

*King
Arthur,
or The
British
Worthy*
(1691).

Dryden, it may be here at once added, was not prevented
by the ill fate of *Albion and Albanius* from writing the
'dramatic opera' to which it had been originally designed
to serve as a prelude. *King Arthur, or The British
Worthy* was performed and printed in 1691, and with the
aid of Purcell's music, proved very successful. It possesses
a certain interest from the fact that its subject was one
which both Milton and Dryden intended to treat as an
epos[1]. But the historical—or quasi-historical—theme is
treated very flimsily in the 'dramatic opera' which the later
of the two great poets actually produced[2]; and the main
interest of the piece, such as it is, turns on the rival passions
of Arthur and the heathen King of Kent for the blind
Emmeline. Her blindness is treated with a mixture of
naïveté and something quite the reverse; and this attempt
in a direction in which few dramatists have ventured with
success, is only noteworthy as a proof that no art in the
poet—or, it may be added, in the actor—can render tolerable
on the stage the analysis of a physical infirmity. This
particular infirmity may indeed occasionally be represented
with great and legitimate effect; but an endeavour to
analyse it appertains to a sphere different from that of the
drama[3]. The conception of Philidel, the fallen but repentant
angel, seems Dryden's own. For the rest, *King Arthur*,
according to its kind, contains a good deal of magical
business—not altogether original. The political significance

much ridiculed by Dryden's enemies, who of course rejoiced in the misfortunes
of his opera.

[1] It is known how what they failed to accomplish was executed by
Blackmore—after his own fashion, 'between the rumbling of his coach's
wheels.' (See Dryden's *Secular Mask*.)

[2] The studies which Dryden professes to have made of 'the rites and
customs of the heathen Saxons' may without want of charity be described
as more or less of a pretence.

[3] I say this with a full remembrance of the grace and purity characterising
the representation—by the only English actress to whom a poetic creation
of this description could within the memory of our generation have been
entrusted without grave hazard—of Sir Theodore Martin's version of the
Danish poet H. Herz's *King Réné's Daughter.*—In *King Arthur*, as in this
modern romantic drama, the heroine recovers her sight in the course of the
action.—Dumbness, whether actual or assumed, is a favourite dramatic
motive (cf. *ante*, p. 156, as to L. Machin's *The Dumb Knight*, and the Fenella
of Scribe and Auber's favourite opera)—dissociated of course from deafness.

of this opera is small ; the tag concerning the future is intentionally short and unhopeful ; the poet, though a certain buoyancy of spirit was to the last an essential element in his nature, was now an avowed malcontent.

After the Revolution of 1688 Dryden produced but few plays. Of these the tragedy of *Don Sebastian* (acted 1690), which is in blank-verse and prose, has received very high praise, and Scott repeatedly pronounces it Dryden's dramatic masterpiece. In one respect it certainly deserves special acknowledgment. Dryden has here, in accordance with the views developed in his last critical essay on the drama [1], carefully and powerfully developed two tragic characters— Sebastian and Dorax. Particular passages in the play, moreover, are indisputably very fine [2]; but as a whole it is, as the author frankly confesses, obnoxious to the charge of lengthiness, especially in the quasi-comic parts, where a thin staple of humour is long drawn-out. Moreover the plot—in which the author grafts upon a story already familiar to the English drama an invention of his own, which has no organic connexion with the opening situation—is intolerably harrowing ; and the dramatic solution attempted, although morally satisfactory, is too artificial to content our sense of probability. And while there is much that is powerful in the progress, as depicted in the play, of the fatal passion of the hero and heroine, the tone, though not the conception, of the close lacks elevation. In general, however, the style of this tragedy, notwithstanding an ingredient of rant in its earlier part, is strong as well as attractive ; and in the serious portions of the action Dryden repeatedly rises to an unusual height of dramatic effect [3].

Don Sebastian (1690).

---

[1] Cf. *ante*, p. 375.

[2] Above all the great scene between Sebastian and Dorax (act iv. sc. 3), which in his *Theatre of the Hindus* (Introduction, p. xli) Professor Wilson instances as an example of what Hindu critics call ' *Dyuti*' (*i. e.* provocation to combat) as a link in a dramatic action, and which he designates as one of ' the most powerful scenes in the English language.'

[3] The plot turns upon the strange story of Sebastian of Portugal, which Massinger had treated in his *Believe as You List* (*ante*, p. 31), and to which Beaumont and Fletcher refer in their *Wit at Several Weapons* (act i. sc. 2). Dryden's invention consists in the fatal passion entertained for one another by Sebastian and his sister, while alike unaware of their mutual

*Amphi-
tryon
(1690).*

In the comedy of *Amphitryon* (acted 1690), for which Dryden made use of both Plautus and Molière, with the addition, by way of a further seasoning, of a subordinate intrigue of his own invention[1], the flame of his genius— though fed by impure materials—once more bursts forth with splendid brightness. On the licentiousness of this long-popular play I need not dwell, since it has become almost proverbial; but the writing must be acknowledged to be admirable, and in parts nothing less than magnificent[2].

*Cleomenes,
the Spartan
Hero
(1692).*

The tragedy of *Cleomenes, the Spartan Hero* (acted 1692) was no doubt intended by its author to continue the line of dramatic composition which he had with so much success adopted in *Don Sebastian.* And the character of Cleomenes[3] himself must be allowed to be worked out with considerable care. That of Cassandra, on the other hand, is not very effective; and the youthful Cleonidas was, as Scott suggests, probably modelled on Hengo in Fletcher's *Bonduca*[4]. The plot, though based on Plutarch, whose *Life* 'in the very words of Creech' is prefixed to the play, is to a great extent original; the supposition that it concealed a political intention was probably nothing more than a delusion on the part

relationship. At the conclusion Sebastian determines to seclude himself in a desert for life. The whole play shows that a desire for extraordinary effects or 'sensations' was ineradicable in Dryden as a dramatist. More than one allusion to the times in which the play was produced will be easily discerned in it (as well of course as in the *Prologue*). (Gibbon, *Decline and Fall*, ch. lxx, *note.* has amused himself by pointing out some ineptitudes in the historical allusions made by the Mufti.) That Dryden's contempt for the rabble was as intense as ever, is not surprising; but it may be worth noticing with what scorn the character of the Mufti is drawn in this tragedy. Dryden was consistent in his hatred of priests even after his change of confession.

[1] The intrigue of Mercury with Phaedra, Alcmena's serving-maid. Judge Gripus is also an innovation of Dryden's.

[2] In the *Letters of Lady Mary Wortley Montagu* (edited by Lord Wharncliffe, 2nd ed., 1837), vol. i. pp. 286–7, occurs a characteristic account of a coarse play on the same subject which Lady Mary had seen at Vienna, and which she thinks 'well worthy the serious attention of Mr. Collier.' She speaks of 'the raptures which Dryden puts into Jupiter's mouth.'—An odd attempt was made as late as 1872 to revive Dryden's *Amphitryon* on the London stage—in a Bowdlerised form which was hardly likely to be enjoyed either by many unacquainted with the play, or by any reader of it.

[3] In the play usually pronounced Cleomēnes.

[4] Cf. *ante*, vol. ii. p. 697.

of Queen Mary's anxious administration, which prohibited
its performance, until certain passages, supposed to reflect
upon the Government, had been removed[1]. As to form, it
may be noted that at the height of several passages the
rimed couplet as it were irresistibly introduces itself. Part
of the fifth act of this play was written by Thomas Southerne,
to whom Dryden, in consequence of an illness, had entrusted
its completion and revision.

Dryden produced one further play, the tragi-comedy of
Love Triumphant, or Nature will Prevail (acted 1694). It
proved wholly unsuccessful—to the credit, it must be
allowed, of the public, justly sick of the dramatic motive of
a supposed incestuous passion proved innocent at last, which
once more forms the theme of the serious plot of this play.
The quasi-comic scenes are altogether ineffective. The more
passionate portions of the dialogue are generally in rime. *Love Triumphant (1694).*

Thus it might seem as if in dramatic composition the
glorious hand—which in certain other branches of literature
continued effective to the last—had after all come to lose
its cunning, before it was stayed by death. Dryden lived,
however, to write what may be regarded as the epilogue
to the entire body of his dramatic works—viz. the *Prologue, Song, Secular Masque and Epilogue for the Pilgrim*,
a play by Fletcher revived for the benefit of the old poet
in the year 1700. The Masque has been already noticed[2];
but attention may here be particularly directed to the Epilogue, and to its reference to Jeremy Collier's recent attack
upon the stage. Its tone is not without the admixture
of banter usual in this species of composition—but a more
than passing significance attaches to the attempt of the
poet, now at the close of his career looking back upon
the dramatic labours of himself and his contemporaries,
to shift the responsibility of their sins against morality *Epilogue, &c. for Fletcher's The Pilgrim (1700).* *Dryden's apology.*

[1] See Narcissus Luttrell's *Brief Relation*, vol. ii. pp. 413 and 422 (under
dates of April 9 and 16, 1692); and cf. Miss Strickland's *Queens of England*
(edn. 1847), vol. xi. p. 277, where Queen Mary is said to have visited
upon Dryden her wrath at the political allusions in his Prologue to
Fletcher's *The Prophetess* (1690); cf. *ante*, vol. ii. p. 727, *note.—Cleomenes*
was revived on the English stage in 1721.

[2] *Ante*, vol. ii. p. 706, *note.*

from the stage and its poets to the Court. The charge which he thus brings against those in the sunshine of whose favour he had formerly craved to bask, may have in it less of generosity than of truth. Moreover, if true, it recoils with the most crushing force upon the poet whose genius made him, more than any other man, responsible for the guardianship of the temple which, under influences however powerful, he actually took part in desecrating. But an avowal of a share in the guilt is implied in the very endeavour to transfer its responsibility. Nor was the mind of Dryden —with all its faults a mind distinguished by real manliness— unequal to a full confession of the wrong of which he knew himself to have been guilty. Not many years previously, he had made such a confession—in words which thrill us to the soul whenever they recur to our memory:

> 'O gracious God! how far have we .
> Profaned thy heavenly gift of Poesy!
> Made prostitute and profligate the Muse,
> Debased to each obscene and impious use,
> Whose harmony was first ordained above
> For tongues of angels and for hymns of love!
> Oh wretched we! why were we hurried down
> This lubric and adulterate age,
> Nay, added fat pollutions of our own,
> To increase the steaming ordures of the stage?
> *What can we say to excuse our second fall*[1] ?'

Dryden's moral aberrations as a dramatist. Indications of a similar feeling of shame are not altogether wanting in the writings of his later days[2]; and it is gratifying to find him in other fields of composition mindful of the truth—homely, no doubt, but full of encouragement for

[1] Ode *To the Pious Memory of Mrs. Anne Killigrew* (published with her poems 1686.)

[2] In the *Life of Lucian* (which Dryden prepared for publication in 1696. though it was not actually printed till after his death) he takes occasion from the charges brought against Lucian for 'writing too lusciously' in his Ἑταιρικοὶ Διάλογοι, to confess: 'Of all men living, I am the most unfit to accuse Lucian, who am so little able to defend myself from the same objection.' And writing to Mrs. Thomas in 1699, he similarly declines 'to arraign' Mrs. Behn, 'who have been myself too much a libertine in my poems; which I shou'd be contented I had time to purge, or to see them fairly burn'd.' (Scott and Saintsbury's *Dryden*, vol. xviii. pp. 71 and 166.) This was all the more generous, if he was acquainted with Mrs. Behn's attack upon 'Mr. Dryden, renegate,' mentioned in *Third Report of the Historical MSS. Commission, Appendix* (1872), p. 235.

great as well as for small capacities—that 'it is never too
late to mend[1].' But no candid admirer of Dryden's in
some respects almost incomparable genius can truthfully
plead on his behalf, that manhood and old age, which
mellowed his literary powers, at the same time refined his
literary morality as a dramatist.   The brilliant style of his
Amphitryon can no more conceal his defiance of the principles of good manners than the crudity of his *Wild Gallant*
can excuse it.   He was no more able than were the puniest
of his rivals or would-be rivals, to resist the temptation of.
painting vice of a particular kind in attractive colours, and
his defence of the leniency with which at times he deals
out dramatic justice to his vicious characters in comedy
is as shallow as he must have known it to be[2].

But while only a perverse misinterpretation of the claims
of genius will excuse in a great writer what it blames in a
small, it would be an altogether oblique view of Dryden as
a dramatist which should treat a defect shared by him
with many others as a distinctive characteristic of his dramatic productions.   As a dramatist he exhibits qualities
raising him above the level of any of his competitors—
though less conspicuously so than in one or two other
branches of literature illustrated by his genius.   The flexibility of that genius—all the more notably, inasmuch as his
first dramatic composition dates from the thirty-first year
of his life—enabled him in both tragedy and comedy to
excel all, or very nearly all, his contemporaries.   In the
former, after a more or less tentative effort of a mixed

Character and range of his dramatic powers.

---

[1] The *Fables* (or tales adopted from Boccaccio and Chaucer, published
in 1700) are upon the whole (though by no means uniformly) characterised
by decency of tone.   Dryden accordingly felt himself secure enough to
deprecate the severity of Collier's attack upon his earlier and really
objectionable works, and to turn the point of his adversary's weapon
with some skill upon that adversary himself.   In short, he insinuates that
'the parson' conveniently collects the offences of the stage, as Byron might
have put it, in an 'appendix.'   See the introductory lines (*Poeta loquitur*)
to *Cymon and Iphigenia*.   In *The Wife of Bath's Tale* in the *Fables* Dryden
adopts a line of defence similar to that taken in the Epilogue to *The Pilgrim*.

[2] See the Preface to *An Evening's Love*, where he argues with characteristic
audacity that 'we make not vicious persons happy, but only as Heaven
makes sinners so; that is, by reclaiming them first from vice.'

character, he threw himself in with the current of a mistaken innovation, to which nothing but his example—not even his own brilliant theoretical sophistries—could have secured the vitality it exhibited. But for the brilliancy of style which he lavished upon them, heroic plays would have remained unremembered by posterity, when, with his abandonment of the species, it had ceased to keep a hold over the age which had given birth to it. In these plays, and even in his later efforts in the tragic drama, he never passed beyond the limits of those themes to which the tragedy of the age had gradually restricted itself; although while binding himself to a more rigid method of construction, he had come to recognise in characterisation the highest task and the surest test of dramatic power [1]. Love and honour were the pivots upon which the mimic world of his tragedies turned, even where, as in a solitary instance, another motive (that of religious devotion) is admitted to an apparent share in the action [2]. In the delineation of these passions he never passed beyond his 'heroic' conceptions of their genesis, and of the laws of their being; but within these limits he was master of his themes. Lee may perhaps be held to have occasionally approached him in his fervent representations of heroic honour and love—but at how considerable an interval may be best seen from the works which they composed jointly— while in the reproduction of the most pathetic moments of amorous sentiment he was probably surpassed by Otway. In his use of far-fetched expedients for the provocation of terror he knew no bounds, often confounding the extraordinary with the powerful, and momentary sensation with enduring effect. His diction was often even more excessive than his action; but the former was the product of a real natural force, which it is difficult to withstand even on

---

[1] One of the latest deliverances of Dryden on the art of tragedy will be found in the *Dedication of the Third Miscellany*, 1693, containing *Translations from Ovid's Metamorphoses* (Scott and Saintsbury's *Dryden*, vol. xii. pp. 53 seqq., in which he declares that 'we trail our plays under the venerable shades of Shakespeare and Jonson,' as colours are trooped in honour of the great dead; and asserts that he could show without difficulty 'that many of the tragedies in the former age amongst us were without comparison beyond those of Sophocles and Euripides.'

[2] See *Tyrannic Love*.

the printed page, and which must have been irresistible when aided by the art of Betterton's 'well-govern'd voice' and manner, and by the efforts of the eminent actors and actresses with whom he was associated. The unequalled impetus of Dryden's tragic eloquence was freely acknowledged by the most resolute of his adversaries[1]. For comedy, on the other hand, Dryden at times expressed a dislike resembling contempt, at times declared himself by nature unfitted. 'I want,' he said, 'that gaiety of humour which is required to it[2];' and 'even in his own partial judgment' he held that some of his contemporaries had outdone him in this branch of the drama[3]. He was, I think, doubly mistaken. Beginning with a reproduction of those Spanish plots which pleased the age, but which in truth amount only to delusive perversions of the real excellences of dramatic construction, he rarely took the trouble to construct a good plot, though he was manifestly capable of such an achievement[4]. That he was unequal to the conception of comic character would (even if he had never written a comedy) be a charge too ludicrous to need refutation; that he succeeded in its dramatic presentation has been sufficiently shown by the examples noticed in the preceding pages, ranging from the excellent high comedy

---

[1] 'Though I will not say,' Shadwell wrote of Dryden in the Preface to *The Humourists* (1671), 'his is the best way of writing, yet, I am sure, his manner of writing is the best that ever was . . . he has more of that in his writing which Plato calls σώφρονα μανίαν, than any other Heroick Poet. And those, who shall go about to imitate him, will be found to flutter and make a noise, but never rise.'

[2] *Defence of an Essay of Dramatic Poesy.*

[3] *Epistle Dedicatory to Aureng-Zebe.*

[4] See *The Spanish Friar.*—I have not thought it necessary to touch, except incidentally, upon the charges of plagiarism, in the matter of both plots and characters, brought against Dryden by Langbaine in his *New Catalogue of English Plays* (1688, surreptitiously issued in the previous year under the title of *Momus Triumphans*), and elaborated in his *Account of the English Dramatick Poets* (1691). As usual, Langbaine has been accused of malignity as well as of dulness for having ventured to fall out with Dryden ; but he is in the habit of giving chapter and verse for his statements, and draws a rather telling contrast between Dryden's occasional arrogance as a critic and his practice as a playwright. It would ill become me to set down Langbaine's labours as futile ; but had he proved his case twice over in this particular instance, the fact would remain that Dryden's genius was capable of giving a new life to what he appropriated, and thus justified the process.

*His pre-
eminence
among the
dramatists
of his age.*

of *Secret Love* to the equally excellent low comedy of *The Spanish Friar.* It is surely strange criticism which considers a third-rate writer like Crowne to have surpassed Dryden in comedy: in truth, there was no rival whom he needed to fear, and only one—his adversary Shadwell—who surpassed him in fertility, though falling far behind him in finish, of dramatic characterisation. The prose dialogue of comedy he had at his command whenever he chose to exert his powers in this direction ; here, as in the dialogue of rimed tragedy, he was without a peer, till the vigour of Wycherley and the brilliant wit of Congreve announced the advent of a new generation of comic dramatists. No one was more ready to welcome them than Dryden, one of the kindliest befrienders of younger talent whom the world of letters has ever known [1]. While recognising the merits of Wycherley as well as those of Etherege and Southerne in terms generously chosen, he addresses Congreve in a strain which breathes, together with magnanimous delight in the merits of his successor, the conscious pride of a legitimate sovereign :

> ' Well had I been deposed if you had reign'd !
> The father had descended for the son,
> For only you are lineal to the throne [2].'

The sway which he thus resigned he had exercised with an authority neither unchallenged nor well guarded by himself. But, taking his dramatic works for all in all, his pre-eminence seems indisputable ; and the Restoration drama in the stricter sense of the term will be best understood and best appreciated by those who consistently regard Dryden as its central figure. He reflects both the faults and the vices of that drama with sufficient distinctness to teach us what to shun ; of its merits and its excellences few are wanting in its foremost representative, or shine elsewhere with so dazzling a brilliancy as that which is the unrivalled distinction of this great master of style.

*Dryden
the repre-
sentative
Restoration
dramatist.*

---

[1] Dryden's son and namesake in 1696 published a play called *The Husband his own Cuckold,* to which his father wrote Preface and Epilogue, while the Prologue was written by Congreve. It was dedicated to Sir Robert Howard. But it failed.

[2] *To my dear friend Mr. Congreve, on his Comedy called the Double-Dealer.*

Before we pass from Dryden to lesser writers, a special
word should be said concerning his *Prologues* and *Epilogues* [1].
The freedom of expression which the stage assumed after
its restoration, naturally extended itself in the fullest
measure to these adjuncts of the drama, which had never
been subject to any strict rules of art.   Soon the Prologues
and Epilogues became, far more uniformly and distinctly
than they had been in any previous period, opportunities
for the dramatist to enter as it were into conversation with
his audience, and to discourse with them not only in a more
or less apologetic tone concerning the play and its author, but
about themselves also, and on whatever topic might suggest
itself for comment—from the politics of the nation to the
foibles of the fashionable fair. Indeed, the play was often left
out of sight altogether, except in so far as it suggested some
handle for personalities or political or social satire ; and the
prologue and epilogue, by acquiring an independence of the
play, grew to depend for applause upon their own wit or
audacity. At the same time, since it was not the poet himself, but one of the actors, or at least as frequently one of
the actresses, who spoke these addresses, they could with
impunity indulge in an outspokenness, such as would scarcely
have been possible under any other combination of circumstances. The authors of *The Rehearsal* satirised 'Bayes''
use of 'personal things'; Jeremy Collier is eloquent on the
licence which the dramatic poets of the age permitted themselves in these Prologues and Epilogues. It is perhaps too
much to say that they corresponded to the parabasis of
Athenian comedy ; for the liberty of comment permitted by
the tastes of the King, or encouraged because of the
advantages to be incidentally derived from it, cannot be
compared to the popular freedom which enabled a poet to
hurl his patriotic hatred in the face of the most powerful
politician of the State.   But, in skilful hands, and with the
help of an acknowledged favourite like Betterton or a spoilt
child like Nell Gwynn, ample scope existed for the exercise,

---

[1] This subject is admirably treated in ch. iii and other parts of 'G. S. B.''s
little volume, *A Study of the Prologue and Epilogue in English Literature*,
already cited.

not only of ingenuity in the devising of these addresses, but
also of didactic and still more of satirical power in their actual
composition.   Thus, one need not wonder that the curiosity
of the audience, and even the vigilance of the authorities,
should at times have directed itself to the Prologue rather
than to the play which followed [1] ; while now and then the
best hit in a performance was unmistakeably made after
the play had been brought to a conclusion.   Dryden nowhere
more prodigally displayed his resources of invention and
expression than in these ephemeral appeals to the fancies,
whims, humours, and scandals of the day—and incidentally
nowhere gave more signal proof of his ineradicable moral
recklessness.   As a rule, his Prologues contain a larger
admixture of the serious element ; but this rule is by no
means unvarying.   In any case, this branch of Dryden's
productivity should not be judged only by the wit and the
occasional strong sense of a few selected specimens, but also
by the versatile fertility of which the whole mass of its
foliage serves as evidence [2].

[1] See the Prologue to *The Rival Ladies* :—

> 'In former days
> Good Prologues were as scarce as now good plays.
> For the reforming poets of our age
> In this first charge spend their poetic rage.
> Expect no more when once the prologue's done;
> The wit is ended ere the play's begun.
> You now have habits, dances, scenes, and rhymes,
> High language often—ay, and sense sometimes.'

Stage Prologues and Epilogues were now as heretofore often written by
popular authors to aid the plays of friends, or for a fee of which the amount
was regulated by custom ; and they were sold as broadsides at the theatres
as part of the attraction of a performance.—'G. S. B.' mentions, in illustration of the melancholy experience of the mutability of all things, that the
Dryden form of prologue, which had so triumphantly superseded the Elisabethan theatrical preface, intended to blow the trumpet of the play like 'the
prologue's prologus' (see *The Trumpeter* in Earle's *Microcosmography*), was in
its turn laughed out of court as a 'useless, necessary thing' in the days of
Fielding. (See his Prologue to *The Debauchees*, 1732.)

[2] *The Dramatic Works of Sir Robert Howard.* Third Edition, 1722. (This
contains the Preface, cited *ante*, p. 355, *note*, to the *Four New Plays* published
in 1665.)   The comedy of *The Blind Lady* was first printed in 1660, in the
edition of the *Poems* to which Dryden prefixed a poetical *Epistle* (see Scott
and Saintsbury, vol. xi).—The biographical notices of Howard and his
brothers in vol. xxviii of *The Dictionary of National Biography* (1891) are by
Mr. A. H. Bullen.

The name of SIR ROBERT HOWARD (1626–1698) chiefly
interests us in connexion with the life and literary labours
of his great brother-in-law ; but it is evident that the
'Crites of the *Essay of Dramatic Poesy* was a man of some
culture as well as of a good deal of pretension.   The active
services in the field of Sir Robert Howard (who was a
younger son of the first Earl of Berkshire) in the days of the
Civil War were rewarded by a place of profit after the
Restoration ; and though he served the interests of King
Charles he was so good a Whig as to be admitted to the
Privy Council after the Revolution.   He retained his seat
in Parliament till the time of his death.   His literary
activity was not confined to his dramatic works ; for besides
a treatise on the State of the King's Revenue and a History
of Religion, he wrote *Historical Observations on the Reigns
of Edward I, II and III, and Richard II*, and a brief
*History of the Reigns of Edward and Richard II, with
Reflections and Characters of their Chief Ministers and
Favourites*.   But though universality seems to have been
'Sir Positive Atall's'[1] foible, it was as a dramatic writer he
above all sought to play a part in the world of letters.   His
dramatic works, however, furnish no evidence of remarkable
creative power.   Of these, besides *The Indian Queen*,
noticed above as written in conjunction with Dryden[2],
three comedies and two tragedies are extant ; the tragedy
of *The Conquest of China by the Tartars*, whose name
'heroically sounds,' and which shortly before Howard's
death Dryden entertained the thought of adapting for the
stage[3], remained unaltered and unprinted.   Among the
comedies, viz. *The Blind Lady, The Surprisal*, and *The
Committee*, the last-named is worth examining, as a curious
picture, or rather caricature, of the manners of the later
Commonwealth period, draw by a hostile hand.   The plot
turns on the rascalities perpetrated by members of Com-
mittees of Sequestration in keeping or turning rightful
owners out of their property for political disaffection ; but

*Sir Robert
Howard
(1626–
1698).*

---

[1] Cf. *ante*, p. 356, *note* 3.   [2] *Ante*, p. 348.

[3] See his letter of September, 1697, 'to his Sons at Rome.'   Dryden
estimated that the task would cost him six weeks, 'with the probable benefit
of an hundred pounds.'

His trage-dies :

The Vestal Virgin, or The Roman Ladies (*pr.* 1665).

The Duke of Lerma (*pr.* 1668).

the attack is made after so coarse a fashion that the edge of the satire is blunted [1]. The play, however, contains some good rough fun. Among Howard's tragedies I may pass by *The Vestal Virgin, or The Roman Ladies* (printed 1665), mostly in rime, but not otherwise remarkable, unless it be for the fact that it has two terminations, for choice, like Suckling's *Aglaura* [2], and confine myself to a brief notice of *The Duke of Lerma* (printed 1668). This play is not devoid of merit, but is chiefly interesting as a protest (only a partial protest however) on Howard's part against the theories of dramatic versification advocated by Dryden [3]. The Epilogue, alluding to the form in which this tragedy is mainly written, describes it as

'A melancholy Plot tied with strong lines.'

In contrast with the abstinence imposed upon the stage in

---

[1] Mr. Day, the Chairman of the Committee, is represented as a vile kind of Tartuffe. The socially ambitious Mrs. Day is better; and one cannot help being amused with the sheepish son Abel Day, and with Obadiah the Clerk to the Committee, whom Teague, the faithful Irishman (a character said by Dibdin, iv. 115, to have been copied from Howard's own Irish servant, and thought by Pepys, *Diary*, June 12, 1663, to be 'beyond imagination'), makes drunk, and causes to sing and 'snuff' in honour of the King. Teague is drawn with much spirit, and has another capital scene in which he 'takes the covenant' by robbing a bookseller of a copy thereof (act ii. sc. 1). For an amusing story as to the application of 'Obadiah' in this play to Dr. Obadiah Walker of Oxford see Cibber's *Apology* (2nd ed), p. 383. 'Teague' seems henceforth to have become the favourite name for the stage Irishman; see Shadwell's *The Amorous Bigot* and its continuation *Teague O'Dively*, and Mrs. Centlivre's *A Wife Well Manag'd*. Swift, writing to Francis Grant in 1734, describes himself as by birth 'a Teague, or an Irishman, or what people please.' (Forster's *Life of Swift*, vol. i. p. 25, *note*.) —When Sir Roger de Coverley was taken by Mr. Spectator to see *The Distrest Mother*, he assured his companion that 'he had not been at the Play for these twenty years. The last I saw,' said Sir Roger, 'was *The Committee*, which I should not have gone to neither, had I not been told before-hand that it was a good Church-of-England Comedy.' (*The Spectator*, No. 335.)—A play entitled *L'Intérieur des Comités révolutionnaires, ou Les Aristides modernes*, attained to great popularity at Paris in 1795, after the close of the Terror. (Muret, *u. s.*, vol. i. p. 145.)

[2] *Ante*, p. 145, and cf. below as to James Howard's 'adaptation' of *Romeo and Juliet*.

[3] In the Preface to this tragedy Howard declines to say 'why he writ this Play partly in Rhyme, partly in Blank Verse';—he had no better reason than 'Chance which waited upon his present fancy,' and 'expects no better a Reason from any Ingenious Person than his Fancy for which he best relishes.' Here we certainly have criticism, as well as authorship, made easy.

earlier times [1], the nature of this plot is striking. It is indeed only partly historical [2]; for the heroine, Lerma's daughter, is I suppose a poetic substitute for the historical Lerma's son the Duke of Uzeda; and most of the incidents reproduced in the drama (certainly that of Lerma obtaining for himself a cardinal's hat as a supreme protection) took place in the reign of the old King (Philip III) and not in that of the new (Philip IV). Yet it is something of a change from the days of James I to find a foreign sovereign quite recently deceased [3] and his Court thus frankly brought upon the stage in the presence of the King before an audience, in which at least one intelligent observer thought the play designed as a reproach to 'our King' himself [4].

Whatever may have been the special intention of this tragedy, its action, though undoubtedly crude in treatment, is interesting and stirring, and the figure of Lerma exhibits some signs of originality of characterisation. The writing, however, though here and there likewise distinguished by a power above what is usual in this author [5], is upon the whole poor. As already observed, though rime is only employed in parts of the piece, these contain some of the most important passages to be found in it [6]. Thus, as in the case of certain of Dryden's later tragedies, the evidence of this play cannot be simply thrown into the scale of either the advocates or the opponents of the 'new way' of tragic

[1] See *ante*, vol. ii. p. 496.

[2] According to the Preface it was an improvement of a play which had been shown to Howard, but of which he retained very little in his own.

[3] Philip IV died in 1665.

[4] See Pepys' *Diary*, February 20, 1668, where he notes firstly that the Prologue was most excellently spoken by 'Knipp and Nell,' secondly that the play was designed 'to reproach our King with his mistresses, that I was troubled with it, and expected it should be interrupted; but it ended all well, which salved all.'

[5] The passionate awakening of Lerma's love for his daughter (at the close of act iv) strikes me as finely conceived; and here is a passage written with real power:

> 'I do believe he knows what he does,
> But like a tired over-hunted Deer
> Treads fatal Paths offer'd by Chance and not
> Design'd by him.' (Act v. sc. 2.)

[6] Cf. act ii. sc. 2; act iii. sc. 2; act v. sc. 2.

writing. In other respects, a discriminating judgment will, I think, find in this tragedy an illustration of the fact that the spirit of the Elisabethan drama was not yet wholly extinct, even in the second-rate writers of the Restoration age.

Edward Howard and James Howard (d. 1698).

Sir Robert's brothers, EDWARD and JAMES HOWARD, were likewise writers of plays. 'Ned' Howard seems to have been unfortunate in the facility with which as a playwright he incurred both satire and reproach, although his play of *The Change of Crowns*, which Pepys saw acted on April 15, 1667, was described by the diarist as the best he ever saw at the King's house, being 'a great play and serious[1].' James Howard's muse seems to have taken a lower flight, to judge from his comedy of *All Mistaken, or The Mad Couple*, in which the manner is as mixed as is the metre[2]. He is, however, best—or worst—remembered by his alteration of *Romeo and Juliet*, to which he gave a 'happy' ending and which was performed in this condition on alternate nights with the Shaksperean original[3].

Elkanah Settle (1648– 1724).

The name of ELKANAH SETTLE (1648–1724) has experienced to the full the fate which frequently befalls minor men of letters who become involved in contentions with their superiors; but although to posterity he is little more than the Doeg of the *Second Part* of *Absalom and Achitophel*, he enjoyed in his day a passing prospect of outshining Dryden in popularity as a dramatist. Having as a youth of eighteen years obtained a certain success with his tragedy of *Cambyses King of Persia*, of which the subject had certainly been chosen by him with engaging frankness, he in 1671 made a most successful venture in *The Empress of Morocco*, a heroic tragedy in rime, which after being performed under circumstances of special *éclat* at Court, was produced by Betterton with much splendour and great success

---

[1] The actor-dramatist Lacy is said to have told him that 'he was more a fool than a poet.' He is not overlooked in *The Rehearsal*; and Oldham, in his *Imitation of Boileau's VIIth Satire* (*Works*, vol. ii. p. 170), mindful perhaps of Lacy's gibe, bids him   'give o'er
        (His) scribbling Itch, and play the Fool no more.'

[2] Reprinted in vol. xv of Hazlitt's *Dodsley*.

[3] Cf. *ante*, vol. ii. p. 117.

on the public stage[1]. A pamphlet[2] was accordingly launched against Settle's tragedy by the dramatist Crowne, with the assistance, it is more instructive than edifying to observe, of both Dryden and the Whig dramatist Shadwell. Settle replied without delay[3]; nor was the warfare closed by the only incident in it of which the memory survives— the attack upon Doeg, 'the *heroically* mad[4].'

Settle's later career as a dramatist had its vicissitudes, which were mixed up with the history of his political manœuvrings. In 1676 was performed his *Ibrahim the Illustrious Bassa*, of which I can give an account at first hand, and which is interesting as founded on Madeleine de Scudéry's *Ibrahim, ou l'Illustre Bassa*, which her brother Georges had reproduced as a play. It must in candour be allowed that Settle's tragedy furnishes a fair example of a heroic play on a French love-story of the accepted type, written in rime, devoid of any trace of poetic afflatus, but on the whole (though exceptions might no doubt be here and there noted) free from rant. In spite of the accumulation of deaths in the last act, and of the pathetically conceived character of the self-sacrificing Asteria, the whole, however, leaves but a tame and commonplace impression behind it. The result is due above all to the flooding of both action and characters by the resistless waters of 'heroic love,' which take every trace of distinctive colour or complexion out of Turk and Persian, Mussulman Roxana and Christian Isabella, alike[5].

In 1680 Settle, finding himself neglected by the Court, to whose patronage he had been introduced by the fickle

---

[1] The drawings published in the 1673 edition of the play enable us to realise the Dorset Garden Theatre and its external magnificence. See Lowe's *Betterton*, p. 112.

[2] *Notes and Observations on the Empress of Morocco.*

[3] *Notes and Observations on the Empress of Morocco Revised.*

[4] Settle's last work was *Reflections on several of Mr. Dryden's Plays* (1687).

[5] The Epilogue puts this latter characteristic with remarkable candour, with evident allusion to the titles of plays by D'Avenant, Dryden, and Settle himself:

'How many has our Rhymer kill'd to-day?
What need of Siege and Conquest in a Play,
When Love can do the work as well as They?
Yet 'tis such Love as you've scarce met before,
Such Love I'm sure as English ground ne'er bore.'

favour of Rochester, entered into a new phase of his career as a Whig, and in the midst of the Exclusion Bill agitation testified to his Protestantism by a drama entitled *The Female Prelate*, on the subject of Pope Joan, which was printed with a dedication to Shaftesbury[1]. He furthermore devised a pageant of The Burning of the Pope 'before Queen Besses' throne at Temple Bar, on the anniversary of her birth-day,' long kept as a Protestant festival. But neither these efforts availed him, nor his return to Toryism after the great agitation had ended in failure, nor his veering back to the Whigs when the Revolution had been accomplished. In the *Dedication* to *The Distressed Innocence, or The Princess of Persia* (a tragedy printed in 1691) he confessed himself ' undone ' by his politics[2]), and he was glad soon afterwards to accept the office of city poet, with which the 'Triumphs' of his later years are chiefly associated. He also, however, continued his labours in the regular drama, and produced a series of tragedies and comedies, including a *Second Part* of *The Empress of Morocco*, entitled *The Heir of Morocco* (1694). Towards the close of his career he sank to humble depths, adapted for Mrs. Mynn's booth at Bartholomew Fair his operatic spectacle of *The Siege of Troy* (originally produced on the stage in 1701), and according to Pope's genial satire, and conscientious annotation, acted the Dragon in a droll called *St. George of England*, performed in the same locality[3].

John Crowne (d. 1703 or post).   One of the most fertile of the dramatists of this period, whose endeavours were about equally divided between tragedy and comedy, and who attained to a certain distinction in both, was JOHN CROWNE[4]. He was the son of a gentleman who is stated on doubtful evidence to have

[1] See an account of it *ap.* Genest (vol. i. pp. 273 *seqq.*), who with his usual impartiality says that, apart from its anachronisms, ' it is very far from a bad Tragedy.'

[2] ' I grew weary of my little Talent in Dramatics, and forsooth must be rambling into politics; and much I have got by it, for, I thank 'em, they have undone me.'

[3] See *Dunciad*, Bk. iii. v. 285, and Pope's *note*.

[4] *The Dramatic Works of John Crowne. With Prefatory Memoir and Notes.* (By James Maidment and W. H. Logan.) 4 vols. 1873-4. See also Mr. Bullen's notice of Crowne in vol. xiii of *The Dictionary of National Biography* (1888).

afterwards become an Independent Minister in Nova Scotia, but whose lands there were taken away from him or his family. Thus Crowne had to rely on himself for his means of subsistence. In 1665 he published a romance entitled *Pandion and Amphigenia*, and a few years later resorted to writing for the stage. He seems to have had no hesitation in changing his political colours in deference to the times, becoming in turn an ardent servant of the Stuart Court and an upholder of the Protestant principles of the Revolution. He seems to have enjoyed the special good-will of King Charles II, and, like other dramatists, to have been in turn patronised and abandoned by Rochester. His masque of *Calisto*[1] was presented at Court in 1675; but the King died before the performance of the comedy which some have considered Crowne's masterpiece, and of which Charles had himself dictated the subject. Altogether Crowne, though usually willing to go half-way towards meeting Fortune, was not a lucky man. His death cannot have taken place before 1683.

His dramatic efforts were extremely varied in style and *His trage-dies:* species. As a writer of tragedy he holds a conspicuous place among the followers of several styles, for he can hardly be said to have a style of his own. Often happy in the choice and ingenious in the construction of his plots, he

---

[1] *Calisto, or The Chaste Nimph*, notwithstanding its attempt to give a decorous version of an indecorous myth, was to say the least an odd masque for presentation at the Court of Charles II (where it was performed by an equally strange medley of actors, including the princesses Mary and Anne, the Duke of Monmouth, two of the King's mistresses, and the pure and high-minded lady who afterwards became Mrs. Godolphin). The Jupiter of the masque conducts himself after a fashion which might almost have been taken for a satirical picture of Charles II's system of government:

> 'All politic cares of every kind
> I'll from my breast remove;
> And will to-day perplex my mind
> With never a thought but love.'

For the rest, this masque is both moral and tedious. The virtue of Calisto, after prevailing against the passion of Jupiter and the detraction of a sister-nymph (Psecas), is finally rewarded by her being requested to 'accept the small dominion of a star.'—Dryden, whose privileges as Poet Laureate were infringed by the employment in his place of Crowne for the composition of a masque, good-naturedly wrote an Epilogue to his rival's production; but even this the influence of Rochester prevented from being spoken.

possesses a certain power of coarse but not ineffective characterisation. But he entirely lacks not only refinement, but elevation of sentiment; and in beauty of form cannot be said to approach Dryden. He is more successful as a writer of blank-verse than of rimed couplets; although, as will be seen, he alternated between the two forms, apparently without entertaining any preference for either.

Juliana, or The Princess of Poland (1671), which calls itself a tragi-comedy, is mainly in blank-verse. It is chiefly remarkable for a wild profusion of action; the plot, however, appears to have no foundation in fact—at all events in Polish history; perhaps the original of the Cardinal ought to be looked for nearer home (in France). The comic character of the Landlord in this play seems to have been considered humorous. History has again very little to do with the so-called *History of Charles the Eighth of France, or The Invasion of Naples by the French* (1672); and indeed this rimed tragedy is no fortunate instance of an endeavour to treat a quasi-historical subject in the form of a 'heroic play.' Such interest as the play excites is absorbed by its wholly fictitious love-story; the action has to be helped on by the apparitions of ghosts; and the versification (although Rochester succeeded in culling from it one flower of extravagance, a passage about 'waves smiling on the sun') is in general bald. *The Destruction of Jerusalem by Titus Vespasian* (1677), another heroic play, in two Parts, was successful—too much so indeed. if its success cost the poet the favour of Rochester. The applause showered on Dryden's *Conquest of Granada* doubtless helped to suggest to Crowne the composition of this work. It was produced after the completion of *The Rehearsal*, thus furnishing a further proof of the fact that this famous burlesque by no means 'killed' heroic plays. It would, however, not have been so easy for the wits to find points of attack in the *Jerusalem* as in the *Granada*; for Crowne usually moves on so low a level that it seems to cost him an effort even to rise into bombast. The quite extraordinary success which attended this commonplace production would remain unaccountable were it not for the expenditure on scenery and

Juliana, or The Princess of Poland (1671).

The History of Charles VIII of France (1672).

The Destruction of Jerusalem, &c. (1677).

effects with which it was decked out, and which the familiar subject of the action cannot but have made doubly enjoyable to the spectators[1]. Crowne's next tragedy, *The Ambitious Statesman, or The Loyal Favourite* (1679), appears to have been specially prized by the author. It is in a different style from that of the preceding play, and in blank-verse. This tragedy is certainly not deficient in vigour, and the plot (which boldly invents a history of the fortunes of Count Bernard VII d'Armagnac after Agincourt[2], and which bears some resemblance to that of Howard's *Duke of Lerma*[3]) is contrived with undeniable skill and effectiveness. Yet in none of Crowne's tragedies is the paucity of poetic touches and the lack of poetic elevation more perceptible than in this work, spirited though it may fairly be called in its general conception. The author seems desirous of reviving to the best of his ability the strong characters of early Elisabethan tragedy, though the 'strong' lines in which their passions found expression in Marlowe and his school are beyond the reach of this *epigonus*. Here and there, however, he indulges in an extravagance of diction beyond that of *Tamerlane* and *The Spanish Tragedy*, and ventures on flights of rant unsurpassed in his own age

The Ambitious Statesman, or The Loyal Favourite (1679).

---

[1] Part I is mainly taken up with the love of a fictitious King of Parthia for the daughter of the Jewish High-Priest, and with the rebellion of the Pharisees (by whom other than Jewish 'Separatists' are obviously signified). In Part II we have the destruction of the city and the loves of Titus and Berenice, treated by Racine in his charming tragedy (to which Crowne makes very contemptuous reference, and which, as noted below, was reproduced by Otway). In Part II, act iii. *ad fin.*, a famous passage from *The Merchant of Venice* is diluted.—As to earlier dramatic treatments of the theme, William Hemings' *The Jews' Tragedy, or Their Fatal and Final Overthrow by Vespatian and Titus his Son*, was printed in 1692. Josephus, who is appealed to as the authority for the story of this drama, appears as a personage in the play. Its principal aim (agreeably to which it contains a large proportion of prose) seems to have been to furnish a realistic picture of the siege. The Epilogue confesses accordingly, that

'The lofty Buskin and the learned Bay
Are not expected to adorn our Play.'

[2] The traditional character, however, of this famous master of mercenaries, who 'estoit tenu pour très cruel homme et tiran et sans pitié' (see a contemporary journal quoted in Schmidt, *Geschichte Frankreichs*, vol. ii. p. 222, *note*), well accords with that of Crowne's Constable.

[3] Cf. *ante*, p. 294.

Thyestes
(1681).

even by the ecstasies of Lee[1]. In *Thyestes* (1681), partly
founded on Seneca's tragedy of that name, which had been
recently again translated into English[2], Crowne introduces
the story of an amour between the children of Atreus and
Thyestes, thus slightly mitigating the revolting impression
made by the main plot, in the unfolding of which the
spectator is spared none of the horrors of the gruesome myth[3].
Thyestes, as well as the two succeeding tragedies, is in
blank-verse ; both of these, together with their successor,
treat subjects derived from classical history.   But, in order
to follow the 'heroic' method of his age, Crowne consistently
gave the rein to his inventive talents in the addition of love-

*Darius,
King of
Persia*
(1688).

plots.   Thus, in *Darius, King of Persia* (1688), instead of
following the estimable example of an earlier quasi-dramatic
treatment of the same subject[4], he allowed his judgment to
be overborne by 'some he much regarded,' 'left out Statira

---

[1] Thus the heroine, when about to precede her lover in death, after sighing
with a profundity which causes him to exclaim,

'Such a groan a breaking sphere would give'—
declares,

> 'I cannot talk or think too much of you ;
> The thoughts you loved me once, will make me think myself
> Above an angel, and this sight of you
> Make me disrelish all the Heavenly visions.
> I say this openly before the world ;
> I scorn to tarry till we meet in death
> *And whisper it behind the globe in private*'—

an odd 'behind the scenes' notion of future bliss.   On the death of the
hero, the King cumulatively observes :

> 'Here falls a Pharaoh's tower, Ephesian temple,
> The cost of ages, wonder of eternity.'

[2] By J. W(right) in 1674.   To this translation (which is in heroics, with
the exception of course of the choruses, parts of the latter being by no
means ill rendered) the author appended a burlesque called *Mock-Thyestes*,
not worthy of notice.   Comparing his 'mimick fare' with 'Heroique Fustian
dressed in metre,' he invites the audience to signify which it prefers, and

> 'Which raises most concern, which most surprise,
> No plot, no characters, or no disguise?'

Jasper Heywood's translation of Seneca's *Thyestes* has been noted, vol. i.
p. 196.   The subject was afterwards treated by Crébillon in his *Atrée*,
criticised at length in La Harpe, *Cours de Littérature*, vol. xv.

[3] Thyestes drinks his son's blood on the stage (in Seneca the fatal banquet
is related by a Nuncius).—The audience seems to have been pleased with
Crowne's play.

[4] By Sir William Alexander (Earl of Stirling); cf. *ante*, vol. ii. p. 624.

and her two daughters [1],' and substituted an extravagant
intrigue of his own device—the innocent love of Bessus'
son for his father's wife Barzane. The remainder of the
play treats of the treason of Bessus and the noble conduct of Darius; and is not altogether uninteresting [2].
In *Regulus* (1692), which contains a large admixture of   *Regulus*
prose, the famous Roman legend is nearly, though not   (1672).
quite, resolved into the story of an amour between
Regulus and Fulvia, needlessly encumbered by reminiscences of Regulus' dead wife, who still more needlessly
appears as a ghost. Though Crowne only here and
there rises to the height which his themes demand, this
tragedy not the less proves that he had in him some
of the elements of a genuine dramatist; and suggests
a creditable appreciation on his part of more vigorous
growths of English tragedy than those which it was in
the main his lot to follow or exemplify [3]. Finally,   *Caligula*
in *Caligula* (1698), written during intervals of serious   (1678).
illness, and therefore to be criticised without severity,
Crowne once more returned to rime. Of this tragedy it
will suffice to say, that though it reveals a praiseworthy
attempt at character-drawing, the baldness of its form in

---

[1] See the Dedication, where Crowne (in testimony of his usual want of
luck) gives an account of the misfortune which befell this play in the sudden
illness of the famous actress Mrs. Barry on the night of its production.

[2] This tragedy might in no inconsiderable measure have been regarded as
an intentional historical parallel, devised by an admirer of King James II,
to the fate and conduct of that monarch—had it been produced a few
months later than was actually the case.

[3] Some real feeling pervades the speech of Regulus, 'I know 't, sweet
Fulvia,' &c. (act v. sc. 1).—The management of the plot, even were the legend
of Regulus to be looked upon as history, is boldly unhistorical, especially
in the part which the 'gallant Xantippus' is made to play. The prose-
scenes, which are quasi-comic, deal with the ambitious intrigues of Asdrubal
at Carthage, which State the poet treats with the utmost scorn (though
we may be sure he intended no side-reference to Holland).—Later
English plays have been written on the story of Regulus; in a French
one by Lucian Arnault (1822) Regulus symbolised the captive Napoleon, and
Carthage the Power which had chained him down (see Muret, *u. s.*, vol. ii.
p. 176). But in dramatic literature this famous story is chiefly memorable
as having entered into the conception of one of Calderon's best-known
dramas, *El Principe Constante* (translated among Mr. D. F. M'Carthy's
Dramas of Calderon, 1853).

general corresponds to the commonplace character of its sentiment [1].

His come-dies :

As a writer of comedy, CROWNE is in my judgment entitled to no high rank. In this as in the other branch of the drama his versatility enabled him to fall in with the prevailing tastes, while his political pliability easily suited itself to the different tempers of the audiences which he desired to gratify. His comic dialogue is fluent both in prose and in verse (when in the latter he resorted to a form which was becoming obsolete). But his range of characters is limited, and no great vigour of humour signalises even the special type produced by him and varied in several of his plays—the character of the 'formal' fool—although its most successful exemplar, *Sir Courtly Nice*, has been held to surpass anything ever accomplished in comedy by Dryden.

The Coun-try Wit (1675).

Crowne's earliest comedy was probably *The Country Wit*, a production of some gaiety and a great deal of coarseness, which derives only part of its plot from Molière [2]. The chief novelty in this play, which is said to have been much liked by King Charles II, is the character of Sir Mannerly Shallow, to some extent (although his grand airs are but country manners) the prototype of the more celebrated Sir Courtly Nice. It may be questioned whether Crowne quite proved his point, viz. that the old-fashioned ways of this solemn 'country gull,' whose simplicity betrays him into the most hopeless of difficulties, are more deserving of satire than those of the town wits with whom he comes into contact. To a later generation the brazen vice of the hero Ramble (who is duly forgiven at the end) may perhaps seem to reflect the folly of the age more strikingly than the silly softness of Sir Mannerly Shallow.

---

[1] Crowne's tragedy treats in part the same subject as that of the German play (by the late 'Friedrich Halm,' a pleasing though not powerful dramatist), *Der Fechter von Ravenna*, a considerable part of which was translated by Sir Theodore Martin in an article in *Fraser's Magazine*, March 1857, since reprinted in his *Essays on the Drama* (1874), where excessive praise is bestowed upon the original—a work which enjoyed a singular ephemeral celebrity.—The plot of Crowne's tragedy (in which Philo Judaeus takes part) adheres more closely to history than is usual with this author.

[2] *Viz.* from *Le Sicilien, ou L'Amour Peintre*, to which Steele was afterwards indebted in his *The Tender Husband*.

City Politiques, which has been regarded as Crowne's earliest comedy, yet has been also stated to have been first printed in 1688, cannot be referred to either so early or so late a date.   Not only are some extant copies of this play undoubtedly dated 1683[1], but even a cursory examination of its contents will leave no doubt as to its purpose of satirising the Whig agitation which extended from the time of the ' Popish Plot ' to that of the Shaftesbury trial[2].   So far as is known, the plot of this piece is original ; on the other hand, it is executed without any attempt to adapt the allusions with which it brims over to the locality (Naples) where its scene is laid.   The thin disguise of the mock disclaimers in the Preface is not intended to prevent the recognition of such personalities as Titus Oates and Stephen Colledge, the Protestant joiner[3] ; while the Whigs are attacked as the fomenters of popular excitement.   *The English Friar, or The Town Spark*, is another comedy with a political intention, being directed against the Court Catholics and their ghostly counsellors in the days of James II.   The plot was clearly suggested—though not more than suggested—by Molière's *Tartuffe*[4].   The main

City Politics (1682 c.).

The English Friar, or The Town Spark (1689).

---

[1] This fact was ascertained by Mr. Bullen at the British Museum.

[2] One of the characters in the play is engaged in writing answers to *Absalom and Achitophel* and *The Medal* under the titles of '*Azariah and Hushai*' and ' *The Medal Revers'd.*'   The latter a designation of one of an actual rejoinder to Dryden, by Samuel Pordage, published in 1681.

[3] They appear as Dr. Panchy (who ' applies himself very much to the Bible; I mean, to kiss it ') and ' the Catholic bricklayer.'   Opinions have differed as to identity of the lawyer Bartholine (whose peculiar way of talking Crowne takes great trouble to explain in the Preface).

[4] In his turn Crowne may have helped to suggest to Cibber the composition of *The Non-Juror* (1717), which however more closely follows *Tartuffe*.   To this refers the sneer in *The Dunciad*, Bk. i. v. 132 : ' The Frippery of crucify'd Molière.' (As to the changes effected by Molière in the character of Tartuffe, who began as a kind of ecclesiastic, and ended as a layman, see V. Cousin, *u. s.*, vol. ii. p. 293, *note*.)   Since the date of *The Non-Juror* falls outside the period to which this book is confined, I may here remark that Cibber's caricature was legitimately designed to expose a real public evil, which threatened to fester like a sore in the commonwealth. The weakness of the satire lies in the fact that, while the general body of the non-jurors included many men of an earnest religiosity which found expression in a grave simplicity of bearing, very few of them can be supposed to have resembled Dr. Wulf in sanctimoniousness of manners.   Indeed, Cibber himself felt this ; see a passage in act ii, descriptive of the

characters are Father Finical and his patron (and all but victim) Lord Stately. The latter exhibits those grand airs which Crowne loved to ridicule[1]; the former (who may have been intended as a portrait of Father Petre), with his mixture of godliness and worse than worldliness, and his power over women, is not altogether ill drawn; but he wears his cloak less artfully than the French hypocrite. In *Sir Courtly Nice, or It Cannot Be* (1685), Crowne, as already stated, has been frequently held to have achieved his comic masterpiece; and the play held the stage for nearly a century. It is however nothing more than a comedy with an extravagantly farcical plot (taken from the *No Pued Esser* (*It Cannot Be*) of Moreto[2], and resembling the plots of Molière's least artistic productions), and with a number of eccentric characters—or the sketches of characters—antithetically mixed. Of these the intriguing scamp Crack was borrowed by Crowne from his original; the Aunt too (who must be allowed to be amusing) has a genuine Duenna touch about her; of Crowne's own invention, however, are

Sir Courtly Nice, or It Cannot Be (1685).

Doctor as unlike the generality of non-jurors. Thus, it was hardly justifiable to transfer to a non-juring layman the outward characteristics habitually associated, on the stage at least, with the opposite pole of religious hypocrisy. In general, this comedy, though besides Dr. Wulf and his friend Sir John Woodvil the sprightly Maria is a well-drawn character, may I think be described as a coarse play, and inferior to some of Cibber's earlier comedies to be noticed below. Concerning the production of *The Non-Juror*, see Doran's *London in the Jacobite Times*, vol. i. pp. 290 *seqq.*, where some allusions in the play are explained.—In 1760 appeared Bickerstaffe's *The Hypocrite*, a new version of *The Non-Juror*, in which by the side of Dr. Cantwell, as the hero was now called, was introduced the new character of Mawworm.

[1] Another character recurring in Crowne is that of Young Ranter, 'a young debauch of Quality'—in other words, a combination of the young man of fashion and the blackguard.

[2] This plot was given to Crowne by King Charles II, to whom 'the first three acts and more' are said to have been regularly submitted, as written scene by scene, up to the time of the King's last illness. See a very curious note cited from Oldmixon's *History of the Stuarts*, *ap.* Burnet, *Own Time* (ed. 1882), vol. ii. p. 464, *note*; where Crowne is stated to have on one of these occasions overheard a most notable conversation between King Charles and the Duke of York.—Crowne afterwards found that the plot of *No Pued Esser* had been already adapted by a previous writer, Sir Thomas St. Serfe, in his *Tarugo's Wiles, or The Coffee-House* (1668), on which Dorset wrote some highly complimentary lines.—A French version of Crowne's play, Dumaniant's *Guerre Ouverte*, is mentioned by Mr. C. A. West.

the choleric cavalier Hothead and the canting Puritan Testimony; and again Surly, a kind of Plain Dealer in speech, and one of the most disgusting figures in the whole range of English comedy, and his antitype Sir Courtly Nice himself. This latter is doubtless a happy example of the effeminate fop; but I cannot regard either this, or any of the other characters, as entitled to superlative praise.

Lastly, in *The Married Beau, or The Curious Impertinent* (1694), which is written in very fluent blank-verse, Crowne followed earlier models—and the play may be regarded as an attempt to return to the style of Fletcher and Shirley. The play is however to be condemned, not so much on account of the dangerous nature of the plot (recurring in other plays), which it borrows from a tale of Cervantes [1], as because of its lubricity of treatment, which is anything but mitigated by the new ending—thoroughly peaceable and thoroughly immoral—there given to a story in itself hardly tolerable on the stage.

The Married Beau, or The Curious Impertinent (1694).

The authors whom it remains to notice may, according to the relatively more notable among their several dramatic productions, be conveniently grouped as tragic and as comic dramatists.

A prominent place among the former is held by NATHANIEL LEE [2]. Born about 1653, as the son of a Presbyterian, afterwards Church of England, divine, who was at one time chaplain to Monck (Albemarle), and educated at Trinity College, Cambridge, he betook himself early to London, where he led a dissolute life under the fitful patronage of Buckingham, Rochester, and their fellows, and for the most part followed the prevailing current of political sentiment and opinion. He appears to have been gifted with considerable natural powers of elocution; but

Other tragic dramatists of the period. Nathaniel Lee (1653 c.–1692).

[1] The *Curioso Impertinente* in *Don Quixote*. See Ticknor, vol. ii. p. 119; and cf. *ante*, vol. ii. p. 683, *note* 2.

[2] *The Dramatic Works of Mr. Nathanael Lee*, 3 vols., 1754. See also Mr. Sidney Lee's notice in vol. xxxii of *The Dictionary of National Biography* (1892), and an Essay on *Lee's Plays* in *The Retrospective Review*, vol. iii. part ii.

he failed as an actor. His great facility as a writer, and the hold which his passionate style gave him upon the public favour, might however have ensured his success in life, had not his excitable temperament and his habits of dissipation combined to bring upon him the catastrophe of madness[1]. For five years he remained in this condition; then he appears to have for a short time recovered the use of his senses, but he died not long afterwards (in 1692) in a drunken fit.

His characteristics as a tragic dramatist. The tragedies of Lee discover noble if not rare gifts; his choice of subjects exhibits a soaring delight in magnificent and imposing historic themes, and is in general felicitous as well as ambitious. In execution he displays an impetuosity in which it is easy to discover the traces of incipient insanity; Dryden, who co-operated with him, speaks of him as one 'who had a great genius for tragedy,' but who, 'following the fury of his natural temper, made every man, and woman too, in his plays stark raging mad; there was not a sober person to be had for love or money[2].' But, as one of his critics has observed[3], there is 'method in his madness' and his 'frenzy is the frenzy of a poet.' In bombast he may almost be said to be without an equal— but a real passion often burns beneath the heap of words superimposed upon it. In versification Lee was a follower of Dryden—whose example prompted him both to adopt the use of rime, and from 1677 onwards to abandon it.

His Nero, Emperor of Rome (1675). Sophonisba, or Hannibal's Overthrow (1676). Thus, his earliest play, the tragedy of *Nero, Emperor of Rome* (acted 1675), is mainly, though not entirely, in rime, and his second, *Sophonisba, or Hannibal's Overthrow* (acted 1676), entirely so. Of these the former may be passed by as an unhistorical medley of historical personages; the latter is a version, far from enjoyable, of a favourite subject of our English tragic drama[4]. Besides

---

[1] It is to be feared that it would not be difficult to find parallels to his unhappy fate. One of them seems to have been the mental collapse of the Spanish dramatist Montalvan, 'the first-born of Lope de Vega's genius. (Ticknor, vol. iii. p. 314.)

[2] See *A Parallel of Poetry and Painting, u. s.*, p. 320.

[3] In *The Retrospective Review, u. s.*

[4] Cf. *ante*, vol. ii. p. 480, as to Marston's *The Wonder of Women, or Sophonisba*.

the story of Sophonisbe—treated here with the utmost freedom—Lee has availed himself of the tradition of Hannibal's passion for a Capuan lady ; but the love-sick Hannibal of this ' heroic play ' is altogether unendurable[1]. ' Praecipitandus est liber Spiritus' is the characteristic motto of this tragedy; but the spirit that moves both it and of its successor, *Gloriana, or The Court of Augustus Caesar* (acted 1676), likewise in rime, is compounded of artificiality and extravagance[2]. In *The Rival Queens, or Alexander the Great* (acted 1677), however, Lee achieved a work which was splendidly successful, and which deserves to live. The subject of this tragedy is the jealousy conceived by Alexander's first wife, the passionate and vindictive Roxana, against his second, the mild and gentle Statira ; and, stirring in itself[3], this theme is indisputably here treated not only with great dramatic skill, but with considerable poetic power. There is no reason for denying that passages in *The Rival Queens* exhibit the bombast to which Lee inclined, and that the catastrophe, Alexander's death, is managed with a hazardous audacity such as only a really great actor could save from toppling over into the ridiculous; but I must confess to having been unable to read this tragedy without genuine admiration for the fervour which hurries it irresistibly along in its impetuous course[4]. It is mainly

Gloriana, or The Court of Augustus (1676). *The Rival Queens, or Alexander the Great* (1677).

---

[1] The authorities for this tradition will be found in a note to *Hannibal*, a historical drama of unusual interest by the late Professor Nichol (1873). —Lee's heroine, named Rosalinda (!), is a prisoner in the Roman camp, and appears in boy's clothes at the battle of Zama, where she is killed. This event is foretold in a witchcraft scene; but the witchcraft is not borrowed from that in Marston's *Sophonisba*.

[2] The main plot of this tragedy turns on the love of Caesario for Gloriana, Pompey's daughter, whom the jealous passion of Augustus keeps confined ! Julia and Ovid are of course introduced.

[3] Probably (I have not seen more than a summary of the romance) founded upon part of Calprenède's *Cassandre*.

[4] Colley Cibber, who testifies to the unparalleled popularity of this play and did homage to it by a parody called *The Rival Queans, with the Humours of Alexander The Great* (1710), which likewise had an unusually protracted life, makes some pointed remarks on Lee's tragedy. After quoting a ' rhapsody of vain-glory' from it, he observes that ' when these flowing Numbers came from the Mouth of a Betterton, the Multitude no more desired Sense to them, than our musical *Connoisseurs* think it essential in the celebrate Airs of an Italian opera.' (*Apology*, R. W. Lowe's edition,

Mithridates 1678).

Theo- dosius, or The Force of Love 1680).

Caesar Borgia (1680).

Lucius Junius Brutus (1681).

written in blank-verse; and the same is also the metre of the tragedies of *Mithridates King of Pontus* (acted 1678) and *Theodosius, or The Force of Love* (acted 1680), though the latter has occasional passages in rime, including the striking night-soliloquy of Varanes [1]. *Mithridates* is a mere story of love and lust, provided with a quasi-historical back- ground. In *Caesar Borgia* (acted 1680)—also in blank-verse —the poet could not easily add to the horrors of his theme ; and he even deserves our gratitude for having spared us the personal introduction of Pope Alexander VI. But though his plot (the terrible story of the murder of the Duke of Gandia by his brother Caesar) is historical, the same cannot be said of the use made by him of that old bugbear of English theatrical audiences, Macchiavelli, who figures as the villain proper of the piece [2]. The play forms one of the most outrageous attempts of Restoration tragedy to revive the worst horrors of the Elisabethan drama in the days of its crudity and in those of its decay; and the language is fre- quently as outrageous as the theme—consisting, to borrow a phrase from the play, of ' volleys of revenge [3].' On *Caesar Borgia* followed in 1681, likewise in blank-verse, the tragedy of *Lucius Junius Brutus, Father of his Country*. This tragedy, which after the third night of its performance was stopped by authority as an ' anti-monarchical' play [4], is

vol. i. pp. 105 *seqq.*)—*The Rival Queens* remained a favourite play of the English stage till the days of Edmund Kean ; and many revised versions of it were published, among them one by John P. Kemble.—Several lines from this play have passed into familiar quotations, especially one which is fre- quently misquoted ('When Greeks join'd Greeks, then was the Tug of War.' Act iv).—The lines beginning 'See the Conquering Hero comes' (introduced by Handel from his *Joshua* into his *Judas Maccabeus*), are stated by Mr. Lee to have found their way into a late acting edition of *The Rival Queens*.

[1] See act v. sc. 2.—The subject of this tragedy is the same as that of Massinger's *The Emperor of the East* (*ante*, p. 29).

[2] He says (act iv) :

     'Well could I curse away a Winter's Night,
     Though standing naked on a Mountain's Top,
     And think it but a Minute spent in Sport.'

[3] The heroine Bellamira is strangled on the stage ; the rest of the main characters are poisoned.—Borgia's ravings at the conclusion are in Lee's most advanced style.

[4] Dibdin, vol. iv. p. 187. *The Duke of Guise* seems to have been written

stated to be partly founded on Mlle. de Scudéry's romance of *Clélie*. It is very ambitious in design, beginning with the death of Lucrece and occupied chiefly with Brutus' treatment of his sons, one of whom is married to Teraminta, a natural daughter of Tarquin. This tragedy is devoid neither of bombast nor of pathos [1], but in the speeches of Brutus Lee proves unequal to his task, and the interval becomes apparent which even as to mere power of execution separates Elisabethan from Restoration tragedy [2]. In *Constantine the Great* (acted 1684) the same method is adopted of treating a quasi-historical subject. Although the tragedy begins with the vision of the Cross, it soon becomes a mere drama of erotic passion, turning on the love of father and son for the same woman [3]. There remain two other plays from the hand of this fertile but hasty author, of very different merit. *The Princess of Cleve* (acted in 1681) is very appropriately described by Lee in the Dedication as 'this Farce, Comedy, Tragedy, or mere Play.' Founded on the once famous French romance of the same name by Madame La Fayette, it envelopes a more than hazardous sentimental situation [4] in ribald comedy of almost unequalled grossness [5]. *The Massacre of Paris*, on the other hand, seems to me one of the best of Lee's plays.

Constantine the Great (1684).

The Princess of Cleve (1681).

The Massacre of Paris (1690).

partly with a view to removing the impression created by the reflexions on King Charles II which had been thought discoverable in Lee's previous play.

[1] See for the latter Titus' speech to Teraminta (act iii *ad fin.*), but even here the beauty of the passage is spoilt.

[2] Lee's treatment of the subject contrasts very strongly with that adopted in Ponsard's *Lucrèce* (1843), a work of considerable significance in the history of the modern French drama, and noticeable on its own account because of the chaste and scholarly conduct of a story which lends itself readily to florid rhetorical ornamentation.

[3] The *historical* episode here reproduced bears some resemblance to the *unhistorical* story of *Don Carlos*, which (as narrated by the Abbé St. Réal) furnished Otway (cf. *infra*) and afterwards Schiller with the plots, or part of the plots, of their tragedies. In Lee's tragedy Arius conducts himself as a thorough villain, and in the end is thrown into a poisoned bath prepared by him for his victims —a catastrophe not very different from that of Marlowe's *Jew of Malta*.

[4] In his *Cours de Litterature Dramatique*, vol. iv. sect. lxvii, M. Saint-Marc Girardin has commented on the ethical significance of the main situation of this romance, where a wife, in order to claim her husband's protection against herself, avows to him her love for another man.

[5] In this play occurs a passage in which the character of Rochester is drawn under the name of Rosidore (act i. sc. 2).

Of this tragedy, which Lee had had by him some time in MS., but which was not produced till 1690, two scenes had been inserted in the *Duke of Guise*[1]. It is less disfigured by rant than the generality of his plays, though this element is by no means altogether absent; and the action is both perspicuous in its management and spirited in its conduct. Moreover, the amorous intrigue is in this instance subsidiary only, and heightens, instead of merely absorbing, the effect of the whole. Nor is it possible to part from this author without pointing out that, as typically characteristic of him, the constant extravagance of his diction is even less noticeable than is the uniform extravagance of his imagination; it might be said of his personages that they are mad even before they go mad (as they often do); and none of our later tragic poets has dwelt so persistently on images of lust and wantonness. Lee had in him some genuine fire of passion, but it burnt with an impure flame.

Lee's extra-vagance.

THOMAS OTWAY[2]—'the tender Otway' as he has been not inappropriately called[3]—deserves a more than passing notice in the literary history of the Restoration age. Passages in his life remind us of the brief and broken career of Marlowe, to whose mightier and manlier genius however that of Otway bears little resemblance. The weakness of his moral nature prevented him from gathering up his wasting strength, and the miseries of his existence, due in part to this moral weakness, overcame him, partly in the form of exhausting want, partly in that of enervating debauchery, so that on the mere threshold of manhood he sank into a premature grave. Had it been otherwise, the record of his literary career might tell of something more

Thomas Otway (1651–1685).

---

[1] Cf. *ante*, p. 378.

[2] *The Works of Thomas Otway. With Notes and Life.* By Thomas Thornton. 3 vols., 1813.—An edition of his *Works* in 2 vols., 1812, contains a sketch of his life, enlarged from that by Johnson in the *Lives of the Poets*.—Mr. E. W. Gosse's admirable essay on *Thomas Otway*, which first appeared in *The Cornhill Magazine* for December, 1877, is reprinted in his *Seventeenth Century Studies*.

[3] See Collins' *Ode to Pity*, in a celebrated passage which, as Mr. Gosse points out, contains a topographical mistake.

than one or two isolated achievements of rare excellence amidst a succession of imperfect attempts ; and the story of his personal life might not have to be designated one of the most pitiful and melancholy chapters of English literary biography.

Born in 1651 at Trotton, near Midhurst, in Sussex, and educated at Christ Church, Oxford, Thomas Otway was left penniless by his father's death. Mrs. Aphra Behn good-naturedly furnished the young man with a part in her tragedy of *The Forced Marriage*, but as was natural enough, he broke down and was permanently spoilt for an actor [1].' But he had mixed in good society at Oxford, and his pleasant manners and literary talents attracted to him the goodwill and patronage of the young men of fashion of the Court—above all of Lord Plymouth, one of the King's sons. In the midst of dissipations he composed his first —and indisputably worst—tragedy, *Alcibiades* (acted 1675), the plot of which has been said to be taken from Cornelius Nepos and Plutarch, but resembles their narratives chiefly in the way in which a nightmare resembles the incidents chaotically crowded into it [2]. In the death of the hero, how-ever, the dramatist shows the sure perception of stage-effect of which his plays give constant proof. The part of Druxilla was played by Mrs. Barry, the beautiful young actress who was henceforth to exercise an irresistible fascination upon Otway. *Alcibiades* is a not very successful experiment in rimed verse; the same form is perhaps more effectively [3] employed in Otway's second play, the better-known tragedy of *Don Carlos*, produced (in 1676) under the immediate

His life and works.

His Alcibiades (1675).

Don Carlos (1676).

---

[1] R. Lowe, *Betterton*, p. 273 (from Downes).

[2] The central figure is Timandra, who is beloved not only by Alcibiades, himself here a model Athenian, but also by Theramenes 'the now Athenian general,' and by Agis King of Sparta. Tissaphernes startles us by presenting himself not as a Persian satrap, but as an old Spartan general.—The plot, which is absurd in the extreme, ends by Elysium opening to receive Timandra, while the Spirits recite verses not devoid of a reminiscence of the Witches in *Macbeth*. On the other hand, the death of Alcibiades must have been dramatically very impressive.

[3] I am not inclined to go so far as Mr. Gosse, who thinks that we should be justified in calling *Don Carlos* the best English tragedy in rime, and considers its verse of its kind, ' supple ' and ' strong.'

patronage of Rochester, who happened at this time to have grown tired of protecting the efforts of Crowne [1]. The play is however not without real merits. But the subject (borrowed from a French historical novel by St. Réal, the source of the myth upon which the genius of Schiller afterwards stamped a wide popular currency [2]) is excellently chosen. And though towards the close the execution lapses into excess, a multiplicity of incident and an interesting variety of characters are upon the whole managed with great skill; so that, in view of the general dearth, in the drama of this age, of plots possessed of a similar combination of external and intrinsic interest, the extraordinary success of *Don Carlos* cannot be regarded as at all wonderful. This tragedy was dedicated to the Duke of York; but Otway's active patron at this time was Rochester—whose transfer of his goodwill from Elkanah Settle is said to have excited the jealousy of the elder dramatist to such a degree as to cause him to challenge his rival to a duel. To his patron Rochester Otway hastened to dedicate his next two plays, mere versions of French originals, the tragedy of *Titus and Berenice* and the farce of *The Cheats of Scapin* (both acted 1677) [3]; whereupon he was in his turn abandoned by the fickle profligate, and afterwards mercilessly ridiculed by him in some of the most disgusting lines of a disgusting lampoon, doubtless written ' with ease ' by this fit leader of a ' mob of gentlemen.'

Titus and Berenice (1677). *The Cheats of Scapin* (1677).

---

[1] Cf. *ante*, p. 399.

[2] The resemblance between Schiller's and Otway's plays, though doubtless only arising from this community of source, is most striking—not only in many of the characters and situations, but also in some individual scenes. The hypothesis of an acquaintance on the part of Schiller with Otway's play is denied by J. Löwenberg, *Ueber Otway und Schiller's Don Carlos* (Lippstadt, 1887). The character of the Marquis Posa appears in both plays; but Schiller does not, like Otway, introduce Don John of Austria ('Austria,' as Philip most inappropriately calls him). A fine dramatic contrast is obtained by the juxtaposition of the two kinsmen. The close of Otway's play, which resembles that of *Hamlet* (manifest reminiscences of *Othello* and *King Lear* occur elsewhere), is furiously tragical; and the King, whom history would not allow the author to kill, instead (according to the stage-direction) ' Runs off Raving Mad.'—It is to be regretted that the play should have been accompanied by an Epilogue containing a ribald reference to a scandal about Dryden.

[3] From Racine's *Bérénice* and Molière's *Les Fourberies de Scapin*.

Shortly before the production of his comedy of *Friend-* *ship in Fashion* (1678), an unpleasant work bespeaking the cynical mood in which it was doubtless written, Otway at last succeeded in obtaining, through his earlier patron, the Earl of Plymouth, a cornetcy of horse in the force at that time about to start for Flanders under the Duke of Monmouth. But unfortunately for the unhappy adventurer, the troops of which his regiment formed part were disbanded after the briefest period of service, their pay was doled out to them in an unsatisfactory and comparatively valueless shape, and Otway was again reduced to poverty and distress. The farcical comedy of *The Soldier's Fortune,* though not printed till 1681, was very probably produced some two or three years earlier; but this I may in any case pass over. In the Epilogue to his next play, *The History* *and Fall of Caius Marius* (1680), Otway refers to his brief and unlucky military career. This tragedy, which is nothing short of a monstrous plagiarism [1], was obviously produced in haste; but it is creditable to the public taste, vitiated as it was and wholly callous to any desecration of the masterpieces of the national drama, that such a demand upon its patience was regarded as intolerable.

In the same year—in the midst of his troubles—Otway at last produced a work not unworthy of his genius. His life and work had now for some time been under the influence of a gifted actress but unworthy woman, whose favours were bestowed upon his former patron Rochester. Mrs. Barry, whom the poet loved with an unrequited passion, impersonated his chief female tragic characters, and doubtless largely inspired him in their creation. One of her greatest theatrical triumphs was achieved in the character of Monimia in the tragedy of *The Orphan, or The Unhappy* *Marriage* (1680), and the eye of love had no doubt detected the capacities which could give reality to the heart-breaking pathos of its later portions. The situation in which Mrs. Barry—and Mrs. Siddons after her—drew forth tears so abundantly, is after all only one of a distress caused by a brutal deception at which our gorge rises; and the source

---

[1] *Viz.* of *Romeo and Juliet.* The details may, for very shame, be omitted.

of pity seems vitiated by the wanton cruelty of such a story. But there can be no doubt that these once famous scenes reveal the power of genuine feeling, and agitate spectator or reader by the excitement of strong personal emotion. The story, which Otway took over from a publication of his own times [1], is unsuited for dramatic treatment, helped on as it is towards its catastrophe by misapprehension and confusion of persons; moreover, it is disfigured by a pruriency of treatment which, after on one occasion arising the wrath of the descendants of the Puritans [2], has at last banished it from the English stage. But the result remains that, even as we read the play in cold blood, nothing can stay the flow of our compassion for the innocent victim of guilt and mischance; and that the true charm of melting tenderness here for the first time exhibited by Otway still clings to the favourite passages of this once celebrated play [3]. It is noticeable that *The Orphan*, the pathetic cadence of whose metre came home to the audience as with a new force, is written in blank-verse.

Venice Preserved, or a Plot Discovered (1682).

In *Venice Preserved, or A Plot Discovered* (1682), a side-reference, although in truth not a very skilful one, is perceptible to the system of partisan manœuvres built up by the Whigs on the fictitious basis of the 'Popish Plot' and its 'discovery.' And the buffoon character of Antonio, whose scenes cast a gross blemish upon Otway's tragic masterpiece, was, as the Prologue clearly indicates, intended in ridicule of Shaftesbury, whom Otway had already attacked in his discreditable *rifacimento*, called *Caius Marius*. This infusion of political virulence into his 'historical' tragedy could not but detract from its artistic

[1] *Viz.* a pamphlet called *English Adventures*, published in 1667. One of the personages in the story is Charles Brandon Duke of Suffolk. This was already pointed out by Langbaine; see also Cooke, *Memoirs of Foote*, vol. iii. pp. 1 *seqq.*

[2] An amateur performance of *The Orphan* at Boston gave rise to the Massachusetts Act prohibiting all stage performances. (See Lecky, *History of England in the Eighteenth Century*, vol. ii. p. 18.)

[3] I may include in these Monimia's speech early in the play (act ii. sc. 1: 'Man therefore was a Lord-like creature made,' &c.), in reading which we almost seem to hear the undulations of voice that would make such a passage irresistible, if spoken by an actress suited to the part.

effect, and indeed is so grossly contrived as to give offence to any unprejudiced mind. The subject proper of the play was, as in the case of *Don Carlos*, furnished by the Abbé St. Réal, who in 1674 seems to have published the first literary account that had reached the world at large of the strange conspiracy which in 1618 had, by the policy of the signiory, under circumstances purposely left in darkness, menaced the safety if not the very existence of the Venetian Republic [1]. One of the speeches in the play, that of the conspirator Renault, who directs the procedure of the outbreak [2], seems to be translated *verbatim* from the French historical writer. The general interest of the plot is considerable, and there can be no doubt but that it is enhanced by the scene in which the action takes place. Otway, like St. Réal himself, appreciated the influence upon the imagination of their public of the associations of locality, to which landscape and tradition, history and contemporary gossip were alike contributory. As in *Don Carlos* the Spanish Court, still supposed by honest English hearts to be capable of most deeds of darkness [3], had furnished a suitable background to a picture of intrigue and murder, so in *Venice Preserved* the scene was appropriately laid in a State whose mysteries still formed part of its accepted system of government, and occupied the imagination of many generations of visitors to the beautiful and luxurious city. It is not surprising that there should be much in Otway's play (particularly near the beginning) which at once reminds the reader of *Othello* ; but it possesses quite enough of originality to allow us to pass by the undoubted fact of these reminiscences. The three principal dramatic personages in *Venice*

---

[1] Sismondi in his *History of the Italian Republics* notes the determination of the Council of Ten to preserve as long as possible the ' silence of terror.' —The main difficulty as to this conspiracy consists in the question whether at the bottom of it lay a deliberate design on the part of the Spanish Government, or merely the inflated vanity of the Spanish Viceroy of Naples and the Spanish Ambassador at Venice, the Duke of Ossuna and the Marquis of Bedmar. The Frenchman Giacomo Pierre was the chief of its numerous agents, taken from a class of men of whom the lagunes and their hospitality were prolific. See H. E. Brown, *Venice, an Historical Sketch* (1893), pp. 403, *seqq.*

[2] Act iii. sc. 2.

[3] See *e. g.* Sir Robert Howard's *The Duke of Lerma* (*ante*, p. 394).

Preserved are drawn with great, though perhaps not with equal, skill and vigour. The settled determination of Pierre contrasts effectively with the weakness of Jaffier, who after joining in the conspiracy is persuaded by Belvidera to save the State by revealing his knowledge of the design. He afterwards seeks to atone for this betrayal by sacrificing himself for his friend ; and at last stabs both himself and Pierre in Roman fashion, thus deluding the scaffold of its double prey. To my mind the terrors of this scene are in no respect out of accord with the general conception and character of so gloomy a tragedy ; but the madness of Belvidera and the apparition of the ghosts of Pierre and Jaffier overburden a mind already overdone with horrors. The most striking and characteristic beauty of *Venice Preserved*, however, consists beyond a doubt in the exquisitely natural tenderness of the love-scenes between Jaffier and Belvidera, and in the consummate art of the great scene in which she saves her father and the State [1]. This tragedy is, like its predecessors, written in blank-verse, with a slight intermixture of prose chiefly to accommodate the comic vein of Antonio.

The Atheist (1684).

Otway's end.

After *Venice Preserved* Otway produced no further drama, except *The Atheist, or The Second Part of The Soldier's Fortune* (acted 1684) [2]. But neither pathetic tragedies [3] nor coarse comedies—though alike suited to the taste of the age,—neither ignoble efforts of political partisanship nor open panegyric (which in his poem of *Windsor Forest* Otway

---

[1] Act iv. sc. 2. Dryden, generous as usual, and at the same time discriminating in his praise, singles out the 'real passion' in *Venice Preserved* as its chief title to commendation. 'I will not,' he says, 'defend everything in' the play ; 'but I must bear this testimony . . . that the passions are truly touched in it . . . nature is there, which is the greatest beauty.' And Pope described Otway's talent of 'writing so movingly' as 'a talent of nature.' (See *A Parallel of Poetry and Painting, u. s.*, pp. 325–326 and *note*.)

[2] It has the coarseness of all Otway's comedies ; but there is some humour in the notion of the *père prodigue* in this play. The 'Atheist' himself, I am sorry to say, being asked of what religion he is, replies: 'Of the religion of the Inner-Temple, the common-law religion.' It is refreshing to find him saluted as 'Iniquity,' like a Vice in an old morality.

[3] The copy-right of *Venice Preserved* is said to have been purchased by a bookseller for £15. Southerne is said to have sold that of *The Spartan Dame* for £120. 'Plays have their fates.'

lavished upon the recently deceased Charles II and his successor), could avail him. Debt and distress weighed him down ; and in the obscure retreat of an ale-house on Tower Hill he spent the last days of his unhappy existence, which ended on April 15, 1685,—it was said by his choking himself with a piece of bread that charity had enabled him to purchase [1]. From a life for the most part wretched and throughout ill-regulated it would be futile to look for perfect poetic fruit. Yet—if his comedies be left aside—such is the self-educating power of real genius, even where its range is limited, that it is possible to trace in Otway's tragic productions a progress from crude beginnings to achievements not wholly unworthy of his most characteristic gifts. His unhappy passion for Mrs. Barry may have aided him in casting off the bombast that had disfigured his earlier works, and in coming to rely for his chief dramatic effects upon the power which was natural to him, of appealing directly to the tender emotions of the human heart. It is no shame to him that the emotion of pity long continued to respond to the appeal of his masterpieces when played on the popular stage, and that the same kind of response should be evoked by them in the modern reader who is willing to surrender himself to the dictates of his natural feelings [2]. And at least, sincerely though we may regret his literary sins as well as his moral errors, we shall find something besides pity to bestow upon the poet who created Monimia and Belvidera.

Progressive developement of his tragic genius.

THOMAS SOUTHERNE [3] (1660–1746) should not be passed over among the tragic poets of this age, between which and the next he forms a notable connecting link. In the earlier part of his career as a dramatist he was much associated

Thomas Southerne (1660–1746).

[1] The actual circumstances of his death are variously reported; see Johnson's *Life.*—He was said to have left behind him four acts of a tragedy, with which an attempt was made in 1719 to identify a play called *Heroic Friendship,* then for the first time published—an attempt which so high a critical authority as Mr. Gosse considers not wholly unworthy of credit.

[2] Gay, in his *Trivia, c.* iii. *v.* 561, commemorates the 'saunt'ring Prentices' who 'o'er Otway weep.' But such popular instincts are not invariably misleading.

[3] *Plays written by Thomas Southerne. With an Account of the Life and Writings of the Author.* 3 vols., 1774.—See also my notice of Southerne in vol. liii of *The Dictionary of National Biography* (1898).

with Dryden, who wrote the Prologues for his first and second pieces (and the Epilogue for the first), and who, besides in 1692 entrusting to him the revision and completion of his tragedy of *Cleomenes*[1], praised him as the Terence of English comedy. Just half a century later,—in lines which touch on his Irish birth, his successful theatrical career, his happy disposition and his simple piety—Pope congratulated the poets' Nestor (as he had long since been called) on 'his fair account' having

'run
Without a blot to eighty-one[2].'

It ran yet four years further ; and, according to Warton, Southerne who had 'lived the longest, died the richest of our poets[3].' Altogether,—and not only because a long life ending with honour is always agreeable to contemplate,— Southerne's career stands in pleasing contrast to the turbulent lives of too many of our Restoration dramatists.

The Loyal Brother, or The Persian Prince (1682). Of Southerne's plays, the tragedy of *The Loyal Brother, or The Persian Prince*, produced in 1682, and founded on a novel called *Tachmas, Prince of Persia*, contains, in the character of Semanthe, some indications of the pathetic power which was Southerne's most distinctive gift as a dramatic writer. The play, as may have been guessed from its title in conjunction with its date, was intended to compliment the Duke of York, whom during his subsequent brief reign Southerne served in arms[4] ; the villain Ismael is one of the many contemporary dramatic characters supposed to cover an attack upon Shaftesbury. *The Loyal Brother* is written in blank-verse, but the rabble of citizens, and their

---

[1] Cf. *ante*, p. 385.

[2] *To Thomas Southern, on his Birth-day,* 1742. (Pope's *Works*, Elwin and Courthope's edition, vol. iv. p. 496.)

[3] Pope, in the lines referred to, speaks of Southerne as—

'sent from heaven to raise
The price of prologues and of plays.'

He was said to have paid Dryden a fee of ten, instead of the usual five, guineas for the Prologue to his first play, and, by insisting on an extension of author's rights, to have made the sum of £500 out of his tragedy *The Spartan Dame.*

[4] He held an ensigncy, and then a captain's commission, in the Princess Anne's regiment from 1685 to 1688 or 1689.

wives who love fireworks, cast ridicule upon themselves in
prose.   Four comedies followed, in whose favour it is not *Comedies.*
possible to say much, viz. *The Disappointment, or The Mother
in Fashion* (1684), founded in part on *The Curious Impertinent* in *Don Quixote*; *Sir Antony Love, or The Rambling
Lady* (1691); *The Wives' Excuse, or Cuckolds make themselves* (1692), which, though unlike the much grosser previous
play a failure on the stage, justifies the praise of Dryden by
its very amusing depiction of contemporary manners[1]; and
The Maid's Last Prayer; or Any, rather than Fail (1692)[2].
The last three of these comedies are entirely in prose.

The first of Southerne's plays which furnished him with
an opportunity of revealing the true nature of dramatic
power that he possessed, was *The Fatal Marriage, or The
Innocent Adultery* (1694).   The pathetic plot of this play,
which is founded on Mrs. Behn's novel of *The Nun, or the
Fair Vow-Breaker*, may be described as a dramatic treatment of the motive familiar to modern readers from
Tennyson's *Enoch Arden* and a larger number of other
narrative or dramatic versions than it would be worth while
to enumerate.   After continuing to command popular favour
during the life-time of its author, this tragedy was in 1757
revived by Garrick with great success ; nor can we wonder
that it should have suited the highly-sentimental tastes of
this later age[3].   Yet it would be unjust to Southerne, and it
would obscure the continuity in the history of the English

---

[1] See the 'music-meeting' in act. i which begins with a scene in 'the
outward Room in the Music-meeting; several Footmen at Hazard, some
rising from Play.' This act forms a sort of side-piece to the last act of
Shirley's *The Ball* (*ante*, p. 107).

[2] The device of the previous play is here repeated in Sir Symphony's
music-meeting in act v, where practical jokes are played as well as music.
The song in this scene ('Tell me no more I am deceiv'd'), written by
Congreve, is supposed to have been his earliest acknowledged production.—
There is considerable humour in the twaddle of Lord Malepert and of his aunt,
Lady Susan, the unfortunate heroine of this sarcastically named comedy.

[3] Garrick removed as 'immoral' the comic scenes, including the disgraceful
one borrowed from Fletcher's *The Night-Walker* (*ante*, vol. ii. p. 740).—As
late as 1775—the date of the production of Sheridan's *Rivals—The Innocent
Adultery* was a work which the Lydia Languishes of the day borrowed from
the circulating library at Bath. (Act i. sc. 2.)—A long series of revivals of
The Fatal Marriage, under the title of *Isabella*, is mentioned by Genest,
closing with the year 1729.

seventeenth-century drama, which, however partial and imperfect, should not be overlooked, were we to ignore the remnant of Elisabethan intensity noticeable in the passage, where the thought transiently occurs to Isabella of murdering her first husband on his unexpected return, and in the scene of her lapse into madness [1]. The tragedy of *Oroonoko, or The Royal Slave*, likewise founded on a prose-work of Mrs. Behn's, the *History of the Royal Slave*, which in its turn was founded on historical fact, rivalled its predecessor in the endurance of its popularity [2], but can hardly be rated at the same value as a dramatic work. Mrs. Behn, who had a kind heart, gave proof in addition of some praiseworthy freedom of spirit in commending to the public of her age the virtues of a negro slave; but, leaving her tale out of the question, we cannot allow much merit to the play (which is written in a mixture of prose and blank-verse) except in the way of occasional fine lines and fine sentiments. But considering the novelty of its theme, and of its choice of hero, there is nothing surprising in a popularity which established itself as a tradition [3].

Oroonoko, or The Royal Slave (1696).

The Fate of Capua (1700).

In his next two plays, Southerne turned to tragic themes of a more generally accepted cast. *The Fate of Capua*, for which Dryden within less than a month of his death com-

---

[1] Acts iv and v.

[2] It was altered in 1759 by Hawkesworth, who followed Garrick in doing Southerne's reputation a service by suppressing his comic scenes.

[3] See Scott and Saintsbury's *Dryden*, vol. xviii. p. 179.—The hero of Mrs. Behn's novel and Southerne's tragedy, the noble Oroonoko, is, so far as I am aware, the original ancestor of a long line of descendants, with whom English fiction both on and off the stage has since become sufficiently familiarised. He is a Pagan full of all the Christian virtues who, after being dragged from his native kingdom in Africa into slavery on a West-Indian island, is there, after an unsuccessful attempt at revolt, cruelly put to death.—The passage,

'Do pity me,
Pity's akin to love,'

(act ii. sc. 2) has passed into a proverb. It is not very easy to bear with the stageyness of such passages as that in which the high-souled negro is prevailed upon to allow himself to be called Caesar. And near the end of the play Oroonoko soars to a sentiment of almost sublime absurdity:

'*Stan.* He has kill'd the Governor, and stabb'd himself.
Oroon. 'Tis as it should be now: I have sent his Ghost
To be a Witness to that Happiness
In the next World, which he denied us here.'

posed Prologue and Epilogue, is a fine blank-verse tragedy, which adequately treats an admirably chosen theme—viz. the self-immolation of the Senators of Capua before the surrender to Rome of the rival city which had so long adhered to the cause of Hannibal.   But this was insufficient for the public ; and the play was not successful.   It was followed by *The Spartan Dame* (1719), founded on Plutarch's *Life of Agis*, which cannot on the whole be pronounced its equal. This tragedy, which Southerne had commenced early in his career, but had laid aside by reason of the dangerousness of its subject, was, when actually published by him, for similar reasons weakened by large omissions.   Southerne's last play, the comedy of *Money's the Mistress*, acted in 1726, may be passed by, although it possesses some curious points.   Its plot is taken from the Countess Dunois' *The Lady's Travels into Spain*, and suits a novel better than a drama ; the scene is laid in Tangier, which had long ceased to be an English possession ; and the characters are unsympathetic. The thin gold of Southerne's fine talent had been beaten out in the tragedies of his manhood.

The Spartan Dame (1719).

Money's the Mistress (1726).

Hardly any other names of note remain to connect the tragic drama of the Restoration and Revolution with that of the 'Augustan' age.   A link of this sort may however be found in GEORGE GRANVILLE (from 1711) LORD LANSDOWNE [1] (1667 *circ.*–1735), the patron of Pope's early efforts—'Granville the polite,' whose unselfish amiability would entitle him to be remembered with equal propriety, in his character of a man of letters at all events, as Granville the modest.   Besides some harmless love-poetry which does not concern us here [2], and two not inelegant

George Granville, Lord Lansdowne (1667 *circ.*– 1735).

---

[1] *The Genuine Works in Verse and Prose of the Right Hon. George Granville, Lord Lansdowne.* 3 vols., 1736.—Granville, who had remained in retirement under William III, held office under Anne, and was one of the twelve Peers created by Oxford in 1711 on a memorable political occasion.   After the accession of George I he was confined for two years in the Tower, and soon after his release 'rallied' to the reigning family, who were reconciled to him, probably through the good offices of Mrs. Howard.   (See *Suffolk Letters*, vol. i. p. 228, *note*.)   He went abroad again in 1722, and resided in France for ten years.   He took no part in public affairs after his return, and died in 1735.

[2] In *The British Enchanters* (act iii. sc. 3) 'a Captive Lover' invokes the

contributions to the operatic drama [1], Granville produced,

His Heroic Love (1698).

in 1698, a tragedy, *Heroick Love, or The Cruel Separation*, to which Prologues were written by two eminent men respectively representative of two different ages—Dryden and Henry St. John (afterwards Lord Bolingbroke). This play, though written in blank-verse, may so far be regarded as a signal example of 'heroic' tragedy, that its whole action tends to turn on the one passion of love—the 'universal passion' truly of the tragic dramatists of this period. We here find 'True Love, Heroic Love,' defined as the affection which sacrifices itself for its object; and the heroine 'Chruseis' is described as

'the brightest Pattern of Heroic Love
And perfect Virtue, that the World e'er knew [2].'

For the rest, the story of Chryseis and Briseis is treated by Granville with a certain ingenuity, and with a degree of sentimental pathos to which Homer certainly remained a stranger. But though this tragedy is not altogether without merit—for the passion of Chryseis is touching, even though the craft used by Ulysses in arousing her jealousy cannot be described as profound—the love-sick King Agamemnon sinks into something very like a parody of passion, and is in no sense what he calls 'a gainer' by having exchanged his Homeric for a 'heroic' personality.

His comedies.

As a writer of comedy, Granville cannot be said to shine. His *Once a Lover and Always a Lover* (1736), which appears from the Preface to be a revised version of a juvenile piece, *The She-Gallants* (1696), has some resemblance to Congreve in style, with touches of the gaiety as well as of the licence of the great master [3]. Granville is, however, unequal to vigorous drawing of character. The comedy of *The Jew of Venice*, a version of *The Merchant* far from credit-

fictitious name of the lady to whom the author's early erotics were addressed by a song beginning,

'The happiest Mortals once were we;
I lov'd Mira, Mira me.'

[1] Cf. as to *The British Enchanters,* which was one of these, *ante,* p. 323.

[2] See the speech of Chruseis, act iii. sc. 2, and that of Ulysses, act v. sc. 2.

[3] Sir Toby Tickle, in whom, as the Preface shows, the author took pride as a character at once free from indecency and typical of the spirit of libertine gaiety that lingers in an old man, is really a colourless figure.

able to Granville's literary taste, has been mentioned in an earlier connexion [1].

Pope's name, as in truth the dominant one in his literary era, may be allowed to link with the mention of one of his early patrons those of two writers with whom, in different ways, he was constantly at war. This war was one of brave and bitter words—of which, so far as the attention of posterity is concerned, Pope's incomparable neatness of satirical invective usually secured to him the last. But of the two writers in question, one enjoyed a measure of contemporary consideration which goes very far towards accounting for Pope's anxiety to anticipate any comparison between their respective attempts in the same branch of literary composition [2]; while to the diligence and candour of the other it is possible to render justice, notwithstanding the vengeance which he brought down upon himself by falling foul in succession of the foremost wits of a brilliant, but signally quarrelsome, literary age.

AMBROSE PHILIPS (1675 c.–1740), although he published three tragedies [3], is as a dramatist remembered by one of these only, or rather perhaps on account of the celebrity acquired by the *Epilogue* bestowed upon it by the master-spirit of the little literary senate in which Philips had enrolled himself. The characteristically sentimental title of *The Distrest Mother* (acted in 1711) was not intended to conceal the fact that this tragedy was a version of the *Andromaque* of Racine ; but the efforts of Steele and Addison to buoy up its theatrical success have succeeded in securing to it a

Ambrose Philips (1675 c.– 1740).

---

[1] See *ante*, vol. i. p. 514.—The tragedies of another of Pope's patrons, as conspicuous for vanity as Granville is for modesty—viz. John Sheffield, Duke of Buckinghamshire—which likewise consisted in adaptations of Shakspere for the worse, and are noticed as such, *ib.* p. 515—fall in date a little outside the range of the present work.

[2] Pope's ironical comparison between the *Pastorals* of Ambrose Philips and his own may not uncharitably be held to have been suggested by an apprehension that the world might be disposed to compare the two efforts seriously.

[3] The titles of his remaining tragedies were *The Briton* and *Humfrey Duke of Gloucester*. The *Three Tragedies* were jointly printed under this designation in 1725.

place among the remembered productions of our dramatic literature [1].

John Dennis (1657–1733).

The redoubtable JOHN DENNIS [2] (1657–1733), who as a literary critic by no means deserves the contempt heaped on him by Pope, likewise endeavoured, by a series of works more or less original, to help to arrest that 'declension of Poetry' which he deplored as the antecedent of the down-fall of 'Liberty of Empire [3].' Among these, his dramatic efforts alone call for notice here. Beginning with a comedy judiciously mingling patriotism and party-spirit, *A Plot and No Plot, or Jacobite Credulity* (1697), which met with little success [4], he produced (in 1699) *Rinaldo and Armida*, a tragedy from Tasso, and in 1700, *Iphigenia*, founded on Euripides, which proved alike unfortunate; although the Prologue to the latter introduced the Genius of England, with a patriotic protest against the sway of Opera. Dennis has met with so hard a measure of judgment, that it may be well to state that his *Iphigenia* is free from absurdity, although its picture of the madness of Orestes is quite inadequate. In 1704 followed the tragedy of *Liberty Asserted,* which was successful, doubtless by dint of its direct appeal to national animosity and pride, the subject

---

[1] See *The Spectator*, No. 290, for a notice of the play by Steele (who had written the Prologue to it), supposed to be due to 'my friend Will Honey-comb's' having taken Mr. Spectator to a reading of it; and cf. Nos. 335 *seqq.* for the ingeniously contrived correspondence on the subject of the Epilogue to the tragedy, which Sir Roger de Coverley thought so incon-gruous—as well he might, with regard in particular to the lines telling how Hector—
> 'did commodiously on his wedding-day;
> While I, his relict, made at one bold fling
> Myself a princess, and *young Sty* a King.'

This Epilogue, attributed to Budgell, was, as already Dr. Johnson revealed, really written by Addison.—*The Distressed Mother* is reprinted in vol. i of *The Modern British Drama*.

[2] *The Select Works of John Dennis*, 2 vols., 1718. Talfourd's article on *John Dennis's Works* in *The Retrospective Review*, vol. i. part ii, confines itself to a notice of his labours as a critic, and of his alteration of *Coriolanus*. Cf. *ante*, vol. i. p. 524, concerning Dennis' views of Shakspere.

[3] See his *Essay on the Opera*, cited *ante*, p. 321, *note* 3.

[4] Bull senior and Bull junior (his son, just arrived from France) are the chief characters in this play.

being the war of the French and the Hurons against the Iroquois assisted by the English. After adapting *The Merry Wives of Windsor* and *Coriolanus* without advantage to anybody or anything concerned in either process, and adding to these at least one 'original' failure in *Gibraltar, or The Spanish Adventure* (1705), he brought out in 1709 his last drama, the tragedy of *Appius and Virginia*. It failed like so many other of his plays, but it remains unforgotten, owing to a satirical allusion by Pope, which was the beginning of many troubles,—and to an anecdote connected with the withdrawal of the play, which has given rise to the now proverbial phrase of 'stolen thunder[1].' Dennis not inaptly described *Appius and Virginia* by two epithets applicable to himself, when he called it 'this rough manly play.'

His Appius and Virginia (1709).

A few other names may be mentioned of authors of this age who wrote tragedies of one or other of the types of which the more conspicuous examples have been previously discussed. We do not know to which of these types, if to any, belonged the plays composed by JOHN EVELYN (1620–1706), which he read to Pepys, but of which no traces remain[2]. Among the adapters of Shaksperean tragedies were NAHUM TATE (1652–1715), who after continuing Dryden's great satire against the leader of the Whigs and the adversary of the claims of the Duke of York became the poet-laureate of William and Mary. Tate, who is more generally remembered in association with Brady as the reviser of the poets Sternhold and Hopkins, before adapting *Richard III*

Other tragic dramatists.

John Evelyn (1620–1706).

Nahum Tate (1652–1715).

---

[1] See *Essay on Criticism*, v. 584. The anecdote of Dennis' indignant exclamation on finding the new kind of thunder invented by himself, which had been set free by the withdrawal of *Appius and Virginia*, employed in *Macbeth*, is told by Dibdin, vol. iv. p. 357, and elsewhere. Though it may contain apocryphal elements, the story, like the thunder, is too good to be lost.—Virginius in this play seems to have been Betterton's last original part. Dennis is the 'Sir Tremendous' of Pope, Arbuthnot, and Gay's wretched farce *Three Hours after Marriage* (1717)—which gave rise to Pope's quarrel with Colley Cibber, and was the final cause of the substitution of the latter for Theobald as the hero of *The Dunciad*. See Cibber's *Apology*.—Besides the plays mentioned, Dennis produced a masque, *Orpheus and Euridice* (1709).

[2] See Pepys' *Diary*, November 5, 1665. Pepys thought the plays 'very good,' but not so excellent as their author seemed to 'conceit them to be.'

(1681), *Coriolanus* (1682), and *King Lear* (1687), as well as Fletcher's *Island Princess* (1687) and Webster's *White Devil* under the title of *Injur'd Love, or The Cruel Husband* (1707), and laying hands upon the works of other earlier dramatists of great or of mediocre repute[1], produced in his earlier days a tragedy—which is also called an opera— called *Brutus of Alba* (1678) inspired by Vergil, and a second, *The Loyal General* (1680), of which the originality has *Charles* not been disproved[2]. CHARLES GILDON (1665–1724), one *Gildon* of the Whig hacks who were the favourite objects of *(1665–* Pope's venomous invective, besides re-casting *Measure for* *1724).* *Measure*[3], produced among writings of almost every sort a sheaf of tragedies, partly founded on the efforts of previous *John Old-* writers, from Euripides to Lee[4]. A Whig author of more *mixon* substantial equipment, but who was aspersed with the same *(1673–* contempt from the same source, JOHN OLDMIXON (1673– *1742).* 1742), before he began his laborious career as a historical and political writer, essayed the paths of the drama, and, in addition to some attempts at pastoral and opera, produced a tragedy, called *The Governor of Cyprus* (1703), which (though it introduces a Moor) has no concern with Othello, and is founded on a contemporary novel[5].

John The most famous of all the prose romances of this period *Banks.* of Western literature supplied its theme, and lent its title, to the last of the series of tragedies perpetrated by JOHN BANKS[6]. His earlier dramatic efforts, with the exception

[1] Upon Chapman and Jonson in his *Cuckold's Haven, or An Alderman no Conjuror* (1685) and Cokayne in his *A Duke and no Duke* (1685).

[2] Genest, vol. i. p. 282, is inclined to think that the plot was borrowed from some romance, inasmuch as 'we seldom or never meet with a King of Greece' (a character in this play) 'except in a romance, or on the stage.'

[3] Cf. *ante*, vol. i. p. 514; cf. *ib.*, p. 524.

[4] Gildon is more generally remembered for what he said of others, than for what he copied from them. His *New Rehearsal, or Bayes the Younger* (1714), directed against the plays of Rowe, also fell foul of Pope. In 1699 Gildon put forth an enlarged edition of Langbaine's *Account of the Dramatick Poets*, as to which cf. *ante*, p. 389, *note* 4.

[5] *The Governour of Cyprus, or The Loves of Virotto and Dorothea.* See Genest, vol. x. p. 280.

[6] See a short notice of him by Mr. Gosse in vol. iii of *The Dictionary of National Biography* (1885). Of *Cyrus the Great* I speak from personal acquaintance.

of *The Unhappy Favourite* (1682), which treated the story of
Essex, appear to have been unsuccessful, although aspiring
high in the choice of their themes[1]; but his *Virtue Betrayed*
(1692), on the story of Anne Bullen, long kept the stage.
The last of his plays was *Cyrus the Great, or The Tragedy*   *His Cyrus*
of Love (1696), on a perusal of which I am obliged to base   *the Great*
                                                              (1696).
my opinion of his dramatic powers.   I see no reason for
differing from the judgment of the actors, who are said in
the first instance to have refused to perform the play.   In
Banks' blood-and-thunder version of a portion of the gentle
French author's romance no trace of refinement remains;
and this 'Tragedy of Love' (as it calls itself at the close),
with its ranting and raving declamation, its ghosts and its
charnel-house ending[2], severely appeals, like all such con-
coctions, to the sensations of the moment.

Another dramatist whose career—not perhaps altogether   *Edward*
unfortunately for him—was covered by that of Dryden, was   *Ravenscroft*
                                                           (d. 1692).
EDWARD RAVENSCROFT (*d.* 1692).   Although he adven-
tured, and as he opined with notable effect, an adaptation of
Titus Andronicus[3], Ravenscroft's activity chiefly lay in the
direction of the comic drama[4].   But, besides a tragi-comedy
on the perennial theme of *King Edgar and Alfreda* (1677),
he likewise produced in the latter part of his career a tragedy
entitled *The Italian Husband* (1697; printed 1698).   He
thought it a rather notable achievement to have constructed
this play in three acts; but they suffice for the working out of
its simple plot of adultery and revenge[5].   In point of fact,

---

[1] *The Rival Kings*, in emulation of Lee's *The Rival Queens; The Destruction
of Troy; The Innocent Usurper* (Lady Jane Grey), which was (perhaps
excusably) not allowed to be performed; *The Island Queens* reproduced as
The Albion Queens.

[2] 'Cyrus taking Abradatas' hand, offering to put it to his mouth, it comes
from the Body; Ponthea places it back again,' and explaining how much
trouble it had taken her to compose her Lord out of the remains scattered
about the battlefields, asks to be allowed to die in peace by his side.

[3] Cf. *ante*, vol. ii. p. 58.

[4] See below; and cf. my brief notice of Ravenscroft in vol. xlvii of *The
Dictionary of National Biography* (1896).   Dryden's quarrel with Ravenscroft
has inevitably served to keep the name of the latter alive, and has perhaps
directed an excess of attention to his plagiarisms.

[5] It is stated to be taken from a horrible tale in a collection by Thomas

it illustrates a not very uncommon experience,—viz. that of a play, theatrically effective, which reveals no trace of an attempt at characterisation, and no thought of style. Far different is the case of two tragic poets, whose literary history extends into a period beyond my limits, but neither of whom I should like to leave unmentioned. JOHN
John Hughes (1667–1720). HUGHES (1677–1720), who assisted Addison in his *Cato*, wrote no tragedy of his own before the death of Queen Anne, except a juvenile work that has never been published [1] ; and his only other contribution to the literature of the stage was the opera *Calypso and Telemachus* (1712). But the fine quality of his powers as a tragic dramatist was not long afterwards—in 1720—attested by his justly-celebrated play of *The Siege of Damascus*, for the plot of which he was unmistakeably indebted to D'Avenant's *The Siege* [2].
Aaron Hill (1685–1750). AARON HILL (1685–1750), although an author of very eccentric genius, whose pen was said to have treated every subject from the Creation to the Day of Judgment (both inclusive), had in him a nobility of soul which shut out anything impure or mean from his literary efforts [3]. The earliest only of his many tragedies—*Elfrid, or The Fair Inconstant* —falls within the scope of this book ; like *Clavigo* and *La Dame aux Camellias*, it was averred by the author to have been written within a week; perhaps the familiarity of the subject added wings to an inborn audacity [4].

Wright of Peterhouse, called *The Glory of God's Revenge against Murther and Adultery* (1685). The situation at the beginning of act ii of Ravenscroft's tragedy bears a certain resemblance to the famous scene (act v. sc. 1) in Rowe's *The Fair Penitent*. The *dénouement* is imagined with a strong sense of realistic effect.

[1] *Amalasont, Queen of the Goths.*

[2] Cf. *ante*, p. 329. Swift and Pope indulged in sneers at Hughes, who must be allowed to have incurred considerable hazard by remaining so respectable a Whig; but, whatever the wits might say, he had elevation of style.

[3] Aaron Hill's life is full of interest, and in many ways typifies the intellectual activity of the eighteenth century. His poem on *The Art of Acting* appeared in 1746, and the substance of it was afterwards elaborated by the author in a prose *Essay*. His connexion with the theatre and theatrical management, however, belongs to a much earlier part of his career; in the course of this period he wrote the libretto of *Rinaldo*, the first opera composed by Handel in England (1716).

[4] For an account of this play see Genest, vol. ii. p. 432.

I add a mention of some further names of writers by whom *Other tragic writers.* tragedies were produced in this period. WILLIAM MOUNT-FORT (*d.* 1692) was a celebrated actor, and his tragic death is justly remembered as casting a glaring light on the unhappy connexion between the stage and the dissolute manners of the age. The most interesting of his dramatic efforts, however, stands apart from my theme, and could hardly have been thought by himself likely to secure to him remembrance in literary history[1]. PETER ANTHONY MOTTEUX (1660–1718), whose active career in his adopted country as a man of letters[2] and playwright came to a malign end, wrote among many plays of more or less mixed species a tragedy, *Beauty in Distress* (1698). WILLIAM JOYNER (1622–1706), who as a convert to the Church of Rome had accompanied Lord Glamorgan on his critical mission to Ireland, was the author of *The Roman Empress*, a play acted with applause in 1671 and supposed by Langbaine to have been intended to treat, under changed names, the story of Constantine the Great, his wife and his son. Dryden wrote the Prologue, and Tate the Epilogue, to *The Mistakes, or The False Report* (1691) by JOSEPH HARRIS, an actor-dramatist upon whom this tragedy was rumoured to have been wrongly fathered, but who also produced other plays. THOMAS SCOTT'S *The Unhappy Kindness, or A Fruitless Revenge* (1697), was an alteration of Fletcher's *A Wife for a Month*. CHARLES HOPKINS' three tragedies, *Pyrrhus, King of Epious* (1695), to which Congreve wrote a Prologue, *Boadicea, Queen of Britain* (1697), and *Friendship Improved, or The Female Warrior* (1697), were so far as is known original works of an author the promise of whose powers was early wasted[3]. And, to end a very miscellaneous list,

---

[1] Some years before his death Mountfort brought out at Dorset Garden a farce called *The Life and Death of Doctor Faustus* (printed in 1697), a curious *farrago* of Marlowe and harlequinade, which must, however, have materially helped to keep alive the remembrance of a poetic theme of inexhaustible capabilities. See O. Francke's edition (Heilbronn, 1886), with its very instructive Introduction.

[2] His translation of *Don Quixote* long held its own.

[3] See Scott and Saintsbury's *Dryden*, vol. xviii. p. 161. Hopkins was the son of the Bishop of Derry, and served in King William's Irish wars.

it may be noticed that among the female authors who in this age obtained a literary reputation several were active as tragic dramatists. The list includes MRS. APHRA BEHN, to whom it will be necessary to return below, and MRS. MANLEY (*d.* 1724), the great society novelist of an age to which she should not be too severely condemned for having held up a mirror. Of her cleverness there can be no doubt, and if she had little consideration for the good fame of others, she had at least the courage of her intentions, and held her own not only by the fear she inspired. She wrote in this period two tragedies and one comedy; the former consisting of *The Royal Mischief* (1696) and *Almyna, or The Arabian Vow* (1707)[1]. MRS. PIX (1660–1720 *c.*), by birth Mary Griffith, came before the world as a tragic dramatist in the same year—1696—as the redoubtable Mrs. Manley, with the tragedy of *Ibrahim, the Thirteenth Emperor of the Turks*[2]; in 1698 followed *Queen Catharine,* and in 1701 *The Double Distress.* She was much associated with another female authoress of more attractive personality, to whom as to herself Congreve extended his goodwill. The tragedies of Catharine Cockburn who afterwards became MRS. TROTTER (1679–1749) belong to the earlier period of her literary life ; the latter, together with the history of her philosophic doubts, is exempt from notice here. Her *Agnes de Castro* appeared in 1695 ; her *Fatal Friendship* in 1698 ; and her *Revolutions of Sweden,* in which she is said to have been indebted to Congreve's advice, in 1706[3].

I have thought it permissible to reserve, for the conclusion of this necessarily incomplete outline of the history of English tragedy in the period reviewed in the present chapter, two names of eminence—the one in our dramatic literature, the other in our national literature at large.

---

[1] *Lucius, the first Christian King of Britain,* followed in 1720. All these plays are in the Dyce Library.

[2] ' When it was too late,' says Mr. Gosse, ' she discovered that she should have written "Ibrahim the Twelfth".'

[3] I have had no opportunity of acquainting myself with any of her plays except her comedy of *Love at a Loss, or Most Votes Carry It* (1701), which impresses me favourably by an unartificial sprightliness (if such a combination be thought possible) of tone.

NICHOLAS ROWE (1674–1718)[1] deserves to be remem- *Nicholas*
bered as a tragic dramatist on grounds more solid than *Rowe*
those which entitle him to an ' esteem ' such as too many of *(1674–
1718).*
his contemporaries have failed to secure. The success of
his literary career, which may be held to have culminated in
his appointment (just after the close of our period) to the
Poet-Laureateship, was due in part to his personal presence,
breeding, and training,— in part to his assiduous service in
the interest of the dominant political party to which he
remained consistently attached,—and very largely to the
versatility of his talents and to the modesty with which he
bore the successes of a singularly prosperous career. He
lived in one of those literary periods where a lively
interest in foreign works of note goes far towards conferring
distinction at home ; and he was so apt a translator, that his
Lucan might almost be described as the most popular of
his works. But posterity holds in most kindly remembrance
his unselfish interest in the greatest of our national poets,
and the stimulating influence exerted by his labour of love
upon the subsequent progress of the study of Shakspere's
life and works [2]. Rowe's general characteristics as a man of
letters reflect themselves with sufficient distinctness in his
tragic dramas, which in a single respect only—but that
a very important one—surpass the endeavours of the
foremost among his predecessors [3]. In dramatic power, as *His*
exhibiting itself in characterisation, he cannot be said to *qualities*
as a tragic
have excelled. Of a genuinely poetic touch he shows few *dramatist.*
signs. His plays are still occupied almost entirely with
themes of ' heroic love ' ; on this pivot everything is made to
turn, whatever other passions may be nominally brought
into play. In the invention of situations exciting terror or
pity Rowe is fertile and skilful ; he is fond of night-scenes,
and of all the outward machinery of awe and gloom. But
he rarely exhibits any natural force even in his most

---

[1] *The Works of Nicholas Rowe, Esq.*, 3 vols. (Third Edition, 1733.)
[2] Cf. *ante*, vol. i. p. 526.
[3] Rowe's solitary comedy, *The Biter* (1704), is quite worthless. Its scene
is laid among the ' humours ' of Croydon fair; its chief characters consist of
caricatures of an East India merchant, an old widow in search of a new
husband, and a ' biter,' or amateur of jokes, practical and other.

effective passages, and is wanting in impetus or in aspiring ardour, where some exceptional movement of the kind seems to be demanded by his theme. His most distinctive and most praiseworthy feature lies in the greater degree of refinement to which in expression if not in sentiment he has attained. Rowe is indeed far from being an English Racine; his style is too tame to rise to the dignified beauty and exquisite grace proper to the great French tragedian; but he is at least subject to none of those grosser influences which depressed the higher impulses of so many dramatists whose creative genius was not inferior to his own.

These characteristics will be found to recur with little variation in Rowe's five earlier tragedies, which, like their two successors, are written in blank-verse, though 'the ends of acts'—and occasionally of scenes or speeches—' still jingle into rhyme [1].' They may therefore for the most part be rapidly enumerated. In *The Ambitious Step-Mother* (1700) we are introduced to one of those Oriental palace-intrigues of which heroic tragedy was so fond. A plot against the elder brother's right to the throne is formed by the mother of the younger—Artemisa—whose politic practices bring about a large number of deaths, although she herself is left alive at the close. The story of this play is as good of its kind as anything to be found in Rowe; and in the self-sacrificing death of Cleone there is a touch of pathos [2]. *Tamerlane* (1702), the play upon which its author is said to have 'valued himself most,' chiefly interests us as treating one of the most famous themes of the Elisabethan drama. But most assuredly this Tamerlane would have caused supreme astonishment to Marlowe. In the place of the truculent hero of the old tragedy, with his 'high astounding terms,' we are here met by a calm, tolerant, nay philosophic prince, who discusses the common merits of varying forms of religion in a tone resembling that of Nathan the Wise, and whom the severest of personal trials hardly suffice to move from his temperate calm. Rowe, as he informs us, designed in this piece to draw two parallels —one between Tamerlane and William the Deliverer, the

His The Ambitious Step-Mother (1700).

Tamerlane (1702).

---

[1] Prologue to *Jane Shore.*   [2] Act iv. sc. 3.

other between Bajazet and Lewis XIV. As to Bajazet, inasmuch as he remains a prisoner all through the play and as under the circumstances of his position he behaves like a madman, he can hardly be held to be a parallel to anybody but himself[1]; as to Tamerlane, Gibbon's sneer disposes of the appropriateness of the comparison[2]. The plot is altogether without dramatic probability; everything as usual resolves itself into a love-story ; but even here the poet fails to rise to the height of his own situations; his efforts indeed are perceptible, but to borrow a phrase which he appears to affect, ' it wo' not be.' The next among Rowe's tragedies is by far the most celebrated of their number[3]. But in my opinion *The Fair Penitent* (1703), while sharing the general features that are so attractive in the works of Rowe, is not indebted for its extraordinary success to any special merit. It is to be feared that this success was not unconnected with the ghastly device of the first scene of the last act, where the unhappy heroine is discovered ' in a room hung with Black; on one side Lothario' (her seducer)'s ' Body on a Bier[4]; on the other, a Table, with a Skull and other Bones, a Book and a Lamp on it.' It would be an error to suppose that this play, the idea of which is borrowed from Massinger and Field's *The Fatal Dowry*[5], shows any sustained endeavour to trace the purifying power of penitence, or to rival the tender pathos of such an Elisabethan tragedy as Heywood's *A Woman Killed with Kindness*. Until she is brought face to face with her doom, the unhappy Calista fails to excite our sympathy[6], although ' the false

The Fair Penitent (1703).

---

[1] Fielding in a note to his *Tom Thumb* (act ii. sc. 1) very cleverly contrives at once to twit Rowe with the bombast of his Bajazet, and to compliment him on the general (comparative) moderation of his tragic diction.

[2] 'Except in Rowe's fifth of November play' (*Tamerlane* was for more than a century annually performed on this twofold Protestant anniversary) 'I did not expect to hear of Timour's amiable moderation.' (*Decline and Fall*, ch. lxv, *note*.)

[3] Genest enumerates a long series of revivals on the London stage, continuing till near the date of the publication of his work. The play was repeatedly translated into French ; and in 1780 Goethe and Corona Schroeter acted in Seckendorff's *Kallisto*, founded on a German adaptation of Rowe's tragedy. (Düntzer's *Life of Goethe*, English Translation, vol. i. pp. 385 *note*, and 390.)

[4] ' Is this that haughty, gallant, gay Lothario ?'   [5] *Ante*, p. 39.

[6] How poor is the soliloquy (act iii. sc. 1), where instead of awakening

Lothario' may excite our loathing. Nor is the plot managed with any great expenditure of skill. Its cardinal points are the dropping of a letter and an overhearing ; on the other hand, a certain attraction may have been found in the novelty of a purely domestic theme, and in the concentration of the action upon a very small number of persons— *Ulysses* less even than that which is usual in Rowe's plays. *Ulysses* (1705). (1705) may be coupled with Granville's *Heroic Love*[1] as a 'heroic' version of Homer. The plot pursues its path with a sort of relentless logic ; but it is difficult to follow the solution of the complex problem with decent vigilance. Eurymachus King of Samos loves Penelope ; Telemachus secretly marries Semanthe, a daughter of Eurymachus ; on his father discovering himself, Telemachus kills Eurymachus ; the Samians and Ithacans rise against Ulysses ; and Semanthe, by falsely accusing another of Penelope's suitors (Antinous) of her father's death, saves Ulysses and Telemachus from the wrath of their adversaries. Neither Ulysses himself, nor any of the other characters, is in the slightest degree interesting ; so that we have no recognition to spare for the perverse ingenuity which has foisted a commonplace intrigue into the broad course of the loved Homeric epos[2]. Even so, however, the familiar names lend a certain *The Royal* degree of interest to this production, as compared with *The* *Convert* *Royal Convert* (1707), where we have to make shift with (1707). Hengist the son of Hengist, his brother Aribert[3], the Christian maiden Ethelinda, the jealous Rodogune, and other Early English unrealities. The story is again one of fraternal rivalry in love ; Hengist being enamoured of his

---

sympathy by dwelling on her own misery, she enters into a general exposition of women's wrongs. In act iv. sc. 1, where the fatal discovery finally takes place, Calista's outburst of anguish can find vent only in five nouns substantive :

'Distraction! Fury! Sorrow! Shame! and Death!'

[1] *Ante*, p. 424.

[2] 'Minerva' appears as a *dea ex machinâ* rather early in the play (act iii. sc. 1).

[3] Gibbon, whose notices of Rowe illustrate the literary attention secured by this dramatist, surmises (ch. xxxviii and *note*) that he may have borrowed the character and situation of Rodogune from *Procopius*—no such Princess being mentioned by English writers.

brother's secret wife, whom the jealousy of Rodogune brings (*coram populo*) to the rack. The scene, however, where the Christian Ethelinda discourses to her Aribert—about to suffer death in her company—on the consolations of the Christian faith [1], reveals an elevation of sentiment to which Rowe rarely attains, and I cannot but think this passage superior to any but a few to be found in English tragedies attempting to treat the great theme of Christian martyrdom.

In Rowe's last two plays, *The Tragedy of Jane Shore* (1714) and *The Tragedy of the Lady Jane Gray* (1715), the latter of which properly falls outside the range of this work [2], he sought, to some extent at least, to follow a model whom he had done much to bring into honour. That as a critic of Shakspere he should still have been beset by the prejudices and hasty generalisations of his age, was a short-coming which none but a short-sighted and ungenerous judgment could deem discreditable to him. In the Prologue to his first play the utterly unwarranted assertion is made that Shakspere excelled in male characters only [3]; and, though it was precisely in female characterisation that Rowe in his latest plays still strove more especially to shine, he now professed to write in the style of the author whose merits he had thus early commended to the public, though with more warmth than completeness of judgment [4]. It must,

Jane Shore (1714) *and Lady Jane Grey* (1715).

---

[1] Act v. sc. 2.

[2] It was produced early in the reign of George I, to whom and whose family play and Epilogue contain pointed—not to say forced—allusions. In her dying moments Lady Jane Grey beseeches Heaven to send 'in Its due season the Hero who may save Its Altars from the Rage of Rome,' and adds a prayer that the Protestant succession may be kept up by a son with virtues equal to his father's. The Epilogue, with a still greater stretch of ingenuity, compares the self-sacrifice of the future Queen Caroline in 'adopting our Britain' to that of Queen Jane in dying for it.

[3] 'Shakespear, whose Genius, to itself a Law,
    Could Men in every Height of Nature draw,
    And copied all but Women that he saw.'
        Prologue to *The Ambitious Step-Mother*.
This reads like an imperfect reminiscence of Dryden's dictum that 'Shakespeare writ better betwixt man and man; Fletcher betwixt man and woman: consequently the one described friendship better, the other love: yet Shakespeare taught Fletcher to write love; and Juliet and Desdemona are originals.' (*The Grounds of Criticism in Tragedy*.)

[4] See the Prologue to *Jane Shore*, which, on the title-page, professes to be 'written in Imitation of Shakespear's Style.'

however, be observed that he did not proceed very far in the direction which he had thus shown himself inclined to look. In outward form no essential difference is perceptible between these two tragedies and their predecessors by the same hand, although the dialogue is marked by a higher degree of animation (irrespectively of the intermixture of a few 'by my halidomes' and 'by the Roods'). The subjects of these two plays are however happily chosen, and treated with natural dignity as well as with genuine feeling: so that in spirit if not in form Rowe certainly approaches Shakspere more nearly in these than in his remaining works. *Jane Shore*, though on the same theme and in part adopting the same treatment as that which it had received in Thomas Heywood's *Edward IV*[1], was apparently written in ignorance of that early play ; *Lady Jane Gray* owed something —but according to the author, very little—to some rough beginnings of a play on the same subject by a contemporary dramatist named Edmund Smith[2]. The sentiment of Rowe's tragedy is unequivocally Protestant ; but a wholesome breath of patriotic feeling pervades both this tragedy and its predecessor ; while the pathetic scenes, especially in *Jane Shore*, are admirably effective [3]. Both plays are therefore to be pronounced successful efforts in a sphere of tragic composition to which this author was naturally and legitimately attracted, and to which he brought the advantages of a trained experience and a natural judgment.

Lady Jane Grey, reading Plato's *Phaedon* before the news of her downfall comes upon her, irresistibly recalls the hero of the last tragedy to which I propose to refer in the

---

[1] Cf. *ante*, vol. ii. p. 555, and see *ib.* p. 557 *note*, as to *Jane Shore's* earlier appearances on the stage.—Rowe's tragedy would appear to have caused the reprinting, in the year 1717, of the song of *Jane Shore's Ghost*, to the tune of *Live with me*. (See Halliwell's *Notices of Popular Histories*, p. 38, in *The Percy Society's Publications*, vol. xxiii.)

[2] *The Innocent Usurper*, by John Banks (1694) treating the same subject, has been mentioned *ante*, p. 429, *note* 1.

[3] *Jane Shore* was accordingly frequently acted in the past and in the present century; and supplied a pathetic part to Mrs. Siddons. It was also translated into French. The late Mr. Wells produced a play on the subject in 1876.

present chapter. But *Cato*, the single dramatic composition of its illustrious author worthy of remembrance [1], is far from representing any intention on his part to co-operate with Rowe in bringing about a return to life and nature in English tragedy by a closer adherence to the example of Shakspere. JOSEPH ADDISON (1672–1719) had a warm admiration for Shakspere as a 'great natural genius [2],' and there are passages in his critical writings which prove him to have entered more closely into the great master's art than this commonplace conception might seem to imply. But as a productive dramatist he cannot be said to have added greatly to the lustre of a name in literature, as well as the political life of the age to which he belonged. His *His Cato.* tragedy of *Cato* was not originally destined for the stage. Addison had first thought of the subject before he left Oxford, had written the greater part of the tragedy on his travels, and had kept it in an unfinished state among his papers for seven years. He affirms that it was only by the persuasion of his friends that he was induced to let it try its fortune upon the stage, where (furnished with a Prologue by Pope and an Epilogue by Garth) it was first performed on April 14, 1713 [2].

The time at which *Cato* was thus produced was a season *Circum-* of the utmost political excitement, and a very critical period *stances of* in our history. Only eleven days previously—on April 3 *its produc-* —the news of the definitive conclusion of the Treaty of *tion (April* Utrecht had reached London. For the Tories this event *17,1713).*

---

[1] His opera of *Rosamond* (1707) has been incidentally mentioned *ante*, p. 323, *note*; his farce of *The Drummer, or The Haunted House* (1716), in which William Harrison is held to have co-operated with him, is almost equally frigid and (although Steele wrote that to mention its failure was to 'say a much harder thing of the stage than of the comedy') undeniably feeble. The character of Vellum in this play was stated by Addison to have been taken from that of the steward Savil in Beaumont and Fletcher's *The Scornful Lady* (*ante*, vol. ii. p. 668). As to Steele's criticism of *The Drummer* and its bearings on Addison's qualifications for dramatic composition, see Mr. Austin Dobson's *Richard Steele*, p. 188 ; and cf. as to this play Mr. W. E. A. Axon's *The Literary History of the Comedy of the Drummer* (Manchester, 1895). For an account of the actual occurrences on which the story of the play was taken, and the literature connected with it, see a note to *Memoir of Philip, Second Earl of Chesterfield* (1829), pp. 24–5 ; and cf. Pepys' *Diary* under date June 15, 1663, *et al.*

[2] See *The Spectator*, No. 160.

signified the consummation of their peace-policy, pursued
under great difficulties, although with a balance of public
sympathies in its favour; for the Whigs it involved the
sacrifice of many (though not as they maintained all) of
the results gained on the battle-fields of Europe, chiefly
by the genius of the great general Marlborough, who
after so long enjoying their confidence, had recently been
relegated by their opponents to what was very like a
splendid exile. A play on a subject of high classical
dignity, intended by Addison to bring English tragedy
into more perfect accordance with the purity of ancient
models, was by his friends seized upon for a political
party demonstration on an unprecedented scale[1]. It was
hoped, as Macaulay puts it [2], that 'the public would
discover some analogy between the followers of Caesar and
the Tories, between Sempronius and the apostate Whigs,
and between Cato, struggling to the last for the liberties of
Rome, and the band of patriots who still stood firm round
Halifax and Wharton.' The Tories, whether or not touched
in their consciences by Stamp Act and cognate reminiscences, were wise enough to adopt the contrary course to
that followed by their adversaries in the case of Sacheverell [3];
the theatre was accordingly filled with the adherents of
each party, alike determined to interpret the play as a compliment to themselves and their leaders. 'The numerous
and violent party-claps,' Pope wrote to his patron Sir
William Trumbull, 'of the Whig party on the one side of
the house were echoed back by the Tories on the other . .
and . . after all the applauses of the opposite faction, Lord
Bolingbroke sent for Booth, who played Cato, into his box,
and presented him with fifty guineas in acknowledgment
(as he expressed it) for defending the cause of liberty so

---

[1] Party performances—'bespoken' or otherwise set on foot—appear to
have been a fashion of the period.—See *The Wentworth Papers* in a letter
from Lady to Lord Strafford, dated December, 1711, in which she writes:
'There is a Play at Drury lain for all the Whigg toasts . . . I would have
had my sister Betty gon, because she is a Whigg.'

[2] Essay on *The Life and Writings of Addison*.

[3] In a contemporary letter (quoted in Macknight's *Life of Bolingbroke*,
p. 330, *note*) the Whigs are said to have expected from *Cato* an effect equal
to that of Sacheverell's sermon and trial.

well against a perpetual dictator [1].' The play ran during an entire month, and afterwards enjoyed a supplementary triumph at Oxford [2]. The criticisms of Dennis failed to destroy the popularity of the play ; which was performed at intervals down into the present century [3].

When we view this famous tragedy as it now lies dead and cold before us, and examine it, as we needs must, on its own merits, there remains surprisingly little to account for its unprecedented success. *Cato* is full of effective commonplaces, many of which are to this day current as familiar quotations ; but otherwise it would be difficult to find in it any distinguishing feature. Voltaire extolled it as the first English *tragédie raisonnable, i.e.* as the first in which the Rules had been observed with perfect obedience to them as based upon reason [4] ; but Dennis had some grounds for his remark, that by observing the Unity of Place the author had only contrived to render the action impossible. For, in order to accommodate his incidents to the Rules, Addison was obliged to exclude much that was essential to the action, while he included much that is not only non-essential but disturbing. It would be difficult to mention a drama in which the amatory episodes are more decidedly tedious and intrusive. Not less than six lovers appear in the piece, and at the close, as Schlegel points out, Cato, before dying, feels himself called upon like a good father in a comedy to arrange a brace of marriages. Moreover, with the exception of these arrangements, the hero of the tragedy is given nothing to do ; and where an original feature is added, its introduction is inopportune—thus, the apprehension expressed by Cato that he has been too hasty

Its characteristics as a drama.

[1] In allusion to the efforts at one time made by Marlborough to obtain a patent as Captain-General *for life.*

[2] For an account of this see Cibber's *Apology.* Addison generously gave all the profits of the play to the managers.

[3] The latest performance mentioned by Genest took place in 1811.

[4] Gottsched, the chief of the French school in Germany, composed *Der Sterbende Cato* (1732), in which he availed himself of the works of Addison and Deschamps. (Goedeke, *Grundriss,* i. 542.) The tragedy had been previously translated into Italian by A. M. Salvini (1714). Cf. Walker's *Historical Memoir on the Italian Stage* ; and see *ib.* the Appendices, *On the Cato of Addison and on the Catone of Metastasio,* and as to the short drama *Catone Uticense.*

in committing suicide, seems quite out of harmony with his Stoic opinions. Macaulay with his usual courage defends *Cato*, but cannot say more on its behalf than that it 'contains excellent dialogue and declamation, and that among plays fashioned on the French model, it must be allowed to rank high.' But even to this praise certain exceptions might with justice be taken. The language, like every page that came from Addison's pen, is transparently pure; but where can it be said to approach the grandeur of *Cinna*, or to sparkle like that pure stream from the Castalian fount which permeates the dramas of Racine, even when they fall short of the highest excellence within his reach? And if excellent dialogue means a lifelike interchange of speech—is even so much as this to be found in *Cato*? The popularity of Addison's tragedy was due in part to purely adventitious causes, in part to the singular esteem in which its author was held, and to the literary pre-eminence which he had already reached,—in some measure also, but in a proportionately small one, to its merits of purity of style and nobility of sentiment. Such as *Cato* was, it helped to make English tragedy pursue more resolutely than before the path into which it had unfortunately entered. We had now, it was thought, proved that we too could produce master-pieces in the Classical style; and any further acceptance of the traditions of the Elisabethan drama, however much the direct effectiveness of its creations might commend it to continued favour on the stage, could only mean retrogression. Thus, the play which Addison had written and which Voltaire eulogised, marks no doubt with incontestable definiteness an epoch in the history of English tragedy; but this epoch was one of decay, holding out no prospect of recovery by any signs easily admitting of interpretation.

Comedy.
Sir George Etheredge (1634-5 c.- 1691 c.)

Among the earlier comic dramatists of the Restoration period the first mention is justly due to SIR GEORGE ETHEREDGE[1] (born, according to computation from a

---

[1] *The Works of Sir George Etheredge—Plays and Poems.* Edited with Introduction by A. W. Verity, 1888. See also Mr. E. W. Gosse's admirable essay on Etheredge which first appeared in *The Cornhill Magazine* for March 1881, and is reprinted in his *Seventeenth Century Studies*.

passage in Dryden's *Epistle* to him[1] in 1635 or the following year, and stated early in 1691 to have 'died lately'). The extreme paucity of the extant biographical data concerning Etheredge indicates how very restricted was the publicity commanded in his day by the doings of a man about town, who caught the fancy of the time by the ease and gaiety of his dramatic writing, and whose familiarity with the language and manners of foreign countries (or perhaps I should be safer in saying, of France) recommended him for diplomatic employment during the three or four years that preceded the Revolution. Etheredge, whose earlier two plays date from the first decade of Charles II's reign, produced his third and last in the middle of the second ; of his life in England we know nothing further except that he was concerned in a disgraceful 'skirmish' with the watch, ending in the death of one of the revellers, and that not long afterwards he married a fortune and was knighted in consequence. In 1685 he was appointed to the post of resident at Ratisbon, where the Germanic Diet then provided opportunities to minor diplomatists according to their kind; as to Etheredge's doings of which the records are not calendared among our State-papers, a recently discovered *Letterbook* of his supplies information sufficient to serve as a commentary upon Dryden's waggish *Epistle*[2]. After the Revolution he seems to have fluttered back to Paris, where he died.

Etheredge's comedies possess, in their chronological progression, both importance and interest, as furnishing early—probably the earliest—examples of a style of comic dialogue which was of natural growth, and which owed much less than might at first sight be supposed to French examples. No doubt, Molière and other French dramatists with whose works Etheredge was familiar had initiated him into the uses of a light and graceful style. But he not the

---

[1] *Epistle IX* (vol. xi). It is in the same metre (and tone) as Etheredge's two letters to the Earl of Middleton, who had preceded him at Ratisbon.

[2] The *Letterbook*, of which Mr. Gosse was the first to make use, was discovered in the MS. room of the British Museum by Mr. Edward Scott.—Mr. Verity informs me that in 1896 he paid a visit to the Theological College (formerly the Scots' College of St. James) at Ratisbon, where Etheredge's library was said to be preserved, and actually found there several books with a notice in each that it had belonged to him.

less deserves credit for having, as he proceeded, modelled his diction not on the traditions of the exhausted English stage, but on the conversation of the society in which he lived, although no doubt animating his dialogue by more wit than that conversation can be supposed to have habitually displayed.　He wrote as a man of the world for men and women of the world, who flocked to his plays to see themselves in his comic mirror, and pointed the way to the style of English comedy, of which Congreve afterwards shone as the acknowledged master.　Of characterisation few traces are preceptible in Etheredge's comedies; and in this respect too he anticipated Congreve.　Thus, to quote a criticism of Dryden's which appears to have been intended for the earlier rather than for the later writer, 'being too witty himself, he could draw nothing but wits in a comedy of his; even his fools were infected with the disease of their author.　They overflowed with smart repartee, and were only distinguished from the intended wits by being called coxcombs, though'—as Dryden holds—'they deserved not so scandalous a name.'　An inevitable result of the limitations of Etheredge's dramatic workmanship was its imitability;—perhaps it may seem unfair to him to insist upon the fact, but it is I think true nevertheless, that the fine gentlemen and fops of Colley Cibber, who have been described as 'well-finished copies from the paintings of Etheredge,' are altogether, and not merely in point of elaboration, superior to their originals.

His comedies : The Comical Revenge, or Love in a Tub (1664).

Etheredge's first play, *The Comical Revenge, or Love in a Tub* (1664), was written in a mixture of prose and rimed couplets, and was therefore the earliest regular play in which the use of rime was actually attempted, unless its isolated application by Dryden in two passages of *The Rival Ladies* (1663) be taken into account[1].　Etheredge therefore was courageous enough to carry out in a regular comedy the innovation which D'Avenant had employed in an 'operatic' entertainment, and on behalf of which Dryden had argued; but there is no reason for attributing the success of the play to this element in its composition[2].

[1] See Gosse, *Seventeenth Century Studies*, p. 238.　Cf. *ante*, pp. 317, 347.

[2] Lord Chesterfield (*Letters to his Friends*, 1779, vol. iv. pp. 363–4), arguing

Their success was doubtless due to the realism of its prose scenes; although, as it seems to me, their excellence has been over-rated both in these latter days and when they were originally placed upon the boards[1]. The chief comic character is Sir Frederick Frollick's impudent French valet Dufoy,—a figure which has been no doubt justly held by Mr. Gosse to have been suggested to Etheredge by the Mascarille of Molière's early comedies[2]. The chief comic incident in the play is of a purely farcical sort.

She Wou'd, if She Cou'd (1668), was expected with extraordinary curiosity[3], and seems for a time at least to have met with the utmost success, although for some reason Etheredge could not during several years be prevailed upon to produce another play. In the ease and brightness of the dialogues which is throughout in prose, this comedy represents a distinct advance upon its predecessor; but the picture of life here offered amounts to little more than a breathless succession of passages of intrigue, which differ little if at all from one another; and among the characters we can hardly be said to be introduced to any one really distinctive type[4].

She Would, if She Could (1668).

against the monstrosity of using rimed verse as the vehicle of dialogue in comedy, says that in *Love in a Tub* Etheredge introduced 'the capital characters speaking in rhyme; but the public was offended at this insult offered to common sense, and, as an equitable avenger, irrevocably damned the piece.' Downes is the authority for its success; and Pepys saw it both in 1666 and in 1668.

[1] Mr. Gosse says that 'in the underplot, the gay, realistic scenes which give the play its sub-title . . ., Etheredge virtually founded English comedy, as it was successively understood by Congreve, Goldsmith, and Sheridan.'— In Roger North's *Life of the Lord Keeper Guilford* (*Lives of the Norths*, ed. 1826, vol. ii. pp. 232-3), the 'very action' of this comedy is said to be based on an affair of which the hero or victim was a Mr. Charles Crompton, a supposed natural son of Sir Henry North of Mildenhall.

[2] *L'Étourdi* (1658), *Le Dépit Amoureux* (1658), and *Les Précieuses Ridicules* (1659).

[3] See Pepys' *Diary*, February 6, 1668, where on the occasion of the first performance '1000 people' are said to have been 'put back that could not have room in the pit.'

[4] The following passage in this play (act ii. sc. 1) fairly describes the kind of life led by Etheredge's heroes, and the atmosphere in which the action of his comedies moves: 'Truly, you seem to be Men of great Employment, that are every Moment rattling from the Eating-Houses to the Play-houses, from the Play-houses to the Mulberry-Garden, that live in a perpetual

In *The Man of Mode, or Sir Fopling Flutter*, which was produced in 1676 with an Epilogue by Dryden, and was afterwards dedicated to the Duchess of York, Etheredge, whom Rochester and others had urged to put some of his superfluity of 'fancy, sense, judgment and wit' into yet one further play[1], undoubtedly reached his highest point of excellence as a comic writer. We have here a fully elaborated character in the celebrated personage of the hero 'the freshest Fool in town,' who deserves remembrance as one of the eldest and best-drawn of the long family of would-be-Parisian English fops who have embellished our comic stage[2]. And it would be unjust to deny that the humour of the conception is kept within bounds, so as to have deserved to fascinate the critics as well as delight the society to whom it came so closely home.

Sir Charles Sedley (1639 c.– 1728 c.). Even more signally honoured by his contemporaries—and perhaps with better reason, though little remains of him to warrant their praises—was SIR CHARLES SEDLEY[3] (1639 *circ.*–1701). King Charles II, whose notice he attracted

hurry.'—I may be wrong in not attaching importance to Mr. Gosse's suggestion, which seems to me far-fetched, that the movement of this comedy is founded upon a reminiscence of *Tartuffe* (1667).

[1] *A Session of the Poets.*

[2] Fopling is mentioned with other characters by 'gentle George' as 'charming the pit' in Dryden's *Mac Flecknoe*. Here is a specimen of his literary coxcombry :

'*Sir Fopling.* Writing, Madam, is a mechanic part of wit. A Gentleman should never go beyond a Song or a Billet.

Harriet. Bussié was a Gentleman.

Sir Fopling. Who, D'Ambois?

Medley. Was there ever such a brisk Blockhead?

Harriet. Not D'Ambois, Sir, but Rabutin. He who writ the Loves of France.

Sir Fopling. That may be, Madam : many Gentlemen do things that are below 'em.' (Act iv. sc. 1.)

In the amusing *Letter to Sir George Etherege*, already mentioned, Dryden is likewise highly complimentary to his friend's comic wit. In his lines to Congreve, he briefly extols the 'courtship' of Etheredge.—The title of Marvell's *Mr. Smirke, or The Divine in Mode* (published in 1676) seems to have been due to *The Man of Mode* (where Mr. Smirk, a parson, appears as a subordinate character).

[3] *The Works of Sir Charles Sedley in Prose and Verse.* With [extremely brief] Memoirs of the Author's Life. 2 vols., 1778.—See also my biographical notice of Sedley in vol. li of *The Dictionary of National Biography* (1897).

soon after the Restoration, told him that ' Nature had given
him a patent to be Apollo's viceroy.' Buckingham spoke
of his ' witchcraft '; Shadwell testified to the extraordinary
wit of his conversation as well as to his literary merits;
Rochester attributed to him

> ' that prevailing, gentle art
> That can with a resistless charm impart
> The loosest wishes to the chastest heart';

and Dryden, who saluted him as the Tibullus of his age[1],
ensured him a lasting remembrance as the Lisideius of the
Essay of Dramatic Poesy. Sedley, as it is needless to adduce
evidence to prove, was commonly accounted one of the
most notorious profligates of the most dissolute period of
Charles II's reign; but he was a capable politician of
moderate views, and gained distinction in more than one
branch of literature.   His lyrics[2] contain occasional turns
of a felicitous and engaging simplicity, such as is not
generally observable in his plays; and he wrote a facile and
clear style as a prose pamphleteer.

Sedley's plays comprise two tragedies and three comedies, *His tra-*
of which the former may be very briefly dismissed. *Antony* *gedies.*
and Cleopatra (1667, reprinted in 1702 under the title of
Beauty the Conqueror, or The Death of Marc Antony) was,
in Shadwell's opinion, ' the only Tragedy (except two of
Jonson's and one of Shakespear's) wherein Romans are
made to speak and do like Romans.' Nothing more frigid
and feeble than this ' heroic tragedy' (in rimed couplets)
could well be imagined; it is as unworthy of comparison
with Dryden's as it is with Shakspere's play on the subject[3].
Sedley's play is the latest example of the English rimed heroic
drama[4]; a large proportion of triplets being, according to his
wont, interfused.   His other tragedy, *The Tyrant King of*

---

[1] See the *Epistle Dedicatory* to *The Assignation.*
[2] They include the pretty song, ' Phillis is my only joy.'
[3] The action, which as to *extent* is conducted on the same plan as Dryden's
(cf. *ante*, p. 372), is managed without skill; and Antony takes a most un-
conscionable time dying (through two scenes).   The length to which the
catastrophe is carried was probably the reason for the sub-title under which
the play was reprinted.   What interest the play possesses, lies chiefly in
the part of Octavia; but the rhetoric nowhere rises to passion, although the
dialogue is here and there epigrammatically pointed.
[4] See Gosse, *Seventeenth Century Studies*, p. 236.

Crete (1702), is nothing more than an alteration of Henry Killigrew's *Pallantus and Eudora* (1653)[1]. It is in blank verse.

His Comedies: The Mulberry Garden (1668).

Of the comedies, *The Mulberry Garden* (1668), which is partly founded on Molière's *L'École des Maris*, is, like Etheredge's *The Comical Revenge*, written in a mixture of prose and heroic couplets, and resembles that author's *She Would if She Could* in its 'rambling' character—to use an adjective of frequent occurrence in Sedley's piece[2]. *The Mulberry Garden*, which is supposed to play about the time of Monck's declaration in favour of the Restoration, is in my judgment a very worthless example of the class of comedy to which it belongs.

Bellamira, or The Mistress (1687).

Bellamira, or The Mistress (1687), founded on the *Eunuchus* of Terence, is the most licentious, but also from a literary point of view, the most successful of Sedley's plays. Nor in truth can the picture of the *faux ménage* of Bellamira[3], notwithstanding the grossness of the situation, be censured as altogether unwholesome satire. Finally, *The Grumbler*, printed in 1702, but not acted till many years after the author's death[4], was a mere translation or adaptation from Brueys and Palaprat's *Le Grondeur*. The character of Grichard, which was the invention of Brueys, is in the English version all but devoid of humour, and not even distantly approaches the immortal Croker of Goldsmith's *The Good-natured Man*.

The Grumbler (*pr.* 1702).

A word of notice may likewise be given to the comedies

---

[1] *Ante*, p. 163. Langbaine thinks that the resemblance to *Pallantus and Eudora* would be found greater than to *The Conspiracy* (1638) of which this was a revised reproduction.

[2] One of the scenes of *She Would, if She Could* (act ii. sc. 1) is laid in the Mulberry Garden.—Pepys, who 'could not be reconciled' to Sedley's play, finding in it 'only here and there an independent piece of wit, and that is all,' as in duty bound visited the Mulberry Garden itself, and found it 'a very silly place, worse than Spring-garden, and but little company in it, only a wilderness here that is somewhat pretty.' (Its site was that of the present Buckingham Palace.) See Pepys' *Diary*, May 20, 1668.

[3] The character is supposed by Genest (vol. i. p. 453) to have been pointed at the Duchess of Cleveland, with an incidental allusion to her amour with Churchill.

[4] It was brought out as a farce at Drury Lane in 1754, and this or the original was again adapted by Goldsmith for Quick's benefit.

which remain to us from the hand of JOHN LACY[1] (who
died in 1681), though it was as an actor rather than as an
author that he acquired his chief celebrity. He appears
to have begun his London life in 1631 by apprenticing
himself to Ogilby[2] in his capacity of dancing-master; nor
is it unlikely that the pupil imbibed from his teacher some
literary tastes or ambitions into the bargain. During the
Civil War, Lacy held a commission in the Royal army, and
gained an experience which he afterwards turned to account
for his extremely realistic comedy of *The Old Troop*. After
the Restoration he returned to the stage, where he became
an established favourite, and at times presumed upon the
goodwill which he enjoyed[3]. He died in 1681.

John Lacy (d. 1681), actor and dramatist.

   Lacy's comedies—both those which are adaptations and
those which are so far as we know original—possess a certain
interest as showing what kind of entertainment so experienced
a comedian thought most likely to suit the tastes of the
public for whom he catered. While he delighted the King
and Court by his performances, and was in at least one
prominent instance equally successful as a tutor of his art
(Nell Gwynn is said to have owed to him her first instruction
as an actress), in the style and general character of his productions he consulted the tastes not only of the exalted
personages to whom some of his plays are dedicated, but
also of his 'friends of th' upper region[4]' in the playhouse.
In other words, he is uniformly and unblushingly coarse, and
whatever he has of wit is lost in his grossness. *The Dumb
Lady, or The Farrier made Physician* (1669) is concocted

His adapta-tions.

   [1] *The Dramatic Works of John Lacy, Comedian.* With Prefatory Memoir
and Notes. (By James Maidment and W. H. Logan.) 1875.
   [2] Cf. *ante*, p. 96.
   [3] See Pepys' *Diary*, April 15 and 16, 1667, as to the King's annoyance at
the liberties taken by Lacy in the part of a country-gentleman come up to
Court, in Edward Howard's *The Change of Crowns* (*ante*, p. 396). Lacy
was arrested, and the company prohibited from acting. On his release he
insulted Howard and a fresh interdict was laid on the company.
   [4] See the rather happy Prologue to *The Old Troop*, which appeals to the
'gods' as against the critics in 'box and pit.' Let the latter deal with 'their
match, their Dryden wit,' the present poet is 'for the censure' of different
judges:
           'Let wits and poets keep their proper stations;
           He writes to th' terms, I to the long vacations.'

out of Molière's *Le Médecin malgré lui* and the same
author's *L'Amour Médecin*. *Sauny the Scot, or The Taming
of the Shrew* (1667) is a less endurable adaptation of Shakspere, whose Grumio Lacy has converted into a Scotch—or
would-be Scotch—serving-man, and the close of whose
comedy he has 'strengthened' by an incident probably
suggested by the last scene of Fletcher's *The Woman's
Prize, or The Tamer Tamed* [1]. In *The Old Troop, or
Monsieur Raggou* (1665), of which Langbaine rather unreasonably suspects the originality, Lacy is quite on native
ground, and paints (or daubs) a picture probably not wholly
unlike an aspect of life which he had had good opportunities
of studying during the Civil Wars. The humours of a
troop of Royalist soldiers, with its Plunder-Master-General,
its French cook Monsieur Raggou [2], and its other appen-
dages, are contrasted with the terrors of the country folk,
raised to a climax by the threat of cannibalistic requisitions [3],
and with the organised hypocrisy of a Roundhead garrison.
The whole furnishes a sufficient illustration of the extent to
which, at the commencement of the reign of Charles II, the
nation had grown sick of soldiers and soldiering; manifestly,
the public was prepared to applaud even a very unflattering
sketch of the art of war. *Sir Hercules Buffoon, or The
Poetical Squire* (printed 1684) is Lacy's most ambitious
effort. In the chief personage of the play he has made
something like an attempt at an original character—*viz.*
that of an insolent lying braggart, with an egregious fool of
a more ordinary type for his son. But though not alto-

*His The
Old Troop,
or Monsieur
Raggou
(1665).*

*Sir Her-
cules Buf-
foon, or
The Poeti-
cal Squire
(1684).*

---

[1] Cf. *ante*, vol. i. p. 514; and vol. ii. p. 709.

[2] Monsieur Raggou's notion of the considerations which should regulate
the purchase of a gentleman's apparel is economical enough to admit of
quotation : 'Buy shart!—who see my shart?'

[3] Captain Wildrake, in Scott's *Woodstock*, vol. ii. ch. 2, refers to 'Lacy, who
was an old play-actor, and a lieutenant in ours,' as having made 'drollery'
on the supposed requisition of 'roasted babes or stewed sucklings'; and in
a note Scott quotes the scene from act iii of *The Old Troop*, which, as he
says, Swift had not perhaps forgotten, when recommending 'the eating of the
children of the poor as a mode of relieving the distress of their parents.'
Gibbon (ch. lviii and *note*) speaks of the 'cannibal hunger' of the Crusaders
as having been 'sometimes real, more frequently an artifice or a lie,' intended
to terrify the infidels.

gether devoid of wit[1], the comic parts of the play possess only relative merit, while the serious action exhibits very little of either power or pathos[2].

Concerning EDWARD RAVENSCROFT, already noticed among the tragic dramatists of the period[3], little need be added as a writer of comedies, in which capacity he first came before the public, with the play which proved the occasion of his quarrel with Dryden. *Mamamouchi, or The Citizen turned Gentleman* (1671) was founded on Molière's *Le Bourgeois Gentilhomme*, with a side-indebtedness to his *Monsieur de Pourceaugnac*; and proved an unmistakeable success. From the latter comedy were also taken two scenes in *The Careless Lovers* (1673). And so in a better comedy, *The Wrangling Lovers, or The Invisible Mistress* (1676) and *Scaramouch* (1677), and again in the outrageously farcical *The London Cuckolds*, the action of which was taken from half-a-dozen sources, but was not the less acceptable to its annual city patrons, and in a few other more decorous compositions, Ravenscroft unblushingly continued his system of literary conveyance. He was a denizen of that theatrical back-alley in Grub Street, which leads its literary life without thinking much evil except of those who criticise its conditions. Then, as is not unnatural, a Ravenscroft turns against a Dryden, frankly unconscious of the difference between them.

Edward Ravenscroft (d. 1692).

PETER ANTHONY MOTTEUX'S numerous plays[4] included one or two comedies, but the larger number belonged to one or other of the mixed dramatic speech with which the facile Frenchman—whose linguistic abilities must have been considerable—was largely instrumental in familiarising the English public of the day.

Peter Anthony Motteux (1660– 1718).

---

[1] A specimen will suffice to indicate its level. Sir Hercules confesses he would 'rather be thought an Atheist than not a Wit.' It is indeed, says his uncle the Alderman, 'impossible to part those two sins.' 'The truth is,' remarks Sir Hercules, 'they are linked together like sausages.' 'Ay,' is the reply, 'and they will fry together like sausages one day.'

[2] A wicked uncle tries to defraud his nieces—one of whom talks a guileless Yorkshire—of their inheritance, in order to secure it for his daughters. But he is defeated by the virtuous exertions of his own offspring.

[3] Cf. *ante*, p. 429.   [4] Cf. *ante*, p. 431.

If the authors enumerated in the last pages may—probably with little injustice to any one of them—be described as having 'trod the stage loosely,' what remains to be said of an authoress who shared with them the applause of their age? 'The divine Astræa,' Mrs. APHRA BEHN (1640– 1689)[1], was the writer of comedies which, in conjunction with her other plays, are too numerous to mention ; but some of them at least deserve a signal share of the censure which has loosely attached itself to her literary activity as a whole. For she was a novelist who, besides writing much that one would desire to forget, at times, as in her *Oroonoko*[2], displayed a high spirit worthy of praise, and for lyrical poetry some of the songs interspersed in her plays show her to have possessed a genuine gift[3]. In addition, she was a busy pamphleteer ; indeed she had at one time been employed by the Government of Charles II as a political agent or spy in Holland, nor was it until she found her services in this capacity left unpaid, that she resorted to the profession of letters. In this profession she in her lifetime certainly held a leading position ; and in truth not many among those who associated with her, and whose names are mentioned with honour, where hers is waived aside as unfit for such company, could have afforded to throw stones at her reputation. As usual, Dryden was magnanimous enough to recall this fact, in words written many years after her death[4]. But although, as Sir Walter Scott with

---

[1] *Plays Written by the Late Ingenious Mrs. Behn.* (Pearson's Reprint.) 4 vols., 1871.   [2] *Ante*, p. 422.

[3] See the song 'Love in fantastick Triumph sat,' which opens the tragedy of *Aldelazar, or The Men's Revenge*, an adaptation of *Lust's Dominion* (*ante*, vol. i. p. 360).

[4] They have been already cited. Writing to Mrs. Elizabeth Thomas in 1699, he expressed his certainty that she would avoid the licence which Mrs. Behn allowed herself, 'of writeing loosely, and giveing, if I may have leave to say so, some scandall to the modesty of her sex. I confess, I am the last man who ought, in justice, to arraign her, who have been my self too much a libertine in most of my poems ; which I shou'd be well contented I had time either to purge, or to see them fairly burn'd.' (Dryden's *Works*, edd. Scott and Saintsbury, vol. xviii. p. 166.) Sir Walter Scott mentions in a note to this passage that an aged lady, a relation of his, 'assured him that in the polite society of her youth, in which she held a distinguished place,' the plays and novels of Mrs. Aphra Behn were accounted proper reading ; and 'she added, with some humour, it was not till after a long interval, when

his usual inimitable kindliness of humour pointed out
with regard to this very writer, much of the change which
her literary reputation has undergone must be placed to
the account of an advance in manners, while not a little of
her literary infamy is due to the sting of Pope, the treatment her name has experienced cannot in candour be said
to be undeserved. That one of the very grossest offenders
against decency, by a licence which seems directly designed
both to inflame and to shock, should have been a woman,
may have been her misfortune; but this plain fact goes far
towards justifying the obloquy which has been the grave
of her literary reputation. Nearly all Mrs. Behn's plays—
fifteen out of seventeen—were written before the Revolution of 1688. Her earliest tragedy, *The Young King*,
remained unperformed and unprinted; it is said to have
been based on one of the novels of La Calprenède. In her
first comedy, *The Amorous Prince* (1671), she struck the
vein which she worked with so conspicuous an energy, and
of which such later comedies as *The Roundheads* (1682) and
The Rover, or The Banished Cavaliers (1677 and 1681)
may be cited as examples[1]. Several of her plays are
versions of previous French or English works; others may
be original; and not a few of them, as it seems to me,
entitle their authoress to the praise of uncommon ingenuity
in the contrivance of stage-situations, so that it would be
quite unjust to attribute her theatrical popularity to the
licentiousness which made so many of her plays attractive
to their audiences. But it is not necessary to enter upon
an analysis of her dramatic productions, in order to show
that the judgment usually passed upon them may admit
of qualifications, although the reproach cannot be lifted
that justly rests upon her name.

Mrs. Behn was, as noted above[2], by no means the only *Other*
female dramatist of her age; but I need not pause on *female comic dramatists.*

she looked into them, at the age of seventy, that she was shocked with their
indecorum.'

[1] Of these and other plays of Mrs. Behn the reader who may prefer to
obtain some knowledge of her comedy at second-hand, will find a brief
notice in vol. i of *The Retrospective Review*.   [2] *Ante*, p. 432.

Mrs. MANLEY'S solitary comedy, *The Lost Lover, or The Jealous Husband*, performed without success in 1696; or on the comedies of Mrs. PIX, among which *The Innocent Mistress* (1696) is written under the influence of Etheredge, from whose *Man of Mode* some of its incidents seem borrowed, and of Congreve, most of whose comedies had by this time been produced. 'The celebrated Mrs. Centlivre' will be briefly noticed nearer the close of this chapter.

Thomas D'Urfey (1653–1723).

The literary nadir of Restoration comedy—and indeed of the Restoration drama in general—was perhaps (though a positive assertion would be hazardous) reached in THOMAS D'URFEY (1653–1723). Of distinguished literary descent—for his uncle Honoré d'Urfé was the author of the famous *Astrée*—he seems to have derived from his French blood a persistent amiability, which Tom Brown failed to upset and Jeremy Collier could scarcely disturb. Nor can it be denied that his songs amused four successive monarchs and their lieges, in the houses of the nobility, on the race-course, in the tavern, and in the theatre[1]. His dramatic activity proper, however, calls for no detailed review. He adapted, or borrowed from, Shakspere, Chapman, Marston, Beaumont and Fletcher, Shirley, Marmion, Dryden, and doubtless many others, besides occasionally attempting original works; and he wrote altogether twenty-nine plays which were acted, and three which were not, comprising tragedies, comedies, operas serious and comical, and burlesques and extravaganzas under divers designations[2]. He appears to have given a large amount of pleasure to great and small in his day—which was a long one—and to have been no very

---

[1] See Mr. J. W. Elsworth's admirable sketch of him in vol. xvi of *The Dictionary of National Biography* (1888).

[2] His *New Operas* (1721) comprise a sequel to *The Rehearsal* entitled *The Two Queens of Brentford, or Bayes no Poetaster*, containing some allusions to the South Sea excitement (the Epilogue is a Trialogue between the Sun, the Rain, and the North Wind, under the names of Mississippi, Directius, and Bubble); a tragedy, *The Grecian Heroine, or The Fate of Tyranny* (written 1718), which is in blank-verse and ends with a blessing on 'the happy Revolution'; and a trashy opera, *Ariadne, or The Triumph of Bacchus*, in a variety of metres. These are the only plays of his which I remember to have seen.

conspicuous sinner against a propriety which could hardly be expected to form part of his stock-in-trade.

It has been the unenviable lot of THOMAS SHADWELL[1] (1640–1692) to be remembered by later ages chiefly as the butt of some of Dryden's most ruthless wit. Formerly friends and literary associates[2], they had been separated by politics; and when Dryden had produced his masterpieces of political satire in the *First Part of Absalom and Achitophel* and *The Medal* (with a prose *Epistle to the Whigs*), Shadwell retorted with a now forgotten answer, *The Medal of John Bayes,* and with a prose *Epistle to the Tories.* Dryden's revenge was *Mac Flecknoe, or A Satire on the True Blue Protestant Poet, T. S.*, and the grosser caricature of Og in the *Second Part of Absalom and Achitophel.* It was not however in vain that Shadwell (to borrow the pious eloquence of his son) had in his dramas 'studied to serve his Country, rather than raise himself by the low Arts then in Practice'; for 'he succeeded so well in his Design, as to merit the Honour of being made Poet Laureat and Historiographer Royal upon the Revolution by King William and Queen Mary.' Nor can it be denied that, as times went, he had deserved the reversion of the rather dusty laurel. He lived only a year or two to enjoy it; but on his death, which took place in 1692[3], he found a resting-place in Westminster Abbey, where the critical spirit or the political resentment of

Thomas Shadwell (1640–1692).

His life and politics.

---

[1] *The Dramatic Works of Thomas Shadwell. With a Prefatory Memoir by his Son.* 4 vols., 1720. The memoir is in part rather naïvely written, as where the younger Shadwell says of his father: 'He had not only a strict Sense of Honour and Morality, but likewise (particularly in his latter days) a true Sense of Religion too.'—A good account of Shadwell's plays will be found in *The Retrospective Review* (Second Series, vol. ii).

[2] Shadwell joined Crowne and Dryden in the attack upon Settle's *The Empress of Morocco* (1673); cf. *ante*, p. 397; in 1676 Dryden was spoken of by Shadwell in the Preface to his *The Humorists* as the author's friend; in 1679 he wrote a prologue for Shadwell's *The True Widow.*

[3] It was attributed to an overdose of the drug to which Dryden had not spared an allusion in the character of Og.—I do not know why Miss Strickland should call Shadwell specifically 'Mary's laureate.' He had sung her husband's and her own coming into England in an Ode apiece.

a Tory prelate had to content itself with revising his epitaph [1].

His The Sullen Lovers, or The Imper- tinents (1668).
In the Preface to his first comedy, *The Sullen Lovers, or The Impertinents* (1668), which is founded on *Les Fâcheux* of Molière, Shadwell extols Ben Jonson as 'the Man, of all the World, I most admire for his Excellency in Dramatick Poetry.' In his next comedy, *The Humourists* (1671), he appears as a genuine imitator of the old master for whom, in the Preface, he again avows his reverence [2]. All the characters are succinctly defined in the list of *dramatis personae*.

The Humour- ists (1671).

The Virtuoso (1676).
The same model is followed in *The Virtuoso* (1676), which is in part a very amusing comedy. Among the chief characters are Snarl, who conceals his disreputable present under the cloak of angry laudations of the past [3],—Sir Formal Trifle, a concoctor of absurdly pedantic phrases, after inditing which he expressed a hope (aside) that he has been 'florid and precise,'—Sir Nicholas Gimcrack the Virtuoso, whose 'scientific' vagaries remind us that we are in the early days of the Royal Society satirised by Butler [4],—and Sir Samuel Hartly, who claims to rank as a wit by virtue of a free expenditure of bluster and 'by-words [5].'

Epsom Wells (1675).
Another comedy in the Jonsonian style is *Epsom Wells* (1675), although the resemblance to *Bartholomew Fair* (noted by Dibdin [6]) is not very strong. The most amusing

---

[1] Part of it, as originally written by Shadwell's son, ran :

> 'Majori enim sibi laudi duxit
>   Bonus Civis haberi
> Quam Principibus Poetis inseri.'

[2] 'Nor let false friends seduce thy mind to fame
  By arrogating Jonson's hostile name;

. . . .

  Thou art my blood, where Jonson has no part :
  What share have we in nature or in art?'   *Mac Flecknoe.*

[3] Thus he will not see plays, for 'he thanks God, he has seen 'em at Blackfriars.'

[4] Sir Nicholas learns the art of natation on a table—'I content myself with the speculative part of swimming, I care not for the Practic. I seldom bring anything to Use; 'tis not my way. Knowledge is my ultimate end.' (Act ii.)—A pleasant allusion to this quip will be found in Dr. Aikin and Mrs. Barbauld's *Evenings at Home.*

[5] *e. g.* 'Hey! pull away, Rogues; in the twinkling of a Bed-staff: a witty way I have of expressing myself.'

[6] Vol. iv. p. 181.

character in the piece is Clodpate, the London-hating country-gentleman, well defined in the *dramatis personae* as 'a hearty, true English coxcomb.' But *Epsom Wells* can hardly be described as more than a comedy of manners— while its coarseness is utterly revolting[1].

Passing by certain of Shadwell's plays which can in no sense claim to be called original[2],—together with the comedy of *A True Widow* (1679), noteworthy only for the odd picture which it introduces on the stage of the stage itself[3], and that of *The Woman-Captain* (1680)[4],—we come

A True Widow (1679).

The Woman-Captain (1680).

---

[1] Dryden, in *Mac Flecknoe*, insinuates that Sedley (who wrote the Prologue to this play) 'loaded with wit' Shadwell's 'hungry Epsom prose'; but there seems no foundation for the charge. Shadwell in acknowledging Sedley's revision of *The True Widow* expresses a wish that all his plays had had the same advantage.—In his *Character of St. Evremont* (*Works*, edd. Scott and Saintsbury, vol. xviii. p. 16 and *note*), Dryden says that he 'gave to some of our coarsest poets a reputation abroad which they never had at home.' In his *Remarks on English Comedy* (1677) St. Evremont had singled out *Epsom Wells* for a complimentary reference.

[2] The 'tragi-comedy' of *The Royal Shepherdess* appears to have been merely a revision of the work of another author (Fountain). *Psyche*, a 'tragedy' (1674), should rather be called an opera. The author says in the Preface: 'I had rather be author of one Scene of Comedy, like some of Ben Jonson's, than of all the best Plays of this kind, that have been, or ever shall be written.' The story is the old one from Apuleius, with 'a few externals' borrowed from Molière; the writing is devoid of merit. *The Libertine*, a tragedy (1676), purports to be derived from *Il Ateista Fulminato*,—the source of part of Cokayne's Ovid (cf. *ante*, p. 488),—but appears to contain details not in Molière, with whose *Le Festin de Pierre* Shadwell must of course have been also acquainted (cf. *ante*, p. 315, *note*). Don John's comic servant Jacomo has the familiar features of Leporello (Sganarelle in Molière). The play is sensational enough to satisfy the robustest appetite, and its most exciting scene impressed itself upon the popular imagination : ''tis like eating with the Ghost in *The Libertine*,' says Novel in Wycherley's *The Plain Dealer* (act ii. sc. 1). *The Miser* (1671) had been avowedly founded on Molière, though Shadwell considers himself to have added so much that he 'may call more than half the play his own.' (Fielding's *The Miser* (1733) was likewise based on *L'Avare*.) *The History of Timon of Athens, the Man-Hater* (1678) is Shakspere's tragedy, which, says Shadwell, 'I can truly say, I have made into a play.' (Cf. *ante*, vol. ii. p. 180.)

[3] In act iv, where (with less elaboration, however, than in the first act of M. Edmond Rostand's clever *Cyrano de Bergerac*) a play-house is represented and part of a play within the play is acted. 'Several young Coxcombs fool with the Orange-Women.' Prig proposes a game at 'Lang-trilloo' 'in the Box.' Women come in masked.

[4] A popular play, revived in 1744 under the title of *The Prodigal*. Unless I mistake, this comedy is indebted to Fletcher and Shirley's *The Night-Walker* (*ante*, vol. ii. p. 740).

to a production by Shadwell, curious for more than one reason. *The Lancashire Witches and Tegue O'Divelly the Irish Priest* (1681) was directed not only against the Roman Catholics (the 'Popish Plot' is constantly referred to), but also against a particular type of clergymen of the Church of England, represented by the 'Foolish, Knavish, Popish, Arrogant, Insolent, yet, for his Interest, Slavish' chaplain Smerk [1]. Of course in the Preface any desire of reflecting upon the Church is disclaimed [2]; but the intention is obvious, particularly inasmuch as a protest on behalf of tolerance towards the Dissenters is introduced. Secondly, the comedy is interesting as illustrating the popular belief in witchcraft, which the author evidently in his heart shares [3]. Thirdly, it contains one of the earliest, though as has been seen not altogether the earliest [4], Irishman of the comic stage, in the character of the villainous priest. Shadwell re-introduced it in the comedy of *The Amorous Bigot, with the Second Part of Tegue O'Divelly* (1690).

All Shadwell's remaining plays are examples of the species in which he chiefly excelled. But to describe *The*

[1] The name, to which Marvell had given a wide currency, is of course taken from a character in Etheredge's *The Man of Mode* (cf. *ante*, p. 446). Shadwell's and King William's wish, as Bishop Croft's and Marvell's had been in different times, was clearly to promote a more catholic sentiment in matters of religion than suited their times.

[2] Shadwell points to the fact that Smerk is disgraced in the play. He does not think it worth while to disclaim animosity against the Church of Rome, though Tegue is a vile rascal.—Much of the play was struck out by authority; hence the passages which have the chief historical interest for us are now printed in italics. Cf. Morley, *First Sketch*, p. 676.

[3] The priest Tegue tries to exorcise the witches 'per Melchisedec, per Bethlehem Gabor, per omne quod exit in *um*, seu Graecum sive Latinum,'— but to no purpose. In his Preface, Shadwell modestly disclaims the hope of equalling Shakspere 'in fancy' in the magical part of the play. Though he declares himself incredulous, he manifestly treats witchcraft as a reality. *The Spectator* (No. 141, in a paper by Steele, of which however the substance consisted of a letter by Hughes) very manfully exposed this fatalism in a letter written in a spirit of friendliness towards the play.—Shadwell doubtless had no wish to rise above the prejudices of his age. For illustrations of the popular belief in witchcraft in the reign of Charles II, which obliged judges to direct juries to convict, in order to avoid popular disturbances, see *Autobiography of Roger North* (*Lives of the Norths*, edn. 1890), vol. iii. pp. 130-2.—For the rest, Shadwell had read up a good many books; but the poetry in the play is altogether contemptible.

[4] Cf. *ante*, p. 393, as to Sir R. Howard's *The Committee*.

Squire of Alsatia (1688) as a comedy in the style of Jonson
seems to imply higher praise than is called for ; it is rather
in the style of Jonson's imitator Cartwright, whose *Ordinary*
it something resembles in conception.   Shadwell deserves
some credit for having in this lively and vigorous play
sought to brand a real social evil, which indeed was not
long afterwards removed by statute. The 'Squire of Alsatia'
is a young heir whom the rascally denizens of that locality
have enticed into their clutches, whence he is ultimately
rescued.   The fight between the 'Alsatians' and the
Templars at the Whitefriars gate of the Temple gives a
curious picture of scenes which really disgraced the London
of the day ; and the cant talked by the inhabitants of the
sacred precinct may invite the study of specialists [1]. *Bury-*
Fair (1689) flies at less dangerous game, its chief ridicule
being directed against the folly of the English *Précieuses*
ridicules of the day [2]. *Bartholomew Fair* doubtless suggested the background of this comedy—the fair at Bury
St. Edmunds. *The Scowrers* (1693) combines social with
political satire, food for the latter being found in the person
of a foolish Jacobite alderman who glories in King Lewis,—
while a social nuisance of the age is depicted by the band of
boon-companions and swaggerers, whose chief is in the end
converted, much to the disgust of his old crew. Finally,
in the posthumous *The Volunteers, or The Stock Jobbers*
(acted 1692), Shadwell comes as near to comedy of character

The Squire
of Alsatia
(1688).

Bury Fair
(1689).

The
Scourers
(1693).

The Volun-
teers, or
The Stock-
Jobbers
(1692).

[1] A glossary is considerably appended in the younger Shadwell's edition.
—As to the plot of this play both Dibdin and Genest compare the *Adelphi.*—
Richard Cumberland, when accused of having borrowed the story of his
The Choleric Man from *The Squire of Alsatia,* denied having ever seen that
play, but acknowledged his obligations to Terence. (See the Dedication
—' To Detraction '—of *The Choleric Man.*)

[2] Shadwell is stated to have been indebted in this play, not only to Molière's
comedy, but also (and very largely) to the Duke of Newcastle's *The*
Triumphant Widow. In Shadwell, Mrs. Fantast's French tastes and French
vocables are diverting enough. ('Heroick Numbers upon Love and Honour
are most ravissant, most surprenant, and a Tragedy is so Touchant! I die at
a Tragedy ; I'll swear I do.') Oldwit too, who recites 'pretty things' like
Sir Benjamin Backbite, is an amusing representative of the *laudator temporis*
acti—a character dramatists have frequently taken a natural pleasure in
ridiculing—he ' was a Critic at Blackfriars, but at Cambridge, none so great
as I with Jack Cleveland,' &c.—Shadwell spent a year at King Edward's
School, Bury St. Edmunds, before proceeding to Caius College.

as in any of his plays. While the Jobbers or projectors for patents constitute good side-figures, a clever contrast is presented between the rough old Cavalier officer and the Anabaptist Cromwellian veteran 'very stout and godly, but somewhat Immoral' (he has been a brave soldier in his day, but now 'turns a penny in the way of Stock-jobbing '). Besides these, we have the 'most luxurious effeminate Volunteer' Sir Nicholas Dainty and the 'ugly sub-Beau' Sir Timothy Kastril, who are equally men of their time in their mortal hatred of war[1]. Unfortunately, however, this play is disfigured by very gross indecency.

Shadwell's character-istics as a dramatist.
Posterity is not obliged to imitate Shadwell's disappointed adversaries in grudging him the recognition earned by his consistent and useful support of a cause which commended itself to many fine minds and clear intelligences, although its popularity in the world of letters and on the stage was naturally enough of tardy growth[2]. No very close scrutiny need even be applied to the substance of his boast, that he should not be afraid of these adversaries—

'till they have shown you more Variety
Of natural, unstol'n Comedy than he[3].'

As a matter of fact, he so well fitted to himself much that he had taken over from previous writers as to be fairly entitled to claim it as part of his own equipment; and in the invention of comic characters he was often original.

Shadwell and Ben Jonson.
With Ben Jonson, whom he manifestly thought that he followed at no immeasurable distance, he had in common something of the old dramatist's industry; something of his humour; and more of his healthiness of spirit. If Shadwell is often gross and indecent, it has been observed, I think truly, that he is not profane[4]; and if he altogether lacks

Shadwell's merits and shortcom-ings.

---

[1] Sir Timothy is not a Jacobite 'nor a Williamite neither'; ''tis all one to me who reigns, if I can keep my 2000 Pound a year, and enjoy myself with the Ladies.'—Queen Mary is appealed to, *per contra*, as an example of a heroic woman 'who sets her heart on one who may be lost in every *rencontre.*'

[2]   'Loyal writers of the last two Reigns,
Who tir'd their Pens for Popery and Chains,
Grumble at the Reward of all his Pains.'
Prologue to *The Scourers.*

[3] *Ib.*

[4] Genest, vol. ii. p. 41.

elevation of spirit, he is by no means deficient in moral purpose. As a comedian of manners he is obviously often truthful as well as vivid; but his grain is coarse, and brutal though the manners and sentiments of his age most assuredly were in many respects, they can hardly have been so uniformly brutal as he represents them. He did little or nothing to advance his art; but his vigour of comic invention, his hatred of political shams and social abuses, and his healthy antagonism to much that really endangered the national future, contributed to arrest the decay which was overtaking English comedy by reason of its lack both of intellectual breadth and of moral fibre. But the artistic pleasure is scant that is to be derived from the comic pictures in which he faithfully reproduces many of the unattractive features of his age.

In WILLIAM WYCHERLEY[1] (1640–1715) we at last meet with a comic dramatist of real and unmistakeable power. His contemporaries variously praised his careful workmanship and his facile genius[2]; but they were at one in extolling

William Wycherley (1640–1715).

---

[1] Wycherley's plays were, together with those of Congreve, Vanbrugh, and Farquhar, edited by Leigh Hunt in 1840. Few essays on a period of dramatic literature are better known than that of Macaulay occasioned by this publication, which contains both biographical and critical notices. In the case of Wycherley, Leigh Hunt's edition points out the sources of several of his plots, scenes, or characters.—See also Dr. J. Klette, *William Wycherley's Leben und dramatische Werke, mit besonderer Berücksichtigung von Wycherley als Plagiator Molière's* (Münster, 1883).

[2] Rochester, in his Imitation of one of Horace's *Epistles*, bestows on Wycherley the epithet of 'slow' (which Pope repeated), and says that he

'earns hard whate'er he gains;
He wants no Judgment, and he spares no Pains.'

An opposite view of Wycherley's method of workmanship is maintained by Granville (Lord Lansdowne) in *A Letter with a Character of Mr. Wycherley*, Lansdowne's *Works*, vol. ii. pp. 108 *seqq.* 'In him,' it is observed in the same letter, 'every Syllable, every Thought is masculine.' See also Dryden's Preface to *The State of Innocence*. Wycherley, who before going to Oxford had spent some time in France, where he was much noticed by the celebrated Duchess of Montausier (Julia de Rambouillet), was introduced into English Court circles by a very different kind of Duchess,—Lady Castlemaine, with whom his relations were extremely intimate. In 1672 he served in the naval war against the Dutch, and some time afterwards King Charles II proposed to appoint him tutor to his son the Duke of Richmond. But the proposal fell through in consequence of Wycherley's marriage in 1680 to the Countess of

the masculine boldness which (in allusion to the name of the hero of his most successful comedy) obtained for him the honourable sobriquet of 'Manly' Wycherley. It may however be well to reduce the compliment implied in the epithet to narrower dimensions. The general characteristics of Wycherley as a dramatist may I think be summed up as follows. His merits lie in the vigour with which his characters are drawn, the clearness with which they stand out from one another, and the naturalness with which he both constructs his plots and chooses his language. As for his plots, they are rarely original, and in the main based upon Molière; but Wycherley neither borrows without reflexion, nor combines without care. The wit of his dialogue is less sparkling and spontaneous than that of Congreve's or of Vanbrugh's; he is, as Leigh Hunt says, somewhat heavy as well as brawny in his step, and he lacks in general the gaiety of spirit which is the most charming phase of comic humour. On the other hand, he excels in satire of an intenser kind; his sarcasms are as keen as they are cruel; and the cynicism of his wit cannot prevent us from acknowledging its power. But while he ruthlessly uncloaks the vices of his age, his own moral tone is affected by their influence to as deplorable a degree as is that of the most light-hearted and unthinking of the dramatists contemporary with him. Macaulay[1] is within the mark in

His salient characteristics as a dramatist.

Drogheda. After her death he underwent an imprisonment for debt which lasted several years, but he was liberated towards the close of the reign of King James II, who, after witnessing a performance of *The Plain-Dealer*, conferred a pension on its author. King James liked to hear his own system of government described as 'Plain Dealing'; indeed, the phrase must have become a cant phrase of politics, for in 1716 we find Rowe in the Prologue to Mrs. Centlivre's *The Cruel Gift* complimenting the then Prince of Wales, who was present at the author's benefit, by bidding the spectators

'In his each Feature Truth and Candour trace,
And read Plain Dealing written in his Face.'

See also the opening passage of the Preface to Arbuthnot's *History of John Bull* (1712). If Pope's account be trustworthy—it is known how the intimacy between the curiously assorted pair suffered from the severity with which the young poet had revised the poems entrusted to him for the purpose by the veteran—Wycherley, who as a young man had left the Church of Rome (in which he was born), returned to it before his death. He died in 1715, a few days after he had contracted a second marriage.

[1] *History of England*, ch. vii.

describing him as 'the most licentious writer of a singularly licentious and hard-hearted school.'

Of Wycherley's comedies the earliest, *Love in a Wood, or St. James' Park* (1672), is in the style of Etheredge and Sedley,—indeed *The Mulberry Garden* of the latter (1668) has been justly held to have suggested this play[1]. Its satire on manners is, however, perhaps more incisive and contemptuous than theirs; and, in contrast to the fantastic figures of Sedley's production, it already exhibits signs of a realistic vigour capable of taking us back from the Restoration writers to Elisabethans like Middleton. In the construction of his plot Wycherley made use of two of Molière's comedies, *L'École des Maris* and *L'École des Femmes*, the former of which had previously supplied Sedley with the opening of *The Mulberry Garden*[2]. The mixture of respectable and the reverse of respectable characters in *Love in a Wood* is however so puzzling that few will care to take the trouble of drawing accurate distinctions. Dapperwit is the fool, and Alderman Tripe the deserving victim, of this comedy.

The Gentleman Dancing-Master (1672) resembles Molière in manner more than any other of Wycherley's plays; indeed its intrigue has been compared to that of *L'École des Femmes*, but, in accordance with this author's general method of working, the resemblance is by no means close. The English work may be described as a capital farce, written with genuine vigour and freshness of humour; and to my mind this is by far the most agreeable of Wycherley's plays. The contrast between the starched father who affects the Spaniard and the foolish young man who assumes the airs and speech of a Frenchman is fairly amusing, and may possibly have been even more so at the time of the production of the play, supposing it to have contained personalities at which we can now only guess; but in any case the fun of the action is excellent. In carrying on his intrigue in the disguise of a dancing-master, the lover is

Love in a Wood, or St. James' Park (acted by 1671).

The Gentleman Dancing-Master (acted 1672).

[1] As Dr. Klette (p. 41) points out, the Prologue seems to imply that the writer expected to be blamed as a plagiary:

'He e'en is come to suffer here to-day
For counterfeiting (as you judge) a play.'

[2] *Ib.* pp. 46 and 71 *seqq.*

protected both by his rival and the lady's father against the suspicions of an old aunt; and the dancing-lesson scenes (suggested by Calderon's *El Maestro de Danzar*), if not very refined, are as good as anything of the sort in modern comedy or farce[1].

The Country Wife (acted 1673).

The two remaining plays of Wycherley are the most characteristic among their author's works. *The Country Wife* (1673) in its plot (which again seems indebted to two of Molière's comedies for its groundwork[2]) reaches the extremity of the revolting; yet one cannot wonder at the long-enduring popularity the play enjoyed upon the stage[3]. For not only is it written with considerable spirit, besides being seasoned with that cynicism to which Wycherley was so ready to give vent[4]; but it contains one character—of the *fausse ingénue* type—which naturally lends itself to the art of a good actress of a particular bent of talent[5]. But it was indeed a 'frank age' to which such a play would be introduced upon the stage[6]. In *The Plain-Dealer* (1674) the cynicism of Wycherley has reached its acme. It begins with

The Plain-Dealer (acted 1675 or 1676).

[1] The impudence of the Epilogue is at all events in perfect keeping with the character of the personage who speaks it.

[2] *Viz. L'École des Maris* and *L'École des Femmes*. The main motive is of course traceable to the *Eunuchus* of Terence.

[3] It held the stage during the earlier half of the century, and was in 1765 revived in a shortened form. (Genest, vol. v. p. 69.)

[4] A specimen or two will suffice to illustrate it:
'*Horner.* Ay, your arrantest cheat is your trustee or executor; your jealous man, the greatest cuckold; your churchman the greatest atheist; and your noisy pert rogue of a wit, the greatest fop, dullest ass, and worst company.' (Act i. sc. 1.)
'*Sir Jasper.* Woman, made for man's companion—
'*Horner.* So is that soft, gentle, tame and more noble creature a spaniel, and has all their tricks; can fawn, lie down, suffer beating, and fawn the more; barks at your friends when they come to see you. . . . And all the difference is, the spaniel's the more faithful animal, and fawns but upon one master.' (Act ii. sc. 1.)
'*Sparkish.* I can deny you nothing: for though I have known thee a great while, never go, if I do not love thee as well as a new acquaintance.' (Act iii. sc. 2.)

[5] Mrs. Pinchwife was a popular character of Mrs. Jordan's.

[6] Cf. act iii. sc. 2. The remarks on *The Country Wife* in *The Plain-Dealer* (act ii. sc. 1) can hardly be called a defence.—Steele in No. iii of *The Tatler* (1709), while praising the literary qualities of *The Country Wife*, temperately reproves its immorality. (See Mr. Austin Dobson's *Richard Steele*, p. 97.)

the Prologue[1], where 'the coarse dauber of the coming scenes' announces his intention 'to follow life and nature only,' to 'display you as you are,' to exhibit his 'fine lady' as 'a mercenary jilt,' and his 'men of wit and pleasure' as 'dull rogues,' while he

> 'draws a friend only to custom just,
> And makes him naturally break his trust.'

And it continues down to the 'moral' at the close:

> 'Yet for my sake, let no one e'er confide
> In tears or oaths, in love or friend untried.'

As for the plot of this famous comedy, it is not less horrible than the chief character, Manly the 'Plain-Dealer,' is revolting. The repulsiveness of the story, and of its *dénouement*, is such as to make description irksome; but the character of the hero may be judged by contrasting it with the original—if it can be so called—which suggested it, viz. the noble hero of Molière's immortal *Misanthrope*. Manly is a naval captain who comes to shore with a rooted hatred of mankind, to which he gives vent on every occasion and in terms such as would justify his being shipped off again at the public cost. Even apart from the monstrous revenge which he takes upon the cause of his misanthropy, he is a brutal antitype of the noble and honourable Alceste whom Molière—perhaps introducing here and there a touch of saddened consciousness of self—has drawn with so much humour and so much tenderness. Such a character could only be tolerated—and admired—by a society which knew itself to be vile, and took pleasure in hearing itself called so to its face. I need quote no examples of the scalp-hunting misanthropy which seemed philosophy in the eyes of the bad world to which it was preached; nor reproduce in detail the invectives of this new Timon of the reigns of Charles II and James II—a denouncer of vice who is in himself

---

[1] Or, indeed, in the printed play with the Dedication, which contains a not unwarranted sarcasm against the dramatists of the age as fond of 'talking to you of the rules of writing (like the French authors), to show you and my reader I understand 'em, in my epistle, lest neither of you should find it out by the play.'

as coarse and loathsome as is the very vice denounced by him [1].

In speaking of this comedy, it would neither be possible nor desirable to keep asunder the moral and the literary points of view. The picture of society which *The Plain-Dealer* offers is not altogether a false one, nor is the operation of such a world as that which surrounds Manly upon such a character as Manly's misrepresented. Neither therefore as a comedy of manners nor as a comedy of character—and it may justly lay claim to the latter and higher rank—can this remarkable drama be properly said to fail. To us its effect is utterly revolting, because of the absence of all moral relief, without which few dramatic characters are endurable—least of all a type so repugnant to ordinary human feeling as that of the man resolved to hate his kind. *Wycherley's social satire.* But working within the limits of his own horizon, with nothing perceptible to him beyond a vicious world hateful on account of the palpable grossness of its outward pretences, Wycherley must in this play be allowed to have given proofs of genuine force and of essential originality, and to have produced what is indisputably one of the most powerful dramas of its age [2]. To no other of his dramatic works

[1] I cannot think that Taine, in his *Histoire de la Littérature Anglaise* (livre iii. chap. 1), has at all exaggerated the impression which this ' modèle d'une brute déclarée et énergique' makes upon the mind of a modern reader.—A scene in this play (act ii. sc. 1) is in part translated from Molière's *La Critique de l'École des Femmes*. The Comtesse in Racine's *Les Plaideurs* is thought to have furnished Wycherley with the first hint of that amusing personage, the Widow Blackacre. Dr. Klette points out that the circumstances of the discovery of Fidelia in the closing scene may have been derived by Wycherley direct from Bandello's story which has been noticed among the possible indirect sources of *Twelfth Night* (*ante*, vol. ii. p. 143), and that the notion of the duel may have been suggested by the famous Shrewsbury-Buckingham affair.—The origin of the term Plain-Dealer (cf. *ante*, p. 461, *note*) would seem to be due to a game at cards called Plain-Dealing, described by Charles Cotton in *The Complete Gamester* (1680). Cf. S. W. Singer, *Researches into the History of Playing Cards* (1816), Appendix, p. 345.

[2] The whole of *The Plain-Dealer* must be said to be admirably written; and even the most revolting scene of the play displays singular dramatic power. Some of the witticisms have an almost proverbial ring—see *e. g.* Manly's estimate of the value of a lord's title (act i. sc. 1), which recalls Burns: Olivia's description of the coxcomb Mr. Novel, ' who rather than not rail will rail at the dead, whom none speak ill of; rather than not flatter, will flatter the poets of the age, whom none will flatter ' (act ii. sc. 1); and

can a similar praise be given. *The Country Wife* indeed forms a notable attempt at painting the life of the age as one of uncontrolled self-indulgence; it is a satire upon the very name of virtue, to the mere conception of which the society here depicted is an absolute stranger. The plot is that of an extravagant farce, but of one which plays under the ordinary conditions of everyday life, enveloped and disguised by no Utopian or burlesque imaginings. Lawless lust running riot in a real—not an imaginary —sphere of contemporary life fills a canvas, from which we turn aside with a sense of nausea; and it is only when we remember that the life painted by Wycherley was not the life of the nation that we recover from our wonder how a society which could be thus represented should ever have risen out of its decay.

The foremost position among the comic dramatists of the later Stuart period is beyond all dispute due to WILLIAM CONGREVE [1] (1670–1729). In life he received more than his proper share of praise and recognition. The literary leaders of his times vied with personages of the highest rank in acknowledging his eminence. In Halifax (Montagu) he found a patron who provided him with a modest sinecure at the very commencement of his literary career, and gradually added or substituted other offices of the same sort, which ensured him a life of comfort, without exacting in return so much as a political pamphlet or poem. Female rank and beauty smiled upon him in the persons of the second Duchess of Marlborough and of Mrs. Bracegirdle, whose respective favours were at the last so very unequally requited. Dryden addressed him in an *Epistle* [2] which, notwithstanding the

William Congreve (1670-1729).

Eliza's confession as to her sex: 'All wise observers understand us now-a-days, as they do dreams, almanacs, and Dutch gazettes, by the contrary' (act ii. sc. 1).

[1] Congreve's plays are most easily accessible in the joint edition by Leigh Hunt (1840) mentioned above under Wycherley; a convenient reprint of their text has recently appeared in the *Mermaid* Series, with notes by Mr. A. C. Ewald (1887). See also Mr. E. W. Gosse's *Life of William Congreve* in the *Great Writers* Series (1888); and Dr. D. Schmid, *William Congreve, sein Leben und seine Lustspiele* (Vienna and Leipzig, 1897).

[2] *To my dear Friend, Mr. Congreve, on his Comedy called The Double-Dealer.* (*Works*, vol. xi.)

audacious exaggeration of its flattery, it is difficult to read
without emotion—so generous is the spirit of this tribute
from the old writer to the young.   Steele, Swift, and Pope
honoured and loved him, and the last-named dedicated to
him his translation of the *Iliad*. Voltaire paid a memorable
visit to him in his old age as a great English man of letters
—although Congreve deprecated the title, and preferred to
be regarded as a gentleman.   And when after more than
a quarter of a century of literary inertia he passed away, a
pompous funeral and a grave in Westminster Abbey finally
testified to the honour in which his name continued to be
held[1].   Nor, perhaps, is there any great difficulty in understanding the secondary causes of the quick growth of his
literary reputation, or in accounting for its long endurance.
In the first place, neither his literary success[2] nor his personal prosperity ever suffered interruption ; with the exception of ill-health there was no drawback to the even progress
of his life—and the world looks with favour on such a career.
A personal charm of manner must unmistakeably have
contributed its influence towards making Congreve liked
and loved.   Finally, it must not be forgotten that, when
Dryden besought his young friend to 'shade those laurels
which descended to him,' and for many a year afterwards, no
promise was visible of any competitor for the succession.
Congreve's name shone with unequalled brilliancy among
the names of living English poets, till the youthful heir
seated himself on the vacant throne.   And the combination
of literary qualities in Congreve which had first dazzled the
contemporaries of his early manhood in the days when
Dryden was growing old and Pope was still a child, was
alike splendid and uncommon.

Congreve's
wit.
          Among these qualities one has always justly been
regarded as pre-eminent.   Congreve is indisputably one
of the very wittiest of English writers.   No doubt, even
when this praise has been unreservedly accorded to a comic
dramatist—for it is as such alone that Congreve can be held

----

[1] See *A Poem to the Memory of William Congreve*. By James Thomson.
Edited, with a Preface and Notes, for the Percy Society, by P. Cunningham. (*Publications*, vol. vi, 1843.)

to have really excelled—the highest praise has not been given. 'Wit,' he says himself in a letter well deserving of attention [1], 'is often mistaken for humour'; 'the saying of humorous things does not distinguish characters; for every person in a Comedy may be allow'd to speak them. From a witty man they are expected; and even a fool may be permitted to stumble on 'em by chance. Tho' I make a difference betwixt Wit and Humour, yet I do not think that humorous characters exclude Wit: No, but the manner of Wit should be adapted to the Humour.' Congreve, therefore, recognised as a danger incident to an abundance of wit the possibility of its injuriously affecting the drawing of characters, and of its obscuring that clear distinction between them which is indispensable in the best kind of comedy. This danger he cannot be said to have altogether escaped; and the unbroken and unmitigated brilliancy of his dialogue, which enraptured his own age, must be censured as a fault of excess by those who are no longer under the influence of a transitory fashion. It should at the same time not be overlooked that Congreve's grace and ease of style, as distinguished from its brilliancy and wittiness, contribute to the charm of his prose and make it enjoyable like that of only the very best of contemporary English writers; and that, though these qualities are not always separable from, they should not in consequence be confounded with, one another [2]. In brilliancy of wit he is the

---

[1] See Congreve's letter to Dennis *Concerning Humour in Comedy*, dated July 10, 1695 (in *Select Works of John Dennis*, vol. ii. p. 514).—In the same spirit Sheffield Duke of Buckinghamshire in his *Essay on Poetry* (*temp.* Charles II) had written:

> 'Another fault which often may befall
> Is, when the wit of some great poet shall
> So overflow, that is, be none at all,
> That ev'n his fools speak sense, as if possess'd,
> And each by inspiration breaks his jest.
> If once the justness of each part be lost,
> Well we may laugh, but at the poet's cost.
> That silly thing men call *sheerwit* avoid,
> With which our age so nauseously is cloy'd;
> *Humour* is all; wit should be only brought
> To turn agreeably some proper thought.'

Cf. *ante*, p. 444, as to Etheredge.

[2] Cf. Gosse, *Life of Congreve*, p. 184.

superior of all his predecessors and contemporaries of the post-Restoration period, among whom Dryden and perhaps Vanbrugh alone approached him, and Sheridan is his only successor. In ease of dialogue he far surpasses Wycherley; Vanbrugh, and still more Farquhar, lack the element of grace which he possesses ; while Etheredge and the rest— even Dryden—fall short of him in polish as writers of comic prose. Congreve is therefore to be regarded as an artist of rare as well as genuine gifts—the more so that he understood how to conceal his art. For it would be a mistake to suppose that effects such as he produced can be the result of a mere copying of the very happiest examples furnished by actual life. This error, into which second-rate comic dramatists are only too prone to fall, was not one of which Congreve was likely to be guilty[1]. It may be added that the lyrics occasionally inserted by Congreve in his plays are at times brighter and conciser than those which are found in most contemporary comedies[2], and that the blank verse of his solitary tragedy is not wanting in harmony of cadences.

His other merits as a comic dramatist. Congreve possessed other gifts as a comic dramatist besides those of style, though in this direction only was his endowment superlative. He possessed a power of inventing character to which, as will be seen, two at least of his comedies[3] very distinctly testify; and in the construction of plots, although he possessed a very thorough familiarity with Molière and other French comic dramatists, he displayed an independence[4] of workmanship which contrasts with the rude methods of appropriation practised by many of his contemporaries, and even with the assimilating processes of Wycherley.

The comedies of Congreve are but few in number ; they vary, however, from one another in more respects than one. But, although they are not uniformly devoid of moral

---

[1] 'I believe,' he says in the letter to Dennis already quoted, 'if a Poet should start a Dialogue of any length, from the Extempore Discourse of the two Wittiest Men upon Earth, he would find the Scene but coldly receiv'd by the Town.'

[2] See *e. g.* Gavot's song in *The Old Bachelor,* act ii. sc. 9.

[3] *The Double-Dealer* and *The Way of the World.*

[4] Cf. Schmid, *u. s.,* pp. 40–1.

purpose, not one of them can be pronounced free from gross and intentional indecency, or undegraded by a deplorable frivolity of tone. The good-breeding of Congreve proved no sufficient safeguard against his falling in with the worst tastes of the age which he enchanted ; and the utmost that can be urged on his behalf is that he instinctively avoids the brutality of Wycherley, and that even to a modern reader he seems less coarse than either Vanbrugh or Farquhar. Yet it is a melancholy reflexion that a writer of such gifts and capable of exercising so great a power over his age should only, when essaying the branch of his art for which he was least fitted, have risen to the height of a desire to prove that 'a Play may be with industry so disposed (in spite of the licentious practice of the modern theatre) as to become sometimes an innocent and not unprofitable entertainment[1].' As a matter of fact, it was Congreve's fate to suffer severely for the sins of the comic drama of his age,—both when he found himself, as was but just and reasonable, held up to censure as one of its leading representatives, and when he came forward, as in duty bound, in the character of its champion. No doubt can exist that but for the catastrophe which he had helped to provoke, his career as a dramatist would have been a far more productive one[2].

His indecency.

Congreve's earliest comedy, *The Old Bachelor* (1693), which he appears to have brought with him to London, and which received some kindly finishing touches from Dryden, Southerne, and Arthur Maynwaring, met with an extraordinary success[3]. The writing here is already excellent, and distinguished, especially by its lightness, from anything that had preceded it in the post-Restoration drama. The majority of the leading characters, however, contain nothing quite

His comedies : The Old Bachelor (acted and printed 1693).

---

[1] See the Dedication to *The Mourning Bride.*

[2] See below as to Jeremy Collier's *Short View*, and as to Congreve's share in the controversy which followed.

[3] Dryden, among whose weaknesses jealousy against possible rivals had no place, returned this comedy, which had been submitted to his judgment, with the remark that it was the best first play ever brought under his notice; and Charles Montagu (Halifax) immediately rewarded the author with a commissionership for licensing hackney-coaches. *The Old Bachelor* was acted as late as 1789.

original; it would be easy to find in Molière or elsewhere prototypes or analogues of Heartwell, who sets up for a misogynist but is in reality a victim to female wiles, of the blustering coward Captain Bluffe, and of the demure but deep Mrs. Fondlewife. Yet these in company with a number of other personages furnish an abundant variety, and the action is both brisk and diverting[1]. Morally, both the plots of which the play is composed are objectionable; but the dramatic life in this comedy is unmistakeable, and more than any other quality justified a success so rarely achieved by the work of a novice hand.

The Double-Dealer (acted and printed 1693).

Its successor, *The Double-Dealer* (1693), justifies the assertion in Dryden's generous but extravagant lines on this play, that its author, and only he, was ' lineal to the throne[2].' Notwithstanding certain repulsive features in the action, this is undoubtedly one of the best comedies in our dramatic literature; but it failed at first to please the public, although welcomed with enthusiasm by the best judges[3]. Perhaps the badness of some of the bad people in this play was beyond the popular notion of the endurable; but there is no accounting for such judgments, and the *Plain-Dealer* had been much liked[4]. Congreve claims the credit of complete originality for this plot[5], which is constructed with extreme skill, and declares his desire to have been to render it as strong as possible because it was single. He

[1] The very numerous proportion of 'scenes' in each act is worth observing in Congreve. Stage-management must have been in a state of high perfection to allow of his plays being performed with success.

[2] The same compliment was generously paid to Congreve by Southerne; see his lines in Scott and Saintsbury's *Dryden*, vol. xi.

[3] Queen Mary, who seems to have been gifted with the family insight into a good play, helped the *The Double-Dealer* by an early ' command.'

[4] No modern dramatist of genius has better understood the Parisian public than the late Alexander Dumas the younger; yet the fascinating volume of *Notes* on his principal plays just published (forming vol. viii of his *Théâtre Complet*) shows how impossible it was even for him at times to overcome the caprices of audiences, whose applause on other occasions he conquered by storm.

[5] As observed above, Congreve's plots and characters frequently suggest reminiscences, which should not however be set down as anything more than this. So J. C. Walker has pointed out, that act iii. sc. 8 of *The Double-Dealer* recalls a scene in Macchiavelli's *Mandragola*, where Messir Nicia corresponds to Sir Paul Plyant.

has certainly shown that no kind of comedy is in reality so effective as that in which the action is *one*, but which, as in this instance, presents unexpected turns to the very last[1]. The characters are not many, but well distinguished ; the interest however concentrates itself on two of the most effective pictures of villainous cunning and evil passion ever conceived by a comic dramatist—Maskwell and Lady Touchwood. Neither of these exceeds the proportions befitting a comedy ; yet the execution cannot be said to fall short of the conception in real power—especially in the case of Maskwell, the key to whose system of conduct is furnished by the motto of the play borrowed from Terence[2]: 'he tells the truth to both sides and contrives to cheat them both.' In the writing we are already struck by the wonderful lightness and naturalness of the dialogue as well as by the brilliancy of wit shown in a constant play of repartee[3]. It should be added, that although this comedy contains episodes of the most blameworthy character, the issue of the main plot is entirely on the side of virtue ; the defeat of the artful Maskwell and the shameless Lady Touchwood in truth offers a singularly powerful dramatic illustration, such as the stage may legitimately pride itself on having repeatedly supplied both before and after *Hamlet*, of the encouraging fact that Truth will out at last.

Love for Love (1695) is a very amusing comedy, which kept possession of the stage with no long intermission till Hazlitt's day[4]. Among the variety of characters contained in it, the preference will perhaps be given to Jeremy, one of those witty 'gentlemen's gentlemen' whom Congreve bequeathed to Sheridan and to modern comedy at large[5].

Love for Love (printed 1695).

---

[1] The conclusion of act iv and the *dénouement* in act v seem to me equally excellent.

[2] 'Vera dicendo ambos fallere.'

[3] See *e.g.* act iii. sc. 10, which will at once recall Sheridan.

[4] *Love for Love* had the honour of being noticed in the first number of *The Tatler* as a play which by its success promised well for a renewal of the public interest in the drama so largely usurped of late by opera.

[5] He has 'the seeds of rhetoric and oratory in his head.' 'I have,' he says, 'been taught at Cambridge'; on which the beau Tattle observes, 'Ay! 'tis well enough for a servant to be bred at a university ; but the education is a little too pedantic for a gentleman.' Tattle was not forgotten by Sheridan

The would-be astrologer Foresight seemingly carries us back to an earlier age of the drama; but the belief in palmistry and astrology had by no means expired before Free-thinking began to come into fashion. Several of the other characters are highly diverting [1]; but parts of this play are indelicate enough to have been thought so more than a century ago [2]. Nor can one help remarking that the unselfish constancy of Valentine is looked upon as a miracle even by his quick-witted lady-love, Angelica.

Love for Love, intended to begin an established connexion between the foremost comic dramatist of the day and a venture of great importance in the history of the London stage [3], had exhibited Congreve at the height of his reputation, and unmistakeably in full possession of the powers to which he owed it. He followed it up by the production of his solitary tragedy, of which immediately, and which was to prove the most signal of his theatrical successes. Before he once more—and as it proved for the last time—came before the world as a comic dramatist, Jeremy Collier had launched his bolt against the offences of the contemporary stage, and Congreve, who had not been spared in the attack, had thought himself bound in honour to take part in the defence. It was therefore at a time of inevitable depression—both in the general condition of the theatre and in his personal relations to it [4]—that he brought out his last comedy, *The Way of the World*.

when he wrote *The School for Scandal*—see particularly act i. sc. 13; but Sheridan may be described as a follower of Congreve and Vanbrugh.

[1] Miss Prue and Ben are an amusing couple—country-girl and sea-monster.—Valentine's mock madness is entertaining; with Congreve a madman is of course as witty as everybody else. 'I'll tell you one thing,' he remarks to the lawyer Buckram. 'It's a question that would puzzle an arithmetician if you should ask him whether the Bible saves more souls in Westminster Abbey, or damns more in Westminster Hall; for my part, I am Truth, and can't tell; I have very few acquaintance.' *Sir Sampson*. 'Body o' me, he talks sensibly in his madness! has he no intervals?' *Jeremy*. 'Very short, sir.' (Act iv. sc. 7.)—Mr. Gosse directs attention to Ben Legend, as the earliest of 'a long line of stage-sailors.'

[2] Evelina and Miss Mirran were much shocked by it. (See Miss Burney's *Evelina*, Letter xx.)

[3] The opening of Lincoln's Inn Fields by a company of leading actors, headed by Betterton, independently of the Royal Patentees of Drury Lane.

[4] When his *Double-Dealer* was revived on March 4, 1699, these words

Congreve was manifestly conscious of the hazard which he ran in producing *The Way of the World* (1700); but he met it with spirit, and perhaps in some measure succeeded in disguising part at least of the issue to himself. At all events, he was resolved to adhere to his own conceptions of comedy, without paying much more regard to the ordinary tastes of its patrons than to the recent diatribes of its censors. His intention in his present play was, as he states in the *Dedication*, to substitute for the gross fools of ordinary comedy, who 'instead of moving our mirth ought very often to excite our compassion,' some characters 'which should appear ridiculous, not so much through a natural folly (which is incorrigible and therefore not proper for the stage) as through an affected wit which, at the same time that it is affected, is also false.' The difficulty, as he says, is that hasty judges in face of the scene will often take false wit for true, and prove unable to distinguish between a Witwoud and a Truewit. The result of this endeavour was naturally enough to impair the attractiveness of the play for the many by rendering it more interesting to the few—so that, as Dryden records, it 'had but moderate success, though it deserved much better[1].' *The Way of the World* impresses the modern reader as a bitter satire, though the author was true to himself in the elegance of his handling[2]. If the character of Lady Wishfort is almost too offensive for comedy[3], Witwoud is as diverting as he is original—a man afflicted by a perfect cacoëthes of feeble repartee—'I cannot help it, madam,' he says, 'though it is against myself.' And in Millamont and Mirabell he has excelled the brilliancy of all his previous raillery of social types and their deviations from sense and law, giving the

---

were added in the playbill—involving a twofold innovation, for no author's name had previously been included in such an announcement : 'Written by Mr. Congreve ; with several expressions omitted.' (Gosse, *u. s.*, p. 191.)

[1] See Dryden's letter to Mrs. Steward, March 12, 1700 (Scott and Saintsbury's *Dryden*, vol. xviii. p. 177).

[2] 'Satire, he thinks, you ought not to expect :
    For so reform'd a town who dare correct.' (*Prologue.*)

[3] Her 'Cabal-Night' (see act. iv), as Mr. Gosse remarks, 'is the direct original of Sheridan's *School for Scandal*; but in some ways the earlier picture is the more biting, the more disdainful.'

place of distinction to the lady[1]. With the failure of this play on the stage, Congreve's career as a dramatist virtually came to a close.

*His tra-
gedy, The
Mourning
Bride
(1697).*
Congreve's long-celebrated tragedy of *The Mourning Bride* dates from 1697, the year previous to that of Jeremy Collier's denunciation. This play, written in blank verse[2], is a love-tragedy with a plot, so far as is known of Congreve's own invention, which unfolds itself with dignity in the romantic region of Granada. The last act, how-ever, is full of sensational effects—except that at the close, after a succession of deaths, the happy union of Almeria and Osmyn-Alphonso seems like an anti-climax, and finds suitable expression in the tame conventionality of the closing couplets of the tragedy[3]. It contains, however, some well-written passages, among them the description of the cathedral surrounded by its tombs which in a much-quoted passage of Boswell's *Life*[4] Dr. Johnson is stated to have extolled as the finest poetical passage he had ever read,—'he recollected none in Shakespeare equal to it.' The impressiveness of the lines depends, however, on the external circumstances of the situation ; and if as Johnson, by way of completely disconcerting Shakspere's apologist

---

[1] 'The higher the comedy, the more prominent the part women enjoy in it. . . . In Congreve's *Way of the World,* Millamont overshadows Mirabell, the sprightliest male figure in English comedy.' See George Meredith, *An Essay on Comedy and the Uses of the Comic Spirit* (1877), p. 29; and cf. *ib.* pp. 35 *seqq.,* for a fuller criticism of the play.—Act iv. sc. 5 is specially delectable, where a declaration *à la mode* takes place between the pair, both the lady and the gentleman being, like Arthur Pendennis and Blanche Amory, solely anxious to secure the conditions of perfect freedom and mutual tolerance, under which they are prepared to make one another happy.—The waiting-maids in this comedy are even more amusing than is usual with Congreve.

[2] See Mr. Gosse's observations (*u. s.,* p. 92) on the blank verse of *The Mourning Bride,* which he considers to have been modelled on Milton's, and to have been in its turn followed in Thomson's.

[3] Alphonso permits himself a hope that he and his beloved may

'Still in the paths of honour persevere
And not from past or present ills despair;
For blessings ever wait on virtuous deeds ;
And though a late, a sure reward succeeds.'

[4] Vol. ii. p. 85 of Dr. G. Birkbeck Hill's edition (1887), where see the editor's note showing with sufficient fulness that Johnson's comparative estimate of the two poets, and his opinion of *The Mourning Bride* as a whole, were quite in accordance with those approved by modern criticism.

Garrick, went on to assert, ' Congreve has *nature*,' he has certainly in this instance failed to reveal any of its deeper recesses [1]. In general, being unequal to really sustained flights of passion, the author has to take refuge in rant, and Lee himself could hardly have surpassed some of his attempts of this description [2]. In brief, we may agree with Lessing, that Congreve's solitary attempt in tragic poetry proves this field to have lain outside the natural range of his talents ; or, if we prefer to put it so, we may assent to the opinion of Swift's *quidnunc* (rather than to that of Swift himself), that tragic composition ' quite lost ' so essentially comic a genius [3]. Congreve was associated with Vanbrugh and Walsh in the adaptation of Molière's *Monsieur de Pourceaugnac*, to which their version attached the sub-title of *Squire Trelooby* (1704); and he was also the author of a masque *The Judgment of Paris* (1701), and of an opera, *Semele* [4]; but neither of the two latter was ever represented on the stage.

Less brilliant than Congreve, and altogether his inferior both as a dramatist and as a wit, Sir JOHN VANBRUGH (1666 *circ.*–1726) is in my opinion unsurpassed by any of our post-Restoration writers of comedy in the vivacity, gaiety, and ease of his prose dialogue. Moreover, he enriched the comic stage by one supremely ludicrous character which, except in so far as Etheredge's Sir Fopling Flutter may have a claim to its parentage, may fairly be called new, viz. the admirable Lord Foppington of *The Relapse*; and

Sir John Vanbrugh (1666 circ.– 1726).

Characteristics of his comedy.

[1] Almeria's exclamation on the appearance of Osmyn from among the tombs in the scene following closely upon this (act ii. sc. 2) is a rather too obvious reminiscence of *Hamlet* :

'Angels, and all the host of heaven, support me ! '

[2] See especially the conclusion of the great scene (act iii. sc. 6), and Almeria's offer to clothe the rotten bones of her lover (supposed to be dead) with her own flesh.

[3] See the lines from Swift to Congreve, which, as Forster in his *Life of Swift* (vol. i. p. 69) shows, must have been written when Swift knew that such an effort as *The Mourning Bride* was impending.

[4] The former of these is short and commonplace ; *Semele*, though also a mere trifle, is a well-conceived and executed production of its kind. The admixture of short rhythmic lines in both this *Semele* and Schiller's little drama suggests the possibility of the German poet's having cast a passing glance at Congreve's opera ; but no real resemblance exists between the two pieces.

he invented some others which are almost equally extravagant and almost equally true to life. He borrowed with skill while he constructed with ease, and must altogether be allowed to be one of the most entertaining dramatists of his age. His morality might be averred to sink below that of Congreve—could it be said to sink at all; for such is the levity of this author that it is difficult to weigh even his sins in any very serious balance. The utter frivolity of the later Stuart comedy has no more signal representative than Vanbrugh, though, as it happened, he was very far from being a mere man of pleasure [1].

The Relapse, or Virtue in Danger (1697).

Vanbrugh, it may be unhesitatingly affirmed, never surpassed his earliest effort as a comic dramatist [2]. *The Relapse, or Virtue in Danger* (1697) seems to have been written as a sequel to Colley Cibber's *Love's Last Shift, or The Fool in Fashion* (1696), in which Sir Novelty Fashion, the first in Cibber's series of fops, appears, and the erring Loveless is reclaimed by his virtuous wife Amanda. Whatever may be thought of the morality of Cibber's play, it would be difficult to point to a more recklessly immoral production than this of Vanbrugh's, notwithstanding the triumphant final assertion of the strength of female virtue in the person of the wronged and tempted wife [3]. Her faithless husband goes scotfree for his sins ; nor is there any pretence at excusing the unblushing effrontery of the picture. But it must be allowed that after the first scene has in hastily but not ill-written blank-verse exposed the situation, the prose dialogue of the remainder moves with contagious gaiety and spirit. The bye-plot of Lord Foppington (the ennobled Sir Novelty), his brother Tom Fashion, their joint bride Miss Hoyden and her father Sir Tunbelly Clumsey, is one of the most amusing things in later

---

[1] He is known to fame as the architect of Blenheim and other mansions; and filled the offices of comptroller of the royal works, and surveyor of the works at Greenwich Hospital under George I, by whom he was knighted.

[2] All his plays are said to have appeared anonymously, as the mere diversions of his life ; and *The Relapse* is stated to have been written in six weeks.

[3] *The Relapse* was one of the plays selected by Jeremy Collier for special analysis and reprobation. Farquhar replied by *A Short Vindication of The Relapse and The Provok'd Wife, from immodesty and prophaneness. By the author.* (1698.)

English comedy, and so good as to have borne reproduction by Sheridan in his *A Trip to Scarborough*. Lord Foppington I am inclined to pronounce the best fop ever brought on the stage—unsurpassed and unsurpassable, and admirable from first to last. The 'natural sprauts' of his lordship's 'brain' entitle him to such a pre-eminence; there is not an inch of him that is not consistent with the whole[1].

The Provoked Wife (1697), though not so supremely amusing as its predecessor, displays a considerable *vis comica*; but the realism here is at times of a very gross character. Sir John Brute, who thoroughly deserves his name, may probably have been only too true a picture of actual life; but it is impossible to look upon him without the disgust he excites in his wife. Lady Fanciful cannot be ranked as an equal of Lord Foppington; but her French fille-de-chambre is a type drawn direct from nature. *The False Friend* (1702), of which the scene is laid in Spain, is clearly taken from a foreign—probably in the first instance from a French[2]—original; it is a comedy of intrigue, with a well-contrived though hardly novel plot. The Prologue ingeniously avows the author's object to be, instead of reforming the stage all at once, to 'steal the immorality' of plays away. If so, he addresses himself to the first step in his task after the most cautious fashion. In *The Confederacy* (1705) Vanbrugh is quite at home again. The plot of this play, which might be called 'the adventures of a necklace,' is very clever if not original[3], and the dialogue is

The Provoked Wife (1697).

The False Friend (1702).

The Confederacy (1705).

---

[1] '*Amanda*. . . . 'tis I think the inside of a book should recommend it most to us.

'*Lord Foppington*. That, I confess, I am not altogether so fand of. Far to mind the inside of a book, is to entertain one's self with the forced product of another man's brain. Now I think a man of quality and breeding may be much better diverted with the natural Sprauts of his own.' (Act ii. sc. 1.) This scene and act i. sc. 3 are supremely excellent.—As to the dialect put into the mouth of Lord Foppington, 'long after it had ceased to be spoken in fashionable circles,' see a note to Macaulay's *History of England*, chap. iii, where it is stated that 'Lord Sunderland was a great master of this court tune, as Roger North calls it; and Titus Oates affected it in the hope of passing for a fine gentleman.'—Voltaire Gallicised Lord Foppington as *Le Comte de Boursouffle*.

[2] French words are very oddly left in the text.

[3] It is said to be founded on one of D'Ancourt's pieces.

distinguished by the author's usual vivacity. Dick Amlet
and his mother make a choice pair, and Flippanta the
lady's-maid is a fine specimen of the effrontery of her kind.
The morality of this comedy is on Vanbrugh's usual level,
which may be described as about the lowest to which
English comedy has ever sunk ; and the rascally Dick is
made perfectly happy at the close. *The Mistake* (1705) is
a comedy of intrigue, playing in Spain, taken in part from
Molière's *Le Dépit Amoureux* [1]. It is amusing as a whole,
but the comic servants, Lopez and Sancho and the waiting-
maid Jacinta are familiar types, while the bravo Toledo
and the tutor Metaphrastus [2] recall respectively the swordsmen and the pedants of earlier comedy. Vanbrugh likewise translated from the French a farce by D'Ancourt,
under the title of *The Country House* (1705), which is not
striking ; and left behind him an unfinished comedy,
A Journey to London, to which a fifth act was added
by Colley Cibber, who produced the play under the title of
The Provoked Husband (1728). The idea of the comedy is
novel and instructive [3] ; but I cannot think that upon the
whole this fragment exhibits the sparkling vivacity of most
of Vanbrugh's previous works. Among these I have not
mentioned his *Æsop* (1697)—a very clever version of Boursault's *Ésope à la Ville,* of which however it proved unable

*The Mis-
take* (1705).

*The Coun-
try House*
(1705).
*A Journey
to London
(unfinished).*

Æsop
(1697).

---

[1] Vanbrugh translated two other of Molière's plays ; cf. *ante,* p. 4, note.

[2] See act v. sc. 1, and act ii. sc. 1.

[3] A country-gentleman who has spent a large sum on his election for
the borough of *Gobble-guinea* comes to town as a parliament-man, in the
expectation of a place of £1000 a year from the noble lord at the head of the
Government in requital of his exertions. He brings his whole family
with him—and his wife very nearly verifies the prediction of his morose
uncle that ' before her husband has got five pound by a speech at Westminster, she will have lost five hundred at cards and dice in the parish of
St. James.' There is something in the satire on ' political ambition ' of the kind
exemplified in this play which gives it a character of its own. ' Humphry,'
says the M.P. to his son, ' perhaps you'll be a senator in time, as your father
is now ; when you are, remember your country ; spare nothing for the good
of your country ; and when you come home at the end of the sessions, you
will find yourself so adored, that your country will come and dine with
you every day in the week.' (Act iii. sc. 1.) From a note to the *Memoirs of
Sir John Reresby,* p. 413, by their last editor, Mr. J. J. Cartwright, it
appears that Yorkshire tradition identified the Sir Francis Headpiece of this
comedy with Sir Thomas Yarburgh, twice M.P. for Pontefract, whose grand-
daughter was married to Vanbrugh.

to equal the success [1]. This 'moral lecture,' as Leigh Hunt calls it, can scarcely be called a comedy, but deserves much praise for the brightness of its execution [2]. Vanbrugh also adapted Fletcher's *Pilgrim* for the stage of his own day, on a memorable occasion previously noticed (1700) [3].

Were it not, perhaps, for one of his plays, GEORGE FARQUHAR (1678–1707)[4] would hardly deserve to be ranked by the side—not of Congreve and Wycherley, but even of Vanbrugh. Farquhar, an Irishman by birth and early in life an actor on the Dublin stage (he afterwards served in the army), seems to have bestowed some attention upon the theory as well as the practice of the comic drama [5], and to have had a keen eye towards finding new expedients with

George Farquhar (1678–1707). His merits and defects.

---

[1] 'The French,' says Vanbrugh, 'have more mercury in their heads' than we.

[2] The following is its scheme—for it cannot be properly said to possess a plot. Learchus, in his admiration for Æsop, forces his daughter to bestow her hand upon the sage, who at the last moment renounces it in favour of her youthful lover. A succession of personages—including the country-gentleman Sir Polidorus Hogstye (Vanbrugh's own invention)—arrive to consult the ill-favoured old philosopher, who conveys his counsel by reciting to them a series of fables. Some of these are admirably versified ; see *e. g.* that in act i. sc. 1, concerning the nightingale who would be a linnet till she

> 'Spoil'd her voice, she strain'd her throat,
> She did, as learned women do,
>   Till every thing
>   That heard her sing
> Would run away from her—as I from you.'

' Pray speak,' Æsop has previously remarked to Hortensia, to whom this fable is addressed, ' that you may be understood ; language was designed for it, indeed it was.' The dialogue is altogether very light and amusing ; see *e. g.* Learchus' defence of his tyrannical treatment of his daughter—'I speak as a father ' (act v. sc. 1)—a passage with which Mr. J. L. Toole must have become at some time acquainted.   Part II of *Æsop*, added by Vanbrugh to the original, consists of three scenes only—the first being occupied with theatrical politics. The closing fable recited by the Beau to cap Æsop is a fair specimen of Vanbrugh's moral philosophy.

[3] *Ante*, vol. ii. p. 706, *note* 1.

[4] *The Dramatic Works of George Farquhar* have been separately edited, with Life and Notes, by the late A. C. Ewald.

[5] Leigh Hunt quotes from Farquhar's *Discourse upon Comedy in reference to the English Stage*, published by him in a miscellaneous volume (1702) which may have helped him to a commission. The extract, however, contains nothing that is very striking.

which to supplement the familiar methods of gratifying the public palate.   He is happy in the description of a wider range of manners than that commanded by Vanbrugh ; but his dialogue is in general less gay and sparkling, and while his morality is no better than that of the most reckless of his contemporaries, he has a coarseness of fibre which renders him more offensive to a refined ear.   The vivacity of his dramatic invention is however indisputable ; and the freshness of mind which enabled him to widen the range of popular comedy in his last two plays entitles him to mention among the more distinguished authors of our later comic drama.

Love and a Bottle (1698).

His earliest play, *Love and a Bottle* (1698), while in parts extremely gross in tone, and altogether coarse in treatment, is fluent rather than sparkling in its dialogue.   In some degree this comedy recalls *The Plain-Dealer* ; but the brutality of its principal personage is of a less complex kind [1].   Farquhar's idea of a hero, indicated already in this play [2], is more fully developed in his *The Constant Couple, or A Trip to the Jubilee* (1700) and its sequel *Sir Harry Wildair* (1701).   So much of plot as the former of these plays possesses, Farquhar seems to have taken from a kind of scandalous novel, imitated from Scarron, in the authorship or concoction of which he had been himself concerned [3].   It is, however, unnecessary to trace the adventures of Lady Lurewell either to their literary or to their probable historical source. Both plays doubtless derived their popularity from the figure of Sir Harry Wildair, for which Farquhar [4] with a kind of mock modesty takes credit.   In this character, whatever scope it may have provided for lively acting, the element of utter impudence reigns paramount ; nor is the manner of the impudence, to my mind, especially agreeable.

The Constant Couple, or A Trip to the Jubilee (1700).

[1] In Leanthe (disguised as a page) I can perceive nothing pathetic except her situation.   There is nothing particularly fresh or pleasing in the humour of the country-gull Mockmode, who after trying to learn fencing and dancing, and seeking the friendship of the poet Lyric (who burlesques Lee and tragedy in general), is finally fooled into and out of a mock marriage.

[2] ' *Leanthe.* How charming would virtue look in him, whose behaviour can add a grace to the unseemliness of vice! ' (act iii. sc. 1.)

[3] *The Adventures of Covent Garden* (1699).

[4] See the Dedication to *The Inconstant.*

But what fascinates one generation is not necessarily irresistible to another.   On the whole, *Sir Harry Wildair* is
perhaps happier than the earlier play ; but the design—which
is to exhibit the hero as all but absolutely incorrigibile [1]
—can hardly be borne with, and is moreover in its essence the
reverse of comic.   Parts of this play are, however, decidedly
entertaining.   Sir Harry's supposed brother (really his wife
in disguise) makes an amusing figure, which once more
illustrates the not very edifying views held by the world of
fashion and its mirror, the comic stage, as to the university
education of the age.   But though the dialogue of this comedy
is vivacious and occasionally witty [2], it must as a whole, notwithstanding its termination, be described as utterly bad in
spirit, and as furnishing a signal example of the degradation
which the English comic drama had by this time reached.
For *The Inconstant, or The Way to Win Him* (1703) Farquhar 'took the hint from Fletcher's *Wild-Goose-Chase* [3],
and to those who say, that I have spoiled the original, I
wish no other injury, but that they would say it again.'
Fletcher's play was theatrically one of the most brilliantly
successful of its author's comedies ; but Farquhar's version
cannot be denied the praise of being both brisk and entertaining ; and the fifth act (founded on fact) adds an ingenious
contrivance of the author's own.   There was moreover some
boldness in laying the scene in Paris ; although the manners,
such as they are, differ in no wise from those of the English
comedy of this age in general ; and Young Mirabel is a

Sir Harry Wildair (1701).

The Inconstant, or The Way to Win Him (1703).

[1] His wife, supposed dead, appears to him as a ghost, without disturbing
his equanimity.   On her declaring herself alive, he is at first gently incredulous, but soon reconciles himself to his happiness, and concludes the
play with ' the definition of a good wife, in the character of my own.'

[2] Lady Lurewell reappears in this play as the fashionable card-playing
wife of the unfortunate Standard—or rather he appears as her husband (' you
may have the honour,' says little Banter, ' of being called the lady's husband ;
but you will never find in any author, either ancient or modern, that she's
called Mr. Standard's wife ').   In accordance with the ' patriotic ' tone
observable in the comedy of this period, the French Marquis is a card-sharper :
' Fortune,' he says, ' give de Anglisman de riches, but nature give de
Franceman de politique to correct de unequal distribution.'   ' Monsieur le
Marquis ' must have been an ancestor of Lessing's ' le Chevalier Riccaut de
la Marlinière, Seigneur de Pret-au-val, de la Branche de Prensd'or.'

[3] *Ante*, vol. ii. p. 707.

mere reproduction of Sir Harry Wildair.   It is striking, that even an idea like that of *The Wild-Goose-Chase* should suffice to give, so to speak, more body to this play than most contemporary comedies possess.

The Twin-Rivals (1705).   In the Preface to *The Twin-Rivals* (1705) the author announces his intention of taking advantage of the success of Collier's attack upon the theatre, so as to 'make the stage flourish by virtue of that satire by which' its assailant 'thought to suppress it.'   Farquhar can however hardly be said to move very easily in his moral enterprise.   This comedy is, to say the least, quite as coarse as anything he had previously written, while the virtuous characters are not very interesting [1].   The notion of making the villain of the action a humpback is presumably meant as a tribute to morality. Teague, the Irish servant, is fairly amusing.   In *The Re-*

The Recruiting Officer (1706).   *cruiting Officer* (1706) the author sought to break fresh ground.   The comedy, dedicated 'to all friends round the Wrekin,' was intended as a sketch of country (Shropshire) manners, as well as of the humours of the recruiting system. From both points of view the attempt was legitimate and novel, and attaches a certain historical interest to the picture in which it resulted.   But the colours are in this comedy laid on as coarsely as in the lowest scenes of our eighteenth-century novels; there is little to choose between Captain Plume and Sergeant Kite, and hardly more between the young ladies

The Beaux' Stratagem (1707).   and the country wenches of Shropshire [2].   In *The Beaux' Stratagem* (1707) Farquhar achieved his master-piece.   This comedy, justly the most celebrated of his plays and destined to an enduring life on the stage, deserved its success in the first instance by the cleverness of the plot, which is ingenious without being improbable.   Some of the incidents, indeed, are of dubious import, including one at the close,—a separation by mutual consent,—which throws a glaring light on

[1] Dr. A. Brandl, *Zu Lillo's Kaufmann von London* in *Vierteljahrsschrift für Litteraturgeschichte*, vol. iii (1890), p. 54, points out that George Barnwell's faithful and virtuous friend Trueman shares name and character with the Trueman of *The Twin Rivals*, and that the conduct of the one personage closely resembles that of the other.

[2] As to the originals of the personages figuring in this comedy see W. Cooke's *Memoirs of Foote*, vol. ii. p. 223.

the view taken by the author and his age of the sanctity of the marriage-tie. But the comedy is also an excellent picture of manners. The inn with its rascally landlord and highwaymen-guests and the country-house into which the Beau is carried in a fainting-fit, stand before us as scenes from real life ; and some of the characters are drawn with much humour and spirit. The most successful conception is that of Archer, who pretends to be the valet of his friend the Beau, but carries on adventures on his own account. This became one of Garrick's most famous parts ; and indeed the easy volubility of the pretended servant furnishes an admirable opportunity [1] for a fine actor of light comedy. Altogether this play is written in the happiest of veins ; and may be regarded as the prototype of Goldsmith's *She Stoops to Conquer*, like which it hovers rather doubtfully on the borders—not always easy to determine—of comedy and farce.

Dramatists whose career extends beyond the reign of Anne.

Colley Cibber (1671–1757).

The three dramatic authors who remain to be mentioned all continued their literary activity beyond the beginning of the Georgian age of our history, so that only a part of it falls within the range of the present survey. COLLEY CIBBER [2] (1671–1757), whose *Apology for his Life* furnishes a contemporary view, unique of its kind, of a remarkable period of English stage history, gained applause on the boards as an actor before he made his first attempt as an author. His first play, *Love's Last Shift*, was produced in 1696 ; he afterwards became for a considerable time joint patentee and principal manager of Drury Lane—he was, as a satirist put it, Chancellor Cibber of the Court of Appeal for Authors, while his two colleagues sat only for form's sake ; in 1730 he was appointed poet laureate ; and in 1732 he retired from his connexion with the theatre, though he

---

[1] See especially act iii. sc. 3, the scene to which the phrase 'brother Scrub' owes its origin.—This comedy likewise introduces an Irishman (a priest).

[2] *The Dramatic Works of Colley Cibber.* 4 vols., 1760.—The best edition of the *Apology* is that of Mr. R. W. Lowe, with Notes and Supplement (2 vols., 1889). An appreciative notice of this autobiography will be found in *The Retrospective Review*, vol. i. part ii.

appeared as an actor as late as 1745.   In the latter capacity
he had gained great applause in his early days, particularly
as a representative of fops ; and it was a figure of this description which forms the most amusing character—the first

His Love's
Last Shift,
or The Fool
in Fashion
(1696).

of a long series—in his earliest play.   Of *Love's Last Shift,*
or The Fool in Fashion (1696) Cibber acknowledges Congreve's criticism to have been just, that 'it had only in it
a great many things that were *like* wit, that in reality were
not wit [1].'   Already, however, in this comedy a moral purpose is to be recognised ; indeed, the author attributes its
enduring success to 'the moral delight received from its
fable [2].'   There is no reason to disbelieve the honesty of
purpose which Cibber claims for himself as an author ; he
always wished, he says, to give profit as well as delight,
to make 'the *utile dulci*' [*sic*] his aim, and to 'have the
interest and honour of virtue in view [3].'   Passing by three

Other
earlier
plays
(1702).

comedies, *Woman's Wit, or The Lady in Fashion* (1697)—
part of which was afterwards reproduced in *The Schoolboy*
(1702)—*Love Makes a Man, or The Fop's Fortune* (1700),
partly founded on Fletcher [4], and the brisk *She Wou'd and*
She Wou'd Not, or The Kind Impostor (1703), taken from
a Spanish source, as well as the commonplace tragedy in
blank-verse, *Perolla and Izidora* (1706), which treats of an
episode of the Second Punic War and is founded on Lord
Orrery's novel of *Parthenissa*, we come to a comedy of
indisputable excellence.   No critic capable of discerning

The Care-
less Hus-
band
(1704).

real merit ought to 'deny praise' to *The Careless Husband*
(1704).   In the Dedication to this play Cibber modestly
avows his intention of seeking to reform by example the
coarseness of contemporary comedy and to produce what
may be fit entertainment for People of Quality, 'especially
the Ladies.' *The Careless Husband* doubtless contains things
which may seem out of harmony with this intention, and
the principal situation would justly be resented by a modern
audience [5].   But the purpose of this play is genuinely

---

[1] *Apology*, vol. i. p. 220.   [2] *Ib.*   [3] *Ib.*, p. 266.
[4] *The Custom of the Country* and *The Elder Brother.*
[5] According to a note by Croker to Boswell's *Life of Johnson* (Birkbeck
Hill's edition, vol. i. p. 174), every scene of *The Careless Husband* had been

moral—viz. to exhibit the triumph of pure long-suffering affection, when its object is a man not spoilt at heart. There is true pathos in the character of Lady Easy, and one may forgive her husband as one forgives Fielding's heroes, or Steele in actual life. It cannot be justly said that such a picture is an apology for vice, though doubtless it fails to treat vice from the loftiest of standpoints. The execution is upon the whole admirable; and the quarrels of Lady Betty Modish and Lord Morelove, with Lord Foppington and Lady Graveairs intervening, are in the best style of later English comedy. Lady Betty in particular is a most delightful coquette—with a heart; and the Lord Foppington of this play, who is not a mere *replica* of Vanbrugh's developement of Cibber's Sir Novelty, is one of the best easy-going fools ever invented[1]. *The Lady's Stake, or The Wife's Resentment* (1707) is a kind of *pendant* to *The Careless Husband,* its moral being the maxim that it is by love and not by angry jealousy that a wife should keep her husband to her side. Although the play has merit of its kind, and the under-plot of the triumph of Mrs. Conquest over her rival, whether or not original, is indisputably amusing, yet this comedy is not equal to its predecessor; and in truth Cibber's social philosophy, though well-intentioned and certainly on the side of morality, cannot be extolled as possessed of a very masculine character. We are already approaching the age of sentimental comedy.

The remaining plays produced by Cibber in this period being chiefly adaptations, call for no notice[2].

The Lady's Last Stake, or The Wife's Resentment (1707).

submitted by Cibber to Mrs. Brett (formerly Lady Macclesfield), the reputed mother of Richard Savage. She is said to have suggested from her experience the 'well-wrought' scene in the play, to which reference is made in the text.

[1] After carrying on a desperate flirtation with Lady Betty, he willingly resigns her to her lover, merely observing: 'I am struck dumb with the Deliberation of her Assurance; and do not positively remember that the *Non-Chalence* of my Temper ever had so bright an Occasion to shew itself before.' His phraseology has a few flowers to add to those which decorate the speech of his namesake, 'sun-burn me,' &c. When invited by Lady Betty to fall foul of 'everything that is not Gallant and Fashionable,' he is 'transported'; 'for if ever I was oblig'd to Nature for any tolerable Qualification, 'twas positively the Talent of being exuberantly pleasant upon this subject.'

[2] They include *Richard III* (1700); cf. vol. i. p. 515; *The Double Gallant,*

Mrs. Cent-
livre
(1667–
1723).

The
Perjured
Husband,
or The Ad-
ventures of
Venice
(1700).

Of the numerous plays of MRS. CENTLIVRE[1] (1667–1723) the great majority were produced before the death of Queen Anne; a very few words will, however, suffice with regard to them.

Her first dramatic effort was a tragedy in blank-verse, *The Perjur'd Husband, or The Adventures of Venice* (1700); but she only on a single occasion returned to this branch of composition, which may be assumed to have lain outside the range of her talents. Her early tragedy is without a touch of poetry, but is fairly successful in the conduct of a sufficiently straightforward action[2].

Character-
istics of her
comedies.

Her comedies, whether original or not,—for several of these borrow their plots from foreign sources[3],—bear all

or *The Sick Lady's Cure* (1707), made up, as Cibber confesses in his *Apology* (vol. ii. p. 3), 'of what little was tolerable in two or three others,' and soon laid aside as 'poetical lumber'; and *The Comical Lovers* (1707), which consisted (see *ib.*, p. 5) of ' the Comic Scenes of Dryden's *Marriage à la Mode* and of his *Maiden Queen*' put together. *Xerxes* (1699) is not included in my edition.—As to the most celebrated of Cibber's later plays, *The Non-Juror*, cf. *ante*, p. 405, *note* 4. His *The Refusal, or The Ladies' Philosophy* (1721), an adaptation of Molière's *Les Femmes Savantes*, with its character of the South Sea Director, Sir Gilbert Wrangle, has a similar historical interest. Cibber's alterations of Shakspere furnished Fielding with a subject of satire in *The Historical Register* for the year 1736, where Cibber appears under the name of Ground-Ivy: '*King John* as now writ will not do—But a word in your ear, I will make him do.' (Act iii. sc. 2.)

[1] *The Dramatic Works of the celebrated Mrs. Centlivre, with a New Account of her Life.* (Reprint.) 3 vols., 1872.—Her maiden name was Susanna Freeman, and her early adventures resembled those of a page-heroine of later Elisabethan comedy. Her successive married names were Fox, Caroll, and Centlivre. (See note to *The Dunciad*, vol. ii. p. 411, in Elwin and Court-hope's edition of Pope's *Works*, vol. iv. p. 338.)

[2] A wife in disguise kills her rival; the husband by mistake kills the wife; and the lover of the rival kills the husband. The comic under-plot, though praised by Genest, seems to me commonplace.—Mrs. Centlivre's other tragedy, *The Cruel Gift*, was not produced till 1716. The terrific situation of the last act, which in some measure recalls the climax of the old play of *Tancred and Gismunda*, finds an unexpected solution, and all ends happily. (Cf. vol. i. p. 214, and *note*. Besides the English dramatic versions of the story there noticed I am enabled to mention a very interesting one dating from the seventeenth century, which Mr. I. Gollancz is now engaged in editing.)

[3] Thus, *The Gamester* (1705) is a prose version of Jean-François Regnard's comedy of *Le Joueur* (printed in Jules Janin's *Chefs d'œuvre Dramatiques du XVIIIme Siècle*, vol. i) to which therefore the merit of the effective plot belongs;—unless, as has been alleged, Regnard in his turn had derived the idea of his piece from Dufresnoy's *Le Chevalier Joueur*. The gambling-scene, which is vigorously realistic, is however original; and the Marquis is turned

an unmistakeable family likeness to one another. Their
authoress needed no indulgence as a playwright on the score
of her sex; for not one among the dramatists contemporary with her better understood the construction of light
comic actions, or the use of those conventional figures of
comedy which irresistibly appeal to the mirthful instincts of
a popular audience. Inasmuch as she had no hesitation in re-
sorting to the broadest expedients of farce, she was sure of
the immediate effect which was all that her ambition desired;
for she never flattered herself, as she confesses, 'that anything
she was capable of doing could support the Stage[1].' In
one instance, however, she virtually invented a personage of
really novel humour; and in another she devised a character
to which the genius of a great actor ensured a long-
enduring life on the boards. Marplot in *The Busy-Body*
and Don Felix in *The Wonder* are creations upon which any
comic dramatist might look back with satisfaction; and on
the former, indeed, Mrs. Centlivre relies as conferring a real
title to popular favour[2]. As a rule, however, her characters
are little more than thin outlines left to the actor to fill
up. This cavil applies particularly to those of her comedies
which are to all intents and purposes mere pictures of
manners. Such is *The Beau's Duel, or A Soldier for the
Ladies* (1704), in which we are introduced to Sir William
Mode, one of the fops in whom the comedy of this period
abounds, distinguished only by a few novelties in the way of
asseverations, such as 'enfeeble me!' An ampler measure
of fun will be found in the character of Ogle, who 'fancies
every Body is in Love with him'; and the duel between the

*The Beau's
Duel, or
A Soldier
for the
Ladies
(1704).*

by Mrs. Centlivre (a good Whig) into the patriotic caricature of a supposed
Frenchman.—In *Love's Contrivance, or Le Médecin malgré Lui* (1703)·'some
scenes I confess are partly taken from Molière.'—Of *The Perplex'd Lovers*
(1712) 'most of the plot' is avowedly taken from a Spanish play; '*The Stolen
Heiress, or The Salamanca Doctor Outwitted* (1702) and the excellent comedy of
The Wonder (1714) were likewise very probably derived from Spanish originals.
   [1] Preface to *The Man's Bewitch'd*.
   [2] See the Prologue to the same comedy:
            'Tho' here and there, a Scene should fail to take,
            Yet spare her for the Busy-Body's sake.'
The Man's Bewitch'd (1709) is a farcical comedy in some degree resembling
The Beaux' Stratagem of Farquhar, but far inferior to it.

pair is a good bit of farce [1]. Mrs. Plotwell, a portrait probably drawn from life, and the most ' convincing' personage
in the piece, is at the same time the least respectable. *Basset-
Table* [2] (1706) can hardly be said to have a plot ; but the
characters, though mere sketches, together make up an
entertaining group ; among them Lady Reveller, who turns
night into day, and keeps the basset-table at which she is
ready to ruin her acquaintances, together with Mrs. Sago,
the doting druggist's wife, and Valeria, a F.R.S. in petticoats, but with feelings to spare for a lover as well as for
a *lumbricus laetus*. In *Love at a Venture* (1706), on the
other hand, the plot is happy—turning on the impudence
of an admirer of the fair sex in general, who in order to
carry on his courtship of two ladies at the same time, pretends to be two gentlemen at once, and engages in a third
intrigue into the bargain. But the personages are here again
the conventional figures of contemporary comedy. In *The
Busy-Body* (1709) and its continuation, *Marplot in Lisbon*
(1710), we meet, as already suggested, with an original
character of genuine humour ; for Marplot differs from Mar-
All and from his original, the hero of Molière's *L'Étourdi*,
by committing a succession of exploits in action as well as
in speech. He is the parent of that long-lived favourite of
our own days, Paul Pry [3], and some of his unexpected
apparitions—especially one down the chimney—are irresistibly ludicrous. Among Mrs. Centlivre's other plays, so
far as they fall within the period of my survey, I need only
once more mention *The Wonder, or A Woman Keeps a
Secret* (1714), of which the plot centres in a happy contrivance, familiar to the later stage, whereby a lover's jealousy suspects a rival in an innocent gentleman, whose real
magnet is another lady amicably concealed in her fair friend's
house. The struggle between love and jealousy in Don Felix,
in conjunction with his ready subservience to Violante's most
daring device, furnished Garrick with the materials for one of

Side notes:

The Basset-Table (1706).

Love at a Venture (1706).

The Busy-Body (1709), *and Marplot in Lisbon* (1710).

The Wonder, or A Woman Keeps a Secret (1714).

---

[1] Act ii. sc. 3.

[2] ' *Thursday.—The Bassette Table*' is the title of one of the *Town Eclogues* of Lady Mary Wortley Montagu, written in 1715.

[3] 'Nay 'tis only I, Colonel ; don't be angry, you forgot your Snuff-box ; and I thought you would want it ; so I brought it you, that's all, Sir,' &c.

his most conspicuous successes. Among Mrs. Centlivre's later comedies, *A Bold Stroke for a Wife* (1718) is remembered on account of the famous *quiproquo* of 'the real Simon Pure' and the indignity to which he is subjected by the ruthless Colonel Fainwell's assumption of his name and character; while the farce of *A Gotham Election* (1715) is worth mentioning as a dramatic illustration of a phase of English life to which the political events of the time were giving unprecedented prominence [1].

Mrs. Centlivre's dialogue is fluent and easy rather than sparkling; and of wit she displays few traces. Both in style and in the contrivance of situations she habitually sinks to the lowest level of our post-Restoration drama, exhibiting no trace of sympathy with the better and purer tone which was gradually gaining ground in English comedy. That her latest play, *The Artifice* (1722), should contain a slight element of sentimental comedy in the blank-verse spoken by the injured Louisa, is an obvious concession to fashion. The moral tone of this authoress is not a whit superior to that of 'Astraea' herself.

Thus it is with a certain sense of satisfaction, which I think will be shared by other students of our national dramatic literature, that having closed the list of the tragic poets of this age with the name of Addison, I end the list of contemporary writers of comedy with another name, inseparably connected in the history of our literature with that of his beloved friend and associate. To the spirit that animated the work carried on hand in hand by Addison and his faithful helpmate SIR RICHARD STEELE [2] (1671–1729), the plays left to us by the latter bear emphatic testimony [3].

[1] It was in 1710 and 1715, says T. Wright in his *Caricature History of the Georges*, that English parliamentary elections 'first took that character of turbulence and acrimony which for more than a century destroyed the peace and tranquillity of our country towns.'—The subject was again dramatically treated by Fielding in his *Pasquin* (1736).

[2] *The Dramatic Works of Sir Richard Steele, Knt.* 1760.—I rejoice to be able to refer the reader to Mr. Austin Dobson's admirable memoir of Steele in the *English Worthies* Series (1886).

[3] See the Dedication of *The Tender Husband* to Addison: 'I should not offer it to you as such' (*i.e.* as 'no improper memorial of an inviolable Friendship') 'had I not been very careful to avoid every thing that might

In his Dedication of them to the Duchess of Hamilton he declares that 'in writing Plays, not to displease such whose Minds are filled with the worthiest Ideas of what is Laudable in real Life, is much more than to escape the Censure of such as are more inclined to observe the Conduct of the characters, as they are part of a Dramatic Entertainment.' In a word, he is in his plays, as in every other composition that came from his hand, a designedly moral writer; and the occasional licences of expression which he permits himself are noticeable only as furnishing a useful test as to how much in the manners of a comedy of this—or indeed of any— period should be attributed to the writer, and how much to his age. The resolution which in the Preface to one of his plays[1] he announces of counteracting the evil tendency of the stage 'to draw Occasion of Mirth from those Images which the Religion of our Country tells us we ought to tremble at with Horror,' is pursued by him with unswerving stedfastness; and here as elsewhere he devotes his talents to the service of virtue and wisdom, and to the denunciation of vice and folly, profanity and ignorance. What Gay so admirably said of Steele's writings in general, although no doubt with a special reference to the extraordinary popularity achieved by *The Tatler*, applies likewise to the dramatic compositions which had for the most part preceded that famous periodical in date of publication.

'It would have been a jest, some time since, for a man to have asserted that anything witty could be said in praise of a married state, or that Devotion and Virtue were any way necessary to the character of a Fine Gentleman. . . . Instead of complying with the false sentiments or vicious tastes of the Age—either in morality, criticism or good-breeding—he has boldly assured them, that they were altogether in the wrong; and commanded them, with an authority which perfectly well became him, to surrender themselves to his arguments for Virtue and Good Sense. It is incredible to conceive the effect his writings have had upon the Town; how many thousand follies they have either quite banished or given a very

look ill-natur'd, immoral or prejudicial to what the better Part of Mankind hold Sacred and Honourable.'

[1] *The Lying Lover.*

great check to! how much countenance they have added to Virtue and Religion! how many people they have rendered happy, by showing them it was their own faults if they were not so[1]!'

It must, at the same time, in comparing the general char- *His humour.* acteristics of Steele's plays with those of his non-dramatic prose writings, be allowed that in the former his humour, although both gay and fresh, is at times rather thin. But the quality of refinement suffers from too close a contrast with its opposite; and we cannot wonder that in Steele it should at times fail to satisfy even critics more appreciative than John Dennis. For the rest, besides being one of the *His politics.* kindest of men, Christians, and good fellows, Steele was not only an ardent patriot, but a strong war Whig, and in his plays, as elsewhere, there is no mistaking his eager and unfaltering political partisanship.

In pursuing the moral and social aims of which, to his *Steele the real founder of sentimental comedy.* enduring honour, he never allowed himself to lose sight, Steele as a dramatist came to mistake the true means and methods of the comic drama. His own comic genius lacked the sustained vigour which is required by the stage; and his artistic sense was too keen altogether to have left him unconscious of his inability to satisfy his moral purpose by holding up to ridicule with unflagging persistence those human vices and follies which are the proper subjects of comedy. He therefore called in sentiment to the aid of humour. Availing himself of the reaction against the grosser methods of provoking laughter and amusement which had set in as part of the general reaction against the licence of the Restoration age[2], he took a hint from Colley Cibber, who so carefully watched the currents of the public taste, and became the real founder of that Sentimental Comedy which during a period lying beyond the range of

[1] See Gay's tract, addressed in 1711 'To a Friend in the Country,' and entitled *The Present State of Wit*, cited by Mr. Austin Dobson, *u. s.*, pp. 123 *seqq.*

[2] It is curious that the masterpiece of the Chinese drama (*Pi-Pa-Ki*, or *The Story of the Lute*), which is at the same time one of the most touching of sentimental plays, should be stated to have been originally designed with a view to producing a reaction against the immorality of the dramatic productions at the time in fashion.

these volumes exercised so strong and, on the whole, so far from salutary an influence upon the progress of our dramatic literature. There is no reason for attributing Steele's innovation to any foreign literary influence[1]; on the other hand it would be unjust to hold his tentative beginnings responsible for the futility of successors who, being altogether deficient in any kind of comic power, in the end came to abandon even the semblance of true comic intention. In so far however as their aberrations followed the lines into which he was the first to cause English comedy consciously to deviate, Steele must be held to have contributed to the decline of the English drama, and in particular to the sinking of the sap in that branch of it to which his plays both nominally and in their general design belong.

The Funeral, or Grief à-la-Mode (1702).

The Funeral, or Grief à-la-Mode (1702) has a good intrigue, and is written with vivacity. Lady Harriot presents a pleasant picture of a pure merry-hearted girl; and the honest steward Mr. Trusty is the earliest example of a type which became familiar to the stage and of which Sheridan's Rowley is the best-known specimen. There are also at least two scenes of broad humour—that introducing the ragged soldiers in act iv, and the scene in the last act, where the widow prepares for the funeral of her late lamented husband, while her friend Tattleaid administers consolation after her kind, with her mouth full of pins[2].

---

[1] The introduction of sentimental comedy (*la comédie larmoyante*) in France is usually ascribed to Nivelle de la Chaussée—'*le sage et modeste La Chaussée*'—the earliest of whose plays appeared a few years after Steele's death. As in England, so in France, and at a later date, mainly through Lessing's influence, in Germany, sentimental comedy and the domestic drama ('the two worst varieties,' says Grillparzer, 'that exist') were inextricably mixed up with one another. The attractions of the combined species are of a kind against which criticism will in the future as in the past often protest unheard; for it is not often that a Zadig comes into power at Babylon. (Zadig, when prime-minister, 'faisait représenter des tragédies où l'on pleurait, et des comédies où l'on riait; ce qui était passé de mode depuis longtemps, et ce qu'il fit renaître parcequ'il avait du goût.')

[2] 'Hark ye, Hussey,' is the Widow's request to her friend, 'if you should outlive me, as I hope you won't, take care I an't buried in Flannel, 'twould never become me, I'm sure.' Pope adapted this allusion to the cruel statute 30 Charles II, cap. 3, in a well-known couplet of his *Moral Essays*. (The statute is referred to as 'the woollen act' in the Prologue to Dryden and Lee's *Œdipus*.)

Already in this comedy the sentiment is slightly obtrusive, but not to the same extent as in Steele's later plays [1].

Steele's next comedy, *The Lying Lover, or The Ladies' Friendship* (1703) announces itself as 'a stranger on the stage; his sire de Vega'—but it was in truth taken from Corneille, who in his turn had borrowed the idea of his play from another Spanish dramatist, contemporary with Lope [2]. Young Bookwit (Corneille's Dorante and Foote's Young Wilding) is therefore not an original character. He is however too entertaining a type to be too narrowly scrutinised in any respect; and the final cause of the character almost seems to be its suitability to the genius of an English actor of our own times.

The serious portion of the plot [3] of *The Lying Lover* is Steele's own invention, and renders this play remarkable as the first instance of Sentimental Comedy proper. The origin of the mistake here committed is to be sought in a distrust of the means by which Comedy works, as if they were insufficient for the production of the requisite dramatic effect. Instead of contenting himself with making vice and folly ridiculous, the author applies himself to provoking a response from the emotion of pity. Such a response is not likely to be refused to his kindly and tender touch; but his resort to an expedient outside the range of the proper resources of Comedy announces the approaching virtual extinction of that species in our dramatic literature.

The moral of *The Tender Husband, or The Accomplish'd Fools* (1705) is one which must have been congenial enough to its soft-hearted and uxorious author, although *The*

---

[1] The Preface to *The Funeral* should not be overlooked; the comment on W. W. the embalmer's advertisement is as good of its kind as anything in *The Tatler*.

[2] The original of Corneille's *Menteur* was Ruiz de Alarcon's *Verdad Sospechosa*; but Corneille at first thought this play to be by Lope. (Cf. Ticknor, vol. ii. p. 335.) *Le Menteur* had been translated already in 1661 under the title of *The Mistaken Beauty, or The Liar*. Foote likewise professed to have taken his *The Lyar* (1762) from Lope de Vega; he had certainly seen Steele's comedy. (Cf. Genest, vol. iv. p. 649.) Goldoni composed an Italian prose version of *Le Menteur*, which he thought a good comedy, but susceptible of the infusion of a much greater degree of humour into its principal character. (*Memoirs of Goldoni, English Translation*, vol. i. p. 377.)

[3] It is marked off from the rest by being written in blank-verse.

Careless Husband of Cibber, acted in the previous year, had probably suggested its employment as a dramatic motive. In Steele's comedy, the maxim that love lies at the root of duty, and that on no other basis will it prove possible to establish happiness between man and wife, is pleasantly worked out, though perhaps with a want of that fulness of treatment which we frequently desiderate in this delightful author. The character of Miss Biddy—as to her own unceasing satisfaction she is named, being a worshipper of the heroes of romance, ' Philocles, Artaxerxes, Oroondates and the rest of the Heroick Lovers '—is extremely entertaining[1].

The Conscious Lovers (1722).

The last of Steele's comedies, *The Conscious Lovers*, was not produced till 1722, and therefore falls outside the limits of this survey. Its original title seems to have been *The Unfashionable Lovers*. In this play, although its plot is founded on the *Andria* of Terence, we obviously already have a comedy of which the main interest is sentimental; indeed, the story of Indiana and of Bevil's virtuous love for her might have served as a subject for an Iffland or a Kotzebue[2]. But though Steele was thus directing dramatic literature

[1] She desires, like Lydia Languish in *The Rivals*, to be wooed and won in something out of the humdrum way. ' I am almost of Opinion, that had Oroondates been as pressing as Clerimont, *Cassandra* had been but a pocket-book. It looks so ordinary, to go out at a Door to be married—Indeed, I ought to be taken out of a Window, and run away with.' (Act iv.)—In the charming essay on Mrs. Lennox's *The Female Quixote, or The Adventures of Arabella* (1752), in his *Eighteenth Century Vignettes* (1st series, 1892, p. 64), Mr. Austin Dobson says that the heroine of that famous romance has her prototypes in the *Précieuses Ridicules* and in Steele's Biddy Tipkin.

[2] Young Mr. Bevil is a hero deserving of the highest respect, and his resistance to the temptation of fighting a duel with his friend (for the sake of which episode Steele declares the whole play to have been written) constitutes a courageous protest on the part of the author against a vicious and senseless practice. But now and then the virtue of his hero approaches those borders which in drama and novel it is so difficult for a good young man to avoid,— the borders of priggishness; as when he bows the music-master to the door, and subsequently explains to the admiring Indiana his desire to do honour to superior talent in an inferior position. Old Humphrey is the conventional figure of the trusty old family servant; on the other hand, there is real freshness and humour—without the least touch of impropriety—in the loves of Tom (Bevil's servant) and Phillis (Lucinda's maid). Tom's description of their Pyramus-and-Thisbe sorrows while he was cleaning the windows outside and she in, is in Steele's happiest manner. Mr. Dobson, *Richard Steele*, p. 208, shows that it must have been *calqué sur le vif*, since Steele had first printed it in *The Guardian* as an actual experience.

into a path sure to end in artificiality and weakness, his last play, like its predecessors—and like everything he wrote—shows his steady adherence to the guiding principle of his literary life. The homage which he consistently paid to virtue, never constrained him to do violence to nature. Steele and Addison[1] were in truth the literary champions who confronted and drove back from its vantage-ground the shameless immorality which had so long flaunted its insolent attractions on the surface of English society, and which might in the end have destroyed some of the noblest elements of the national life. If in Addison's tragedy and in Steele's comedies respectively traces are still observable of the affectation of Heroic Virtue and of the licence of Restoration mirth, this could hardly have been otherwise, and the inner consistency of all their literary labours remains unimpaired. How little could it be foreseen that the success of what seemed the lightest and the most fleeting among their productions was signally to advance another literary growth, destined to inherit much of the popular vigour, the human interests, and the high aspirations, of our old drama! The importance of *The Tatler* and *The Spectator* for the history of the English novel belongs, however, to another field of enquiry.

Consistency between Steele and Addison's plays and their essays.

It has been seen in what respects and in what measure our drama had before the outbreak of the Civil War declined from the height to which it had been raised by the great masters of earlier days. When it had once more recovered possession of that arena with which no living drama can dispense, our dramatists could not possibly be expected to return altogether into the ancient paths, unaffected by the influences, native and foreign, in operation around them. The contemporaries of the Restoration were at once too far removed in time from the great Elisabethans, and too near them, for such an attempt to have been feasible on their part. They were moreover—

Concluding remarks on the later Stuart drama.

---

[1] Readers of Fielding will remember Parson Adams' opinion of Steele's last comedy and its distinguished tragic contemporary : 'I never heard of any plays fit for a Christian to read, but *Cato* and *The Conscious Lovers* ; and, I must own, in the latter there are some things almost solemn enough for a sermon.'

in some respects for good, in more for evil—too conscious of the necessity of maintaining an intimate relation between the drama and the existing currents of literature and society to be willing to engage in any attempt to archaise their form of art.   Such a return it was left to a much later period of our literature to essay, when the Romantic School endeavoured either to bridge or to leap the gulf interposed between present and past.

Conditions under which it might have become a legitimate developement of the Elisabethan.

While, however, an absolute return to the past was out of the question, no reason existed why a legitimate developement should not be hoped and striven for.   Had the Restoration drama and that of the ensuing period been in true sympathy with the Elisabethan, a future of this kind lay before it.   But to convert such a prospect into possession, the new drama must likewise have been in sympathy with those qualities in the Elisabethan which had formed part of its very life and being,—must have proved true in spirit if not in the letter to the higher purposes of the dramatic art, to the nobler tendencies of the national life, and to the eternal demands of moral law.   Because, while

The later Stuart drama untrue to these conditions.

following its own courses, our dramatic literature in the later Stuart period was as a whole untrue to these traditions, and never altogether recovered from the aberrations in one direction or another to which it had abandoned itself, its history is that of a decay such as no brilliancy, either borrowed or original, can conceal.

Marked separation between tragedy and comedy.

Owing in part no doubt to the influence of the French theatre, the separation between tragedy and comedy became so marked in our post-Restoration drama, that in the large majority of instances the style and manner of a play suffice of themselves to determine the branch to which it claims to belong.   Indeed, this separation is even more emphatic in the English than in the French drama itself, where the same metrical form serves for tragedy and for the higher kind of comedy, while our comic dramatists, with the exception of a very few experiments, confine themselves to the use of prose [1].

[1] The single instance of a comedy in (blank) verse in this period is, so far as I know, Crowne's *The Married Beau* (*ante*, p. 407).   Sir George Etheredge's *The Comical Revenge* and Dryden's *The Rival-Ladies* are tragi-comedies, in which the alternation of metre and prose corresponds to that of the themes.

And it is significant that when, towards the close of the period under review, an attempt is made to introduce into comedy an element of sentiment—and morality—to which she had long been a stranger, the use of verse simultaneously endeavours to re-assert itself. But throughout the earlier part of this period, although the term 'tragi-comedy' has not yet altogether fallen out of use, the mixed species which combines tragic with comic scenes is but little cultivated; and tragedy gathers her robes around her with a more self-conscious fear of their coming into contact with the flying skirts of her sister.

It therefore seemed on the whole admissible, as well as convenient, except in the instance of particular writers who like Dryden are of equal importance for the history of both tragedy and of comedy, to consider the progress of each of these branches of our dramatic literature separately, though the influences to which they were subjected were necessarily in many cases identical; and the same course may be pursued in these few concluding observations. The phases through *Summary* which English tragedy successively passed in the time from *of the history of* the Restoration to the death of Queen Anne cannot always *tragedy in* be kept distinct from one another; and it would be quite *this period.* futile to attempt to do so by the guidance of the theories *Critical theories* and principles at different times professed by the several *not con-* dramatists. Following the example of Corneille, they *sistently followed* eagerly sought to come before the public as masters of the *by their* theory of their art as well as of its practice. From Dryden *authors.* and Howard to Granville and Congreve we have a constant succession of critic-dramatists, not to mention writers such as Rymer[1], Gildon[2], and Dennis[3], whose fame—or notoriety—as critics has completely overshadowed the memory of their efforts as writers of plays. But while announcing, in forms variously modified, their adherence to this or that principle of dramatic construction or execution, while declaring in favour of the Unity of Action, or indicating the extent to which they would allow themselves to depart

No reference need of course be made to the couplets which, as Mr. Trapwit would say, 'inculcate a particular moral at the end of every act.'

[1] Cf. *ante*, vol. i. pp. 522 *seqq.*

[2] Cf. *ante*, p. 428.   [3] Cf. *ante*, p. 426.

from the Unity of Time or of Place, the dramatists were in general only seeking to reconcile the exigences of literary taste and fashion with the demands and traditions of the national genius. The former largely pointed to foreign models ; but since it was impossible to follow these implicitly, at all events in the first instance, the critical humour of the age was well suited by the introduction and temporary maintenance of what Sir Walter Scott[1] justly describes as 'certain romantic whimsical limitations of the dramatic art.' But a steadfast adherence to principles, or even to the semblance of principles, was as little the order of the day in the literary as in the political world ; nor had the influence of the old masters of the national drama by any means wholly died out. So long as any dramatic power whatever remained in our tragic poets, points of contact with Elisabethan tragedy were sure to be discovered ; —indeed such are easily noticeable even in the highly artificial composition which at the close of this period was hailed as the 'first reasonable English tragedy,' and which might have seemed designed to bring the national tragic drama to a solemn euthanasia.

The more clearly distinguishable of the phases referred to in the history of English tragedy in the period of its decay have been sufficiently illustrated in the preceding

Heroic plays.

pages. By the King's command, the loyal Lord Orrery was supposed to have set up the standard of Heroic Plays, round which the brilliant example of Dryden for a time rallied the efforts of contemporary tragic poets, and though, as has been seen, certain tentative efforts had been previously made by other dramatic writers in the same direction, it was upon Dryden that alone depended the recognition and respect that would be paid to the gorgeous banner. The new species—for such it certainly pretended to be—commended itself by its novel choice of themes, to a large extent supplied by recent French romance, by its novel garb of rime, likewise introduced into the English drama from France (for to speak of re-introduction would

[1] See his *Essay on the Drama*, first published in the *Encyclopaedia Britannica*.

be misleading), and by its claim to rise 'as far above the ordinary proportion of the stage' as a heroic poem soars 'beyond the common words and actions of human life[1].' But the themes which to the patient readers of Scudéry novels might seem of their nature inexhaustible, could not long suffice for the satisfaction of theatrical audiences, however select in composition; and the form, as attempted to be permanently established, was doomed to remain an exotic that failed to strike root in the soil. Dryden, to begin with, claimed for the English tragic muse the right to combine her native inheritance of freedom with these newly-imported acquisitions. Subsequently, undismayed by the ridicule which had seized upon the extravagances of the new style together with other materials of satire ready to hand, rather than upon the pretended principles of the new style itself, he again insisted upon the superior freedom which according to his view it permitted; and all but anticipated in earnest the mock boast supplied by 'a friend' to Fielding's tragic poet, that the muse

Develope-ment of the species by Dryden.

'can make what ne'er was made before:
Can search the realms of Fancy, and create
What never came into the brain of Fate[2].'

But while the foremost tragic poet thus invited Tragedy to rival the sensuous effects (without disdaining the mechanical aids) of Opera, the moral sameness of the tragic themes and of the sentiments round which those themes revolved, prepared for this transient phase of dramatic composition a speedier extinction than that to which by their form and their matter the 'heroic plays' had condemned themselves. A desire for change once more prevailed. In the last of his noteworthier disquisitions on the tragic drama Dryden is found once more labouring to reconcile the supposed demands of dramatic theory with his dramatic instincts; while at the same time he endeavoured to give expression to his views by essaying—nor essaying ignobly—to rival Shakspere on his own ground. But although after this he produced one or two works of

[1] See Dryden's *Essay on Heroic Plays.*
[2] *Pasquin* (act iii).

merit and interest by virtue of their tragic characterisation, he was in truth already growing weary of the stage itself; and though he had put a decisive end to the species of the rimed heroic drama, he failed to point the way effectively or enduringly to a legitimate and living new developement of English tragedy.

Lee.

Among the other tragic poets of this period, Lee had been subject to the same influences as Dryden. Like Dryden, he allowed political partisanship to intrude upon the stage;—but to this ugly chapter in the history of the Restoration drama I need not again advert. In the outward form of his tragedies he accommodated himself to Dryden's practice; the rhetorical character of his genius made him even less capable of cultivating his art in broader and freer growths, but its energy raises him above the level of a mere

Otway.

imitator. Otway, the most gifted tragic poet of the younger generation contemporary with Dryden, brought back into English tragedy a breath of the Elisabethan days. In addition to a keen insight into the dramatic excellence of themes, he possessed a real gift of tragic pathos; but he lacked the self-restraint which genius itself can rarely forego, and his efforts were as incomplete as his end was premature.

Decline of tragedy.

Neither Southerne nor Rowe, though each of them was possessed of certain dramatic qualities out of the common, nor any of their contemporaries, are worthy of being compared as tragic poets to Lee and Otway; to Congreve's solitary tragedy one is tempted to apply an emblem of Quarles', 'Tinnit—inane est'; and thus the English tragic drama could no longer rely on itself for the determination of its future course. Rymer, Gildon, and Langbaine were not the men to settle it by their canons of criticism, or by their cavils against particular tragic poets; and the censures which had made themselves audible in these and other writers were swallowed up in judgments of a wider significance. The excesses of a long and turbulent period of the English drama had, as will be more especially noted with reference to comedy, produced their inevitable reaction; the Sovereigns who followed upon the Revolution— the good Queen Mary in particular, albeit a friend of the

theatre—had exercised a real if not very potent influence
in favour of good manners and decorum; the offences of
the stage had been exposed with force and spirit by a
censor to whom the world of letters and even the idle world
had been obliged to listen; and elsewhere, while De Foe
was inculcating the lessons of a sound homespun morality
in pamphlet upon pamphlet, Steele and Addison were by
their constant appeals to all the kindliest and more refined
associations to be found in the life of the men and the
women around them, binding faster the alliance between
good manners and good morals. When genius—which
takes its own course and finds its own style,—has nothing
to say in the matter, influences such as these will always
operate in favour of forms of composition bound down by
rules which exclude licence, and which even vigilantly control freedom, of manner. Under the agency of not wholly
dissimilar causes, French tragedy itself had sacrificed much
of its earlier vigour and passion for the sake of qualities
more acceptable to the 'reformed' Court of Lewis XIV.
Such a model might well commend itself to Addison's
tranquil hand; and the transition, if transition it can be
called, was easy from Rowe to Addison. Hesitatingly he
allowed his revised college-exercise to take its chance
upon the stage. Dennis might cavil, but Voltaire approved; *Extinction*
and though 'some senseless trifling tales, as that of *Othello*,' *of English*
might still continue 'impiously to assume the sacred name of *national*
Tragedy[1],' though Rowe and Addison themselves might con- *tragedy as*
a literary
tribute, in their generation, towards vindicating the honour *growth.*
of the greatest of the Elisabethans, and though, so long as
the stage endured, hope could never become utterly extinct,
—as a literary growth English national tragedy was dead.

'For modern comedy,' says the critic who so loudly *Comedy.*
deplored the aberrations of English tragedy from the
Aristotelian rules, 'doubtless our English are the best in
the world'; and so far as the dramatic literature of this
age is concerned, there can be no question but that from
a purely literary point of view the sum-total of its comic

[1] Rymer.

Its contact with the times.

works must be rated at a far higher value than that of its tragic. It was impossible that comedy should as completely as tragedy seek to cut itself off from its native soil, in an age whose tendencies and manners furnished to the muse of mirth so promising a field of materials. The dominant reaction against Puritanism could nowhere find so direct and facile expression as in the productions of the comic stage; and in proportion as the times were poor in imaginative genius, and out of sympathy with many ideal currents of thought and sentiment which experience seemed to have proved illusory, English comedy became more and more a drama of real life. Different styles indeed continued

Extinction of romantic comedy and cognate species.

even here to find representatives in different writers. The spirit of the old romantic comedy had long ago fled; the airy fancies of Shakspere could not inspire to similar flights in so gross an atmosphere; even such an imitation as Suckling's *Goblins* found no imitators; even the graceful artificialities of the pastoral drama could not--except here and there in a translation—be revived in an age which had learnt to laugh at the shepherds of Arcadia as the age of Cervantes had learnt to laugh at Amadis de Gaul[1]. The very masque was no longer a species of Court entertainment capable of competing with more simply sensuous attractions; it has been seen how little of poetry remained in an isolated endeavour like Crowne's *Calisto*. The attempts of Shadwell and one or two others in the direction of poetic comedy were neither uniformly original, nor otherwise worthy of a more than passing notice; what elements of this description admitted of being combined with the comic drama were absorbed by the hybrid species of the opera and the ballet, on which there is no reason

Perfection in this period of comic prose dialogue.

further to dwell. On the other hand, to the prose dialogue of our Restoration comedy must be directly traced the quick growth in the Restoration age of an English prose style distinguished by an ease, an elasticity, and a grace formerly unknown to our literature—a growth attributable to a combination of influences, but above all to the incomparable

---

[1] See an account in *The Retrospective Review*, vol. vii. part ii, of *The Extravagant Shepherd* (' a *Don Quixote* of pastoral poetry ') published in 1654.

flexibility of the greatest writer of the age, who found as
it were an instrument ready to his hand. The stage,
which had reflected the world in so many things, at last
began to reproduce its actual speech, and the art of a great
master of style such as Congreve, taking this actual speech
as its material, could in its turn transform it into so choice
a texture of diction that it is without a rival in the literature of English prose.

No new species of the comic drama proper formed itself *Licence of*
in this period, although towards its close may be noticed *political*
the beginnings of modern English farce. The introduc- *comment.*
tion—with a violence hitherto unknown—of elements of
political and religious partisanship exercised no important
influence upon the progress of English comedy as a literary
species, though as a matter of course their admission could
not otherwise than render its mirth coarser, and infuse into it
an extraneous element of cruelty of purpose. Soon after the
close of this period comedy was to venture upon an unprecedented degree of licence in this direction, and thereby to
bring about a legislation for the partial control of the stage
which was well warranted by sound principles of government,
and which, it is to be hoped, no mistaken notions of liberty
will ever induce a democratic legislature to reverse.

With the help of Spanish and French plays, to which *English*
they continued to resort through the whole of this period, *and foreign*
our dramatists found little difficulty in obtaining the *comedy.*
materials for comic plots, and in varying the figures on
which they concentrated their chief comic efforts. But
they generally found that the complicated Spanish plots,
whether simplified or not, required to be supported by
characters of native English directness ; and they had
perhaps unfortunately convinced themselves that a single
French plot would not suffice for an effective English
comedy. At the same time the higher efforts of French
comedy of character, as well as the refinements of style
natural to the best of their models, were alike accommodated to the ruder appetites and the grosser tastes of their
patrons. They often succeeded, as they almost invariably
boasted to have done, in strengthening the borrowed texture

Prevailing immorality of English comedy. of their plays ; and never added comic humour without at the same time adding coarseness of their own. Yet, even thus, the true vigour of English comedy might have remained unimpaired, had these authors remembered that, so long as they essayed the task of exposing the follies and the ridiculous vices even of a particular age, they could not dispense with a moral standard of which the best of that age had retained a consciousness. Such a writer as Shadwell had caught something not only of the art, but of the spirit of Ben Jonson ; but Shadwell in most of his works was like the rest of his earlier contemporaries, and like the brilliant group which succeeded them, usually content to take his tone of moral sentiment from the reckless sphere of society for which he wrote. This deliberate ignoring of moral tone and purpose is the true cause of the failure of our post-Restoration comic dramatists, as a body, to satisfy the demands from which it was impossible for their art to hold aloof. They essayed—or pretended—to draw character as well as to paint manners ; but so entirely caught were they in the toils of the vicious manners of their age, that they forfeited the guidance of an ethical standard. They had not yet made the discovery, reserved for a later generation, that an aesthetical standard may serve as a substitute ; or they would have added self-deception to self-indulgence. Thus they proved in the main unequal to the higher purposes and the more strenuous tasks of comedy ; and choosing those paths by which a comic dramatist is at all times only too easily able to commend himself to the favours of his immediate public, they achieved little as interpreters of those contrarieties of human nature and life which it is the supreme function of their art to illustrate, and did much by their 'pleasantry to countenance and cherish' the social and moral decay at which it behoved them to point the finger of scorn [1].

[1] '*Epicurus.* I suspect, Menander, that you enjoy the follies of men in our rotten state as flies enjoy fruit in its decay.

Menander. What can we do with such men as those about us better than laugh at them ?

Epicurus. Nothing with them, but much by keeping apart. If they laugh at each other for their weaknesses and their vices, these countenanced

Pedantry alone would insist upon the application of a moral standard, or of the requirement of a moral purpose, to the extravagance of a professed romantic fancy or to the centrifugal design of a sheer farce. Such structures as these are alike reared on the quicksands of unreality, over which who would hesitate to pass in a lightsome moment? It would be absurd to pause in order to reconcile such fancies or humours to the moral laws that govern the solid actual world, or even to raise an objection to the presentment of these laws in a perverted or inverted form.

But there can be no question of conceding an analogous *This immo-* licence to comedy proper—and least of all to a form of *rality not* comedy which proposes to bring before us men and women *or unreal.* not only as they are, but as they are in the particular time and place in which the spectators of the play are accustomed to seek and find them. Charles Lamb's famous apology for the licence of Restoration comedy condemns itself as a hopeless paradox even without the help of the incandescent commonsense of Macaulay[1]. The question is not whether either in the later Stuart days, or possibly in times nearer to our own, many a spectator and spectatress of stage wantonness may have taken comfort to themselves from its inevitable finality and obvious illusoriness. The same easy belief that if reader, spectator or hearer is made happy for the moment, all must be well, is habitually indulged in other spheres of art— literary, pictorial, musical. But in face of the footlights we are a little too near to actual life for such idle fancies. The theatre has always been candid enough to wait upon the wishes, and to reflect the preferences, of its patrons; and to dramatic literature at all events we may safely apply Ben Jonson's saying as to literature at large: ' There cannot be one colour of the mind, another

and cherished by pleasantry, will become habitual and increase.' Walter Savage Landor, *Menander and Epicurus* (*Imaginary Conversations, First Series, Works*, vol. ii. p. 256). This passage seems to me to contain the whole question of the ' social ' drama (with or without a problem) in a nutshell.

[1] See his Essay *On the Comic Dramatists of the Restoration.*

of the wit. . . . So that we may conclude wheresoever manners and fashions are corrupted, language is. It imitates the public riot[1].' And in the case of the public before which Dryden and his contemporaries, and in the days of his old age Congreve and the younger generation of dramatists, brought their comedies, we know only too well that it recognised, and had ample reason for recognising, in the productions of the comic stage a faithful reflexion of what from day to day it witnessed and approved and practised. The view of wedded life, for instance—and my only reason for singling out the subject is that our later Stuart comedy returns to it with the persistency of Epicurus' fly buzzing back to the spoilt peach—which the comedy of this age complacently illustrates, is no other than that which the Restoration period succeeded in making fashionable for a time that long outlasted its general defiance of the decencies of social relations. On the stage poor Lord Malapert complains, 'But that 'tis not the fashion to be fond of one's Wife, I verily believe I could say a great many soft things to her[2]'; Mrs. Frail apprises us, that 'there is no creature perfectly civil but a husband. For in a little time he grows rude only to his wife, and that is the highest good breeding, for it begets his civility to other people[3]'; and 'the very scribble-scrabbles of the city,' we learn elsewhere, 'have got into the way of despising their wives[4].' In the world which naturally wished to see itself represented at its worst, but which brought with it its own criteria of verisimilitude, society was, to borrow the expression of a dispassionate judge, fast falling into the same 'bizarre condition,' and into the same 'strange aberration of ways of thought.' A new paragraph had been tacitly added to the liturgical enumeration of the uses of marriage—and its gist was the convenience of the institution as covering sin abroad[5].

No further observations are needed by way of introduction here to a final mention of the serious indictment which was

---

[1] *Discoveries* (*De Corruptelâ Morum*).
[2] Southerne, *The Maid's Last Prayer*, act iv. sc. 1.
[3] Congreve, *Love for Love*, act i. sc. 13.
[4] Rowe, *The Biter*, act i. sc. 1.
[5] St. Marc-Girardin, *u. s.*, vol. v. sect. lxxiv.

brought against the later Stuart comedy already in its own
days, which its foremost representatives were either unwilling
or unable to repel, and the substance of which no genial
sophistry or unseasonable leniency of later times will succeed in invalidating.   In the course of this work reference
has been made to many assaults which at various times it
was the fate of the English stage to undergo at the hands
of its self-constituted censors.   But not one of these Puritan
diatribes— from *The School of Abuse* to *Histrio-mastix*—
was delivered with so much concentrated force, was based
on evidence so difficult to dispute or minimise, or was
attended with so immediate and unmistakeable an effect,
as the non-juring clergyman Jeremy Collier's *A Short
View of the Immorality and Profaneness of the English
Stage*, published in 1698.   Jeremy Collier, who in a different
sphere of action had already given very uncommon proofs
of high courage and power of endurance, would doubtless
not have shrunk from the least promising and popular
of literary crusades, but as it proved public feeling was
found to be on his side.   It is true that the Revolution
which put an end to the Restoration *régime* had made no
visible change for the better in the moral tone of the
English stage any more than in that of the society which
it reflected; but as the new reign went on, as the unaffected
piety and wifely devotion of Queen Mary exerted their
influence, and as the picture of unbridled licence which had
so long been offered by the palace of an English king began
to fade from remembrance [1], a social reaction in favour of
moral restraint and order undoubtedly set in.   The old
Puritan feeling was not yet dead in England, but it was
a spirit at once more catholic and more rational which as
I think informed the movement of which about the middle
of the last decade of the century we observe the earliest
signs [2].   Gradually, signs of it began to make themselves

*Anti-
theatrical
publica-
tions.*

*Jeremy
Collier and
his prede-
cessors.*

---

[1] ' His majestie yesterday checkt a young lord for swearing within his
hearing ; telling him the court should give good examples, and reformation
should begin there first, and then others would follow.'   Narcissus Luttrell's
Brief Relation, vol. ii. p. 346, under date January 8, 1692.

[2] Many illustrations might be given of the survival of Puritan sentiment ;
one may be cited from Evelyn's *Diary* (October 25, 1695), where he relates

perceptible in literature. But slight importance, however, is to be attached to Sir Richard Blackmore's endeavour to cure the public taste for immoral plays by means of moral epics—in the first instance by his *Prince Arthur* (1695), which he prefaced by an invective against stage-poets and their licence, which made some palpable allusions to Dryden[1]. Probably stimulated by this attack, George Merriton, a literary barrister of ability and insight, printed in 1698 a pamphlet on *Immorality, Debauchery, and Profaneness Exposed*[2]. The City Poet followed up his previous attack at a later date in a *Satire upon Wit* (1699), which drew down upon him two contemptuous rejoinders from Dryden, mainly however confined to reflexions upon Blackmore's literary character[3]. But it was not by so ill-equipped a champion, nor by the interested cavils of a would-be literary rival such as Milbourne against a particular tendency of Dryden's dramatic satire[4], that the cause of a reformation of the drama asserted itself. It had found a champion of real mark in Jeremy Collier, of whose famous work it will be worth while to give a brief account in a note[5].

that the blind old Sir Samuel Morland ' had newly buried £200 worth of music-books six feet under ground, being, as he said, love-songs and vanity.' One of Queen Mary's proclamations against vice and immorality, addressed to Justices of the Peace in the last year of her life (1694), is thought to have caused Colley Cibber to be careful in furnishing his *Love's Last Shift* with a moral purpose (*ante*, p. 486; cf. Aloys Brandl, *u. s.*, p. 51).—A significant illustration of the general tendency to which I have adverted is supplied by '*An Account of the Societies for Reformation of Manners, with a Persuasion to Persons of all Ranks to be zealous and diligent in promoting the execution of the Laws against Profaneness and Debauchery*' (1699).

[1] The passage is cited in Scott's *Life of Dryden* (Scott and Saintsbury's edition, vol. i. p. 351, *note*).

[2] See E. W. Gosse, *Life of Congreve*, p. 101. Mr. Gosse's account of the Collier controversy is particularly full and interesting.—Merriton wrote besides many books on legal and cognate subjects, a humorous poem on *The Praise of Yorkshire Ale*, with a *Dialogue* in the Yorkshire dialect. His brother Thomas dedicated to him his tragedy of *Love and War* (printed in 1658) ; he also wrote a tragi-comedy, *The Wandering Lover* (printed in the same year), as ' several times privately acted.'

[3] See the Preface to Dryden's *Fables*, and the Prologue to *The Pilgrim* (where Blackmore is gibbeted as 'Quack Maurus'); and cf. Scott's *Life of Dryden, u. s.*

[4] Milbourne, in his *Notes on Dryden's Virgil* (to which he ventured to oppose a translation of his own), appears to have attacked Dryden for his abuse of priests. See Scott's *Life of Dryden, u. s.*, p. 338.

[5] Jeremy Collier states the object of his essay with naked simplicity :

The force of much of Jeremy Collier's invective, which *Effects of the Short View.*
was impaired neither by intemperance of language nor by

'Being convinc'd that nothing has gone further in Debauching the Age than the Stage-Poets and Play-House, I thought I could not employ my Time better than by writing against them.' His diatribe divides itself into five parts—to which is added by way of appendix a view of the Opinion of the Pagans, of the Church, and State concerning the Stage. This display of learning may be passed by, as falling very far short of Prynne's, and contributing little to the more immediate purpose of the book. Unlike Prynne, Jeremy Collier had not shrunk from acquiring an intimate acquaintance with the subjects of his invective, and illustrated the charges which he brought against plays and playwriters by quotations and direct references. These charges comprise, firstly, the Immodesty of the Stage, which, as Collier argues, is a fault in behaviour as well as in religion. He asks how it comes to pass that those liberties which disoblige so much in conversation, should entertain upon the stage? He visits with particular censure the scandalous Prologues and Epilogues, which have not even the supposed justification or fiction. He rejects any appeal on the part of the comic dramatists to the examples of Plautus, in whom it is only the immodest characters who speak immodestly, while even these are Vestal Virgins as compared with the ladies of the modern stage,—or of Terence, whose general propriety he is justified in asserting. Aristophanes, though superior in some respects by reason of his abstinence from particular themes, condemns himself as an authority to be appealed to by the modern stage, for his scandalous liberty is accounted for by the fact that he is a downright atheist, while though his buffoonery is often too strong for his judgment, in his lucid intervals he condemns his own practice. (All this must be allowed to be but poor criticism, which may be commended to the supporters of a modern theory as to Aristophanes' gradual lapse into irreligion.) Collier's remarks on the Elisabethan drama show more soundness, though he here picks and chooses rather arbitrarily; but on the whole his first chapter sustains the double argument, that the immodesty of the modern stage is intolerable, and that no precedent can be found for it.

The Second Chapter, on 'The Profaneness of the Stage,' is more open to exceptions. Its first section, on 'Their Cursing and Swearing,' is not devoid of exaggerations, and occasionally suggests the defence 'I' fac's no oath' (cf. *The Alchemist*, act i. sc. 1). In his second section, on 'Their Abuse of Religion and Holy Scripture,' Collier shows himself eager to accumulate doubtful evidence in addition to such as is indisputably in point.

The Third Chapter, 'The Clergy Abus'd by the Stage,' carries us into the range of personal as well as moral grievance ; and though there is too much colour for the charge of a design on the part of the dramatists to bring the clergy as such into hatred and contempt (cf. *ante,* p. 299, *note*), it is always easier to suggest than to prove a charge of malice prepense. Colley Cibber (*The Careless Husband*, act v) accordingly makes a happy rejoinder in observing that ' since the late short-sighted View of plays, Vice may go on and prosper, the Stage dares hardly shew a vicious Person speaking like himself, for fear of being call'd profane for exposing him. 'Tis hard indeed, when People won't distinguish between what's meant for Contempt, and what for Example.' The ground Collier here takes is therefore unsafe, though the suspicion which suggested this topic of attack cannot be described as a hallucination.

any other symptom of inferior breeding, was irresistible; and although few literary manifestoes of the kind have been more abundantly answered, or answered by abler pens, the strength of his case was such that it may be said to have ensured him the victory at the outset. The controversy may be said to have continued during nearly a generation, when it was brought to a conclusion and consummation by William Law's *The Absolute Unlawfulness of the Stage Entertainment fully demonstrated* (1726)[1]. The first noteworthy incident in it was the publication, still in the earlier half of the year 1698, of *A Vindication of the Stage*, which Mr. Gosse thinks was written by Wycherley with the design of letting it be supposed that Congreve was the author, and which treated the whole subject with a lightness often highly expedient in a quarrel of this sort, but misplaced on the present occasion, when expressions of sympathy and approval were reaching Collier from

In the charge of the Fourth Chapter, that 'the Stage-Poets make their Principal Personages Vicious, and reward them at the End of the Play,' is bluntly expressed one of the chief moral sins of the dramatists of this period, which Dryden in the Preface to his *An Evening's Love* had in vain attempted sophistically to elude. It is a sin of which, as has been incidentally noted (*ante*, vol. ii. p. 519), our earlier drama had rarely made itself guilty; but from which, as the preceding review of plays has shown, it is impossible to acquit many of the dramatists of the later Stuart period. The chapter concludes with instances of the offences of the stage against good manners, the last of which—its audacious treatment of ' Quality'—will not strike most readers as greatly aggravating its guiltiness. Cowley had by anticipation answered something at least of the spirit of this charge when he contended (in the Preface to *Cutter of Coleman-Street*) that ' it has been the perpetual Privilege of Satyre and Comedy, to pluck their Vices and Follies, though not their Persons, out of the Sanctuary of any Title.'

The Fifth Chapter, in fine, subjects four plays (Dryden's *Amphitryon* and *King Arthur*, D'Urfey's *Don Quixote*, and Vanbrugh's *The Relapse*) to a special comment to which the first and the last of them at all events must be allowed to be peculiarly obnoxious.

The Conclusion, which adverts to the encouragement of vicious tendencies and manners by the stage in general, and points clearly to the remedy of its suppression, has no special importance for the history of the drama in this particular period.

[1] Law was not a man of compromise, and in his disciple John Byrom's *Diary* (April 18, 1737) he is reported to have described stage-entertainments as worship of the Devil.—Strictly speaking, Law cannot be said to have had the ' last word'; for his treatise was answered in the same year by John Dennis in his *The Stage Defended from Scripture, reason, experience, and the common-sense of mankind, for* 2000 *years*.

various quarters, including the King himself[1]. In the very month in which the *Vindication* appeared, the Middlesex justices gave proof of the excitement of the public temper by 'not only presenting the playhouses, but also Mr. Congreve, for writing *The Double Dealer*, D'Urfey for *Don Quixote*,' and the printers of these plays, and added an expression of opinion against the frequenting of the playhouses by women in masks, as 'tending much to debauchery and immorality[2].' Meanwhile, the defenders were hastening to the front; Edward Filmer, the author of a tragedy called *The Unnatural Brother*[3], with the first of a series of elaborate replies; John Dennis, with a sensible argument on the fundamental question really involved in Collier's invective, *The Usefulness of the Stage*; Vanbrugh, with *A Short Vindication of The Relapse and The Provok'd Wife*,—the two comedies of his own which the censor had selected for special castigation. In June, Dryden gave the first sign of his consciousness of an exposure which as he knew meant a condemnation of so much of his life's work; but his tone was one of remonstrance against the excess of the invective, rather than of a protest against the foundations on which it rests[4]. When, a year later, in again referring to the charge, Dryden attempted to balance admission and denial, he criticised Collier with tact and temper, allowing that 'in many things he has treated me justly,' but denying— and rightly denying—that he has judged impartially betwixt the former age and us[5].' And when, at the very

[1] It is stated that by order of William III a *nolle prosequi* relieved Jeremy Collier from all further fear of proceedings against him as a political offender.

[2] Narcissus Luttrell's *Brief Relation*, vol. iv. p. 379, under date May 12, 1698.

[3] It was founded on the *Cassandre* of Calprenède, and had been printed in the previous year, 1697.

[4] See the '*Epistle* (xiv) to my friend Mr. Motteux on his tragedy called *Beauty in Distress*,' published in 1698. There is a certain pathos already in the measure of submission implied in the lines:

> 'Were they content to prune the lavish vine
> Of straggling branches, and improve the wine,
> Who but a madman would his thoughts defend?
> All would submit; for all but fools will mend.'

[5] See the Preface to *The Fables*. Dryden adds, anticipating the phrase of

close of his career, Dryden once more touched upon the fatal indictment[1], it was in order to admit its substantial truth. It was plain that 'the parson,' whether or not he had 'stretched a point too far,' had in the poet's judgment hit the blot; and Dryden's farewell to the controversy became him better than his share in any previous stage of it. Congreve, who as early as July, 1698, had put forth his *Amendments of Mr. Collier's False and Imperfect Citations*, had, by one of those unlucky accidents which at times result from what is significantly called 'a false position,' entirely mistaken the tone and bearing which the circumstances of the controversy imposed upon him as the foremost representative of the writers whose good manners had been impugned with their morals; and a shower of retorts attempted to make his blunder manifest to him. In the midst of these the author of the *Short View* thought it necessary to follow up his original publication with a *Defence*, which has not generally been held to have improved his case[2]. In truth, the position in which he stood after the dramatists of the age, both great and small, had in vain hurled spear and javelin against his shield of morality and truth, had been proved impregnable. From this time forward a marked change becomes visible both in the attitude of Court, Government, and of a section at least of the ruling classes, towards the stage, and in its own consciousness of the purposes and the restrictions proper to the exercise of its art. The censorship of the Master of the Revels began to be exercised more strictly[3]; actors were prosecuted

his later reference, that his assailant 'has lost ground at the latter end of the day by pursuing his point too far, like the Prince of Condé at Senneph; from immoral plays to no plays, *ab abusu ad usum, non valet consequentia.*' —Mr. Gosse points out that in *Cymon and Iphigenia* the author of these judicious remarks cannot forbear from turning round upon his adversary in vehement anger; but for this he will be readily forgiven.

[1] *Epilogue* to *The Pilgrim.*

[2] The *Defence of the Short View* bears the date 1699; the *Second Defence* (1700) was in reply to James Drake's *The Ancient and Modern Stages Surveyed.*

[3] See Lecky's *History of England in the Eighteenth Century,* vol. i. p. 539, where will be found further information on the subject of the repression of stage immorality.

for the use of profane language, and the playhouses were once more presented as nuisances by the grand-jury[1]; the admission of women wearing masks into any of the theatres was prohibited[2]; and Convocation occupied itself with the condition of the stage as a matter of moment to be pressed upon the consideration of the Crown[3]. The comic poets, who had always been more or less aware of their sins[4], now began with uneasy hilarity to allude in their prologues to the reformation which had come over the spirit of the town[5]. Writers like Mrs. Centlivre became very anxious to reclaim their sinners with much emphasis in the fifth act; and Colley Cibber, while adopting the same facile process of escaping from both dramatic and moral complications[6], may fairly be credited with the moral intention which he claims to have kept in view throughout his career as a dramatist. Steele, as has been seen, pursued a still more definite moral aim in his comedies; and though he mistook the proper task of comedy in seeking to elevate its ends, the purification of the manners and with them of the morals of the comic stage had now begun in earnest, and the social evil against which Jeremy Collier had contended had been virtually overcome. *Beginnings of sentimental comedy.*

English comedy, unlike English tragedy, had still a creative future before it, which it forms no part of my present task to discuss. Both what was weakest and what was brightest in the English comedy of the eighteenth century *Later growths of English comedy.*

[1] See Narcissus Luttrell's *Brief Relation*, vol. iv. pp. 713 and 720 (under the dates November 30, and December 19, 1700).

[2] *Ib.*, p. 711 (November 26, 1700).

[3] This was in 1711. In 1708 Swift had included in his *Project for the Advancement of Religion* 'a scheme for correcting the immorality of the stage by the establishment of a censorship exercised by men of wit, learning and virtue.' (See Forster's *Life of Swift*, vol. i. p. 217.)

[4] If proof of this were needed, one might point to passages where women are actually bantered for witnessing comedies by the comic writers themselves! The half-hypocritical prologues of earlier times, of which it may in general be said that they protest far too much, had long gone out of fashion —the age was in truth, in Wycherley's phrase, a 'frank' one.

[5] See the Prologue to Congreve's *The Way of the World*; Vanbrugh seems to allude to the same change in the Prologue to his *Æsop*; see also the Prologue to his *The False Friend*.

[6] See Scott's *Essay on the Drama* for some happy remarks on the Fifth Acts of these dramatists.

may be alike regarded as a natural developement of phenomena which have been noted in this chapter. Sentimental
comedy begins with Steele, if not already with Colley
Cibber, whose good intentions without their wit were inherited by Kelly and all the other writers who prided themselves on making the stage 'a school of morality[1].' Nor
is there anything essentially new in the dramatic style of
Fielding—even in his burlesques he merely follows in
the footsteps of *The Rehearsal*, though the combination of
political with literary satire is audaciously fresh ; Goldsmith has a predecessor in Farquhar ; and the most brilliant
writer of later English comedy, Sheridan, is but the lineal
Achieve- successor of Congreve and the adapter of Vanbrugh. In
ments of the period from the Restoration to the death of Queen
English Anne our drama had achieved no master-pieces of comedy
comedy in of character worthy to be placed by the side of those of
this period. Jonson and his contemporaries, or by the side of the
noblest creations of Molière. It had however displayed
a great flexibility and promptitude in adapting and modifying the favourite types of our own and of foreign schools
of comedy ; and if it had confined itself to a limited range
in choosing its

> 'Ardentes juvenes, raptasque in amore puellas,
> Elususque senes, agilesque per omnia servos[2]'—

yet it had extended the range of characters of affectation,
and in one direction—from Etheredge and Dryden to Vanbrugh and Cibber—had produced a type which may be
called its own, the fop of the modern English stage. In
general, our comedy had mirrored with unprecedented ease
and faithfulness the manners of the class it addressed ; and
while more abundantly than conscientiously availing itself
of the aid of both foreign and native sources, it cannot
be said to have owed to these the main elements of its

---

[1] See Kelly's *False Delicacy, ad fin.*—It has been well said of Schroeder,
who, later in the century, engaged in a similar attempt in Germany, that 'he
forgot that it is the business of pedagogues of the school and the pulpit to
preach morality; the object of the theatre is, not like theirs, to improve men,
but to ennoble them.' (F. L. Schmidt, *Denkwürdigkeiten*, vol. ii. p. 36.)

[2] Manilius of Menander's comedy, quoted by Donaldson, *Theatre of the
Greeks*, p. 201.

dramatic effectiveness. Without altogether avoiding the danger of sacrificing distinction of character to brilliancy of diction, our comic dramatists had accomplished an unprecedented advance in the treatment of their chosen form—prose dialogue. If in ease and grace the comic prose of Dryden surpasses that of his earlier contemporaries—with the exception perhaps of Etheredge—he had in this respect been in his turn outshone by Congreve. No further names need be mentioned to show that the dialogue form of English comedy had been perfected to a degree which the predecessors of this master of style had failed to reach, and which none of his successors has surpassed. Prose had been permanently made the vehicle of dramatic speech in English comedy, whence (to the indignation of Dr. Johnson) it was even to encroach upon the domain of her serious sister. Nor can there be any doubt but that to the example *Comedy* of the dialogue of our comic drama the prose of Addison and *and the* Steele, and that of our great novelists who preceded them, *novel.* owed much of its facility, its variety, and its power of expressing with spontaneous readiness the rapid play of wit and the subtler as well as the broader touches of humour.

The history of the English drama in the period of *Conclusion.* which this chapter has treated illustrates the truth that there are two forces which no dramatic literature can neglect with impunity—the national traditions on which the greatness of that literature is founded, and the enduring principles of moral law and order. Because, swayed at one time by fashion, at another obsequious to artificial and arbitrary canons of literary taste, our tragic poets had ceased to tread the paths which the traditions of the great Elisathan age had marked out for them, this period witnessed the decay of English tragedy—a decay followed by its all but absolute extinction as a living literary form. Because, again, intent only upon suiting the vicious licence of their public, the contemporary comic dramatists bade defiance to the principles in which they well knew the moral government of human society to be rooted, their creations have failed to command either the esteem or the attention of the lovers of our national literature. What was designed to attract, has ended by repelling ; and works abounding in talent—here and there even instinct with genius—are all but consigned to oblivion by the judgment of posterity, on account of the very features which were intended to ensure to them a rapid and commanding success.

Of all forms of literary art the drama can least reckon without its responsibilities. So long as it remains true to these, it need fear neither adversary nor rival.

APPENDIX.

Page 142, note 3 (*Mrs. Carroll, afterwards Centlivre*).

Mrs. Carroll, mentioned as adaptor of May's comedy, *The Heir*, is better known under her later married name of Mrs. Centlivre, with which she first signed a play in 1709. Cf. p. 488, note 3.

Page 144 (*Sir John Suckling*).

I intended to have directed attention to Dr. Hermann Schwarz' essay on this writer (Halle, 1881), whose activity touched so many sides of the life and literature of his times.

Page 249 (*French actors in London*, 1635).

In a letter to the *Athenaeum*, dated July 25, 1891, Mr. Swinburne suggests that '*Mélise*, a French comedy,' acted in 1635 by French players at the Cockpit in Whitehall, was Corneille's first dramatic work, the comedy of *Mélite*, dated 1625, but apparently not acted till 1629. It had previously been supposed to be a comic pastoral called *La Melize*, performed at Paris in 1633.

INDEX

(The small figures refer to the Notes.)

Abbott, Dr., his *Shakespearian Grammar*, ii. 51[3].

Abdelazar, by Mrs. Aphra Behn, ii. 467[7]; an adaptation of *Lust's Dominion*, iii. 326[5].

Abdicated Prince, The, iii. 294[3].

Abel Drugger, the character of, ii. 369[1].

Abelard, Hilarius a pupil of, i. 38.

Aberdeen, the religious drama performed at, i. 55.

Abraham's Sacrifice, a translation from Beza by Arthur Golding, i. 172[1].

Abraham and Isaac, the East-Anglian play of, i. 79[1]; the isolated miracle-play of, i. 91; *Sacrifice of*, in the York plays, i. 69; the isolated miracle-play at Dublin, i. 92.

Abrame and Lotte, an early play, i. 172.

Absolome, an early play, i. 172[1].

Absurda Comica, by Andreas Gryphius, i. 545.

Academical plays of early Stuart times, iii. 174 *et seq.*

Accolti, Bernardo, his *Virginia*, i. 210, ii. 119.

Achademios, a comedy by Skelton, i. 130.

Achilles, by Boyer: see *Victim, The.*

Acolastus, by W. Fullonius, i. 253.

Actor's Vindication, by T. Heywood, ii. 551[3].

Actors, the close contact of the professions of playwrights and, i. 448; companies, a list of early Elisabethan, 451[4], 452[1]; consolidated, i. 468; familiarity and good fellowship among, i. 470; continental companies of, i. 472; companies under James I and Charles I, iii. 230, 231; at the time of the Revolution, iii. 278 *et seq.*; at the Restoration, iii. 283.

Actresses, almost unheard of before the Restoration, iii. 248, 251 *et seq.*; at the Restoration, iii. 285.

Adaptations and Performances of Shakespearean Plays, list of, by Baron G. Vincke, i. 513[1].

Addison as a critic of Shakspere, i. 534; his opera, *Rosamond*, iii. 323[1]; his *Cato*, iii. 439.

Adélaïde du Guesclin, by Voltaire, i. 536[1].

Adelphi, by Terence, *The Scornful Lady* taken from, ii. 669.

Adone, by Marini, i. 276[1].

Adoration of the Shepherds, The, in the Coventry plays, i. 88.

Adventures of Five Hours, The, by Sir Samuel Tuke, iii. 305.

Aemilia, by 'Cecill' of St. John's, Cambridge, iii. 184.

Aeneid, Phaer's translation of, i. 189; Surrey's translation of, i. 203.

Aeschylus, early Christian dramas modelled on, i. 4; the tragedies and comedies of, i. 159[1].

Aesop, by Vanbrugh, iii. 480.

Agamemnon, Seneca's, translated by John Studley, i. 195; Dekker and Chettle's, ii. 467.

Aglaura, by Sir John Suckling, iii. 145.

Agnes de Castro, by Mrs. Trotter, iii. 432.

Agony and the Betrayal, The, one of the York plays, i. 67[3].

Agrippina, by Cyramo de Bergerac, compared with Shakspere's *Hamlet*, i. 534.

Aicard, J., his *Davenant*, iii. 166[4].

Ajax and Ulysses, an early English tragedy, i. 208.

Alaham, by Lord Brooke, ii. 615.

Alarcon, Ruiz de, influence of his

comedies, iii. 303 ; his *Verdad Sospechosa*, Corneille's obligations to, iii. 495 [2].

Alarum against Usurers, by Thomas Lodge, i. 410.

Alarum for London, co-authorship of, attributed to Marlowe, i. 360.

Albert of Stade, his *Troilus*, ii. 150.

Albertus Wallenstein, by Henry Glapthorne, synopsis of, iii. 152.

Albin's Triumph, a masque by A. Townshend, iii. 192.

Albion and Albanius, Dryden's opera, iii. 323 ; synopsis of, iii. 380.

Albion's England, by William Warner, i. 200, 266 [1].

Albovine, King of the Lombards, The Tragedy of, by Sir W. D'Avenant, ii. 505 [1] ; observations on, iii. 169.

Albumazar, by J. Tomkis, attributed to Shakspere, ii. 211 ; synopsis of, iii. 179, 180, 184.

Albyon Knight, a political morality, i. 139.

Alcazar, Battle of, The, by Peele, i. 368, 370.

Alcestis, the, of Euripides, the nature of, i. 210.

Alchemist, The, by Ben Jonson, remarks on, ii. 367, 404.

Alchemists in Elisabeth's time, ii. 368 [1].

Alcibiades, by T. Otway, synopsis of, iii. 413.

Alcida, Greene's Metamorphosis, by Robert Greene, i. 389.

Alcmaeon, an early English tragedy, i. 208.

Aldelazar, by Mrs. Aphra Behn, iii. 452 [3].

Aleman, Mateo, his *Guzman*, Fletcher's obligations to, ii. 720 ; Beaumont and Fletcher's obligations to, ii. 753.

Alexander, William, Earl of Stirling, his version of *Julius Caesar*, ii. 138 ; the dramatic works of, ii. 623 ; 'Monarchic Tragedies,' ii. 624.

Alexander and Lodowick, by Martin Slater, ii. 578 [2], 608 [2].

Alexandraean Tragedy, The, by Lord Stirling, ii. 624.

Alfonso von Ferrara, by Schroeder, a version of Massinger's *Duke of Milan*, iii. 15 [2].

Alfred, King, his translation of Boëthius, i. 11.

All Fooles, by Chapman, synopsis of, ii. 434.

All for Love, Dryden's, compared with Shakspere's *Antony and Cleopatra*, i. 513, 520 [3], ii. 187 ; observations on, iii. 372.

All Mistaken, by James Howard, iii. 396.

All's Lost by Lust, by William Rowley, ii. 544.

All's One, ii. 231.

All's Well that Ends Well, Shakspere's, Lord Lafeu an impersonation of John Lyly, i. 274 [3] ; reference to Essex and Elisabeth in, ii. 33 [3] ; versification of, ii. 49 [2] ; observations on, ii. 117-119.

Allegory, treatment of, in early works, i. 103, 104 [1].

Alleyn, Edward, his parts in Marlowe's plays, i. 315, 338 ; Collier's *Memoirs of*, i. 396 [1] ; the contemporary influences surrounding, i. 450, 469.

Almanzor and Almahide, by Dryden, remarks on, iii. 359.

Almonde for a Parrott, An, authorship attributed to John Lyly, i. 273 [1] ; attributed to Thomas Nashe, i. 420, 461 [2], 465 [4].

Almyna, by Mrs. Manley, iii. 432.

Alphonsus, Emperor of Germany, by Chapman, synopsis of, ii. 427.

Alphonsus King of Arragon, Comicall History of, by Robert Greene, i. 393.

Altemira, by Lord Orrery, iii. 344.

Amadis de Gaule, A. Munday's translation of, i. 431.

Amalasont, Queen of the Goths, an unpublished play by T. Hughes, iii. 430.

Amantes de Cartago, Los, compared with Marston's *Sophonisba*, ii. 483 [3].

Ambitious Statesman, The, by J. Crowne, iii. 401.

Ambitious Step-Mother, The, by Nicholas Rowe, iii. 434.

Amboyna, by Dryden, iii. 367.

Ambrosius Martin, Life of, by T. Heywood, ii. 555.

Amends for Ladies, by Field, Mary Frith impersonated in, ii. 519 [2] ; observations on, iii. 50.

American Shaksperean criticism, i. 571.

Amicizia, by Nardi, i. 228.

Aminta, by Tasso, i. 231, ii. 382.

Amor, honor, y poder, by Calderon, ii. 222 [1].

Amores, Ovid's, Marlowe's translation of, i. 314.

Amorous Bigot, The, by Shadwell, iii. 458.

Amorous Fantasme, The, from Quinault, by Sir W. Lower, iii. 291.

Amorous Prince, by Mrs. Behn, an adaptation of *City Night-Cap*, iii. 326 [5].

Amorous War, The, by Jasper Mayne, synopsis of, iii. 141.

Amorous Widow, The, Betterton's adaptation of Molière's *George Dandin*, iii. 315 [1].

l'Amour Médecin, Molière's, Lacy's adaptation of, iii. 450.

Ampère, J. J., his *César*, ii. 142.

Amphitruo, the, of Plautus, reproduced by Vitalis Blesensis, i. 9 [1]; the nature of, i. 210; *Jacke Juggler* founded on, i. 249.

Amphitryon, by Dryden, iii. 384.

Amyntas, by T. Randolph, synopsis of, iii. 135.

Anatomie of Absurditie, The, by Thomas Nashe, i. 419, 461 [2].

Anatomie of Abuses, The, by Philip Stubbes, i. 460.

Anatomie of Lovers Flatteries, The, by Robert Greene, i. 387 [1].

Anatomy of Melancholy, The, by Burton, reference to Shakspere in, i. 500.

Ancient Critical Essays upon English Poets and Poesy, edited by Haselwood, i. 268 [2].

Andria, the, of Terence, edited by Notker Labeo, i. 8; an English version of, i. 253.

Andromana, a play attributed to James Shirley, iii. 120.

Andromaque, by Racine, Ambrose Philips' translation of, iii. 315 [1].

Andronicus, an early play, ii. 57.

Andronicus Comnenius, by Wilson, ii. 58, iii. 338.

Anfitrione, by Pomponio Leto, i. 228.

Angels and the Shepherds, The, in the Chester plays, i. 67 [4].

Angry Catharine, Comedy of the (Die böse Katharina), by Christian Weise, i. 545.

Annals, Stowe's, i. 446 [1].

Anne, Queen of James I, her patronage of the stage, iii. 217.

Anne, Queen, and the stage, iii. 296.

Annunciacio, The, in the Towneley plays, i. 73.

Annunciation, The, one of the York plays, i. 67.

Anonymous plays of the later Elisabethan period, ii. 608 *et seq.*

Antichrist, one of the Chester plays, i. 83.

Antigone, by T. May, a synopsis of, iii. 143.

Anti-masque, the, ii. 392.

Antiphonies in the Mass, i. 33.

Antipodes, The, by R. Brome, iii. 127 [7]; remarks on, iii. 130.

Antiquary, The, by S. Marmion, iii. 147, 148.

Antonio and Mellida, by Marston, ii. 477.

Antonio's Revenge (Part II of Antonio and Mellida), ii. 478.

Antony and Cleopatra, Shakspere's, Dryden's treatment of the theme, i. 513; versification of, ii. 49 [2], 51 [2]; observations on the play, ii. 185–187; Dryden's obligations to, iii. 372.

Antony and Cleopatra, by Sir Charles Sedley, iii. 447.

Anything for a Quiet Life, by Middleton, ii. 523.

Apius and Virginia, i. 142; *The tragical comedy of*, by R. B., i. 204.

Apocryphal Gospels of James, and of *Nicodemus*, used in York plays, i. 67.

Apollinaris, the tragedies and comedies of, i. 4.

Apollo's Shroving, an academical play, iii. 183.

Apollonius and Silla, by Bandello, ii. 81.

Apologetic Dialogue, added to Jonson's *Poetaster*, ii. 361.

Apologie of Pierce Pennilesse, by T. Nashe: see *Strange Newes*.

Apologie of the Schole of Abuse, by Stephen Gosson, i. 410 [3].

Apology for Actors, by T. Heywood, i. 471 [1], ii. 552.

Apology for his Life, by Colley Cibber, iii. 485.

Apology for Poetry, Sidney's, i. 267.

Appearance of Our Lady to Thomas, The, one of the York plays, i. 70.

Appius and Virginia, by Webster, notice of, iii. 62; Betterton's version of, iii. 326 [4]; by J. Dennis, iii. 427.

Appleton, Sir Richard, possibly uncle of T. Heywood, ii. 551 [1].

Apprentice's Prize, The, a non-extant play by T. Heywood, ii. 583.

Arabian Nights, Shakspere's obligation to, in *The Taming of a Shrew*, ii. 94.

Arbasto, by Robert Greene, i. 387.

Arber, Prof. E., on the Marprelate controversy, i. 463 [1]; his *Transcripts of the Stationers' Registers*, ii. 45 [2]; on the *Parnassus Plays*, ii. 633 [1].

Arcades, Milton's masque, iii. 197.

Arcadia, Sidney's, i. 266 [1], 442 [3]; the style of, compared with that of *Euphues*, i. 276; Shakspere's obligation to, ii. 81; Day's obligations to, ii. 595 *et seq.*

Arcadia, The, by Shirley, notice of, iii. 102.

Archer, Francis, the reputed murderer of Marlowe, i. 317 [1].

Archer, Mr. W., his translation of Brandes' *William Shakespeare*, i. 562 [2].

Arden, Robert, Shakspere's maternal grandfather, his family and descendants, ii. 5 [1]; Agnes, ii. 6; Mary, ii. 6.

Arden of Feversham, synopsis of the play, ii. 217–219.

Aretino, P., his comedies, i. 229.

Argalus and Parthenia, by Henry Glapthorne, iii. 151.

Argenti, Agostino, his *Lo Sfortunato*, ii. 381.

Ariadne, by T. D'Urfey, iii. 454 [2].

Ariodante and Genevora, an early English tragedy, i. 217; Shakspere's possible obligations to, ii. 133.

Ariosto, L., his comedies, i. 229; his *I Suppositi* anglicised by George Gascoigne, i. 262, ii. 95.

Aristippus, by T. Randolph, iii. 132.

Aristophanes, his *Plutus* performed in Greek before Elisabeth, i. 190; Jonson's obligations to, in his *Staple of News*, ii. 374.

Aristotle, on the distinction between tragedy and comedy, i. 159.

Arlecchino, the, of Italian comedy, i. 229, 230.

Armas de la Hermosura, Las, by Calderon, ii. 189.

Armin, Robert, his life and works, i. 4, 35.

Arne, Dr., his music to Dalton's adaptation of *Comus*, iii. 199 [1].

Arraignment of Paris, The, by Nicholas Udall, i. 254; by George Peele, i. 366; attributed to Shakspere, iii. 211.

Arte of English Poesie, The, by George Puttenham, i. 268, 442 [4].

Arthur, King, by Dryden, iii. 382.

Artifice, The, by Mrs. Centlivre, iii. 491.

Arviragus and Philicia, by L. Carlell, iii. 160, 161.

Ascencio Domini, The, one of the Towneley plays, i. 76.

Ascension, The, one of the Chester plays, i. 82 [2].

Ascham, Roger, on Seneca's position among classic writers, i. 190; on Buchanan's tragedies, i. 194 [1]; on the theme of the *Morte d'Arthur*, i. 219.

Aschbach, J., on Hrotsvitha's comedies, i. 7 [3].

Ashe, T., his *Lectures and Notes on Shakspere*, i. 566 [2].

Asinari, Federico, his *Gismonda*, i. 214 [3].

Asinaria, the, by Plautus, brought out by Pomponio Leto, i. 228.

Assignation, The, by Dryden, iii. 366.

Assumption and Coronation of the Virgin, The, one of the York plays, i. 70; one of the Chester plays, i. 84.

Assumption, The, in the Coventry plays, i. 89.

Astrologo, Il, by G.-B. della Porta, iii. 180.

As You Find It, a play by the third Earl of Orrery, iii. 344 [4].

As You Like It, Shakspere's, his obligations to Lodge's *Rosalynde* in, i. 412; Shakspere erroneously supposed to have acted in, ii. 21; versification of, ii. 49 [2]; observations on the play, ii. 128–132.

Atellanae, origin of the, i. 14, 229 [1].

Atheist, The, by T. Otway, iii. 418.

Atheist's Tragedy, The, attributed to Marlowe, i. 315 [1]; by Cyril Tourneur, synopsis of, iii. 67.

Athelwold: see *Elfrid*.

Atrée, by Crébillon, a version of Seneca's *Thyestes*, iii. 402 [2].

Aubigny, Esmé Stuart, Lord de, a patron of Ben Jonson's, ii. 314.

Aubrey, on Shakspere's early manhood, ii. 12, 13; on his acting, ii. 21.

Augustine, St., on Menander's comedy, i. 14.

Aulularia, the, of Plautus, connexion of the *Querolus* with, i. 6.

Aureng-Zebe, by Dryden, notice of, iii. 370.

Ausonius, D. Magnus, the *Ludus septem Sapientium* attributed to, i. 5 [3].

Avisa, Henry Willobie's, identification of 'W. S.' and of 'H. W.' in, ii. 26.

Avranches, Bishop of, *see* John of Bayeux.

Ayrer, Jacob, influence of his plays on English dramatists, i. 474; influence of Shakspere's works on, i. 545; his *Beautiful Phoenicia*, Shakspere's obligations to, ii. 133; his *Fair Sidea* compared with Shakspere's *Tempest*, ii. 195.

Bacon, Francis, co-author of *The Misfortunes of Arthur*, i. 219; probable relations with Shakspere, i. 504; the Bacon-Shakspere craze, i. 504 [1], 571, 572; his masques, &c., ii. 628.

Bacon, Miss Delia, an upholder of the Bacon-Shakspere craze, i. 571.

Bailey, Sir W. H., on *Shakspere and Montaigne*, ii. 10 [1], 160

Baker, Mr. G. P., his edition of Lyly's *Endymion*, i. 270 [1], 289 [2].

Baker, Sir Richard, his *Theatrum Triumphans*, iii. 245 [1].

Balaam and his Ass, one of the Chester plays, i. 79.

Balaam and Jehoshaphat, by John of Antioch, i. 121; Shakspere's obligations to, ii. 111.

Baldock, Robert de, in *Edward II*, i. 350, 352.

Bale, Bishop, his authorship of the last extant English miracle-play, i. 52; the sacred plays of, i. 97; his *Kyng Johan*, i. 142, ii. 102; his life and works, i. 173; significance of his Chronicle History for the progress of the English drama, i. 218.

Ball, The, by Chapman and Shirley, ii. 444; notice of, iii. 107.

Ballet, the, institution of, iii. 324.

Bame, Richard, his aspersions on Marlowe, i. 317.

Bancroft, Richard, Archbishop, his part in the Marprelate controversy, i. 465.

Bandello, Matteo, his *Romeo and Juliet*, i. 213, ii. 114; his *Apollonius and Silla*, ii. 81; Shakspere's possible obligations to, in *Much Ado about Nothing*, ii. 133; Beaumont and Fletcher's obligations to, ii. 752.

Banished Duke, The, iii. 294 [3].

Banks, John, his adaptation of La Calprenède's *Cassandra*, iii. 309 [2]; *Grand Cyrus, ib.*; his dramatic works, iii. 428, 429; *The Unhappy Favourite*, iii. 429; *Virtue Betrayed*, iii. 429; *Cyrus the Great*, iii. 429.

Barabas, the character of, in Marlowe's *Jew of Malta*, stage-successors of, i. 345 [1].

Barack, K.A., his edition of Hrotsvitha's comedies, i. 7 [3].

Baret, Eugène, his translation of selections from Lope de Vega, ii. 754 [2].

Baretti, Joseph, on Shakspere and Voltaire, i. 539.

Barklay, Alexander, on the popularity of minstrels and jugglers, i. 27; his *Ship of Fooles*, i. 103, 234.

Barksted, W., his *Mirrha* and *Hiren*, ii. 481.

Barlow, Jerome, his and William Roy's polemical verse and Dialogues, i. 235.

Barnard, Lady, ii. 41.

Barnefield, Richard, his estimate of Shakspere, i. 495 [1]; some of Shakspere's Sonnets published in works of, ii. 25 [3].

Barnes, Barnaby, his *Devil's Charter*, notice of, ii. 626.

Barneveld, John de, literature concerning, ii. 716 [4].

Baron, R., his *Mirza*, iii. 149 [1], 289; his *History of Donquixot*, iii. 290.

Barrons Wars, The, by Michael Drayton, i. 437.

Barrowe, Henry, his part in the Marprelate controversy, i. 463 [1], 464 [2, 3].

Barry, Lodowick, his *Ram Alley* compared with Middleton's *A Trick to catch the Old One*, ii. 516, iii. 157.

Barry, Mrs., Restoration actress, iii. 285 [4]; Otway's connexion with, iii. 415, 419.

Bartholomew Fair, by Ben Jonson, account of the play, ii. 369, 405.

Bashful Lover, The, by Massinger, a synopsis of, iii. 36.

Basoche, les Farces de la, i. 22; moralities of the, i. 107.

Basse, William, his tribute to Shakspere, i. 498.

Basset-Table, The, by Mrs. Centlivre, iii. 490.

Bassingbourne, Cambridgeshire, the play of *St. George* at, i. 50 [1]; *The Harrowing of Hell* performed at, i. 55.

Baston, Robert, his plays, i. 51 [2].

Batchelars Banquet, The, by Dekker, ii. 455.

Bath, miracle plays acted at, i. 56 [2].

Battle of, see under *Alcazar, Hexham*.

Baudissin, Count Wolf v., his share in the Schlegel-Tieck translation of Shakspere, i. 556; his translation of Fletcher's *The Elder Brother*, ii. 736 [2].

Bayes, the character of, in *The Rehearsal*, iii. 363.

Bayle, P., his appreciation of Shakspere, i. 560.

Baynes, Prof. T., on Shakspere's education, ii. 10 [1].

Bazin, M., on the Chinese theatre, iii. 251 [1].

Beau's Duel, The, by Mrs. Centlivre, iii. 489.

Beau's Stratagem, The, by Farquhar, iii. 484.

Beaumont, Francis, Ben Jonson's relations with, ii. 329. (*See below*, Beaumont and Fletcher.)

Beaumont, Sir John, his poems, ii. 649.

Beaumont and Fletcher, their contemporary reputation compared with Shakspere's, i. 509; their dramatic works, ii. 643–763; life of John Fletcher, ii. 646; life of Francis Beaumont, ii. 649; their literary partnership, ii.

653; their plays, ii. 661 *et seq.*; *Woman-Hater*, ii. 662; *The Faithful Shepherdess*, ii. 663; *Four Plays in One*, ii. 666; *The Scornful Lady*, ii. 668; *Philaster*, ii. 669; *The Maid's Tragedy*, ii. 672; *A King and no King*, ii. 676; *The Knight of the Burning Pestle*, ii. 679; *The Coxcomb*, ii. 682; *Cupid's Revenge*, ii. 684; *The Captain*, ii. 686; *The Honest Man's Fortune*, ii. 687; *The Knight of Malta*, ii. 688; *Thierry and Theodoret*, ii. 689; *Love's Cure*, ii. 691; *Wit at Several Weapons*, ii. 692; *Love's Pilgrimage*, ii. 693.

Plays by Fletcher only, ii. 695 *et seq.*; *Wit without Money*, ii. 695; *Bonduca*, ii. 696: *Valentinian*, ii. 698; *The Loyal Subject*, ii. 699; *The Mad Lover*, ii. 701; *The Humorous Lieutenant*, ii. 702; *Women Pleased*, ii. 703; *The Island Princess*, ii. 704; *The Pilgrim*, ii. 705; *The Wild-Goose-Chase*, ii. 707; *Monsieur Thomas*, ii. 708; *The Woman's Prize*, ii. 709; *A Wife for a Month*, ii. 711; *Rule a Wife*, &c., ii. 711; *The Chances*, ii. 712.

Plays by Fletcher and others, not Beaumont, ii. 713 *et seq.*; *The Queen of Corinth*, ii. 714; *The Double Marriage*, ii. 715; *Sir John van Olden-Barneveld*, ii. 716; *The False One*, ii. 718; *The Little French Lawyer*, ii. 720; *The Custom of the Country*, ii. 721; *The Lawes of Candy*, ii. 723; *The Spanish Curate*, ii. 723; *The Beggar's Bush*, ii. 725; *The Prophetess*, ii. 727; *The Sea Voyage*, ii. 728; *The Maid in the Mill*, ii. 729; *The Lovers' Progress*, ii. 730; *The Nice Valour*, ii. 732; *The Bloody Brother*, ii. 734; *The Elder Brother*, ii. 736; *The Fair Maid of the Inn*, ii. 737; *The Noble Gentleman*, ii. 738; *The Night-Walker*, ii. 740.

Other plays, extant or non-extant, connected with Beaumont or Fletcher, ii. 741 *et seq.*; *The Faithful Friends*, ii. 741; *The Two Noble Kinsmen*, ii. 743; *Henry VIII*, ii. 746.

Fletcher's share in other plays, ii. 747; lost plays by Fletcher, ii. 748; Beaumont and Fletcher's productivity, ii. 748; range and source of their subjects, ii. 751; their supposed familiarity with Spanish literature, ii. 752; and with Lope de Vega in particular, ii. 754; early popularity of, ii. 756; their defects, ii. 757; their range

of characters, ii. 759; Beaumont and Fletcher as dramatists, ii. 759; not above their age, ii. 762; Massinger's collaboration with, iii. 5; adaptations of their plays, iii. 326 [3].

Beautiful Phoenicia, The, by Jacob Ayrer, Shakspere's obligations to, ii. 133.

Beauty in a Trance, a non-extant play by Ford, iii. 86.

Beauty in Distress, by Peter Motteux, iii. 431.

Beauty the Conqueror, by Sir Charles Sedley, iii. 447.

Beauvais, Vincent de, his *Speculum Historiale*, ii. 111.

Beccari, Agostino, his *Il Sagrifizio*, ii. 381.

Beeston's Company, temporarily prohibited, iii. 246 [1].

Beggar of Bethnal Green, The, by Sheridan Knowles, ii. 599 [5].

Beggars' Bush, The, by Fletcher, ii. 725.

Behn, Mrs. Aphra, her *Abdelazar*, ii. 467 [7]; her adaptation of La Calprenède's *Cléopâtre*, iii. 309 [2]; her *Amorous Prince*, an adaptation of Davenport's *City Night-Cap*, iii. 326 [5]; other adaptations by, *ib.*; her dramatic works, iii. 432; her comedies, iii. 452.

Believe as You List, by Massinger, synopsis of, iii. 31.

Bellamira, by Sir Charles Sedley, iii. 448.

Belleforest, his novel containing the story of *Hamlet*, ii. 163 *et seq.*

Bellenden, his English edition of Boece's *Historia Scotorum*, ii. 172.

'Belle Savage,' the, Ludgate Hill, early plays acted at, i. 455.

Bellum Grammaticale, a Latin play by Spense, produced at Oxford, ii. 631 [1]; iii. 187.

Belman of London, The, by Dekker, ii. 454 [1].

Belphegor, by John Wilson, iii. 338.

Bendixen, Dr., his translation of Hrotsvitha's comedies, i. 7 [3].

Benedictines, the, influence of, on art in religion, i. 6.

Benoît de Sainte More, his *Destruction de Troyes*, ii. 151.

Beolco, Angelo, the originator of the typical figures of the *commedia dell' arte*, i. 230.

Beowulf, the jongleur in, i. 19 [1].

Berardo, G., his version of Plautus' *Mostellaria*, ii. 566 [3].

Bergerac, Cyrano de, his *Agrippina* and Shakspere's *Hamlet*, i. 534.

Bergersdorff, R., on Shakspere's education, ii. 10 [1].

Berkeley, Sir William, his *Lost Lady*, iii. 163; *Cornelia* attributed to, iii. 163, 164.

Berkenhead, J., on the literary partnership of Beaumont and Fletcher, ii. 657 [1].

Bermudas, the, reference to, in *The Tempest*, ii. 196, 197.

Bernays, Jacob, on Aristotle's conception of tragedy, i. 159 [3].

Bernays, Michael, on the Schlegel-Tieck Shakspere, i. 554.

Berners, John Bourchier, Lord, his comedy *Ite in vineam*, i. 219.

Bernhardi, W., on Greene's works, i. 379 [3]; on *Locrine*, ii. 219.

Bestiaries, i. 78 [1].

Bethersden, Kent, *Ludi Beatae Christinae* at, i. 50 [1]; *The Harrowing of Hell* performed at, i. 55.

Betraying of Christ, The, one of the Coventry plays, i. 88.

Betterton, Thomas, Shaksperean actor, i. 511, 515; his *Life*, by R. Lowe, i. 511 [1], 526; his impersonation of Pericles, ii. 185; his *Prophetess*, ii. 727 [3]; iii. 326 [3]; his adaptation of Webster's *Appius and Virginia*, iii. 62 [3], 326 [4]; his adaptation of Molière's *George Dandin*, iii. 315 [1]; *Appius and Virginia* and *The Roman Virgin*, iii. 326 [4]; his version of *Henry IV*, iii. 326 [1].

Beumelburg, Dr. H., on Alexander (Lord Stirling), ii. 623 [3].

Beverley, the religious drama performed at, i. 55.

Beverley Plays, the, i. 65 [2], 70.

Beverley, Peter, his translation of *Orlando Furioso*, i. 217 [2].

Beza (T. de Bèze), his *Tragedie of Abraham's Sacrifice*, i. 112 [1]; his *Abraham's Sacrifice* translated by Arthur Golding, i. 172 [1].

Bibbiena, Cardinal de: *see* Divizio, Bernardo.

Bible, the, Shakspere's familiarity with, ii. 11.

Bickerstaffe, Isaac, his *The Padlock*, ii. 725 [2].

Birch, Dr., his discovery of Jonson's letter to Earl of Salisbury, ii. 312.

Bird in a Cage, The, by Shirley, iii. 108.

Birde, W.: *see* Bourne, W.

Birdwood, Dr. H. M., on the Plague in London, i. 575, 576.

Birth of Merlin, The, attributed to Shakspere and Rowley, i. 220 [1], ii. 210; synopsis of the play, ii. 243–245.

Biter, The, by Nicholas Rowe, iii. 433 [3].

Black, J., his translation of Schlegel's *Lectures on Dramatic Art and Literature*, i. 557 [1].

Black Booke, The, by Middleton, ii. 494.

Blackfriars Theatre, the, i. 458, ii. 19, 27, 29, iii. 232 [5]; at the Restoration, iii. 283.

Blackmore, Sir Richard, his *Prince Arthur* and its purpose, iii. 510.

Black Prince, The, by Lord Orrery, iii. 343.

Blades, Mr. W., his *Shakspere and Typography*, i. 505 [4], ii. 13 [4].

Blair, Hugh, his edition of Shakspere, i. 529.

Blew, Mr. J., his edition of Dekker's *Sir Thomas Wyat*, ii. 468.

Blind Beggar of Alexandria, by Chapman, ii. 432.

Blind Beggar of Bednal-Green, by John Day, ii. 599.

Blind Lady, The, by Sir R. Howard, iii. 393.

Bliss, Dr., on Heywood's *Play of the Wether*, i. 246 [1].

Blomefylde, Miles, authorship of *The Conversion of St. Paul* attributed to, i. 93.

Bloody Brother, The, by Fletcher, Jonson, and others, ii. 734.

Bloody Duke, The, iii. 294 [3].

Blount, Edward, publisher of Lyly's plays, i. 273.

Blount and Jaggard, publishers of the *Henry VI* plays, ii. 59.

Blurt, Master-Constable, by Middleton, ii. 502.

Boadicea, by Hopkins, and other versions, ii. 697 [3], iii. 431.

Bobadil, Ben Jonson's character of, ii. 345.

Boccaccio, G., influence of the school of, on early English drama, i. 213, 217 [4]; his version of *All's Well that Ends Well*, ii. 119; his *Filostrato*, ii. 152; Shakspere's indebtedness to his *Decamerone* in *Cymbeline*, ii. 190.

Boccalini, Trajano, his *Bagguagli di Parnaso*, ii. 634 [2].

Bodenham, John, his estimate of Shakspere, i. 495 [1].

Bodmer, J. J., his mention of Shakspere as 'Sasper,' i. 546.

Boece, Hector, his *Historia Scotorum*, ii. 172.

Boëthius' *Consolation of Philosophy*, translated by King Alfred, i. 11.

Boileau-Despréaux, N., his satirical dialogue *Les Héros de Roman*, iii. 310.

Boisteau, P., his *Romeo and Juliet*, i. 213.
Boito, his libretto of Verdi's *Falstaff*, ii. 138.
Bojardo, his *Timone*, i. 228, ii. 110.
Bold Beachams, The, a non-extant play by T. Heywood, ii. 583.
Bold Stroke for a Wife, A, by Mrs. Centlivre, iii. 491.
Bolte, Dr. J., discovered Tieck's translation of *Mucedorus*, ii. 226; on the various treatments of subject of Jonson's *Sejanus*, ii. 339 [2, 3].
Bondman, The, by Massinger, iii. 16.
Bonduca, by Fletcher, ii. 696.
Bonen, W., *The Crafty Merchant* attributed to, iii. 148 [1].
Bonner, Bishop, forbids performances of plays in his diocese, i. 54; mentioned in *Cambises*, i. 205.
Boorde, Andrew, his *Merry Tales of the Mad Men of Gotham*, ii. 610 [3].
Booth, Mrs., her adaptation of Fletcher's *Little French Lawyer*, ii. 720 [3].
Borck, C. W. v., his translation of *Julius Caesar*, i. 546, 547.
Borlase, his description of the Cornish ' Rounds,' i. 56 [1].
Borne, W. : *see* Bourne, W.
Boston Public Library, the Shakspere autograph in, ii. 3 [1].
Boswell, James, the younger, his edition of Malone's *Shakspere*, i. 505 [2]; his *Variorum* edition of Shakspere, i. 533.
Bottom, Hazlitt on the character of, ii. 279 [1].
Bourchier, John : *see* Berners, Lord.
Bourgeois Gentilhomme, Le, by Molière, Ravenscroft's adaptation of, iii. 315 [1], 451.
Bourne, W., his and S. Rowley's plays, ii. 546; his additions to Marlowe's *Dr. Faustus*, i. 329 [3].
Boutevilain, the jongleur, i. 20.
Bowge of Courte, The, by Skelton, i. 103.
Bowyer, William, his *The Valiant Scot*, iii. 159.
Boy Bishop, election of, i. 22.
Boyer, Abel, his translation of Racine's *Iphigénie*, iii. 315 [1].
Boyle, Roger : *see* Orrery, Earl of.
Boyle, Mr. Robert, on *Pericles*, ii. 183, 184; on *Henry VIII*, ii. 206; on *The Two Noble Kinsmen*, ii. 242; on the respective contributions of Beaumont and Fletcher in their conjoint plays, ii. 658 *et seq.*; on Fletcher's *Sir John Van Olden-Barnavelt*, ii. 716 [4]; on *A New Way to Pay Old Debts*, ii. 747 [2]; on Massinger, iii. 2 [1].

Boyle, W. : *see* Bourne, W.
Boys, acting companies of, i. 452 [1], 467.
Bracegirdle, Mrs., a Restoration actress, iii. 285 [4].
Brackley, Lord, his parts in masques, iii. 192 [5].
Bräker, Ulrich, on Shakspere, i. 552 [2].
Brambs, J. G., his edition of the Χριστὸς πάσχων, i. 4 [3].
Brandes, Dr. Georg, his Shaksperean criticism, i. 562 ; his *Life* of Shakspere, ii. 1 [1].
Brandl, Dr. Alois, on tragedy in all its phases, i. 210 [5].
Brandon, S., his *Virtuous Octavia*, ii. 187.
Brant, Sebastian, author of the original *Ship of Fooles*, i. 103, 234.
Brennoralt, by Sir John Suckling, synopsis of, iii. 146.
Brewer, Antony, his *Lovesick King*, iii. 174, 175; *Country Girl*, iii. 175 [1]; adaptations by Leanerd from, iii. 326 [5].
Brewer, Dr., on Southampton's intimacy with Shakspere and his works, ii. 33 [1].
Brewer, Thomas, author of a prose tract, *The Merry Devil of Edmonton*, ii. 233, iii. 175.
Breymann, Professor H., and Dr. A. Wagner, their forthcoming edition of Marlowe's works, i. 313 [3], 329 [1].
Bridal, The, by Sheridan Knowles, ii. 674 [1].
Bridals, The, by the Duchess of Newcastle, iii. 335 [4].
Bridges, Dr., Dean of Salisbury, authorship of *Gammer Gurton's Needle* attributed to, i. 260 [3].
Bristol, Earl of: *see* Digby, George.
Bristol Tragedy, The, a non-extant play by Day, ii. 591 [3].
Bristowe Merchant, The, by Dekker and Ford, iii. 75.
Britannia Triumphans, a masque by Sir W. D'Avenant, iii. 173.
British Enchanters, by George Granville, the operatic element in, iii. 323.
Broghill, Lord, *see* Orrery (iii. 343 [2]).
Broken Heart, The, by Ford, synopsis of, iii. 79.
Brome, the play of *Abraham and Isaac* discovered at, i. 91.
Brome, Richard, his and T. Heywood's *Late Lancashire Witches*, ii. 575; the idea of his *Jovial Crew* taken from *The Beggars' Bush*, ii. 726 [2]; his dramatic works, iii. 125–131; his lines on the folio of Suckling's *Aglaura*, iii. 145 [2].

Bromefield, William, his additions to Mayne's *City-Match*, iii. 141 [2].

Brooke, Arthur, his *Romeo and Juliet*, i. 213, ii. 114.

Brooke, Christopher, his tribute to Shakspere, i. 497.

Brooke, Henry, his *Antony and Cleopatra*, ii. 187.

Brooke, Lord, his tragedies, ii. 614; *Alaham*, ii. 615; *Mustapha*, ii. 616.

Brookes, S., his *Melanthe*, iii. 184.

Brothers, The, by Shirley, iii. 104.

Brown, J. M., on Greene's works, i. 379 [3]; on treatments of the subject of the *Parnassus Plays*, ii. 634 [2].

Browne, Robert, his continental company of players, i. 472.

Browning, Robert, his *Caliban upon Setebos*, ii. 200.

Brunne, Robert de, on translations of French *gestes*, i. 27 [1]; his translation of the *Manuel des Pechiez*, i. 52.

Bruno, Archbishop of Cologne, influence of Hrotsvitha's plays on, i. 7 [1]; his influence on the revival of religion, i. 8.

Brunswick, Henry Julius, Duke of, his plays and patronage of players, i. 473.

Brutus, Voltaire's, i. 535.

Brutus, by Duke of Buckingham, ii. 141.

Brutus of Alba, by Tate, iii. 428.

Bryan, George, one of Leicester's players, i. 472 [1].

Buchanan, George, his tragedies, i. 193, 194.

Buckhurst, Lord, Puttenham's commendation of the works of, i. 268. (*See also* Sackville.)

Buckingham (George Villiers), Duke of, his *Rehearsal*, iii. 362.

Buckinghamshire (John Sheffield), Duke of, his plays of *Caesar* and *Brutus*, ii. 141.

Bülow, Dr. G. von, his edition of *The Diary of the Duke of Stettin*, ii. 452 [2].

Bürger, G. A., as a translator, i. 555.

Bulaeus (C. E. du Boulay), on the *Ludus de S. Katharina*, i. 10.

Bull, the, inn in Bishopsgate Street, early plays acted at, i. 455.

Bullen, Mr. A. H., his edition of Marlowe's works, i. 313 [3]; his edition of George Peele's works, i. 363 [1]; his edition of *Arden of Feversham*, ii. 217 [1]; *Two Tragedies in One*, ii. 219; his edition of *Sir Gyles Goosecappe*, ii. 412 [1]; on Chapman's *Alphonsus*, ii. 429 [1]; on Dekker's works, ii. 451; his edition of Marston's works, ii. 472 [1]; his edition of Middleton's works, ii. 493 [1]; on *The Old Law*, ii.

502 [1]; *Game of Chess*, ii. 529 [3]; his introduction to S. Rowley's *Noble Souldier*, ii. 545 [2]; his discovery of T. Heywood's *Captives*, ii. 567, 568; *Dick of Devonshire*, ii. 583; his edition of Day's works, ii. 589 [2]; on Day as the author of the *Parnassus Plays*, ii. 640 [2]; on Fletcher's *Sir John Van Olden-Barnavelt*, ii. 716 [4]; his edition of the works of Thomas Campion, iii. 189–192.

Bulleyn, William, his *Dialogue of Death*, i. 236.

Bulthaupt, H., on *Timon of Athens*, ii. 179.

Bunnett, Miss, her translation of Gervinus' *Shakspere*, i. 558.

Bunyan, his possible acquaintance with Jonson's *Bartholomew Fair*, ii. 371 [5].

Burbage, James, one of Leicester's players, i. 457 [2]; his play-house, i. 458; his connexion with the Blackfriars' theatre, ii. 19.

Burbage, Richard, the contemporary influences surrounding, i. 450, 454 [1], 469; at the Blackfriars' theatre, ii. 27; at the Globe theatre, ii. 29; a friend of Shakspere, ii. 34, 35.

Burges, Sir J. Bland, his adaptation of Massinger's *City Madam*, iii. 34 [2].

Burghley, Lord, his interest in John Lyly, i. 271; a patron of Peele, i. 364; his intervention in the Marprelate controversy, i. 466.

Burial and Resurrection of Christ, The, the miracle-play of, i. 96.

Buriall of Christ, The, part of the Newcastle cycle, i. 91.

Buriall of our Lady St. Mary the Virgin, The, part of the Newcastle cycle, i. 91.

Burlador de Sevilla, El, by Tirso de Molina, iii. 303 [3].

Burlesque, the, distinction between the extravaganza and, i. 161.

Burning of John Huss, The, by Ralph Radcliffe, i. 170, 474 [2].

Burton, Robert, his tribute to Shakspere, i. 500.

Bury-Fair, by Shadwell, iii. 459.

Bussy d'Ambois, by Chapman, synopsis of, ii. 414.

Busy-Body, The, by Mrs. Centlivre, iii. 490.

Butler, Samuel, his share in Buckingham's *Rehearsal*, iii. 363.

Cædmon, allegorical elements in his *Paraphrase*, i. 102.

Caesar, by the Duke of Buckinghamshire, ii. 141.

Caesar and Pompey, by Chapman, ii. 140; account of, ii. 425.

Caesar in Egypt, by Cibber, ii. 141; an adaptation of Fletcher's *The False One*, ii. 719[1].

Caesar's Fall, a play by Munday, Webster, and others, iii. 52.

Caesar Borgia, by N. Lee, iii. 410.

Caius Marius, by Otway, a version of *Romeo and Juliet*, iii. 326[1]; notice of, iii. 415.

Calandria, by Bernardo Divizio, i. 228.

Calderon, P. de la Barca, his version of *Dr. Faustus*, in *El Magico Prodigioso*, i. 330; Schlegel's translation of, i. 558; his version of *Coriolanus*, ii. 189; his *Amor, honor y poder*, ii. 222[1]; the influence of his dramatic works, iii. 304, 305; translations from, iii. 305.

Caleb Shillock his Prophecie, ii. 107.

Caliban, the character of, ii. 199.

Caligula, by J. Crowne, iii. 403.

Calista and Meliboea, by Cota and de Rojas, i. 232; English version of, i. 249.

Calisto, by Crowne, Princess Mary's part in, iii. 295[4], 399.

Calprenède, his *Édouard III*, ii. 222[1]; his dramas and their influence, iii. 309; adaptations of, iii. 309[2].

Calthorpe, Martin, Mayor of London, Peele's pageant for, i. 368[1].

Calvert, Charles, his production of *Henry V*, ii. 264[2].

Calypso and Telemachus, by J. Hughes, iii. 430.

Cambises King of Percia, &c., an early tragedy, by Thomas Preston, i. 142, 205.

Cambridge, the religious drama performed at, i. 56; plays acted at, in later Elisabethan times, ii. 631; plays at, during James I's visits to, iii. 184.

'Cambridge Shakespeare,' the, i. 570.

Cambyses, by Settle, iii. 396.

Camden, William, his estimate of Shakspere, i. 495[1]; a friend of Ben Jonson, ii. 299.

Camden Society, the, i. 570.

Camilla, an Italian opera translated by McSwiney, iii. 322[1].

Campanella, Thomas, his *Civitas Solis*, ii. 199.

Campaspe, by John Lyly, i. 293.

Campbell, Lord, on Shakspere's legal acquirements, ii. 13[2].

Campbell, Thomas, his appreciation of Shakspere, i. 568.

Campeggi, Ridolfo, his *Gismonda*, i. 214[3].

Campion, Edmund, Munday's pamphlets on, i. 431.

Campion, Thomas, his masques, iii. 189–192.

Canaan's Calamity, ascribed to Dekker, ii. 453.

Canterbury, religious plays performed at, i. 57.

Capell, Edward, his edition of Shakspere, i. 526, 532; on *Edward III*, ii. 222.

Capgrave, John, Marlowe's obligations to, i. 350[2].

Capricious Lady, by W. Cooke, taken from *The Scornful Lady*, ii. 669[1].

Captain, The, by Beaumont and Fletcher, ii. 686.

Captain Mario, Stephen Gosson on, i. 217, 263.

Captain Thomas Stukely, Famous History of the Life and Death of, i. 370[3].

Captain Underwit, attributed to James Shirley, iii. 120.

Captives, The, by T. Heywood, ii. 567.

Captivity, a tragedy by Landivio, i. 169.

Capture of Cesena, The, an early Italian play, i. 169.

Caractacus, a version of *Bonduca*, by J. R. Planché, ii. 697[2]; Mason's, ii. 697[3].

Cardenio, The, History of, attributed to Shakspere and Fletcher, ii. 213, 743.

Cardenio und Celinde, by Andreas Gryphius, ii. 213[3].

Cardinal, The, by Shirley, iii. 98.

Careless Husband, The, by Colley Cibber, iii. 486.

Careless Lovers, The, by Ravenscroft, iii. 451.

Carew, Richard, on the Guary miracles, i. 56[1].

Carew, Thomas, his masque, *Coelum Britannicum*, iii. 192.

Carey, Sir George, his connexion with Nashe, i. 423[3].

Carlell, Lodovick, Lodge's *Wounds of Civil War* assigned to, i. 416[3]; a patron of Dekker, ii. 455[2]; his dramatic works, iii. 160, 161; his translation of Corneille's *Héraclius*, iii. 315[1].

Carnarvon, Lord, a patron of Massinger, iii. 7.

Carretto, Galeotto del, his *Sofonisba*, i. 169[4].

Carri, the, i. 227.

Carrière, Moritz, on Shakspere's *Tempest*, ii. 194.

Carroll, Mrs. (Mrs. Centlivre), her adaptation of May's *Heir*, iii. 142[3], 488[3].

Cartwright, Thomas, his position towards the Marprelate controversy, i. 463.

Cartwright, William, his estimation of Shakspere, i. 510 [1]; on Fletcher, ii. 657 [5]; his works, iii. 137-140; *Royal Slave*, iii. 138; *Lady Errant*, iii. 139; *The Siege*, iii. 139; *The Ordinary*, iii. 139.

Caryl, John, his translation of Molière's *L'École des Femmes*, iii. 315 [1].

Case is Altered, The, by Ben Jonson, i. 346; account of the play, ii. 350.

Cassandre, by La Calprenède, Banks' adaptation of, iii. 309 [2]; Lee's obligations to, *ib.*

Castara, by W. Habington, iii. 149.

Castell of Perseverance, The, one of the 'Macro' Moralities, i. 113.

Castelvines y Monteses, Los, by Lope de Vega, ii. 116.

Catherina II, Empress, her *Pretty Basketful of Linen*, ii. 137.

Catilina, Voltaire's, ii. 340 [3].

Catiline his Conspiracy, by Ben Jonson, notice of, ii. 339, 402.

Catiline's Conspiracies, by Stephen Gosson, i. 208, 209, 460 [1], ii. 340.

Cato, by Joseph Addison, account of, iii. 439.

Catuelan, Count de, and Letourneur's *Shakspere*, i. 538.

Cavendish, *see* Newcastle.

Cawarden, Sir Thomas, appointed Magister Jocorum Revellorum et Mascorum, i. 152.

Caxton, William, his translation of le Fèvre's *Troy*, ii. 152.

Cayet, P. V. de, Chapman's obligations to, ii. 423.

Cefalo, by Niccolo dà Correggio, ii. 381.

Celebration of Charis, A, by Ben Jonson, ii. 331.

Celestina, The, by Cota and Rojas, i. 232; earliest English version of, i. 249.

Celtes, Conrad, his edition of Hrotsvitha's Comedies, i. 7 [3].

Cent Nouvelles Nouvelles, an English translation of, i. 217 [4].

Centlivre, Mrs., her adaptation of Regnard's *Joueur*, iii. 316 [1]; her dramatic works, iii. 488-491; *The Perjured Husband*, iii. 488; *The Beau's Duel*, iii. 489; *The Basset-Table*, iii. 490; *Love at a Venture*, iii. 490; *The Busy-Body* and *Marplot in Lisbon*, iii. 490; *The Wonder*, iii. 490; later plays, iii. 491. (*See also under* Carroll.)

Centurie of Prayse, Shakespeare's, edited by Dr. Ingleby, i. 491 [1] *et seqq.*

Cervantes, Saavedra, M. de, his influence on the Spanish drama, i. 232; Middleton's obligations to in *The Spanish Gipsy*, ii. 508; his *Viage del Parnaso*, ii. 634 [2]; Beaumont and Fletcher's obligations to, ii. 752.

César, a tragedy by Jacques Grévin, i. 207 [1].

César, Scènes Historiques, by J. J. Ampère, ii. 142.

Cespedes, Gonzalo de, Fletcher's obligations to his *Gerardo*, ii. 724; Beaumont and Fletcher's obligations to, ii. 753.

Chabot, by Chapman and Shirley, account of, ii. 444.

Challenge at Tilt, A, a masque by Ben Jonson, ii. 395.

Challenge for Beauty, A, by T. Heywood, ii. 570.

Chalmers, George, his edition of Lyndsay's Poetical Works, i. 132 [1].

Chamberlayne, William, his *Pharonnida*, iii. 289; *Love's Victory*, iii. 289.

Chances, The, by Fletcher, notice of, ii. 712.

Chandos portrait of Shakspere, the, ii. 42.

Change of Crowns, The, by Edward Howard, iii. 396.

Changeling, The, by Middleton and W. Rowley, ii. 511.

Changes, The, by Shirley, iii. 105.

Chanones Yemannes Tale, The, the alchemists in, ii. 368 [1].

Chansons de Geste, origin of, i. 18.

Chapel Children, the, an acting company, i. 452 [1], 469.

Chapman, George, his tribute to Marlowe, i. 318; his *Caesar and Pompey*, ii. 140; *The Second Maiden's Tragedy* assigned to, ii. 212; his disgrace, and his connexion with Ben Jonson, ii. 311, 326 [1]; second imprisonment of, ii. 312; possible reference to, in Jonson's *Poetaster*, ii. 360; his life, ii. 409-13; his *Homer* and other translations, ii. 411; theatrical experiences, ii. 412; character, ii. 413; his dramatic works, ii. 414-50; *Bussy d'Ambois* and *The Revenge of Bussy d'Ambois*, ii. 414; *The Conspiracy* and *Tragedie of Byron*, ii. 421; *Caesar and Pompey*, ii. 425; *Alphonsus*, ii. 427; *Revenge for Honour*, ii. 431; *The Blind Beggar of Alexandria*, ii. 432; *An Humorous Day's Mirth*, ii. 433; *All Fooles*, ii. 434; *The Gentleman Usher*, ii. 435; *Monsieur d'Olive*, ii. 437; *May-Day*, ii. 440; *The Widdowes Teares*, ii. 440; *Masque of the Middle Temple*,

ii. 441; plays of which he was part-author, ii. 441; *Eastward Hoe*, ii. 442; *The Ball*, ii. 444, iii. 107; *Chabot*, ii. 444; plays attributed to, ii. 446; as a dramatist, ii. 447; his learning, ii. 449; his versification, ii. 450; his *Masque of the Middle Temple* compared with Beaumont's, ii. 650[3]; adaptations of his plays, iii. 326[2].

Charles the Great, his influence on the revival of religion, i. 8.

Charles I, his estimation of Shakspere, i. 510[1]; Ben Jonson's relations with, ii. 320; effect of his influence on the Drama, iii. 218, 229.

Charles II and the stage, iii. 300.

Charles VIII of France, The History of, by J. Crowne, iii. 400.

Charles IX, by M. J. de Chénier, i. 355[3].

Chasles, Philarète, on Shakspere, i. 561.

Chaste Maid in Cheapside, A, by Middleton, a synopsis of, ii. 521.

Chaucer, his *Romaunt of the Rose*, allegorical elements in, i. 103; his use of the words tragedy and comedy, i. 159[1]; his version of Boccaccio's *Filostrato*, ii. 152; on the alchemists in his *Chanones Yemannes Tale*, ii. 368[1]; Beaumont and Fletcher's obligations to, ii. 752.

Cheats, The, by John Wilson, iii. 338.

Cheats of Scapin, The, by Otway, iii. 315[1], 414.

Chénier, M. J. de, his *Charles IX*, i. 355[3].

Cherea, Francesco, his comedies, i. 229[1].

Chester, performances of the religious drama at, i. 56; *Robert Cicill* acted at, i. 170.

Chester Plays, The, i. 54; their connexion with the *Mystère de vieil Testament*, i. 58[2]; performance of, i. 59; pageants comprising, i. 59; a synopsis of, i. 76–84; similarity to the *Cursor Mundi*, i. 77.

Chester, Robert, his *Love's Martyr*, ii. 31.

Chettle, Henry, publisher of *A Groatsworth of Wit* by Robert Greene, i. 316, 391[4]; his life and works, i. 426; his collaboration with Munday in *The Downfall* and *The Death of Robert Earl of Huntington*, i. 432, 433; his tribute to Shakspere in *Kind Hart's Dreame*, i. 492[1], 496; his *Hoffman*, ii. 162; his and others' *Patient Grissil*, ii. 466; *Henry I*, ii. 466; *Earl Godwin*, ii. 467; his and

Dekker's *Troilus and Cressida*, ii. 467; *Robert of Scots*, ii. 467; *The Conquest of Brute* attributed to Day and, ii. 591.

Child, Mr. C. G., on John Lyly, i. 273[4].

Chinese stage, legislation as to the, i. 235[3]; women's parts on the, iii. 251[1].

Chit-Chat, a comedy by Thomas Killigrew (the younger), iii. 165[2].

Chloridia, Jonson and Inigo Jones' failure in, ii. 379[1], 397.

Christ, by Cynewulf, allegorical elements in, i. 102.

Christ and Satan, poem on, connexion with Cædmon's *Paraphrase*, i. 12.

Christ Betrayed, in the Chester plays, i. 80.

Christ's Entry into Jerusalem, in the Chester plays, i. 80.

Christ's Teares over Jerusalem, Thomas Nashe on London in, i. 402[1], 421.

Christian turn'd Turk, The, by Robert Daborne, iii. 155.

Christmas his Masque, by Ben Jonson, ii. 395.

Χριστὸς πάσχων, authorship of, i. 4.

Christus Patiens, by Hugo Grotius, connexion with the Χριστὸς πάσχων, i. 5[1]; George Sandys' version of, and Milton's scheme of dramatic treatment of, iii. 202.

Chronicle History, Bishop Bale and the origin of the, i. 173, 218.

Chronicle Histories, decline of, i. 479.

Chronicle of Edward I: see *Edward I*.

Chronicle of Histories, by R. Fabyan, i. 349.

Chrysanaleia, i. 148.

Churchill, Charles, his *Rosciad*, i. 541[2].

Cibber, Colley, his adaptation of Shakspere's *Richard III*, i. 515, ii. 100; his *Caesar in Egypt*, ii. 141, 719[1]; on *The Maid's Tragedy*, ii. 673[2]; his *Rival Forts*, ii. 693[4]; his impersonation of Bayes in *The Rehearsal*, iii. 363[4]; his *Non-Juror*, iii. 405[4]; his quarrel with Pope, iii. 427[1]; his dramatic works, iii. 485–487; *Love's Last Shift*, iii. 486; earlier plays, iii. 486; *The Careless Husband*, iii. 486; *The Lady's Last Stake*, iii. 487.

Ciceronis Amor, Tullies Love, by Robert Greene, i. 390.

Cid, Le, by Corneille, Rutter's translation of, iii. 315[1].

Cinthio, Giraldi, his plays and novels, i. 213, 216; his *Dido*, i. 357[1]; his version of Bandello's *Apollonius and Silla*, ii. 81; his *Hecatommithi*, ii. 154, 168; his *Epitia*, ii. 154; Fletcher's

obligations to his *Hecatommithi*, ii.
723; Beaumont and Fletcher's obligations to, ii. 752.

Cipio Africanus, an early English play,
i. 208.

Circe, a tragedy by Charles D'Avenant,
iii. 331[3].

Citharistae, in England, i. 27.

City Heiress, The, by Mrs. Behn, an
adaptation of *Mad World my Masters*,
iii. 326[5].

City Madam, The, by Massinger, notice
of, iii. 34.

City Nightcap, The, by R. Davenport,
notice of, iii. 158; adapted by Mrs.
Behn, iii. 326[5].

City Politics, by J. Crowne, iii. 405.

City Wit, The, by R. Brome, iii. 127[1],
128.

Civil Wars, The, by S. Daniel, ii.
617.

Civil Wars in France, The, by Dekker
and Drayton, ii. 467.

Civitas Solis, by Campanella, ii. 199.

Civitatis Amor, a masque by Middleton,
ii. 498[1].

Claracilla, by T. Killigrew (the elder),
iii. 166.

Clarendon, Lord, his *Life* of Thomas
May, iii. 142[2].

Clark, W. G., and Mr. Aldis Wright,
their 'Cambridge' edition of Shakspere, i. 570.

Classical drama, the, efforts to restore,
iii. 302.

Classical models, early Christian dramas
founded on, i. 4.

Clayton, Thomas, the musical composer of Addison's *Rosamond*, iii.
323[1].

Cleander, by Massinger, ii. 731.

Clement, St., of Alexandria, his fragment of Ezechiel's *Exodus*, i. 3[1].

Cleomenes, by Dryden, account of, iii.
384, 385.

Cleopatra, by S. Daniel, i. 436[3], ii.
186; notice of, ii. 618.

Cleopatra, by T. May, iii. 143.

Cléopâtre, by La Calprenède, Mrs. Behn's
adaptation of, iii. 309[2]; Lee's adaptation of, iii. 309[2].

Cléopatre Captive, early French tragedy,
by Étienne Jodelle, i. 193, 207[1].

Clergy, the, rivalry between the histriones and, in the miracle-plays, &c.,
i. 47[1], 51.

Clifford, Martin, his share in Buckingham's *Rehearsal*, iii. 363.

Clowns, in early Elisabethan comedy,
i. 485.

Club-Law, by G. Ruggle, produced at
Cambridge, ii. 632.

Clytaemnestra, by Timotheus of Gaza,
i. 5[2].

Cockayne, Sir Aston, on the connexion
between Fletcher and Massinger, iii. 5[1],
11[1]; plays published by him during
the Protectorate, iii. 287; *Dianea*;
Masque at Brethie; *The Obstinate
Lady*, iii. 287; *Trappolin Creduto
Principe*, iii. 288; *The Tragedy of
Ovid*, iii. 288.

Cockpit theatre, the, iii. 232[5], 249[4]; at
the Restoration, iii. 282, 283 *et seq.*

Codrington, Robert, supposed translator
of *Ignoramus*, iii. 185.

Coelum Britannicum, a masque by
Thomas Carew, iii. 192.

Cohn, A., his *Shakespeare in Germany*,
i. 544[2].

Coleridge, S. T., his Shaksperean criticism, i. 565; on *Pericles*, ii. 181; his
version of *The Winter's Tale* in
Zapolya, ii. 193; on Beaumont and
Fletcher, ii. 643[1], 645, 756[1]; his
edition of Massinger, iii. 2[1].

Colet, Dean, prohibits the clergy from
playing and acting, i. 53.

Colin Clout's Come Home Again,
Spenser's impersonation of Peele in,
i. 367; tribute to Shakspere in, i. 493.

Coliphizatio, the, one of the Towneley
plays, i. 75.

Collier, Jeremy, his criticisms on Shakspere, i. 524; on Vanbrugh's *Relapse*,
iii. 478[3]; his anti-theatrical publications, iii. 509 *et seq.*; his *Short View*,
&c., iii. 511; his *Defence*, &c., iii.
514[2].

Collier, J. Payne, his *History of Dramatic Poetry and Annals of the English Stage*, i. 1[1]; on the Chester
plays, i. 76; his edition of *The Harrowing of Hell*, i. 90[1]; of *The Sacrifice of Abraham*, at Dublin, i. 92;
editor of Woodes' *Conflict of Conscience*, i. 138; on *Robert Cicill*, i.
170[1]; his edition of Bale's *Kyng
Johan*, i. 177[1]; his edition of Thynn's
Debate, i. 237[3]; his edition of early
copies of *History of Patient Grissil*,
i. 429[4]; his edition of Munday's
works, i. 431[1]; his edition of Armin's
Nest of Ninnies, i. 435[3]; edition
of Northbrooke's *Treatise against
Dicing, Dancing, vain Plays*, &c.,
i. 459[1]; of Gosson's *Schoole of Abuse*,
i. 459[3]; his edition of Christopher
Brookes' poems, i. 497[1]; his edition
of Coleridge's Shakspere lectures, i.

566; his Shaksperean criticism, i. 569, 570; his *Life of Shakspere*, ii. 1 [1]; on the relations between Ben Jonson and Shakspere, ii. 303 [3]; on Chapman's *Eastward Hoe*, ii. 311 [1]; his editions of T. Heywood's plays, ii. 550 [3], 558 [1] *et seq.*

Collier of Croydon, The, by Crowley, i. 134 [1].

Collins, Dr. Churton, his edition of Cyril Tourneur's works, iii. 66 [1].

Collins, William, on Shakspere's male characters, i. 529 [1].

Colman, George, the elder, his version of *Bonduca*, ii. 697 [2].

Colonel, The: see *Siege, The.*

Combe, John, his legacy to Shakspere, ii. 39.

Combe, Thomas, his family and descendants, ii. 5 [1].

Combe, William, ii. 39.

Comedia von König Edwarto, by Jacob Ayrer, i. 545 [1].

Comedie or Interlude treating upon the Historie of Jacob and Esau, i. 112 [1].

Comedy, distinctions between Tragedy and, i. 158 *et seq.*; the developement of, in England, i. 225; in France and Italy, i. 226; in Spain, i. 231; in Germany, i. 232; examples of early English, i. 234; in the hands of Shakspere's predecessors, i. 484; of character, at early Stuart period, iii. 260; of manners, iii. 274; writers of, in later Stuart times, iii. 442 *et seq.*; sentimental, Steele the founder of, iii. 493; summary of history of, in the later Stuart period, iii. 503 *et seq.*; characteristics of, iii. 504; English and foreign comedy, iii. 505; immorality of English, iii. 506; later growths of, iii. 515; achievements of, iii. 516; comedy and the novel, iii. 517.

Comedy of Errors, The, Shakspere's, possibly acted before Elisabeth, ii. 27; versification, ii. 49 [1]; observations on the play, ii. 74-76.

Comedy of Humours, The, the question of the identity of, ii. 303, 304.

Comic Gallant, The, by John Dennis, an adaptation of Shakspere's *Merry Wives*, i. 515, ii. 137.

Comicall History, &c.: see *Alphonsus*, &c.

Comical Lovers, The, by Colley Cibber, iii. 487 [2].

Comical Revenge, The, by Sir George Etheredge, notice of, iii. 444.

Comines, P. de, compared with Froissart, i. 171.

Comme Il Vous Plaira, George Sand's adaptation of *As You Like It*, ii. 130.

Commedia dell' arte, later developements of the, i. 229, ii. 274.

Commedie, the early, in Italy, i. 227.

Committee, The, by Sir R. Howard, iii. 393.

Committee-Man Curried, The, by S. Sheppard, iii. 292 [2].

Common Conditions, i. 142.

Commonwealth, the condition of the stage during the, iii. 277; plays published during, iii. 286; dramatic works in derision of, iii. 292 [3].

Comoedia Bubionis, by Vitalis Blesensis, i. 9 [1].

Comoedia von Vincentio Ladislao, by Duke Henry Julius, i. 545 [1].

Comoedia von zweyen Brüdern auss Syracus, by Jacob Ayrer, i. 545 [1].

Complaint of Elstred, by Lodge, ii. 220.

Complaynt of Rosamund, by S. Daniel, ii. 619.

Comus, Milton's obligation to Peele's *Old Wives' Tale*, i. 373; compared with Fletcher's *Faithful Shepherdess*, ii. 663 [3]; synopsis of, iii. 197–201.

Conceited Pedler, The, by T. Randolph, synopsis of, iii. 132, 133.

Condell, Henry, his and John Heminge's first folio edition of Shakspere, i. 499; his share in Burbage's new Globe theatre, ii. 29; a friend of Shakspere's, ii. 35.

Conde Lucanor, El, by Don Juan Manuel, compared with *Taming of a Shrew*, ii. 95.

Confederacy, The, by Vanbrugh, account of, iii. 479.

Conference of Pleasure, a series of masques by Francis Bacon, ii. 628.

Confessio Amantis, by Gower, allegorical elements in, i. 103.

Conflict of Conscience, The, a morality by Nathaniel Woodes, i. 138.

Confrérie de la Passion, the, religious plays performed by, i. 107.

Congreve, William, his *Old Bachelor*, ii. 725 [2], iii. 471; his dramatic works, iii. 467–477; his wit, iii. 468; *The Double-Dealer*, iii. 472; *Love for Love*, iii. 473; *The Way of the World*, iii. 475; *The Mourning Bride*, iii. 476; his attack on Collier, iii. 514.

Conquest of Brute, a non-extant play by Day and Chettle, ii. 591.

Conquest of China by the Tartars, The, by Sir R. Howard, iii. 393.

Conquest of Granada, The, by Dryden, account of, iii. 359.

Conquest of Spain, The, adapted from W. Rowley's *All's Lost,* ii. 544.

Conrad, H., on Greene's works, i. 379 [3].

Conrad of Würzburg, his *Trojan War,* ii. 151.

Conscious Lovers, The, by Steele, a synopsis of, iii. 496.

Consolation of Philosophy, The, by Boëthius, translated by King Alfred, i. 11.

Conspiracie of Charles Duke of Byron, The, by Chapman, a synopsis of, ii. 421.

Conspiracy, The, by Killigrew, iii. 163.

Constable, Henry, the contemporaries of, i. 442.

Constant Couple, The, by Farquhar, a synopsis of, iii. 482.

Constant Maid, The, by Shirley, notice of, iii. 114.

Constantine the Great, by N. Lee, iii. 411.

Contention between Liberality and Prodigality, The, a morality, i. 135.

Contention betwixt a Wife, a Widow and a Maid, The, by Sir John Davies, i. 227 [2].

Contention betwixt Yorke and Lancaster, &c., *The,* ii. 59.

Contention for Honour and Riches, The, by Shirley, a synopsis of, iii. 101.

Contention of Ajax and Ulysses, The, by Shirley, iii. 101 [2].

Conti, Antonio, his *Giulio Cesare,* ii. 141; and *Marco Bruto,* ii. 142.

Contrasti, early Italian farces, i. 227.

Convent of Pleasure, The, by the Duchess of Newcastle, iii. 335.

Conversations with Drummond, Ben Jonson's, ii. 296 [1], 317, 331.

Conversion of Saul, The, one of the Digby Mysteries, i. 60 [2], 93.

Cook, Captain Henry, his music to D'Avenant's entertainments, iii. 281 [2].

Cooke, Edward, his *Love's Triumph,* iii. 295 [1].

Cooke, John, the dramatic works of, ii. 608, 609; *Greene's Tu-Quoque,* ii. 608; *How a Man may chuse a Good Wife,* &c., ii. 608, 609.

Cooke, W., his *Capricious Lady,* taken from *The Scornful Lady,* ii. 669 [1].

Cooper, Thomas, his part in the Marprelate controversy, i. 463 [2].

Cooper, W. D., his edition of *Gorboduc,* i. 198 [3].

Cooper's Hill, a poem by Sir John Denham, iii. 148.

Corbet, Richard (afterwards Bishop), Ben Jonson's visit to, ii. 319.

Coriolanus, Shakspere's, adapted by John Dennis, i. 515; versification of,

ii. 49 [2], 51 [2]; observations on the play, ii. 187–189; Tate's adaptation of, iii. 428.

Corneille, Pierre, compared with Shakspere, i. 537; Sir W. Lower's translations from, iii. 290; influence of his works, iii. 313; adaptations of, iii. 315 [1], 352.

Corneille, Thomas, adaptations of, iii. 315 [1].

Cornelia, a non-extant play ascribed to Sir W. Berkeley, iii. 163, 164.

Cornelia, by Kyd: see *Pompey the Great.*

Cornelianum Dolum, a Latin comedy ascribed to T. Randolph, iii. 136.

Cornélie, by R. Garnier, Kyd's translation of, i. 304.

Corney, Mr. Bolton, on Day as the author of the *Parnassus Plays,* ii. 640 [2].

Cornwall, the miracle-plays of, i. 56 [1].

Cornwall, Barry, his edition of Ben Jonson's works, with memoir, ii. 296 [1], 401 [1].

Coronation, The, by Shirley, ii. 747; notice of, iii. 112.

Coronation of Our Lady, The, one of the York plays, i. 70.

Corpus Christi, institution of, i. 46, 52, 54.

Corpus Christi plays, the Beverley, i. 70; the Newcastle-on-Tyne, i. 70.

Correggio, Niccolo dà, his *Cefalo,* ii. 381.

Coryate, Thomas, his travels satirised in Fletcher's *Queen of Corinth,* ii. 714 [4].

Cota, Rodrigo, his *entremeses,* i. 232.

Cotton, Charles, his translation of Corneille's *Horace,* iii. 315 [1]; *Nicomède,* iii. 315 [1].

Cotton, Sir Robert, Ben Jonson's relations with, ii. 326 [2].

Countercuffe given to Martin Junior, a contribution to the Marprelate controversy, i. 465 [5].

Country Captaine, The, by the Duke of Newcastle, iii. 333.

Country Girl, The, by Antony, or Thomas, Brewer, iii. 175 [1].

Country House, The, by Vanbrugh, iii. 480.

Country Wife, The, by Wycherley, iii. 464.

Country Wit, The, by J. Crowne, iii. 404.

Courageous Turk, The, by T. Goffe, iii. 159.

Court Beggar, The, by R. Brome, iii. 127 [2], 128.

Court Secret, The, by Shirley, iii. 119.

Courthope, Mr. W. J., his *History of English Poetry*, i. 104 [1].

Courtlie Controversie of Cupid's Cautels, published by Sir Henry Wotton, i. 309.

Covent Garden theatre, the first, iii. 284 [3].

Covent Garden Weeded, by R. Brome, iii. 128.

Coventry, religious plays performed at, i. 56.

Coventry plays, the, pageants comprising, i. 59, 60 [4], 61 [1] *et seqq.*; a synopsis of, i. 84–89; characters in, i. 89; allegorical characters, i. 106.

Coverley, Sir Roger, at Howard's *Committee*, iii. 394 [1].

Cowley, Abraham, his plays, iii. 164; *Naufragium Joculare*, iii. 187; his place among his contemporaries, iii. 327; *Cutter of Coleman Street*, iii. 327.

Cox, Captain, his play *Impatient Poverty*, i. 144 [5].

Cox, Robert, his drolls, iii. 280.

Cox of Collumpton, attributed to Day and Haughton, ii. 591 [3].

Coxcomb, The, by Beaumont and Fletcher, a synopsis of, ii. 682.

Crafty Merchant, The, attributed to Shackerley Marmion, iii. 148 [1].

Craven, Lord, a patron of Ford, iii. 72.

Creatio, the, one of the Towneley plays, i. 73.

Creation and Fall, and Death of Abel, The, one of the Chester plays, i. 77.

Creation and the Fall of Lucifer, The, one of the York plays, i. 67.

Crébillon, P. J. de, his *Atrée*, a version of Seneca's *Thyestes*, iii. 402 [2].

Credo, the, in the Chester plays, i. 82 [2].

Creed play, the, of York, i. 66, 97, 98.

Crispin and Crispianus, performed at Dublin, i. 50 [1]; W. Rowley's obligations to, ii. 545.

Croesus, by Lord Stirling, ii. 624.

Croker, Crofton, his edition of Massinger's *Believe as You List*, iii. 31 [3].

Croly, G., his *Catiline*, ii. 340 [3].

Cromwell, The Life and Death of Thomas, Lord, attributed to Shakspere, ii. 210; a synopsis of the play, ii. 234, 235.

Cromwell, Oliver: *see* Protectorate.

'Cross Keys,' the, Gracious (Gracechurch) Street, early plays acted at, i. 455.

Crossley, Mr. James, his edition of Potts' *Witches of Lancaster*, ii. 576 [2].

Crowley, Robert, his *Collier of Croydon*, i. 134 [1].

Crowne, John, his *Calisto*, Princess Mary's part in, iii. 295 [4]; his dramatic works, iii. 398–407; *Juliana*, iii. 400; *Charles VIII of France*, iii. 400; *The Destruction of Jerusalem*, iii. 400; *The Ambitious Statesman*, iii. 401; *Thyestes*, iii. 402; *Darius*, iii. 402; *Regulus*, iii. 403; *Caligula*, iii. 403; *The Country Wit*, iii. 404; *City Politics*, iii. 405; *The English Friar*, iii. 405; *Sir Courtly Nice*, iii. 406; *The Married Beau*, iii. 407.

Croxton, the Sacrament play designed to be played at, i. 98.

Crucifixio, the, one of the Towneley plays, i. 75; one of the Chester plays, i. 81.

Cruel Brother, The, by Sir W. D'Avenant, iii. 170.

Cruel Detter, The, by W. Wager, i. 137 [1].

Cruel Gift, The, by Mrs. Centlivre, iii. 488 [2].

Cruelties of the Spaniards in Peru, The, by Sir W. D'Avenant, iii. 282.

Cuckold's Haven, Tate's version of *Eastward Ho!* iii. 326 [2].

Cumberland, R., his version of *Timon of Athens*, ii. 180; his adaptation of Massinger's *Duke of Milan*, iii. 15 [2].

Cunliffe, Dr. J. W., on *The Influence of Seneca upon Elizabethan Tragedy*, i. 194 [2].

Cunningham, Lt.-Col. F., his edition of Marlowe, i. 313 [3]; his edition of Massinger, iii. 2 [1], 31 [3].

Cupid and Death, a masque by James Shirley, iii. 93, 101 [2].

Cupid's Banishment, a masque by Robert White, iii. 192.

Cupid's Mistress, by T. Heywood, ii. 582.

Cupid's Revenge, by Beaumont and Fletcher, synopsis of, ii. 684.

Cure for a Cuckold, A, by Webster and W. Rowley, synopsis of, iii. 54.

Curioso Impertinente, Il, compared with *The Coxcomb*, ii. 683.

'Curré, Jérôme,' a pseudonym of Voltaire, i. 537 [2].

Cursor Mundi, the MSS. of, i. 65; similarity to the Chester plays, i. 77.

Curtain theatre, the, iii. 232 [5].

Custom of the Country, The, by Fletcher, synopsis of, ii. 721.

Cuthbert Cutpurse, the character of, i. 111.

Cutter of Coleman Street, by Cowley, iii. 327.

Cymbeline, Shakspere's, D'Urfey's adaptation of, i. 514; versification of, ii. 49 [1], 51 [2]; observations on the play, ii. 189-191.

Cynewulf, allegorical elements in his *Christ*, i. 102.

Cynthia's Revels, by Ben Jonson, its euphuistic tendencies, i. 285 [2]; supposed insults contained in, ii. 307; account of the play, ii. 352, 403.

Cyprian Academy, The, by R. Baron, iii. 290[1].

Cyprian of Antioch, the story of, and *Doctor Faustus*, i. 330.

Cyrus the Great, J. Banks' adaptation of La Calprenède's *Grand Cyrus*, iii. 309 [2]; account of, iii. 429.

Daborne, R., his *Machiavell and the Devil*, i. 339 [3]; his connexion with Fletcher, ii. 747; his works, iii. 155.

Dalton, J., his adaptation of Milton's *Comus*, iii. 199 [1].

Dame Sirith, the old English tale of, i. 237.

Damoiselle, The, by R. Brome, iii. 127 [4], 128.

Damon and Pithias, by Richard Edwardes, i. 210, 211.

Dance of Macabre, The, by Lydgate, i. 50 [3].

Dance of the Sevin Deidly Synnis, by Dunbar, i. 113 [4].

Dancer, John, his translation of *Pastor Fido*, iii. 303 [1]; his and Charles Cotton's translation of Corneille's *Nicomède*, iii. 315 [1]; of Quinault's *Agrippa*, iii. 315 [1].

Daniel, The History of, by Hilarius, i. 38.

Daniel, Mr. P. A., on *Henry V*, ii. 126; on *The Birth of Merlin*, ii. 243.

Daniel, Samuel, his place in literature, i. 436 [3], 442; his *Complaint of Rosamund*, i. 437; his *Cleopatra*, ii. 186; possible impersonation of, in Jonson's *Bartholomew Fair*, ii. 371; relations with Ben Jonson, ii. 391 [4]; his literary and dramatic works, ii. 617–623; his *Defence of Rhyme*, origin of, iii. 190 [3].

Daphne, by Ottavio Rinuccini, the first Italian opera, iii. 321 [1].

Dares Phrygius, his history of the Trojan war, ii. 149 *et seq.*

Darius, by Lord Stirling, ii. 624.

Darius, by J. Crowne, account of, iii. 402.

Darius, King, an early religious play, i. 112 [1].

Darley, George, his edition of Beaumont and Fletcher, ii. 643 [1].

Daudet, M. Léon A., his *Voyage de Shakespeare*, ii. 19 [3].

D'Avenant, Charles, his *Circe*, iii. 331 [3].

D'Avenant, Sir William, his estimate of Shakspere, i. 508; Shakspere's plays acted by his company, i. 512, 513; Shakspere's alleged relationship to, ii. 41; his version of *The Tempest*, in *Gondibert*, ii. 200, 331, 352; his *Albovine*, ii. 505 [1], iii. 169; his prologue to Beaumont's *Woman Hater*, ii. 662; to Fletcher's *Faithful Shepherdess*, ii. 663; his dramatic works, iii. 166–173; his life, iii. 166, 167; his ideas on dramatic composition, ii. 167–169; *The Cruel Brother*, iii. 170; *The Just Italian*, iii. 170; *The Platonic Lovers*, iii. 170; *Wits*, iii. 171; *Love and Honour*, iii. 172; *The Unfortunate Lovers*, iii. 172; *The Siege*, iii. 173; *News from Plymouth*, iii. 173; *The Fair Favourite*, iii. 173; *The Distresses*, iii. 173; his masques, iii. 173; his devices, iii. 281; *The Siege of Rhodes*, iii. 282, 328; *The Cruelties of Spaniards in Peru*, iii. 282; *The History of Sir Francis Drake*, iii. 283; *The Playhouse to be Let*, iii. 283 [2], 330; his company of actors at the Restoration, iii. 283, 284; plays by, published during the Protectorate, iii. 286; his *Rivals* taken from *The Two Noble Kinsmen*, iii. 326 [3]; his later plays, iii. 328-331; *The Siege*, iii. 329; his adaptations of old plays, iii. 330; his position as a dramatist, iii. 331.

Davenant, a play by J. Aicard, iii. 166 [4].

Davenport, R., two non-extant plays, *Henry I* and *Henry II*, attributed to Shakspere and, ii. 213; his works, iii. 157, 158; Mrs. Behn's adaptation of his *City Night-Cap*, iii. 326 [5]; Ravenscroft's adaptations from, iii. 326 [5].

David and Bethsabe: see *Love of King David*.

Davies, John, of Hereford, the contemporaries of, i. 442; his tribute to Shakspere in *The Scourge of Folly*, i. 496; on Shakspere's acting, ii. 21; on Brooke's *Mustapha*, ii. 615 [3].

Davies, Sir John, his *Contention*, i. 227 [2].

Day, John, part-author of Chettle and Dekker's *Spanish Moor's Tragedy* and of *Jane Shore*, i. 428 [5], 430, ii. 466; part-author of *Travels of Three English Brothers*, ii. 183, 600; his works, ii. 589-604; his life and labours, ii.

590; non-extant plays by, ii. 591; *Peregrinatio Scholastica*, ii. 592; *The Parliament of Bees*, ii. 593; *The Ile of Guls*, ii. 595; *Humour out of Breath*, ii. 596; *Law-Tricks*, ii. 598; *The Blind Beggar of Bednal-Green*, ii. 599; as a dramatist, ii. 603; the *Parnassus Plays* attributed to, ii. 640.

Dead Tearme, The, by Dekker, ii. 453[9].

Death and Buriall of Martin Marprelate, The, Will Summer mentioned in, i. 423[4].

Death of Mary, The, one of the York plays, i. 70.

Death of Robert Earl of Huntington, by Anthony Munday, i. 432.

Debate between Follie and Love, The, by Robert Greene, i. 246[2].

Debate between Pride and Lowliness, The, by Francis Thynn, i. 237[3], 384[2].

Debate of the Body and the Soul, The, i. 12, 25[1].

Debate of the Carpenter's Tools, The, i. 25[1].

Decamerone, the, by Boccaccio, Shakspere's indebtedness to, in *Cymbeline*, ii. 119, 190.

Dedekind, F., his *Grobianus*, ii. 455[4].

De Educatione Liberorum, Plutarch's, Lyly's adaptation of, i. 277[1].

De Exilio, Plutarch's, Lyly's adaptation of, i. 277[1].

Defence of the Epilogue, by Dryden, iii. 361.

Defence of Poetry, Music, and Stageplays, by Thomas Lodge, i. 410.

Defence of Ryme, by S. Daniel, ii. 617.

Deimling, Dr. H., his edition of the Chester plays, i. 76[2].

Dekker, Thomas, his pageants, i. 147; on Marlowe's *Dr. Faustus*, i. 329; his *Seven Deadly Sinnes of London*, i. 335[1]; his *Olde Fortunatus*, i. 337; his mention of Peele in *A Knight's Conjuring*, i. 365; joint-author with Chettle's *Patient Grissil* and of *The Spanish Moor's Tragedy*, i. 428[5]; his *Satiro-Mastix* attributed to Shakspere, ii. 212; Ben Jonson's quarrel with, ii. 307, 325, 356; his dramatic works, ii. 450–472; his life, ii. 452; *The Shoe-makers' Holiday*, ii. 456; *Olde Fortunatus*, ii. 457; *Satiro-Mastix*, ii. 459; *The Honest Whore*, ii. 462; *The Whore of Babylon*, ii. 463; *If it be not good, the Devil is in it*, ii. 465; *Match me in London*, ii. 465; *The Wonder of a Kingdom*, ii. 466; his pageants, ii. 466; *Patient Grissil*, ii. 466;

various historical plays of which he was part-author, ii. 466; *The Spanish Moor's Tragedy*, ii. 467; *Sir Thomas Wyat*, ii. 468; *Westward Hoe* and *Northward Hoe*, ii. 469; *The Roaring Girl*, ii. 469, 519; *The Virgin Martyr*, ii. 469, iii. 3, 12; *The Witch of Edmonton*, ii. 470, iii. 74; *The Sun's Darling*, ii. 470, iii. 75; as a dramatist, ii. 470; authorship of *The Noble Souldier* attributed to, ii. 549; *The Spanish Fig* attributed to, ii. 550[1]; Webster's collaboration with, iii. 52; *The Weakest Goeth to the Wall*, iii. 55; his collaboration with Ford, iii. 74.

Delavigne, Casimir, his *Les Enfants d'Édouard*, ii. 100.

Delectable History of Forbonius and Prisceria, The, by Thomas Lodge, i. 411.

Delirus, by Accius Paulus, i. 5[3].

Delius, N., on Dryden's adaptations of Shakspere, i. 514[4]; his Shaksperean criticism, i. 559; on the classical ingredients of Shakspere's writings, ii. 10[1]; on *Timon of Athens*, ii. 179; on *Pericles*, ii. 182; on *Coriolanus*, ii. 189; on *Cymbeline*, ii. 191; on *The Winter's Tale*, ii. 192; *Henry VIII*, ii. 207; on doubtful Shaksperean plays, ii. 213[4]; his edition of *Edward III*, ii. 221[2]; of *Mucedorus*, ii. 225[3]; edition of *Faire Em*, ii. 235[2].

Deliverance of the Children of Israel, The, part of the Newcastle cycle, i. 91.

Delivery of Susannah, The, by Ralph Radcliffe, i. 170[2].

Demetrius and Enanthe: see *Humorous Lieutenant*.

Denham, Henry, his pamphlet in opposition to the drama, i. 460.

Denham, Sir John, his works, iii. 148, 149; *Cooper's Hill*, iii. 148; *The Sophy*, iii. 148, 149.

Dennis, John, his adaptations of Shakspere's *Merry Wives* and *Coriolanus*, i. 514, 515; his reply to Rymer's Shaksperean criticisms, i. 524; his version of *The Merry Wives*, entitled *The Comical Gallant*, ii. 137; his *Plot and No Plot*, iii. 295[6], 426; on Italian Operas, iii. 321[3]; his dramatic works, iii. 426, 427; *Iphigenia*, iii. 426; *Rinaldo*, iii. 426; *Liberty Asserted*, iii. 426; *Appius and Virginia*, iii. 427; his *Vindication* of the stage, iii. 512[1], 513.

Departed Soul's Address to the Body, The, translated by J. M. Kemble, i. 12[3].

Derby, Lord: *see* Strange, Lord.

Descensus Astraeae, a pageant, by Peele, i. 147, 368, 377.

Deschamps, E., his *Macbeth*, i. 561 [2].

Deserving Favourite, The, by Lodowick Carlell, notice of, iii. 160.

De Silva, on Elisabeth's patronage of the drama, i. 451 [3], 501 [1].

Desputizon du Croisié et du Descroisié, by Rutebeuf, i. 21 [1].

Destouches, P. N., his *Dissipateur*, probably indebted to *Timon of Athens*, ii. 180.

Destruction of Jerusalem, The, by J. Crowne, synopsis of, iii. 400.

Device of an Indian Prince, The, a masque attributed to Bacon, ii. 629 [2].

Device of the Pageant for Martin Calthorpe, Mayor, by Peele, i. 368 [1].

Device of the Pageant borne before Woolstone Dixie, by Peele, i. 368, 377.

Devil, the, treatment of the character in moralities, i. 109.

Devil, The, and his Dame, by W. Haughton, i. 263 [1]; synopsis of, ii. 606.

Devil, The, is an Ass, by Ben Jonson, the 'vice' characters in, i. 110, 115 [2], 331 [2]; synopsis of the play, ii. 372, 404.

Devil, The, of Dowgate, supposed to be identical with *Wit at several Weapons*, ii. 693; attributed to Fletcher, ii. 740 [3], 748 [1].

Devil's Charter, The, i. 331 [2]; by Barnaby Barnes, notice of, ii. 626.

Devil's Law-Case, The, by Webster, notice of, iii. 61.

Devil Tavern, the, Ben Jonson a frequenter of, ii. 319, 321.

Devonshire harvest-plays, i. 144 [1].

Dial of Princes, The, by Sir Thomas North, i. 280.

Dialogue between Love and an Old Man, i. 231.

Dialogue between Watkyn and Jeffroye, by Roy and Barlow, i. 235 [1].

Dialogue of Death, The, by William Bulleyn, i. 236.

Dialogue of Gentylnes and Nobilitye, by John Rastell, i. 237.

Dialogue of Wit and Folly, by John Heywood, i. 236, 247.

Dialogue-Literature, German, i. 232; English, i. 234; early forms of *estrifs*, i. 25 [1].

Dialogues, the, of Gregory the Great, i. 12; by T. Heywood, ii. 584.

Diana Enamorada, by Jorge de Montemayor, ii. 80.

Diary of the Duke of Stettin, mention of boy actors in, i. 453 [2].

Dicke of Devonshire, attributed to T. Heywood, ii. 583; attributed to Shirley, iii. 104.

Diderot, his appreciation of Shakspere, i. 560.

Dido, various treatments of the theme, i. 357 [1].

Dido, by Dr. W. Gager, i. 364.

Dido, Queen of Carthage, The Tragedy of, by Marlowe, i. 356.

Dido, Queen of Carthage, by Thomas Nashe, i. 423.

Didon se sacrifiant, by Jodelle, i. 357 [1].

Didone, by A. de Pazzi, i. 357 [1].

Diest, Peter van, his version of *Everyman*, i. 120.

Digby, George, Earl of Bristol, his dramatic works, iii. 305; *Elvira*, iii. 305.

Digby Mysteries, the Office of the Sepulchre in, i. 35 [1]; 'Conversion of Saul' in, i. 60 [3]; a synopsis of, i. 92.

Digges, Leonard, his tribute to Shakspere in the first Folio, i. 499.

Disappointment, The, by T. Southerne, iii. 421.

Disciplinati, i. 33.

Discours sur la Tragédie, by Voltaire, i. 535.

Discours sur Shakespeare et sur M. de Voltaire, by Joseph Baretti, i. 539.

Discourse of English Poesie, A, by William Webbe, i. 268; on John Lyly, i. 273 [4].

Discoverie of Witchcraft, The, by Reginald Scot, Middleton's obligations to, ii. 507.

Discoveries, Ben Jonson's, ii. 331; his portrait of himself in, ii. 333.

Disguises, The, a non-extant play attributed to Chapman, ii. 410.

Disinterested Love, an adaptation of Massinger's *Bashful Lover*, attributed to Thomas Hull, iii. 36 [1].

Disobedient Child, The, by Thomas Ingelend, i. 250.

Disputatio inter Mariam et Crucem, a dialogue, i. 25 [1].

Disputation in the Temple, The, one of the Coventry plays, i. 86.

D'Israeli, Isaac, on the Marprelate controversy, i. 463 [1].

Distressed Innocence, The, by Settle, iii. 398.

Distresses, The, by Sir W. D'Avenant, iii. 173.

Distrest Mother, The, Ambrose Philips' translation of Racine's *Andromaque*, iii. 315 [1], 425.

Dives and Lazarus, by Ralph Radcliffe, i. 170 [2].

Divine Comedian: see *Soul's Warfare*.
Divizio, Bernardo, his *Calandria*, i. 228.
Dixie, Woolston, Lord Mayor of London, Peele's pageant for, i. 368, 377.
Dobson, Mr. Austin, his Memoir of Steele, iii. 491 [2].
Doctor Faustus, The Life and Death of, a ballad, i. 329.
Doctor Faustus, The Tragical History of, by Marlowe, i. 328, 332, 396; Dekker's additions to, ii. 453, 467, 468; compared with Barnes' *Divil's Charter*, ii. 627; W. Mountfort's adaptation of, i. 337 [4], iii. 326 [5], 431 [1].
Doctors of Dullhead College, The, a droll after *Monsieur Thomas*, ii. 708 [2].
Dolce, Ludovico, Gascoigne's *Jocasta* indebted to the *Phoenissae* of, i. 209; his *Dido*, i. 357 [1].
Donaldson, Dr. J. W., his conception of the tragic, i. 159 [3], 161 [2].
Don Carlos, by T. Otway, account of, iii. 413.
Don Quixote, compared with *The Knight of the Burning Pestle*, ii. 679.
Donquixot, The History of, a play assigned to Robert Baron, iii. 290.
Don Sebastian, by Dryden, a synopsis of, iii. 383.
Donna Diana, a version of Moreto's *Desden con el Desden*, iii. 304 [1].
Donne, C. F., on *Arden of Feversham*, ii. 217.
Donne, John, his satires, i. 442.
Donne, W. Bodham, on the neglect of Shakspere early in eighteenth century, i. 525 [2]; on Beaumont and Fletcher, ii. 643 [1], 645.
Donovan, T., on Shakspere's Histories, ii. 259 [2].
Doomsday, one of the Chester plays, i. 83; one of the Coventry plays, i. 89.
Doran, Dr., on Mrs. Montagu and her writings, i. 539 [3].
Dorastus and Fawnia, by R. Greene: see *Pandosto*.
Double-Dealer, The, by Congreve, account of, iii. 472.
Double Distress, The, by Mrs. Pix, iii. 432.
Double Falsehood, The, attributed to Shirley, i. 528 [2], ii. 743 [3], iii. 120; attributed by Theobald to Shakspere, ii. 212.
Double Gallant, The, by Colley Cibber, iii. 487 [2].
Double Marriage, The, by Fletcher, notice of, ii. 715.
Double PP, The, by Dekker, ii. 455.
Doubtful Heir, The, by Shirley, notice of, iii. 116.

Douce, on the Towneley plays, i. 71.
Dowden, Prof., on Shakspere's *Othello*, ii. 167.
Downfall of Robert Earl of Huntington, by Anthony Munday, i. 432.
Drake, Nathan, his Shaksperean criticism, i. 569, ii. 1 [1]; his *Ancient and Modern Stages*, iii. 514.
Drama, the English. Origin of, i. 1–157; early Christian, i. 3; classical influence on, i. 4, 5; emanating from monasteries, i. 8; no English dramatic literature before the Norman Conquest, i. 11; influence of the Roman stage, i. 13; decay of Roman drama, i. 15; jongleurs and minstrels in England, i. 23; beginnings of English drama, i. 24; main source of the modern drama, i. 29; the mystery-drama, i. 36, 41; emancipation of the drama from the Church, i. 43; the religious drama in England, i. 48; performances by the laity, i. 54, 573; names given to religious plays, i. 57; collective plays, i. 57, 58 *et seq.*; isolated miracle-plays, i. 89; moralities, i. 99–143, 573; pageants, i. 143; court entertainments, i. 148; masques, i. 150.
Beginnings of the regular, i. 158–269; tragic and comic drama, i. 158; transition from the morality to the drama, i. 165; early Italian drama, i. 168; isolated English secular plays of an early date, i. 169; origin of chronicle history, i. 173; translations of plays, i. 189; influence of the classic authors on Renascence literature, i. 193; English tragedy, i. 197; plays on Romance subjects, i. 212, 574; play-subjects from national history, i. 218; comedy, i. 225; dialogue literature, i. 232; interludes, i. 237; transition from moralities, i. 238; Heywood's interludes, i. 238; influence of Plautus and Terence on Renascence comedy, i. 251; summary of beginning of tragedy and comedy, i. 264.
Shakspere's Predecessors (John Lyly to Michael Drayton), i. 270–486; summary of Shakspere's predecessors, i. 438 *et seq.*; nationalising of Elisabethan literature by the drama, i. 444; summary of history of early-Elisabethan stage, i. 450; literary attacks upon the drama, i. 458; Marprelate controversy, i. 462; intercourse between the German and English theatre, i. 471; technical arrangements of the

early stage, i. 475; tragedy, i. 480; comedy, i. 484.

Shakspere, general survey of developement of his fame and influence, i. 487–572; life, ii. 1–43; his dramatic works, ii. 43–295.

Ben Jonson, ii. 296–407.

Later Elisabethans (G. Chapman to S. Daniel), ii. 408–627; masques, &c., ii. 627; academical drama, ii. 630; Parnassus plays, ii. 633.

Beaumont and Fletcher, ii. 643–763.

End of the old, iii. 1–276; review of period from Shakspere to Civil War, iii. 206; historical aspects of the period, iii. 207; public feeling, as reflected in the drama, towards foreign nations, iii. 211; James I, iii. 217; Charles I, iii. 218; national religion, iii. 219; society, iii. 220; refinement in manners, iii. 226; the stage under James I and Charles I, iii. 229; legislation and the stage, iii. 233; attitude of Puritanism towards the stage, iii. 236; anti-theatrical literature, iii. 239; the Revolution, iii. 245; theatres closed, iii. 247; the art of acting, iii. 248; scenery and costume, iii. 254; summary of literary history of drama at this period, iii. 257; national historical drama, iii. 259; comedy of character, iii. 260; moral decline, iii. 262; influence of contemporary foreign drama, iii. 264; summary of achievements of national drama in this period, iii. 269; pre-eminent writers, iii. 269; Jonson and his school, the merits and defects of their achievements, iii. 270; comedy, iii. 274; masque, iii. 274; verse, iii. 274; prose, iii. 275.

Later Stuart Drama, iii. 277 *et seq.*; the stage during the Civil War, iii. 277; during the Protectorate, iii. 280; at the Restoration, iii. 283; art of acting, iii. 285; plays published in Commonwealth, iii. 286; effect of Restoration, iii. 291; court of Charles II and its influence, iii. 300; influence of foreign dramatic literatures on our own, iii. 301; Italian drama, iii. 302; Spanish drama, iii. 303; French drama, iii. 306; Molière and English comedy, iii. 318; the Opera, iii. 320; the Ballet, iii. 324; dramatists who wrote both before and after Restoration, iii. 326; Dryden and Restoration writers, iii. 345; dramatists whose careers extend beyond the reign of Anne, iii.

485; concluding remarks on later Stuart drama, iii. 497; tragedy, iii. 499; heroic plays, iii. 500; comedy, iii. 503; anti-theatrical publications, iii. 509; Jeremy Collier, iii. 509; later growths of comedy, iii. 515; comedy and the novel, iii. 517; conclusion, iii. 517.

Dramatic Poesy, On, Dryden's dialogue, i. 520 [3].

Draper's Pageant, the, at Coventry, i. 61 [5].

Drayton, Michael, on the styles of Lyly and Sidney, i. 279 [1]; his tribute to Marlowe, i. 317, 318; joint-author of *First Part of Sir John Oldcastle,* i. 432; his works, i. 436, 442; *Epistle to H. Reynolds* and the literary criticism in, i. 443 [2]; his tribute to Shakspere, in his *Poets and Poësie,* i. 500; *Sir Thomas More* attributed to Lodge and, ii. 215; his and others' *Henry I,* ii. 466; *Earl Godwin,* ii. 467; *Sir Piers Exton,* ii. 467; his and Dekker's *Civil Wars in France,* ii. 467.

Dream of Pilate's Wife, The, and Jesus before Pilate, a York play, i. 61 [2].

Dream of Scipio, The, Chaucer's indebtedness to, i. 103.

Droeshout, Martin, his engraving of Shakspere, ii. 42.

Drolleries, their origin, iii. 324 [1].

'Drolls,' definition of, i. 574; performed during the Revolutionary times, iii. 280.

Drousiano, extempore Italian actor, i. 230 [1].

Drue, Thomas, a collaborator with R. Davenport, iii. 158.

Drummer, The, by Addison and Harrison, iii. 439 [1].

Drummond, William, of Hawthornden, his estimate of Shakspere, i. 495 [1]; Jonson's *Conversations* with, published by Gifford, ii. 296 [1]; Jonson's visit to, ii. 316; Jonson's conversations with, ii. 317, 331.

Drury Lane theatres: *see* Cockpit; Theatre Royal.

Dryden, John, his adaptations of Shakspere's plays, i. 512, 513; his criticisms on, 516–518, 520; his critical writings, i. 520 [3]; his version of *Troilus and Cressida,* entitled *Truth found too Late,* ii. 153, iii. 374; his *All for Love,* ii. 187, iii. 372; on Ben Jonson's humour, ii. 405, 406 [1]; on Chapman's *Bussy d'Ambois,* ii. 419, 420 [1]; on Heywood, Shirley, &c., iii. 587 [1]; on Beaumont and Fletcher, ii. 643 [1], 645; his additions to

Fletcher's *Pilgrim*, ii. 705; his *Spanish Friar*, ii. 725 [2]; on Tomkis' *Albumazar*, iii. 179 [4]; his obligations to La Calprenède, iii. 309 [2]; to Quinault, iii. 315 [1]; to Corneille, iii. 315 [1]; his opera, *Albion*, iii. 323, 380; his plays, iii. 345–392; *Wild Gallant*, iii. 346; *Rival Ladies*, iii. 347; *Indian Queen*, iii. 348; *Indian Emperor*, iii. 349; *Secret Love*, iii. 350; *Sir Martin Mar-All*, iii. 351; *The Tempest*, iii. 352; *An Evening's Love*, iii. 352; *Essay of Dramatic Poesy*, iii. 353; Howard's reply, iii. 356; Dryden's *Defence*, iii. 356; *Tyrannic Love*, iii. 358; *Almanzor and Almahide*, iii. 359; *The Conquest of Granada*, iii. 360; *Defence of the Epilogue*, iii. 361; *The Rehearsal*, iii. 362; *Of Heroic Plays*, iii. 365; *The Assignation*, iii. 366; *Marriage à-la-Mode*, iii. 366; *Amboyna*, iii. 367; *The State of Innocence*, iii. 368; *Aureng-Zebe*, iii. 370: he abandons rime, iii. 37; *Limberham*, iii. 373; *Œdipus*, iii. 373; *On the Grounds of Criticism in Tragedy*, iii. 375; *The Spanish Friar*, iii. 376; *Duke of Guise*, iii. 377; *King Arthur*, iii. 382; *Don Sebastian*, iii. 383; *Amphitryon*, iii. 384; *Cleomenes*, iii. 384; *Love Triumphant*, iii. 385; Epilogue, &c., for Fletcher's *Pilgrim*, iii. 385; his apology for his licentiousness as a dramatist, iii. 385; his dramatic powers, iii. 387; the representative Restoration dramatist, iii. 390; his Prologues and Epilogues, iii. 391; his developement of Heroic plays, iii. 501; his apology and vindication, iii. 513.

Du Bartas, G. de S., Lodge's summary of poem of, i. 415.

Du Bec, Abbé, his *History of Tamburlaine*, i. 322 [3].

Dublin, religious plays performed at, i. 56; *The Sacrifice of Abraham* discovered at, i. 92; *Play of the Sacrament* at, i. 98.

Duchesne, André, his edition of Hilarius' plays, i. 37.

Duchess of Fernandina, The, a non-extant play by H. Glapthorne, iii. 153.

Duchess of Malfi, The, by Webster, a synopsis of, iii. 59.

Ducis, J., his version of *Hamlet* and other Shaksperean plays, i. 537, 538.

Duclos, C. P., on the Roman pantomime and its influence, i. 17.

Duke, The, by Shirley, iii. 118.

Duke, The, and the Devil, an adaptation of Cockayne's *Trappolin*, iii. 288 [2].

Duke Humphrey, a play, non-extant, attributed to Shakspere, ii. 212.

Duke of Guise, The, by Henry Shirley, i. 355 [3].

Duke of Guise, The, by Dryden and Lee, a synopsis of, iii. 377.

Duke of Lerma, The, by Sir R. Howard, iii. 394.

Duke of Milan, The, by Massinger, a synopsis of, iii. 14.

Duke of Milan, The, and the Marquis of Mantua, an early English tragedy, i. 217.

Duke's Mistress, The, by Shirley, a synopsis of, iii. 97.

Dulcitius, by Hrotsvitha, i. 7.

Dumas, Alexandre, the elder, and Paul Meurice, their *Hamlet*, i. 561 [2].

Dumb Knight, The, by Machin and Markham, a synopsis of, iii. 156.

Dumb Lady, The, by John Lacy, iii. 449.

Dunbar, William, his *Dance of the Sevin Deidly Synnis*, i. 113 [4].

D'Urfé, Honoré, his influence on contemporary literature, iii. 307, 308.

D'Urfey, Thomas, his *Injured Princess*, an adaptation of Shakspere's *Cymbeline*, i. 514; on Chapman's *Bussy d'Ambois*, ii. 420 [1]; his adaptation of Fletcher's *Monsieur Thomas*, ii. 708 [2]; his reproduction of Fletcher's *Noble Gentleman*, ii. 739 [1]; his version of *The Sea Voyage*, iii. 326 [3]; his *Two Queens of Brentford*, iii. 363 [2]; his dramatic works, iii. 454, 455.

Dutch Courtezan, The, by Marston, i. 402 [1]; a synopsis of, ii. 486.

Dutton's acting company, i. 451 [4].

Dyce, Alexander, his edition of Skelton's works, i. 128; his edition of Marlowe's works, i. 313 [3]; on Marlowe's obligation to *Henry VI* plays, i. 349 [1]; his edition of George Peele's works, i. 363 [1]; of R. Greene's works, i. 379 [3]; his edition of *Kemp's Nine Daies Wonder*, i. 472 [1]; his Shaksperean criticism, i. 569, 570; his *Life* of Shakspere, ii. 1 [1]; his edition of *Sir Thomas More*, ii. 214 [1]; his edition of Middleton, ii. 493 [1], 517; his edition of Porter's *Two Angry Women*, ii. 604 [2]; of Beaumont and Fletcher, ii. 643 [1], 645; of Webster's works, iii. 51 [2]; of Ford's works, iii. 71 [1]; of Shirley's works, iii. 89 [1].

Eades, Dr. Richard, his version of *Julius Caesar*, ii. 140.

Earl Godwin, by Dekker and others, ii. 467.

Eastern Mystery, the, i. 36 [1], 37 [2], 46.

Eastward Hoe, by Chapman, unfortunate results of, ii. 311 ; account of, ii. 441 ; Tate's version of, iii. 326 [2].

Ebert, Professor, on the *farces* and the *sotties*, i. 22 [1]; on the use of the vernacular in popular mysteries, i. 41 [1].

Ebsworth, J. W., on drolls, iii. 280 [1]; his edition of *Westminster Drolleries*, iii. 324 [1].

Ecatompathia, by Thomas Watson, i. 310.

Eccerinis, by Alberto Mussato, i. 168.

Eclogues, by Juan de la Enzina, i. 232.

École des Femmes, La, by Molière, translated by Carlyl, iii. 315 [1]; Wycherley's version of, iii. 463.

École des Maris, La, Molière's, Wycherley's version of, iii. 463.

Eden's *West and East Indies*, Shakspere's acquaintance with, ii. 196.

Edgar, a tragedy by Thomas Rymer, i. 523 [2]; ii. 610 [2].

Edgar and Alfreda, King, by E. Ravenscroft, iii. 429.

Edinburgh, religious plays performed at, i. 55.

Edward I, The Famous Chronicle History of, by Peele, i. 348, 368.

Edward II, The History of, by Lord Falkland, i. 350 [3].

Edward II, The Troublesome Raigne and Lamentable Death of, by Marlowe, i. 347.

Edward III, attributed to Marlowe and Shakspere, i. 359, 360; attributed to Shakspere, ii. 210; synopsis of the play, ii. 221–225.

Edward IV, by T. Heywood, notice of, ii. 555.

Edward VI, his comedy, *The Whore of Babylon*, i. 136 [2].

Edward and Alfreda, King, by Ravenscroft, ii. 610 [2].

Edwardes, Richard, his plays, i. 211 ; authorship of *Misogonus* assigned to, i. 260; Puttenham's commendation of the works of, i. 268.

Edwards, H. Sutherland, on the English Opera, iii. 320 [3].

Egerton, Thomas, his performances in masques, iii. 192 [5].

Egloga Pescatoria, by Sannazaro, ii. 380 [3].

Egmont, Goethe's, Shaksperean influences apparent in, i. 552.

Eikonoklastes, Milton's reference in, to Shakspere's *Richard III*, i. 519.

Elder Brother, The, by Fletcher, notice of, ii. 736.

Eleanor, Queen, the legend of the 'sinking' of, i. 369 [2], 370 [1].

Elegy on Death of Hugh Atwell, by W. Rowley, ii. 542 [5].

Elfrid, by Aaron Hill, ii. 610 [2], iii. 430.

Elfrida, by Mason, ii. 610 [2].

Eliote, J., his *Greene et Lylli*, i. 408.

Elisa, by Philip Waimer, ii. 222.

Elisa Dido, by C. de Virues, i. 357 [1].

Elisabeth, Queen, plays patronised by, i. 154; impetus given to literature in the reign of, i. 265 ; her relations with John Lyly, i. 273, 274; as Cynthia in *Endimion*, i. 291 ; her influence on contemporary literature, i. 440, 445, 450; her relations with Shakspere, i. 501 ; Shakspere's position at the death of, ii. 36 ; her relations with Ben Jonson, ii. 306.

Ellis, Mr. Havelock, his edition of Marlowe's works, i. 313 [3]; his edition of Middleton's best works, ii. 493 [1].

Elton, Mr. Oliver, on Michael Drayton, i. 437 [1]; his translation of Saxo-Grammaticus, ii. 165.

Elvira, by George Digby, iii. 305.

Elze, Dr. Karl, his *Life of Shakspere*, i. 559, ii. 1 [1]; his *Alexandrines in The Winter's Tale and Richard II*, ii. 52 [1]; his edition of *Hamlet*, ii. 157 ; on Shakspere's *Henry VIII*, ii. 203 ; on Jonson's masques, ii. 392 [1]; his edition of Chapman's *Alphonsus*, ii. 428 [1], 430 [1], 450 [2]; his edition of S. Rowley's *When You See Me*, &c., ii. 547 [3]; his essay on D'Avenant, iii. 166 [3].

Emblems, Quarles', iii. 286 [3].

Emilia Galotti, similarity to *Apius and Virginia*, i. 204.

Emission of the Holy Ghost, The, one of the Chester plays, i. 82.

Empeños de Seis Horas, by Calderon, Sir Samuel Tuke's adaptation of, iii. 305.

Emperor of the East, The, by Massinger, synopsis of, iii. 29.

Empiric, The, a droll, ii. 369 [1].

Empress of Morocco, by Settle, iii. 396.

Enchanted Island, The, a ballad, ii. 195.

Enchanted Lovers, The, by Sir W. Lower, iii. 291.

Encomium Moriae, the, of Erasmus, translated by John Wilson, iii. 337.

Endightment against Mother Masse, The, i. 235.

Endimion, by John Lyly, edited by Mr. G. P. Baker, i. 270 [1]; synopsis of,

i. 287, 289; date of publication, i. 574; compared with Shakspere's *Midsummer Night's Dream*, ii. 88.

Enfans sans souci, the *sotties* of the, i. 107.

Enfants d'Édouard, Les, by Casimir Delavigne, ii. 100.

Engaños, Los, by Lope de Rueda, ii. 75.

England's Elisabeth, by T. Heywood, ii. 554.

Englande's Mourning Garment, by Henry Chettle, i. 427.

English Friar, The, by J. Crowne, account of, iii. 405.

English Grammar, Ben Jonson's, ii. 331.

English Monarch, The, by Rymer : see *Edgar*.

English-Moor, The, by R. Brome, iii. 129.

English Romayne Life, The, by Anthony Munday, i. 431.

English Traveller, The, by T. Heywood, a synopsis of, ii. 565.

Englishmen for my Money, by Haughton, i. 428[5]; notice of, ii. 605.

Entertainment at the Opening of the New River, The, a masque by Middleton, ii. 495[3].

Entertainment of the two Kings, &c., The, a masque by Ben Jonson, ii. 394.

Entertainment of King James and Queen Anne, The, a masque by Ben Jonson, ii. 394.

Entremeses, in Spain, i. 231 ; definition of, i. 574.

Entremets, a kind of French pageant, i. 146[2].

Entry into Jerusalem on an Ass, The, one of the York plays, i. 67[1].

Enzina, Juan de la, his *Representaciones*, i. 232.

Epicoene, or The Silent Woman, by Ben Jonson, account of the play, ii. 364, 404.

Epigrammes, J. Weever's, reference to Shakspere in, i. 495.

Epigrams, Ben Jonson's, ii. 330.

Epigrams upon Proverbs, by John Heywood, i. 240.

Epilogue, The Defence of the, by Dryden, iii. 361.

Epilogues, Shakspere's use of, ii. 291 ; by T. Heywood, ii. 585 ; in early Stuart drama, ii. 256 ; examples of, from Dryden's plays, iii. 391.

Epistle to H. Reynolds, by Drayton, his literary criticisms in, i. 443[2].

Epistolae farcitae, the, i. 41[1].

Epitia, the, by Giraldi Cinthio, i. 213[2], 216[2], ii. 154.

Epsom Wells, by Shadwell, account of, iii. 456.

Equall Match, An, after Fletcher's *Rule a Wife*, &c., ii. 712[2].

Erasmus, the dialogues of, i. 233.

Eromena, a version of Chamberlayne's *Pharonnida*, iii. 289[1].

'Errors,' Elisabethan meaning of the word, ii. 75.

Éryphile, by Voltaire, Shaksperean influence visible in, i. 536[1].

Eschenburg, J. J., his completion of Wieland's translation of Shakspere, i. 547 ; his translations of doubtful Shaksperean plays, ii. 210.

Ésope à la Ville, Boursault's, Vanbrugh's version of, iii. 480.

Essay of Dramatic Poesie, by Dryden, iii. 353 ; Howard's reply to, iii. 356 ; Dryden's *Defence of*, iii. 356.

Essex, Earl of, his Irish expedition, Shakspere's references to, ii. 33 ; plays on the career of, iii. 429[1].

Estrif, a form of dialogue, examples of, i. 25[1].

Etheredge, Sir George, his dramatic works, iii. 442–446 ; *The Comical Revenge*, iii. 444 ; *She Would if she Could*, iii. 445; *The Man of Mode*, iii. 446.

Étourdi, Le, Molière's, translated by the Duke of Newcastle, and adapted by Dryden, iii. 334, 351.

Eucharist, the, regarded as a mystical liturgy, i. 29.

Eufemia, by Lope de Rueda, ii. 191.

Eunuch, The : see *Fatal Contrast*.

Eunuchus, the, of Terence, Sedley's obligations to, iii. 448.

Euphues, the Anatomy of Wit, by John Lyly, i. 272.

Euphues and his England, by John Lyly, biographical data from, i. 271 ; an account of, i. 272, 274.

Euphues and his Ephoebus, by John Lyly, an adaptation of Plutarch's *De Educatione Liberorum*, i. 277[1].

Euphues his Censure to Philautus, by Robert Greene, i. 386, 388.

Euphues' Shadow, the battaile of the sences, i. 413.

Euphuism, John Lyly and, i. 274 *et seqq.*

Euripides, early Christian dramas modelled on, i. 4 ; the tragedies and comedies of, i. 159[1]; Seneca's obligations to, i. 190.

Eusebius, his fragment of Ezechiel's *Exodus*, i. 3[1].

Eutychianus, the supposed narrator of the story of *Theophilus*, i. 330.

Evelyn, John, on Shakspere's plays, i. 516[1]; his dramatic writings, iii. 427.

Evening's Love, An, Dryden's adaptation of Corneille's *Feint Astrologue,* iii. 315[1], 352.

Every-man, a morality, i. 119.

Every Man in his Humour, by Ben Jonson, Shakspere an actor in, ii. 21; account of the play, ii. 344, 404.

Every Man out of his Humour, by Ben Jonson, account of, ii. 346, 404.

Ewald, A. C., his edition of Congreve's plays, iii. 467[1]; Farquhar's, iii. 481[4].

Examination of the Mass, by Dr. William Turner, i. 235.

Example, The, by Shirley, notice of, iii. 111.

Exodus, The, of Ezechiel, i. 3.

Expostulation with Inigo Jones, An, by Ben Jonson, ii. 371[1], 391[2].

Extempore actors, i. 230[1]; Tarlton, i. 454[1]; French and Italian players, i. 471[2].

Extractio Animarum ab Inferno, one of the Towneley plays, i. 75.

Extravaganza, distinction between burlesque and, i. 161.

Ezechias in English, by Nicholas Udall, i. 255.

Ezechiel, *The Exodus* of, i. 3.

Ezekiel, one of the Chester plays, i. 83.

Fables, Dryden's collection of, iii. 387[1].

Fabulae Atellanae, the, i. 14.

Fabyan, Robert, *Concordance of Histories,* i. 171; his *Chronicle of Histories,* i. 349.

Faerie Queene, The, the procession of the Sins in, i. 113[4]; historical influences during composition of, i. 442[2]; compared with Fletcher's *Faithful Shepherdess,* ii. 664.

Faire Em, attributed to Shakspere, ii. 210; synopsis of the play, iii. 235–237.

Fair Favourite, The, by Sir W. D'Avenant, iii. 173.

Fair Maid of Bristol, The, ii. 219, 591[3].

Fair Maid of the Exchange, The, by T. Heywood, ii. 572.

Fair Maid of the Inn, The, by Fletcher, ii. 737.

Faire Maid of the West, The, by T. Heywood, ii. 566.

Fair Penitent, The, by Nicholas Rowe, iii. 435.

Faire Quarrell, A, by Middleton and W. Rowley, ii. 509.

Fair Sidea, The, by Jacob Ayrer, compared with Shakspere's *Tempest,* ii. 195.

Fairholt, F. W., on London pageants, i. 146[3]; his edition of Lyly's works, i. 270[1].

Fairy Knight, The, by Dekker and Ford, ii. 470, iii. 75.

Faithful Friends, The, attributed to Beaumont and Fletcher, ii. 741.

Faithful General, The, by M. N., an adaptation of *The Loyal Subject,* ii. 699[2].

Faithful Servant, The: see *Grateful Servant.*

Faithful Shepherdess, The, by Fletcher, compared with *The Tempest,* ii. 198; criticism of, ii. 663.

Falkland, Henry (first) Lord, his *History of Edward II,* i. 350[3].

Falkland, Henry (third) Lord, his *Marriage Night,* iii. 335, 336.

Fall of Mortimer, The, a fragmentary play by Ben Jonson, ii. 343.

False Friend, The, by Vanbrugh, notice of, iii. 479.

False Heir, The, by Kirkman, taken from *The Scornful Lady,* ii. 669[1].

False One, The, by Fletcher and Massinger, ii. 187; synopsis of, ii. 718.

Falstaff's Wedding, by Kenrick, ii. 124.

Familie of Love, The, by Middleton, account of, ii. 517.

Famous Historie: see under *Edward I*; *Capt. Thomas Stukely,* &c., &c.

Famous Tragedie: see under *Rich Jew of Malta,* &c.

Fancies Chaste and Noble, The, by Ford, notice of, iii. 83.

Fanshawe, Sir Richard, his translations from Mendoza, iii. 306.

Farce, origin of the, i. 21, 22; the, of the *Enfans sans souci,* i. 107; the modern meaning of, i. 161.

Farces de la Basoche, the influence of the, on early English comedy, i. 226.

Farewell to Folly, by Robert Greene, i. 381[2], 392.

Farewell to Sir J. Norris and Sir Francis Drake, a poem by Peele, i. 364, 393[2].

Farmer, Dr., his assistance offered to Johnson in his edition of Shakspere, i. 532.

Farquhar, George, his *Inconstant,* an adaptation of Fletcher's *Wild-Goose-Chase,* ii. 707[4]; his version of *The Wild-Goose-Chase,* iii. 326[3]; his dramatic works, iii. 481–485; *Love and a Bottle,* iii. 482; *The Constant Couple,* iii. 482; *Sir Harry Wildair,*

iii. 483; *The Inconstant*, iii. 483; *The Twin-Rivals*, iii. 484; *The Recruiting Officer*, iii. 484; *The Beaux' Stratagem*, iii. 484.

Farrar, Dean, on *The Spanish Tragedy*, by Kyd, i. 306 [2]; on the classical ingredients in Shakspere's writings, ii. 10 [1].

Farsa, the Italian, i. 14, 226.

Fastnachtsspiele, in Germany, i. 232, 233.

Fastolf, Sir John, and the character of Falstaff, ii. 123.

Fatal Contrast, The, by W. Heminge, iii. 161.

Fatal Dowry, The, by Massinger and Field, iii. 39.

Fatal Marriage, The, by T. Southerne, iii. 421.

Fate of Capua, The, by T. Southerne, iii. 422.

Father Hubburd's Tales, by Middleton, ii. 494.

Father's Own Son: see *Monsieur Thomas*.

Faucit, Helen (Lady Martin), her Shaksperean criticisms, i. 569 [2].

Fault in Friendship, A, by R. Brome and Benjamin Jonson (junior), iii. 126.

Faust, Dr. E. K. R., on R. Brome, iii. 126 [1].

Faustbuch, the, i. 332.

Fechter von Ravenna, Der, by 'Friedrich Halm,' iii. 404 [1].

Feint Astrologue, Le, by Corneille, Dryden's adaptation of, iii. 315 [1], 352.

Feis, Mr. Jacob, on *Hamlet* and Shakspere's obligations to Montaigne, ii. 160, 162; on references to Shakspere in Jonson's *Poetaster*, ii. 357 [2].

Felix and Philomena, The History of, compared with Shakspere's *Two Gentlemen*, ii. 81.

Feltham, Owen, his estimation of Shakspere, i. 510 [1].

Female Prelate, The, by Settle, iii. 398.

Female Wits, The, by the Duchess of Newcastle, iii. 335 [4].

Femmes Savantes, Les, Molière's, Cibber's adaptation of, iii. 487 [2].

Fenton, Elijah, his share in Pope's edition of Shakspere, i. 527; his *Mariamne*, iii. 344 [3].

Fernow, Dr. H., his essay on *The Three Lords and Three Ladies of London*, i. 344 [4].

Ferrers, George, Master of the Pastimes of Edward VI, i. 152.

Ferrex and Porrex, Haughton's version of, i. 428 [5], ii. 605 [1]: see *Gorboduc*.

Ferriar, Dr. John, on Massinger, iii. 2 [1].

Ferrys, Edward, Puttenham's commendation of the works of, i. 268.

Festin de Pierre, Le, by Molière, iii. 303 [3].

Fêtes de l'âne, i. 21, 22.

Fidele and Fortunio, by A. Munday, i. 431.

Fides, Spes, et Charitas, by Hrotsvitha, i. 7.

Field, Mr. Barron, his editions of T. Heywood's plays, ii. 550 [3], 556 [1] *et seq.*

Field, John, his pamphlet in opposition to the drama, i. 461 [3].

Field, Nathaniel, one of the Children of the Chapel, ii. 356 [2]; his *Amends for Ladies*, Mary Frith impersonated in, ii. 519 [2]; his connexion with Fletcher, ii. 747; *The Jeweller of Amsterdam*, ii. 748; his and Massinger's *Fatal Dowry*, iii. 39; his dramatic works, iii. 47; *A Woman is a Weather-Cock*, iii. 48; *Amends for Ladies*, iii. 50.

Field, Richard, printer of Skakspere's *Venus and Adonis*, ii. 24 [2].

Fiestas de Aranjuez, by Mendoza, Fanshawe's translation of, iii. 306 [1].

Fig for Momus, A, i. 414.

Filmer, E., his *Vindication of the Stage*, iii. 513.

Fine Companion, A, by S. Marmion, notice of, iii. 147.

Finsbury Fields, the *Theatre* at, i. 458.

Filostrato, by Boccaccio, ii. 152.

Fiorentino, Giovanni, his *Il Pecorone*, Shakspere's obligation to, ii. 108.

First Part of: see under *Selimus*; *Sir John Oldcastle*, &c.

Fischerin, Die, Goethe's, ii. 380 [3].

Fisher, Dr. Jasper, his *Fuimus Troes*, a synopsis of, iii. 182.

Fisher's Folly, ii. 732 [2].

Fitch, Mr. R., editor of *The Story of the Creation*, part of the Norwich cycle, i. 91 [1].

Fitton, Mary, supposed to be the heroine of Shakspere's *Sonnets*, ii. 764.

Fitzgerald, Edward, on Shakspere's sub-title to *Twelfth Night*, ii. 144.

Fitz-Stephen, William, on the miracle-plays performed in London, i. 49.

Flagellants, the, i. 33.

Flanders, pageants in, i. 146.

Fleay, Mr. F. G., his *Chronicle History of the English Stage*, i. 1 [1]; on Bale's *Kynge Johan*, i. 178; on *Chronicle Histories*, i. 222; on Kyd's productions, i. 303 [2]; his edition of Marlowe's *Edward II*, i. 347 [1]; on Marlowe's *Dido*, i. 357 [1]; on plays attributed to Marlowe, i. 359, 360; on Michael Drayton, i. 437 [1] *et seq.*; on early Elisabethan acting companies, i. 451 [4]; on the Marprelate controversy, i. 466 [1]; his *Life of Shakspere*, ii. 1 [1]; on Shakspere's first literary efforts, ii. 22 [1]; his *Chronicle History of Shakspeare*, ii. 44 [1]; on Shakspere's versification, ii. 48 [1], 49 [2]; on *Troilus and Cressida*, ii. 146; on *Hamlet*, ii. 158; on *Timon of Athens*, ii. 179; on *Pericles*, ii. 182, 184; on authorship of *Sir Thomas More*, ii. 215; on *Edward III*, ii. 223; on *The Second Maiden's Tragedy*, ii. 446 [2]; on the Middleton-Rowley plays, ii. 499; on the *Parnassus Plays*, ii. 633 [1]; on the respective contributions of Beaumont and Fletcher in their conjoint plays, ii. 658 *et seq.*; on Fletcher's *Sir John Van Olden-Barnavelt*, ii. 716 [1]; on Massinger, iii. 2 [1].

Flecknoe, Richard, on Beaumont and Fletcher's female characters, ii. 758 [1]; his *Short Discourse of the English Stage*, iii. 354.

Flemish Mystery-plays, i. 46.

Fletcher, John, on tragi-comedy, i. 210 [5]; Shakspere's relations with, i. 500; his *Faithful Shepherdess*, compared with *The Tempest*, ii. 198; his *Sea Voyage*, ii. 200; *Henry VIII* attributed to, ii. 206, iii. 38; *The Two Noble Kinsmen* attributed to Shakspere and, ii. 210, iii. 38; his and Shirley's *Love's Pilgrimage*, ii. 213; *The History of Cardenio* attributed to Shakspere and, ii. 213; his and Shakspere's *Two Noble Kinsmen*, ii. 237; possibly part-author in Middleton's *Widow*, ii. 520; Ben Jonson's relations with, ii. 326 [1], 329; his connexion with Massinger, iii. 4; plays by Massinger and, iii. 37; *Very Woman*, iii. 38; a share in Shirley's *Coronation* attributed to, iii. 112. (*See principally under* Beaumont and Fletcher.)

Fletcher, Phineas, his *Sicelides*, ii. 380 [3]; synopsis of, iii. 180–182.

Fletcher, Phineas and Giles, the poetical works of, ii. 646, 647.

Floating Island, The, by Dr. P. Strode, iii. 182.

Florio, John, his translation of Montaigne's Essay *Of the Caniballes*, ii. 199.

Flower, Francis, joint-author of *The Misfortunes of Arthur*, i. 219.

'*Focasse*,' by Martin Slater, ii. 608 [2].

Foljambe, Sir Francis, a patron of Massinger, iii. 11 [1].

Folz, Hans, his *Fastnachtsspiele*, i. 233 [1].

Fontaine-Malherbe, Count, and Letourneur's *Shakspere*, i. 538.

Fool would be a Favourite, The, by L. Carlell, iii. 160.

Fool's Preferment, A, by D'Urfey, a reproduction of Fletcher's *Noble Gentleman*, ii. 739 [1].

Fools, Shakspere's, ii. 283.

Foot out of the Snare, by John Gee, Middleton's obligations to, ii. 529 [8].

For the Honour of Wales, a masque by Ben Jonson, ii. 396.

Forbonius and Prisceria: see *Delectable History of*.

Ford, John, his *Lover's Melancholy* assigned to Shakspere, ii. 211; his and others' *Witch of Edmonton*, ii. 470, iii. 74; *The Sun's Darling*, ii. 470; *The Fairy Knight*, ii. 470; Mr. Swinburne's essay on, ii. 470 [1]; his dramatic works, iii. 71–89; collaborated plays, iii. 74; *The Murder of a Son upon a Mother*, iii. 76; *The Lover's Melancholy*, iii. 76; '*Tis Pity She's a Whore*, iii. 77; *The Broken Heart*, iii. 79; *Love's Sacrifice*, iii. 81: *Fancies Chaste and Noble*, iii. 83; *The Lady's Trial*, iii. 83; *Perkin Warbeck*, iii. 84; lost plays by, iii. 86; as a dramatist, iii. 86.

Forest, The, Ben Jonson's, ii. 330.

Foreste, The, by Fortescue. i. 322.

Forman, Simon, on *Cymbeline*, ii. 190; on *The Winter's Tale*, ii. 192.

Forrest, W., his version of *Dr. Faustus*, i. 330; his *Second Gresyld*, i. 429 [4].

Fortitude of Judith, The, by Ralph Radcliffe, i. 170 [2].

Fortunate Isles, The, a masque by Ben Jonson, ii. 397.

Fortunatus, Dekker's obligation to the old *Volksbuch* on, ii. 457; Hans Sachs' version of the subject of, ii. 458 [1].

Fortune theatre, the, iii. 232 [5], 249 [4].

Fortune by Land and Sea, by T. Heywood and W. Rowley, ii. 243 [5]; account of, ii. 569.

Fortune in her Wits, by Charles Johnson, iii. 187 [2].

Four Birdes of Noah's Arke, The, by Dekker, ii. 455 [6].

Foure Letters, by Gabriel Harvey, i. 382 [3], 383; reference to Tarlton in, i. 454 [1].

Four P's, The, &c., an interlude by John Heywood, i. 244.

Four Plays in One, by Beaumont and Fletcher, synopsis of, ii. 666.

Four Prentices of London, The, by T. Heywood, account of, ii. 559.

Fourberies de Scapin, Les, by Molière, adapted by Otway, iii. 315 [1].

Francesco's Fortunes, by Robert Greene, i. 381 [2], 391.

Fraunce, Abraham, his English translation of Tasso's *Aminta*, ii. 384 [2].

Freeman, Thomas, his tribute to Shakspere in *Runne and a Great Caste*, i. 496.

French, Mr. S. Russell, his *Life* of Shakspere, ii. 1 [1], ii. 13 [4]; on allegorical meanings in *Hamlet*, ii. 161.

French drama, the, influence of the Roman pantomime on, i. 18; jongleurs and mimes, i. 18–21; the use of French in Hilarius' works, i. 38, 39; in the Towneley plays, i. 71; in the Chester plays, i. 76 [3]; the beginnings of, i. 21; mysteries, i. 35 [3]; pageants, i. 146 [2]; early comedy, i. 226; early influence of Shakspere on, i. 533, 534, 576; French versions of Shakspere, i. 535; nineteenth-century criticisms on, i. 560; in the earlier half of the seventeenth century, iii. 265; its influence on the later Stuart dramatic literature, iii. 306.

Frere, Mr. W. H., editor of *The Winchester Tropes*, i. 573.

Freund, F., on Shakspere's knowledge of jurisprudence, ii. 13 [2].

Freytag, Gustav, on the distinction between tragedy and comedy, i. 159 [1]; his *Technik des Dramas*, ii. 289 [1], 290 [1]; his *Journalisten*, ii. 374 [5].

Friar Bacon and Friar Bungay, by Greene, the 'vice' a personage in, i. 111 [1], 396; compared with *A Knacke to Know*, &c., ii. 610 [2]; Middleton's prologue and epilogue to, ii. 495 [1].

Friar Bakon's Prophesie, i. 397 [1].

Friar Rush, Jonson's probable obligations to, ii. 372; Dekker's obligations to, ii. 465.

Friendship Improved, by C. Hopkins, iii. 431.

Friendship in Fashion, by T. Otway, notice of, iii. 415.

Frith, Mary, alluded to in *Twelfth Night*, ii. 145; personified in *The Roaring Girle*, ii. 519 [2].

Froissart, Jean, compared with Comines, i. 171; the plot of *Edward III* taken from, ii. 221, 222.

Frottola, the, i. 227.

Fuerza de la Sangre, La, by Cervantes, plays derived from, ii. 508.

Fuimus Troes, by J. Fisher, a synopsis of, iii. 182.

Fulbeck, William, joint-author of *The Misfortunes of Arthur*, i. 219.

Fuller, Thomas, criticisms on Shakspere, i. 522; on Ben Jonson's humour, ii. 406 [2]; his *Holy Warre*, Heywood's obligations to, in *The Four Prentices*, ii. 559.

Fullerton, Mr. R. M., his *Merlin, a Dramatic Poem*, ii. 245 [1].

Fullonius, William, his *Acolastus*, i. 253.

Fulwel, Ulpian, his *Like wil to Like*, &c., i. 134; possible author of *The History of the Collier*, i. 263.

Funeral, The, by Steele, account of, iii. 494.

Furness, Mr. Howard, his *New Variorum* edition of Shakspere, i. 571; on date of *As You Like It*, ii. 129; his *New Variorum* edition of *Hamlet*, ii. 157 *et seq.*

Furnivall, Dr., his edition of the Digby Mysteries, i. 92 [3]; his edition of *Mary Magdalene*, i. 95 [1]; on Thomas Lodge, i. 410 [4]; his Shaksperean research, i. 570; his *Life* of Shakspere, ii. 1 [1]; on the versification of Shakspere's plays, ii. 49 [1]; on the chronology of Shakspere's plays, ii. 54 [1]; on *Edward III*, ii. 223.

Fust, Johann, erroneously identified with Dr. Faustus, iii. 331.

Gaedertz, Dr., on Canon John de Witt's papers concerning the Swan theatre, i. 458 [4].

Gager, William, his *Dido*, i. 357 [1]; his *Rivales*, i. 364, ii. 631 [1]; his controversy with Rainoldes on Stage-plays, i. 506 [3].

Gainsford, T., his *History of Perkin Warbeck*, iii. 85.

Gairdner, Mr. James, his essay on Perkin Warbeck, iii. 85 [1].

Gaisford and Dübner's edition of Ezechiel's *Exodus*, i. 3 [1].

Gallathea, by John Lyly, i. 296; Lyly's attack upon the alchemists in, ii. 368 [1].

Game of Chess, The, by Middleton, political significance of, ii. 496; a synopsis of, ii. 524–536.

Gamester, The, by Shirley, account of, iii. 109.

Gamester, The, by Mrs. Centlivre, an adaptation of Regnard's *Le Joueur*, iii. 315 [1], 488 [3].

Gammer Gurton's Needle, authorship attributed to (Bishop) Still, i. 260; account of, i. 261.

Gardiner, Bishop, protests against *Kynge Johan*, i. 179.

Gardiner, Dr. S. R., on Massinger, iii. 2 [1]; his edition of *Documents of proceedings against William Prynne*, iii. 244 [2].

Garlande of Laurell, The, by Skelton, i. 130.

Garnett, Dr. R., on Dryden's Shaksperean criticisms, i. 518 [1].

Garnier, Robert, his *Cornélie*, Kyd's translation of, i. 304; his *Marc Antoine*, ii. 186.

Garrick, David, his acting edition of Shakspere's *Hamlet*, i. 515; his career, i. 540, 563 [1]; his impersonation of Abel Drugger in *The Alchemist*, ii. 369 [1]; his adaptation of Fletcher's *A King and No King*, ii. 676 [4]; of Fletcher's *Chances*, ii. 712 [3]; his adaptation of Shirley's *Gamester*, iii. 109 [3]; his impersonation of Bayes in *The Rehearsal*, iii. 363 [4].

Garve, Christian, on Shakspere's mad characters, ii. 295 [1].

Gascoigne, George, his masques, i. 155 [2]; his *Jocasta*, i. 209; his *Supposes*, i. 262; his treatment of the plot of Peele's *Arraignment of Paris*, i. 366; his *Spoyle of Antwerp*, ii. 211 [3]; his *Masque for Viscount Montacute*, ii. 388 [1].

Gaudersheim, the Benedictine Convent of: *see* Hrotsvitha.

Gay, John, his share in Pope's edition of Shakspere, i. 527; on Steele and his influence, iii. 492, 493 [1].

Gay Goss Hawk, The, compared with story of *Romeo and Juliet*, ii. 116.

Gee, John, Middleton's obligations to in his *Game of Chess*, 529 [3].

Genée, R., his discovery of a MS. of Marlowe's *Edward II*, i. 347 [1].

General, The, ascribed to Lord Orrery, iii. 345.

General History of Women, The, by T. Heywood, ii. 554.

Generous Portugal, The, an adaptation of Fletcher's *Island Princess*, ii. 704 [3].

Genest, John, his *Account of the English Stage*, i. 1 [1].

Gentleman, Francis, his *Tobacconist*, ii. 369 [1].

Gentleman Dancing Master, The, by W. Wycherley, iii. 463.

Gentleman Usher, The, by Chapman, ii. 435.

Gentleman of Venice, The, by Shirley, iii. 117.

Geoffrey, Abbot of St. Albans, and the *Ludus de S. Katharina*, i. 10, 49.

Geoffroy, J. L., on Shakspere and Voltaire, i. 539.

George-a-Greene, the Pinner of Wakefield, attributed to Greene and Peele, i. 403, 404; to Lodge, i. 418; attributed to Shakspere, ii. 211.

George Dandin, by Molière, adapted by Betterton, iii. 315 [1].

George Scanderbage, The True History of, attributed to Marlowe, i. 360.

German theatre, intercourse of the, with the early Elisabethan, i. 471.

Germany, mysteries in, i. 46; early comedy of, i. 232; recognition of Shakspere's genius in, i. 544 *et seq.*

Gernutus a Jew, ii. 106.

Gervinus, G. G., his Shaksperean criticism, i. 558.

Gesta Grayorum, masques comprising, ii. 628 [3].

Gesta Romanorum, the story of the Jew of Venice in the, ii. 108.

Gesta Stephani, the, ii. 212.

Gestours, origin of the, i. 18.

Geta, by Vitalis Blesensis, i. 9 [1].

Ghost of Richard III, The, by C. Brooke, tribute to Shakspere in, i. 497 [1].

Gibbon, Edward, on Shakspere's classical knowledge, ii. 10 [1].

Gibraltar, by J. Dennis, iii. 427.

Gifford, William, his edition of Massinger, iii. 2 [1]; his edition of Ben Jonson's works, ii. 296 [1]; on Ben Jonson's attitude towards Shakspere, ii. 327; his edition of Ford's works, iii. 71 [1].

Gilchrist, O., on Ben Jonson's attitude towards Shakspere, ii. 327.

Gildon, Charles, his adaptation of Shakspere's *Measure for Measure*, i. 514; his criticisms on Shakspere, i. 522, 524; his dramatic works, iii. 428.

Gill, Alexander, his attack on Jonson's *Magnetic Lady*, ii. 378.

Ginecocratia, by G. Puttenham, i. 442 [4].

Gipsies Metamorphosed, The, a masque by Ben Jonson, ii. 396.

Girish, John Michael, his German translation of Jonson's *Sejanus*, ii. 339.

Gismonda, various treatments of the theme, i. 214 [3].

Gismonde of Salerno: see *Tancred and Gismunda*.

Gitanilla, La, by Cervantes, plays derived from, ii. 508.

Giudati, the, i. 227.

Giulietta e Romeo, by Cesare della Valle, ii. 117.

Giulio Cesare, by Antonio Conti, ii. 141.

Glapthorne, Henry, his *Parracide*, ii. 432[1]; works of, iii. 151–155; *Argalus and Parthenia*, iii. 151; *The Ladies' Privilege*, iii. 151; *Albertus Wallenstein*, iii. 152; *The Hollander*, iii. 153; *Wit in a Constable*, iii. 153; *The Lady Mother*, iii. 154.

Glaucus and Silla, Most Pithie and Pleasant Historie of, by T. Lodge, i. 412[2].

Globe theatre, the old, i. 458; the new, ii. 29, 37, 38; the burning of, in 1613, ii. 201, iii. 232[5], 249[4].

Gloriana, Lee's adaptation of La Calprenède's *Cléopâtre*, iii. 309[2], 409.

Glossary of Shakspere's Plays, by Richard Warner, i. 533[3].

Glover, Richard, his *Boadicea*, ii. 697[3].

Goblins, The, by Suckling, derived from *The Tempest*, ii. 200; account of, iii. 144.

God's Plea for Nineveh, by T. Reeve, i. 402[1].

God's Promises, by Bishop Bale, i. 175.

Godfrey of Viterbo, his version of *Pericles* in his Pantheon, ii. 184.

Godly Queene Hester, the 'vice' character in, i. 110, 112[1].

Goedeke, Dr. K., his edition of *Everyman*, i. 119[2]; his edition of the Duke of Brunswick's plays, i. 476[6].

Goethe, J. W. von, on tragedy, i. 159[3]; on Shakspere, i. 552; his *Fischerin*, ii. 380[3].

Götz von Berlichingen, Goethe's, the Shaksperean influences apparent in, i. 552.

Goffe, Thomas, his *Raging Turk*, i. 405[3]; *The Second Maiden's Tragedy* assigned to, ii. 212; his dramatic works, iii. 158, 159.

Golden Age Restored, The, a masque by Ben Jonson, ii. 395.

Golden Garland of Princely Delights, The, ii. 57.

Golden Legend, The, the story of *Doctor Faustus* introduced into, i. 330; Shakspere's obligations to, ii. 111.

Golden, Silver, Brazen and Iron Ages, by T. Heywood, synopsis of, ii. 578.

Golding, Arthur, his translation of Beza's *Abraham's Sacrifice*, i. 172[1].

Goldoni, Carlo, his version of *Le Menteur*, iii. 495[2].

Gollancz, Mr. I., on the authorship of the *Parnassus Plays*, ii. 640.

Gomberville, M. le R. de, his *Polexandre*, iii. 309.

Gondibert, by D'Avenant, a version of *The Tempest*, ii. 200, iii. 166, 167.

Gondomar: see *Game of Chess*, by Middleton (ii. 529[3]).

Gongora, Luis de, his literary style, i. 276.

Gongorism, i. 276.

Gonzaga, Curzio, his treatment of *Gli Ingannati*, ii. 143.

Goodman's Fields theatre, the, iii. 284[3].

Gorboduc, the earliest English tragedy, i. 198.

Gordon, Mr. James, his edition of the Towneley plays, i. 71[1].

Gosse, Mr. Edmund, his edition of Lodge's works, i. 409[1]; on Webster, iii. 51[2]; his edition of a selection of Shirley's plays, iii. 89[1]; on Chamberlayne's *Pharonnida*, iii. 289[1]; on Thomas Otway, iii. 412[2]; on Etheredge, iii. 442[1]; his *Life of Congreve*, iii. 467[1].

Gosson, Stephen, his *Catiline's Conspiracies*, i. 208, ii. 340; his *Captain Mario*, i. 217, 263; his opposition to the drama, i. 267; on Marlowe's *Jew of Malta*, i. 344; his *School of Abuse* and its opponents, i. 409, 410; his works against stage-plays, i. 459.

Gotham Election, A, by Mrs. Centlivre, iii. 491.

Gottsched, J. C., on Shakspere, i. 547; his *Der Sterbende Cato*, iii. 441[4].

Governor of Cyprus, The, by John Oldmixon, iii. 428.

Gower, John, his *Confessio Amantis*, allegorical elements in, i. 103; indebtedness of Shakspere's *Pericles* to, ii. 184.

Grafton, Richard, his Continuation of Halle's works, ii. 260[1].

Grand Cyrus, Le, by La Calprenède, Dryden's obligations to, iii. 309[2]; Banks' adaptation of, iii. 309[2].

Grandisson, Bishop, his opposition to the drama, i. 573.

Granville, George, his adaptation of Shakspere's *Merchant of Venice*, i. 514, ii. 112; his opera, *British Enchanters*, iii. 323; his dramatic works, iii. 423–425; *Heroic Love*, iii. 424; his comedies, iii. 424, 425.

Grateful Servant, The, by Shirley, account of, iii. 105.

Great Duke of Florence, The, by Massinger, compared with *A Knacke to Knowe a Knave*, ii. 610[2]; notice of, iii. 28.

Grecian Heroine, The, by T. D'Urfey, iii. 454[2].

Green, Mr. H., on *Shakspere and the Emblem Writers*, ii. 185.

Green, John, the clown, i. 382³; his *Of a King in Cyprus*, ii. 108.

Greene, Robert, his *Friar Bacon and Friar Bungay*, the 'vice' a personage in, i. 111¹; his *Quip for an Upstart Courtier*, i. 237³; an imitator of John Lyly, i. 281; his pamphlet to Marlowe and others, *A Groatsworth of Wit*, i. 316; on *Tamberlaine*, i. 328¹; his reference to Machiavelli, i. 339³; his admonitions to Peele in *A Groatsworth of Wit*, i. 365; his life, i. 379; his prose, i. 385 *seqq.*; his plays, i. 393 *seqq.*; *Alphonsus*, i. 393; *Orlando Furioso*, i. 395; *Friar Bacon and Friar Bungay*, i. 396; *James IV*, i. 400; *A Looking Glasse for London*, i. 402; plays attributed to, i. 403; *George-a-Greene*, i. 403, 404; *Selimus* attributed to him, i. 405; his position as a dramatist, i. 407; his treatment of tragic themes, i. 482; his aspersions on Shakspere in *A Groatsworth of Wit*, i. 491; his relations with Shakspere, ii. 22; *Titus Andronicus* attributed to, ii. 56; theory of his connexion with the *Henry VI* plays, ii. 60, 66, 73; his *Euphues, his Censure to Philautus*, ii. 147; his *Pandosto* compared with *Winter's Tale*, ii. 192; his *George-a-Greene*, ii. 211; *Faire Em* attributed to, ii. 235.

Greene, Thomas, his *Poet's Vision*, i. 382³, 502¹.

Greene et Lylli, by J. Eliote, i. 408.

Greene's Arcadia: see *Menaphon*.

Greene's Mourning Garment: see *Mourning Garment*.

Greene's Tu Quoque, by John Cooke, i. 370³; account of, ii. 608.

Greene's Vision, i. 383¹.

Greenstreet, Mr. J., on Shakspere's connexion with Burbage's company, ii. 38³.

Greenwood, John, his part in the Marprelate controversy, i. 464³.

Gregorovius, F., on the Roman pantomime, i. 18¹.

Gregory of Antioch, the Χριστὸς πάσχων attributed to, i. 4.

Gregory the Great, Pope, his *Dialogues*, i. 12; the Mass in the time of, i. 29.

Gregory the Nazianzene, St., the Χριστὸς πάσχων attributed to, i. 4.

Gregory IX, Pope, on performance of dramatic spectacles in churches, i. 52.

Gresset, J. B. L., his *Édouard III*, ii. 222¹.

Greville, Sir Fulke: see Brooke, Lord.

Grévin, J., his *Mort de César*, ii. 140, 625⁵.

Grillparzer, F., Shakspere's influence on, i. 554¹.

Grim the Collier of Croydon, i. 263¹; identified as Haughton's *Devil and his Dame*, ii. 606.

Grindal, Archbishop, suppression of Paternoster plays by, i. 97; his opposition to the stage, i. 456.

Griseldis, by 'Friedrich Halm,' i. 429³.

Grisélidis, by MM. Silvestre and Morand, i. 429³.

Groatsworth of Wit, A, Greene's pamphlet addressed to Marlowe and others, i. 316; admonitions to Peele, i. 365; personal reminiscences of the author in, i. 380³ *et seq.*, 391; edited by Chettle, i. 426; aspersions on Shakspere in, i. 491.

Grobianus, Dedekind's, ii. 455⁴.

Grondeur, Le, by Brueys and Palaprat, Sir Charles Sedley's adaptation of, iii. 448.

Grosart, Dr. A. B., his edition of Bale's *Temptacyon of our Lorde*, i. 176¹; his edition of Greene's works, 379³; on the authorship of *Selimus*, i. 405; his edition of Nashe's works, i. 418³; his edition of Dekker's non-dramatic works, ii. 450³; his edition of Barksted's *Mirrha* and *Hiren*, ii. 481²; his edition of Lord Brooke's works, ii. 614²; of S. Daniel's works, ii. 618²; on Alexander (Lord Stirling), ii. 623³; his edition of Sir John Beaumont's poems, ii. 649; his edition of Phineas Fletcher's works, iii. 180⁴.

Grosteste, Bishop Robert, and the Feast of Fools, i. 22; the *Manuel des Pechiez* attributed to, i. 52.

Grotius, Hugo, his *Christus Patiens* and the Χριστὸς πάσχων, i. 5¹; iii. 202.

Groto, Luigi, his *Hadriana*, ii. 115.

Grounds of Criticism in Tragedy, On the, by Dryden, iii. 375.

Grumbler, The, by Sir Charles Sedley, iii. 448.

Gryphius, Andreas, his *Absurda Comtca*, i. 545; his *Cardenio und Celinde*, ii. 213³.

'G. S. B.', on *Prologues and Epilogues*, iii. 391¹, 392¹.

Guardian, The, by Abraham Cowley, iii. 164¹, 327.

Guardian, The, by Massinger, account of, iii. 35.

Guarini, G. B., his *Pastor Fido*, i. 231, ii. 382 ; Fletcher's obligations to, ii. 664 ; Beaumont and Fletcher's obligations to, ii. 752.

Guary miracles, the, acted in Cornwall, i. 56 [1].

Guevara, Antonio de, Lyly's obligations to, i. 280.

Guevara, L. de, his treatment of the story of *Tamburlaine*, i. 322 [1].

Guido della Colonna, his version of the Trojan war, ii. 151.

Guilevile, Guillaume de, his *Pèlerinage de l'Homme*, ii. 634 [2].

Guise, The, a play attributed to Massinger, iii. 52 [1].

Guise, The, by Webster, i. 355 [3].

Guizot, F. P. G., on Shakspere, i. 561 ; on Shakspere's comedy, ii. 277 [1].

Gul's Hornebooke, The, by Dekker, ii. 453 [8], 455.

Gunpowder Plot, the, Jonson's connexion with the enquiry into, ii. 312.

Guy Earl of Warwick, a non-extant play by Dekker and Day, ii. 592 [2].

Guzman, F. de, his *Triunfos Morales*, ii. 667 [2].

Guzman, by Lord Orrery, iii. 345.

Gwydonius, the Carde of Fancie, by Robert Greene, i. 387.

Habington, W., his dramatic works, iii. 149, 150 ; *Queene of Arragon*, iii. 150.

Hacket, John, his Latin play, *Loiola*, iii. 186 [1].

Hadriana, Luigi Groto's tragedy of, compared with *Romeo and Juliet*, ii. 115.

Hakluyt, R., his *Voyages and Discoveries*, i. 442.

Hales, Dr. J., on the *Parnassus Plays*, ii. 633 [1].

Hales, John, of Eton, his estimate of Shakspere, i. 508.

Haliblude, The, an early Scotch play, i. 131.

Hall, Bishop, on John Lyly, i. 274 [2]; his challenge to Lodge, i. 414; his contemporaries, i. 442 ; his *Satires*, i. 468, ii. 474 [3]; his invective against clowns, i. 485 [1]; his quarrel with Marston, ii. 474.

Hall, Dr. Fitzedward, his edition of Lyndsay's *Satyre of the Thrie Estaits*, i. 132 [1].

Hall, Dr. John, a son-in-law of Shakspere, ii. 16, 39 ; Susanna, ii. 41 ; Elisabeth, ii. 41.

Hall, J., his *Royal Merchant*, an adaptation of Fletcher's *Beggars' Bush*, ii. 726 [2].

Hall, Thomas, his version of *Timon of Athens*, ii. 180.

Halle, E., the dialogue mentioned in his *Chronicle*, i. 237 ; his historical works compared with Holinshed's, ii. 260 [1].

Halliwell, Edward, authorship of a Latin *Dido* attributed to, i. 357 [1].

Halliwell-Phillipps, Mr. J. O., his edition of *The Harrowing of Hell*, i. 90 [1]; of Redford's *Wyt and Science*, i. 127 [3]; of *The Triall of Treasure*, i. 133 ; of *Marriage of Wit and Wisdom*, i. 135 [1]; of Ingelend's *Disobedient Child*, i. 250 [1]; of *Tarlton's Jests*, i. 435 [3], 454 [1]; his Shaksperean criticism, i. 569, 570; his *Life* of Shakspere, ii. 1 [1]; his edition of Marston's works, ii. 472 [1]; of Day's *Humour out of Breath*, ii. 596; of the droll, *Merry Conceits of Bottom*, &c., iii. 280 [1].

'Halm,' 'Friedrich,' his *Griseldis*, i. 429 [3]; his *Fechter von Ravenna*, iii. 404 [1].

Halpin, Mr. N. J., on John Lyly's *Endimion*, i. 290.

Hamburger Dramaturgie, Lessing's, i. 548.

Hamlet, an early play, non-extant, attributed to Thomas Kyd, i. 312.

Hamlet, Shakspere's, Garrick's acting edition, i. 515 ; and the *Agrippina* of Bergerac, i. 534 ; J. Ducis' version, i. 537 ; Goethe's criticism on, i. 552 ; de Vigny's version, i. 561 [2]; Dumas' version, i. 561 [2]; Ireland's forgery, i. 564 ; probable date of first performance of, ii. 37 ; Shakspere's representation of the Ghost in, ii. 21, 22 ; versification of, ii. 49 [2]; a synopsis of the play, ii. 156-167 ; Shakspere's *chef-d'œuvre*, ii. 294 ; Marston's obligations to, ii. 478 [2]; compared with Cyril Tourneur's *Revenger's Tragedy*, iii. 69.

Handel, G. F., his music to Aaron Hill's *Rinaldo*, iii. 322 [1].

Handlyng Synne, on miracle-plays, i. 52.

Hanging of Antioch, The, a play, i. 153.

Hanmer, Sir Thomas, his edition of Shakspere, i. 529.

Hannibal, by John Nichol, iii. 409 [1].

Harde Shifte for Husbands, by S. Rowley, ii. 546.

Hardwick, Archdeacon, his edition of the *Passion of St. George*, i. 13 [1].

Harris, Joseph, his *Mistakes*, iii. 431.

Harrison, William, his *Chronologie*, on the prohibition of plays in 1572, i. 457; his historical works, ii. 260 [1].

Harrison, William, his and Addison's *Drummer*, iii. 439 [1].

Harrowing of Hell, The, earliest extant religious drama, i. 25; performed at Winchester, i. 55; in the Chester plays, i. 81; the isolated play of the, i. 90; in the York plays, i. 90 [1]; in the Towneley plays, i. 90 [1].

Harry I, The Life and Death of, i. 224.

Harry V, a play mentioned by Henslowe, ii. 125.

Harry VI, ii. 58.

Hart, William, brother-in-law of Shakspere, ii. 8, 16, 39.

Harvey, Gabriel, his relations with John Lyly, i. 272, 273; impersonation of, in *Endimion*, i. 293 [1]; his relations with Marlowe, i. 316 [1]; on Robert Greene, in his *Foure Letters*, i. 382 [3], 383, 384; on Thomas Nashe, i. 419 [2], 420; his *Letter-Book*, edited by E. J. L. Scott, i. 420 [4]; his enumeration of Fools in *Pierce's Supererogation*, i. 423 [4]; his influence on contemporary literature, i. 443; on Tarlton's works, i. 454 [1]; his reference to *Hamlet*, ii. 160.

Harvey, Richard, his part in the Marprelate controversy, i. 465 [4].

Haslewood, Joseph, his edition of *Ancient Critical Essays upon English Poets and Poesy*, i. 268 [3].

Hathaway, Anne, her marriage with Shakspere, ii. 14.

Hathwaye, R., joint-author of *First Part of Sir John Oldcastle*, i. 434; nothing known of him personally, ii. 15 [1]; his dramatic works, ii. 607.

Hatton, Sir Christopher, supposed joint-author of *Tancred and Gismunda*, i. 214 [1]; a patron of Thomas Randolph, iii. 134 [2].

Haughton, W., possible author of *Grim the Collier of Croydon*, i. 263; co-author in Chettle's *Patient Grissil*, i. 428, ii. 466; his joint-play with Day, non-extant, of *Thomas Merry*, ii. 219; *The Spanish Moor*, ii. 467; a collaborator of John Day, ii. 591; their plays, ii. 591 [3]; *The Blind Beggar*, ii. 599; his dramatic works, ii. 605, 606; *Englishmen for my Money*, a synopsis of, ii. 605; *The Devil and his Dame*, ii. 606.

Hausted, Peter, on Lyly, in his *Senile Odium*, i. 283 [1]; his *Senile Odium*, iii. 187, 188; *Rival Friends*, iii. 188.

Have with you to Saffron Walden, by Thomas Nashe, i. 273 [2], 420.

Hawes, Stephen, his *Pastime of Pleasure*, allegorical elements in, i. 103.

Hawkins, J. S., his edition of the Digby mysteries, i. 92 [3]; his edition of Ruggle's *Ignoramus*, iii. 183 [1].

Hay any work for Cooper, a Martin Marprelate tract, i. 462 [1].

Haymarket theatre, the, built by Sir John Vanbrugh, iii. 284 [3].

Hayward, Sir John, his *History of Henry IV*, ii. 102.

Hazlitt, William, his Shaksperean criticisms, i. 568; on Shakspere's character of Bottom, ii. 279 [1].

Hazlitt, Mr. W. C., his edition of doubtful Shaksperean plays, ii. 213 [4]; his edition of Webster's works, iii. 51 [2]; his edition of works of Thomas Randolph, iii. 131 [1]; of Sir John Suckling, iii. 144 [1].

Heard, Mr. F. F., on Shakspere's legal acquirements, ii. 13 [2].

Heautontimorumenos, the, Terence's, Chapman's obligations to, ii. 434.

Hecatommithi, by Giraldo Cinthio, story of *Measure for Measure* in, ii. 154; story of *Othello* in, ii. 168.

Hector of Germany, disputed authorship of, ii. 607.

Heir, The, by T. May, notice of, iii. 142.

Heir of Morocco, The, by Settle, iii. 398.

Hekastus, a comedy by Macropedius, i. 120.

Heminge, John, joint-editor of the First Folio of Shakspere, i. 499; his share in Burbage's new Globe theatre, ii. 29; a friend of Shakspere, ii. 35.

Heminge, William, his *Fatal Contrast*, iii. 161; *The Jew's Tragedy*, iii. 162.

Henges, a play perhaps identical with Middleton's *Mayor of Quinborough*, ii. 500 [4].

Henrietta Maria, Queen, her patronage of the stage, iii. 218.

Henry I, a play, non-extant, attributed to Shakspere and Davenport, ii. 213, iii. 158.

Henry II, a play, non-extant, attributed to Shakspere and Davenport, ii. 213, iii. 158.

Henry IV, Shakspere's, versification of, ii. 49 [2]; observations on the play, *Parts I and II*, ii. 120–124; Betterton's version of, iii. 326 [1].

Henry V, Aaron Hill's, ii. 128.

Henry V, The Famous Victories of, date of performance of, i. 187 [2]; authorship assigned to Tarleton, i. 222; Shakspere's obligations to, ii. 121, 125.

Henry V, The History of, by Lord Orrery, ii. 128; a synopsis of, iii. 342.

Henry V, Shakspere's, allusion to the Globe theatre in the prologue, ii. 29 [1]; to Essex's Irish expedition, ii. 33; versification of, ii. 49 [2]; observations on the play, ii. 125–128; as a type of Shakspere's Histories, ii. 264.

Henry VI, old plays on, i. 348; Marlowe's authorship of, i. 358; Peele's share in authorship of the early plays on, i. 374; Greene's claims to authorship of, i. 407; Lodge's claims, i. 418; Shakspere an actor in, ii. 21; and possibly part-author, ii. 23 [2].

Henry VI, Shakspere's, versification of, ii. 49 [2]; remarks on, ii. 58–74.

Henry VIII, the stage patronised by, i. 152.

Henry VIII, Shakspere's, his reference to the fate of Essex in, ii. 33; versification of, ii. 49 [2]; observations on the play, ii. 201–209; the prologue to, ii. 291 [3]; compared with S. Rowley's *When You see Me*, &c., ii. 547; attributed to Fletcher, Massinger, and Shakspere, ii. 746; on the authorship of, ii. 765; Massinger's share in, iii. 38.

Henry Julius, Duke of Brunswick, influence of Shakspere's works on, i. 545; his *Vincentius Ladislaus*, ii. 133, 134.

Hense, Dr. C. C., on Euphuism, i. 270 [1], 276 [4]; on Shakspere's *Tempest*, ii. 200; on Shakspere's mad characters, ii. 295 [4].

Henslowe, Philip, his acting company, i. 469; Shakspere's connexion with, ii. 20, 22.

Henslowe's Diary, fabricated entry as to *Dr. Faustus* in, i. 321 [3], 329; *The Jew of Malta*, i. 338; *Matchavell*, i. 339 [3]; *The Spanish Moor's Tragedy* (*Lust's Dominion*), i. 360 [3]; Peele's plays, i. 374 [3]; information as to Greene's plays in, i. 404 [1]; as to Nashe's plays, i. 425; as to Henry Chettle's works, i. 427 [3]; as to Michael Drayton, i. 437; as to *Titus Andronicus*, ii. 57; the *Henry VI* plays, ii. 58; *Phillipo and Hewpolyto*, ii. 80; *The Merchant of Venice*, ii. 105; *Henry V*, ii. 125; *Julius Caesar*, ii.

140; *Troilus and Cressida*, ii. 147; *Hamlet*, ii. 162; possible reference to Jonson's *Every Man in his Humour*, ii. 303; references to Jonson's co-operation with Dekker and Chettle, ii. 307 [3]; Chapman mentioned in, ii. 410; as to the *Comodey of Humers*, ii. 433 [1]; *All Fooles*, ii. 434 [3]; references to Dekker, ii. 453, 454 *et seq.*; to *Olde Fortunatus*, ii. 458; *The Honest Whore*, ii. 462 [1]; reference to Marston, ii. 475; Middleton, ii. 495, 500 [4]; T. Heywood, ii. 551; John Day, ii. 591; some of the minor playwrights mentioned in, ii. 604 *et seqq.*

Heptameron of Civil Discourses, by George Whetstone, i. 216.

Heraclius, a non-extant play attributed to Carlell, iii. 161 [1], 315 [1].

Hercules, by Slater, i. 193 [1], ii. 578 [2], 608 [2].

Hercules Furens, the, of Seneca, translated by Jasper Heywood, i. 195.

Hercules Oetaeus, the, of Seneca, translated by John Studley, i. 195; translated by Queen Elisabeth, i. 209.

Herder, J. G. von, his Shaksperean criticisms, i. 551.

Herford, Capt. Ivan J. A., on the Laude of the Italian mass, i. 33 [3].

Herford, Prof. C. H., on German dialogue literature, i. 233; on Marlowe's authorship of *Tamburlaine*, i. 322; on Greene's works, i. 379 [3]; on Robert Greene and his works, i. 388 [5], 392; on the Marprelate controversy, i. 464 [5]; on the connexion between the German and early Elisabethan stages, i. 473 [7]; on *Much Ado About Nothing*, ii. 134; his edition of *The Two Noble Kinsmen*, ii. 237 [2].

Herman, Guillaume, the works of, i. 10 [2], 25, 42, 51, 105.

Hero and Leander, by Marlowe, i. 315, 320; compared with Shakspere's *Venus and Adonis*, ii. 24.

Hero and Leander, by Sir R. Stapylton, notice of, iii. 336.

Herod and Antipater, by Markham and Sampson, iii. 156.

Herod and Mariamne, by S. Pordage, iii. 344 [3].

Herod the Great, by Lord Orrery, notice of, iii. 344.

Heroic Friendship, attributed to Otway, iii. 419 [1].

Heroic Love, by G. Granville, notice of, iii. 424.

Heroic Plays, their origin and development, iii. 500 *et seq.*

Heroic Plays, Of, Dryden's Essay, iii. 365.

Heroicall Epistles, by Michael Drayton, i. 437.

Hertzberg, Dr. W. A. B., on the versification of Shakspere, ii. 49 ; on *Troilus and Cressida,* ii. 148.

Herz, Henrik, his *King Réné's Daughter,* iii. 382 ³.

Hexham, The Battle of, attributed to Barnaby Barnes, ii. 627.

Heybridge, in Essex, *Harrowing of Hell* performed at, i. 55.

Heyes, printer of *The Merchant of Venice,* ii. 105.

Heywood, Jasper, his translations of Seneca, i. 195, 196.

Heywood, John, his *Interludes,* reference to the Coventry plays in, i. 84 ; his *Play of the Wether,* the 'vice' character in, i. 110 ⁴; his allegory, *The Spider and the Flie,* i. 136 ³; his *Dialogue of Wit and Folly,* i. 236 ; his *Interludes,* i. 238 *et seq.*; his mention of Will Summer, i. 423 ⁴.

Heywood, Thomas, on moralities, i. 141 ¹; his pageants, i. 147 ; his tribute to Marlowe, i. 319 ; his revision of Marlowe's *Jew of Malta,* i. 338 ²; on his contemporaries' familiar names, i. 469; his tribute to Shakspere in his *Hierarchie,* i. 500 ; Richard III in his *Edward IV,* ii. 100 ; *Cromwell* attributed to, ii. 234 ; his *Fortune by Land and Sea,* ii. 243, 569 ; his and others' *Sir Thomas Wyat,* ii. 468 ; his dramatic works, ii. 550–589 ; his life, ii. 551 ; *Apology for Actors,* ii. 552 ; as a play-wright, ii. 552 ; his non-dramatic works, ii. 554 ; *Edward IV,* ii. 555 ; *If You Know not me,* &c., ii. 558 ; *The Four Prentices of London,* ii. 559 ; *The Royal King and Loyal Subject,* ii. 560 ; *A Woman Killed with Kindness,* ii. 562 ; *The English Traveller,* ii. 565 ; *The Fair Maid of the West,* ii. 566 ; *The Captives,* ii. 567 ; *A Challenge for Beauty,* ii. 570 ; *A Maidenhead Well Lost,* ii. 571 ; *The Fair Maid of the Exchange,* ii. 572 ; *The Wise Woman of Hogsdon,* ii. 574 ; *The Late Lancashire Witches,* ii. 575 ; *The Golden, Silver, Brazen, and Iron Ages,* ii. 578 ; *The Rape of Lucrece,* ii. 581 ; *Love's Mistress,* ii. 582 ; non-extant plays by, ii. 583 ; pageants, ii. 584 ; prologues and epilogues, ii. 585 ; as a dramatist, ii. 585 ; 'a prose Shakspere,' ii. 587.

Hickson, Mr. S., on *The Two Noble Kinsmen,* ii. 239 ³.

Hierarchy of the Blessed Angels, The, by T. Heywood, familiar names of contemporaries enumerated in, i. 470 ; reference to Shakspere in, i. 500, ii. 554.

Higgenett, Randell, authorship of the Chester plays assigned to, i. 76.

Hilarion : *see* Prodromus.

Hilarius, his *Ludus super Iconia S. Nicolai,* i. 9 ²; the works of, i. 24 ; the plays of, i. 37.

Hilaro-tragedies, the, of Rhinthon of Tarentum, i. 210.

Hill, Aaron, his *Henry V,* ii. 128 ; his *Elfrid,* ii. 610 ²; his opera, *Rinaldo,* iii. 322¹; his dramatic works, iii. 430.

Hill, Dr. G. Birkbeck, his edition of Congreve's *Mourning Bride,* iii. 476 ⁴.

Hippolytus, the, of Seneca, translated by John Studley, i. 195.

Historia de Bello Africano, i. 370 ³.

Historia Scotorum, by Hector Boece, story of Macbeth in, ii. 172.

History of England, by S. Daniel, ii. 617.

History of Error, A, an early comedy, i. 263.

History of the Collier, The, i. 263.

History of the Foure Sonnes of Fabyous, The, an early English play, i. 208.

History of : see under *Jobe; Orlando Furioso; James IV; Robert second Duke of Normandy; Edward I; Edward II; Glaucus and Silla; Alphonsus; Friar Bacon,* &c., &c.

Histrio-Mastix, by Prynne, i. 507 ¹, iii. 240; Marston's share in, ii. 489.

Histriones, origin of, i. 16, 17 ; anglicised, i. 28, 48 ; interdicted, i. 50.

Hock Tuesday : *see* Hox Tuesday.

Hoffman, by Henry Chettle, i. 427 ; similarity to *Hamlet,* ii. 162.

Hog hath lost his Pearl, The, by Robert Tailor, iii. 157.

Holinshed, R., his *Chronicles,* Marlowe's obligation to, i. 350 ; the source of *Henry IV,* ii. 121; of *Henry V,* ii. 125; of *Macbeth,* ii. 172; of *King Lear,* ii. 176 ; of *Cymbeline,* ii. 190 ; of *Henry VIII,* ii. 207; of *Locrine,* ii. 200 ; of *Edward III,* ii. 222; Shakspere's general indebtedness to, ii. 260; Fletcher's *Bonduca* taken from, ii. 697.

Holland's Leaguer, by S. Marmion, a synopsis of, iii. 147.

Hollander, The, by Henry Glapthorne, iii. 153.

Holophernes, a play, i. 153.

Holyday, Barton, his *Technogamia,* iii. 176-178.

Homer, Chapman's, ii. 411.

Homulus, a Latin version of *Everyman,* by Christian Ischyrius, i. 120.

Honest Man's Fortune, The, by Beaumont and Fletcher, account of, ii. 687.

Honest Whore, The, by Dekker, account of, ii. 462.

Honoria and Mammon, by Shirley, notice of, iii. 101.

Honour of a London Prentice, a ballad, ii. 679.

Honour of the Garter, The, by George Peele, i. 365.

Honour of Women, attributed to Fletcher, ii. 748 [1]; ascribed to Massinger, iii. 9 [1].

Honourable Historie of : see under *Friar Bacon,* &c.

Hooft, P., his Senecan dramas, i. 193 [5].

Hope theatre, the, i. 458.

Hopkins, Charles, his *Boadicea,* ii. 697 [3]; his dramatic works, iii. 431.

Horace, by Corneille, Mrs. Catharine Philips' translation of, iii. 315 [1]; Charles Cotton's translation of, iii. 315 [1].

Horace's *Art of Poetry,* Jonson's translation of, ii. 330.

Horatius, translated from Corneille by Sir W. Lower, iii. 290.

Horestes, New interlude of Vice concerning, by John Pickering, i. 207, 208.

Horn, Franz, his Shaksperean criticism, i. 558.

Hornby, Mr. J., on the proceedings of the Council connected with Middleton's *Game of Chess,* ii. 497 [1].

Horne, R. H., his *Death of Marlowe,* i. 319; his adaptation of *The Honest Man's Fortune,* ii. 688.

Hoskyns, Serjeant John, a friend of Ben Jonson, ii. 321 [5].

How a Man may Chuse a Good Wife, &c., an anonymous play, notice of, ii. 608.

Howard, Edward, his plays, iii. 396.

Howard, James, his plays, iii. 396; his version of *Romeo and Juliet,* iii. 326 [1].

Howard, Sir Robert, his and Dryden's *Indian Queen,* iii. 348; his reply to Dryden's *Essay of Dramatic Poetry,* iii. 356; his dramatic works, iii. 393–396; his tragedies, iii. 394.

Howell, James, on Ben Jonson's dramatic works, ii. 334 [1].

Howes, Edmund, his estimate of Shakspere, i. 495 [1].

Hox Tuesday Play, i, 144.

Hrotsvitha, the comedies of, i. 6; moralities by, i. 101; her version of the story of *Theophilus,* i. 330.

Hudibras, the reflexion of the spirit of the times in, iii. 296 [1].

Hudson, H.N., his edition of Shakspere, i. 571.

Hue and Cry after Cupid, The, a masque by Ben Jonson, ii. 392 [2], 394.

Hübsch, G., his edition of Dekker's *Henry I,* ii. 466.

Hughes, John, his dramatic works, iii. 430.

Hughes, Thomas, his *Misfortunes of Arthur,* i. 218.

Hugo, F. V., his translation of Marlowe's *Dr. Faustus,* i. 329 [1]; on Shakspere, i. 561.

Hull, Thomas, an adaptation of Massinger's *Bashful Lover* attributed to, iii. 36 [1].

Humbert, C., his *Molière, Shakspeare und die deutsche Kritik,* ii. 275 [2].

Humfrey Duke of Gloucester, by Ambrose Philips, ii. 213 [1].

Humorous Courtier, The, by Shirley, iii. 118.

Humorous Dayes Myrth, by Chapman, ii. 433.

Humorous Lieutenant, The, by Fletcher, ii. 702.

Humorous Lovers, The, by the Duke of Newcastle, iii. 333.

Humour out of Breath, by John Day, ii. 596.

Humourists, The, by Shadwell, iii. 456.

Hunsdon, Lord, the patron of Lord Strange's acting company, ii. 26.

Hunt, Leigh, his edition of the plays of Wycherley, Congreve, Vanbrugh, and Farquhar, iii. 461 [1].

Hunter, Joseph, his Shaksperean criticism, i. 569; his *Life* of Shakspere, ii. 1 [1]; on Shakspere's *Tempest,* ii. 197.

Hunting of Cupid, The, by Peele, i. 368.

Huon and Auberon, ii. 85.

Husband his own Cuckold, The, by the younger Dryden, iii. 390 [1].

Hutten, Ulrich von, his dialogues, i. 233.

Hycke-Scorner, a morality, i. 118.

Hyde Park, by Shirley, account of, iii. 106.

Hymen's Holiday, by W. Rowley, ii. 546.

Hymen's Triumph, by S. Daniel, notice of, ii. 622.

Hymenaei, a masque by Ben Jonson, ii. 391 [1], 394.

Hyppolito and Isabella, Middleton's obligations to, ii. 512.

Ibrahim, by Mrs. Pix, iii. 432.
Ibrahim, Settle's adaptation of La Calprenède's *l'Illustre Bassa*, iii. 309 [2]; account of, iii. 396.
If this be not a Good Play, &c., by Dekker, compared with Jonson's *The Devil is an Ass*, ii. 372; quotation from, ii. 452 [1]; account of, ii. 465.
If You Know not Me, &c., by T. Heywood, notice of, ii. 558.
Ignoramus, by G. Ruggle, account of, iii. 183–187.
Ile of Guls, The, by John Day, notice of, ii. 595.
Iliad, Chapman's translation : see *Homer*.
Illustre Bassa, Le, by La Calprenède, Settle's adaptation of, iii. 309 [2].
Imposture, The, by Shirley, notice of, iii. 117.
Impostures of Thomas a Beckett, Of the, by Bishop Bale, i. 175.
Inconstant, The, by Farquhar, an adaptation of Fletcher's *Wild-Goose-Chase*, ii. 707 [4], iii. 326 [3]; notice of, iii. 483.
Indian drama, its treatment of the theme of *Hamlet*, ii. 165; women's parts in, iii. 251 [1]; plagiarism in, iii. 268 [2]; comparisons between themes of, and of plays by Dryden, iii. 376 [3], 383 [2].
Indian Emperor, The, by Dryden, notice of, iii. 349.
Indian legend, the theme of *King Lear* in, ii. 176.
Indian Queen, The, by Dryden and Sir R. Howard, notice of, iii. 348.
Ingannati, Gli, Shakspere's obligations to, in *Twelfth Night*, ii. 142, 143.
Ingelend, Thomas, his *Disobedient Child*, i. 250.
Ingleby, Dr. C. M., his pamphlet, *Was Thomas Lodge an Author?* i. 410 [4]; editor of *Shakspere Allusion Books*, i. 426 [2]; his *Shakespeare's Centurie of Prayse*, i. 491 [1]; his Shaksperean criticism, i. 569.
Ingram, Dr. J. K., on Shaksperean verse-tests, ii. 51 [1].
Injur'd Love, by Tate, iii. 428.
Injured Princess, The, by D'Urfey, an adaptation of Shakspere's *Cymbeline*, i. 514.
Inner Temple Masque, The, by Middleton, ii. 537.
Innocent Mistress, The, by Mrs. Manley, iii. 454.

Insatiate Countess, The, by Marston, a synopsis of, ii. 481.
Interlude, An, for a christening, by Ben Jonson, ii. 397.
Interlude of Youth, The, i. 126.
Interludes, a name given to moralities and early plays acted by professional performers, i. 108; early, i. 237; John Heywood's, i. 242 *seqq.*; Shakspere's use of, ii. 292.
Interludium de clerico et puella, the, i. 237.
Intimes, Les, by V. Sardou, ii. 377 [3].
Intrighi d'Amore, Gli, Shakspere's obligation to, in *A Midsummer Night's Dream*, ii. 85.
Invader of his Country, The, by John Dennis, an adaptation of Shakspere's *Coriolanus*, i. 515.
Invocation to Calliope, a poem by Beaumont and Fletcher, ii. 650.
Iphigenia, an early English tragedy, i. 208.
Iphigenia, by J. Dennis, iii. 426.
Iphigenias, Peele's version of one of the Euripidean, i. 364.
Iphigénie, by Racine, translated by A. Boyer, iii. 315 [1]; by C. Johnson, iii. 315 [1].
Iphis and Ianthe, a play, non-extant, attributed to Shakspere, ii. 213.
Ireland, William Henry, his literary forgeries, i. 563.
Irish Masque, The, by Ben Jonson, ii. 395 [1].
Irving, Dr. D., on *The History of Scottish Poetry*, i. 131.
Iscanus, Josephus, his *De Bello Trojano*, ii. 150.
Ischyrius, Christian, his *Homulus*, i. 120.
Island Princess, The, by Fletcher, a synopsis of, ii. 704; Tate's version of, iii. 326 [3], 428.
Isle of Dogs, The, by Thomas Nashe, i. 425.
Isle of Gulls : see *Ile of Guls*.
Italian drama, mysteries, i. 33 [3], 46; pageants, i. 146 [2]; the early, and its actors, i. 168; influence of the, on early English tragedies, i. 212 *et seq.*; early comedy, i. 226; at early Stuart period, iii. 264; its influence on later Stuart writers, iii. 302; opera, at later Stuart period, iii. 321.
Italian Husband, The, by E. Ravenscroft, iii. 429.
Italian Tragedy, The, by Day, ii. 591 [3].
Ite in vineam, a comedy, by Lord Berners, i. 219 [4].

Jack Drum's Entertainment, a satire on Ben Jonson, attributed to Marston, ii. 308.

Jack Juggler, the 'vice' a character in, i. 110 [1], 249.

Jack Strawe, The Life and Death of, by Peele, ii. 104 ; notice of, ii. 611.

Jacob, T. E., his edition of *The Birth of Merlin*, ii. 243 [3].

Jacob and Esau, a Northumbrian play, i. 74. (See also *Comedie of*.)

Jaggard, W., surreptitious publication of some of Shakspere's *Sonnets* by, ii. 25.

James I, his relations with Shakspere, i. 501 ; Shakspere's position at the accession of, ii. 36 ; his relations with Ben Jonson, ii. 309 ; his visits to Cambridge, and his delight at Ruggle's *Ignoramus*, iii. 184, 185 ; effect of his influence on drama, iii. 217, 221, 229.

James IV, The Scottish Historie of, by Robert Greene, i. 400 ; joint-authorship of, attributed to Lodge, i. 418.

Jameson, Mrs., her Shaksperean criticism, i. 569.

Jamieson, Mr. T. H., his edition of *The Ship of Fools*, i. 236 [2].

Jane Shore, by Chettle and Day, i. 428 [5].

Jane Shore, by Nicholas Rowe, account of, iii. 437.

Jane Shore, the ballad of, and various plays with the story of, ii. 557 [1].

Jansen, Cornelius, his portrait of Shakspere, ii. 42.

Jeaffreson, Mr. J. C., indictment against Ben Jonson at his first imprisonment discovered by, ii. 304 [3].

Jealous Lovers, The, by T. Randolph, iii. 133.

Jeronimo, The First Part of, i. 305 [1], 307, 308.

Jesters, in England, i. 27.

Jeux, the popular, origin of French farce, i. 21.

Jeux du Martire St. Étienne, the, i. 94 [1].

Jeux-partis, the, i. 21 [3].

Jeweller of Amsterdam, The, a nonextant play attributed to Fletcher, ii. 748.

Jew of Malta, The, by Marlowe, synopsis of, i. 337 *seqq.*; and *The Merchant of Venice*, i. 343–7, ii. 106 ; T. Heywood's revision of, ii. 584.

Jew of Venice, The, by George Granville (Lord Lansdowne), an adaptation of Shakspere's play, i. 514, iii. 424.

Jew of Venice, The, by Thomas Dekker, ii. 105.

Jew's Tragedy, The, by W. Heminge, iii. 162.

Jews, in Elisabethan England, i. 343.

Jigs, in Elisabethan theatres, definition of, i. 476.

Job, A History of, attributed to R. Greene, i. 407.

Job's Sufferings, by Ralph Radcliffe, i. 170 [2].

Jocasta, by George Gascoigne, i. 209, 262.

Joculatores, origin of the, i. 17.

Jodelle, Étienne, his *Cléopatre Captive* i. 193, 207 [1]; his *Didon se sacrifiant*, i. 357 [1]; his version of *Antony and Cleopatra*, ii. 186.

Johan Baptyste, by Bishop Bale, i. 176.

Johan, Kyng, by Bishop Bale, i. 142, 175, 177, ii. 102.

Johannes Baptista, one of the Towneley plays, i. 72.

John of Antioch, his *Barlaam and Jehoshaphat*, i. 121.

John of Bayeux, on *tableaux* in the liturgy, i. 34.

John of Damascus, the authorship of *Barlaam and Jehoshaphat* assigned to, i. 121.

John of Salisbury, his anathema on mimes and minstrels, i. 24.

John, King, Shakspere's, versification in, ii. 49 [2]; account of the play, ii. 100–102.

John, King, and Matilda, by R. Davenport, iii. 158.

John, King of England, The Troublesome Raigne of, &c., i. 185, 187 ; attributed to Marlowe, i. 359 ; to Greene, i. 407 ; to Lodge, i. 418.

John a Kent and John a Cumber, by Anthony Munday, i. 432.

John Bon and Mast' Parson, a dialogue, i. 235.

Johnson, Charles, his *Wife's Relief*, iii. 109 ; his *Fortune in her Wits*, iii. 187 [2]; his translation of Racine's *Iphigénie*, iii. 315 [1].

Johnson, Gerard, his statue of Shakspere, ii. 42.

Johnson, Samuel, his edition of Shakspere, i. 529 ; on the Unities, i. 530.

Jonas, by Ralph Radcliffe, i. 170 [2].

Jones, Mr. H. A., his *Patient Grizzle*, i. 429 [3].

Jones, Inigo, Ben Jonson a collaborator of, ii. 319, 320, 325, 391 ; possible impersonation of, in Jonson's *Bartholomew Fair*, ii. 371 ; his and Ben Jonson's masques, ii. 393 [2] *et seq.*

Jongleurs, origin of the, in France, i. 18 ;

in England, i. 20, 27 ; their influence on the drama in France, i. 21.

Jonson, Ben, on poetic laws, i. 2 ; his *Devil is an Ass*, i. 110, 115 [2]; on Skelton's works, i. 128 [4]; his tribute to John Lyly, i. 273 [4]; his obligations to *Euphues*, i. 282 [1], 285 [2]; his 'additions' to *The Spanish Tragedy*, i. 305; his tribute to Marlowe, i. 318; on Marlowe's diction, i. 327 [4], 328 [1]; references to Machiavelli, i. 339 [3]; his *The Case is Altered*, i. 346; on Anthony Munday, i. 432 [1]; on Michael Drayton in his *Underwoods*, i. 438; his tribute to Shakspere in the first Folio, i. 499, 509; on the Unities, and rules of the Greek drama, i. 531 [2]; a friend and associate of Shakspere, ii. 34; his references to *The Tempest*, ii. 199, 200. His dramatic works, ii. 269 *et seq.*; his literary fame, ii. 296; editions of his works, &c., ii. 296 [1]; life, ii. 298; first imprisonment, ii. 304; Queen Elisabeth and, ii. 306; habits and means, ii. 307; quarrel with Dekker and Marston, ii. 307; James I and, ii. 309; his masques and entertainments, ii. 309; voluntary imprisonment, ii. 311; Jonson and Chapman's second imprisonment, ii. 312; Jonson's connexion with the Gunpowder Plot, ii. 312; his career as a dramatic poet, ii. 312; patrons, ii. 314; his library, ii. 314; his taverns, ii. 313; his journeys to France and to Scotland, ii. 315; his visit to Drummond, ii. 316; his return to the stage, ii. 319; his death, ii. 321; traits of character, ii. 321; Shakspere and, ii. 326; Beaumont and Fletcher and, ii. 329; his non-dramatic works, ii. 330; his learning, ii. 331. Classification of his dramatic works, ii. 334; historical tragedies, ii. 335; *Sejanus his Fall*, ii. 336; *Catiline his Conspiracy*, ii. 339; *The Fall of Mortimer*, ii. 343; comedies, ii. 343; *Every Man in his Humour*, ii. 344; *Every Man out of his Humour*, ii. 346; *The Case is Altered*, ii. 350; *Cynthia's Revels*, ii. 352; *The Poetaster*, ii. 356; *Volpone, or the Fox*, ii. 361; *Epicoene, or the Silent Woman*, ii. 364; *The Alchemist*, ii. 367; *Bartholomew Fair*, ii. 369; *The Devil is an Ass*, ii. 372; *The Staple of News*, ii. 374; *The New Inn*, ii. 375; *The Magnetic Lady*, ii. 377; *Tale of a Tub*, ii. 378; his pastoral

dramas: *The Sad Shepherd*, ii. 379, 384; *The May Lord*, ii. 386; his masques, ii. 387; his character as a dramatist, ii. 394; his experience and observation of life, ii. 399; elevation of purpose, ii. 400; his humour, ii. 402; his pervading consciousness, ii. 405; his and others' *Eastward Hoe*, account of, ii. 441; his and others' *Robert of Scots*, ii. 467; *The Page of Plymouth*, ii. 467; possibly part-author in Middleton's *Widow*, ii. 520; his *Discourse of Poesie*, written against J. Campion and S. Daniel, ii. 617; on Fletcher, ii. 648, 650; his *New Inn* partly inserted in *Love's Pilgrimage*, ii. 694; his and Fletcher's *Bloody Brother*, ii. 734; his connexion with Fletcher, ii. 747; with R. Brome, iii. 126; his general literary influence, iii. 270; achievements of Jonson and his contemporaries, iii. 270 *et seq.*; his connexion with Shadwell, iii. 460.

Jonsonus Virbius, edited by Gifford, ii. 296 [1], 322 [1].

Joseph's Trouble about Mary, one of the York plays, i. 67 [3].

Josephus, Lodge's translations of, i. 415.

Joshua, by S. Rowley and W. Bourne, ii. 546.

Joueur, Le, by Regnard, Mrs. Centlivre's adaptation of, iii. 315 [1], 488 [3].

Journalisten, Die, by G. Freytag, ii. 374 [5].

Journey to London, A, by Vanbrugh, iii. 480.

Jovial Crew, by Brome, after Fletcher's *Beggars' Bush*, ii. 726 [2]; notice of, iii. 130.

Joyner, William, his dramatic works, iii. 431.

Judas, by W. Bourne and S. Rowley, ii. 546.

Judgment Day, The, in the York plays, i. 70.

Judgment of Paris, The, a masque by Congreve, iii. 477.

Juditium, the, one of the Towneley plays, i. 73, 76.

Jugglers, in England, i. 27, 50.

Julia Agrippina, by T. May, account of, iii. 143.

Juliana, by J. Crowne, notice of, iii. 400.

Julius and Hippolyta, ii. 80.

Julius Caesar, a Latin play by T. May, iii. 143.

Julius Caesar, by Lord Stirling, ii. 624.

Julius Caesar, Shakspere's, John Sheffield, Duke of Buckinghamshire's adaptation, i. 515; French versions, i. 536,

ii. 141, 142; Goethe's version, i. 553; versification of, ii. 49 [2]; observations on the play, ii. 138–142.

Julius Sesyar, an early play, i. 207.

Jusserand, M. J. J., on the legend of St. Catharine, i. 10 [2]; on R. Greene's prose tracts, i. 379 [3]; his *Shakespeare en France sous l'Ancien Régime*, i. 575.

Just Italian, The, by Sir W. D'Avenant, iii. 170.

Kalidasa, the *Sakontala* of, ii. 119.

Kallisto, by Baron K. S. von Seckendorff, founded on N. Rowe's *Tamerlane*, iii. 435 [3].

Katherine and Petruchio, an adaptation by Garrick of *The Taming of the Shrew*, ii. 96.

Kelly, an impostor satirised in *The Alchemist*, ii. 368 [3].

Kemble, Fanny, her 'Shakspere readings,' i. 558.

Kemble, J. M., his edition of *The Departed Soul's Address to the Body*, i. 12 [3].

Kemble, John and Charles, their renderings of Shaksperean characters, i. 563.

Kemp's Nine Daies Wonder, edited by Dyce, i. 472 [1].

Kempe, William, successor of Tarlton, i. 454 [1]; in the Netherlands, i. 472 [1]; his association with Shakspere, ii. 18 [1]; his part in *A Knacke to Knowe a Knave*, ii. 610.

Ken, Bishop, on St. Gregory the Nazianzene, i. 4 [2].

Kendal, religious plays performed at, i. 55.

Kenilworth, the great festivities at, i. 145, 155.

Kenrick, William, his *Falstaff's Wedding*, ii. 124.

Kett, Francis, possible influence of, on Marlowe, i. 314 [1].

Kilkenny, Bale's plays acted at, i. 175.

Killigrew, Dr. Henry, iii. 283 [6]; play by, published during the Commonwealth, iii. 286; his *Conspiracy*, iii. 163.

Killigrew, Thomas (the elder), his dramatic works, iii. 165, 166; his company of actors at the Restoration, iii. 283, 284; play by, published during the Commonwealth, iii. 286.

Killigrew, Thomas (the younger), his *Chit-Chat*, iii. 165 [2].

Kind Hart's Dreame, by Chettle, i. 426; reference to Shakspere in, i. 492 [1].

King and No King, A, by Beaumont and Fletcher, account of, ii. 676.

King John (also *Arthur, Lear, Edward, Darius, Cambises*, &c.): see under *John, Arthur, Lear*, &c.

King Réné's Daughter, by H. Herz, iii. 382 [3].

Kingsley, Dr. G. H., discoverer of the Brome play of *Abraham and Isaac*, i. 91.

Kinnaird, Douglas, his *Merchant of Bruges*, adapted from *Beggars' Bush*, ii. 726 [2].

'Kinsayder,' 'William,' Marston's *nom de plume*, ii. 474.

Kinwelmarsh, Francis, joint-author of *Jocasta*, i. 209.

Kirke, John, on classical ghosts, i. 192 [1]; his *Seven Champions of Christendom*, iii. 100 [1].

Kirkman, Francis, on authorship of *The Arraignment of Paris*, ii. 211; his *False Heir*, taken from *The Scornful Lady*, ii. 669 [1]; publisher of Webster's *Thracian Wonder*, iii. 55; his collection of drolls, iii. 280 [1].

Klein, J. L., on early Italian and Spanish mysteries, i. 46 [1]; on Shakspere's *Othello*, ii. 169.

Kleist, Heinrich v., his *Zerbrochener Krug*, i. 261 [2].

Klette, Dr. J., on Wycherley, iii. 461 [1].

Klinger, F. M. von, on Shakspere, i. 551.

Knack to Know an Honest Man, A, ii. 611 [1].

Knacke to Knowe a Knave, A, an anonymous play, account of, i. 142, ii. 609, 610.

Knight, Charles, his Shaksperean research, i. 569, 570; his *Life* of Shakspere, ii. 1 [1]; on *Hamlet*, ii. 158; on *Timon of Athens*, ii. 179; his edition of doubtful Shaksperean plays, ii. 213 [4].

Knight of Malta, The, by Beaumont and Fletcher, account of, ii. 688.

Knight of the Burning Pestle, The, by Beaumont and Fletcher, ii. 679.

Knight's Conjuring, A, by Dekker, i. 365, ii. 455.

Knowles, Sheridan, his *Beggar of Bethnal Green*, ii. 599 [5]; his *Bridal*, ii. 674 [1]; his adaptation of Fletcher's *Noble Gentleman*, ii. 739 [1].

Koberstein, A., on Shakspere in Germany, i. 547, 551 [4].

König, W., jun., on Voltaire and Shakspere, i. 535; on Shakspere's education, ii. 10 [1]; on Shakspere's Histories, ii. 259 [1].

Koepke, R., on Hrotsvitha's comedies, i. 7 [3].

Koeppel, E., on Ben Jonson, ii. 296 [1]; on Chapman's play-sources, ii. 408 [1], 423 [1] *et seq.*; on the sources of the plays of Beaumont and Fletcher, ii. 643 [1]; on Massinger's plays, iii. 2 [1].

Kongehl, Michael, his treatment of Shaksperean subjects, i. 546.

Kruse, Heinrich, his *Mädchen v. Byzanz*, iii. 139 [2].

Kyd, Thomas, his life and works, i. 303; his relations with Marlowe, i. 317; *Titus Andronicus*, attributed to, ii. 55; his *Spanish Tragedy* compared with *Hamlet*, ii. 164.

Kyng Johan : see *Johan, Kyng*.

Lacy, John, his *Sauny the Scot*, an adaptation of Shakspere's *Taming of the Shrew*, i. 514; his dramatic works, iii. 449-451; *Dumb Lady*, iii. 449; *Old Troop*, iii. 450; *Sir Hercules Buffoon*, iii. 450.

Ladies à-la-Mode, a non-extant play attributed to Dryden, iii. 353 [2].

Ladies' Priviledge, The, by Henry Glapthorne, account of, iii. 151.

Lady Alimony, iii. 170 [5].

Lady Contemplation, by the Duchess of Newcastle, iii. 335 [5].

Lady-Errant, The, by W. Cartwright, notice of, iii. 139.

Lady Fitzwater's Nightingale : see *Philomela*.

Lady Jane, by Dekker and others, ii. 468.

Lady Jane Grey, Tragedy of, by Nicholas Rowe, iii. 437.

Lady Mother, The, attributed to Henry Glapthorne, iii. 154.

Lady of May, The, by Sidney, i. 268 [1].

Lady of Pleasure, The, by Shirley, iii. 114.

Lady's Last Stake, The, by Colley Cibber, iii. 487.

Lady's Trial, The, by Ford, iii. 73; a synopsis of, iii. 83.

Laemmerhirt, Dr., on George Peele, i. 363 [1].

La Fayette, Mme. de, her works and their influence, iii. 309.

La Harpe, J. F. de, on Shakspere and Voltaire, i. 539.

Laing, D., on Lodge's works, i. 409 [1]; his edition of Jonson's and Drummond's *Conversations*, ii. 296 [1].

L'Allegro, Milton's reference to Shakspere in, i. 519 [1].

Lamb, Charles, on Marlowe's *Edward II*, i. 351 [2]; his Shaksperean criticisms, i. 567; the *Tales*, i. 568; on Dekker's works, ii. 451, 463 [2]; on Middleton's *Witch*, ii. 505, 506; *A Faire Quarrell*, ii. 509; on Heywood's *Fair Maid of the Exchange*, ii. 572, 587; on Day's *Parliament of Bees*, ii. 593; on Porter's *Two Angry Women*, ii. 604; on Beaumont and Fletcher, ii. 645; on *Four Playes in One*, ii. 668.

Lame Commonwealth, The, after Fletcher's *Beggars' Bush*, ii. 726 [2].

Lamentacion for the decease of the Mass, by Roy and Barlow, i. 235 [1].

Lancashire dialect, Mr. G. Milner on, ii. 578 [1].

Lancashire Witches, The, by J. Heywood and Brome, i. 331 [2].

Lancashire Witches, The, by Shadwell, account of, iii. 458.

Lancaster, religious plays performed at, i. 55.

Landivio, his tragedy of *Captivity*, i. 169.

Landlady, The, after Fletcher's *Chances*, ii. 712 [3].

Landmann, Dr. F., on Euphuism, i. 276 [4].

Landor, Walter Savage, his *Citation and Examination of William Shakespeare*, ii. 16 [4].

Laneham, R., on the Kenilworth pageants, i. 155 [2].

Langbaine, G., criticisms on Shakspere, i. 522; on *Two Wise Men*, ii. 447; his criticisms on Dryden, iii. 389 [4].

Langton, Etienne (Stephen), the works of, i. 10 [2], 25, 42, 51, 105.

Lankveld : *see* Macropedius.

Lansdowne, Lord: *see* Granville, G.

Lanthorne and Candlelight, by Dekker, ii. 454 [1], 456.

Laodicea, Bishop of, identified with the dramatist Apollinaris, i. 4.

Laplace, his *Théâtre Anglais*, i. 536, 537.

Larum for London, A, attributed to Shakspere, ii. 211.

La Taille, Jacques de, his *Darius*, ii. 625 [5].

Late Lancashire Witches, The, by T. Heywood and Brome, a synopsis of, ii. 575.

Latham, Mr. Baldwin, on the Plague in London, i. 576.

Latimer, Bishop, his *Sermons*, comparison of London to Nineveh in, i. 402 [1].

Laude, the Italian, in the Mass, i. 33 [3].

Laudesi, the, i. 33.

Law, William, his anti-theatrical publications, iii. 512.

Law Against Lovers, The, an adaptation by D'Avenant, i. 513.

Lawes, Henry, his music to Cartwright's *Royal Slave*, iii. 138; his music to Strode's *Floating Island*, iii. 182; to Carew's *Coelum Britannicum*, iii. 192; his music to Milton's *Arcades*, iii. 197; to *Comus*, iii. 198, 199; to D'Avenant's *Siege of Rhodes*, &c., iii. 281[2].

Laws of Candy, The, by Fletcher, account of, ii. 723.

Law-Tricks, by John Day, account of, ii. 598.

Lazarus, one of the Chester plays, i. 80 (see *Suscitatio Lazari*).

Leanerd, John, his adaptations of Brewer and Middleton's works, iii. 326[4].

Lear, King, Shakspere's, Ducis' version of, i. 538; Ireland's forgery, i. 564; probable date of production of, ii. 37; versification of, ii. 49[2]; observations on the play, ii. 174–177; Tate's version of, iii. 326[1], 428.

Lecky, Mr. W. H., on early Scottish drama, i. 131.

Lee, Miss Margaret, her edition of *Narcissus*, ii. 642[2].

Lee, Nathaniel, his adaptations of La Calprenède's *Cléopâtre, Pharamond*, and *Cassandre*, iii. 309[2]; his and Dryden's *Œdipus*, iii. 373; his and Dryden's *Duke of Guise*, iii. 377; his *Massacre of Paris*, iii. 378; his dramatic works, iii. 407–412; *Nero*, iii. 408; *Sophonisba*, iii. 408; *Gloriana*, iii. 409; *The Rival Queens*, iii. 409; *Mithridates*, iii. 410; *Theodosius*, iii. 410; *Caesar Borgia*, iii. 410; *Lucius Junius Brutus*, iii. 410; *Constantine the Great*, iii. 411; *The Princess of Cleve*, iii. 411; *The Massacre of Paris*, iii. 411; his influence as a dramatist, iii. 502.

Lee, Mr. Sidney, on the heroine of Shakspere's *Sonnets*, ii. 764.

'Lee,' 'Vernon,' his *Euphorion*, on the English drama and the Italian Renascence, iii. 215[1].

Leeds, the religious drama performed at, i. 55.

Le Fèvre, Raoul, his *Recueil des Histoires de Troyes*, ii. 152.

Legend of Piers Gaveston, The, by Michael Drayton, i. 437.

Legenda Aurea, the, by Jacobus Voragine, i. 120.

Legends, the literature of, i. 437.

Legge, Dr. Thomas, his *Richardus Tertius*, ii. 97.

Leicester, the Earl of, his patronage of plays, i. 156; his impersonation in Lyly's *Endimion*, i. 291.

Leicester, the religious drama performed at, i. 56.

Leisewitz, J. A., on Shakspere, i. 551.

Leland, John, on early English historians and writers, i. 171[1].

Lennox, Mrs., her *Shakespear Illustrated*, i. 530[1].

Lenten Stuffe, by Thomas Nashe, i. 419[1], 421, 425[2].

Lenz, J. M. R., on Shakspere, i. 551, 552.

Leon, Melchior de, Fletcher's obligations to his *Conquista de las Moluccas*, ii. 705.

Leonico, Angelo, his *Soldato*, ii. 228[4].

Leopold Shakspere, The, ii. 1[1], 49[1], 54[1].

Lessing, G. E., on tragedy, i. 159[3]; his eminence in Shaksperean criticism, i. 544, 547.

Leto, Pomponio, his comedies, i. 228.

Letourneur, Pierre, his French edition of Shakspere, i. 538.

Letter to the Gentlemen Students of both Universities, by Thomas Nashe, i. 390, 396[3].

Levellers, The, Levelled, by Needham, iii. 292[3].

Lewes, G. H., on Beaumont and Fletcher's obligations to Spanish literature, ii. 753[6].

Lewis the Pious, his attitude towards the mimes, i. 16.

Liber Alani de Planctu Naturae, allegorical figures in, i. 25[1].

Libertine, The, by Shadwell, iii. 457[2].

Liberty Asserted, by J. Dennis, iii. 426.

Life of: see under *Doctor Faustus; William Longbeard; Capt. Thomas Stukely*, &c.

Like wil to Like quod the Devel to the Colier, by Ulpian Fulwel, i. 134.

Lillie de Tristibus, addressed by John Lyly to Elisabeth, i. 273.

Lillo, George, his adaptation of *Arden of Feversham*, ii. 217.

Limberham, by Dryden, iii. 373.

Lincoln, Earl of, a character in Greene's *Friar Bacon*, i. 398[2].

Lincoln's Inn Fields theatres, iii. 284, 284[3].

Lindo Don Diego, El, by Moreto, iii. 304[1].

Ling, Nicholas, printer of fourth Quarto of *Hamlet*, ii. 157.

Lingua, attributed to John Tomkis, synopsis of, iii. 174–176.

Lista, Don Alberto, on Lope de Vega, ii. 754 [2].

Litany, the, a part of the Mass, i. 33.

Little French Lawyer, The, by Fletcher, notice of, ii. 720.

Littledale, Mr. H., his edition of Fletcher's *Two Noble Kinsmen*, ii. 237 [2], 745 [1].

Liturgy, original meaning of the term, i. 29 ; symbolism in the liturgy of the Mass, i. 30; dramatic element of, i. 32 ; the developement of, i. 33 ; processions in, i. 33 ; introduction of *tableaux* into, i. 34.

Livy, his influence on early English play-wrights, i. 208.

Lochlomond Pastoral, a fragment by Ben Jonson, ii. 319.

Lock, Matthew, his early operatic compositions, iii. 323, 330.

Lockhart, J. G., his collaboration with Scott in editing Shakspere, i. 568 [2].

Locrine, authorship of attributed to Marlowe, i. 360; attributed to Shakspere, ii. 210; account of, ii. 219–221.

Lodge, Thomas, an imitator of John Lyly, i. 281 ; his and Greene's *Looking Glasse for London and England*, i. 402, 411 ; his life and works, i. 409 ; *Wounds of Civil War*, i. 416; possible part-author of the *Henry VI* plays, ii. 73 ; his *Rosalynde*, Shakspere's obligations to, ii. 129 ; *Mucedorus* attributed to, ii. 226 ; *Sir Thomas More* attributed to Drayton and, ii. 215 ; his *Complaint of Elstred*, ii. 220.

Logan : *see* Maidment and.

Lohenstein, Daniel Casper von, his *Cleopatra*, ii. 187.

Loiola, a Latin play by John (Bishop) Hacket, iii. 186 [1].

London, religious plays performed in, i. 49, 56 ; pageants, i. 146 ; exhortations to the citizens of, in early literature, i. 402 [1] ; its centralisation an important influence on the earlier Stuart drama, iii. 221, 222.

London Cuckolds, The, by Edgar Ravenscroft, iii. 451.

London Prodigal, The, attributed to Shakspere, ii. 210 ; account of the play, ii. 228, 229.

London's Jus Honorarium, and other pageants, by T. Heywood, ii. 584.

Longer thou livest, &c., by W. Wager, i. 137.

Looke About You, an anonymous play, ii. 611.

Looking Glasse for London and England, A, by Robert Greene and Thomas Lodge, i. 402, 411, 413 [2], 414, 417.

Lopez, Dr. Roderigo, hanged for treason, i. 345, ii. 107.

Lord's Masque, The, by T. Campion, iii. 191.

Lost Lady, The, by Sir W. Berkeley, iii. 163.

Lost Lover, by Mrs. Manley, iii. 454.

Lot and Abraham, Histories of, one of the Chester plays, i. 78.

Love, James, his version of *Timon of Athens*, ii. 180.

Love and a Bottle, by Farquhar, notice of, iii. 482.

Love and Honour, by Sir W. D'Avenant, notice of, iii. 172.

Love and Revenge : see *Fatal Contrast*.

Love at a Loss, by Mrs. Trotter, iii. 432 [3].

Love at a Venture, by Mrs. Centlivre, iii. 490.

Love Despised, taken from *Cupid's Revenge*, ii. 684.

Love for Love, by Congreve, notice of, iii. 473.

Love Freed from Ignorance and Folly, a masque by Ben Jonson, ii. 395.

Love in a Wood, by W. Wycherley, notice of, iii. 463.

Love Makes a Man, by Colley Cibber, iii. 486.

Love of King David and Fair Bethsabe, The, by Peele, i. 376.

Love Restored, a masque by Ben Jonson, ii. 385 [2], 395.

Love-Sick Court, The, by R. Brome, iii. 127 [5], 129.

Love-sick King, The, by Antony Brewer, iii. 174, 175.

Love-Tricks, by Shirley, iii. 103.

Love Triumphant, by Dryden, iii. 385.

Love unloved, labour ill lost, a poem, ii. 77, 78.

Love's Contrivance, by Mrs. Centlivre, iii. 488 [3].

Love's Cruelty, by Shirley, iii. 97.

Love's Cure, by Beaumont and Fletcher, a synopsis of, ii. 691.

Love's Labour's Lost, Shakspere's, Gongora impersonated in, i. 276 ; Lenz's translation, i. 551 [5] ; one of Shakspere's first efforts, ii. 22 ; versification of, ii. 48 [1], 49 [1] ; remarks on the play, ii. 76–79 ; a typical Shaksperean comedy, ii. 273.

Love's Labour's Won, Shakspere part-author of, ii. 22 [1].

Love's Last Shift, by Colley Cibber, notice of, iii. 486.

Love's Martyr, by Robert Chester, Shakspere's contribution to, ii. 31.

Love's Metamorphosis, by John Lyly, i. 301.

Love's Mistresse, by T. Heywood, notice of, ii. 582.

Love's Pilgrimage, by Fletcher and others, original source of plot, ii. 213; notice of, ii. 693.

Love's Riddle, by Abraham Cowley, iii. 164[1].

Love's Sacrifice, by Ford, iii. 81.

Love's Triumph, a masque by Ben Jonson, ii. 397.

Love's Triumph, by Edward Cooke, iii. 295[1].

Love's Victory, by W. Chamberlayne, iii. 289.

Love's Welcome at Bolsover, a masque by Ben Jonson, ii. 391[3], 397.

Love's Welcome at Welbeck, a masque by Ben Jonson, iii. 397.

Lovelace, Richard, his *Scholar*, iii. 164; *Soldier*, iii. 164.

Lover's Complaint, A, Shakspere's authorship of, ii. 32.

Lover's Melancholy, The, Ford's, assigned to Shakspere, ii. 211; account of, iii. 76.

Lover's Progress, The, by Fletcher, account of, ii. 730.

Lovers Made Men, a masque by Ben Jonson, ii. 396.

Lowder, Mr. Charles, on the Oberammergau play, i. 63[1].

Lowe, Mr. Robert W., his *Thomas Betterton*, i. 511[1]; his edition of Colley Cibber's *Apology*, iii. 486[2].

Lower, Sir William, his dramatic works, iii. 290, 292; *Phoenix in her Flames*, iii. 290; translations by, iii. 290; *Enchanted Lovers*, iii. 291; *Amorous Fantasme*, iii. 291.

Lowin, John, his rendering of Falstaff, ii. 137; an actor and innkeeper, iii. 278[1].

Loyal Brother, The, by T. Southerne, iii. 420.

Loyal Citizens, The, taken from *Cupid's Revenge*, ii. 684.

Loyal General, The, by Tate, iii. 428.

Loyal Subject, The, by Fletcher, a synopsis of, ii. 699.

Lucian, Heywood's selections from, ii. 554[1], 585; Jasper Mayne's translations of, iii. 140.

Lucian, Life of, by Dryden, iii. 386[2].

Lucifer, by Vondel, iii. 380.

Lucifer, The Fall of, one of the Chester plays, i. 77.

Lucius, by Mrs. Manley, iii. 432[1].

Lucius Junius Brutus, by N. Lee, iii. 410.

Lucrèce, by Ponsard, iii. 411[2].

Lucy, Sir Thomas, ii. 5[1]; and the deer-stealing story, ii. 17.

Ludi Beatae Christinae, the, at Bethersden, Kent, i. 50[1].

Ludus Coventriae s. Ludus Corpus Christi (Coventry plays), i. 84.

Ludus de S. Katharina, performed at Dunstable, i. 10, 48, 49.

Ludus Septem Sapientium, attributed to D. Magnus Ausonius, i. 5[3].

Ludus super Iconia S. Nicolai, by Hilarius, i. 9[2], 40.

Lüders, F., on Shakspere's prologues and epilogues, ii. 290, 291.

Lusores, in England, i. 27.

Lust's Dominion, authorship attributed to Marlowe, i. 360; identified as Chettle's *Spanish Moor's Tragedy*, i. 428[5]; attributed to Dekker, ii. 467; Day's possible share in, ii. 591[4]; Mrs. Behn's adaptation of, iii. 326[5].

Lusty Juventus, by R. Wever, i. 124; the play within the play of *Sir Thomas More*, ii. 216[1].

Lusty London, by George Puttenham, i. 442[4].

Lyar, The, by Foote, iii. 495[2].

Lycophron, early Christian dramas modelled on, i. 4.

Lydgate, John, on jugglers and minstrels, i. 50, 50[3]; his pageants, i. 53; on Henry V's pageant, i. 147[2]; his *Troy-Booke*, ii. 152.

Lying Lover, The, by Steele, an adaptation of Corneille's *Menteur*, iii. 315[1]; a synopsis of, iii. 495.

Lyly, John, his life, i. 271; his works, i. 274; his prose, i. 282; his verse, i. 286; his dramatic works, i. 286; plays ascribed to, i. 302; his influence on contemporary literature, i. 443; on the Marprelate controversy in *A Pappe with an Hatchet*, i. 464[4], 465[5]; original genius of, i. 478; his *Endimion*, date of publication, i. 574; his influence on Shakspere's comedies, ii. 273; his attack on the alchemists in *Gallathea*, ii. 368[1].

Lyndsay, Sir David, his *Satyre of the Thrie Estaits*, i. 131, 537; his *Philotus*, i. 131[1].

Mabbe, James, his edition of the *Celestina*, i. 232[1].

Mabillon, J., on Hilarius and his plays, i. 37.

Macaulay, Mr. G. C., on Beaumont, ii. 643[1].

Macbeth, Shakspere's, Ducis' version of, i. 538; Schiller's version, i. 553; Deschamps' version, i. 561[2]; first performance of, ii. 37; versification of, ii. 49[2], 51[2]; observations on the play, ii. 170–173; compared with Middleton's *Witch*, ii. 505; Milton's scheme for dramatic treatment of, iii. 202[1]; D'Avenant's version of Shakspere's, Lock's music to, iii. 323, 330.

Machiavell and the Devil, by R. Daborne, i. 339[3].

Machiavelli, N., his comedies, i. 229; his appearances in Elisabethan literature, i. 339[3]; his *History of Florence*, Middleton's obligations to, ii. 505.

Machiavellus, by D. Wiburne, i. 339[3]; produced at Cambridge, ii. 632.

Machin, Lewis, a collaborator of Gervase Markham in *The Dumb Knight*, iii. 155.

Mackenzie, Henry, his Shaksperean criticisms, i. 563.

M᷄Laughlin, Prof. E. T., his edition of Marlowe's *Edward II*, i. 347[1].

Macray, Mr. W. D., his edition of *The Parnassus Plays*, ii. 633[1].

Macready, W. C., his appearance in Sheridan Knowles' *Bridal*, ii. 674[1]; his revival of *Comus*, iii. 199[1].

'Macro Moralities,' the, i. 113[3], 116[1].

Macropedius, author of *Hekastus*, i. 120.

M᷄Swiney, his opera, *Camilla*, iii. 322[1].

Mactacio Abel, one of the Towneley plays, i. 73.

Mad Couple Well Matched, A, by R. Brome, iii. 128.

Mad Lover, The, by Fletcher, a synopsis of, ii. 701.

Mad Men of Gotham, Merry Tales of the, attributed to Andrew Boorde, ii. 610[3].

Mad Pranks of Merry Moll, The, by John Day, a non-extant work, ii. 592.

Mad World, My Masters, A, by Middleton, i. 441, ii. 518; an adaptation by Mrs. Behn, iii. 326[5].

Madcap, The, attributed to Barnaby Barnes, ii. 627.

Mador, King of Britain, attributed to Beaumont, ii. 743.

Mädchen von Byzanz, Das, by H. Kruse, iii. 139[2].

Mähly, J., on Poliziano's *Orfeo*, i. 231[1].

Maerlant, on the Story of Troy, ii. 151.

Magi, the, in the Chester plays, i. 80.

Magico Prodigioso, El, by Calderon, i. 330.

Magnetic Lady, The, or Humours Reconciled, by Ben Jonson, a synopsis of, ii. 377.

Magnin, A., his translation of Hrotsvitha's comedies, i. 7[3].

Magnon, J., his *Seianus*, ii. 339.

Magnus Herodes, one of the Towneley plays, i. 71.

Magnyfycence, by John Skelton, i. 128.

Mahomet, a play attributed to Peele, i. 374.

Maid in the Mill, The, by Fletcher and W. Rowley, notice of, ii. 729.

Maid of Honour, The, by Massinger, notice of, iii. 19.

Maid's Last Prayer, The, by T. Southerne, iii. 421.

Maid's Metamorphosis, The, attributed to John Lyly, i. 302.

Maid's Revenge, The, by Shirley, notice of, iii. 95.

Maid's Tragedy, The, by Beaumont and Fletcher, account of, ii. 672; Waller's version of, iii. 326[3].

Maiden's Holiday, The, authorship of, attributed to Marlowe, i. 360; attributed to Day and Marlowe, ii. 591[?].

Maidenhead Well Lost, A, by T. Heywood, notice of, iii. 571.

Maidment, James, and W. H. Logan, Messrs., their edition of the works of Shackerley Marmion, iii. 146[1]; of Sir William D'Avenant, iii. 166[3]; of John Wilson's plays, iii. 337[2]; of John Crowne's works, iii. 398[4]; of John Lacy's works, iii. 449[1].

Maine, Jasper, on the literary partnership of Beaumont and Fletcher, ii. 657[1].

Maître Pathelin, acted by the Basoche, i. 226[3].

Malam, Mr. John, on Shakspere's marriage, ii. 14.

Malcontent, The, by Marston, dedicated to Ben Jonson, ii. 310; by Webster and Marston, account of, ii. 483; Webster's revision of, iii. 52.

Mall, Dr. E., his edition of *The Harrowing of Hell*, i. 90[1].

Malone, Edmund, on the authorship of *Tamburlaine*, i. 321; on the relations between Elisabeth and Shakspere, i. 502[1]; his edition of Shakspere, i. 532; his *Shakspeare*, i. 505[2] *et seq.*; his *Inquiry* into the Ireland MSS., i. 565; his Shaksperean biographical data, ii. 1[1]; the chronology of Shakspere's plays deduced from his *Life* of *Shakspeare*, ii. 54 [1]; on *Measure for Measure*, ii. 153, 154; on *Coriolanus*, ii. 189; on doubtful Shaksperean plays, ii. 210; on *Locrine*, ii. 219.

Mamamouchi, by Edward Ravenscroft, iii. 451.

Mamillia, a Mirror or Looking-Glass for the Ladies of England, by Robert Greene, i. 381, 386.

Man of Mode, The, by Sir George Etheredge, account of, iii. 446.

Mankind, a morality, i. 116.

Manley, Mrs., her dramatic works, iii. 432, 454.

Manningham, John, his *Diary*, mention of *Twelfth Night* in, ii. 142.

Manningtree, religious plays performed at, i. 56 [2].

Man's Master, The, by D'Avenant, iii. 330.

Manuel, Don Juan, his *El Conde Lucanor*, ii. 95.

Manuel, Nicholas, his *Sickness of the Mass*, i. 235 [1].

Manuel des Pechiez, Le, i. 52.

Map, Walter, his writings, i. 25.

Marco Aurelio, El Libro de, by Guevara, i. 280.

Marco Bruto, by Conti, ii. 142.

Margarite of America, A, by T. Lodge, i. 414.

Mariamne, by E. Fenton, iii. 344 [3].

Marie Magdalen's Lamentations, by Gervase Markham, i. 88.

Marinism, i. 275, 276 [1].

Marius and Sylla, Lodge's: see *Wounds of Civil War*.

Markham, Gervase, authorship of *Marie Magdalen's Lamentations* attributed to, i. 88; his works, iii. 155, 156.

Marlowe, Christopher (or Kit), his life, i. 313; his reputation among his contemporaries, i. 317; non-dramatic works, i. 320; *Tamburlaine*, i. 321; *Doctor Faustus*, i. 329; *Jew of Malta*, i. 337; *Edward II*, i. 347; *Massacre at Paris*, i. 354; *Dido*, i. 356; plays attributed to, i. 358; summary, i. 360; his treatment of tragic themes, i. 482; his influence on Shakspere, ii. 23; possibly author of *Titus Andronicus*, ii. 56; the *Henry VI* plays attributed to, ii. 66, 73; *Richard III* partly attributed to, ii. 99; *Locrine* assigned to, ii. 220; *Edward III* assigned to, ii. 223; *The Maiden's Holiday* attributed to Day and, ii. 591 [2].

Marmion, Shackerley, his works, iii. 146–148; *Holland's Leaguer*, iii. 147; *The Fine Companion*, iii. 147; *The Antiquary*, iii. 147, 148; *The Crafty Merchant*, iii. 148 [1].

Marmontel, J. F., his version of *Antony and Cleopatra*, ii. 186.

Marplot in Lisbon, by Mrs. Centlivre, notice of, iii. 490.

Mar-Prelate controversy, the, John Lyly's part in, i. 272; Thomas Nashe's part in, i. 419; Munday's part in, i. 432 [1]; effect on contemporary literature, i. 442 [1]; an account of, i. 462; authorities on, i. 463 [1]; Martin Mar-Prelate on the stage, i. 465.

Marriage à-la-Mode, by Dryden, account of, iii. 366.

Marriage Night, The, by Henry Lord Falkland, iii. 335, 336.

Marriage of Wit and Wisdom, The, a morality, i. 135.

Marriage of Witte and Science, The, a morality, i. 134.

Married Beau, The, by J. Crowne, iii. 407.

Marshal Osrick, a non-extant play by T. Heywood, ii. 560 [4].

Marshall, Mr. Frank A., on *Hamlet*, ii. 167.

Marston, John, his obligations to Lyly, i. 285; his *Dutch Courtezan*, i. 402 [1], ii. 486; Ben Jonson's quarrel with, ii. 307, 325, 356; their reconciliation, ii. 310; his disgrace together with Chapman and Ben Jonson, ii. 311; his and others' *Eastward Hoe*, account of, ii. 441, 489; his dramatic works, ii. 472–493; his life, ii. 474; his quarrel with Ben Jonson, ii. 475, 476, 489; *Antonio and Mellida*, ii. 477; *Antonio's Revenge*, ii. 478; *The Wonder of Women*, ii. 480; *The Insatiate Countess*, ii. 481; *The Malcontent*, ii. 483; *Parasitaster*, ii. 485; *What you Will*, ii. 488; *Histriomastix*, ii. 489; *Jack Drum*, ii. 490; as a dramatist, ii. 491; Webster's collaboration with in *The Malcontent*, iii. 52.

Marston, Dr. Westland, his version of Moreto's *Desden con el Desden*, iii. 304 [1].

Martelli, L., his *Tullia*, i. 169 [4].

Martin, Lady, on Shakspere's Rosalind, ii. 132. (*See* Faucit, Helen.)

Martin, Sir Theodore, his version of H. Herz's *King René's Daughter*, iii. 382 [3].

Martyr'd Souldier, The, by Henry Shirley, iii. 157.

Marvell, Andrew, his *Rehearsal Transposed*, iii. 363 [3]; his *Tom May's Death*, iii. 142 [2].

'Marvels,' a synonym of 'miracles,' i. 57 [3].

Mary Magdalene, the play of, i. 57.

Mary Magdalene, one of the Digby mysteries, i. 88 [1], 94, 95 [2].

Mary Magdalene, The Repentance of, by Wager, the 'vice' a character in, i. 110 [1], 112 [1].

Mary I, Queen, introduced into the play *Respublica,* i. 136; plays prohibited by, i. 153.

Mary II, her patronage of the stage, iii. 295; and her influence on the drama, iii. 509 [2].

Masaker of France, The, identified as *The Guise,* by Webster, i. 355 [3].

Maskell, W., his *History of the Marprelate Controversy,* i. 463 [1].

Mason, John Monck, on various editions of Shakspere, i. 533; on Beaumont and Fletcher, ii. 643 [1]; his edition of Massinger, iii. 2 [1].

Mason, William, his *Elfrida,* ii. 610 [2]; his *Caractacus,* ii. 697 [3].

Masque of Augurs, The, by Ben Jonson, ii. 396.

Masque of Beauty, The, by Ben Jonson, ii. 394.

Masque of Blackness, The, by Ben Jonson, first performance of, ii. 310, 394.

Masque of Cupid, The, by Middleton, ii. 495.

Masque of Flowers, The, iii. 192.

Masque of Inner Temple, &c., *The,* by Beaumont, ii. 650.

Masque of Lethe, The, by Ben Jonson, ii. 396.

Masque of Owls, The, performed at Kenilworth, i. 145, ii. 397.

Masque of Queens, The, by Jonson, i. 331 [2], ii. 392 [2], 394.

Masque of the Middle Temple, The, by Chapman, ii. 441.

Masque presented at Brethie, by Sir Aston Cockayne, iii. 194 [1].

Masques, i. 150; Shakspere's use of, ii. 292. By Ben Jonson, ii. 387; his success as a writer of, ii. 389; characteristics of, ii. 391; lyrical passages, ii. 393; a list of, ii. 393 [2]–397. Of the later Elisabethan period, ii. 627; prevalence of drama over, ii. 629; by Sir W. D'Avenant, iii. 173; examples of, in reigns of James I and Charles I, iii. 188 *et seq.*; Milton's productions in the sphere of, iii. 195 *et seq.*; general view of, at early Stuart period, iii. 274.

Masques and Triumphs, Francis Bacon on, i. 219.

Mass, the dramatic element in the, i. 29, 32.

Massacre of Paris, The, by Marlowe, i. 354.

Massacre of Paris, The, by N. Lee, iii. 378, 411.

Massey, Gerald, on Shakspere's *Sonnets,* as bearing on his married life, ii. 15 [2]; on Shakspere's *Henry VIII,* ii. 203.

Massinger, Philip, part-authorship of *Henry VIII* attributed to, ii. 206, 746, iii. 38; *The Second Maiden's Tragedy* assigned to, ii. 212; *The Double Falsehood* assigned to, ii. 212; *Two Noble Kinsmen* attributed to, ii. 242, iii. 38; his and Dekker's *Virgin Martyr,* ii. 469, ii. 12; his additions to Middleton's *Old Law,* ii. 501; his obligations to Middleton's *A Trick to Catch the Old-One,* ii. 516. His collaboration with Fletcher, possibly in *The Captain,* ii. 686; *The Honest Man's Fortune,* ii. 687; *Love's Pilgrimage,* ii. 693; *The Queen of Corinth,* ii. 714; *The Double Marriage,* ii. 715; *Sir John Olden-Barneveld,* ii. 716; *The False One,* ii. 718; *The Little French Lawyer,* ii. 720; *The Custom of the Country,* ii. 721; *The Laws of Candy,* ii. 723; *The Spanish Curate,* ii. 724; *The Beggars' Bush,* ii. 725; *The Prophetess,* ii. 727; *The Sea-Voyage,* ii. 728; *The Lover's Progress,* ii. 730; *The Elder Brother,* ii. 736; *The Fair Maid of the Inn,* ii. 737; *The Orator,* ii. 747 [2]; *The Jeweller of Amsterdam,* ii. 748. His dramatic works, iii. 1–47; his life, iii. 2; Fletcher and, iii. 4; his patrons, iii. 6; his friendship with other dramatists, iii. 9, 10; religious and political tone, iii. 10; character, iii. 11; his plays, iii. 12 *et seq.*; *The Duke of Milan,* iii. 14; *The Unnatural Combat,* iii. 15; *The Bondman,* iii. 16; *The Renegado,* iii. 17; *The Parliament of Love,* iii. 18; *The Maid of Honour,* iii. 19; *A New Way to Pay Old Debts,* iii. 21; *The Roman Actor,* iii. 25; *The Picture,* iii. 27; *The Great Duke of Florence,* iii. 28; *The Emperor of the East,* iii. 29; *Believe as You List,* iii. 31; *The City Madam,* iii. 34; *The Guardian,* iii. 35; *The Bashful Lover,* iii. 36. Joint plays by Massinger and others, iii. 37; *A Very Woman,* iii. 38; *The Fatal Dowry,* iii. 39; *The Old Law,* iii. 41. His moral earnestness, iii. 41; defects,

iii. 42; diction, iii. 45; Shakspere and, iii. 45; choice of subjects, iii. 46.

Masson, Prof. David, on Ben Jonson's Scotch tour, ii. 317 [1]; his *Life of Milton*, iii. 196 [1] *et seq.*

Master Antony, a play ascribed to Lord Orrery, iii. 345.

Match at Midnight, A, attributed to Middleton, ii. 536.

Match mee in London, by Dekker, account of, ii. 465.

Match or no Match, A, by S. Rowley, ii. 546.

Matchavell, a play produced by Henslowe, i. 339 [3].

Matrimonial Trouble, The, by the Duchess of Newcastle, iii. 335 [5].

Matthew, Mr. F. D., his edition of Wyclif, i. 97 [2].

Matthieu, Pierre, Chapman's obligations to, ii. 423.

Mawe, The, a play mentioned by Henslowe, ii. 465 [4].

May, Thomas, his works, iii. 142–144; *The Heir*, iii. 142; *The Old Couple*, iii. 143; *Antigone*, iii. 143; *Cleopatra*, iii. 143; *Julia Agrippina*, iii. 143; *Julius Caesar*, iii. 143; *Nero*, iii. 143.

May Lord, The, a non-extant pastoral by Ben Jonson, ii. 380, 386.

Mayday, by Chapman, obligation to *Promos and Cassandra* in, i. 217; account of, ii. 440.

Mayne, Jasper, his estimate of Shakspere, i. 508; his works, iii. 140–142; *The City-Match*, iii. 141; *The Amorous War*, iii. 141.

Mayor of Quinborough, The, by Middleton, account of, ii. 499.

Measure for Measure, Shakspere's, the story borrowed from Whetstone's *Promos and Cassandra*, i. 216; D'Avenant's adaptation of, i. 513; Gildon's adaptation of, i. 514, iii. 428; first performance of, ii. 37; versification of, ii. 49 [2]; observations on the play, ii. 153–156.

Medal of John Bayes, A, by T. Shadwell, iii. 455.

Medbourne, M., his translation of Molière's *Le Tartuffe*, iii. 315 [1].

Medea, the, of Seneca, translated by John Studley, i. 195.

Médecin malgré lui, Le, Molière's, Lacy's adaptation of, iii. 450; Mrs. Centlivre's adaptation of, iii. 488 [3].

Medwell, Henry, his morality *Nature*, i. 113 [4], 117.

Meissner, J., on Shakspere's *Tempest*, ii. 195.

Melanthe, by S. Brookes, iii. 184.

Melibeus, by Ralph Radcliffe, i. 170.

Mélite, by Corneille, an early performance of, in London, iii. 519.

Menaechmi, the, of Plautus, English adaptation of, i. 263; Joseph Ayrer's adaptation of, i. 545 [1]; Shakspere's obligation to, in his *Comedy of Errors*, ii. 75.

Menaechmi taken out of Plautus, by W. W. (possibly William Warner), i. 263, ii. 74.

Menander, Apollinaris' dramas partly modelled on, i. 4; comedy of, i. 14.

Menaphon, Greene's letter prefixed to, i. 380 [1], 389, 390; Nashe's preface to, i. 386, 419.

Mendoza, A. de, Sir R. Fanshawe's translations from, iii. 306.

Menecmi, I, by Pomponio Leto, i. 228.

Menestrels, origin of the, i. 18.

Menteur, Le, Corneille's, Steele's version of, iii. 315 [1], 495 [2].

Merchant of Bruges: see *Royal Merchant*.

Merchant of Venice, The, Shakspere's, his obligation to Marlowe's *Jew of Malta*, i. 343; George Granville's adaptation of, i. 514; versification of, ii. 49 [2]; observations on the play, ii. 105–112; an example of Shaksperean comedy, ii. 282.

Merchant's Wedding, The, by J. R. Planché, his indebtedness to W. Rowley in, ii. 544 [6], iii. 141 [2].

Mercury Vindicated, a masque on the alchemists by Jonson, ii. 368 [1], 395.

Meredith, Mr. George, on comedy, iii. 476 [1].

Meres, Francis, his eulogy on John Lyly in *Wit's Treasury*, i. 273 [4]; his *Palladis Tamia*, references to death of Peele in, i. 366; on the Greene and Harvey quarrel, in his *Palladis Tamia*, i. 384; on R. Wilson, in his *Palladis Tamia*, i. 435; his criticisms on the early Elisabethan literature, i. 443 [2]; his tribute to Shakspere in *Palladis Tamia*, i. 494; on Shakspere's early sonnets, ii. 25; on his popularity, ii. 28; chronology of Shakspere's plays inferred from, ii. 45, 54 [1]; on *Henry IV*, ii. 120; his mention of Ben Jonson in the *Palladis Tamia*, ii. 304 [2]; Chapman mentioned in, ii. 410; on Marston, ii. 475.

Merie, The Tragedie of, attributed to Day and Haughton, ii. 591 [3].

Merivale, C. (Dean), on the Roman pantomimes, i. 15 [1].

Merlin, a Dramatic Poem, by R. M. Fullerton, ii. 245 [1].

Mermaid Tavern, the, Ben Jonson's haunt, ii. 314 [3].

Merry conceited Jests of George Peele, i. 365.

Merry Conceits of Bottom, the Weaver, a droll, iii. 280 [1].

Merry Devil of Edmonton, The, i. 331 [2]; attributed to Michael Drayton, i. 473 [3]; attributed to Shakspere, ii. 210; a synopsis of the play, ii. 232–234.

Merry Wives of Windsor, Shakspere's, adapted by John Dennis, i. 514; versification, ii. 49 [2]; observations on the play, ii. 135–138; John Dennis' adaptation of, iii. 427.

Mery Geste of Robyn Hoode, i. 144 [3].

Mery Play between Johan the Husbande, Tyb the Wife, and Syr Jhon the Priest, an interlude by John Heywood, i. 243.

Mery Play between the Pardoner and the Frere, the Curate and Neybour Pratte, by John Heywood, i. 242.

Messallina, Roman Emperesse, The Tragedie of, by Nathaniel Richards, iii. 162.

Metanoia, by Greene, i. 389 [6].

Metamorphoses, the, of Ovid, Shakspere's obligation to, 85, 193.

Metamorphosis of Pigmalion's Image, The, by Marston, ii. 474.

Metastasio, P. B., his *Dido*, i. 357 [1].

Meurice, Paul, and A. Dumas, their *Hamlet*, i. 561 [2].

Mexia, Pedro, his *Silva*, i. 322.

Mézières, A., on Shakspere, i. 561 [1].

Michaelmas Term, by Middleton, account of, ii. 514.

Microcosmus, a masque by T. Nabbes, iii. 195.

Micro-cynicon, by 'T. M. Gent.,' ii. 494.

Middleton, Thomas, his epitaph on R. Burbage, i. 35 [1]; a collaborator with Michael Drayton, i. 437; his *Mad World*, i. 441 [1]; his description of French and Italian players in *The Spanish Gipsy*, i. 471 [2]; and Dekker, their *Roaring Girle*, ii. 145, 469; his *Witch*, ii. 171, 504; his *Puritan Maid*, ii. 230 [2]; *The Birth of Merlin* attributed to, ii. 243; his life and works, ii. 493–540; non-dramatic works, ii. 493; activity of, ii. 495; political significance of his *Game of Chess*, ii. 496; *The Mayor of Quinborough*, ii. 499; *The Old Law*, ii. 501; *Blurt*, ii. 502; *The Phoenix*, ii. 503; *More Dissemblers*, ii. 507; *The Spanish Gipsy*,

ii. 508; *A Fair Quarrel*, ii. 509; *Changeling*, ii. 511; *Women beware Women*, ii. 512; *Michaelmas Term*, ii. 514; *A Trick to Catch the Old-One*, ii. 516; *The Family of Love*, ii. 517; *Your five Gallants*, ii. 518; *A Mad World*, ii. 518; *The Roaring Girle*, ii. 519; *The Widow*, ii. 520; *A Chaste Maid in Cheapside*, ii. 521; *Anything for a Quiet Life*, ii. 523; *No Wit, No Help like a Woman's*, ii. 523; *A Game at Chess*, ii. 524; historical antecedents of the production of the play, ii. 524; plays ascribed to, ii. 536; his pageants and masques, ii. 537; his merits as a dramatist, ii. 538; his comedies of English life, ii. 539; his and Fletcher's *The Nice Valour*, ii. 732; *The Noble Gentleman*, ii. 738; connexion with Fletcher, ii. 747; his *Widow*, ii. 747 [2]; Leanerd's adaptations from, iii. 326 [5]; Mrs. Behn's adaptations, iii. 326 [5].

Middleton, Sir Thomas, and Sir Hugh, masques produced by the poet Middleton in honour of, ii. 495 [3].

Midsummer Night's Dream, A, Shakspere's, a play by Gryphius after, i. 545; Shakspere's first version, ii. 23 [1]; versification, ii. 49 [2]; observations on the play, ii. 82–89; a typical Shaksperean comedy, ii. 273, 279; Purcell's music to, iii. 323.

Miles Gloriosus, the, of Plautus, adapted by N. Udall in his *Ralph Roister Doister*, i. 256.

Millington, Thomas, printer of the *Henry VI* plays, ii. 59.

Milner, Mr. G., on the Lancashire dialect in verse, ii. 578 [1].

Milton, John, his idea of a drama on the *Christus Patiens*, i. 5 [1]; his obligations in *Comus* to Peele's *Old Wives' Tale*, i. 373; his criticism of Shakspere's works, ii. 518; his *Comus* and its dramatic connexion, iii. 195; his life, iii. 196; *Arcades*, iii. 197; *Comus*, iii. 197–201; his dramatic designs, iii. 201; *Christus Patiens*, iii. 202; *Macbeth*, iii. 202; *Samson Agonistes*, iii. 203; the protest latent in his *Samson Agonistes*, iii. 326.

Mimes, origin of the, i. 16, 17; in England, i. 27.

Mind, Will, and Understanding, part of the Digby MS., i. 92 [3].

Mingo Revulgo, Couplets of, i. 231.

Ministeriales, origin of the, i. 18.

Minna von Barnhelm, Lessing's, i. 548.

Minstrels in England, i. 23, 50.

Miracle-plays, origin of, i. 41, 42, 57.

Miracle de Théophile, Le, by Rutebeuf, i. 21.

Miracolo de Nostra Donna, Il, the version of *Dr. Faustus* in, i. 330.

Mirror, favourite use of the term, in titles of early works, i. 402 [1].

Mirror, The, an adaptation of Randolph's *Muses' Looking-Glasse*, iii. 134 [3].

Mirror for Magistrates, A, Thomas Norton's contribution to, i. 200.

Mirror of Monsters, A, by William Rankine, i. 461.

Mirza, by Robert Baron, iii. 149 [1], 289.

Misanthropos, a version of Lucian's *Timon*, by T. Heywood, ii. 585.

Miser, The, by Shadwell, iii. 457 [2].

Miseries of Inforst Marriage, by George Wilkins, ii. 183; notice of, ii. 607; adapted by Mrs. Behn, iii. 326 [5].

Misfortunes of Arthur, The, by Thomas Hughes, i. 218.

Misogonus, authorship of, attributed to R. Edwardes, i. 211 [1], 259.

Miss Sara Sampson, Lessing's, ii. 228 [4].

Missa : *see* Mass.

Missa pro Fidelibus Defunctis, the, i. 74 [2].

Mistake, The, by Vanbrugh, notice of, iii. 480.

Mistakes, The, by Joseph Harris, iii. 431.

Mistère de Sainte Cathérine, Le, i. 10.

Mist's Journal, Theobald's Shaksperean contributions to, i. 528.

Mithridates, by N. Lee, iii. 410.

Mock Testator, The, an adaptation of Fletcher's *Spanish Curate*, ii. 724 [3].

Moffat, Thomas, *The Peace Maker* and another pamphlet ascribed to, ii. 494.

Molière, J. B. P. de, his *Précieuses Ridicules*, iii. 309, 314, 318; Jonson compared with, in his *Epicoene*, ii. 365; his *Festin de Pierre*, iii. 303 [3]; Wycherley's obligations to, iii. 462.

Molina, Tirso de, influence of his comedies, iii. 303.

Moltke, M., his edition of doubtful Shaksperean plays, ii. 213 [4]; edition of *Edward III*, ii. 221 [2].

Mommsen, Tycho, on *Romeo and Juliet*, ii. 114; on *Hamlet*, ii. 158; his edition of Wilkins' *Pericles*, ii. 183.

Monarchicke Tragedies, The, of Sir William Alexander (Lord Stirling), ii. 624.

Monastery, The, by Sir W. Scott, his caricature of Gongora in, i. 276.

Money's the Mistress, by T. Southerne, iii. 423.

Monsieur d'Olive, by Chapman, account of, ii. 437.

Monsieur de Pourceaugnac, by Molière, translated by Vanbrugh, and adapted by Ravenscroft, iii. 315 [1]; Congreve, Vanbrugh, and Walsh's version, iii. 477.

Monsieur Thomas, by Fletcher, a synopsis of, ii. 708.

Montaigne, M. E. de, Shakspere's obligations to, ii. 160; his essay on Canibals, ii. 199.

Montagu, Mrs., on Shakspere, i. 539; on Garrick, i. 541 [1].

Montague, W., his *Shepherd's Paradise*, a play in which Queen Henrietta Maria took part, iii. 244.

Montemayor, Jorge de, his *Diana Enamorada* and Shakspere's *Two Gentlemen of Verona*, ii. 80.

Montgomery, Earl of, a patron of Shakspere, i. 503; a patron of Massinger, iii. 6.

Moor, Sir Thomas de la, his narrative of the resignation of Edward II, i. 349.

Moralité Nouvelle des Enfans de Maintenant, i. 131 [2].

'Moralities,' origin of, i. 41, 42, 58; a description of, i. 99; their origin, i. 100; early developement, i. 105; French moralities, i. 107; English moralities, i. 108; concrete elements in, i. 111; of the reign of Henry VI, i. 113; early Tudor, i. 117; Renascence, i. 126; later Tudor, i. 133; bearing on religious controversy, i. 136; political, i. 139; resembling comedy and tragedy, i. 141; tragic and comic elements in, i. 162; transition from, to regular drama, i. 238.

Morality of Wisdom, Who is Christ, A, part of the Digby MS., i. 92 [3], 114.

Morando, the Tritameron of Love, by Robert Greene, i. 387 [5].

More, Sir Thomas, his *Utopia*, a species of dialogues, i. 235; his 'pageants,' i. 148 [3]; his *History of Edward V and Richard III*, ii. 96; his *Utopia*, Shakspere's obligations to, ii. 199.

More Dissemblers besides Women, by Middleton, account of, ii. 507.

Moreto, Augustin, his comedies and his influence, iii. 304; Crowne's version of his *No Pued Esser*, iii. 406.

Morgan, M'Namara, his *Philoclea*, iii. 102 [3].

Morgann, Maurice, his *Essay on Character of Falstaff*, i. 540, ii. 123.

Morhoff, D. G., his mention of Shakspere, i. 546.

Morley, Henry, on John of Salisbury's condemnation of mimes, i. 24 [1]; his essay on Euphuism, i. 275.

Morley, Lord : *see* Parker, Henry.

Mort de César, La, by Voltaire, i. 536, ii. 141 ; by Royou, ii. 142 ; by J. Grévin, ii. 140, 625 [5].

Morte d'Arthur, La, the foundation of *The Misfortunes of Arthur,* i. 219.

Mortimeriados, by Michael Drayton, i. 437.

Moschus, J. Roseveldt's, the story of the *Jew of Venice* in, ii. 109.

Moses and the Two Tables, one of the Coventry plays, i. 86.

Most Lamentable Tragedy : see *Titus and Andronicus.*

Most Pithie and Pleasant Historie : see under *Glaucus and Silla.*

Mostellaria, the, of Plautus, Jonson's obligations to, in *The Alchemist,* ii. 368 ; T. Heywood's obligations to, ii. 566.

Mother Bombie, by John Lyly, i. 300.

Motteux, Peter Anthony de, Shakspere's influence on the works of, i. 534 ; his adaptation of *The Island Princess,* ii. 704 [3]; his dramatic works, iii. 431 ; his comedies, iii. 451.

Moulton, Dr. R. G., *Shakespeare as a Dramatic Artist,* ii. 288 [1].

Mountebank's Masque, The, attributed to Marston, ii. 477.

Mountfort, W., his version of *Dr. Faustus,* i. 337 [4], iii. 326 [5]; his *Edward III,* ii. 222 [1]; his part in Chapman's *Bussy d'Ambois,* ii. 420 [1]; his dramatic efforts, iii. 431.

Mourning Bride, The, by Congreve, account of, iii. 476.

Mourning Garment, The, by Greene, impersonation of the author in, i. 380 [3], 381 [2], 391.

Mucedorus, attributed to Thomas Lodge, i. 418 ; attributed to Shakspere, ii. 210 ; account of the play, ii. 225–227.

Much Ado About Nothing, Shakspere's, D'Avenant's adaptation of, i. 513 ; versification, ii. 49 [2]; observations on the play, ii. 132–134.

Müller, 'Maler,' on Shakspere, i. 551.

Müller, W., his translation of Marlowe's *Dr. Faustus,* i. 329 [1].

Mulberry Garden, The, by Sir Charles Sedley, iii. 448.

Muley surnamed Abdelmilech, i. 370.

Mullinger, Mr. J. Bass, on Ruggle's *Ignoramus,* iii. 183 [1].

Munday, Anthony, his pageants, i. 147, 148 [1]; his life and labours, i. 431 ; his part in the Marprelate controversy, i. 465 ; Ben Jonson's attack upon, ii. 325, 352 ; his and Webster's *Caesar's Fall,* iii. 52.

Murderus Mychaell, The History of, ii. 219 [2].

Murray, Sir James, offence given to, by Chapman's *Eastward Hoe,* ii. 311.

Murther of the Sonn upon the Mother, The, a non-extant play by Webster and Ford, iii. 52, 76.

Musaeus, his *Hero and Leander,* paraphrased by Marlowe, i. 320.

Muses' Looking-Glasse, The, by T. Randolph, synopsis of, iii. 134.

Mussato, Alberto, his *Eccerinis,* i. 168.

Mustapha, by La Calprenède, Orrery's adaptation of, iii. 309 [2]; account of, iii. 343.

Mustapha, by Lord Brooke, account of, ii. 616.

Mutius Scevola, an early English play, i. 208.

Mydas, by John Lyly, i. 297.

Myddleton, W., printer of *The Four P's,* i. 244.

Myngo, an early Spanish comedy, i. 231 [2].

Mystère, the, in France, i. 42 [1].

Mystère du Vieil Testament, Le, its connexion with the Chester plays, i. 58, 76, 79 [1].

Mystery, the, origin of, i. 29 ; the liturgical mystery, i. 36 ; popular mystery, i. 40 ; distinguished from miracle-plays and 'moralities,' i. 41 ; the collective mystery, i. 41, 58 ; peculiarities of speech in, i. 43 ; of various nations, i. 46 ; name not in use in England, i. 57 [3]; collective, i. 57, 58 ; the performance, i. 58 ; the spectators, i. 62 ; the literary features, i. 63 ; similarity between the Chester plays and the French, i. 76 ; tragic and comic elements in, i. 164.

Nabbes, Thomas, his estimate of Shakspere, i. 508 ; his masques, iii. 194 ; his plays, iii. 194 [2].

Names, proper, the origin of the custom of using designations of virtues as, i. 101.

Narcissus, an early English tragedy, i. 208 ; a late Elisabethan play acted at Oxford, notice of, ii. 641.

Nardi, J., his *Amicizia,* i. 228.

Nashe, Thomas, on the Manningtree moralities, i. 141 [1]; authorship of *Pappe with a Hatchet* assigned to, i. 272; his reply to Lyly's *Pappe with a Hatchett*, i. 273 [2]; on Kyd, i. 312 [1]; his relations with Marlowe, i. 316 [1], 319; authorship of *Tamburlaine* assigned to, i. 321; his reference to Machiavelli, i. 339 [3]; joint authorship of Marlowe's *Dido*, i. 356; his tribute to Peele, i. 365; on Robert Greene, in his *Strange Newes*, i. 383 [3]; his *Letter to the Gentlemen Students of both Universities*, i. 390, 396 [3]; on London and Nineveh, in *Christ's Teares over Jerusalem*, i. 402 [1]; his life and prose works, i. 418; his dramatic works, i. 423; his *Isle of Dogs*, i. 425, ii. 41; his part in the Marprelate controversy, i. 465 [4, 5].

Nature, a morality by Medwell, i. 113 [4], 117.

Nature of the Four Elements, The, ascribed to Rastell, i. 126.

Naufragium Joculare, by Abraham Cowley, iii. 164 [1]; notice of, iii. 187.

Needham, Marchamont, his *Levellers Levelled*, iii. 292 [2].

Neptune's Triumph, a masque by Ben Jonson, ii. 397.

Nero, ascribed to T. May, notice of, iii. 143.

Nero, by N. Lee, iii. 408.

Nerulos, J. R., his comedies, ii. 374 [5].

Nest of Ninnies, A, by R. Armin, i. 435 [3].

Never too Late, by Greene, impersonation of author in, i. 380 [3], 381 [2], 391.

Neville, Alexander, his translation of Seneca's *Oedipus*, i. 195.

Neville, H., his *Shuffling, Cutting and Dealing*, &c., iii. 292 [2].

New Academy, The, by R. Brome, iii. 128.

New Custome, a morality, i. 137.

New Inn, The, or The Light Heart, by Ben Jonson, notice of, ii. 375; partly inserted in *Love's Pilgrimage*, ii. 694.

New Operas, by T. D'Urfey, iii. 454 [2].

New Playe of Robyn Hoode, The, i. 144 [3].

New Shakspere Society, the, i. 570.

New Shreds of the Old Snare, by John Gee, Middleton's obligations to, ii. 529 [3].

New Trick to Cheat the Divell, A, by R. Davenport, iii. 158.

New Way to Pay Old Debts, A, Massinger's obligations to Middleton in, ii. 516; attributed to Fletcher, ii. 747 [2]; synopsis of, iii. 21.

New Wonder, A, a Woman never Vexed, by William Rowley, notice of, ii. 543.

Newcastle-on-Tyne, the religious drama performed at, i. 55; the plays of, i. 70; the play of *Noah's Ark* at, i. 91.

Newcastle, Duke of, a patron of Ben Jonson, ii. 321; his connexion with Shirley, iii. 92; his plays, iii. 332, 333.

Newcastle, Margaret, Duchess of, her plays, iii. 332–334, 335.

Newdigate-Newdegate, Lady, her *Anne and Mary Fytton*, ii. 764.

Newington Butts theatre, the, i. 458, 575.

News from Plymouth, by Sir W. D'Avenant, iii. 173.

News from the Moon, a masque by Ben Jonson, ii. 317 [2], 374 [5], 396.

News out of Purgatorie, Tarlton's, Shakspere's obligations to, ii. 137.

Newton, Thomas, his translation of Seneca's *Thebais*, i. 195; his career, i. 196.

Nice Valour, The, by Fletcher and Middleton, account of, ii. 732.

Nice Wanton, The, a morality, i. 142.

Nichol, Prof. John, his *Hannibal*, iii. 409 [1].

Nicholson, Dr. Brinsley, on Nashe's *Summer's Last Will*, i. 423 [3]; on clowns in early Elisabethan literature, i. 485 [1]; on *Henry V*, ii. 126.

Nicolai, Otto, his opera, *Die Lustigen Weiber von Windsor*, ii. 138.

Nicomède, by Corneille, translated by Cotton and Dancer, iii. 315 [1].

Night-Walker, The, by Fletcher and Shirley, account of, ii. 740.

Nigromansir, by Skelton, i. 109 [2], 130.

Nine Books of Women, by T. Heywood, ii. 554.

Nixon, Anthony, his *Three English Brothers*, ii. 600.

Noah and his Wife, in the York plays, i. 68.

Noah's Ark, the isolated miracle-play of, i. 91.

Noah's Flood, in the Chester plays, i. 78.

Noble Gentleman, The, by Fletcher and another, notice of, ii. 738.

Noble Souldier, The, by S. R., ii. 423 [2]; attributed to S. Rowley and Dekker, notice of, ii. 549.

Noble Stranger, by Lewis Sharpe, notice of, iii. 162.

Noble Trial, The, perhaps identical with Glapthorne's *Paraside*, iii. 154 [1].

Nobleman, The, a non-extant play by Cyril Tourneur, iii. 66, 67.

Nobody and Somebody, author unknown, i. 436.

Nodier, Charles, his appreciation of Shakspere, i. 561.

Non-Juror, The, by Cibber, iii. 405 [4].

Norris, Mr. E., his translation of the Cornish miracle-plays, i. 56 [1].

North, Sir Thomas, his *Dial of Princes*, i. 280; his contemporaries, i. 442; his *Plutarch*, Shakspere's obligations to, ii. 140, 180, 186, 188.

Northbrooke, John, his opposition to the drama, i. 267, 459.

Northern Lass, The, by Richard Brome, iii. 126, 128.

Northumberland, Earl of, a patron of Peele's, i. 364.

Northward Hoe, by Dekker and others, ii. 469; Webster's share in, iii. 52, 54.

Norton, Thomas, co-author of *Gorboduc*, i. 199.

Norwich, religious plays performed at, i. 55; the *Adam and Eve* play at, i. 91.

No Siempre lo Peor, &c., by Calderon, Digby's adaptation of, iii. 305.

Nostel, near Wakefield, the Friars of, i. 72.

Notable Discovery of Cosenage, A, by Greene, impersonation of author in, i. 380 [3].

Notker, Balbulus, author of the ' Sequences,' i. 8 [2].

Notker, Labeo, editor of Terence's *Andria*, i. 8.

Notti piacevoli, by Straparola, Shakspere's obligation to, in *The Taming of the Shrew*, ii. 95, 137.

Novella, The, by R. Brome, iii. 127 [3], 129.

No Wit, no Help like a Woman's, by Middleton, ii. 523.

No Wit to a Woman's, Shirley's adaptation of Middleton's play, ii. 523 [2].

Nuce, Thomas, his translation of Seneca's *Octavia*, i. 195; his career, i. 196.

Nueva era de Dios, y Tamerlan de Persia, La, by Guevara, i. 322 [1].

Nugatores, origin of the, i. 16.

Oberammergau Play, the, i. 47, 81 [1]; Mr. Charles Lowder on, i. 63 [1]; former division of, i. 85 [1].

Oberon the Fairy Prince, a masque by Ben Jonson, ii. 395.

Obstinate Lady, The, by Cockayne, iii. 287.

Octavia, the, of Seneca, translated by Thomas Nuce, i. 195.

Odyssey, the, Chapman's translation: *see* Homer.

Oedipus, the, of Seneca, translated by Alexander Neville, i. 195.

Oedipus, by Dryden and Lee, iii. 373.

Of a King in Cyprus, produced by John Green, ii. 108.

Old Bachelor, The, by Congreve, ii. 725 [2]; account of, iii. 471.

Old Couple, The, by T. May, notice of, iii. 143.

Olde Fortunatus, by Dekker, i. 337; account of, ii. 457 [1].

Old Law, The, by Middleton and others, account of, ii. 501; Massinger's share in, iii. 41.

Old Troop, The, by John Lacy, notice of, iii. 450.

Old Wives' Tale, The, by Peele, i. 372.

Oldcastle, Sir John, the character of, ii. 121, 122.

Oldmixon, John, his dramatic works, iii. 428.

Oliphant, E. H., on Beaumont and Fletcher, ii. 660.

Once a Lover and Always a Lover, by G. Granville, iii. 424.

Opera, the, beginnings of in England, iii. 320 *et seq.*; D'Avenant's attempts at, iii. 328-330.

Opitz, Martin, effect of his writings on German literature, i. 546.

Opportunity, The, by Shirley, account of, iii. 112.

Orator, The, attributed to Fletcher, ii. 747 [2].

Orbecche, the, by Giraldi Cinthio, i. 213 [2], 220 [4].

Ordinary, The, by W. Cartwright, account of, iii. 139.

Ordish, Mr. T. Fairman, his *Early London Theatres*, i. 455 [1], 458 [2].

Orestes, The Tragedie of, by T. Goffe, iii. 159.

Orfeo, by Agnolo Poliziano, i. 231, ii. 381.

Orlando Furioso, the, *Ariodante and Geneuora* taken from, i. 217 [2].

Orlando Furioso, The Historie of, by Robert Greene, i. 395.

Oroonoko, by T. Southerne, account of, iii. 422.

Orphan, The, by T. Otway, account of, iii. 415.

Orpharion, by Robert Greene, i. 391.

Orpheus and Euridice, a masque by J. Dennis, iii. 427 [1].

Orrery, Roger Boyle (Lord Broghill), first Earl of, his *History of Henry V*, ii. 128; his adaptation of La Calprenède's *Mustapha*, iii. 309 [2]; his plays,

iii. 340–345; his heroic plays, iii. 340; *Henry V*, iii. 342; *Mustapha*, iii. 343; *Black Prince*, iii. 343; *Tryphon*, iii. 344; *Herod the Great*, iii. 344; *Altemira*, iii. 344; *Guzman*, iii. 345; plays attributed to, iii. 345.

Orrery, Charles Boyle, third Earl of, his *As you find It*, iii. 344[4].

Osborne, Dorothy, reference to Shakspere in her *Letters*, i. 510[1].

Osmond the Great Turk, by L. Carlell, iii. 160.

Othello, Shakspere's, French version, i. 537[3], 538; first performance of, ii. 37; versification of, ii. 49[2]; observations on the play, ii. 167–170.

Otto the Great, Hrotsvitha's works in honour of, i. 7; his influence on the revival of religion, i. 8.

Otway, Thomas, his obligations to St. Réal, iii. 309[2]; his adaptation of Molière's *Les Fourberies de Scapin*, iii. 315[1]; version of *Romeo and Juliet*, iii. 326[1]; his influence, iii. 502.

Overthrow of Stage-plays, The, by Dr. Rainolds, i. 376[2], 506[3].

Ovid, Lyly's obligations to, i. 284; Marlowe's translation of his *Amores*, i. 314; his *Metamorphoses*, Shakspere's obligation to, ii. 10[1], 185, 193.

Ovid, The Tragedy of, by Sir Aston Cockayne, iii. 288[2].

Owl and the Nightingale, The, i. 25[1].

Oxford, Earl of, Puttenham's commendation of the works of, i. 268; his comedies, i. 475[1].

Oxford, plays performed at, in Elisabethan times, ii. 631[1].

Oxford University Press annotated editions of Shakspere, i. 570.

Padlock, The, by Bickerstaffe, ii. 725[2].

Page of Plymouth. The, by Dekker and Jonson, ii. 467.

Pageant of Holy Trinity, The, i. 58[1].

Pageants, i. 56, 143–148; by Lydgate, i. 53; by Dekker, ii. 466; by T. Heywood, ii. 584.

Pageants, The, of St. Fabyan, St. Sebastian, St. Botolf, of the Holy Trinity, i. 50[1].

Paget, Sir William, his use of the word 'farce,' i. 227[1].

Painfull Adventures of Pericles, The, by George Wilkins, ii. 183.

Palamon and Arcyte, by Richard Edwardes, i. 211.

Palatinate, the question of the fate of the, iii. 209; English popular interest in the, iii. 212.

Pallace of Pleasure, The, by Paynter, i. 217[4]; compared with *All's Well that Ends Well*, ii. 119; the story of *Timon of Athens* in, ii. 180; Beaumont and Fletcher's obligations to, ii. 752.

Palladis Tamia, by Francis Meres, reference to death of Peele in, i. 366; on the Greene and Harvey quarrel in, i. 384; Meres' mention of R. Wilson in, i. 435[2]; the author's criticisms on early Elisabethan literature, i. 443[2]; Meres' reference to Shakspere in, i. 494; testimony to Shakspere's popularity in, ii. 28; chronology of plays inferred from, ii. 45, 54[1]; on *Henry IV*, ii. 120; Meres' mention of Ben Jonson in, ii. 304[2]; Chapman mentioned in, ii. 410.

Pallantus and Eudora: see *Conspiracy*.

Palsgrave, John, printer of Fullonius' *Acolastus*, i. 253.

Pammachii tragoediae, Bale's translation of the, i. 174.

Pan's Anniversary, a masque by Ben Jonson, ii. 397.

Pandosto, the Triumph of Time, by Robert Greene, i. 388; Shakspere's obligations to, in *The Winter's Tale*, ii. 192.

Pantomime, Roman, origin of, i. 14.

Paphnutius, by Hrotsvitha, i. 7.

Pappe with a Hatchet, A, authorship assigned to John Lyly and Thomas Nashe, i. 272; reference to the Marprelate controversy in, i. 464[4], 465[5].

Parabosco, G., his *Il Viluppo*, compared with Shakspere's *Two Gentlemen*, ii. 81.

Paraclete, the monastery of, i. 38.

Paradyse of Daynty Deuises, The, contributed to by Jasper Heywood, i. 195.

Paraphrase, The, by Cædmon, allegorical elements in, i. 102.

Paraphrase of St. John, The, of Erasmus, translated by Queen Mary, i. 254.

Paraphrase of St. Luke, The, of Erasmus, translated by Nicholas Udall, i. 254.

Parasitaster, by Marston, synopsis of, ii. 485.

Pardoner, the character of the, in Heywood's Interlude, i. 243.

Parfre's Candlemas Day, one of the Digby mysteries, i. 92.

Paris, Matthew, on the *Ludus de S. Katharina*, i. 10, 49; on city pageants, i. 146.

Paris and Vienna, an early English tragedy, i. 208.

Parker, Henry (Lord Morley), his comedies and tragedies, i. 170[2].

Parliament of Bees, The, by John Day, account of, ii. 593.

Parliament of Love, The, by Massinger, account of, iii. 18.

Parnassus Plays, the, reference to Nashe in, i. 426; criticism on Shakspere in, i. 498; synopsis of, ii. 633–640; *The Pilgrimage*, ii. 634; *The Return*, I, ii. 636; *The Return*, II, ii. 637; authorship of, ii. 640.

Parracide, The, by Henry Glapthorne, ii. 432 [1], iii. 153.

Parson's Wedding, The, by T. Killigrew (the elder), iii. 166; acted entirely by women, iii. 285 [4].

Parthenissa, a romance by Lord Orrery, iii. 341.

Partures, i. 21 [3].

Pasos, definition of, i. 574.

Pasquier, Étienne, Chapman and Shirley's obligations to his *Recherches*, ii. 445.

Passion, the, one of the Chester plays, i. 76 [3], 81.

Passion of St. George, The, i. 12; edited by Archdeacon Hardwick, i. 13 [1].

Passionate Lovers, The, by L. Carlell, iii. 161.

Passionate Pilgrim, The, a collection of poems, i. 320; some of Shakspere's Sonnets printed in, ii. 25.

Passionate Shepherd to his Love, The, by Marlowe, i. 315 [3], 320.

Pastime of Pleasure, The, by Stephen Hawes, allegorical element in, i. 103.

Paston, Walter, his life at the Universities, i. 167 [2].

Pastor Fido, Il, by Guarini, i. 231, ii. 382; Fletcher's obligations to, ii. 664.

Pastoral drama, early Italian, i. 231; origin of, ii. 380; Italian, ii. 381; Tasso's *Aminta*, ii. 382; Guarini's *Pastor Fido*, ii. 382; the modern, ii. 383; Elisabethan, ii. 384; Spanish, ii. 384 [1]; general view of, at early Stuart period, iii. 274.

Paternoster plays, i. 97; of York, i. 66.

Pathomachia, an allegorical prosedrama, iii. 195.

Patient Grisilde, by Ralph Radcliffe, i. 170.

Patient Grissil, The Pleasant Comedie of, by Henry Chettle, i. 428; by Dekker and others, ii. 466.

Patient Grizzle, by H. A. Jones, i. 429 [3].

Patterne of Painful Adventures, by Laurence Twine, *Pericles* taken from, ii. 184.

Paulus, Accius, the *Delirus* by, i. 5 [3].

Pauses, a name given to moralities, i. 108.

Pavier, Thomas, publisher of the *Henry VI* plays, ii. 59.

Pavy, Salathiel, one of the Children of the Chapel, ii. 354 [1], 356 [2].

Paynter: see under *Pallace of Pleasure*.

Pazzi, A. de, his *Didone*, i. 357 [1].

Peace-Maker, The, a pamphlet ascribed to Middleton, ii. 494.

Pearl, The, allegorical elements in, i. 103.

Pearson, Mr. J., his reprint of T. Heywood's dramatic works, ii. 550 [3]; of Henry Glapthorne's works, iii. 151 [1].

Pecorone, Il, by G. Fiorentino, Shakspere's obligation to, ii. 108.

Peele, George, his tribute to Marlowe, i. 317; on *Tamburlaine*, i. 328 [1]; his *Famous Chronicle History of Edward I*, i. 348, 351; his life and works, i. 363; *Arraignment of Paris*, i. 366; *Battle of Alcazar*, i. 370; *Old Wives' Tale*, i. 372; plays attributed to, i. 374; pageants, i. 377; his position as a dramatist, i. 378; Shakspere's collaboration with, ii. 22 [1]; the *Henry VI* plays attributed to, ii. 66, 73; *Tale of Troy*, compared with *Troilus and Cressida*, ii. 148; his *Arraignment of Paris*, ii. 211; *Locrine* attributed to, ii. 220; his *Life and Death of Jack Straw*, ii. 104; *Alphonsus* attributed to, ii. 428 [3].

Pèlerinage de l'Homme, Le, by de Guilevile, ii. 634 [2].

Pembroke, Countess of, her *Tragedie of Antonie*, ii. 187; her *Tragedie of Antonie* and Daniel's *Cleopatra*, ii. 618, 619.

Pembroke, Earl of, a patron of Shakspere, i. 503, ii. 26, 32, 33; a patron of Ben Jonson, ii. 314; Massinger's connexion with, iii. 2, 3.

Penates, The, occasion of first performance of Ben Jonson's masque of, ii. 310, 394.

Penelope's Web, by Robert Greene, i. 388.

Penley, S., his edition of Marlowe's *Jew of Malta*, i. 337 [5].

Penry, John, his part in the Marprelate controversy, i. 463 [1], 464 [1–3].

Pensées de Shakspeare, by Charles Nodier, i. 561.

Pepys, S., his Diary and its references to Shakspere's plays, i. 512, 516 [1]; on the performance of Jonson's *Bartholomew Fair*, ii. 370 [1]; the plays he saw, ii. 645; his music to a song in D'Avenant's *Siege of Rhodes*, iii. 329 [2].

Percy Society, the, i. 570.
Peregrinatio Scholastica, by John Day, ii. 592, 634 [2].
Peregrini, the, one of the Towneley plays, i. 76.
Peregrino en su Patria, by Lope de Vega, Fletcher's obligations to, ii. 705.
Pericles, probably Shakspere's first play, ii. 23 [2], 181; versification of, ii. 49 [2]; observations on the play, ii. 180–185.
Perimedes the Blacksmith, by Robert Greene, i. 388, 396 [3].
Perjured Husband, The, by Mrs. Centlivre, notice of, iii. 488.
Perkin Warbeck, Chronicle History of, by Ford, account of, iii. 84.
Pernassus Plays: see *Parnassus Plays*.
Perolla and Izidora, by Colley Cibber, iii. 486.
Perondinus, his life of Timour, i. 322.
Perplex'd Lovers, The, by Mrs. Centlivre, iii. 488 [3].
Perron, Cardinal de, Ben Jonson's acquaintance with, ii. 315.
Perseus and Anthomeris, an early English tragedy, i. 208.
Person, Robert, one of Leicester's players, i. 472.
Perymus and Thesbye, ii. 86.
Peters, Hugh, erroneously supposed to have been a member of Shakspere's company, ii. 35 [1].
Petite Pallace of Pettie his Pleasure, by George Pettie, i. 281.
Petowe, H., his tribute to Marlowe, i. 318.
Petrarch, his *Philologia*, i. 228.
Petrarchisti, the, the style of, i. 274.
Petronius, his *Satyricon*, Chapman's obligations to, ii. 441.
Pettie, George, the style of his *Petite Pallace*, i. 281.
Phaer, Thomas, his translation of the *Aeneid*, i. 189 [1].
Phaeton, by Dekker, ii. 453, 470.
Pharamond, by La Calprenède, Lee's adaptation of, iii. 309 [2].
Pharao, one of the Towneley plays, i. 74.
Pharonnida, by W. Chamberlayne, iii. 289.
Phelan, James, on Massinger, iii. 2 [1].
Philaster, by Beaumont and Fletcher, a synopsis of, ii. 669.
Philippson, J. H., on Ezechiel's *Exodus*, i. 3 [1].
Philips, Ambrose, his *Humfrey Duke of Gloucester*, ii. 213 [1]; his translation of Racine's *Andromaque*, iii. 315 [1]; his dramatic works, iii. 425, 426.

Philips, Augustine, his share in Burbage's new Globe theatre, ii. 29.
Philips, Mrs. Catharine ('Orinda'), her translations of Corneille's *Horace* and *Pompée*, iii. 315 [1].
Phillipo and Hewpolyto, ii. 80.
Phillips, Edward, his tribute to Shakspere in the *Theatrum Poetarum*, i. 519 [1].
Phillis, by Thomas Lodge, i. 414.
Philoclea, by M'Namara Morgan, iii. 102 [3].
Philologia, Petrarch's, i. 228.
Philomela, by Robert Greene, i. 391.
Philostrate, his theory of the distinction between tragedy and comedy, i. 159.
Philotas, by S. Daniel, a synopsis of, ii. 619.
Philotus, by Lyndsay, i. 131 [1].
Phlyacographies, i. 210 [4].
Phoenissae, the, of Euripides, adaptation of, in Gascoigne's *Jocasta*, i. 209.
Phoenix theatre, the, iii. 249 [4].
Phoenix, The, by Middleton, a synopsis of, ii. 503.
Phoenix in her Flames, The, by Sir William Lower, a synopsis of, iii. 290.
Physiologus, i. 102.
Piccinino, Jacopo, tragedy commemorating the death of, i. 169.
Pickburn and Brereton, Messrs., their edition of Ford's *Perkin Warbeck*, iii. 84.
Pickering, John, his *New interlude of Vice concerning Horestes*, i. 207, 208.
Ficture, The, by Massinger, a synopsis of, iii. 27.
Pierce Pennilesse his Supplication to the Divell, i. 420, 421.
Pierce's Supererogation, by Gabriel Harvey, his eulogy on John Lyly, i. 273 [1]; mention of Will Summer in, i. 423 [4].
Piers Gaveston: see *Legend of*.
Piers Plowman, definition of a minstrel in, i. 23; on 'miracles,' i. 53; allegorical elements in, i. 103.
Pike-harnes, a character in the Towneley plays, i. 73.
Pilate's Wife's Dream, one of the Coventry plays, i. 87.
Pilgrim, The, by Fletcher, notice of, ii. 705; Vanbrugh's version of, iii. 326 [3]; Dryden's Epilogue to, iii. 385.
Pilgrimage of the Sowle, The, ii. 634 [2].
Pilgrimage to Parnassus, The, synopsis of, ii. 634.
Piner of Wiackefelld, The, i. 404 [1].
Pi-Pa-Ki, a Chinese play, its moral purpose, iii. 493 [2].

Pix, Mrs., her dramatic works, iii. 432, 454.

Plague, the, in London, i. 574, 575.

Plain Dealer, The, by Wycherley, account of, iii. 464.

Plaine Percevall, a contribution to the Marprelate controversy attributed to Richard Harvey, i. 465 [4].

Planché, J. R., his indebtedness to W. Rowley in his *Merchant's Wedding*, ii. 544 [6]; his *Caractacus*, ii. 697 [2]; his adaptation of Mayne's *City-Match*, iii. 141 [2].

Planetomachia, by Robert Greene, i. 380 [2], 388.

Platen, Count A. von, his *Verhängnissvolle Gabel*, i. 261 [2].

Plato (comic poet), probable beginnings of his work as a playwright, i. 449 [1].

Platonick Lovers, The, by Sir W. D'Avenant, a synopsis of, iii. 170.

Plaudite, the Roman, ii. 291.

Plautus, the *Querolus* formerly attributed to, i. 6; reproduction of his *Amphitruo* by Vitalis Blesensis, i. 9 [1]; as a model of Renascence comedy, i. 251; Ayrer's obligations to, i. 545 [1]; his *Mostellaria*, Jonson's obligations to, in *The Alchemist*, ii. 368; T. Heywood's obligations to his *Mostellaria*, ii. 566; *Rudens*, ii. 568; Ruggle's obligations to the *Pseudolus*, iii. 186.

Play of Love, The, by John Heywood, i. 247.

Play of the Sacrament, The, at Dublin, i. 98.

Play of the Wether, The, by John Heywood, the 'vice' a character in, i. 110 [4], 246; Will Summer mentioned in, i. 423 [4].

Playe of Playes, The, a morality, i. 140 [1].

Players: *see under* Actors.

Playhouse to be Let, The, a comedy by Sir W. D'Avenant, iii. 283 [2], 330.

Plays confuted in Five Actions, by Stephen Gosson, i. 217, 410, 459.

Plays, religious, original designations of, i. 57; collective series of, i. 58; method of performance, i. 58.

Pleasant Comedie: see under *Patient Grissil*; *Taming of a Shrew*, &c.

Pleasure Reconciled to Virtue, a masque by Ben Jonson, ii. 396.

Pliny, Lyly's obligations to, i. 277.

Plot and No Plot, A, by John Dennis, iii. 295 [6], 426.

Plutarch, Lyly's obligations to, i. 277 [1]; Shakspere's knowledge of, ii. 10 [1]; Shakspere's indebtedness to in *Julius Caesar*, ii. 140; possibly in *Timon of Athens*, ii. 180; in *Antony and Cleopatra*, ii. 186; in *Coriolanus*, ii. 188; in his Roman tragedies, ii. 271.

Plutarch's Lives, Shakspere's acquaintance with, ii. 84.

Plutus, the, of Aristophanes, compared with early French moralities, i. 108; performed in Greek before Elisabeth, i. 190; Jonson's obligations to in his *Staple of News*, ii. 374; a translation of, attributed to Randolph, iii. 136.

Poems in divers Humors, by R. Barnfield, Shakspere's sonnets in, ii. 25 [3].

Poet's Vision and a Prince's Glorie, A, by Thomas Greene, i. 382 [3], 502 [1].

Poetaster, The, by Ben Jonson, the objects of the satire in, ii. 308; account of the play, ii. 356, 403.

Poets and Poësie, by Drayton, his tribute to Shakspere in, i. 500.

Politian: *see* Poliziano.

Politician, The, by Shirley, account of, iii. 97.

Politique Father, The, iii. 97 [2].

Poliziano, Agnolo, his *Orfeo*, i. 231, ii. 381.

Pollard, Mr. A. W., his edition of *The Harrowing of Hell*, i. 90 [1].

Polydore Virgil, his history of England, i. 171.

Polyeuctes the Martyr, a translation from Corneille by Sir W. Lower, iii. 290.

Polyhymnia, a poem by Peele, i. 368.

Polyolbion, by Michael Drayton, i. 438.

Pompée, by Corneille, Mrs. Catharine Philips' translation of, iii. 315 [1].

Pompey the Great, his faire Cornelias Tragedie, by Thomas Kyd, i. 304.

Ponsard, F., his *Lucrèce*, ii. 411 [2].

Poole, John, his adaptation of Shirley's *Gamester*, iii. 109 [3].

Poor Man's Comfort, The, by Robert Daborne, iii. 155.

Poor Man's Talent, The, by Thomas Lodge, i. 415.

Pope, A., his edition of Shakspere, i. 527; his opinion and prophecy of Garrick's talent, i. 541; on *The Two Noble Kinsmen*, ii. 238 [1]; on Chapman's *Bussy d'Ambois*, iii. 420 [1]; his quarrel with Cibber, iii. 427 [1].

Pope, Thomas, one of Leicester's players, i. 472 [1].

Pordage, S., his *Herod and Mariamne*, iii. 344 [3].

Porta, G.-B. della, his *l'Astrologo*, iii. 180; *Trappolaria*, iii. 186.

Porta Pietatis, a pageant by T. Heywood, ii. 584.

Porter, Henry, his dramatic works, ii. 604, 605; *Two Angry Women*, ii. 604.

Porto, Luigi da, his *Romeo and Juliet*, i. 213; his *Historia di due nobili Amanti*, ii. 115.

Pott, Mrs. Henry, her Baconian-Shakspere craze, i. 504 ¹, 571, 572.

Potter, A. Claghorn, his bibliography of Beaumont and Fletcher, ii. 643 ¹.

Potts, T., his *Witches of Lancaster*, ii. 575 ⁵.

Précieuses Ridicules, Les, Molière's, iii. 309.

Précieux, the, i. 276.

Preston, religious plays performed at, i. 55.

Preston, Thomas, his *Cambises King of Percia*, i. 205.

Pretty Basketful of Linen, A, by Empress Catherina II, ii. 137.

Prichard, J Cowles, on Shakspere's intellectual nationality, i. 560 ¹.

Prima Pastorum, one of the Towneley plays, i. 73.

Prince Arthur, by Sir Richard Blackmore, iii. 510.

Prince d'Amour, The, a masque by Sir W. D'Avenant, iii. 173.

Princely Mirrour of Peerles Modestie, The, by Robert Greene, i. 387 ⁵.

Princely Pleasures of Kenilworth, The, by R. Gascoigne, i. 155.

Princess, The, by T. Killigrew (the elder), iii. 166.

Princess of Cleve, The, by N. Lee, iii. 411.

Prisoners, The, by T. Killigrew (the elder), iii. 165.

Processus Noë cum Filiis, one of the Towneley plays, i. 73.

Processus Prophetarum, one of the Towneley plays, i. 74.

Processus Talentorum, one of the Towneley plays, i. 75; one of the Coventry plays, 'Pownce Pilate' in, i. 111 ³.

Prodigal Son, The, attributed to Shakspere, ii. 211; version of Shadwell's *Woman-Captain*, iii. 457 ⁴.

Prodromus, Theodore, probable author of the Χριστὸς πάσχων, i. 4.

Projectors, The, by John Wilson, iii. 338.

Prologues, Shakspere's use of, ii. 291; of Jonson's *Poetaster*, compared with that of *Troilus and Cressida*, ii. 361; by T. Heywood, ii. 585; in early Stuart drama, iii. 256; Dryden's, iii. 391.

Promos and Cassandra, by George Whetstone, i. 216.

Prophetess, The, by Fletcher, account of, ii. 727; adaptations of, ii. 727 ³; Betterton's version of, iii. 326 ³; Purcell's music to, iii. 323.

Prosopopeia, attributed to Thomas Lodge, i. 414 ⁴.

Protectorate, the: *see* Commonwealth.

Protevangelium Jacobi, the, the ideas in the Chester plays borrowed from, i. 79 ².

Proverbs, The Book of, a species of morality, i. 100.

Provoked Wife, The, by Vanbrugh, account of, iii. 479.

Prynne, William, his opposition to the drama in his *Histrio-Mastix*, i. 507 ¹, iii. 193, 240.

Pseudolus, the, of Plautus, Ruggle's obligations to, iii. 186.

Psyche, an opera by Shadwell, iii. 457 ².

Purcell, Henry, his music for *Bonduca*, ii. 697 ²; for *Island Princess*, ii. 704 ³; his music to Betterton's *Prophetess*, ii. 727 ³; his early operatic compositions, iii. 323; his music to Dryden's *King Arthur*, iii. 382.

Purification, The, one of the Chester plays, i. 80.

Puritan, The, i. 365 ¹; attributed to Shakspere, ii. 210; synopsis of, ii. 229-231; attributed to Middleton, ii. 536.

Puritan Maid, The, by Middleton, ii. 230 ².

Puteanus of Louvain, his *Comus*, iii. 199 ².

Puttenham, George, on John Skelton, i. 128 ³; his *Arte of English Poesie*, i. 268; the criticisms of, i. 442.

Pyrrhus, by C. Hopkins, iii. 431.

Pythagoras, by Martin Slater, ii. 608 ².

Quarles, Francis, plays by, published during the Protectorate, iii. 286; his *Emblems*, iii. 286 ³.

Queen Catharine, by Mrs. Pix, iii. 432.

Queen Elisabeth, by T. Heywood, ii. 558 ¹.

Queen of Corinth, The, by Fletcher, ii. 714.

Queene of Arragon, The, by W. Habington, iii. 150.

Queen's Arcadia, The, by S. Daniel, ii. 621.

Queen's Exchange, The, by R. Brome, iii. 127 ⁶, 129.

Queen's Masque, The, by T. Heywood, ii. 582.

Queen and Concubine, The, by R. Brome, iii. 129.

Querer per solo querer, by Mendoza, Fanshawe's translation of, iii. 306 [1].

Querolus, the, authorship of, i. 6; reproduction of by Vitalis Blesensis, i. 9 [1].

Quin, James, Garrick's rival, i. 542.

Quinault, Philippe, his works and their influence, iii. 315 [1]; adaptations of, iii. 315 [1].

Quiney, Richard, a son-in-law of Shakspere's, ii. 16, 39; his letter to Shakspere, ii. 31 [1].

Quintus Fabius, an early English play, i. 208.

Quip for an Upstart Courtier, A, by Robert Greene, origin of, i. 237 [3], 384.

Rabagas, by V. Sardou, ii. 374 [5].

Racine, J., influence of his works, iii. 313; adaptations of, iii. 315 [1].

Radcliffe, Ralph, his plays, i. 170; his *Burning of John Huss*, i. 474 [2].

Raging Turk, The, by Thomas Goffe, i. 405 [3], iii. 158.

Raine, Dr. James, his edition of the Towneley plays, i. 71 [1].

Rainoldes (or Reynolds), John (Dean), his *Overthrow of Stage-plays*, i. 376 [2], 506 [3]; his *Triumph of God's Revenge*, Middleton's obligations to, ii. 511, 512.

Raising of Lazarus, The, one of the York plays, i. 70.

Ralegh, Sir Walter, Marlowe's relations with, i. 315 [3], 517; on witchcraft, i. 336 [1]; the patron of Spenser, i. 442; probable relations with Shakspere, i. 504; Ben Jonson governor to a son of, ii. 315.

Ralph Roister Doister, by Nicholas Udall, i. 254; Shakspere's obligation to, in *A Midsummer Night's Dream*, ii. 89.

Ram-Alley, by Lodowick Barry, iii. 157; compared with Middleton's *Trick to Catch*, &c., ii. 516.

Ramsay, Allan, his adaptation of Sir Aston Cockayne's *Trappolin*, iii. 288 [2].

Randle: *see* Higgenett.

Randolph, Thomas, his works, iii. 131–137; *Jealous Lovers*, iii. 133; *Muses Looking-Glasse*, iii. 134; *Amyntas*, iii. 135; plays ascribed to, iii. 137.

Rankine, William, his opposition to the drama, i. 461.

Rape of Lucrece, The, Shakspere's, early references to, i. 493, ii. 24.

Rape of Lucrece, The, T. Heywood's tragedy, ii. 25 [2]; a synopsis of, ii. 581.

Rape of Proserpine, The, a non-extant pastoral drama, by Ben Jonson, ii. 386 [2].

Rare Triumphs of Love and Fortune, The, an early romantic comedy, i. 264; the authorship attributed to Kyd, i. 311.

Rastell, John, *The Nature of the Four Elements* ascribed to, i. 126; his *Dialogue of Gentylnes and Nobilitye*, i. 237; early plays printed by, i. 242, 244, 249.

Ravens Almanacke, The, by Dekker, ii. 453 [7].

Ravenscroft, Edward, his *Titus Andronicus*, ii. 58; his *King Edward and Alfreda*, ii. 610 [2]; his adaptation of *Ignoramus*, iii. 185; his adaptations of Molière's *Monsieur de Pourceaugnac* and *Le Bourgeois Gentilhomme*, iii. 315 [1]; *Titus Andronicus*, iii. 326 [1]; his dramatic works, iii. 429, 430; *Italian Husband*, iii. 429; his comedies, iii. 451.

Rawlins, Thomas, his *Rebellion*, iii. 161.

Razzi, Silvano de, his *Gismonda*, i. 214 [3].

Reading, *Harrowing of Hell* performed at, i. 55.

Rebellion, The, by T. Rawlins. iii. 161.

Recruiting Officer, The, by Farquhar, notice of, iii. 484.

Red Bull theatre, the, iii. 232 [5], 249 [4]; at the Restoration, iii. 283.

Redford's *Wyt and Science*, i. 127.

Reed, Isaac, publisher of the Johnson-Steevens *Shakspeare*, with Marlowe's additions, i. 532; his *Variorum* edition of Shakspere, i. 533.

Reeve, T., *God's Plea for Nineveh*, i. 402 [1].

Refusal, The, by Colley Cibber, iii. 487 [2].

Regnard, J. F., his works and their influence, iii. 315 [1]; adaptations of, iii. 315 [1].

Regulus, by J. Crowne, a synopsis of, iii. 403.

Rehearsal, The, by the Duke of Buckingham and others, in derision of heroic plays, iii. 362.

Rehearsal Transposed, The, by Marvell, iii. 363 [3].

Relapse, The, by Vanbrugh, a synopsis of, iii. 478.

Remorse, Coleridge's, i. 565 [2].

Rémusat, Charles de, his *Saint-Barthélemy*, i. 355 [3].

Renan, Ernest, his *Caliban*, ii. 200.

Renegado, The, by Massinger, a synopsis of, iii. 17.

Repentance of Robert Greene, The, i. 381 [1], 392.

Representaciones, the, of Juan de la Enzina, i. 232

Respublica, a morality, i. 136, 139.

Restauration, The, by G. Villiers, Duke of Buckingham, ii. 670 [3].

Resurrectio, the, one of the Towneley plays, i. 76.

Resurrection, The, performed at Witney, i. 57 [1]; in the Chester plays, i. 76 [3], 82; in the Coventry plays, i. 89.

Résurrection, La, a popular mystery, i. 41.

Returne from Parnassus, The, Marlowe referred to by the author of, i. 318; a tribute to Michael Drayton in, i. 438; Part I, synopsis of, ii. 636; Part II, ii. 637.

Returne of the renowned Cavalerio Pasquil, The, by Thomas Nashe, i. 420; a contribution to the Marprelate controversy, i. 465 [4,5].

Revelations, The, a species of morality, i. 100.

Revenge, Young's, ii. 467 [7].

Revenge for Honour, by Chapman, account of, ii. 431; perhaps identical with Glapthorne's *Paraside*, iii. 154.

Revenge of Bussy d'Ambois, The, by Chapman, account of, ii. 414, 420.

Revenge of Hamlet Prince of Denmark, The, an early play, i. 428.

Revenger's Tragedy, The, by Cyril Tourneur, account of, iii. 69.

Re Vera, by G. Ruggle, a non-extant play, ii. 632 [2].

Revetor, William, bequeaths the *Creed Play* to the York Guild, i. 98.

Revolution, the Great: *see* Commonwealth.

Revolutions of Sweden, The, by Mrs. Trotter, iii. 432.

Reynolds, Frederick, his *Don John*, after Fletcher's *Chances*, ii. 712 [3].

Reynolds, John: *see* Rainoldes.

Rhinthon of Tarentum, his Hilarotragedies, i. 210.

Rhodes, John, his acting company licensed by General Monk, iii. 283.

Rich, Barnabe, his *Historie of Apolonius and Silla*, ii. 143.

Rich Jew of Malta, The Famous Tragedy of the: see *Jew of Malta*.

Richard II, Shakspere's, resemblance to Marlowe's *Edward II*, i. 353; Theobald's adaptation, i. 528 [2]; possible reference to fall of Essex in, ii. 33; versification, ii. 49 [2]; observations on the play, ii. 102–105.

Richard II, The Tragedy of, ii. 103.

Richard III, an early play, i. 224; attributed to Marlowe and Shakspere, i. 360.

Richard III, Shakspere's, Colley Cibber's adaptation of, i. 515, iii. 487 [2]; versification of, ii. 49 [2]; observations on the play, ii. 96–100; as a type of Shakspere's Histories, ii. 261; *Richard III*, by S. Rowley, a non-extant play, ii. 100, 547; Tate's adaptation of, iii. 427.

Richard III, The True Tragedie of, date of performance of, i. 187 [2]; attributed to Thomas Lodge, i. 418, ii. 97.

Richard Crookback, a non-extant play, attributed to Ben Jonson, ii. 343.

Richard Duke of York, The True Tragedie of, i. 348; authorship attributed to Marlowe, i. 358, ii. 59.

Richards, Nathaniel, his *Messallina*, iii. 162.

Richardson, William, on Shakspere, i. 540.

Richardus Tertius, a poem by Dr. T. Legge, ii. 97.

Riches, by Sir J. Bland Burges, an adaptation of Massinger's *City Madam*, iii. 34 [2].

Ridings, i. 147.

Right Woman, The, attributed to Beaumont and Fletcher, ii. 742.

Rightwise, John, authorship of a Latin *Dido* attributed to, i. 357 [1].

Rimbault, E. F., his edition of Dekker's *A Knight's Conjuring*, ii. 455 [3].

Rinaldo, an opera by Aaron Hill, with music by Handel, iii. 322 [1].

Rinaldo and Armida, by J. Dennis, iii. 426.

Rinuccini, Ottavio, his *Daphne*, the first Italian opera, iii. 321 [1].

Rio, A. F., on Shakspere's religion, ii. 41 [4].

Ristori, Adelaida, her 'Lady Macbeth,' i. 561 [2].

Ritson, John, on Steevens' and Malone's editions of Shakspere, i. 533.

Rival Forts, The, by Colley Cibber, ii. 693 [4].

Rival Friends, The, by Peter Hausted, iii. 188.

Rival Kings, The, Banks' adaptation of Calprenède's *Cassandre*, iii. 309 [2].

Rival Ladies, The, by Dryden, a synopsis of, iii. 347.

Rival Queens, The, by Lee, an adaptation of Calprenède's *Cassandre*, iii. 309 [2]; a synopsis of, iii. 409.

Rivales, by W. Gager, i. 364; produced at Oxford, ii. 631 [1].

Rivals, The, by D'Avenant, a version of *Two Noble Kinsmen*, iii. 326 [3] (see *Two Noble Kinsmen*).

Roaring Girle, The, by Middleton and Dekker, their impersonation of Mary Frith in, ii. 145, 469, 519.

Robert Cicill, an early secular play acted at Chester, i. 170.

Robert Second Duke of Normandy, History of, by T. Lodge, i. 413.

Robert II, The King of Scots, a non-extant play by Ben Jonson, Dekker, and others, ii. 343, 467.

Robertes, printer of *Merchant of Venice,* ii. 105.

Robin Hood plays, i. 144 [3].

Robin Hood and the Pinder of Wakefield, i. 404 [2].

Robinson, ' Dickey,' his impersonation of women's parts, ii. 374 [1].

Robinson, T., Middleton's obligations to, in his *Game of Chess,* ii. 529 [3].

Robinson, William, actor, his death, iii. 277 [3].

Robyn Conscience, a dialogue, i. 235.

Rochester, Earl of, his adaptation of Fletcher's *Valentinian,* ii. 698 [1]; a patron of dramatists, iii. 301.

Rogers, Archdeacon, his account of the Chester plays, i. 59 [1].

Rogers, Dr. Charles, his *Earl of Stirling,* ii. 623 [3].

Rojas, Fernando de, his *Calista and Meliboea,* i. 232.

Roman Actor, The, by Massinger, synopsis of, iii. 24–27.

Roman de la Rose, allegorical elements in the, i. 103, ii. 634 [2].

Roman Empress, The, by W. Joyner, iii. 431.

Roman Father, The, Betterton's adaptation of Webster's *Appius and Virginia,* iii. 62.

Roman Virgin, The, by Webster, Betterton's version of, iii. 326 [4].

Rome, pageants in, i. 145 [2].

Romeo and Juliet, early versions of, i. 213.

Romeo and Juliet, Shakspere's, Ducis' version, i. 537; Goethe's version, i. 553; one of Shakspere's first efforts, ii. 22 [1]; versification, ii. 49 [2]; observations on the play, ii. 112-117; versions of, by Otway and J. Howard, iii. 326 [1], 396.

Romeus and Juliet, Tragicall Historye of, by Arthur Brooke, ii. 114.

Rosalind, the character of, ii. 132.

Rosalynde, Euphues' Golden Legacie, by Thomas Lodge, i. 411 ; Shakspere's obligations to, ii. 129.

Rosamond, Addison's opera, iii. 323 [1].

Rosciad, Churchill's, i. 541 [2].

Rose theatre, the, i. 458.

Rosenblüt, Hans, his *Fastnachtsspiele,* i. 233 [1].

Roseveldt, Jacob, his *Moschus,* ii. 109.

Rosmunda, an early Italian tragedy by Rucellai, i. 169.

Rossi, Ernesto, his rendering of Shaksperean characters, i. 561 [2].

Rossum, van, his *Aelius Seianus,* ii. 339.

Roundheads, The, by Mrs. Aphra Behn, iii. 453.

' Rounds,' i. 56 [1].

Rover, The, by Mrs. Aphra Behn, iii. 453.

Rowe, John, his *Tragi-Comoedia* acted at Witney, Oxfordshire, iii. 281 [1].

Rowe, Nicholas, his *Tamerlane,* i. 328 [1], iii. 434 ; his edition of Shakspere, i. 526 ; his ' Life ' of Shakspere, ii. 1 [1]; on Shakspere's acting, ii. 22 ; on the relations between Ben Jonson and Shakspere, ii. 303 ; his dramatic works, iii. 433–438 ; *The Ambitious Step-Mother,* iii. 434 ; *The Fair Penitent,* iii. 435 ; *Ulysses,* iii. 436 ; *The Royal Convert,* iii. 436 ; *Jane Shore,* iii. 437 ; *Lady Jane Grey,* iii. 437.

Rowley, Samuel, his additions to Marlowe's *Faustus,* i. 329 [3]; his *Richard III,* ii. 100 ; his *When You See Me, &c.,* ii. 202, 547 ; *The Noble Souldier* attributed to, ii. 423 [2], 549; his dramatic works, ii. 545-550; as a play-wright, ii. 545.

Rowley, William, part-author of *Travels of Three English Brothers,* ii. 183, 600; possible part-author of *Pericles,* ii. 184 ; and of *Birth of Merlin,* ii. 210, 243 ; his works, ii. 243 [5]; Middleton's collaboration with, ii. 499 ; his additions to Middleton's *Old Law,* ii. 501 ; *Spanish Gipsie,* ii. 508 ; *A Fair Quarrel,* ii. 509 ; *The Changeling,* ii. 511 ; his and Middleton's *World Tost at Tennis,* ii. 537 ; his dramatic works, ii. 540-545 ; as a play-wright, ii. 540, 541 ; *A New Wonder,* ii. 543 ; *All's Lost by Lust,* ii. 544 ; *A Match at Midnight,* ii. 544 ; *A Shoemaker a Gentleman,* ii. 544; *Fortune by Land and Sea,* ii. 569; his and Fletcher's *Maid in the Mill,* ii. 729 ; *The Noble Gentleman,* ii. 738 ; connexion with Fletcher, ii. 747; Webster's collaboration with, ii. 52 ; *A Cure for a Cuckold,* iii. 54 ; *The Thracian Wonder,* iii. 55 ; Ford's, Dekker's and his *Witch of Edmonton,* iii. 74.

Roy, William, his dialogues, i. 235.
Royal Convert, The, by Nicholas Rowe, account of, iii. 436.
Royal Flight, The, iii. 294 [3].
Royall King and Loyall Subject, The, by T. Heywood, notice of, iii. 560.
Royal Master, The, by Shirley, notice of, iii. 115.
Royal Merchant, by J. Hall, an adaptation of *Beggars' Bush,* ii. 726 [2].
Royal Mischief, The, by Mrs. Manley iii. 432.
Royal Shepherdess, The, by Shadwell, iii. 457 [2].
Royal Slave, The, by W. Cartwright, notice of, iii. 138.
Royou, J. C., his *Mort de César,* ii. 142.
Rucellai, G., his *Rosmunda,* i. 169 [4].
Rudens, Plautus', T. Heywood's obligations to, ii. 568.
Rückert, F., as a translator, i. 554.
Rueda, Lope de, his *pasos,* i. 574 ; his *Los Enganos,* ii. 75, 143 ; his *Eufemia,* ii. 191.
Rümelin, Gustav, on *Henry V,* ii. 265 [2].
Ruggle, G., his *Club-Law,* and other plays, ii. 632 ; his *Ignoramus,* iii. 183.
Rule a Wife and Have a Wife, by Fletcher, a synopsis of, ii. 711.
Rule of Reason, The, by Thomas Wilson, i. 256 [1].
Rump, The, by Tatham, iii. 292 [2].
Runne and a Great Caste, by John Davies, tribute to Shakspere in, i. 496.
Rutebeuf, the works of, i. 21 ; his version of the story of *Theophilus,* i. 330.
Rutter, Joseph, his *Shepherd's Holyday,* iii. 162 ; his translation of *Le Cid,* iii. 315 [1].
Ruzante (Angelo Beolco), i. 230.
Rychardes, T., authorship of *Misogonus* assigned to, i. 260.
Rymer, T., criticisms on Shakspere, i. 522, 530 [3] ; his *Edgar,* ii. 610 [2] ; on *The Maid's Tragedy,* ii. 674 [2].

Sachs, Hans, his *Comedie von Hecastus,* i. 120; his comedy on story of Griselda, i. 429 ; his version of *Fortunatus,* ii. 458 [1].
Sachs, Prof. R., on the doubtful Shaksperean plays, ii. 213 [4]; on *Second Maiden's Tragedy,* ii. 672 [1].
Sackful of News, The, a political morality, i. 139.
Sackville, Thomas : *see* Buckhurst, Lord.
Sacrado Passio y Mort de Nostre Senyor Jesu-Crist, i. 46 [1].

Sacrament plays, i. 97, 98.
Sacrificium Cayme and Abell, one of the York plays, i. 68.
Sacrifizio, Il : see *Ingannati, Gli.*
Sad One, The, by Sir John Suckling, notice of, iii. 145.
Sad Shepherd, The, by Jonson, i. 331 [2] ; obligation to Marlowe's *Jew of Malta,* i. 346 [2] ; Waldron's edition of, tribute to Tarlton in, i. 454 [1]; account of the fragmentary play, ii. 379, 384, 407 ; prologue of, ii. 383.
Sagrifizio, Il, by Agostino Beccari, ii. 381.
Saint-Barthélemy, by Charles de Rémusat, i. 355 [3].
St. Botolf : *see under* Pageant.
St. Catharine, plays celebrating legends of, i. 47, 49.
St. Dorothy, plays celebrating legends of, i. 47.
St. Dunstan, the legend of, i. 109 [1].
St. Evremond, influence of Shakspere on works of, i. 534; on Shadwell's *Epsom Wells,* iii. 457 [1].
St. Fabyan : *see under* Pageant.
St. Gallen, the monastery of, literature emanating from, i. 8.
St. George, the play-pageant of, i. 143, 149 ; the play of, at Bassingbourne, i. 50 [1]; at York, i. 66.
St. George of Cappadocia, the play of, at Windsor, i. 50 [1].
St. Gregory : *see* Gregory.
St. Just Church-town, the 'Round' at, i. 56 [1].
St. Katharina : *see* St. Catharine.
St. Marc-Girardin, on Shakspere, ii. 561.
St. Nicholas, early plays on the legends of, i. 37 ; by Hilarius, i. 40.
St. Olave, a stage-play treating of, i. 54.
St. Patrick for Ireland, by Shirley, account of, iii. 99.
St. Paul's, boys of, their acting company, i. 452 [1], 453, 467, 469.
St. Réal, Abbé de, his works and their influence, iii. 309 ; adaptations of, iii. 309 [2].
St. Sebastian : *see under* Pageant.
St. Serfe, his *Tarugo's Wiles,* iii. 406 [2].
Ste. Beuve, C. A., on stage contemporary mechanism, iii. 255 [1].
Saintsbury, Prof. G., on Dryden, iii. 346 [4].
Sakontala, the, of Kalidasa, compared with *All's Well that Ends Well,* ii. 119.
Salernitano, Masaccio, his *Romeo and Juliet,* ii. 116.
Salisbury, Earl of, Jonson's appeal to, ii. 312.

Salisbury Court theatre, at the Restoration, iii. 283, 284.

Salisbury Street, the Private House (theatre) in, iii. 249 [4].

Sallust, Heywood's translation of, ii. 554.

Salmacida Spolia, a masque by Sir W. D'Avenant, iii. 173.

Salmacis and Hermaphroditis, a Latin poem attributed to Beaumont, ii. 650.

Salomon and Saturnus, the dialogues between, i. 12.

Salutacio Elisabeth, one of the Towneley plays, i. 73.

Salutation and the Nativity, The, one of the Chester plays, i. 76 [3], 79 ; one of the Coventry plays, i. 89.

Salvini, A. M., his translation of Addison's *Cato*, iii. 441 [4].

Salvini, Tommaso, his rendering of Shaksperean characters, i. 561 [2].

Sampson, William, a collaborator with Gervase Markham in *Herod and Antipater*, iii. 156.

Sampson, by S. Rowley and Bourne, ii. 546.

Samson Agonistes, Milton's, a synopsis of, iii. 203–206; Milton's protest contained in, iii. 326.

Sand, George, her adaptation of Shakspere's *As You Like It*, ii. 130.

Sandys, George, English version of Grotius' *Christus Patiens* by, i. 5 [1], iii. 202.

Sannazaro, Giacopo, his court-farse, i. 227 ; his *Egloga Pescatoria*, ii. 380 [3].

Sapho and Phao, by John Lyly, i. 295.

Sardou, V., and Moreau, M. M., their version of *Antony and Cleopatra*, ii. 186.

Sardou, V., his *Rabagas*, ii. 374 [5] ; *Intimes*, ii. 377 [3].

Sarrazin, Prof. G., on Kyd and his works, i. 303 [2] ; on *Wily Beguiled*, ii. 612 [4].

'Saspar,' Bodmer's mention of, i. 546.

Satires, by Bishop Joseph Hall, i. 414.

Satiricon, by Petronius Arbiter, Jonson's obligations to, ii. 362.

Satiro-Mastix, Dekker's, attributed to Shakspere, ii. 212 ; a reply to Ben Jonson's *Poetaster*, ii. 308, 356 ; a synopsis of, ii. 459.

Saturae, origin of, i. 14.

Satyr, The, occasion of first performance of Ben Jonson's masque of, ii. 309, 394.

Satyre of the Thrie Estaits, a morality by Lyndsay, i. 131.

Satyricon, the, of Petronius, Chapman's obligations to, ii. 441.

Saul, Tragedy of King, ascribed to Orrery, iii. 345.

Sauny the Scot, by John Lacy, an adaptation of Shakspere's *Taming of the Shrew*, i. 514, iii. 450.

Sawyer, Elisabeth, her appearance in *The Witch of Edmonton*, iii. 74.

Saxo-Grammaticus, his story of Amleth, in the *Historia Danica*, ii. 165.

Scaramouch, by Ravenscroft, iii. 451.

Scenes, the institution of, on the stage, iii. 325, 328.

Scharf, Sir George, on portraits of Shakspere, ii. 42.

Schemers, The, a version of Mayne's *City-Match*, iii. 141 [2].

Schiller, F. von, his fragmentary drama on Perkin Warbeck, iii. 84 ; on Shakspere, i. 553.

Schlegel, August W. v., on *Gorboduc*, i. 201, 202 ; his criticism of *Campaspe*, i. 294; his translation of Shakspere, i. 554; as a critic, i. 556; his *Lectures on Dramatic Art and Literature*, i. 557 ; doubtful Shaksperean plays, ii. 210 ; on *Locrine*, ii. 219 ; on *The London Prodigal*, ii. 228 ; on *The Puritan*, ii. 230; on the anti-masque, ii. 392 ; on Beaumont and Fletcher, ii. 643 [1], 645.

Schlegel, John Elias v., on Shakspere, i. 547, 556.

Schmid, Dr. D., on William Congreve, iii. 467 [1].

Schmidt, Dr. Alexander, his Shakspere Concordance, i. 559.

Scholar, The, by Richard Lovelace, iii. 164.

Schoole of Abuse, The, by Stephen Gosson, his criticisms in, i. 209 [1], 217 [3], 263, 459; its opponents, i. 409.

Schroeder, F. U. L., his company of actors, i. 230 [1]; his rendering of Shaksperean characters, i. 550; his version of Massinger's *Duke of Milan*, iii. 15 [2].

Schurzfleisch, H. L., his edition of Hrotsvitha's comedies, i. 7 [3].

Schwarz, Dr. Herman, on Sir John Suckling, iii. 519.

Science et Anerie, a farce, i. 128.

Scillaes Metamorphosis, by Thomas Lodge, i. 412.

Scop, the, in *Beowulf*, i. 19.

Scornful Lady, The, by Beaumont and Fletcher, account of, ii. 668.

Scot, Reginald, his *Discoverie of Witchcraft*, Middleton's obligations to, ii. 507, 576 [4].

Scotland, early drama in, i. 130, 131.

Scots' Figaries, The, by John Tatham, iii. 160 [1].

Scott, Thomas, his dramatic works, iii. 431.

Scott, Sir Walter, his caricature of Gongora in *The Monastery,* i. 276; his Shaksperean criticisms, i. 569; his criticism of Wilkins' *Miseries of Inforst Marriage,* ii. 607 [3]; his edition of Dryden's works, iii. 346 [1].

Scottish Historie : see under *James IV.*

Scourers, The, by Shadwell, iii. 459.

Scourge of Folly, The, by John Davies, his tribute to Shakspere, i. 496.

Scourge of Villainie, The, by Marston, ii. 474.

Scudéry, Georges de, his sister's romances published under his name, iii. 309.

Scudéry, Madeleine de, her romances and their influence, iii. 309; adaptations of, iii. 309 [2].

Sea Voyage, The, by Fletcher, derived from *The Tempest,* ii. 200; a synopsis of, ii. 728; D'Urfey's version of, iii. 326 [3].

Secco, Nicolo, his *Gl' Inganni,* ii. 143.

Seckendorff, Baron K. S. von, his *Kallisto,* founded on N. Rowe's *Tamerlane,* iii. 435 [3].

Second and Third Blast of Retreat from Plays, The, &c., by Henry Denham, i. 460.

Second Gresyld, The, by William Forrest, i. 429 [4].

Second Maiden's Tragedy, The, attributed to Shakspere, ii. 211, 212, 446, 672 [4].

Secret Love, by Dryden, a synopsis of, iii. 350.

Sedley, Sir Charles, his *Antony and Cleopatra,* ii. 187; his *Tyrant King of Crete,* an adaptation of Killigrew's *Conspiracy,* iii. 163 [1]; his dramatic works, iii. 446–448; *Antony and Cleopatra,* iii. 447; *Mulberry Garden,* iii. 448; *Bellamira,* iii. 448; *The Grumbler,* iii. 448.

Sejanus, Ben Jonson's, Shakspere an actor in, ii. 21; synopsis of, ii. 336, 402.

Selimus, First Part of the Tragicall Raigne of, attributed to R. Greene, i. 405.

Semele, an opera by Congreve, iii. 477.

Semiramis, by Voltaire, i. 536.

Seneca, his influence on early Italian drama, i. 168; popularity in Elisabethan times, i. 189; Renascence writers copying the works of, i. 193 [5]; Lodge's translations of, i. 415; Daniel a deliberate imitator of, ii. 618.

Seneca his tenne Tragedies translated into Englysh, edited by Thomas Newton, i. 194.

Senile Odium, by Peter Hausted, i. 283 [1], iii. 187, 188.

Sepet, M., on the Office of the Foolish Virgins, i. 35 [3].

Sepulchre, the Office of the, i. 34, 35.

Serpedon, History of, an early English tragedy, i. 208.

Serres, J. de, Chapman's obligations to his *Inventaire,* ii. 423.

Seser and Pompie, entered in Henslowe's Diary, ii. 140.

Settle, Elkanah, his adaptation of Beaumont and Fletcher's *Philaster,* ii. 670 [3]; his adaptation of Calprenède's *L'Illustre Bassa,* iii. 309 [2]; his dramatic works, iii. 396–398; *Cambyses,* iii. 396; *The Empress of Morocco,* iii. 396; *Ibrahim,* iii. 397; *The Female Prelate,* iii. 398; *The Distressed Innocence,* iii. 398; *The Heir of Morocco,* iii. 398.

Seubert, A., his German translation of Fletcher's *Wit without Money,* ii. 696 [1].

Seven Champions of Christendom, The, by Kirke, iii. 100 [1].

Seven Deadlie Sins, The, Tarlton's claims to authorship of, i. 454 [1].

Seven Deadly Sinnes of London, The, acted at Manningtree, i. 56 [2].

Seven Deadly Sinnes of London, The, by Dekker, i. 335 [1], ii. 452 [1].

Seven Joys of the Blessed Virgin, The, i. 46 [2].

Sfortunato, Lo, by Agostino Argenti, ii. 381.

Sganarelle, by Molière, translated by Vanbrugh and adapted by others, iii. 315 [1].

Shadwell, Thomas, his version of *Timon of Athens,* ii. 180, iii. 326 [1]; his dramatic works, iii. 455–461; *The Sullen Lovers,* iii. 456; *The Humourists,* iii. 456; *The Virtuoso,* iii. 456; *Epsom Wells,* iii. 456; *The True Widow,* iii. 457; *The Woman-Captain,* iii. 457; *The Lancashire Witches,* iii. 458; *The Amorous Bigot,* iii. 458; *The Squire of Alpasia,* iii. 459; *Bury-Fair,* iii. 459; *The Scourers,* iii. 459; *The Volunteers,* iii. 459; Ben Jonson and, iii. 460.

Shakspere, Edmund, ii. 8, 38; Gilbert,

ii. 7, 35, 38; Hamnet, ii. 15, 29, 41; Henry, ii. 6; Joan, ii. 8, 38; John, ii. 6, 38; Judith, ii. 15, 29, 41; Richard, ii. 6, 8, 38; Susanna, ii. 15, 39, 41.

Shakspere, William, the predecessors of, i. 270 *et seq.*; Euphuistic passages in, i. 279, 281 ³, 285; his tribute to Marlowe, i. 319; references to *Tamburlaine*, i. 328 ¹; references to *Dr. Faustus*, i. 337 ¹; references to Machiavelli, i. 339 ³; obligations to Marlowe's *Jew of Malta*, i. 346 ¹; reference to *Dido*, i. 358 ²; obligations to Munday's *Downfall* and *Death of Robert Earl of Huntington*, i. 434; his acting company, i. 469. A poet for every age and people, i. 487; his contemporaries' opinion of, i. 489; tributes after his death, i. 498; his patrons, i. 501; number of his plays, i. 505; probable small number of copies of First Folio, i. 506; the following Folios, i. 510; his reputation in the Restoration age, i. 511; Milton's opinion of, i. 518; Dryden and his contemporaries on, i. 520. Early editions of, i. 525; Pope's edition, i. 527; Johnson as a critic of, i. 530; Johnson and Steevens' edition, i. 531; his influence on early French literature, i. 533, 575; Voltaire and Shakspere, i. 535; contemporary English criticism on, i. 539; his plays staged in latter half of eighteenth century, i. 540; Garrick, i. 541; early acknowledgement of Shakspere in Germany, i. 544; Lessing on, i. 547; Schroeder, i. 550; Goethe and Schiller, i. 552; Schlegel's translation, i. 554, and Tieck's, i. 556; later German editions, i. 558; French translations, i. 560; Shakspere in other lands, i. 562; the Ireland forgeries, i. 563; new school of English criticism, i. 565; Charles Lamb, i. 567; Hazlitt and Campbell, i. 568; later editions and criticisms, i. 569; American editions and criticisms; i. 571; the Baconian theory craze, i. 571.

Biographical data, ii. 1; his name, ii. 2; his early education, ii. 8; his supposed occupations after leaving school, ii. 12; his marriage, ii. 14; the deer-stealing story, ii. 16; as an actor, ii. 20, 26, 36; early literary productions, ii. 22; *Venus and Adonis* and *Rape of Lucrece*, ii. 42; earlier sonnets, ii.

25, 31, 764; a shareholder in the Globe theatre, ii. 29; *Love's Martyr*, ii. 31; *Lover's Complaint*, ii. 32; patrons and friends, ii. 33: retirement to Stratford, ii. 38; death, ii. 39; his descendants, ii. 41; portraits, ii. 42. Chronological order of the plays, ii. 43; *Titus Andronicus*, ii. 54; *Henry VI*, part I, II and III, ii. 58; *The Comedy of Errors*, ii. 74; *Love's Labour's Lost*, ii. 76; *The Two Gentlemen of Verona*, ii. 79; *A Midsummer Night's Dream*, ii. 82; *The Taming of the Shrew*, ii. 90; *Richard III*, ii. 96; *King John*, ii. 100; *Richard II*, ii. 102; *The Merchant of Venice*, ii. 105; *Romeo and Juliet*, ii. 112; *All's Well that Ends Well*, ii. 117; *Henry IV*, parts I and II, ii. 120; *Henry V*, ii. 125; *As You Like It*, ii. 128; *Much Ado About Nothing*, ii. 132; *The Merry Wives of Windsor*, ii. 135; *Julius Caesar*, ii. 138; *Twelfth Night*, ii. 142; *Troilus and Cressida*, ii. 145; *Measure for Measure*, ii. 153; *Hamlet, Prince of Denmark*, ii. 156; *Othello, the Moor of Venice*, ii. 167; *Macbeth*, ii. 170; *King Lear*, ii. 174; *Timon of Athens*, ii. 177; *Pericles, Prince of Tyre*, ii. 180; *Anthony and Cleopatra*, ii. 185; *Coriolanus*, ii. 187; *Cymbeline*, ii. 189; *The Winter's Tale*, ii. 192; *The Tempest*, ii. 194; *Henry VIII*, ii. 201, 746, 765. Plays ascribed to Shakspere, ii. 209-213; *Sir Thomas More*, ii. 214; *Arden of Feversham*, ii. 217; *Locrine*, ii. 219; *Edward III*, ii. 221; *Mucedorus*, ii. 225; *Sir John Oldcastle*, ii. 228; *The London Prodigal*, ii. 228; *The Puritan*, ii. 229; *A Yorkshire Tragedy*, ii. 231; *The Merry Devil of Edmonton*, ii. 232; *Thomas Cromwell*, ii. 234; *Faire Em*, ii. 235; *The Two Noble Kinsmen*, ii. 237; *The Birth of Merlin*, ii. 243. Shakspere and his times, ii. 247; Spenser, ii. 251; Sidney, ii. 252; his histories, ii. 258; the classification of his plays, ii. 270; his tragedies, ii. 271; his comedies, ii. 272; the names of his comedies, ii. 278; his Fools, ii. 283; his dramatic diction, ii. 284; his use of prose, ii. 286; his versification, ii. 287; construction of his plays, ii. 288; chorus, ii. 291; prologues and epilogues, ii. 291; dumb-show, interludes and masques, ii. 292; *Hamlet* his *chef-*

d'œuvre, ii. 294. Jonson's relations with, ii. 326, 361 [2]; *The Puritan* erroneously attributed to, ii. 536; his supposed connexion with Fletcher, ii. 743; history of Cardenio, ii. 743; *Two Noble Kinsmen*, ii. 743; *Henry VIII*, ii. 746; improbability of his connexion with Massinger, iii. 9, 10, 38; adaptations of his plays, iii. 326 [1].

Sharp, Mr. T., on the performance of the collective miracle-plays, i. 62; his edition of the Digby mysteries, i. 92 [3].

Sharpe, Lewis, his *Noble Stranger*, synopsis of, iii. 162.

Shearman aud Taylor's Pageant at Coventry, i. 60 [4], 71 [4].

Sheffield, John : *see* Buckinghamshire, Duke of.

She-Gallants, The, by G. Granville, iii. 424.

Shepheard's Calender, The, by Spenser, i. 266 [1]; attitude towards the Marprelate controversy in, i. 464 [5]; compared with Fletcher's *Faithful Shepherdess*, ii. 664.

Shepherd, Mr. R. H., his edition of Chapman's works, ii. 408 [1]; of Dekker's works, ii. 450 [3].

Shepherd's Holy-day, The, by J. Rutter, iii. 162.

Shepherd's Paradise, The, by W. Montague, iii. 244 [1].

Shepherds and the Three Kings, The, a Coventry play, i. 63 [2]; in the Digby mysteries, i. 92.

Shepherds' Plays, The, in the Towneley plays, i. 74; in the Chester plays, i. 79.

Sheppard, S., his *Committee-Man Curried*, iii. 292 [2].

Sherley, Sir Anthony, the authorship of Shakspere's plays ascribed to, i. 572.

She Wou'd and She Wou'd Not, by Colley Cibber, iii. 486.

She Would if She Could, by Sir George Etheredge, notice of, iii. 445.

Ship of Fools, The, by Sebastian Brant, its influence on early English comedy, i. 234; A. Barclay's English version of, i. 103.

Shipwright's Play, The, i. 56 [2].

Shirley, Henry, his *Duke of Guise*, i. 355 [3]; his *Martyr'd Souldier*, iii. 157.

Shirley, James, his tribute to Shakspere, i. 500; probable author of *The Double Falsehood*, i. 328 [2], ii. 212; *Love's Pilgrimage*, ii. 213; his and Chapman's *Chabot*, a synopsis of, ii.

444; his and Chapman's *The Ball*, a synopsis of, ii. 444, iii. 107; his adaptation of Middleton's *No Wit like a Woman's*, ii. 523 [2]; his and Fletcher's *Night Walker*, ii. 740; his connexion with Fletcher, ii. 747; his *Coronation*, ii. 747 [1], iii. 112; his connexion with Massinger, iii. 10; his dramatic works, iii. 89–125; his life, iii. 89; his tragedies, iii. 95–102; *The Maid's Revenge*, iii. 95; *The Traitor*, iii. 95; *Love's Cruelty*, iii. 97; *The Duke's Mistress*, iii. 97; *The Politician*, iii. 97; *The Cardinal*, iii. 98; *St. Patrick for Ireland*, iii. 99; *Honoria and Mammon*, iii. 101; *A Contention for Honour and Riches*, iii. 101; *Arcadia*, iii. 102; comedies, iii. 102–119; *Love-Tricks*, iii. 103; *The Wedding*, iii. 103; *The Brothers*, iii. 104; *The Witty Fair One*, iii. 104; *The Changes*, iii. 105; *Hyde Park*, iii. 106; *The Bird in a Cage*, iii. 108; *The Young Admiral*, iii. 108; *The Gamester*, iii. 109; *The Example*, iii. 111; *The Opportunity*, iii. 112; *The Lady of Pleasure*, iii. 114; *The Constant Maid*, iii. 114; *The Royal Master*, iii. 115; *The Doubtful Heir*, iii. 116; *The Gentlemen of Venice*, iii. 117; *The Imposture*, iii. 117; *The Sisters*, iii. 118; *The Humorous Courtier*, iii. 118; *The Court Secret*, iii. 119; plays attributed to, iii. 120; as a dramatist, iii. 120; comic powers, iii. 123; on the decay of the masque, iii. 192; plays by, published during the Protectorate, iii. 286.

Shirley, John, his possible relationship with James Shirley, iii. 94 [1].

Shirley, the adventures of the three brothers, ii. 600 [3].

Shoemakers' Holiday, The, by Dekker, ii. 453; account of, ii. 456.

Shoomaker a Gentleman, A, by William Rowley, ii. 544.

Short Treatise of Stage Playes, A, iii. 240.

Short View of Immorality of English Stage, A, by Jeremy Collier, iii. 509; its effects, iii. 511.

Short View of Tragedy, A, by Thomas Rymer, criticisms on Shakspere in, i. 522.

Shrewsbury, religious plays performed at, i. 56.

Shuffling, Cutting, and Dealing, &c., by Henry Neville, iii. 292 [2].

Sibilla Propheta, one of the Towneley plays, i. 74.
Sicelides, by Phineas Fletcher, ii. 380³; synopsis of, iii. 180–182.
Sickness of the Mass, The, by Nicholas Manuel, i. 235¹.
Siddons, Mrs., her renderings of Shaksperean characters, i. 563.
Sidney, Sir Philip, on *Gorboduc,* i. 202; his *Arcadia,* i. 266¹; his *Apology for Poetry,* i. 267, ii. 613; his *Lady of May,* i. 268¹; his style compared with the Euphuistic, i. 276; his prose works, i. 442; Shakspere's obligation to his *Arcadia,* ii. 81; his supposed impersonation in *Hamlet,* ii. 161; Day's obligations to his *Arcadia,* ii. 595 *et seq.;* Beaumont and Fletcher's obligations to, ii. 752.
Siege, The, by Sir W. D'Avenant, iii. 173, 329.
Siege, The, by W. Cartwright, notice of, iii. 139.
Siege of Damascus, The, by J. Hughes, iii. 430.
Siege of Derry, The, iii. 297³.
Siege and Surrender of Mons, The, iii. 297³.
Siege of Namur, The, iii. 297³.
Siege of Rhodes, The, an entertainment by Sir W. D'Avenant, iii. 281, 282, 328.
Siege of Stirling, The, by Robert Baston, i. 51².
Siege or Batayle of Troye, The, early English poem, ii. 152.
Sigismonda and Guiscardo, published in Dryden's *Fables,* i. 214³.
Sigismund, R., on Shakspere's knowledge of Plutarch, ii. 10¹.
Silva, by Pedro Mexia, i. 322.
Silvestre and Morand, their *Grisélidis,* i. 429³.
Simpleton the Smith, a Droll, iii. 280¹.
Simpson, R., his edition of *Alarum for London,* i. 360⁴; on R. Greene's prose works, i. 379³; on the consolidation of the Elisabethan acting companies, i. 469²; on authorship of *A Larum for London,* ii. 211; his edition of *A Warning for Faire Women,* ii. 212³; on the doubtful Shaksperean plays, ii. 213⁴; *Sir Thomas More,* ii. 214; on *Faire Em,* ii. 235.
Simrock, Karl, his Shaksperean criticism, i. 559; his *Quellen des Shakspeare,* ii. 44¹.
Singer, S. W., his edition of Shakspere, i. 570; his edition of Hall's *Satires,* ii. 474³.

Sir Antony Love, by T. Southerne, iii. 421.
Sir Clyomon and Sir Clamydes, i. 142; authorship attributed to Peele, i. 375.
Sir Courtly Nice, Crowne's, founded on Moreto's *Desden,* iii. 304¹; a synopsis of, iii. 406.
Sir Francis Drake, The History of, by Sir W. D'Avenant, iii. 283.
Sir Gyles Goosecappe, Mr. Bullen's edition of, ii. 412¹.
Sir Harry Wildair, by Farquhar, a synopsis of, iii. 483.
Sir Hercules Buffoon, by John Lacy, iii. 450.
Sir Martin Mar-All, by Dryden, account of, iii. 351.
Sir Martin Skynk, a non-extant play by T. Heywood, ii. 583.
Sir John Oldcastle, First Part of, by Anthony Munday and others, i. 434; erroneously ascribed to Shakspere, ii. 122, 210; notice of the play, ii. 228.
Sir John Van Olden-Barnavelt, by Fletcher, account of, ii. 716.
Sir Piers Exton, by Dekker and others, ii. 467.
Sir Solomon, Caryl's translation of Molière's *L'École des Femmes,* iii. 315¹.
Sir Thomas More, attributed to Shakspere, ii. 23², 210; account of the play, ii. 214–217.
Sir Thomas Wyat, Famous Historie of, by Dekker and others, ii. 468; Webster's share in, iii. 52, 54.
Sisters, The, by Shirley, notice of, iii. 118.
Sixe Bookes Virgidemiarum, by Hall, i. 468.
Skald, the, similarity between the jongleur and, i. 19.
Skeat, Prof. W. W., his edition of *Two Noble Kinsmen,* ii. 237².
Skelton, John, his *Bowge of Courte,* i. 103; his *Nigromansir,* i. 109²; his *Magnyfycence,* &c., i. 128; a character in Munday's *Downfall of Robert Earl of Huntington,* i. 433.
Skinner's Well, Smithfield, early miracle-plays at, i. 55.
Skipworth, Sir William, Fletcher's *Faithful Shepherdess* dedicated to, ii. 663².
Slater, Martin, his *Hercules,* i. 193¹, ii. 578²; his dramatic works, ii. 608.
Slaughter: *see* Slater.
Slaughter of the Innocents, The, one of the Chester plays, i. 80; one of the Coventry plays, i. 88.

Slighted Maid, The, by Sir R. Stapylton, iii. 336.

Smethwicke, John, publisher of Fourth Quarto of *Hamlet,* ii. 157.

Smith, Edmund, his play on the subject of Lady Jane Grey, iii. 438.

Smith, Mr. Henry, an upholder of the Bacon-Shakspere craze, i. 571.

Smith, Miss L. Toulmin, her edition of the *York Plays,* i. 65[1], 66 *et seq.* ; of the Brome play of *Abraham and Isaac,* i. 91[3]; of *Gorboduc,* i. 198[3].

Smith, Mr. Roach, on Shakspere's *Rural Life,* ii. 12[2].

Smith, Wentworth, *Locrine* attributed to, ii. 220; *The Puritan* attributed to, ii. 230[2]; *Cromwell* attributed to, ii. 234; his share in Heywood's *Four Prentices,* ii. 559; his dramatic works, ii. 607; works of his attributed to Shakspere, ii. 607[1].

Socrates, Euripides' obligations to, i. 191.

Soergel, Dr. A., on English masques, ii. 296[1], 387[3] *et seq.*

Sofonisba, by Galeotto del Carretto, i. 169[4]; by Trissino, i. 169[4].

Soldato, by Angelo Leonico, ii. 228[4].

Soldier, The, by Richard Lovelace, iii. 164.

Soldier's Fortune, The, by T. Otway, iii. 415.

Solyman and Perseda, authorship of, attributed to Thomas Kyd, i. 309.

Somers, Sir George, his expedition to the Bermudas, ii. 196.

Somers : see *Summer's Last Will.*

Song of Solomon, The, a species of morality, i. 100.

Sophister, The, an academical play, iii. 183.

Sophocles, the tragedies of, i. 159[1].

Sophonisba, by N. Lee, notice of, iii. 408.

Sophonisba, Marston's : see *Wonder of Women.*

Sophy, The, by Sir John Denham, iii. 148.

Sotternie, the Dutch, i. 233[3].

Sotties, the nature of the, i. 22[1]; of the *enfans sans souci,* i. 107; effect on early English comedy, i. 226.

Soul's Warfare, by Richard Tuke, iii. 305[3].

Southampton, Henry Wriothesley, Earl of, a patron of Shakspere, i. 503, ii. 25, 29[1], 33; possibly the ' H. W.' of Willobie's *Avisa,* ii. 26; Mr. S. Lee on, ii. 764.

Southerne, Thomas, his dramatic works, iii. 419–423; *The Loyal Brother,* iii. 420; some of his comedies, iii. 421 ; *Oronooko,* iii. 422; *The Fate of Capua,*

iii. 422; *The Spartan Dame,* iii. 423; *Money's the Mistress,* iii. 423.

Southey, R., on the introduction by the Benedictines of music into the Church of Rome, i. 6[2].

Southwell, Robert, his reference to Shakspere's *Venus and Adonis,* i. 493[3].

Spalding, Prof. W., on authorship of *The Two Noble Kinsmen,* ii. 238; on Beaumont and Fletcher, &c., ii. 543[1].

Spanish Dramatic Literature, mysteries, i. 46 ; early comedy, i. 231, 574 ; Beaumont and Fletcher's obligations to, ii. 753; at early Stuart period, iii. 265 ; its influence on later Stuart writers, iii. 303.

Spanish Curate, The, by Fletcher, account of, ii. 723.

Spanish Fig, The, attributed to Dekker, ii. 550[1].

Spanish Friar, The, by Dryden, ii. 725[2]; a synopsis of, iii. 376.

Spanish Gipsy, The, Middleton's description of French and Italian players in, i. 471[2]; by Middleton and W. Rowley, account of, ii. 508.

Spanish Lovers, The : see *Distresses, The.*

Spanish Masquerado, The, by Robert Greene, i. 392[3].

Spanish Moor's Tragedy, by Chettle, Day, and Dekker, i. 428[5]; Dekker's share in, ii. 467 ; Day's share in, ii. 591[4].

Spanish Tragedy, The, by Thomas Kyd, i. 303, 305 ; compared with *Hamlet,* ii. 163.

Spanish Viceroy, The, ii. 530[1], 743 ; erroneously attributed to Massinger, iii. 8.

Sparagus Garden, The, by R. Brome, iii. 127[5], 128.

Spartan Dame, The, by T. Southerne, iii. 423.

Speculum Historiale, the, by Vincentius of Beauvais, i. 120 ; Shakspere's obligation to, ii. 111.

Spedding, James, on *Henry VIII,* ii. 205, 765; on *Sir Thomas More,* ii. 214; on Bacon's masques, ii. 628[4], 629.

Speeches at Prince Henry's Barriers, a masque by Ben Jonson, ii. 395.

Speke, Parrot, by Skelton, i. 130.

Spencer, Lord, Ben Jonson a protégé of, ii. 306; his entertainment for Queen Anne (James I), ii. 311.

Spense, his *Bellum Grammaticale,* iii. 187.

Spenser, Edmund, his supposed impersonation of Peele as *Palin,* i. 367 ; the historical influences of his day,

i. 442; attitude towards the Marprelate controversy in *Shepheard's Calendar*, i. 464 [5]; his tribute to Shakspere in *Colin Clout's come home again*, i. 493; his version of *King Lear*, ii. 176; Fletcher's obligations to the *Faerie Queene* in his *Faithful Shepherdess*, ii. 664; Beaumont and Fletcher's obligations to, ii. 752.

Spenser, Gabriel, Ben Jonson's duel with, ii. 304.

Spider and the Flie, The, by John Heywood, i. 136 [3], 240 [1], 241.

Spiera: *see* Spira.

Spiers, Johann, printer of the *Faustbuch*, i. 332.

Spingarn, Mr. J. E., on Lyly's *Endimion*, i. 574.

Spira, Francis, the conversion of, i. 138.

Sponsus, the, or *Play of the Wise and Foolish Virgins*, i. 36.

Spoyle of Antwerp, The, by G. Gascoigne, ii. 211 [3].

Sprat, Dr. T. (Bishop of Rochester), his share in Buckingham's *Rehearsal*, iii. 363.

Squire of Alsatia, The, by Shadwell, iii. 459.

Staël, Mme. de, on Shakspere, i. 561.

Stapfer, G., on Shakspere's classical studies, ii. 10 [1].

Staple of News, The, by Ben Jonson, account of the play, ii. 374, 404.

Stapylton, Sir Robert, his dramatic works, iii. 164; his plays, iii. 336.

State of Innocence, &c., by Dryden, notice of, iii. 368.

Stationers' Registers, data from, with reference to the chronology of Shakspere's plays, ii. 45.

Staunton, H., his edition of Shakspere, i. 570.

Steele, Sir Richard, his version of Corneille's *Menteur*, iii. 315 [1]; his dramatic works, iii. 491–497; his influence, iii. 492; the founder of sentimental comedy, iii. 493; *Funeral*, iii. 494; *Lying Lover*, iii. 495; *Tender Husband*, iii. 495; *Conscious Lovers*, iii. 496; consistency between his and Addison's plays and essays, iii. 497.

Steevens, George, his collaboration with Johnson in his edition of Shakspere, i. 531, 532.

Stephen, Mr. Leslie, on Massinger, iii. 2 [1].

Stephen, History of King, a play, nonextant, attributed to Shakspere, ii. 212.

Step-mother, The, by Sir R. Stapylton, iii. 336.

Steuerwald, W., on the lyrical element in Shakspere, ii. 288.

Still, John, possible author of *Gammer Gurton's Needle*, i. 260.

Stirling, Earl of: *see* Alexander, Sir William.

Stokes, Mr. H. P., on the chronological order of Shakspere's plays, ii. 44 [1].

Stokes, Whitley, editor of *The Play of the Sacrament*, i. 98.

Stolen Heiress, The, by Mrs. Carroll (Mrs. Centlivre), iii. 142 [3], 488 [3].

Stone, W. G., on *Henry V*, ii. 125.

Storojenko, Prof., his *Life of Greene*, i. 379 [3].

Story of the Creation of Eve, The, the isolated miracle-play of, i. 91.

Story of the Lute, see *Pi-Pa-Ki*.

Stow, John, on early miracle-plays, i. 55; Marlowe's obligation to his *Annals*, i. 350; his contemporaries, i. 442; his *Annals*, i. 446.

Strachey, W., his tract on the Bermudas and Shakspere's acquaintance with, ii. 197.

Strange, Lord, his acting company, Shakspere a possible member of, ii. 20.

Strange Newes, by Thomas Nashe, on Robert Greene in, i. 383 [3], 384 [3].

Straparola, G. F., his *Notti piacevoli*, Shakspere's obligation to, in *The Taming of a Shrew*, i. 264, ii. 95, 137.

Strassburg, the religious plays and the rival Indulgences' processions of, i. 47 [1].

Strickland, Miss, on Skelton, i. 128 [4].

Strode, Dr. Philip, his *Floating Island*, iii. 182.

Stuart, Esmé: *see* d'Aubigny, Lord.

Stuart, John, Ben Jonson a guest of, ii. 316.

Stubbes, Philip, his *Anatomie of Abuses*, i. 460.

Studley, John, his translations of Seneca, i. 195.

Stukely, Thomas, impersonations of, i. 370 [3], 371.

'Sturm und Drang' era, the, i. 551.

Suckling, Sir John, his tributes to Shakspere, i. 508; his *Goblins* derived from *The Tempest*, ii. 200; his works, iii. 144–146; *The Goblins*, iii. 144; *Aglaura*, iii. 145; *The Sad One*, iii. 145; *Brennoralt*, iii. 146.

Sullen Lovers, The, by Shadwell, iii. 456.

Summer's Last Will and Testament, by Thomas Nashe, reference to Ingelend's *Disobedient Child* in, i. 250 [1]; Will Summer, Henry VIII's jester, appears in, i. 423, 424.

Sun's Darling, The, a masque by Dekker, Ford, and others, ii. 470, iii. 75.

Supposes, The, by George Gascoigne, i. 262.

Suppositi, I, by Ariosto, adapted by George Gascoigne, i. 262; compared with *Taming of a Shrew,* ii. 95.

Surprisal, The, by Sir R. Howard, iii. 393.

Surrey, Earl of, introduction of blank verse into England by, in his *Aeneid,* i. 203.

Survey of the World, A, by Barton Holyday, iii. 177.

Suscitatio Lazari, by Hilarius, i. 38.

Swan Theatre, the, i. 458; John de Witt's MSS. concerning, i. 458 [4].

Swift, Dean, on immorality of the stage, iii. 515 [3].

Swinburne, Mr. A.C., on Marlowe, i. 313 [3], 359; on Shakspere's biblical knowledge, ii. 11 [2]; his *Locrine,* ii. 220 [2]; his *Study of Ben Jonson,* ii. 296 [1]; his essay on Chapman, ii. 408 [1]; on *Bussy d'Ambois,* ii. 419; *Byron,* ii. 423 [3]; on Chapman's *Alphonsus,* ii. 429 [1]; *The Ball,* ii. 444; *The Second Maiden's Tragedy,* ii. 446; essay on Thomas Dekker, ii. 450 [3], 451; his essay on Ford, ii. 470 [1]; his essay on Middleton, ii. 493 [1]; on Middleton's plays, ii. 539 [3]; his essay on Day, ii. 589 [2]; on Beaumont and Fletcher, ii. 643 [1], 646; on Webster, iii. 51 [2]; on Cyril Tourneur, iii. 66 [1]; on John Ford, iii. 71 [1].

Syceram, Everaert, his translation of *The Spanish Tragedy,* i. 306 [3].

Symonds, J. A., on Euphuism, i. 274 [4]; on Marinism, i. 276 [1]; on Marlowe, i. 313 [3]; on early attempts at Comedy, ii. 273 [1]; his *Ben Jonson,* ii. 296 [1]; on Guarini's *Pastor Fido,* ii. 383 [1]; on Thomas Heywood, ii. 550 [3]; on *Fair Maid of the Exchange,* ii. 572 [5]; edition of some of Webster's works, iii. 51 [2]; on R. Brome, iii. 126 [1].

Symons, Mr. Arthur, his edition of some of Massinger's plays, iii. 2 [1].

Tabarinades, edited by M. C. Louandre, iii. 307 [1].

Tableaux, introduction of, into the liturgy, i. 34; early, in France, i. 146 [2].

Taillefer, his rank and station, i. 19, 20.

Tailor, Robert, *Hog hath lost his Pearl,* iii. 157.

Tale of a Tub, A, by Ben Jonson, account of, ii. 378.

Tale of Troy, The, an early production of Peele's, i. 363, 364.

Talfourd, Sir T. N., on John Dennis, iii. 426 [2].

Tamburlaine the Great, by Marlowe, i. 321; references to, i. 328 [1]; compared with Greene's *Orlando Furioso,* i. 395, 396; ascribed in Phillips' *Theatrum Poetatum,* to Thomas Newton, i. 196 [3].

Tamer Tamed, after Fletcher's *Woman's Prize,* ii. 709 [3].

Tamerlane, a play by Nicholas Rowe, i. 328 [1]; notice of, iii. 434.

Taming of the Shrew, A, an early comedy, i. 264, ii. 89; an early play attributed to Thomas Kyd, i. 312; assigned to Marlowe, i. 359.

Taming of the Shrew, The, Shakspere's, John Lacy's adaptation of, i. 514, iii. 450; Christian Weise's adaptation of, i. 545; versification of, ii. 49 [2]; observations on the play, ii. 90–96.

Tancock, Mr. O. W., his edition of Marlowe's *Edward II,* i. 347 [1].

Tancred and Gismunda, an early tragedy, i. 203 [2], 213.

Tancred and Sigismunda, by Thomson, i. 214 [3].

Tancredo, by Sir Henry Wotton, ii. 383 [1], 632 [5].

Tarleton, Richard, his *Famous Victories of Henry V,* i. 222; his works and position, i. 436, 454 [1].

Tarleton's Newes out of Purgatorie, i. 454 [1]; Shakspere's obligations to, ii. 137.

Tarlton's Jests, R. Armin's connexion with Tarlton, i. 435 [3], 454.

Tarlton's Jigge of a Horse Loade of Fooles, i. 454 [1].

Tarlton's Toyes, i. 454 [1].

Tarletonise, to, origin of the term, i. 454 [1].

Tartuffe, Le, by Molière, translated by Medbourne, iii. 315 [1].

Tarugo's Wiles, by St. Serfe, iii. 406 [2].

Tasso, Torquato, his *Aminta,* i. 231, ii. 382; J. Heywood's obligations to, in *Four Prentices,* ii. 559.

Tate, Nahum, his adaptation of *The Island Princess,* ii. 704 [3], iii. 326 [3]; his version of *King Lear,* iii. 326 [1]; *Cuckold's Haven,* iii. 326 [2]; his dramatic works, iii. 427.

Tatham, J., his *Scots' Figaries,* iii. 160 [1], 164; his play, *The Rump,* iii. 292 [2].

Taverns, Ben Jonson's, ii. 314.

Taylor, John, his tribute to Shakspere,

i. 498 ; his expedition to Scotland, ii. 316 ; his *Heaven's Blessing*, ii. 441[2] ; W. Rowley's contributions to the works of, ii. 542.

Taylor, Joseph, first owner of the Chandos portrait of Shakspere, ii. 42.

Teares of the Muses, Spenser's supposed tribute to Shakspere in, i. 493.

Technogamia, by Barton Holyday, synopsis of, iii. 176-178.

Tempest, The, Shakspere's, Dryden's adaptation of, i. 513, 520[2] ; reference to Pembroke's expedition in, ii. 33 ; first performance of, ii. 37 ; versification of, ii. 48[1], 49[1], 51[2] ; observations on the play, ii. 194-201 ; compared with Fletcher's *Sea-Voyage*, ii. 728 ; Dryden's execution of D'Avenant's design for the adaptation of, iii. 331, 352.

Temple of Love, The, a masque by Sir W. D'Avenant, iii. 173.

Temple Restored, The, a masque by A. Townshend, iii. 192.

Temptacyon of our Lorde, The, by Bishop Bale, i. 176.

Temptation, The, one of the Chester plays, i. 80; one of the Coventry plays, i. 89[1].

Tender Husband, The, by Steele, notice of, iii. 495.

Tennis Court Theatre, the, Lincoln's Inn Fields, iii. 284[3].

Tensons, i. 21[3].

Terence, influence of his writings on Hrotsvitha's comedies, i. 7 ; his *Andria*, edited by Notker Labeo, i. 8 ; as a model of Renascence comedy, i. 251; his *Adelphi*, Beaumont and Fletcher's obligations to, ii. 669 ; Chapman's obligations to his *Heautontimorumenos*, ii. 434.

Terens in English, a version of the *Andria*, i. 253.

Terentius Christianus, &c., i. 7[2].

Terminus et non Terminus, Nashe's part in, i. 419[2].

Terrors of the Night, The, by Thomas Nashe, i. 423[3].

Tertullian's *De Spectaculis*, on the Roman pantomime, i. 16[1].

Testy Lord, The, ii. 673.

Tethys' Festival, by S. Daniel, ii. 623.

Tewkesbury, *The Harrowing of Hell* performed at, i. 55 ; the religious drama at, i. 56.

Theatre Royal, Drury Lane, at the Restoration, iii. 284.

Théâtre Anglais, Le, by Laplace, i. 536.

Theatres, buildings in early Elisabethan times, i. 455[1]; earliest permanent, i. 458 ; site of Newington Butts, i. 575; in reigns of James I and Charles I, iii. 232[5]; closing of, at Revolution, iii. 247.

Theatrum Poetarum, by Edward Phillips, i. 196[3]; tribute to Shakspere in, i. 519[1].

Theatrum Triumphans, by Sir R. Baker, iii. 245[1].

Thebais, the, of Seneca, translated by Thomas Newton, i. 195.

Theobald, Lewis, his edition of Shakspere, i. 528; of *The Double Falsehood*, attributed to Shakspere, ii. 212.

Theodosius, Lee's adaptation of La Calprenède's *Pharamond*, iii. 309[2], 410; Purcell's music to, iii. 323.

Theophilus, the legend of, i. 330.

Thersytes, A New Interlude called, i. 248.

Thierry and Theodoret, The Tragedy of, by Beaumont and Fletcher, account of, ii. 689.

Thimm, F., on the Shaksperean literature of divers lands, i. 562[1].

Thomas Indiae, one of the Towneley plays, i. 76.

Thomas Merry, by Houghton and Day, ii. 219.

Thoms, W. J., on Shakspere a soldier, ii. 13[4].

Thomson, James, his *Tancred and Sigismunda*, i. 421[3]; his *Poem* on Congreve, iii. 468[1].

Thornton, T., his edition of Otway's works, iii. 412[2].

Thou, de : *see* Thuanus.

Thracian Wonder, The, attributed to Webster and W. Rowley, notice of, iii. 55.

Three Estates, A Satire of the, by Lyndsay, i. 573.

Three Kings, The, in the Chester plays, i. 80.

Three Ladies of London, The, by R. W., i. 140[1], 344[1].

Three Laws of Nature, &c., by Bishop Bale, i. 175.

Three Lordes and Three Ladies of London, The, by R. W., i. 140[1], 454[1]; dissertation on, by Dr. H. Fernow, i. 344[4].

Three Merry Boyes, The, a droll after Fletcher's *Bloody Brother*, ii. 734.

Three Miseries of Barbary, The, by George Wilkins, ii. 183.

Throckmorton, Job, his part in the Marprelate controversy, i. 464[3].

Thrush and the Nightingale, The, i. 25[1].

Thuanus, Chapman's obligations to his *Historiae*, ii. 414, 422.

Thümmel, J., on Shakspere's Fools, ii. 283.

Thyest, by Ludwig Uhland, i. 193[5].

Thyestes, the, of Seneca, translated by Jasper Heywood, i. 195, 196.

Thyestes, by J. Crowne, notice of, iii. 402.

Thymelici, late survival of the, i. 17.

Thynn, Francis, his *Debate between Pride and Lowliness*, i. 237[3].

Ticknor, G., his edition of Lope de Vega's works, ii. 754[1],[2].

Tide Tarrieth no Man, by George Walpull, i. 142.

Tieck, L., his completion of Schlegel's translation of Shakspere, i. 556; on doubtful Shaksperean plays, ii. 210, 211; his translation of *Mucedorus*, ii. 226; his translation of Heywood's *Late Lancashire Witches*, ii. 575[4].

Time Vindicated, a masque by Ben Jonson, ii. 396.

Timon of Athens, Shakspere's, versification of, ii. 49[2]; remarks on the play, ii. 177–180; Shadwell's version of, 326[1], 457[2].

Timone, by Bojardo, i. 228, ii. 180.

Timotheus of Gaza, his *Clytaemnestra*, i. 5[2].

Timour, historical account of, i. 322.

Tiptoft, John, Earl of Worcester, influence of the Renascence on, i. 166[1]; a patron of T. Heywood's, ii. 552.

'Tis good sleeping in a whole skin, by W. Wager, i. 137[1].

'Tis pity she's a Whore, by Ford, synopsis of, iii. 77.

Tittmann, Dr. J., his edition of the Duke of Brunswick's plays, i. 476[6].

Tittus and Ondronicus, ii. 57.

Tittus and Vespacia, ii. 57.

Titus Andronicus, authorship attributed to Marlowe, i. 359; attributed to Shakspere, ii. 23[2]; versification of, ii. 49[2]; remarks on the play, ii. 54–58; Ravenscroft's version of, ii. 58, iii. 326[1], 429.

Titus Andronicus, The Most Lamentable Tragedy of, ii. 57.

Titus and Berenice, by T. Otway, iii. 414.

Titus and Gesippus, by Ralph Radcliffe, i. 170.

Tobacconist, The, by Francis Gentleman, ii. 369[1].

Tom Stukely, probably Peele's play of *Battle of Alcazar*, i. 371.

Tom Tiler and his Wife, i. 142.

Tom Tosspot, the character of, i. 111.

Tomkis, or Tomkins, John, his *Albumazar* attributed to Shakspere, ii. 211; *Lingua* attributed to, iii. 174–176; his *Albumazar*, iii. 179, 180.

Tooley, an early comedy, i. 263.

Toolie, an early English play, i. 208.

Torelli, Pomponio, his *Gismonda*, i. 214[3].

Tortores, the, characters in the Towneley plays, i. 75.

Tottel's Miscellany, i. 189.

Tottenham Court, by T. Nabbes, iii. 194[2].

Touchstone for the Time, A, by George Whetstone, i. 461.

Tourneur, Cyril, *Timon of Athens* attributed to, ii. 179; *The Second Maiden's Tragedy* assigned to, ii. 212, 446[2]; his dramatic works, iii. 66–71; *The Atheist's Tragedy*, iii. 67; *The Revenger's Tragedy*, iii. 69.

Town Fop, The, by Mrs. Behn, adapted from *Miseries of Enforced Marriage*, iii. 326[5].

Towneley plays, the, tone of, compared with York plays, i. 66, 69; a description of, i. 71–76.

Townshend, Aurelian, his masques, iii. 192.

Toy-cart, The, an Indian play, compared with Dryden's *Spanish Friar*, iii. 376[3].

Tragedy, distinctions between comedy and, i. 158 *et seq.*; classical influences on early English, i. 189 *et seqq.*; the various phases of, i. 210 *et seqq.*; preference of Shakspere's predecessors for, i. 480; Dryden on, i. 520[3]; writers of, in later Stuart times, iii. 326–442; summary of history of, in the later Stuart period, iii. 499 *et seqq.*

Tragedy, On the Grounds of Criticism in, an essay by Dryden, i. 520[3], 521[1], iii. 375.

Tragicall Raigne of Selimus: see under *Selimus*.

Tragicomedy, definition of, i. 210.

Tragitour, i. 50.

Tragoediae et Comoediae vulgares, by Robert Baston, i. 51[2].

Traitor, The, by Shirley, synopsis of, iii. 95.

Transfiguration, one of the York plays, i. 61[4].

Transitus Mariae, one of the York plays, i. 70.

Translations from the Latin Poets, Ben Jonson's, ii. 330.

Trappolaria, La, by G.-B. della Porta, iii. 186.

Trappolin Creduto Principe, by Sir Aston Cockayne, iii. 288.

Travels of Sir Thomas Herbert, The, Denham's obligations to, iii. 149.

Travels of Three English Brothers Shirley, The, by Day and W. Rowley, and possibly George Wilkins, ii. 183 ; a synopsis of, ii. 600.

Treacheries of the Papists, The, by Bishop Bale, i. 174.

Treatise of Daunces, A, i. 460 [4].

Treatise of the Plague, A, by Thomas Lodge, i. 415.

Trench, Archbishop, on Shakspere's knowledge of Plutarch, ii. 10 [1] ; on *Antony and Cleopatra,* ii. 186.

Trial of Christ, The, at Coventry, i. 61 [1], 88.

Trial of Joseph and Mary, The, in the Coventry plays, i. 86.

Triall of Treasure, The, a morality, i. 133.

Trick for Trick, by D'Urfey, an adaptation of *Monsieur Thomas,* ii. 708 [2].

Trick to Catch the Old-One, A, by Middleton, a synopsis of, ii. 516.

Trimming of Thomas Nashe, The, by Gabriel Harvey, i. 419 [2], 420.

Trissino, G. G., his *Sofonisba,* i. 196 [4].

Triumph of Beauty, The, by Shirley, iii. 101 [2].

Triumph of Faith, The, a Spanish festival-play, i. 355 [2].

Triumph of God's Revenge, &c., by John Reynolds, Middleton's obligations to, ii. 511, 512.

Triumph of Peace, The, a masque by Shirley, iii. 91, 101 [2].

Triumphals, George Puttenham's, i. 442 [4].

Triumphant Widow, The, by the Duke of Newcastle, iii. 333.

Triumphe of Truth, The, a masque by Middleton, ii. 495 [3].

Triumphs, Lord Morley's version of Petrarch's, i. 170 [2].

Triumphs, the, of Beaumont and Fletcher : see *Four Plays in One.*

Triumphs of Love and Fortune, Shakspere's *Cymbeline* compared with, ii. 191.

Triumphs of Old Drapery, The, i. 148.

Triumphs of Truth, of Love, &c., The, masques by Middleton, ii. 537 [2].

Triunfos Morales, by F. de Guzman, ii. 667 [2].

Troades, the, of Seneca, translated by Jasper Heywood, i. 195.

Troicus Britannicus, by T. Heywood, ii. 554.

Troilus and Cressida, by Dekker and Chettle, ii. 467.

Troilus and Cressida, Shakspere's, Dryden's adaptation of, i. 513, 521, iii. 374; observations on the play, ii. 145–153.

' Tropes,' definition of, i. 573.

Trotter, Mrs., her dramatic works, iii. 432.

Trotter, Nicholas, co-author of *The Misfortunes of Arthur,* i. 218.

Troubadours, origin of the, i. 18.

Troublesome Raigne : see under *Edward II ; John,* &c.

Trouvères, origin of the, i. 18.

Trowle, a character in the Chester plays, i. 79.

Troy, early and mediaeval treatments of the story of, ii. 147 *et seq.*

True Tragedie : see under *Richard III; Rich Jew of Malta ; Richard Duke of York,* &c.

True Widow, The, by Shadwell, iii. 457.

Trussebot, the jongleur, i. 20.

Truth Found too Late, by Dryden, a version of *Troilus and Cressida,* ii. 153, iii. 374.

Tryphon, by Lord Orrery, iii. 344.

Tuke, Richard, his *Soul's Warfare,* iii. 305 [3].

Tuke, Sir Samuel, his *Adventures of Five Hours,* iii. 305.

Tullia, by Martelli, i. 169 [4].

Tullies Love, by R. Greene : see *Ciceronis Amor.*

Turkish Mahomet and Hiren the Fair Greek, The, attributed to Peele, i. 374; Dr. Grosart on, ii. 481 [2].

Turner, Dr. W., his *Examination of the Mass,* i. 235.

Twelfth Night, Shakspere's, versification of, ii. 49 [2] ; observations on the play, ii. 142–145.

Twine, Laurence, *Pericles* taken from his *Patterne of Painful Adventures,* ii. 184.

Twin-Rivals, The, by Farquhar, a synopsis of, iii. 484.

Two Angry Women of Abington, The, by Henry Porter, notice of, ii. 604.

Two Gentlemen of Verona, The, Shakspere's, versification of, ii. 49 [1] ; remarks on the play, ii. 79–82; a typical Shaksperean comedy, ii. 273.

Two Noble Kinsmen, The, attributed to Fletcher and Shakspere, ii. 210 ; synopsis of the play, ii. 237–243,

743; Massinger's share in, iii. 38; D'Avenant's version of, iii. 326 [3].

Two Queens of Brentford, The, by Thomas D'Urfey, iii. 363 [2].

Two Tragedies in One, by R. Yarrington, ii, 218, 219; attributed to Day and Haughton, ii. 591 [3].

Two Wise Men, attributed to Chapman, ii. 447.

Tylney, Edmund, his part in the Marprelate controversy, i. 466.

Tyrannic Love, by Dryden, account of, iii. 358.

Tyrant King of Crete, The,· by Sir Charles Sedley, iii. 163 [1], 447, 448.

Tyrrell, H., his edition of *The Two Noble Kinsmen,* ii. 237 [2].

Tzetzes, John, the Χριστὸς πάσχων attributed to, i. 4.

Udall, John, his part in the Marprelate controversy, i. 464 [3].

Udall, Nicholas, his *Ralph Roister Doister,* i. 254.

Uhland, Ludwig, his *Thyest,* i. 193 [5].

Uli, Näbis: see Bräker, Ulrich.

Ulrici, H., on Marlowe's claim for authorship of the *Henry VI* plays, i. 348, 349 [1]; his Shaksperean criticism, i. 558; his *Shakespeare's Dramatic Art,* ii. 44 [1]; on *Troilus and Cressida,* ii. 146; on *Coriolanus,* ii. 188; on Shakspere's Histories, ii. 259 [1].

Ulysses, by Nicholas Rowe, notice of, iii. 436.

Underwoods, Ben Jonson's, ii. 330.

Unfortunate Lovers, The, by Sir W. D'Avenant, notice of, iii. 172.

Unfortunate Mother, The, by T. Nabbes, iii. 194 [2].

Unfortunate Traveller, The, by Thomas Nashe, i. 422.

Unhappy Favourite, The, by John Banks, iii. 429.

Unhappy Kindness, The, by T. Scott, iii. 431.

Universities, the, popularity of the drama at, in Elisabethan times, ii. 630.

University plays: see Academical plays.

Unnatural Combat, The, by Massinger, notice of, iii. 15.

Upon both Marriages of the King, by Bishop Bale, i. 174.

Usurping Tyrant, The, ii. 446 [2].

Uterpendragon, ii. 244 [1].

Utopia, More's, a species of dialogue, i. 235; Shakspere's obligations to, ii. 199.

Valentinian, by Fletcher, account of, ii. 698.

Valiant Scot, The, by W. Bowyer, notice of, iii. 159, 160.

Valiant Welchman, The, attributed to R. Armin, i. 430 [3], 436.

Valle, Cesare della, his *Giulietta e Romeo,* ii. 117.

Vanbrugh, Sir John, his adaptation of Fletcher's *Pilgrim,* ii. 706 [1], iii. 326 [3]; builder of the Haymarket theatre, iii. 284 [3]; his translation of Molière's *Sganarelle,* iii. 315 [1]; of *Monsieur de Pourceaugnac,* iii. 315 [1]; his dramatic works, iii. 477–481; *The Relapse,* iii. 478; *The Provoked Wife,* iii. 479; *The False Friend,* iii. 479; *The Confederacy,* iii. 479; *Mistake,* iii. 480; *The Country House,* iii. 480; *The Journey to London,* iii. 480; *Aesop,* iii. 480; his *Vindication of the Stage,* iii. 513.

Variety, The, by the Duke of Newcastle, iii. 333.

Vatke, T., on Shakspere's *Antony and Cleopatra,* ii. 186.

Vega, Lope de, his influence on Spanish drama, i. 232; his *Castelvines y Monteses,* ii. 116; his fecundity, ii. 553; Fletcher's obligations to his *Peregrino,* ii. 705; Beaumont and Fletcher's obligations to, ii. 752, 754.

Velde, A. von der, his translation of Marlowe's *Dr. Faustus,* i. 329 [1].

Venice Preserved, by T. Otway, a synopsis of, iii. 416.

Venus and Adonis, Shakspere's, ii. 24; Southwell's reference to, i. 493 [3].

Verdad Sospechosa, Alarcon's, Corneille's obligations to, iii. 495 [2].

Verdi, G., his opera of *Falstaff,* ii. 138; of *Othello,* ii. 170.

Verity, Mr. A. W., his edition of *Julius Caesar,* i. 207 [1]; on Milton's estimation of Shakspere, i. 519 [1]; his edition of a selection of T. Heywood's plays, ii. 550 [3], 562 [1] *et seq.*; his edition of the works of Sir George Etheredge, iii. 442 [1].

Vertu, Interlude of, by Skelton, i. 130.

Very Woman, A, by Massinger and Fletcher, iii. 9 [1]; notice of, iii. 38. (See *Right Woman, The.*)

Vestal, The, burnt by Warburton's cook, iii. 153.

Vestal Virgin, The, by Sir R. Howard, iii. 394.

Vice, the, treated as a character in moralities, i. 109.

Victim, The, versions by Boyer and by C. Johnson of Racine's *Iphigénie,* iii. 315 [1].

Vigny, Alfred de, his version of *Hamlet*, i. 561 [2].

Villemain, A. F., on Shakspere, i. 561.

Villiers, G.: *see under* Buckingham, Duke of.

Viluppo, Il, Parabosco's, compared with Shakspere's *Two Gentlemen*, ii. 81.

Vincentius of Beauvais, author of the *Speculum Historiale*, i. 120.

Vincentius Ladislaus, by Henry Julius, Duke of Brunswick, ii. 134.

Vincke, Baron G., on *Adaptations and Performances of Shakesperean Plays*, i. 513 [1]; on the doubtful Shaksperean plays, ii. 213 [4].

Vindication of the Stage, A, attributed to Wycherley, iii. 512.

Virgidemiae, by Marston, ii. 474 [3].

Virgin Martir, The, by Dekker and Massinger, ii. 469; date of publication, &c., iii. 3; account of, iii. 12.

Virgin Queen, The, by Waldron, a sequel to *The Tempest*, ii. 200.

Virgin Widow, The, by Quarles, iii. 286.

Virginia, by Bernardo Accolti, i. 210; compared with *All's Well that Ends Well*, ii. 119.

Virtue Betrayed, by John Banks, iii. 429.

Virtuoso, The, by Shadwell, a synopsis of, iii. 456.

Virtuous Octavia, The, by S. Brandon, ii. 187.

Virues, Cristoval de, his *Elisa Dido*, i. 357 [1].

Vision concerning Piers Plowman: see *Piers Plowman*.

Vision of Delight, The, a masque by Ben Jonson, ii. 396.

Vision of the Twelve Goddesses, The, by S. Daniel, ii. 622, 623.

Visit to Elisabeth, The, one of the Coventry plays, i. 86.

Vitalis Blesensis, the works of, i. 9 [1].

Volpone, or The Fox, by Ben Jonson, synopsis of the play, ii. 361, 404.

Voltaire, F. M. A. de, and Shakspere, i. 535; his criticisms on Shakspere, i. 538; his *Mort de César*, ii. 141; his *Catilina*, ii. 340 [3].

Volunteers, The, by Shadwell, iii. 459.

Vondel, J. van den, his Senecan dramas, i. 193; his *Lucifer*, iii. 380.

Voragine, Jacobus de, his *Golden Legend*, i. 120, ii. 111.

Vortigern and Rowena, Ireland's forgery, i. 565.

Voss, J. H., his translation of Shakspere, i. 556.

Vox Populi, by T. S., Middleton's obligations to, ii. 529 [3].

Wadd, W., on Shakspere's medical knowledge, ii. 13 [3].

Wadeson, Anthony, his *Earl of Gloster*, ii. 612 [1].

Wadington, William of, *Manuel de Pechiez* by, i. 52.

Wager, Lewis, his *Life and Repentance of Mary Magdalene*, i. 110 [1], 112 [1].

Wager, W., his *The longer Thou Livest*, &c., i. 137; and *The Cruel Detter*, i. 137 [1].

Wagner, A., his edition of Marlowe's works, i. 313 [3], 321 [2], 337 [5].

Wagner, Prof. W., his edition of *Doctor Faustus*, i. 329 [1]; of *Edward II*, 347 [1].

Wagnerbuch, the, i. 333 [3].

Waimer, Philip, his *Elisa*, ii. 222.

Walder, Mr. E., on the *History of Shaksperian Criticism*, i. 517.

Waldron, F. G., his edition of Ben Jonson's *Sad Shepherd*, i. 346 [2]; on Tarlton, in his edition of *The Sad Shepherd*, i. 454 [1]; his sequel to *The Tempest*, in *The Virgin Queen*, ii. 200; his inchoate edition of Ben Jonson's works, ii. 296 [1]; his completion of Jonson's *Sad Shepherd*, ii. 386 [1].

Waller, Edmund, on *The Maid's Tragedy*, ii. 673 [2], [3]; his version of *The Maid's Tragedy*, iii. 326 [3].

Walpull, G., 'Courage' in his *Tide Tarrieth no Man*, i. 110, 142.

Walsingham, Sir T., on Richard II's pageant, i. 147; Marlowe's relations with, i. 315.

Wandering Lovers, The: see *Lovers' Progress*.

Warburton, Bishop, his edition of Shakspere, i. 529; on *The Two Noble Kinsmen*, ii. 238 [1].

Warburton, John, the burning of the plays by his cook, iii. 6.

Ward, John, Vicar of Stratford-on-Avon, Shakspere's autograph in the *Diary* of, ii. 3 [1]; as to Shakspere's death, ii. 40 [1].

Ward, Dr. A. W., his edition of Marlowe's *Dr. Faustus*, i. 329 [1], 342 [2]; on the *Parnassus Plays*, ii. 633 [1].

Warncke, K., and L. Proescholdt, edition of *Mucedorus*, ii. 225 [3]; *Faire Em*, ii. 235 [2].

Warner, Richard, his *Glossary* of Shakspere's plays, i. 533 [3].

Warner, William, his *Albion's England*, i. 200, 266 [1]; his contemporaries, i. 442.

Warning for Faire Women, A, by Thomas Lodge, attributed to John Lyly, i. 302, 418, 468³; compared with Shakspere's *Hamlet*, ii. 164; ascribed to Shakspere, ii. 212.

Warton, Thomas, on the rivalry between the *histriones* and the monks, i. 28; his Shaksperean criticism, i. 563.

Watson, Thomas, his collection of sonnets, *Ecatompathia*, i. 310.

Waugh, Edwin, use of Lancashire dialect in his verse, ii. 578¹.

Way of the World, The, by Congreve, account of, iii. 475.

Weakest Goeth to the Wall, The, attributed to Webster and Dekker, a notice of, iii. 55.

Webbe, Alexander, ii. 6.

Webbe, William, his *Discourse of English Poesie*, i. 268; on John Lyly, i. 273⁴.

Webbe, William, Mayor of London, Peele's pageant for, i. 377.

Webster, John, a collaborator with Michael Drayton, i. 437; his estimate of Shakspere, i. 495¹; his and others' *Sir Thomas Wyat*, ii. 468; *Westward Hoe* and *Northward Hoe*, ii. 469; his and Marston's *Malcontent*, ii. 483; mention of, in Henslowe's *Diary*, ii. 604¹; his dramatic works, iii. 51–66; his life, iii. 51; friends and patrons, iii. 52; his puritanical name-sake, iii. 54¹; his plays, iii. 54 *et seq.*; *A Cure for a Cuckold*, iii. 54; *The Thracian Wonder*, iii. 55; *The Weakest Goeth to the Wall*, iii. 55; *The White Devil*, iii. 56; *The Duchess of Malfi*, iii. 59; *The Devil's Law-Case*, iii. 61; *Appius and Virginia*, iii. 62; as a dramatist, iii. 63; Shakspere and, iii. 64; deficient in characterisation, iii. 65; collaboration with Ford, iii. 76; adaptations of his plays, iii. 326⁴.

Wedding, The, by Shirley, notice of, iii. 103.

Weever, John, his estimate of Shakspere, i. 495.

Weise, Christian, his *Comedy of the Angry Catharine*, i. 545.

Weisse, C. F., his *Eduard III*, ii. 222¹.

Well-delivered Judgment of a Female Student, The, ii. 108.

Wely, John de, the murder of, ii. 748.

Werfrith, Bishop of Worcester, translator of Gregory's *Dialogues*, i. 12.

Westminster Drolleries, The, edited by Mr. Ebsworth, iii. 324¹.

Westmoreland rush-bearing, the, i. 144¹.

Westward for Smelts, the version of *Cymbeline* in, ii. 191.

Westward Hoe, by Dekker and others, ii. 469; Webster's share in, iii. 52, 54.

Wever, R., author of the *Lusty Juventus*, i. 124.

Weymouth, Dr. R. F., on Euphuism, i. 276⁴.

Whalley, his edition of Ben Jonson's works, ii. 296¹.

What You Will, by Marston, a synopsis of, ii. 488.

Wheatley, Mr. H. B., his *Samuel Pepys*, i. 512²; his edition of Jonson's *Every Man in his Humour*, with memoir, ii. 296¹.

When You See Me, You Know Me, by S. Rowley, a synopsis of, ii. 547.

Whetstone, George, his *Promos and Cassandra*, i. 216; his opposition to the drama, in *Touchstone for the Times*, i. 461; his play containing the story of Shakspere's *Hamlet*, ii. 154.

White, Mr. Grant, his edition of Shakspere, i. 571, ii. 11¹; on Shakspere's first profession, ii. 13⁴; on Shakspere's metrification, ii. 52²; on Shakspere's Rosalind, ii. 132; Iago, ii. 170.

White, Robert, his masque, *Cupid's Banishment*, iii. 192.

White Devil, The, by Webster, a synopsis of, iii. 56; Tate's adaptation of, iii. 428.

Whitefriars theatre, the, i. 458, iii. 232⁵.

Whitehall and other Poems, by Henry Glapthorne, iii. 155.

Whitelocke, Sir Bulstrode, a patron of D'Avenant's, iii. 281.

Whitgift, his position in the Marprelate controversy, i. 463.

Whore of Babylon, The, a comedy by Edward VI, i. 136².

Whore of Babylon, The, by Dekker, account of, ii. 463.

Wiburne, D., his *Machiavellus*, i. 339³; his *Machiavellus* produced at Cambridge, ii. 632.

Wiclif, on pageants and miracle-plays, i. 53; on the Paternoster play at York, i. 97.

Widdowes Teares, The, by Chapman, a synopsis of, ii. 440.

Widkirk, near Wakefield, the Friars of, probable authors of the Towneley plays, i. 72.

Widow, The, by Middleton and others, ii. 520; attributed to Fletcher and Middleton, ii. 747².

Wieland, C. M., his translation of Shakspere, i. 547.

Wife for a Month, A, by Fletcher, notice of, ii. 711; T. Scott's adaptation of, iii. 431.

Wife's Relief, The, by Charles Johnson, a version of Shirley's *Gamester,* iii. 109 [3].

Wife's Stratagem, The, by Poole, an adaptation of Shirley's *Gamester,* iii. 109 [3].

Wiggin, Miss P. G., on the Middleton-Rowley plays, ii. 499 [2], 539 [2]; on *A Faire Quarrell,* ii. 510 [1]; on Middleton's *Changeling,* ii. 512 [2]; on Middleton's *World Tost at Tennis,* ii. 537 [3].

Wild Gallant, The, by Dryden, iii. 346.

Wild-Goose-Chase, The, by Fletcher, notice of, ii. 707; Farquhar's version of, iii. 326 [3].

Wilhelm Meister, Goethe's criticism of *Hamlet* in, i. 552.

Wilkes, John, his dedication to Jonson's *Fall of Mortimer,* ii. 343.

Wilkins, Dr. A. S., on Christian names taken from designations of virtues, i. 101 [1].

Wilkins, George, possibility of his part-authorship of *Timon of Athens,* ii. 178; his *Pericles,* ii. 183; his share in *Travels of Three English Brothers* Shirley, ii. 600; his dramatic works, ii. 606; *Miseries of Inforst Marriage,* ii. 606; Mrs. Behn's adaptation of his *Miseries of Enforced Marriage,* iii. 326 [5].

William III and the stage, iii. 284 [3], 295.

William Longbeard, Life and Death of, by T. Lodge, i. 414.

William Longsword, by Michael Drayton, i. 438.

Willow Garland, The, a ballad by John Heywood, i. 241.

Wilmot, Robert, his version of *Tancred and Gismunda,* i. 214.

Wilson, John, his plays, iii. 337–340; *The Cheats,* iii. 338; *The Projectors,* iii. 338; *Andronicus,* iii. 339; *Belphegor,* iii. 339.

Wilson, Prof. H.H., on the Hindu theatre, iii. 251 [1], 268 [2]; his comparisons between Dryden's works and the Hindu drama, iii. 376 [3], 383 [2].

Wilson, R., his *Three Ladies of London,* i. 344; co-author of *First Part of Sir John Oldcastle,* i. 434; his works, i. 435; his position, i. 454 [1]; Shakspere's collaboration with, ii. 22 [1]; his *Andronicus Comnenius,* ii. 58;

Faire Em attributed to, ii. 236; his and others' *Earl Godwin,* ii. 467; *Sir Piers Exton,* ii. 467.

Wilson, Thomas, his *Rule of Reason,* i. 256 [1].

Wilton, Marie (Lady Bancroft), ii. 487.

Wily Beguiled, i. 365 [1]; attributed to Peele, i. 374; attributed to Shakspere, ii. 212; account of, ii. 621.

Winchester, *The Harrowing of Hell* performed at, i. 55.

Winchester Tropes, The, edited by W. H. Frere, i. 573.

Winter's Tale, The, Shakspere's, founded on Greene's *Pandosto,* i. 389; Coleridge's play after, i. 565 [2]; versification of, ii. 48 [1], 49 [1], 51 [2]; observations on the play, ii. 192–194; an example of Shaksperean comedy, ii. 281.

Wisdom of Dr. Dodipoll, The, ii. 89.

Wisdom of Solomon Paraphrased, The, by Thomas Middleton, ii. 493, 494.

Wise and Foolish Virgins, The Play of the, i. 35, 36.

Wise Woman of Hogsdon, The, by T. Heywood, a synopsis of, ii. 574.

Wit and Science, by Redford, i. 127.

Wit at several Weapons, by Beaumont and Fletcher, Stukely mentioned in, i. 370 [3]; notice of, ii. 692.

Wit in a Constable, by Henry Glapthorne, iii. 153.

Wit without Money, by Fletcher, notice of, ii. 695.

Wit's Treasury, by Francis Meres, his eulogy on John Lyly, i. 273 [4].

Wits, The, by Sir W. D'Avenant, notice of, iii. 171, 172.

Wits Led by the Nose: see *Love's Victory,* by W. Chamberlayne.

Witch, The, by Middleton, i. 331 [2], ii. 171; account of, ii. 504.

Witch of Edmonton, by Dekker and others, ii. 469, 470; account of, iii. 74.

Witchcraft, popular belief in, in Elisabethan era, i. 331; Ralegh on, i. 336 [1]; the subject of, ignored by Jonson, ii. 367 [4]; belief in, in Elisabethan times, ii. 575, 576 *et seqq.*

Witches of Lancaster, The, by T. Potts, ii. 575 [5].

Wither, George, a caricature of, in *The Cruel Brother,* iii. 170.

Witney, *The Resurrection* performed at, i. 57 [1].

Witty Fair One, The, by Shirley, notice of, iii. 104.

Wives' Excuse, The, by T. Southerne, iii. 421.

Woer, The, an interlude by George Puttenham, i. 442 [4].

Wolsey, Cardinal, prohibits the clergy from play-acting, i. 53.

Woman-Captain, The, by Shadwell, iii. 457.

Woman-hater, The, attributed to Beaumont, notice of, ii. 662.

Woman in the Moone, The, by John Lyly, i. 286.

Woman is a Weathercock, A, by Nathaniel Field, notice of, iii. 48.

Woman Killed with Kindness, by T. Heywood, notice of, ii. 562.

Woman Taken in Adultery, The, one of the York plays, i. 70; one of the Chester plays, i. 80; one of the Coventry plays, i. 88 [1].

Woman's Plot, The, ii. 743 [1]; ascribed to Massinger, iii. 3 [3].

Woman's Prize, The, by Fletcher, notice of, ii. 709.

Woman's Wit, by Colley Cibber, iii. 486.

Women beware Women, by Middleton, notice of, ii. 512.

Women Pleased, by Fletcher, a synopsis of, ii. 703.

Wonder, The, by Mrs. Centlivre, iii. 488 [3]; notice of, iii. 490.

Wonder of a Kingdome, The, by Dekker, ii. 466.

Wonder of Women, The, by Marston, ii. 480.

Wonderfull Yeare, The, by Dekker, ii. 453 [6], 454 [6].

Wood, Anthony à, on John Lyly, i. 271 [2].

Woodes, Nathaniel, his *Conflict of Conscience,* i. 138.

Woodkirk, religious plays performed at, i. 55, 59.

Worcester, Earl of: *see* Tiptoft, John.

Worcester, religious plays performed at, i. 56.

Wordsworth, Bishop Charles, on Shakspere's biblical knowledge, ii. 11 [2].

World and the Child, The, a morality, i. 118.

World Tost at Tennis, The, a masque by Middleton, ii. 498 [1], 537.

Worp, Mr. J. A., on *The Spanish Tragedy,* i. 306 [3].

Worthies of England, The, Fuller on Shakspere in, i. 522.

Wotton, Sir Henry, his Oxford play, *Tancredo,* i. 214 [3], ii. 383 [1], 632 [5]; his publication containing *Courtlie Controversie of Cupid's Cautels,* i. 309;

his letter *re* burning of Globe theatre, ii. 201 ; his *State of Christendom,* ii. 416 [3]; on Tailor's *Hog hath lost his Pearl,* iii. 157 [2].

Wounds of Civil War, The, by Thomas Lodge, i. 411, 414, 416.

Wrangling Lovers, The, by Ravenscroft, iii. 451.

Wright, J., his translation of Seneca's *Thyestes,* iii. 402 [2].

Wright, Thomas, his edition of the *Comoedia Bubionis* and the *Geta* of Vitalis Blesensis, i. 9 [1]; his edition of the Chester plays, i. 12 [1], 76 [2].

Wright, Mr. W. Aldis, editor of the Clarendon Press Series of Shakspere, i. 570.

Wriothesley, Henry : *see* Southampton, Earl of.

Wroughton, his adaptation of Shakspere's *Richard II,* ii. 105.

Wülcker, Prof. R., on Chapman's *Alphonsus,* ii. 429 [1].

Wycherley, William, his plays, iii. 461–467 ; *Love in a Wood,* iii. 463 ; *The Gentleman Dancing-Master,* iii. 463 ; *The Country Wife,* iii. 464; *The Plain-Dealer,* iii. 464; Vindication of the Stage, attributed to, iii. 512.

Wyer, R., printer of *The Play of the Wether,* by John Heywood, i. 246 [1].

Wylley, Thomas, of Yoxford, Suffolk, his plays, i. 136 [1].

Wymondham, Norfolk, religious plays performed at, i. 55.

Yarrington, Robert, his *Two Tragedies in One,* ii. 218, 219 ; the identification of, ii. 591 [3].

Yelverton, Christopher, co-author of Gascoigne's *Jocasta,* i. 209.

York, religious plays performed at, i. 55 ; *The Creed Play* at, i. 98.

York plays, proclamation prior to performance of, i. 59 ; pageants comprising, i. 59, 61 [2] *et seq.*; programme of, i. 60 [2]; synopsis of, i. 65–71.

York and Lancaster, The Contention betwixt, i. 348; authorship attributed to Marlowe, i. 358.

Yorke, Sir John, fined for producing an anti-protestant play, i. 441 [2].

Yorkshire Tragedy, The, attributed to Shakspere, ii. 210 ; a s nopsis of the play, ii. 231, 232.

Young, Edward, his letter *On Original Composition,* i. 551 ; his *Revenge,* ii. 467 [7].

Young Admiral, The, by Shirley, a synopsis of, iii. 108.

Young King, The, by Mrs. Aphra Behn, iii. 453.

Your Five Gallants, by Middleton, ii. 518.

Zaïre, by Voltaire, its obligations to *Othello,* i. 536 [1].

Zapolya, Coleridge's, i. 565 [2]; compared with *The Winter's Tale,* ii. 193.

Zepeda, Romero de, his dramatic adaptation of Cota's *Celestina,* i. 232.

Zingaresche, the, i. 227.

Zorilla, Francisco de Rojas, influence of his comedies, iii. 303.